I AM ERROR

Platform Studies
Nick Montfort and Ian Bogost, editors

Racing the Beam: The Atari Video Computer System, Nick Montfort and Ian Bogost, 2009

Codename Revolution: The Nintendo Wii Platform, Steven E. Jones and George K. Thiruvathukal, 2012

The Future Was Here: The Commodore Amiga, Jimmy Maher, 2012

Flash: Building the Interactive Web, Anastasia Salter and John Murray, 2014

I AM ERROR: The Nintendo Family Computer / Entertainment System Platform, Nathan Altice, 2015

I AM ERROR

The Nintendo Family Computer / Entertainment System Platform

Nathan Altice

The MIT Press Cambridge, Massachusetts London, England

First MIT Press paperback edition, 2017

This book was set in Filosofia by Toppan Best-set Premedia Limited.

Library of Congress Cataloging-in-Publication Data

Altice, Nathan.
    I am error : the Nintendo family computer/entertainment system platform / Nathan Altice.
        pages cm.—(Platform studies)
    Includes bibliographical references and index.
    ISBN 978-0-262-02877-6 (hardcover : alk. paper), 978-0-262-53454-3 (pb.)
1. Nintendo video games.   2. Video games—Design.   3. Nintendo of America Inc.   I. Title.
GV1469.32.A55   2015
2014034284

For Amanda, as always

Contents

Series Foreword

How can someone create a breakthrough game for a mobile phone or a compelling work of art for an immersive 3D environment without understanding that the mobile phone and the 3D environment are different sorts of computing platforms? The best artists, writers, programmers, and designers are well aware of how certain platforms facilitate certain types of computational expression and innovation. Likewise, computer science and engineering has long considered how underlying computing systems can be analyzed and improved. As important as scientific and engineering approaches are, and as significant as work by creative artists has been, there is also much to be learned from the sustained, intensive, humanistic study of digital media. We believe it is time for humanists to seriously consider to the lowest level of computing systems, to understand their relationship to culture and creativity.

The Platform Studies book series has been established to promote the investigation of underlying computing systems and how they enable, constrain, shape and support the creative work that is done on them. The series investigates the foundations of digital media—the computing systems, both hardware and software, that developers and users depend upon for artistic, literary, and gaming development. Books in the series will certainly vary in their approaches, but they will all also share certain features:

• A focus on a single platform or a closely related family of platforms.

• Technical rigor and in-depth investigation of how computing technologies work.

• An awareness of and discussion of how computing platforms exist in a context of culture and society, being developed based on cultural concepts and then contributing to culture in a variety of ways—for instance, by affecting how people perceive computing.

Acknowledgments

A book is a labor that leads to many thanks:

Before all others, I want to thank my wife Amanda for keeping me healthy, happy, and motivated during two years of writing and research. None of this was possible without her. I also owe my parents a special debt for buying my first NES. They are responsible for all of this.

I want to thank my colleague and friend, David Golumbia, for his support, guidance, and enthusiasm, along with the remainder of my dissertation committee—Joshua Eckhardt, Ryan Patton, and Bob Paris—for their thoughtful revisions. Equal thanks go to MIT Press's Douglas Sery and manuscript editor Ariel Baker-Gibbs, and the Platform Studies series editors Nick Montfort and Ian Bogost, whose combined knowledge and patience helped bring this project to bear.

I wish to thank Neal Wyatt for her camaraderie, conversation, and coffee breaks throughout the writing process, Aria Tanner for her excellent (and affordable) Japanese translations, Vera Brown for her friendship (and Dendy), Nate Ayers for his photo editing talents, Matt Schneider for his long-distance reading, Scott Benson for his Game & Watch, Justin Spears for his loaner NES, Nick Wurz for his capture card, David Viens for his invaluable technical revisions, and Steven Jones and George Thiruvathukal for first planting the seed for this project.

This book would not exist without the decades of technical research shared among the members of the *NESDev* community. There are members there who understand the NES far better than I, and likely better than Nintendo's own engineers and programmers. Theirs is a work of dedication and intellectual inquiry, and I thank every member who, knowingly or not, contributed to this book's completion.

I also owe thanks to the members of Nintendo Age, who together comprise a friendly and knowledgeable community. Their forums provide one of the best references for the beginning NES programmer and one of the biggest temptations for expanding my NES collection.

And finally, I want to thank Zac Price, a great friend and a superior *Mega Man 2* player—not superior to me, but to most.

During his quest to find the elusive Island Palace, Link, protagonist from the 1987 Nintendo Entertainment System (NES) videogame *Zelda II: The Adventure of Link*, visits a small house in the Town of Ruto. When Link approaches its sole resident, a portly, bearded fellow in purple attire, the man says, "I AM ERROR." Until Link speaks to another character further along in his quest, any interaction with Error yields the same curious result.

For many players, the cryptic message appeared to be a programming flaw, as if the game's code mistakenly found its way to the graphical surface, replacing the character's name with a diagnostic message. The real cause was less mysterious. In the game's original Japanese script, the man said:

オレノナハ
エラー　ダ・・・

"I am Error" is a passable literal translation, but a more natural read is simply, "My name is Error..."[1] An unlikely character name, perhaps, but that too was part of a poorly translated programmer joke. Link later meets a man named Bagu—a Japanese romanization of "Bug"—who looks identical to Error save for his red tunic. Together, Bug and Error were meant to form a pair of sly computer malfunction references, but the fumbled translation killed the joke and left a generation of NES players thinking the latter's name was more literal than intended.

Error's dialogue has since become an infamous part of the NES's legacy. Despite the accessibility of online FAQs, wikis, and detailed translation notes for the *Zelda* series, articles regularly appear dispelling the myths of the Error error for the players apparently still perplexed by his introduction.[2] Modern games knowingly parody the dialogue. The *Legend of Zelda*–inspired PC game *The Binding of Isaac*, for example, has a hidden room—purposefully framed as a glitch—whose bearded occupant utters the famous line in a cartoon speech balloon.

The NES era was rife with mistranslations. Link's prior adventure in *The Legend of Zelda* was famous for its cryptic and frequently misleading character dialogue. When the old man presented Link with an upgraded sword and said, "MASTER USING IT AND YOU CAN HAVE THIS," many players assumed they could take the blade and practice. Instead, they were meant to return when they had passed a specific heart container threshold. A misplaced letter in *Metal Gear*'s English translation created a comical temporal paradox when the enemy soldiers exclaimed, "I FEEL ASLEEP!!" *after* waking up. Winning a match in *Pro Wrestling* yielded the congratulatory text, "A WINNER IS YOU," proving the translator's heart was in the right place even if their grammar was not. Congratulations in general were a failing point for many NES games, as the lack of an "L" equivalent in the Japanese language led to many "congraturations," "conglaturations," and all variations in between. In some cases, errors became canon, as in *Metroid's* "barrier suit," which was mistranslated as Varia in the U.S. instruction manual and remained as such ever since.[3]

The circumstances of localization—the process wherein games are translated, linguistically and culturally—were much different in the 1980s. Development teams of ten or fewer people worked for a few weeks (in the worst case) or months (in the best case) to produce what we would now call "AAA titles," the big-budget videogames released by the industry's leading publishers.[4] Such was the case with *Super Mario Bros.* and *The Legend of Zelda*, developed concurrently by the same small team for two different media (cartridge and disk, respectively) across a span of months between 1985 and 1986. Compare this to the teams of a hundred or more programmers, sound designers, producers, artists, actors, and animators who work for several years on a single videogame. Of course, the scope of games and their underlying architectures were less complex in the 1980s, but Nintendo's creators also had less time and resources to devote to localization, presuming a game was even slated for release outside Japan.

Yet the same technical concerns that kept development schedules short also limited the quality and content of translation. Even with a completed translation in hand, text replacement was not a trivial cut-and-paste job. The alphanumeric characters onscreen were literally characters, like any other graphic. The letter "A" and the upper half of Mario's head were cut from the same digital cloth; they were both tiles composed of bits that occupied the same memory in ROM. Translation was not just a symbolic act but also a material act: text had to be uncompressed in memory, its tiles redrawn, its characters substituted, its memory limitations reconsidered. If the Japanese text fit cleanly in a hardcoded dialogue box, but the English translation did not, meaning would often be sacrificed for the sake of economy. Why say "My name is" when "I am" gets the same basic point across with six fewer characters?

Any study devoted to Nintendo's first videogame console must necessarily be about translation—not only in a linguistic sense, manifested in Error's dialogue, but in a material sense as well. Translation has real social, economic, and cultural consequences beyond simple misinterpretation; translation takes place between circuits, cartridges, code, and cathode rays just as it does between human actors; and translation is inexorably and inevitably riddled with errors. As Derrida wrote in his "Letter to a Japanese Friend," translation is not "a secondary and derived event in relation to an original language"—in other words, not merely a supplement.[5] Applied to the production of technological objects that must enter cultures, markets, and domestic spaces, that must be made by bodies and touched by bodies, that must be made from rare earths and precious resources, translation does not simply derive meaning from prior sources—translation produces new meanings, new expressions, new bodies, and new objects.

I AM ERROR explores the complex material histories of the Nintendo Entertainment System—and its elder sibling, the Family Computer—that characterized its cultural reception, expressive output, and hardware design. In the 1980s, few NES players knew that their boxy gray videogame console was a cosmetic re-imagining of an older machine known in Japan as the Family Computer. Fewer still understood the machinations necessary to introduce a new console—or an Entertainment System, as Nintendo's marketing team chose to call it—to an American market that had apparently exhausted the videogame fad, ready to move on to the "superior" experience of personal computers. Nintendo, a century-old Japanese company that until a few years prior was primarily known in the United States as the maker of *Donkey Kong* and the Game & Watch, would be the unlikely savior of the dedicated videogame console. Riding the crest of a wave propelled by "next-generation" hardware and superior software like *Super Mario Bros.*, Nintendo would seize the global videogame market with unprecedented force.

But Nintendo's success was equally unlikely based on their console's flaws. The NES's distinctive front-loading cartridge slot, for instance, partly caused the console's infamous blinking screen, leading millions of players to blow into game cartridges as a quick "fix" that inevitably exacerbated the problem. The other cause was a proprietary "lockout chip" exclusive to the NES, meant to wall off piracy and unlicensed developers alike, a hardware tactic that Nintendo developed after such threats had damaged the Family Computer's Disk System peripheral's success in Japan. Such game-disrupting imperfections regularly spell commercial failure for consumer electronics, but players, developers, and software partners alike absorbed the Famicom's/NES's shortcomings into the fabric of gaming culture. Hardware limitations that governed the complexity of graphics and the number of digitized sound channels—or worse, caused sprites to flicker or slowed on-screen action to a crawl—are now part of the living legacy of videogames, referenced by fans and recycled in game design. Contemporary games that aim for nostalgic or "retro" appeal still mimic the console's shortcomings, since they provide quick visual and aural cues to a past era of gaming.

Purposeful malfunctions are a peculiar aesthetic decision in the software industry, where errors and bugs are commonly the bane of programmers. Neither videogames nor word processors nor operating systems nor ATM software nor drone guidance systems should have them, but all inevitably do. In each case, the stakes are successively higher, but programmers' attitudes to them are generally the same. To borrow from Derrida again, glitches operate as a "dangerous supplement" threatening to usurp the integrity of the work as an outside force that originates from within. But users' attitudes toward glitches cover a wide spectrum, dependent upon their nature and severity. A glitch in ATM software that makes the machine inoperable is an inconvenience; one that erringly deducts money from a customer's account is harmful. No game glitch can ruin a household. At their worst, they can make a game unplayable. At their best, they are entry points to new modes of play, exploration, and creative expression.

As Philip Sandifer wrote in his online *Nintendo Project*, "Far from being an aberrant error, the glitch is a central part of the experience of the NES, an era where the games frequently existed on a spectrum between function and breakdown."[6] The minus world does not ruin *Super Mario Bros.* It broadens the play experience, adds mystery, makes code mythic. But the glitch is not just about player experience. It is also a part of the complex function of the machine itself, a means for it to assert its material obstinance. This is the philosophical irony of Error's quote. He is not only erroneously naming himself, but surfacing a paradoxical ontological statement. The NES speaks through Error, naming itself as error. But how can an object be both itself and not itself?

The question is not an empty rhetorical gesture. As we will see throughout the book, a platform is defined less by its positive aspects than by its limits and negations—by what it isn't—situated in the weird liminal spaces that bridge one computational architecture to another. I do not mean that one cannot hold an NES in their hands without risk of its disintegration or that we cannot consult Wikipedia for a list of the console's technical specifications. Indeed, the word platform has an important practical use for this and other studies of its kind. But the deeper we probe into the myriad variations and permutations of Nintendo's console, the less it coheres as a single definable object.

Methodology

It is hard to overstate the NES's importance, both to videogame history and to culture at large. At the peak of their market dominance, the NES and Famicom were in one out of every three homes in the United States and Japan.[7] Even thirty years later, the legacy of the Nintendo's first cartridge-based console looms large in gaming, art, music, graphic design, fashion, literature, and popular culture. But economic landmarks and market superiority are not the focus of this book. There are numerous popular and scholarly texts that focus on the NES and its influence, which tend to fall into a few broad categories: Nintendo's role in the larger history of videogames;[8] Nintendo's corporate history;[9] Nintendo's individual game designers;[10] Nintendo's impact on game players;[11] and Nintendo's iconic videogame characters.[12] However, the NES's importance as a computational platform is widely overlooked.

The NES, of course, was neither the first nor the most technologically advanced home console, but it did mark a transition point in the types of videogames that they could proffer. Its early games were either direct ports of or callbacks to arcade games, designed for short-burst, single-screen play. But within two years, platforming—pioneered in part by Nintendo's own arcade hit *Donkey Kong*—emerged as the dominant genre of the "third generation" of consoles. "Platform" was a catch-all term for any obstacle or structure the player-character had to traverse in order to reach a goal, like the girders that Jumpman scaled to save Pauline from Donkey Kong or the pits and alligators Pitfall Harry had to swing across to reach the hidden gold bars. Later platformers built upon these early prototypes, expanding traversal beyond single screens to elaborate scrolling spaces. Platformers encouraged progressive, long-term play, coherent world design, and narrative development, characteristics antithetical to the arcade's quarter-consuming economy.

Nintendo's console was primed to capitalize on this transition in gameplay style—the Famicom was engineered with hardware-based scrolling, plentiful on-screen sprites, dedicated VRAM, and ample cartridge program ROM. None of these individual technical specs were revolutionary, but in combination they served as the architectural foundation for tile-based worlds tailored to character-based platforming. Even the Famicom controller, with its patented plus pad and dual action buttons, was geared for cardinal movement through 2D space. *Super Mario Bros.*, a landmark in videogame history, became the archetype of the genre, featuring a distinctive world (The Mushroom Kingdom), a memorable protagonist (Mario, the plumber), and a clear narrative goal (rescue the Princess from Bowser)—all novel features for console games at the time. Successors like *Castlevania*, *Mega Man*, *Metroid*, *Contra*, and *Ninja Gaiden* underscored the sophistication of console gaming and paved the way for a new Famicom era.

While Nintendo's console shared architectural similarities with several other machines, including the Atari VCS and the Commodore 64, its expressive capabilities were radically different. And those differences were more significant than sprite sizes or color counts. Historically, media scholars have overemphasized the visual aspect of digital media, a bias that Montfort,[13] Kirschenbaum,[14] and others have called "screen essentialism." Its prevailing assumption is that videogames' primary object of study is what players see onscreen, negating the role of graphics processors, joypads, sound circuitry, and other material concerns in shaping the expressive possibilities of software. *I AM ERROR*, in line with the platform studies methodology first developed in Montfort and Bogost's *Racing the Beam*, adopts a "bottom-up" approach to digital media, unearthing the code- and hardware-level decisions that fundamentally shaped the platform's creative affordances, cultural reception, and styles of play.

I AM ERROR considers videogames and their platforms to be important objects of cultural, material, and personal expression, alongside cinema, dance, painting, theater and other media. It joins the discussion happening in similar burgeoning disciplines—code studies, game studies, computational theory—that engage digital media with critical rigor and descriptive depth. But platform studies is not simply a technical discussion—it also keeps a keen eye on the cultural, social, and economic forces that influence videogames. No platform exists in a vacuum: circuits, code, and console alike are shaped by the currents of history, economics, and culture—just as those currents are shaped in kind.

The book argues for the Famicom's material importance along three interconnected trajectories: first, as a platform directly informed by prevailing trends in arcade, console, and PC design, which in turn influenced the software the platform would support; second, as a pivotal platform in the evolution and popularization of the platformer genre, for which the Famicom's hardware was distinctly suited; and third, as a platform ideally positioned to catalyze console emulation in the 1990s, when both PCs and the Internet reached the necessary maturity to support an emulation ecosystem. With these three trajectories in mind, *I AM ERROR* offers a sustained technical analysis of how the platform was programmed and engineered, from code to silicon, and how those design decisions shaped not only its expressive possibilities, but also the perception of videogames in general. The book also defines the platform not only as a single console, but as a holistic network of objects and texts, including cartridges, controllers, peripherals, marketing materials, play environments, and emulators.

In this light, *I AM ERROR* diverges from the platform studies model by expanding and critiquing the notion of a platform as a stable configuration of hardware and software. As a Japanese product that was later exported to the United States, the Famicom was born in a vastly different cultural context than predecessors like the Atari VCS or Fairchild Channel F, shaped by considerations ranging from the size of Japanese households to the legacy of suspicion that Americans felt toward Japan post–World War II. Thus hardware and software alike underwent a number of translations that prior consoles never did, from the shape and color of the console to the censorship of potentially sensitive religious or political imagery that might offend international audiences. The Famicom's hardware and software were under constant revision, mutating to adapt to new cultures, new play practices, new markets, and new genres.

The NES hardware also reached its commercial obsolescence at a pivotal moment in the history of personal computing. Console emulation became feasible for PCs in the mid-1990s, allowing another important translation to take place—physical hardware, rendered in silicon and plastic, became virtual hardware, rendered in code. The NES was uniquely positioned to make this transition and led the way for the deluge of emulation that took place in the late 1990s. The features built into NES emulators spawned new forms of play, performance, and videogame archiving. Suddenly players could record gameplay movies, save games at any point, play online, alter graphics, load translation patches, and more.

The NES platform blossomed beyond the bounds of hardware, expanding its reach and capabilities past what Nintendo's engineers ever thought possible. There is no single configuration of hardware and software, no single processor, no sound or graphic that defines the Famicom as a platform. It is all and none of them. It is error.

Plan of the Book

I AM ERROR is neither a chronological review of the Famicom's hardware and games nor a history of Nintendo as a corporation. Larger surveys of videogame history are better equipped to furnish comprehensive lists of names, dates, and events.[15] The book is instead structured as a series of "deep dives" into specific hardware and software topics that will illuminate how the platform works at a base technological level. And while *I AM ERROR* covers the full scope of the Famicom's lifespan, it does so to track key developments in its material history along with the broader cultural and technological contexts from which those developments arose. Since Japan, the United States, Europe, and the rest of the world experienced concurrent but staggered trajectories of Famicom/NES development, this hardware focus often demands chronological backtracking.

Similarly, hardware and software examples are not chosen based on their gameplay merits or review metrics, but according to their relevance to the platform-specific topic. Fortunately, some of the best and most critically acclaimed games are also the most interesting to study. *Super Mario Bros.*, for instance, is not only one of the most lauded and bestselling videogames in history, it is also the consummate example of the Famicom's affordances. And despite the game's influence, there has never been a close analysis of how its successful design is tied intimately to the Famicom's Picture Processing Unit and cartridge ROM. Others, like *Gyromite*, *Wild Gunman*, or *Devil World*, while less lauded, offer fascinating glimpses at the Famicom's architectural design.

Chapter 1 ("Family Computer") introduces Nintendo's first cartridge-based console, the Family Computer (or Famicom), along with a few of its key predecessors. The chapter's first half tracks the development of the Famicom hardware, spearheaded by Nintendo engineer Masayuki Uemura, and its trademark industrial design, from case and controller to cartridge and circuits. The chapter's second half provides a detailed overview of the Famicom's computational architecture, including its custom microprocessor and graphical processing capabilities.

Chapter 2 ("Ports") rewinds to Nintendo's first forays into the U.S. arcade market via an ambitious but mistimed failure and the unlikely hit that arose from its ashes. *Donkey Kong* is used as a case study to examine the broader cultural context of Japan's entrance into the Western video-game industry and specifically their software's categorization into the catch-all "novelty games" genre. The chapter also provides a comprehensive technical comparison of arcade *Donkey Kong* to its subsequent Famicom port, a crucial building block in its console future.

Chapter 3 ("Entertainment System") covers the challenging launch of the Nintendo Entertainment System, a hardware translation of the Family Computer suited to the demands of a troubled U.S. videogame market. Two of the console's initial marketing gimmicks—the Robotic Operating Buddy and the Zapper—are profiled in depth alongside the software they supported. Despite their limited use, both peripherals were important links to Nintendo's rich gaming legacy. The chapter concludes with a survey of the inconsistent, and sometimes inexplicable, translations used to transition content from a Japanese to a worldwide audience, ranging from the design and marketing of box artwork to the censorship of "offensive" in-game content.

Chapter 4 ("Platforming") is devoted to a technical exegesis of the seminal Famicom game, *Super Mario Bros.* The chapter delves into the game's source code and analyzes how the Famicom's architecture guided the game's design. Many of the hardware programming concepts introduced in prior chapters—scrolling, metatiles, data compression, attribute tables, palette swaps, sprite o hit—are expanded and explicated through *Super Mario Bros.*'s remarkable object-based software engine. That careful code work is followed by an analysis of the game's unique and sometimes unintended innovations, including player movement beyond world boundaries and the famous "minus world" exploit.

Chapter 5 ("Quick Disk") discusses the Japanese launch of the Family Computer Disk System (FDS), the introduction of Nintendo's proprietary disk format, and their combined effect on the design of the landmark adventure game *The Legend of Zelda*. The chapter examines the FDS's design, media, features, and flaws, and the peripheral's eventual demise in the face of software piracy. The chapter also explores the "miniature gardens" cultivated by *Zelda* and *Super Bros.*' designers as reflections of a tragic ecological crisis facing modern-day Japan.

Chapter 6 ("Expansions") examines the breadth and depth of innovations Famicom developers explored after their "exhaustion" of the stock hardware, the demise of the FDS, and the influx of competitors' "next generation" platforms. The chapter covers the emergence of new genres, hardware mappers meant to expand the Famicom's capabilities, unlicensed cheat devices, and the development and debut of *Dragon Quest*, one of Japan's most influential series and a game whose scope and style were impossible to realize in a standard Famicom cartridge.

Chapter 7 ("2A03") dissects the Famicom's dedicated sound hardware, the Audio Processing Unit (APU), explores its five channels in detail, explains their use in software, and outlines the APU's role in the larger context of synthesis. It also surveys the sound enhancements provided by hardware expansions, including the Famicom Disk System and various extended mapper hardware. Finally, the chapter describes the APU's lasting importance to chiptunes, a music genre dedicated to exploring the sonic boundaries of vintage sound processors.

Chapter 8 ("Tool-Assisted") tracks the Famicom's rebirth through emulation via an analysis of tool-assisted speedruns, a specialized play style devoted to completing games as quickly as possible using software assistance. An overview of emulation's emergence in the 1960s is followed by a history of early NES emulators and their eventual evolution into the modern forms used in tool-assisted play. The chapter concludes with a look at the surprising new forms of play afforded through human/software collaboration and their explicit challenge to the notion of platforms as stable objects of study.

The book's afterword ("Famicom Remix") speculates on Nintendo's future based on its platform past; appendix A ("Famicom/NES Bibliographic Descriptions") issues a practical call for more rigorous enumerative bibliographies for videogames (and digital objects in general) and provides practical models for scholarly and critical use; and appendix B is a glossary of technical terms used throughout the book.

A list of sources concludes the text. I mention it explicitly since, in lieu of citing each Famicom/NES videogame inline or bloating the endnotes unnecessarily, all cited cartridges, disks, and ROMs are instead found here, using the model enumerative format detailed in appendix A.

In October 1981, encouraged by the dual successes of their breakout arcade hit *Donkey Kong* and the Game & Watch LCD handheld games, Nintendo president Hiroshi Yamauchi approached Masayuki Uemura, head of the hardware-focused Nintendo Research & Development 2 (R&D2), to begin work on a home videogame console.[1] Yamauchi knew that arcade games and cheap portables were excellent for short-term profits, but an inexpensive console with interchangeable cartridges could generate profits for years.[2] Atari had proven the model with their long-standing Video Computer System (VCS), the wood-paneled wonder that had dominated the U.S. home console market despite a slew of capable competitors. Yamauchi reasoned that Nintendo could manufacture their own home system, leveraging their popular arcade titles to entice consumers.

Uemura, alongside young engineer Katsuya Nakakawa, researched the feasibility of the console's technical requirements at the budget price Yamauchi demanded: ¥9800, (roughly $40 in 1983).[3] Thanks to Nintendo's recent experience with *Donkey Kong*, it was:

> The conclusion [Nakakawa] came up with was that a domestic game console looked to be a possibility if they IC'd [packaged as an integrated circuit] the Donkey Kong arcade machine's circuits and used them as a base. In the spring of 1982, a concrete development project had begun. The code name of the game console they set out to develop was the GAMECOM.[4]

For nearly a year, GAMECOM was the internal name for Nintendo's first cartridge-based home console.[5] But when Uemura mentioned the name to his wife the following spring, she suggested that if the console was meant to be a "domestic computer that's neither a home computer nor a personal computer," perhaps they should call it a "family computer."[6] And since the Japanese commonly shortened "personal computer" (パーソナル・コンピュータ) to *pasokon* (パソコン), Nintendo's family computer should have a similar nickname. Uemura loved the idea, as did the rest of his team. The Family Computer (ファミリーコンピュータ) released in Japan on July 21, 1983, and was soon after known by its affectionate abbreviation: ファミコン, or Famicom.[7]

As Ms. Uemura intuited, the portmanteau of "family" and "computer" described how Nintendo envisioned the machine to fit into the lives of those who purchased it. "Family" designated the console's range of social functions: Nintendo was bringing its popular arcade titles into the home, to be shared with the family, to become part of the family, and to be played in the family's social space. It would be a "domestic computer" in the most familiar sense. But the console would be more than a simple machine that played variations of ball-and-paddle electronic games—it would also be a powerful computing device, rivaling the *pasokon* that Japanese players were already accustomed to using for home videogame play.

Of course, the Family Computer's idealistic nomenclature was not solely motivated by Nintendo's domestic goodwill. Nintendo was selling a game console, and game consoles were seen as toys, meaning that parents would need to be part of the purchasing decision. Marketing the Family Computer to children would find limited success without the entire family's economic input, as Katayama's 1996 profile of Nintendo explains:

> As the Japanese name, "family computer," shows, the designers had the family market in mind. The product had to be priced so that parents would buy it. No matter how great the games, if mothers thought they were too expensive the machine would never take off. Nintendo therefore aimed for prices that children themselves could afford or at least would be able to convince their parents to lay out.[8]

Juggling Yamauchi's demands of affordability, approachability, and power posed major challenges for the R&D2 team. Not only was Uemura expected to produce a console at bargain prices, but it had to be future-proofed against potential rivals for three years.[9] Moreover, the Family Computer's spec software was *Donkey Kong*, an arcade hit built atop bleeding-edge hardware that cost hundreds of thousands of yen to produce. A cartridge-based machine would not only have to be cheaper, but also more flexible, serving as a platform for *Donkey Kong* and a host of ports to come.

An Unconventional Stone

Uemura grappled with the problem for many months, consulting with the company's arcade engineers to figure out how they might transition *Donkey Kong*'s powerful hardware to an inexpensive home console.[10] Nakakawa's solution to "IC the arcade machine's circuits" was not a simple plug-and-play operation. At the heart of any modern arcade game was a microprocessor. And the choice of that microprocessor had important ramifications in cost and capabilities. An underpowered CPU might hamstring the number of sprites available onscreen, lower the game's palette options, or restrict the audio channel count. Alternately, if a CPU was too complex, it would be costly to manufacture and difficult to program.

In the early 1980s, there were two major players vying for the low-cost microprocessor market: MOS Technology's 6502 and Zilog's Z80. Both 8-bit processors were cheap but powerful, capable of driving a range of videogame consoles, PCs, and arcade games. Japan's arcade industry leaned heavily toward Zilog's microprocessor. The massive hits of the era—*Pac-Man, Galaxian, Galaga*—were all powered by the Z80.

The Family Computer nearly had a Z80 too. In fact, prior to Nintendo's decision to forge ahead with their own console, the Family Computer was nearly a ColecoVision.[11] In the U.S., Atari had maintained a near-deadlock on the emerging home videogame industry with the Atari VCS. However, the unlikely Connecticut Leather Company (Coleco for short), who had previously dabbled in derivative *Pong* clones and electronic handheld games, forged a short-term exclusive licensing agreement with Nintendo to bring *Donkey Kong* to their new console, a Z80-based machine that technologically trumped the elder VCS. The *Kong* partnership benefited both parties, spurring the ColecoVision to impressive first year sales and expanding Nintendo's market reach beyond the arcades.

Nintendo had great admiration for Coleco's port of *Donkey Kong*. Licensing the ColecoVision in Japan would allow Nintendo to develop console versions of its arcade games without a massive upfront investment in research, development, and manufacturing. In *The Golden Age of Videogames*, Roberto Dillon indicates that the two companies were close to a console licensing deal but could not settle on economic terms. In the end, he writes, "negotiations were abandoned when Nintendo declared it would design its own system instead."[12]

Coding for the ColecoVision's Z80 core certainly would have smoothed software conversions. Nintendo's *Radar Scope, Donkey Kong, Donkey Kong Jr., Popeye, and Mario Bros.* cabinets were all Z80-based, so porting to ColecoVision would have been simpler than translating code to a dissimilar microprocessor architecture. There was also the inherent risk of introducing new proprietary hardware to a fledgling videogame market. The less friction there was for third parties (i.e., publishers not directly affiliated with the console manufacturer) to port their games across multiple systems, the better. Without a steady stream of software, a new console was dead in the water. But when negotiations with Coleco broke down, Nintendo decided not only to design their own technologically superior console, but to forgo the Z80 altogether in favor of the 6502. This surprising decision ultimately came down to a mixture of corporate politics, managerial mandate, hardware licensing, manufacturer supply, and competitive strategy.

President Yamauchi had a long-standing reputation as a shrewd but imperious executive, possessing, according to his employees' accounts, an incisive but opaque business sense. Prior to the Famicom's development, for instance, Yamauchi unexpectedly forbade any collaboration between Sharp and Nintendo related to the new console. The order was a jolt for Uemura—Sharp was both his former employer and Nintendo's hardware partner for the Game & Watch. Nonetheless, Yamauchi insisted that Sharp's attention would be detrimentally split if they had to juggle between their handheld line and new console development.[13] With Sharp out of the picture, Uemura found little support from other electronics suppliers. Officially, vendors told him that parts were scarce due to a recent surge in demand for PCs and word processors, but he suspected that they were either reticent to wager on a risky console product—and Nintendo themselves—or had no idea how to produce the machine that Nintendo required.[14]

Uemura and semiconductor manufacturer Ricoh found one another at a fortuitous time. Ricoh had the advanced facilities Nintendo required and were currently only producing at ten percent capacity, an unsustainable shortfall for a large manufacturing operation. Uemura, along with engineers Nakakawa and Masahiro Ohtake, visited the semiconductor factory, where they were met with enthusiasm about a potential partnership. Hiromitsu Yagi, now a Ricoh supervisor, had worked at Mitsubishi in the late 1970s when they had partnered with Nintendo and overseen the chip design for the Color TV Game 6, one of Nintendo's early all-in-one consoles.[15] Uemura pitched the idea of a console made for *Donkey Kong* and, thanks in part to their employees' desire to "take the game home," Ricoh agreed to take on the challenge.[16] However, the per-chip cost necessary to comply with Yamauchi's target price was not feasible at videogame console production numbers. Chip prices drove down at volumes of millions, not tens of thousands, so Nintendo made an extraordinary gamble in guaranteeing Ricoh a three-million chip order over two years.[17] Ricoh agreed to the deal, but feared that Nintendo was headed for an economic catastrophe. If the Famicom flopped, Nintendo would be stuck with millions of unused CPUs.

Chip prices aside, there was a larger roadblock to overcome: Ricoh lacked a manufacturing license for the Z80. As an alternative, they suggested the MOS 6502, a chip that was popular in U.S. and European consoles and PCs. The chip was similar in specs, affordable, and already licensed—a worthwhile replacement, with one caveat: it was virtually unknown among Japan's engineers. Surprisingly, both Uemura and Yamauchi saw this as an advantage, since the tradeoff in engineering complexity would pay off in hardware obfuscation and give Nintendo the competitive lead time they desired. In a 2011 interview with Nintendo president (and former Famicom programmer) Satoru Iwata, Uemura noted that Nintendo's peculiar choice "turned out lucky" for them, since other companies "wouldn't be able to make sense of it."[18]

Uemura's team initially balked at the change, since they too could not make sense of the 6502. Forgoing the familiar Z80 architecture posed major engineering challenges. For one, R&D2 had to build development tools from scratch. And instead of reusing prior source code, they had to tediously reconstruct their arcade games through observation. As Uemura explained, "the work required a lot of patience, including tasks such as watching the game screen and measuring the timing of animations with a stop watch."[19] In April 1983, R&D2 eased their burden when they hired Shuhei Kato, a young engineer who specialized in the 6502. The "Living 6502 Manual," as they called him, spurred on the final surge of software development and sealed Nintendo's microprocessor future.[20]

In the end, the Ricoh partnership satisfied all of Yamauchi's stipulations. Thanks to an inexpensive processor, the console would be cheap (though not on target—the Famicom debuted at ¥14,800, around $60 in 1983). And thanks to an unconventional choice of "stones," as semiconductors were called in Japan, Nintendo had a competitive edge. Reverse engineering the Famicom would prove as troublesome to competitors' engineers as it had for Nintendo's. From the outset, it was clear that Nintendo designed their console with proprietary control in mind. And despite the risk of alienating third parties, they wanted to be the ultimate arbiters of who could and could not develop software for the Famicom—a predilection that would intensify as Nintendo took control of the world-wide videogame market (chapter 3).

The 6502 had one other material advantage: its chip was one-quarter the size of the Z80. As a result, Nintendo's and Ricoh's designers were able to shrink the Famicom's plastic body and further slash the cost of the machine. Compared to contemporaries that used the Z80—ColecoVision, Sega's SG-1000, MSX PCs—the Famicom was more compact and less expensive. The design had both marketing and cultural advantages. The smaller Famicom, garbed in bright red and white plastic, had a toy-like appearance, sure to grab the attention of young children. Moreover, the diminutive size fit the tastes of Japanese consumers and the size of their domestic spaces,[21] making good on the Family Computer name.

With the microprocessor question settled, Nintendo began to work in earnest on the Famicom prototype in late 1982 and soon began courting another U.S. licensing partner. Ever since their entry into the arcade business, Yamauchi had had his sights set on the American videogame market. *Donkey Kong*, its arcade successors, and the Game & Watch were strong starts, but in America, Nintendo was still a minor Japanese player with a "weird foreign name." In a reversal of their aborted negotiations with Coleco, Nintendo decided to license the Famicom to a U.S. partner—one who ironically had their own weird foreign name.

In April 1983, Atari executives flew to Kyoto to inspect demo versions of *Donkey Kong Jr.* and *Popeye* running on prototype hardware.[22] According to Atari's Don Teiser, Nintendo's machine ran the arcade ports with "only minor display glitches."[23] Teiser's memo indicated Atari's interest in the console along with, true to form, a sizable list of President Yamauchi's stipulations (e.g., a minimum two million console order, Atari's limited access to Nintendo's hardware specifications, etc.). But the memo also indicated that he and the other executives present were withholding their true intentions from Nintendo. Atari was shopping for a successor to the aging VCS and its disastrous follow-up, the Atari 5200. While they openly courted Nintendo, internally they were weighing a competing prototype, codenamed MARIA, developed by General Computer Company in Cambridge, MA. This alternative looked to be the "superior machine," according to the memo, but uncertainty regarding the chip's large-scale manufacturing costs kept Atari in talks with Nintendo. In short, they were purposely delaying their decision so they could pick the better machine.

Once again, an international partnership was not meant to be. Although Atari ultimately opted to use MARIA in the Atari 7800 (due in part to Nintendo's impatience with Atari's waffling), grander mitigating circumstances intervened on Nintendo's behalf. By the end of 1983, the U.S. videogame industry collapsed catastrophically (chapter 3). Had Nintendo partnered with Atari, the U.S. Famicom would have likely been collateral damage. Even the promising ColecoVision was among the casualties. Thanks to an economic twist of fate, Nintendo would have to forge ahead alone.

Red, White, and Gold

Readers unfamiliar with the Family Computer might be surprised by its size: it measures 22cm long, 15cm wide, 6cm deep, and weighs approximately 620g. Its curious profile looks more like the torso of a plastic robot than a powerful computing platform. In short, the Famicom looks nothing like the personal computers with which it shared a name.

Nintendo's early consoles—all simple variations of tennis, tabletop, racing, and brick-breaking games—had already experimented with novel, colorful designs. The deep oranges, reds, and yellows of the Color TV series were far afield from the faux wood-paneled furniture style of U.S. consoles, thanks in part to the influence of a young designer named Shigeru Miyamoto. The cherubic Miyamoto is now one of Nintendo's most prominent representatives, widely hailed as one of the greatest innovators in videogame history. He has designed, produced, or directed the lion's share of Nintendo's most prized franchises, from *Donkey Kong* and *Super Mario Bros.* to *Nintendogs* and *Pikmin*. But prior to Miyamoto's industry ascension, he worked as an industrial artist. His first jobs at Nintendo included designs for mahjong labels, playing card stencils (*hanafuda*, or Japanese playing cards, were Nintendo's original gaming industry), arcade cabinet exteriors, and the 1979 console all-in-one Color TV Game Block Breaker (カラーテレビゲームブロック崩し).[24] Miyamoto brought a playful sensibility to his industrial designs, emphasizing simplicity, accessibility, and fun. The bold colors and compact form factors of Nintendo's earlier consoles would carry over to the Family Computer.

While Miyamoto was not directly involved with the Famicom's external design, Uemura was, and the latter established a list of specification guidelines to help shape the console's look. These included the necessity of two controllers, the ability to store them on the console (another legacy of the Color TV consoles), the number of controller buttons, the various ports and power connectors, and the desire to have the cartridge dimensions "be about the same as an analog cassette tape." Curiously, in spite of the console's name, Uemura wanted the Famicom to look like neither a computer nor a toy, but something wholly different.[25] Ricoh's designers concurred. The console should not be judged on looks alone:

> If the system's exterior resembled an audio device, for example, consumers would make judgments on the product's price and value based on preconceptions. [Ricoh] instructed the team to design the exterior in such a way that people wouldn't be able to make snap judgments about it.[26]

While Uemura later admitted that he had failed to realize his design goals, there is no question that the final console stands out from its consumer electronics peers. The Famicom body is replete with ridges and angles. Numerous recessed surfaces, buttons, levers, hinges, and vents combine to form a unique plastic topography (figure 1.1).

The front of the console slopes forward slightly to display a slender aluminum plate printed with the console's name (in English) and the Nintendo logo. Behind the angled surface there are three mechanical switches: reset, power on/off, and a large slider to help children lever the cartridges out of the console's interior.[27] Cartridges are inserted vertically into a narrow slot behind the lever. Since the slot exposes the cartridge card edge connector (and the console's interior), a hinged plastic flap covers the hole when no game is present. Again, Uemura hoped to match the cartridges' dimensions with cassettes so they could be stored in standard tape cases. Cartridges' affinity with cassettes had an important cultural and marketing resonance, due to the recent worldwide success of

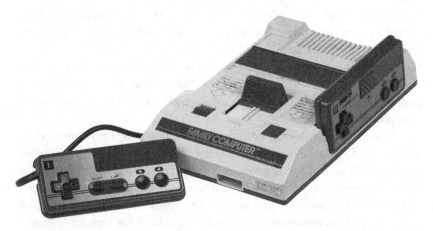

1.1 The Nintendo Family Computer. (Source: Evan Amos, Wikimedia Commons)

Sony's Walkman, which introduced the compact, high-technology Japanese aesthetic to much of the world.[28] "Cassettes" were already a common moniker for game cartridges in Japan, and Nintendo wanted to maintain that material affinity for their software.[29]

As Uemura's guidelines specified, the sides of the Famicom have recessed edges cut to house the console's wired controllers. Both controllers are rounded along the edges but have an additional raised molding around their perimeters that allow them to nest within their respective cradles without falling out. Cords emerge from the controllers on either side—from the upper left on controller I, upper right from controller II—rather than the top. Though the placement looks sleek when the controllers are stored, as there are no cords sprouting from the top, it makes the controllers awkward to hold, since the cords emerge where the hand naturally grips the joypad.

The sole feature of an otherwise barren front edge—a 15-pin expansion port—is evidence of the Famicom's future-proof design.[30] Yamauchi originally requested that the Famicom support a number of computer peripherals, including a cassette storage drive, a keyboard, and a modem, but eventually told his engineers to nix these add-ons in the interest of cost reduction. Furthermore, fewer peripherals made the Family Computer appear less intimidating to new users.[31] Nonetheless, Nintendo had the forethought to leave the expansion port. And indeed, as the Famicom gained popularity, the peripherals excluded from its initial launch were eventually added both by Nintendo and third-party manufacturers. The expansion port would support keyboards, all manner of controllers and joysticks, light guns, 3D glasses, an inflatable motorcycle and punching bag, a drawing tablet, a karaoke microphone, and even a modem.[32]

The Famicom's final distinguishing trademark is its color. While the bulk of its body is white, the switches, logo plate, cartridge slot cover, expansion port plug, controllers, and bottom plate are all painted a rich maroon.[33] The controllers feature two additional accent colors: each of the buttons, their labels, and two thin horizontal decorative lines are painted black and surrounded by a brushed gold face place. The red, white, and gold triumvirate is as iconic in Japan as the gray, black, and red of the NES are in the U.S. and Europe.[34]

Close Playing

The physical forms of computational devices, from mobile phones to room-size server racks, are not benign; they participate in and structure social, personal, cultural, and economic spaces. Upright arcade cabinets, for instance, were played while standing. Their form facilitated fluid movement between machines—players were meant to insert a quarter, play for a short period of time, then move along to the next game. Screens were commonly angled backward to allow players to lean into the cabinet, shielding them from any exterior distractions. If players sat at upright cabinets, they perched on high stools, the common furniture of the pubs and taverns that initially hosted such machines. Cocktail arcade cabinets likewise reflected their social milieu. Their flat, squared surfaces and low profiles resembled tables. Players sat on either side of the machine and looked down at the monitor, which was mounted with the screen facing the ceiling. Unlike the sheltering hood of upright cabinets, cocktail cabinets encouraged social play. Accordingly, cocktail games were commonly programmed either for cooperative play or to rotate between multiple competitors in turns. Players could sit comfortably, rest their drinks on the plexiglass tabletop, and enjoy a videogame together.

When videogames moved into the home, consumers had to be taught how, where, and with whom to play them. In single-television homes, the TV was usually located in the living room, where it could be shared by the family. Since the videogame console required a television, it resided there too. The earliest home consoles featured simple variations on the ball-and-paddle play pioneered by *Tennis for Two*, *Pong*, *Breakout*, and their imitators. Due to both limited technology (i.e., programming a capable artificial opponent) and their arcade heritage, these games normally required two players. The living room, already a site of family gathering, was conducive to social play.

Early commercials for the Magnavox Odyssey, Fairchild Channel F, Coleco Telstar, and other contemporary consoles showed variations on the same themes: this is how the console connects to the television, this is how you select or insert different games, this is how you hold the joystick or paddle, this is how you and your friends and family gather around the television to play.[35] None of these practices were taken for granted. The instructions for play, including the arrangement of bodies and machines, were built into videogame advertisements, manuals, and even product packaging.

The Family Computer, as its name implied, was a console designed for domestic spaces. Two people playing simultaneously were close to both one another and the console, since the wired controllers kept players in close proximity.[36] Smaller televisions and shorter cables meant that videogames were played close to the screen—an ideal spatial configuration for most Japanese homes, which tended to be much smaller than their American counterparts. But in spite of its name, the Famicom was designed to rest on the floor, a table, or a low shelf. PCs in the 1980s comprised several bulky components: a monitor, a case to house the internal processors and memory, a keyboard, disk drive, etc. Computers took up a lot of space. A desktop and chair were best suited for both the size of the machines and long-term computer use, especially typing. The linguistic legacy of the "desktop computer" and the metaphor of the desktop as the default state of the graphical operating system indicate as much.

Had the Famicom ended up looking more like a conventional PC as originally planned, it would have been better suited to the "vertical" orientation of desks and chairs. Uemura considered such a configuration, but he soon realized that most players would not want to use their consoles on desks. A "horizontal" orientation better suited the tastes of Japanese consumers, whom he thought "would probably be lying on the floor or snuggled up inside the *kotatsu* (a foot warmer with a quilt over it) when they played, not sitting in front of a solid, stable desk."[37] Uemura's conclusion seems obvious now, but home videogames in the 1980s were still novel enough that their position in domestic and social space was not yet codified.

In the early 1980s, Japanese consumers were still acclimating to computers' presence in the home, so any added sense of familiarity could ease a product's introduction. The Family Computer joypad was new compared to competitors' controllers, but it was a recognizable interface for the millions of people who had played Nintendo's Game & Watch, the aptly named portable that packed an electronic game, clock, and alarm into a compact handheld enclosure.

Though Game & Watch titles resembled videogames, their simple circuits generated no video signal. Instead, segmented liquid crystal displays, identical to those used in calculators, blinked on and off to produce simple animations. In Nintendo's first Game & Watch title *Ball* (1980), a cartoon man attempted to juggle several balls simultaneously. The man's body, arms, and each individual position of the balls' three possible arcs were LCD segments that could be "lit" to create motion. In a 2010 interview with Satoru Iwata, Game & Watch developer Takehiro Izushi described how calculator circuits could process eight digits with seven segments apiece, so games like *Ball* were limited to those fifty-six segments, plus a few ancillary segments reserved for "decimal points and symbols like the minus sign."[38] The engineering and design innovation was appropriating these segments for use as game objects rather than a calculator's numeric display.

Adhering to the constraints of a calculator LCD created unique design obstacles. As discrete segments, object animations could not deviate beyond their fixed course, nor could they overlap. Since only one segment object could occupy a given portion of the screen, even when unlit, animation was jerky. LCD graphics were thus more akin to the grid of bulbs used to animate sports stadium displays or traffic signs than a console video processor.

Nonetheless, Nintendo devised a remarkable number of gameplay variations from such a restrained palette. Early games like *Octopus* (1981) were based around straightforward objectives like sneaking past an octopus' coiling tentacles to retrieve a treasure chest. As the platform matured, the games grew in complexity, culminating in streamlined conversions of Nintendo's arcade and console games, such as *Donkey Kong* (1982), *Mario Bros.* (1983), and *The Legend of Zelda* (1989). To increase the range of gameplay options, Nintendo added graphics overlays and enlarged the Game & Watch to house two screens (figure 1.2).[39]

Gunpei Yokoi, Nintendo's head of R&D1, led the development of both the Game & Watch concept and its hardware. Yokoi had been a mainstay of Nintendo's games division since he first designed the *Ultra*

1.2 The lower screen of the Game & Watch Multi Screen *Donkey Kong* handheld, the first Nintendo product to feature the "Plus" Button. In its startup state (pictured), one can see the entire spectrum of LCD segments lit simultaneously.

Hand (1966),[40] a collapsible plastic lattice with handles at one end and a pair of rubber cups at the other, meant for grasping small objects. The clever mechanical device, handpicked for production by President Yamauchi, was a big hit for Nintendo, resulting in Yokoi's promotion from maintenance man to toy designer. During his tenure at pre-Famicom Nintendo, Yokoi invented many inspired gadgets: the *Ultra Machine* (1967), an automatic baseball pitching mechanism; an electric *Love Tester* (1969); the *Light Telephone* (1971), a short-range walkie-talkie using photo cells; the *Custom Lion* (1976) light gun target shooting game; the *Chiritorie* (1979), a radio-controlled mini-vacuum; and the mechanical puzzle *Ten Billion* (1980).[41]

Yokoi was instrumental to Nintendo's success, not only due to his inventiveness, but also his influential approach to product design. In a series of interviews published in Japan in 1997, Yokoi articulated his design philosophy as 枯れた技術の水平思考, which translates to English clumsily as "lateral thinking for withered technology."[42] In English, "lateral thinking" denotes a creative, unexpected approach to problem solving, a strategy Yokoi applied to outdated, inexpensive, or otherwise "off-the-shelf" technology. Yokoi famously devised the Game & Watch concept after noticing a train commuter whiling away the time on his pocket calculator.[43] If a simple calculator could engross the man, why not a pocket-sized videogame?

In the 1970s and 1980s portable calculators were a consumer electronics sensation, especially in Japan. In 1972, the so-called "Calculator Wars" were sparked by tremendous sales—over one million in its first ten months—of the Casio Mini, a low-cost, ultra-thin calculator. What was formerly a vestige of Japanese office culture transformed into a mainstream computing device and catalyzed Japanese manufacturers' investments in electronics miniaturization, liquid crystal displays, and solar cells.[44] Though nearly sixty companies entered the war, eventually two main competitors—Sharp and Casio—battled at the front lines. And the stakes were high. According to Johnstone, "By 1980, annual production of calculators topped 120 million units, with the Japanese accounting for just under half the total."[45] Sharp and Casio sparred for a decade, introducing progressively cheaper and smaller models, until Casio struck the death blow in 1983 with a solar-powered calculator measuring 0.8mm thick.[46]

By the time Yokoi saw the salaryman absorbed in his pocket calculator, LCDs and miniaturized ICs were cost-effective enough to use for an affordable handheld gaming system. And though segmented displays were originally devised for displaying ten digits and a few mathematical symbols, they could be creatively repurposed to animate rudimentary game graphics.

Plus Controller

Nintendo has consistently shown an ability to mine engaging games and hardware from obsolete and outdated technologies: *Donkey Kong* arcade units were reworked versions of unsold *Radar Scope* boards (chapter 2); the clunky 3D of the Virtual Boy resurfaced in the Nintendo 3DS; the everyman Mario has worked in professions ranging from doctor to chef; the mechanical *Duck Hunt* rifle resurfaced as the Famicom light gun game *Duck Hunt*; and the gripping cups of the *Ultra Hand* are echoed in the grasping arms of the Robotic Operating Buddy (chapter 3). Unsurprisingly, Yokoi had a hand in each of these projects.[47]

An iconic element of the Famicom controller was a similarly repurposed innovation. Yokoi first devised the "plus controller," as it was originally known, for the Game & Watch conversion of *Donkey Kong* (figure 1.2). The gameplay of many Game & Watch titles took place on a single horizontal axis and thereby required only two buttons for control. In *Ball*, for instance, the player could press a "<LEFT" or "RIGHT>" button, each on its respective side of the handheld, to move the juggler's hands into position. In instances where gameplay required an extended range of motion, the buttons multiplied. In *Egg* (1981), for instance, two stacked pairs of buttons on either side controlled four possible diagonal positions of the wolf's arms. In fact, nearly all Game & Watch titles prior to *Donkey Kong* used four buttons for diagonal movements rather than conventional cardinal directions.[48]

However, arcade *Donkey Kong*'s run-and-jump gameplay required movement along both axes. Jumpman, the proto-Mario character, ran along girders, climbed ladders, and jumped pits and obstacles. To replicate this movement on the Game & Watch, the handheld would have needed five individual buttons—four for directional movement and one for jumping. To prevent uncomfortable button crowding while still accommodating the handheld's small footprint, Yokoi devised a novel control solution for a novel game.

Early console controllers derived from arcade controls, adopting some variation of joystick, paddle, or keypad to varying degrees of success. Atari's iconic VCS joystick, for instance, was ergonomic and easy to use, but its single button foreclosed input complexity of its games. The Intellivision and ColecoVision erred in favor of more buttons, but ended up with intimidating, overwrought controllers that looked more like calculators or remote controls than joysticks. The problem facing all home console manufacturers was that arcade hardware had more leeway in controller design. Since arcade hardware catered to the needs of a single game, their control interface could be built to suit: *Tapper*'s (1983) controller was a beer tap; *Crystal Castles* (1983) provided an embedded track ball to navigate its axonometric architecture; *Super Off Road* (1989) used three conjoined steering wheels and accompanying accelerator pedals; *Skydiver* (1978) featured parachute ripcords as controllers. Home consoles, in contrast, had to sacrifice specialization in favor of generic designs that could accommodate a range of genres. When conventional joysticks were insufficient, publishers provided specialized controllers: wheels, gloves, guns, goggles, microphones, and even balance boards.

Yokoi's "plus" controller, nicknamed after the mathematical symbol it resembles, was an elegant solution that suited both manufacturing and gameplay needs. The flat directional pad took up little space on the handheld, fit comfortably in slim spaces without risk of breaking, provided easy access to all four cardinal directions with a single thumb press, and, most importantly, mapped logically to the two-dimensional spaces presented onscreen.

Uemura initially experimented with disassembled arcade joysticks while prototyping the Famicom's gamepad, but he worried that the joystick would be difficult to fix in place sturdily, break underfoot, or injure children if stepped on. Fortunately, R&D1 member Takao Sawano suggested that they transplant the Game & Watch directional pad.[49] When the rest of the team balked at the idea, Sawano "pulled a lead line out of a Game & Watch and connected it to a Famicom prototype, then invited the development staff to give it a try."[50] Once the team felt the plus controller's responsiveness, they decided to transplant it to the Famicom gamepad, albeit in a slightly larger size.

↑, ↓, ←, →, B, A, Select, Start

Unlike most home consoles, the Family Computer's supplied controllers were not a matched pair. The leftmost Controller I included, from left to right: plus pad, Select, Start, B, and A. Controller II, however, omitted the Select and Start buttons in favor of a late Uemura addition: a tiny microphone and a volume slider. Though the microphone input translated to a simple binary signal internally, meaning that the system could neither interpret pitch nor record audio, it did have a connecting line to the Famicom's audio output, allowing sound to pass through to the television speaker. In a nod to Japan's karaoke craze, Uemura was convinced that players would be entertained "simply by hearing their own voices come out of the television set."[51] Developers apparently were not as entertained, since the microphone saw little use in games.[52] As a result, Nintendo cut the microphone from both a later Famicom revision and the Nintendo Entertainment System.

The asymmetrical controller arrangement, besides further stymying home repairs by making the gamepads non-interchangeable, also meant that player one always controlled menu navigation and pausing—functions conventionally reserved for the Select and Start buttons. This apparently minor detail had interesting ramifications for social play. In Japan, for instance, *Super Mario Bros.* players practiced a technique known as the "Start Kill."[53] When player two, controlling Luigi, would leap over a gap, player one would pause the game mid-jump. Once play resumed, player 2, unable to re-acclimate to their original trajectory, would fall to their death—an early instance of what is now known as "griefing" among videogame players.[54]

The Famicom controllers were also gently rounded on the edges and sized to fit comfortably in a child's hands. Their design allowed easy access to every button with two thumbs—the left drove the plus and Select buttons, while the right bounced between A, B, and Start—leaving the remaining fingers free to grip the controller securely. One of Uemura's stated design goals was to make the controller easy to use while looking at the screen.[55] Though this goal seems commonsense now, designing a controller that could effectively bridge the perceptual divide between hand and eye was a meaningful engineering problem. Arcade cabinets and handheld videogames had their controls and monitor embedded in the same physical housing. Increasing the distance between screen and input device demanded that players develop tactile mastery of the controls in order to keep their eyes fixed to the screen.

As controllers have become more complex, multiplying buttons, joysticks, bumpers, and triggers many times over, this input/output divide has grown more significant. New players unaccustomed to the evolution of controller design face a steep barrier to play. Diverting one's eyes to hunt for a button can spell disaster in a fast-paced, reflex-based videogame. The inherent learning curve required by complex modern controllers partly explains the appeal of simplified and/or integrated control schemes seen in mobile touchscreen devices, the Nintendo Wii, and Xbox Kinect.

By striking a balance between too few and too many buttons, Nintendo designed a controller that favored tactile control and gameplay complexity without alienating new players. But if the Family Computer was meant primarily for arcade ports, why did its controllers stray beyond the plus pad and an action button? Partly we can credit Nintendo's engineering foresight. If the Famicom turned out to be a success, designers would want enough input leeway to represent the vast range of computer game genres. Limiting input to a single button would impose a challenging design restriction.

But there was also a computational reason behind the controller's button arrangement. The Famicom/NES was a member of the so-called "8-bit generation" of videogames, alongside the Sega Master System, Atari 7800, et al. The n-bit designator, while often used misleadingly in the history of videogame marketing,[56] tells us a lot about a console's computing capabilities. Computers make calculations using binary arithmetic, a numerical abstraction meant to mirror the physical states of semiconductor gates, which can either be open or closed. In other words, a computer can only count using two digits: 0 and 1. The 8 in 8-bit refers to the range of possible values the console's CPU can process. Binary is as a base 2 numeral system, so an 8-bit CPU can represent $2^8 = 256$ possible values, or the numbers between %00000000 and %11111111.[57]

However, the eight individual bits comprising a *byte* do not necessarily have to represent numbers. In programming, bits are equally useful as "flags" that signal the current state of a given computational object. But what do binary math and bit flags have to do with the Famicom controller? Consider the range of possible inputs that the controller allows: up, down, left, right, B, A, Select, and Start—eight distinct inputs that may be either pressed or not pressed. The state of the Famicom gamepad at any given time thus fits conveniently in a single byte, making the controller truly 8-bit—both chronologically and computationally.

Scraped to the Die

Removing the Famicom's plastic exterior reveals a dense arrangement of electronic components and integrated circuits packed onto a diminutive PCB.[58] The two most prominent ICs are the Ricoh RP2A03G,[59] which contains both the Central Processing Unit (CPU) and the Audio Processing Unit (APU) in a single package, and the Ricoh RP2C02G, which contains the Picture Processing Unit (PPU), the processor responsible for translating graphical data into video signals that display onscreen. These three processors form the core of the Famicom, handling all of its computational, audio, and graphical tasks.

The 2A03 CPU is not a custom die, but a modified version of the MOS Technology 6502, an 8-bit CPU whose introduction in 1975 transformed the microprocessor market. It was powerful, straightforward to program, and several magnitudes cheaper than its closest competitor—a combination of features that made it overwhelmingly attractive to PC and videogame manufacturers looking to introduce affordable computers to a mass market. Throughout the 1970s and 80s, Atari, Commodore, Apple, and Nintendo all launched successful platforms based on the 6502 architecture. [60]

MOS Technology did not directly manufacture the Famicom CPU. Instead, Ricoh, a "second source" manufacturer, licensed the rights to produce and sell the 6502. And, as its model name suggests, the 2A03 was not simply a stock 6502. In custom microprocessor production, clients routinely cut features in order to reduce individual chip costs. For their VCS, for example, Atari used a 6502 variant dubbed the 6507, a streamlined package that reduced addressable memory to 8KB and eliminated interrupts. With several years' hindsight on their side, Nintendo opted for less drastic revisions. The 2A03's sole subtraction from the stock 6502 was its binary coded decimal mode, or BCD;[61] the most significant addition was the onboard APU (chapter 7).

In 1976, North American corporation Commodore acquired MOS Technology and entered the U.S. PC market with gusto, leveraging their ownership of the inexpensive chip to undercut competitors' prices. CEO Jack Tramiel, whose domestic business interests had been stymied several times by Japanese competitors in the past, aimed to blockade an "invasion" of the U.S. PC and videogame markets after his own unsuccessful challenge of the MSX PC standard in Japan. Despite being a cheaper and technologically superior machine, the Commodore 64 could not compete against MSX's domestic groundswell of third-party support (ironically spearheaded in part by U.S. rival Microsoft).[62] Tramiel decided that if Commodore could not break into the Japanese market, they would retreat and shore up the competitive borders at home instead.

Tramiel's opposition, fueled equally by post-World War II xenophobia and competitive sour grapes, could have caused significant problems for Nintendo. Had Commodore known that Nintendo planned to bring the Famicom to the U.S. in 1985, they might have rejected the 6502 license or inflated the manufacturing price. By working domestically with Ricoh, Nintendo apparently stayed off Commodore's radar, much to the latter's eventual chagrin. After the Famicom's stateside release as the NES (chapter 3), Commodore's engineers were convinced that Nintendo had illegally skirted their microprocessor patents. As Brian Bagnall reports, it took a bit of reverse-engineering to discover Nintendo's "modifications":

[Commodore 64 programmer] Robert Russell investigated the NES, along with one of the original 6502 engineers, Will Mathis. "I remember we had the chip designer of the 6502," recalls Russell. "He scraped the [NES] chip down to the die and took pictures."

The excavation amazed Russell. "The Nintendo core processor was a 6502 designed with the patented technology scraped off," says Russell. "We actually skimmed off the top of the chip inside of it to see what it was, and it was exactly a 6502. We looked at where we had the patents and they had gone in and deleted the circuitry where our patents were."

Although there were changes, the NES microprocessor ran 99% of the 6502 instruction set. "Some things didn't work quite right or took extra cycles," says Russell. [...]

The tenacity of the Japanese was obviously formidable. Russell offers an opinion on why the Japanese elected not to purchase chips from North American sources. "They looked at the patents and realized that we weren't going to let them come over and sell against us," he says.[63]

Ed Logg, veteran arcade programmer for Atari, made a similar observation while working on the ill-fated Tengen port of *Tetris*. Asked about the ease of coding for the NES, he said:

Yeah, it was pretty similar...well, [Nintendo] basically used our patents. They violated Atari's patent while they were suing us, so it was the basic same scrolling algorithm and such. So it was pretty much identical to what we were dealing with. Most of the difficulty came from figuring out what registers and bits did what, and when.[64]

In either case, their discoveries were too late. By the time Russell, Mathis, and Logg could take a close look at its silicon, the NES had already arrived.

Recent reverse-engineering work by the Visual6502 project revealed that Russell's observations were correct.[65] MOS Technology's 1976 patent for their integrated circuit microprocessor specifically covered its ability to "provide decimal results" using a single binary adder, "thus significantly improving the speed of operation without suffering the cost of an additional decimal adder."[66] MOS's innovation saved cycles and manufacturing costs. To avoid either patent infringement or licensing costs, decimal mode had to be excised. However, Nintendo/Ricoh did not fabricate a new chip design based on the 6502—a costly, time-consuming process—nor even remove the circuitry that drove decimal mode. Instead, they made changes "only to the polysilicon mask" by "removing 5 transistors,"[67] disabling decimal mode rather than removing it.[68] In other words, Nintendo physically cut away any patent-infringing functions.

Atari's and Commodore's suspicions of hardware malfeasance were justified, but there is no evidence that Nintendo was trying to clone either company's systems. If anyone had the right to cry foul over intellectual property rights, it was Coleco. Despite their ultimate choice to forgo their Coleco partnership and source an alternative CPU, Nintendo's engineers clearly drew inspiration from the ColecoVision's video display processor (VDP) design. The ColecoVision's TMS9918 VDP (also used in MSX PCs) had several key features that resurfaced in the Famicom PPU: variable sprite size selection, a sprite overflow flag, an interrupt flag, and a special "coincidence flag" that could trigger on sprite collision.[69] Even more convincing were the similarities in graphic processor terminology. The ColecoVision's Pattern Name Tables, Sprite Attribute Table, and Pattern Generator Table resurfaced, with similar functions, as name tables, object attribute memory, and pattern tables in the Famicom. In contrast, beyond general terminology like sprites or VRAM, the Commodore 64's VIC-II VDP shared no such affinities with the Famicom PPU. And the Atari VCS's TIA was a wholly different beast, requiring more explicit coordination with the scanning electron beam than either the Famicom's or C64's graphics processors.[70]

While CPUs are crucial to a console's function, they have an indirect relationship to graphics rendering. When today's videogame players reference the 8-bit style of Famicom and NES games, they are mistakenly crediting central processing with picture processing. It is the PPU that, more than any other component, defines the Famicom's distinctive visual qualities. Nintendo and Ricoh may have made questionable ethical choices while engineering the Famicom, but accusations that the console is a direct theft or clone of prior systems discredits the PPU's (and APU's) crucial contributions to the Famicom's look and sound. Thanks to unlike VDPs, the Famicom, Commodore 64, and Atari VCS are fundamentally different machines. The ColecoVision is the Famicom's true elder sibling, related by looks despite not sharing the same brains.

Mario Tennis

Concealed within their cartridge shells, nearly all Famicom PCBs hold at least two ROM (read-only memory) packages. The first—PRG-ROM—stores the program code, the set of instructions that tell the CPU how and when to execute. The other—CHR-ROM—stores the character tile

1.3 The (inverted) PCB for Family Computer title *Nuts & Milk* features one of the simplest cartridge IC layouts. The 16KB PRG-ROM IC is on the left and the 8KB CHR-ROM IC is on the right. The traces labeled H and V also indicate the game's mirroring setting. (Source: bootgod, NES Cart Database)

patterns the PPU uses to populate the screen with graphics (figure 1.3).[71] In concert, these two ROMs contain the necessary raw materials to form a videogame.

The 6502 has a 16-bit *address bus*, meaning that it can access up to 64KB of memory.[72] However, the address bus size does not make the Famicom a 16-bit machine, since the 2A03's 8-bit *data bus* must construct and convey addresses one byte at a time. The address space is arranged in a specific, unchanging order, commonly called a *memory map*. The memory map is similar to a geographic map, charting the precise locations of inlets and outlets that give the programmer access to all of the console's functions—storage, graphics, audio, controllers, etc. The first 2KB of the CPU's memory map, for instance, are dedicated to the Famicom's internal RAM. Any data that is written to or read from RAM must be accessed through those specific addresses.

Early dedicated consoles either had hardwired game logic, as in *Pong*, or used interchangeable PCBs to reroute internal circuitry, allowing the player to electronically select from a small library of built-in games, as in the Magnavox Odyssey. When the Fairchild Channel F introduced removable ROM cartridges in 1976, the design space for videogames changed radically. Videogame hardware was no longer a closed system, but a proper platform, supporting a host of interchangeable software rather than a handful of games decided in advance by the console's manufacturer.

Relying on cartridges as a game-delivery medium means that a portion of the Famicom's CPU memory map—the final 32KB—is reserved for PRG-ROM. This type of architectural division is fundamental to how a cartridge-based system works. Without a cart inserted, the holistic network necessary to orchestrate a game's code and graphics is incomplete. By offloading the source code and graphics patterns to separate ROM chips, Nintendo left the decisions of how the CPU and PPU would be used up to the programmer. The Famicom has no built-in BIOS or character set, no default software constraints on the look or style of its games.

But there is another important split at work, as the 2A03 reserves none of its memory map for character data. Instead, CHR-ROM is routed to the PPU's address space. Unlike the CPU, the PPU has a 14-bit address bus, so it can access only 16KB of memory, all of which is dedicated to the PPU's various palettes and "tables"—Nintendo's technical nomenclature for the memory locations that hold graphical data. The 8KB of CHR-ROM resident in-cartridge are called *pattern tables*, as they contain the 8x8- or 8x16-pixel patterns that comprise graphics tiles. The remaining 8KB are mapped to *name tables*, *attribute tables*, palette indices, and their respective mirrors.[73]

If we look closely at the PCB in figure 1.3, we see that each IC's traces are sequestered, subdividing the board's sixty pins into roughly equivalent halves. The physical substrate illustrates in silicon the division of labor that takes place when a Famicom cartridge is in play: the CPU executes the program code while the PPU fetches the pattern tables for display. So while the CPU may instruct the PPU to move a tile, update a sprite palette, or cease rendering, it has no direct access to the tile data nor the graphics onscreen. The cartridge's distinct "split architecture" mirrors the Famicom's internal computational division.

Another way to illustrate this point is to execute a decades-old Famicom hardware technique that I call the "cart swap trick."[74] After *Super Mario Bros.*'s release in 1985, Japanese players discovered that they could pause the game, carefully remove the cartridge, insert a *Tennis* cartridge, reset, play a few points, pause, swap back to *Super Mario Bros.*, reset, then resume play by holding A while pressing Start at the title screen. Due to similarities in RAM layout between both games, performing this arcane hardware rite transported Mario to odd variations of the game's fabled "minus world" (chapter 4). However, the trick's result is not as important as the visual artifacts that occur during the interstitial periods when carts are being swapped.

The left image in figure 1.4 shows *Super Mario Bros.* directly before cartridge removal; the right image shows the same screen after the swap (but prior to reset).[75] The underlying tile layout is identical, but the constituent tiles have changed. If you are familiar with the graphics from both

1.4 The "cart swap trick" helps visualize the underlying memory structure of the Famicom and its cartridges. (Source: NES-101 capture)

games, you can see that Mario's body, for instance, is now composed of odd bits of a tennis player, while the pipes are built from fragments of net and court. The Mushroom Kingdom is rebuilt in the image of Wimbledon.

Removing a cartridge while the system is on halts the game, since the CPU can no longer execute instructions from the absent PRG-ROM, but the PPU continues to render graphics. With no CHR-ROM in place, one can actually watch the contents of the PPU dynamic RAM (DRAM) slowly decay as it "forgets" the tiles previously resident on-cart. Once another cartridge is inserted, the PPU dutifully substitutes the new character tiles in place of the old, populating our familiar mosaic with unfamiliar bodies.

The key point is that the 2A03 and 2C02 are independent components, each administering dedicated regions of internal memory. In the absence of new directions from the CPU, the PPU attends to its graphical tasks, fetching tiles and updating the screen until instructed to do otherwise. Dislodging cartridges mid-game has limited gameplay use, but it provides a lovely, albeit glitchy, window into the Famicom's hardware processes.

Patterns, Planes, and Palettes

The PPU divides its 16KB memory map—its Video RAM (VRAM)—into a series of related tables and palette indices, each contributing a crucial part of the data that comprises the tiles we see onscreen. But how are these tables related and what data do they contain?

The first 8KB, known as the pattern tables, are stored in CHR-ROM on the cartridge. Pattern tables contain the elements most recognizable as Famicom graphics, since they store the individual bits that define the 8x8- or 8x16-pixel mosaics we commonly call tiles. The PPU contains two pattern tables, each 4KB in size, which can hold 256 tiles apiece. Each pattern table is dedicated to either *sprites* or *background* tiles. Software emulators like FCEUX arrange the PPU's pattern tables into symmetrical grids that allow us to see the entire contents of CHR-ROM at a glance (figure 1.5).

Visually, sprite and background tiles are identical. In figure 1.5, the pattern tables are stacked side-by-side, divided by a thin center line, with sprites on the left and background tiles on the right. The choice of which tile type goes in which pattern table is up to the programmer, but each table contains either sprites or background tiles exclusively.

Whether sprite or background, each tile in the pattern table is described by sixteen bytes (or 128 bits) of memory. Those individual bits are divided into two 8-byte *bitplanes*, a matrix of binary values wherein

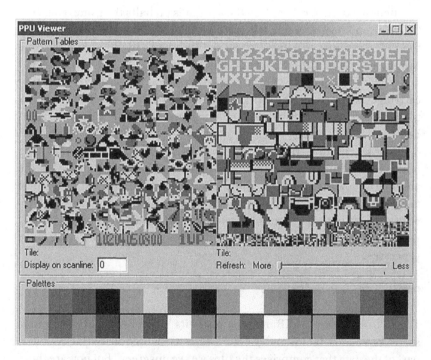

1.5 The contents of *Super Mario Bros.*'s CHR-ROM. Each pattern table contains 256 8x8 tiles. In *Super Mario Bros.*, pattern table 0 (left) contains sprites and pattern table 1 (right) contains background tiles. (Emulator: FCEUX 2.1.5)

each digit represents a single pixel of the final tile. Two bitplanes are necessary because tiles may access up to four colors, so two planes must be "stacked" atop one another to accommodate a 4-bit range of values.

If the Famicom only had four colors total, the two stacked bits from the pattern table bitplanes would be sufficient to describe any tile. However, the Famicom allocates thirty-two bytes of VRAM to eight individual palettes—half devoted to sprites and the other half to background tiles—containing four colors each.[76] In figure 1.5, the eight palettes defined in World 1-1 of *Super Mario Bros.* are arranged along the bottom edge of the PPU Viewer, each divided by a thick black line, with background palettes on top and sprite palettes on the bottom. Every sprite and background tile onscreen may select only one of its four allotted palettes at a time. However, the first (leftmost) color of each four-color block must be identical—shared across all palettes—limiting the PPU to rendering twenty-five individual colors onscreen simultaneously.[77]

In more modern videogame consoles, palette values encode RGB data, the combination of reds, greens, and blues blended to create a composite color. The Famicom, however, uses a hue saturation value (HSV) model based on the NTSC color wheel, which cycles approximately from blue to red to green to cyan.[78] Rather than a mixture profile, the byte stored for each palette slot is a lookup index for sixty-four possible HSV combinations.[79] However, several colors are duplicates (mostly in the black range) and one is technically beyond the NTSC's gamut range, reducing the NES's usable palette to approximately fifty-four colors.[80]

Though the shared color may seem like an arbitrary constraint, it is actually a clever means to "erase" portions of sprite tiles that are meant to be transparent. When a sprite is on top of a background tile, any color bit set to the shared color will permit the underlying background tile to show through. Mario's constituent sprites in *Super Mario Bros.*, for instance, use only three colors, drawn from the bottom left sprite palette seen in figure 1.5: red for his hat and overalls; a muted brown for his hair, eyes, sleeves, and boots; and olive for his skin and overall button. All other pixels in the Mario tiles are set to sky blue, but they render transparent, permitting the background to pass behind his body as he moves.

However, by rendering one color of every sprite palette transparent, each sprite tile is limited to only three colors. Again, in *Super Mario Bros.*, Mario is painted solely with olive, brown, and red; in *The Legend of Zelda*, Link is olive, brown, and lime green; in *Metroid*, Samus Aran is orange, red, and green. But observant Famicom players may notice that many game graphics appear to violate this rule. In *Mega Man 2*, for instance, Mega Man's head clearly uses more than three colors. The secret is sprite stacking. *Mega Man 2*'s programmers used a sprite with a separate palette for the whites of Mega Man's eyes, which sits atop the other sprites that comprise his head. Numerous games use this trick to boost their characters' color count, though it too has drawbacks, since only eight sprites may be visible on a single scanline and sixty-four onscreen simultaneously. Using an additional sprite for Mega Man's eyes sacrifices a slot from both.

Names and Mirrors

CHR-ROM's division into sprite and background tables is not arbitrary— each has a role to play onscreen according to its strengths and weaknesses. Sprites tiles may be positioned freely on the screen, even atop one another, but they sacrifice a color to transparency and face hard limits both on how many may appear in a row and how many may appear onscreen. Background tiles have access to one extra color and can fill the entire screen, but they "move" only via scrolling, may never overlap, and remain fixed to a rigid underlying grid.

That rigid grid is a 32x30 matrix of values known as a name table, a fancy technical name for the game's background layer. However, the name table is not an image stored in memory corresponding to the graphics we see onscreen. Rather, each byte of the name table stores the reference to the appropriate tile in the background pattern table. If the PPU had to store pattern and palette data for every tile of the background, the memory demands would quickly escalate. Referencing each tile by index reduces the memory overhead considerably, allowing background tiles to repeat in long stretches without duplicating each tile's memory "cost." The data is stored once in pattern table memory, then referenced by its pattern number for any subsequent uses.

Though tiles dominated the 8- and 16-bit generations, they were not the sole graphical format. The Atari VCS' Television Interface Adapter (TIA) had no notion of pixels or tiles. It built its playfields and objects scanline by scanline, slimming memory costs to a sliver of what the Famicom would later require, albeit at the expense of graphical fidelity and programmer sanity, since per-scanline rendering required exacting timing and careful code economy.[81] Vector-based graphical systems like those used in the *Asteroids* (1979) arcade cabinet, which also ran on a 6502, and the Vectrex home console (1982) used an electron beam that could draw lines between arbitrary points onscreen rather than being locked to a raster grid. While vector graphics were sharper and less geometrically-constrained than their bitmap counterparts, they also sacrificed the latter's nuances of shading and color, since the display was limited to monochrome line art. In each case, the choice of graphical displays was based on cost and design necessity, rather than a qualitative measure of which was "better" or "worse." For the Famicom's engineers, replicating their arcade games meant importing the same tile-based systems used in *Donkey Kong* and its kin.

Similarly, tile-based graphics were common in the early arcade and console era not because they were the only "natural" way to paint a screen, but because tiles were a particularly efficient means to store and display graphics data in low-memory architectures. For one, tiles eliminated significant graphical redundancy. The opening gameplay screen of *Super Mario Bros.*, for example, predominantly displays blue sky. To paint this sky, the PPU only has to reference one tile from the background pattern table and repeat it as needed. In a modern, "per-pixel" graphical processing unit, each individual pixel would need to be accounted for in memory. Even if we imagined a rudimentary black-and-white videogame that only needed to record whether each pixel was on or off (i.e., using one bit per pixel), accounting for each pixel would require hundreds, thousands, or millions of bits, depending on the resolution of the display. Adding even a handful of additional color possibilities increases the necessary memory by several magnitudes.

Today, that memory escalation makes a minimal impact on cost. 1MB of IC memory in 2014 costs roughly half a cent. But in 1983, that same amount cost approximately $2,000.[82] Nintendo had to use any means possible to keep costs low so their console would be affordable. Every spare byte of savings added up.

The name tables' memory architecture reflects those cost concerns. In the PPU memory map, Nintendo reserved 4KB for four name tables and their accompanying attribute tables. Excluding attribute data, each table was allotted 960 bytes—one byte for each tile reference drawn from the background pattern table. Since each name table comprises an entire screen, multiplying that area by four creates a graphical plane extending beyond the television's border. This is by design—the name tables are arranged contiguously in a 2x2 matrix that the PPU can smoothly track across via its dedicated scrolling registers. Hardware-level scrolling was a powerful feature in 1983, as most arcade and console games were designed for play on a single screen. Arcade titles like *Defender* (1980), *Rally-X* (1980), and *Scramble* (1981) had broken the one-plane barrier a few years earlier, but Nintendo's baked-in scrolling was remarkably forward-thinking for a home console.

Yet despite the four-screen name table layout, Nintendo only allocated 2KB of onboard RAM (technically CIRAM) to store name table data, meaning that only two background planes are unique—the remaining half are mirrors. These are not actual mirrors, reflecting a reverse image across a shared axis, but hardware-level data duplication that produces two identical pairs of name tables. According to how the cartridge is wired (figure 1.3), the name tables are set to either horizontal or vertical mirroring, as pictured below:[83]

```
Horizontal   Vertical
[ A ][ A ]   [ A ][ B ]
[ B ][ B ]   [ A ][ B ]
```

The mirroring setting had important repercussions for scrolling games. With horizontal mirroring set, a character pushing past the right edge of name table A would scroll the left edge of that same background plane into view, breaking the illusion of a seamless space. Pushing toward the bottom edge of name table A, in contrast, would scroll the top edge of B into view, connecting contiguous spaces more naturally. In other words—and somewhat counter-intuitively—horizontal mirroring was best suited for vertical scrolling, and vice-versa. And since mirroring had to be set in advance, developers typically had to settle on a single scrolling direction for the entire game.[84]

Edge Cases

The final component of the PPU's VRAM arsenal is one of the trickiest to grasp, but also one of the most important, since it sets the hard limit for color variety in the background layer. Again, directly following each name table in VRAM is a 64-byte attribute table. The attribute table is like a second grid superimposed atop each name table, grouping its 960 tiles into an 8x8 matrix of 32x32-pixel areas (excluding the final row, which is truncated by half).

The pattern table bitplanes described above contain only two bits of the necessary four to describe a tile's color. The pattern table bits select which of the four colors within a palette a tile will use, but not the individual palette from which those colors are selected. For background tiles, these final bits are supplied by the attribute table. Again, each attribute table has only sixty-four bytes of palette data to allocate to the entire name table, so each attribute byte defines the palette values for one 32x32-pixel area. And since each palette value requires two bits to use in conjunction with the pattern table bits, only four palette values may be assigned within that area. In other words, every 16x16-pixel unit of name table (i.e., 2x2 tiles) may use only one four-color palette.

Though blocking palettes into attribute groups saves hundreds of bytes of memory, it imposes noticeable limits on the shape and granularity of background objects. In general, background graphics are designed to align along attribute table boundaries, making the 2x2-tile square the architectural bedrock of Famicom games. Attentive designers were careful to craft landscapes conducive to square shapes, like the pipes and stairwells in *Super Mario Bros.* or the sharply-edged forests in *The Legend of Zelda.*[85]

Shapes defined by circular or diagonal edges risk so-called "attribute clashes," where the transition between borders of two attribute table entries creates abrupt shifts in color. *Snake Rattle N Roll*, for instance, uses an isometric perspective uncommon on the NES, making its faux three-dimensional terrain appear as if it is diagonal to the player's perspective. The off-axis background is graphically impressive but requires significant palette concessions, since none of the terrain aligns at right angles.

In figure 1.6, you can see obvious attribute clashes along terrain and object edges. The pyramid that abuts the vine-covered platform near the

1.6 A screenshot from *Snake Rattle N Roll* shows abrupt color changes across background attribute boundaries, especially among the pyramids and waterfalls. (Emulator: Macifom 0.16)

center of the screen, for instance, has a portion of its apex colored green to match the vines rather than the adjoining pyramids. Likewise, the tops and faces of waterfalls exhibit sharp transitions between shades of blue, while the gold mechanism near the lower right corner shifts abruptly to green near its base.

Avoiding attribute clashes required either careful planning near attribute boundaries or significant alterations to color and terrain structure. *Solstice* adopts the same isometric perspective as *Snake Rattle N Roll*, for instance, but limits its level palettes to variations of a single color. Doing so sacrifices the overall vibrancy of its levels, but avoids gaudy color mismatches and allows the character sprites to appear that much more vivid against the subdued backdrops. *Metroid* uses a standard side-scrolling view, but pays careful attention to palette choices, keeping radical color changes sequestered by area. Its Brinstar region has vibrant architectures of blue, green, and amber, but never in contiguous blocks. Palettes changes are instead marked by doors or tunnels, giving each area a distinctive visual style.

Since sprites float freely and tap separate palettes, they are often used in atypical ways to bolster the colors capabilities of background tiles. The most common use of this technique is seen in title screens and cutscenes, which require minimal object interactions or player control, freeing sprites to do color touch-up work. Since the title screen is the player's first impression of a game, it is regularly reserved for the game's most complex and detailed artwork.

In figure 1.7, *Contra*'s title screen is shown, via the FCEUX emulator, in three graphical "passes": the far left displays sprites only, the middle background tiles only, and the right the final composite. Without interleaving sprites for the hair, eyes, cigarette, and tank top, *Contra*'s designers would not have been able to create such smooth transitions between colors. They would have either had to reduce the overall color detail of the two characters, square off the character designs, or else leave distracting attribute clashes bordering curves. As we will see in later chapters, Famicom programmers regularly used background and sprite tiles against type. What we often expect to be background is composed of sprites, and vice-versa.

Sprite Adjectives

Similar to how active background tiles are arranged in the PPU's name tables, active sprites have a reserved address space known as Object Attribute Memory (OAM). OAM has slots for sixty-four sprites—the maximum

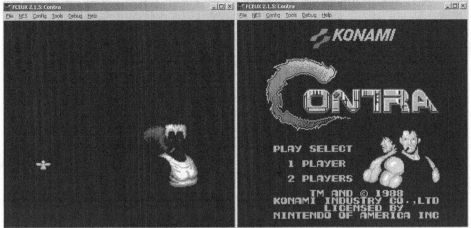

1.7 The *Contra* title screen uses combined sprite (left) and background tiles (middle) to draw more detailed and colorful character portraits (right). (Emulator: FCEUX 2.1.5)

count the PPU can render onscreen simultaneously—occupying 256 bytes of memory. OAM's byte count might seem like overkill considering it stores no actual pattern data, but sprites require more computational overhead to display than background tiles. This is why OAM is called "Object *Attribute* Memory" rather than "Object Memory." The visible sprites are not housed there; rather, OAM stores a *display list* of qualities for each active sprite.

Each sprite's display list is four bytes wide. In sum, the list identifies which sprite from the pattern table will display, its orientation (flipped horizontally or vertically), its priority (above or below background tiles), its screen coordinates, and which sprite palette it will select. Separating the sprites "nouns" (i.e., patterns) from their descriptive "adjectives" (i.e., OAM) is yet another means to mitigate hardware memory costs and eliminate unnecessary redundancy. Like the name tables, multiple OAM slots can reference the same sprite without the need to store multiple copies in pattern memory. This is especially useful in games where multiple objects of the same type display onscreen simultaneously. Furthermore, since there are far fewer sprites than name table tiles, each can access its own palette entry, giving sprites a color advantage over the attribute-bound background tiles.

In OAM, all sixty-four slots are filled at all times, whether with the sprites the programmer intends or with temporary junk data. In many games, especially early Famicom titles, most sprites were not needed onscreen at all times, yet those sprites had to have valid coordinates (i.e., OAM cannot contain a null value). In a pinch, sprites could be toggled on and off, but doing so was an all or nothing affair—sprites were either all visible or all invisible. To strike a compromise between extremes, programmers commonly used "safe areas" around the display's borders to tuck away unneeded objects.

The PPU addresses the screen like a Cartesian graph flipped along its x-axis, with the [0,0] coordinate at the upper left corner. Thus moving a sprite right and down increments its x- and y-coordinates, respectively; moving left and up decrements these coordinates. The key point is that there are no negative coordinates and therefore no means to push a tile past the leftmost and topmost screen borders. However, the Famicom/NES PPU, regardless of region, renders a 256x240 pixel display, while its sprite coordinate positions may contain any valid 8-bit value (i.e., $00-$FF or 0–255). Consequently, pushing a sprite's y-coordinate past $EF (239) hides that tile beyond the PPU's rendering scope.[86]

Misunderstanding OAM's sprite positioning and the PPU's screen perimeter can lead to peculiar graphical artifacts. A common initialization step in Famicom games involved "zeroing out" OAM by manually writing zeroes to all memory locations. Doing so assigned all visible sprites to the first pattern table entry ($00) and shifted their coordinate position to the upper left screen corner. With assurance that there was no unknown garbage data sitting in OAM, the programmer could then assign and position sprites as needed. Unfortunately, many programmers thought this also solved the problem of hiding unused sprites, since many televisions naturally clipped part of the visible frame with *overscan*.

Zeroing OAM is not an airtight sprite hiding technique, since overscan varies from screen to screen, especially in emulation.[87] And since the

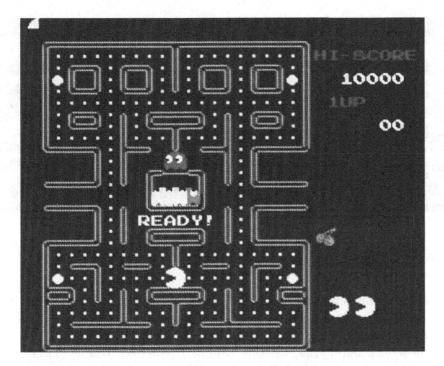

1.8 In Tengen's *Pac-Man*, the unused sprite stack is visible in the upper left corner of the screen. Note that in some emulators that simulate CRT overscan, this portion of the screen may be clipped. (NES-001 CRT capture)

PPU cannot render to negative coordinates, the sprite's upper left pixel nestles in the corner, while its remaining pixels "dangle" into positive coordinate space. Tengen's NES port of *Pac-Man*, for instance, has a conspicuous yellow sprite fragment floating above the upper left side of the maze (figure 1.8). Though the errant graphic appears to be a single tile, it is actually a stack of all OAM sprites not currently in play. To hide the stack properly, *Pac-Man*'s programmers should have pushed the vivisected sprites beyond the lower boundary of the screen rather than relying on overscan to mask their presence.

The lack of non-negative screen coordinates also creates problems for characters that must exit the leftmost screen edge smoothly. Especially in early single-screen arcade games where characters could wrap around edges, characters might find half of their body's sprites clipped at the left edge while emerging from the right. Figure 1.9 shows object coordinate limitations at work in the Famicom port of *Mario Bros*. Mario may approach the left border until his leftmost pixel touches the threshold,

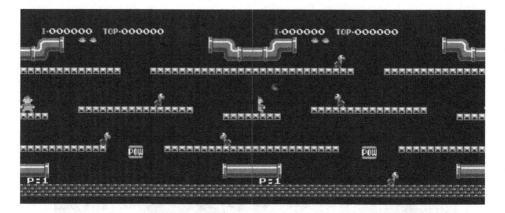

1.9 Without proper masking, single-screen games with wraparound spaces exhibit clipping errors when sprite-based characters approach the left edge of the screen. (Emulator: Nestopia v1.4.1)

but advancing any further chops his body in half. Due to the limits of 8-bit math, subtracting from o causes the sprite to wrap to the rightmost edge of the screen, causing Mario's left half to emerge on the opposite side of the screen. Mario's right half will continue to push toward the left border until its leftmost pixel reaches the threshold, at which point he will fully transition to the right side.

To compensate for such graphical anomalies, the PPU provides a special mask that will hide sprites, background tiles, or both in the screen's leftmost 8-pixel-wide column. When enabled, the mask creates a convincing curtain for sprites to slide behind as they cross the leftmost screen border. As the Famicom aged and single-screen arcade fare gave way to side-scrolling platformers and role-playing games, developers increasingly used this feature to mask scrolling updates and attribute clashes (chapter 6).

The key quality of the Famicom's graphics processor architecture is that no single memory location in VRAM contains the colorful mosaic of tiles we see onscreen. The bit patterns are stored in one location, the palettes in another, the tile positions in another, and palette assignments in yet another. Only at render time do these disparate bits of memory cohere into what we see as graphics. Sequestering data in this way might seem convoluted from a contemporary programmer's perspective, but in an era when memory was measured in hundreds, rather than millions, of bytes, split architectures made good economic sense. Reducing graphical redundancy reduced hardware costs, even if it meant extra legwork for the programmer and the processor. In the end, it doesn't matter if what the player perceives matches what the PPU perceives, so long as the tiles fall into place before the cathode ray sweeps the screen.

Low-Definition Television

Until the recent adoption of high-definition television (HDTV) standards, the dominant display technology of arcade and console videogames was the cathode ray tube (CRT). The CRT's namesake is similar to a vacuum tube—during manufacture, its interior oxygen is burnt away, creating a highly pressurized interior seal.[88] At one end of the tube is a barium-coated cathode that, when heated, emits negatively-charged electrons. Positively charged anodes attract, accelerate, and focus the electrons into a narrow beam. Together these components are known as an electron gun.

The portion of the tube opposite the cathode, which widens considerably to a large curved surface—the television screen—is coated with a luminescent phosphor material. When the electron gun fires at this coating, the phosphor's electrons momentarily become unstable then settle, emitting a photon at a wavelength that human eyes perceive as light.

A beam shot directly down the cathode tube generates a single illuminated point. In order to draw a complete image, the electron beam must be diverted in a predictable, consistent pattern. Along the exterior neck of the tube, magnetic coils deflect the beam's path using alternating voltages. Two electrical signals, each synced to a separate oscillator, play complementary roles in this process: one guides the beam horizontally, the other vertically. The electron gun draws the television image line by line, sweeping the beam left to right and top to bottom, much like a hand composes a letter, repositioning each time it reaches the right margin. Once the "page" is full, the gun resets to the upper-left corner to begin anew. This process repeats dozens of times per second, creating a persistent *raster* of scanlines that compose a moving television image.

Color television requires a more elaborate mechanism. The electron gun multiplies by three, each assigned to a single color: red, green, and blue. The three electron beams are deflected at slightly different angles by a small perforated plate called a *shadow mask*. Each beam then strikes a grouped array of phosphors, known as triads, that emits their assigned color. Television uses triads as additive primaries, meaning that the three colored light sources are blended to produce the desired hue.[89] When all three guns fire at once, for instance, the result is white, while a single gun may light green alone.

1.10 A macro-zoom photo of *The Legend of Zelda*'s key and bomb inventory showing the individual triads of the CRT display. (Source: Author's photo, NES-101)

You can clearly see color triads by ignoring your parents' advice and sitting directly in front of a CRT screen. In figure 1.10, the triads are visible within dozens of miniature columns of rectangles, like so many vertical bricks stacked one atop the other.

The columnar configuration is a result of a PIL, or precision-in-line, tube.[90] In a PIL tube, the electron guns are mounted in a straight line, rather than in a triangle, and the shadow mask is perforated with vertical slots rather than circles.

Triads do not produce the clean, squared pixels we associate with 8-bit videogames. Even at the focal length depicted above, it is impossible to discern individual pixels. Paradoxically, the CRT's flaws contribute to a richer final image. Carefully choosing pixel color and placement creates perceived hues and shades that the PPU does not actually output. The illuminated bleed of CRT triads, caused by the constant excitement and decay of the phosphor coating, both softens the edges of pixels and creates pleasing blends between color borders. The "X"s and numerals above, sourced from *The Legend of Zelda*'s inventory icons, appear to have a golden tint around the upper edges and blue shadows beneath. On an LCD screen or in an emulator, the same tiles are simply white pixels on a black background.

Pixels are the fundamental graphical unit of the PPU, but not of the display. CRT televisions have their own subatomic particles—phosphor triads—that do not adhere to the strict gridded geometries associated with pixel graphics. One or more triads can constitute a single pixel based on the size of display, so CRTs "natively" scale bitmapped graphics. High-definition LCDs, DLPs, and plasmas, on the other hand, have a fixed resolution. As a result, their individual pixels are so small that if we mapped the 256x240-pixel matrix of the Famicom PPU to a modern HDTV, the resulting screen would be miniscule. Therefore, individual pixels must be scaled according to the TV's resolution, resulting in a blurry, distorted image.

Firing Blanks

Before television was a mature technology, the number of times a full vertical scan, or *field*, took place per second was not standardized. When single-digit field rates were the norm, television had noticeable flicker, as the electron gun simply could not generate enough fields per second for persistence of vision to kick in. Field rates progressively improved, but early on a rudimentary form of compression called *interlacing* helped alleviate noticeable flicker.

Interlacing is analogous to "shoelacing"—in the same way that one might alternate laces along the tongue of a shoe in order to secure it tightly, an interlaced image is drawn with alternating scanlines. Though only half the image needs to be drawn at a time, it then takes two full fields of interlaced scanlines to compose a single *frame* of video. Again, due to phosphor's luminous residue, human eyes do not perceive two alternating sets of scanline window shades, but a single composite image. And since the CRT's phosphor luminance bleeds around the edges, it smooths the gaps between scanlines, effectively masking the raster.

Once early television experimenters settled on the minimum threshold of fields necessary to overcome flicker,[91] standard field rates began to emerge around technological, economic, and political interests. The three established standards were NTSC, PAL, and SECAM. The first, a monochrome system named for the National Television System Committee, was adopted in the United States in 1941, then later revised to a color standard in 1954 (called NTSC-2). However, NTSC had color instabilities (necessitating manual hue controls) that European interests sought to improve. Europe adopted the Phase Alternating Line color encoding standard in 1963, eliminating NTSC's hue inefficiencies—with the added benefit of forcing non-European sets out of the domestic television market. The French forged their own path in the early 1960s (also correcting NTSC's color limitations), introducing SECAM, or *Séquentiel couleur à mémoire.*

Though these standards branch into myriad subdivisions that describe precise technical differences, the details relevant to the Famicom involve geographic divisions and their associated field rates. Japan adopted the NTSC standard, which eased the Famicom's later export to the United States. The bulk of Europe and Australia adopted the PAL standard, with pockets of SECAM sprinkled throughout (obviously in France, but also in other parts of Eastern Europe). The discrepancies required a hardware revision for Nintendo's European console launch, so the PAL-compatible NES debuted after the U.S. version with a number of important differences that affected how video displayed.[92]

One modification handled the television standards' differing vertical scan rates. An NTSC television draws its frame at approximately 60 Hz, or sixty individual top-to-bottom electron beam trips per second. The PAL standard is slightly lower—approximately 50 Hz—but the discrepancy has a huge impact on graphics rendering and program timing. Much of the important work of displaying a videogame is done while the electron beam is "at rest," either resetting from drawing a horizontal scanline or resetting to the top after it reaches the bottom. By the time we see the results onscreen, most of the preparation work has been done. Graphics updates are ideally queued and ready prior to each sweep of the electron beam. Those horizontal and vertical "reset periods," or *blanks*, are key to the Famicom's operation.

Image synchronization is a precision art. The electron beam not only deflects at speeds the human eye cannot perceive, but the voltages controlling horizontal and vertical positioning operate at independent frequencies. Those of us alive in the CRT era may remember the delicate choreography required to keep a television's synchronization consistent. "Rolling" images are as common to the CRT generation as compression artifacting is to the flatscreen generation. When the vertical syncing frequency falls out of lockstep, the TV image wraps around the top and bottom borders of the screen, separated by a moving black bar—the vertical blank made visible. Similarly, when horizontal sync goes awry, the image "tears" along jagged diagonals.

Though the vertical and horizontal blank—or VBLANK and HBLANK—describe distances, their importance to programmers is temporal. In other words, it takes time for the gun to travel, and that time is necessary to update or move the proper graphical elements into place before the screen starts to draw again. But it is a slender margin that demands careful preparation. Updating the PPU while the scanline is actively being drawn is a Famicom programming no-no, resulting in noticeable graphical glitches. Any violations to this rule must be done deliberately and with precise timing. The PAL NES's lower refresh rate grants programmers additional affordances: since the gun resets ten fewer times per second, it can make its vertical ascent at a more leisurely pace. The PAL VBLANK is a full fifty scanlines longer than NTSC, granting more time for code to execute.[93]

A PAL television also has more graphical real estate than an NTSC set. This is not a discrepancy of the PPU—on either PAL or NTSC systems, the processor outputs a full 240 scanlines of graphics. The difference stems from overscan, a variation in picture visibility common to CRT displays. Overscan describes the area around the edge of the video frame that is not visible based on variations in the individual monitor, often due to a television's physical bezel or the curve of the cathode ray tube itself. Due to the vacuum inside the CRT, early televisions were tiny, curved, and typically circular, all measures meant to keep the tube from imploding. As manufacturing tolerances improved, shapes resolved into the more familiar rectangular 4:3 aspect ratio, curves decreased, and bezels receded. But this refinement process took decades. Television and videogame producers learned to keep important content away from the edges of the screen, lest it be invisible to some fraction of viewers. On NTSC sets, up to eight pixels of the upper and lower borders of the PPU's output are lost to overscan, reducing its visible scanline count to 224. PAL sets lose a single upper scanline and two pixels on the left and right.

Regional refresh rate differences create an ironic kinship between consoles that share few external similarities. The Family Computer and the U.S. Nintendo Entertainment System do not appear to be blood relatives, but internally they have identical CPUs. Famicom systems play fine on U.S. televisions with the proper step-down transformer and broadcast channel for playback (i.e., channel 2 in Japan is not equivalent to channel 2 in the U.S.). In contrast, PAL NES consoles, which are externally identical to their U.S. brethren, contain a CPU variant known as the Ricoh 2A07. To account for the 10Hz discrepancy in refresh rates, the 2A07 has a slower clock speed (1.66 MHz) than the 2A03 (1.79 MHz). In practical terms, PAL game cartridges played on an NTSC console will both play back faster and have their sound pitched up in frequency (and vice-versa). In some cases, the speed difference is bearable; in others, it renders a game unplayable.

Hobbyist game designers who aim to dabble in Famicom programming are often surprised that its architecture does not support the high-level languages common to modern platforms. The Famicom has no operating system or firmware to boot into; it relies solely on the instructions stored in ROM. Code must be written in assembly language, whose terse syntax is quite different than modern compiled programming languages like C++ or Java. Those languages bear some resemblance to everyday grammar, and even non-programmers can locate recognizable words and parse basic instructions. 6502 assembly, which is a single abstraction layer above machine code, is cryptic in comparison. Each line of code is composed of a three-letter mnemonic, representing an instruction, followed by an associated numeric value or address.

Though I keep the code examples in the book to a minimum, it is worthwhile to understand the basic structure of 6502 assembly, along with a number of common addresses the Famicom uses to get its work done. Unfortunately, there is no "Hello World" program for the Famicom, since it has no straightforward command to output text to screen, much less a built-in character set. Letters are tiles like any other graphic. Displaying text requires creating custom bitmap letterforms, waiting for the Famicom to initialize, clearing the contents of RAM, routing the background graphics to the screen, setting the palettes, and so on. I do not have the space to devote to a full code example, but a small excerpt can help us understand the general look and feel of Famicom programming. Displaying a background color is one of the simpler tasks one can program, so we will walk through a few steps of that process. The following code sets the PPU background color to green:

```
LDA  #$3F
STA  $2006
LDA  #00
STA  $2006
LDA  #$2A
STA  $2007
```

Again, the three-letter mnemonics on the left are instructions for the CPU, and the numbers to their right either designate addresses or specific numeric values. (If the dollar signs seem strange, rest assured that they are a common programmer prefix for hexadecimal values, not the cost of the instructions.) Hexadecimal is a base 16 numeral system. In our common base 10 (or decimal) system, we count from 0 to 9, then move to the tens place, repeat until we require a hundreds place, and so on. Binary, which counts with only 1s and 0s, is a base 2 system. Base 16, as we might expect, counts each digit place up to sixteen. Since we do not have single-digit symbols to represent numbers above 9, the six digits places between 10 and 15 use letters A through F.[94] The $3F value above works out to $3x16^1 + 15x16^0$, or 63, in base 10 notation.

All data in the Famicom is moved via *registers*, or hardware memory locations. Any in-game math, physics, AI, graphics, and sound synthesis is controlled by moving data to and from a handful of registers, including three of the CPU's special registers: the accumulator, x, and y. The code snippet above uses the accumulator—the primary register used for adding, subtracting, and comparing numbers—to pass a number of values to the PPU. $2006 is one of the 16-bit hexadecimal addresses of the Famicom's PPU I/O control registers. Changing the color of the background is a graphical job, so the CPU must send data to the PPU via designated addresses so it can act on that data appropriately.

The first four statements do the following: LDA stands for "LoaD Accumulator" with the value that follows. In this case, it is the hexadecimal value $3F (the "#" symbol tells the assembler to load the numeric value, rather than the value stored at that address). $3F is only the first half of a 16-bit address mapped in PPU memory, so we must load and STore the Accumulator (STA) twice in the I/O control register to designate the proper destination. Via four commands, we have readied the PPU to receive data at address $3F00, the location in memory where background palette information is stored. With our data destination set, we can then pass along information via the PPU data port, located at register $2007. To do so, we load the accumulator with a color value ($2A, or green) then store that value at $2007. In sum, the CPU tells the PPU, "I have the value for green and I would like you to store it in your palette at the requested address."

As this short example illustrates, trivial procedures in today's programming languages require significant legwork in assembly. There are few shortcuts, even for simple tasks. Today's programmers might think coding in such a manner is ludicrous. In most cases, they are right. But assembly language's close relationship to its processing infrastructure grants programmers unprecedented hardware control, since there is little abstraction between code and silicon. And once one understands the locations and behaviors of a handful of registers, extraordinary things can happen onscreen.

Jump button makes Jumpman jump.

— *Donkey Kong* arcade cabinet instructions (1981)

When Uemura and his R&D2 team first played *Galaxian*, they were astounded. Namco's hit 1979 arcade space shooter was clearly indebted to the look and structure of *Space Invaders*, Taito's landmark hit from the prior year, but it updated its predecessor's formula with individually dive-bombing aliens, colorful sprites representing distinct enemy types, and a backdrop of scrolling stars. Nintendo's R&D1 had attempted their own alien invasion game in 1979 with *Space Fever*, but it was a minor tweak of the *Space Invaders* formula, adding color and three selectable alien patterns. Uemura knew Nintendo could match Taito's and Namco's successes, but to do so, they would need to push their next game's realism even further. And better realism would require better hardware.[1]

With an ambitious design in mind, R&D2 tasked Japanese television equipment manufacturer Ikegami Tshushinki to produce the sophisticated circuitry for what would become *Radar Scope*.[2] The results were impressive. *Radar Scope* coupled a unique vanishing point perspective with alien sprites that appeared to scale in size as they dove toward the player. Nintendo also upped the ante on *Galaxian*'s scrolling stars with a feature they advertised as "curvature of field." A dedicated chip drew the "3-Dimensional Vectors"—an onscreen grid—and twinkling stars (driven by the sound board's noise generator) atop a gradient backdrop of black and deep blue.[3] The net effect was a shimmering depth unmatched by other space shooters, promising to position the player in "first-person" view of the action.[4] The audio hardware was equally sophisticated, featuring "supernatural 'Laser Sound'" and, in certain board revisions, in-game speech.[5] Nintendo and Ikegami Tshushinki threw all of their technical muscle at the project, but the audio-visual marvels came at a significant expense. *Radar Scope* cost ¥1,000,000, a hefty price tag for an arcade game.

It is unclear whether *Radar Scope* reached *Galaxian*-level popularity in Japan, but according to Nintendo of America's (NOA) then-president Minoru Arakawa, it was second in popularity only to Namco's monolithic hit *Pac-Man* (1980).[6] Whether this was true or not, the young president was eager to debut a Nintendo hit in the States—Nintendo had recently established their first U.S. office in New York and President Yamauchi was watching Arakawa's decisions closely. Confident of the space shooter's success, Arakawa requested a shipment of three thousand arcade cabinets from Osaka. Unfortunately, after the months-long shipping wait, any buzz preceding *Radar Scope*'s arrival had faded, and players were apparently unimpressed by the game's harsh sounds and perspectival rehash of *Space Invaders*.[7] Without the luster of cutting edge hardware, *Radar Scope* was left to rely on its derivative gameplay, a drawback that no amount of field curvature could mask. American arcade owners showed little interest, nor did players. *Radar Scope* was not the stunning debut Arakawa had hoped for; NOA sold only one third of their order.

As surplus cabinets lingered in NOA's warehouse, Arakawa scrambled for a solution. *Radar Scope* had sold enough to cover its manufacture and transportation costs, but Arakawa and his staff were working strictly on commission. Breaking even on costs meant no actual income for himself or his staff. As resources dwindled, Arakawa turned to Nintendo headquarters for aid. President Yamauchi quickly devised a plan to resurrect the unsold cabinets. In March 1981, he tapped R&D1 lead Gunpei Yokoi and junior industrial designer Shigeru Miyamoto to produce a *Radar Scope* conversion kit.

Conversion kits were common in the arcade era. A game's popularity was subject to unpredictable player tastes, so lackluster titles might lose their appeal after a few weeks. When games no longer drew players' quarters, they were removed from the arcade floor to make room for newer cabinets—only a rare few hung around for months or years. To combat the inevitable ebb in popularity, arcade manufacturers devised kits to update hardware without the need to replace the entire cabinet. This solution was an obvious boon to arcade owners, since shipping, installation, and maintenance cost a fraction of an entirely new machine. A single cabinet could last for several years. Namco's space shooter *Galaga* (1981), for instance, hosted multiple conversions, including *Bosconian* (1981), *Dig Dug* (1982), *Xevious* (1982), and *Super Xevious* (1984). Updated ROM chips reworked the gameplay and graphics while the existing CPU, sound hardware, and monitor were left intact. With a fresh set of decals and an updated marquee, *Radar Scope* became a brand new game.

Novelty Games

Yokoi and Miyamoto had little time to design and engineer their *Radar Scope* conversion kit. Rather than trying to compete with state-of-the-art technology while mimicking the gameplay of a well-worn genre, they thought innovative style and rich characters would attract players, regardless of technical specs. They opted to use the scenario for a *Popeye* game they had originally planned for a Game & Watch handheld, drawing on the cartoon's familiar love triangle—Popeye, Bluto, and Olive Oyl—for both character motivation and spatial structure: Bluto would hold Olive captive at the top of the screen while Popeye would start at the bottom and work upward to rescue her.

However, Nintendo failed to secure the license from Popeye's rights holder, King Features, halting the designers' plans in the pre-production phase.[8] According to Yokoi:

> Pretty early on we had decided that Popeye would go on the bottom of the screen and Bluto would be on the top, thus establishing the framework for the game, but we would later discover that we wouldn't be able to get the rights to use the characters after all. With no other options, we decided to keep the content of the game as it was and just change the characters. And so it was that those characters became Mario, Donkey Kong, and Princess Peach.[9]

Miyamoto's replacement designs were one-to-one translations of the copyrighted characters: Bluto became a sizable ape named Donkey Kong, Olive Oyl became the slender damsel eventually named Pauline, and a squat carpenter named Jumpman stood in for underdog hero Popeye. And even after the character swaps, *Popeye* continued to be an inspirational resource, as Yokoi explained:

> There was an episode in the cartoon show for Popeye in which Olive was sleepwalking and wandered around a construction site. Whenever she was about to lose her footing, miraculously enough another

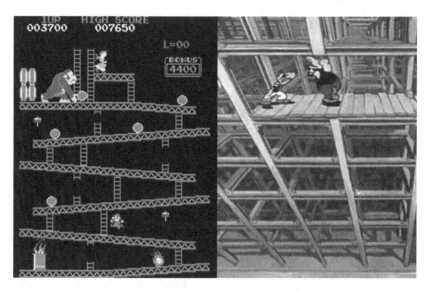

2.1 A cropped still from the 1934 *Popeye* short (right) that directly inspired *Donkey Kong*'s characters and setting, as seen in the opening construction site—or "girders"—stage (left). (Emulator: MAME)

platform would come out of nowhere and support her, and this left quite an impression on me. So we figured by using a construction site as the setting, there would be all kinds of things we could do, and thus chose that as the setting for our Popeye game.[10]

The referenced episode is a 1934 *Popeye* short called "A Dream Walking," wherein Olive Oyl falls asleep and wanders into a poorly-guarded construction site.[11] As she sleepwalks across a series of perilous beams and girders, Popeye and Bluto pummel one another as they race to save her. The germ of a game idea was there, inspired by a veritable "platform cartoon" (figure 2.1).

Yokoi's and Miyamoto's reworked conversion became *Donkey Kong* (1981), whose lighthearted cartoon design, inspired setting, and innovative gameplay were a marked departure from the sci-fi and military fare that populated arcades in the late 1970s. *Donkey Kong*, at heart, is a running and jumping game. The player takes the role of Jumpman, an apt descriptor for his and the player's shared duties. Donkey Kong has abducted Jumpman's girlfriend, hauling her Fay Wray-style up endless elevated construction sites. Kong resides at the top, hurling obstacles downward as Jumpman makes his way to the top. When and if Jumpman reaches the screen's zenith, Kong snatches Pauline and climbs a ladder to the next stage. The same scenario repeats on two additional stages, one dominated by elevators and springs and another by cement pies and conveyor belts. On the fourth and final screen, Jumpman must remove a series of rivets holding the center platforms in place. If he succeeds, the girders collapse, Kong plummets headlong to the bottom, and the lovers reunite. After a brief respite, the game loops to a more difficult version of the opening stage and Jumpman embarks once again on his Sisyphean task.

Donkey Kong's spartan love story, played out in four distinct stages, added a miniature narrative structure that Miyamoto later attributed to comic storytelling:

> Thinking back, I would say that although it wasn't done consciously, I ended up designing *Donkey Kong* like a traditional Japanese four-panel manga comic strip. That way of telling a story in four distinct parts seemed natural to me, so I created four separate screens from the opening to the conclusion.[12]

Miyamoto's mini-narrative allowed players to work toward both higher scores and the culmination of Jumpman's quest. Additionally, each stage required a distinct strategy. The opening "construction site" stage was jump-heavy, as barrels poured erratically over girder edges and down the same ladders that Jumpman clambered up. The "elevator" stage, in contrast, required patient timing to maneuver the rise and fall of the narrow elevators, since Jumpman was not a competent Fallman; any plunge larger than his height resulted in death. The "cement factory" stage threw Jumpman's momentum into disarray, as ladders shifted height and conveyor belts changed direction beneath his feet.

Like many innovative games of the arcade era, *Donkey Kong*'s play style demanded a new genre. In the early 1980s, videogame magazines waffled between a number of generic descriptors, from "climbing" and "jumping" games to "level" and "ladder" games. Many settled on the least inventive of the lot: "Kong-style games." More curious was the "novelty games" category used to describe the influx of (mostly Japanese) titles with colorful, cartoon-inspired sprites and gameplay that focused more on a character's nimble movements than their fighting arsenal. The reviews supplement in the March 1983 issue of *Computer & Video Games* pegged two Japanese titles—*Donkey Kong* and *Frogger*—as key progenitors of a genre whose stylistic differentiator was "cuteness": "Good graphics are by definition crucial to the success of novelty games. The characters must be cute or plausible, well-defined, and above all central to the general theme of the game."[13] The "novelty" descriptor functioned more as a catch-all non-category than a credible genre, and it frequently described blatant rip-offs rather than games that were "novel" in their own right. In the same issue, for instance, *Computer & Video Games* listed a number of novelty PC titles like *Pogoman* and *Hopper*, whose lineages were not difficult to guess.

The "novelty" designator carried two distinct and somewhat contradictory connotations. "Novelty" was newness, a unique approach, a style gamers had not seen before. *Donkey Kong* and its ilk felt fresh in comparison to war, sports, and science fiction titles. Guiding a frog across a busy intersection or dining on ghosts with a sentient yellow circle was far afield from shooting Alien Invader X with Spaceship Y. But "novelty" was also niche, an eccentric or even spurious outsider. This is the sense in which novelty games served as the miscellaneous bin for a number of games that resisted categorization. *Frogger* and *Donkey Kong* were not similar in the same way that *Galaxian* and *Galaga* were, so critics relied on a common visual style instead of concrete gameplay similarities. In Steve Bloom's 1982 book-length survey of the arcade field, *Video Invaders*, his introduction to *Donkey Kong* highlighted the conflicting senses of genuine excitement for the game's uniqueness and near-disdain for its foreignness:

> Donkey Kong is another bizarre cartoon game, courtesy of Japan. While we in America continue to invent new and improved methods of exploring outer space and obliterating all we find there, our Eastern rivals' seemingly frivolous comic mentality keeps spilling over into their design of video games.[14]

Japanese videogames fulfilled both aspects of novelty in the U.S.-dominated videogame market. They were outsiders in an industry they did not create, a sentiment echoed in the "*Invaders*" half of the book title quoted above. Yet the popularity of Japanese games was proving that they had appeal beyond their native country.

In *Power-Up*, an insightful look into the Japanese revival of the American post-crash videogame industry, Chris Kohler argues that Nintendo's games, "*are not products or models of our culture. They are products and models of Japanese culture*, the 'action and reaction' of the Japanese population, presented nearly unaltered for our consumption."[15] In other words, Japan was not selling American culture; Japan was selling Japanese culture, with little or no filter. The underlying assumption is that unmediated Japanese culture would be appealing to the West based on its exoticism, a reflection of a people wholly other from them. This is a longstanding Western conception of the Japanese people, what Susan Napier calls "the embodiment of a variety of fantasies" that throughout history has elicited fear, respect, admiration, fascination, desire, and suspicion.[16]

Part of Kohler's assertion is formal: the exaggerated proportions common in manga were well-suited to the limitations of early videogame hardware. Realism was tough to convey in a four-color, 16x16 block of pixels. Cartoons, however, where exaggeration and abstraction are the norm, made the transition easily. Simplified color and form conformed well to the crudity of palettes and pixels in the early videogame era. Jumpman's visage and wardrobe, for instance, were largely determined by hardware limitations: a cap obviated the need for animated hair, a mustache defined an otherwise indistinct face, and overalls made fashion sense when one had to rely on only two colors to sell an outfit. Kohler also emphasizes how Japan's distinct cultural interest in visual storytelling translated easily to the videogame medium. Japan was a society cultivated around images, from woodblock prints, Bunraku puppetry, and Noh theater, to manga and anime. Unlike in America, where comic books were child's fare, graphic storytelling in Japan ran the gamut of age and interests, from cartoons to pornography. In all regards, Japan's was a culture primed for the transition to the vivid cartoon worlds and characters of videogames.

Kohler is correct in the broad view. Nintendo undeniably helped ease the Western world into Japanese culture as a result of the monolithic popularity of their characters and consoles. And the exoticism of foreign products certainly played a part. Non-Japanese players could see, hear, and feel the novel influence of Eastern culture in the games' designs, as the uncertainty of genre labeling suggests. But to say their products were "nearly unaltered for our consumption" ignores the complexity of a decades-long cultural exchange taking place between Japan and the West, as well as the deliberate linguistic and cultural translations made in Japanese media prior to their export. In many cases, the Japanese origins of cartoons, comics, and videogames were obscured, or more generally labeled as "foreign" rather than specifically Japanese. And the precedents for Japanese media in America were extensive enough that we cannot credit videogames alone with initiating the cultural handshake between East and West.

Even prior to the flood of videogames in the early 1980s, Japanese media had been gradually finding an audience on Western shores. Beginning in 1961, the first Japanese animated films—*Magic Boy* (MGM), *Panda and the Magic Serpent* (Globe Pictures), and *Alakazam the Great* (American-International Pictures)—were shown in American theaters. These "test cases" for American audiences followed the Disney model of adapted folktales for children, featuring humans with a cast of adorable animal companions. Though their stories were sourced from Asian lore, any references to the films' foreign origin were scrubbed. These and subsequent films were commercial failures, so American distributors shifted their efforts to television and 16mm rental markets. Throughout the 1960s and 1970s, Japanese animated shows like *Astro Boy*, *Gigantor*, *Kimba the White Lion*, and *Speed Racer* debuted on American television in local syndications, but the shows' foreign heritage was ambiguous when scrunched between children's fare from Filmation and Hanna-Barbera. As the production of American kid-friendly cartoons increased and more stringent rules regarding violence in children's programming appeared, Japanese animation became largely sequestered to networks catering to Japanese communities.

As journalist Fred Patten documents in *Watching Anime, Reading Manga*, a series of important events reversed Japanese animation's success in America.[17] New sci-fi series like *Brave Raideen* (1976) debuted, featuring teen heroes piloting enormous robots. These action- and drama-heavy cartoons appealed to an audience older than the usual Hanna-Barbera set. The serendipitous arrival of the *Star Wars* phenomenon further bolstered interest in any space adventure-themed animation, comics, and toys. There was also a concurrent shift in the tone and audience of American superhero comics in the 1960s and 1970s. The Golden Age of superheroes was making way for a new Silver Age, offering edgier interpretations of familiar favorites (e.g., Batman and Superman) and new, modern characters targeted for an older audience (e.g., Spider-Man and the X-Men). Finally, the introduction of consumer video cassette recorders (VCRs) around 1975 created an inexpensive means to record, share, and distribute Japanese films and television shows among fans.

This synergy of social, cultural, and technological changes continued to coalesce. America's youth counterculture movement sought edgier forms of art and pop culture that circulated outside mainstream norms. Racial tolerance was shifting. The generation that thirty years before had inaugurated atomic warfare against a Japanese enemy gave way to sons and daughters more receptive to cultural exchange. The time was right for Japan's cultural entrance in the West.

By the early 1980s, Japanese media had seeped into all corners of pop culture: the Cartoon/Fantasy Organization formed in Los Angeles, the first fan group to cater specifically to anime;[18] Japanese animated films and cartoons were screened at comic book and sci-fi conventions; fanzines devoted to "Japanimation" and manga were published; an influx of Japanese sci-fi and robot toys were hitting American shelves; translations of popular manga were sold in U.S. comic shops; and some of Japan's artistic luminaries, like *Astro Boy* creator Osamu Tezuka, were meeting with fans in America.[19] By the time *Donkey Kong* debuted in 1981, there was already a modest but enthusiastic fan base for Japanese media, centered around the same adolescent, teen, and twenty-something demographics that would flock to videogame arcades. There was a reason the early crop of Japanese games were labeled "cartoon" games—they resembled the first Japanese medium that made an impact on Western pop culture.

And just as anime's foreign pedigree was hidden from American viewers in the early 1960s, Japanese creators (and their American distributors) modified, edited, or outright censored their media in accordance with Western tastes, even as their work gained increasing acceptance outside of Japan. In the 1980s, popular sci-fi anime series *Space Cruiser Yamato* and *Macross* were brought to American television, respectively, as *Star Blazers* and *Robotech*. Some revisions were benign, like the titles or character names—certainly Derek Wildstar was more palatable to American children than his original name, Susumu Kodai. Other more significant changes reflected divergent cultural attitudes toward sexuality or vice. Dr. Sano's predilection for alcohol, for instance, was whitewashed in his transformation to the good-humored Dr. Sane, while transgender character Lance "Yellow Dancer" Belmont's appearance was explained away through plot contrivances that cast him as a secret agent "disguising" himself in drag.

Robotech was also subject to drastic structural changes, as anime scholar Antonia Levi explains:

> The long, drawn out stills used to convey moments of extreme emotion or heroism were shortened, and the sound track was changed. Flaws and contradictions in the heroes' personalities were softened. The deaths of some significant characters were covered up. And just to put the final kiss of death on the whole production, the networks persisted in scheduling them at times suitable for children.[20]

As Levi implies, some of these changes were due to divergent audiences. In Japan, *Macross* was not a children's show—in America, nearly all cartoons were children's fare, so they had to be cut accordingly.

The same attention to potentially problematic structure, content, or form applied to videogames. Kohler remarks on the ambivalent cultural status of Japanese videogames, many of which were designed with English text: "Video games in general were a contemporary American invention, and there was nothing that clearly labeled newcomer Nintendo as Japanese."[21] But he also reveals a litany of cultural translations necessary to soften videogames' Japanese roots prior to their introduction to Western markets: among them, the original manga drawings from *Western Gun* arcade cabinets were not used for American release; *Pac-Man's* original onomatopoeic name *Puck-Man* was altered to discourage arcade vandals; and NES games were scrubbed of potentially racist or religiously inflammatory content prior to American release.[22] Time and again, Japanese videogame companies were surgically strategic in their modifications for non-Japanese audiences. Nintendo was no exception—they were acutely aware of their cultural product and its potential Western reception, from their industrial design to outright censorship (chapter 3). This does not discredit Japan's cultural contributions nor valorize "Western" versus "Eastern" design, whatever those broad classifications might mean. But it is crucial to recognize that calculated (and miscalculated) translations were taking place on either side as part of a complex cultural exchange, crossing borders of language, custom, technology, economics, and politics.

And the flow of cultural commerce was not one-sided. Osamu Tezuka, widely considered the father of anime, was inspired in equal measure by both Japanese wartime propaganda films and Disney animation. Though Tezuka's and Disney's content and style were considerably different, Tezuka was dubbed "the Walt Disney of Japan."[23] The same fans in the 1970s who were copying and trading shows among themselves were establishing international connections, swapping cartoons with Japanese science fiction fans hungry for American fare like *Star Trek* and *Battlestar Galactica*.[24] The shared NTSC standard between the U.S. and Japan helped facilitate the exchange (and equally hampered anime's expansion to PAL markets). Many of the first Japanese videogame consoles mimicked or licensed Western machines, like Nintendo's own *Pong* clone Color TV-Game 15 (1977) or Atari's Japanese version of the VCS, the Atari 2800 (1983).[25] The Japanese likewise picked and chose from a range of foreign inspirations for their game designs, from medieval knights to Western gunfights.

Consider the odd amalgam of Western influences in *Donkey Kong*. The most obvious is *King Kong*, the 1933 RKO film directed by Merian C. Cooper and Ernest B. Schoedsack, featuring an enormous gorilla displaced from his native land and put on spectacular display in metropolitan New York. The original theatrical poster featured a familiar pose: Kong perched atop a tall structure, clutching Fay Wray, the helpless damsel in a pink dress. Yet Pauline is no short-cropped flapper. Her long hair, ankle-length dress, and blue heeled boots are distinctly 19th-century American Western, a genre sensibility already rehearsed by Nintendo in their early Wild West-themed arcade game *Sheriff* (1979). Pauline's attire, coupled with the damsel-in-distress trope, also evokes the silent film serials of the 1910s, like the tied-to-the-train-tracks classic *The Perils of Pauline*.[26] Meanwhile, Mario (named after NOA's landlord) is a workaday anachronism, an unlikely Italian hero who relies on agility and carpentry tools to survive. Weirder still, when Mario dies, a halo—the symbol of Christian saints and angels—floats above his supine body.

Some were not so keen to forgive *Donkey Kong*'s similarities to a Western cinematic icon. Universal Studios famously threatened Nintendo of America with copyright infringement, claiming that the game's name, ape, and premise were identical to *King Kong*.[27] Universal tried to strong-arm Nintendo into a settlement, hoping the U.S. newcomer would surrender to Universal's formidable legal team. Nintendo stood strong and Universal sued. In a grand twist of irony, it was revealed that Universal had no legal claim to King Kong—in fact, in order to remake the 1933 film, Universal had successfully argued in court in 1975 that RKO no longer owned the character. Kong was public domain.

Universal's shaky ownership claims notwithstanding, Nintendo would have prevailed. The New York Circuit Court of Appeals ruled in 1984 that the game's premise fell under parody, thanks again to its "cartoon" sensibilities:

> The district court conducted a visual inspection of both the *Donkey Kong* game and the *King Kong* movies and stated that the differences between them were "great." It found the *Donkey Kong* game "comical" and the Donkey Kong gorilla character "farcical, childlike and non-sexual." In contrast, the court described the King Kong character and story as "a ferocious gorilla in quest of a beautiful woman." The court summarized that "*Donkey Kong* creates a totally different concept and feel from the drama of *King Kong*" and that "at best, *Donkey Kong* is a parody of *King Kong*." Indeed, the fact that *Donkey Kong* so obviously

parodies the *King Kong* theme strongly contributes to dispelling confusion on the part of consumers.[28]

For his part, Miyamoto deposed that the *Donkey Kong* name was a translation error, meant to convey a meaning closer to "stubborn monkey" than any allusion to the classic film.[29] He claimed that when he looked up "stubborn" in a Japanese/English dictionary, it read "donkey," while "kong" was a general term for any large ape.[30] Since then, the true origin of the game's title circulates among numerous apocryphal tales. Regardless, the irony came full circle in 2010, when Nintendo attempted to legally trademark the phrase, "It's on like Donkey Kong."[31]

Today we tend to gloss the patent absurdity of *Donkey Kong* and its characters because they have been so tightly woven into the fabric of videogame culture, but when we survey the broad reach of its cultural quotations and allusions, we find that it is a strikingly weird media object. Nintendo's games had an uncanny familiarity to American audiences and the decades of pop cultural exchange leading up to *Donkey Kong*'s release paved the way for its success, though not without an initial measure of trepidation. The Japanese were adopting an industry from the West, infusing it with their own traditions, combining it with their own interpretations of Western culture, then translating it back again into a novel, de-contextualized pastiche. This complex process continued to foster the same mix of attraction and puzzlement that struck players encountering *Donkey Kong* for the first time. And eventually, as the Japanese style became more familiar, works like *Kong* changed from "novelty games" to simply *videogames*.

Kong at Home

In the early 1980s, arcade machines were the lead platform for cutting-edge videogame technology, since they benefited from dedicated hardware: processors, memory, sound chips, cabinets, and control interfaces built to suit the needs of each game (or a handful of similar games). *Marble Madness*'s pseudo-3D graphics and control scheme demanded a different hardware configuration—from increased ROM space to a "rollerball" input device—than, say, the two-dimensional, single-joystick play of *Pac-Man*. Home consoles and computers were underpowered in comparison, especially cartridge-based systems and consumer PCs that tried to provide flexible platforms for a range of software. By the time microprocessors were cheap enough to mass market inside an affordable console package, arcade technology had moved ahead by leaps and bounds. Though cabinets were expensive to design, manufacture, and ship, they could make up for the large upfront costs through volume sales. Hundreds of players might cycle through a single game each day, eventually earning the arcade owner enough revenue to recoup costs, one quarter at a time.

Despite the technology gap, arcade games still made their way to home consoles. The process of translating game software from one platform to another is commonly called *porting*. Thirty years ago there were multitudes of PC platforms, confusing hardware forks within a single company (e.g., the Atari 2600/5200/7800/400/800/ST), and region-specific manufacturers. It was common for an arcade hit like *Pac-Man* to receive ports for a dozen or more PCs and consoles—not to mention tabletop toys, watches, board games, and the like.[32] Arcade ports ran the gamut from near-perfect to abysmal, with cuts and concessions made according to each platform's affordances. Porting has never been a magical process whereby a programmer copies the game's source from one machine and simply compiles it on another. At a time when computers were coded "close to the hardware" in assembly language, the internal architectures of two competing platforms had a drastic impact on the visual results.

Assembly language in itself is not a codified grammar—it is more like a common base for a variety of dialects, each specific to a particular CPU family. In the same way that someone does not speak the Romance language, but rather speaks French or Spanish, one also does not code assembly, but instead 6502 assembly or Z80 assembly. In other words, assembly language is tied to its architecture. There will be similarities between "regional dialects," perhaps a few identical "words," but no clean one-to-one translation. Even identical cross-platform syntax cannot account for the differences in, say, how a video processor draws to the screen, available sprite sizes, palette variety, or even the number and configuration of buttons on a controller. Source code notwithstanding, how does one translate the complex multi-button control scheme of *Defender* (1980) to the single-button joystick of the Atari VCS? These were the types of problems all programmers faced when tackling cross-platform ports.

When arcade developers were slow to deliver ports, third parties picked up the slack. Especially in Europe, where the scope and variety of low-cost PCs overshadowed the burgeoning home console market, games inspired by or directly copied from arcade hits came fast and furious, from professional and amateur programmers alike. British magazine *CRASH*, who published one of the first references to "platform games" (chapter 4) in their "Living Guide to Spectrum Software," often ran reviews of *Kong* clones clearly "inspired" by Nintendo's hit game. In

CRASH's blurb on *Killer Kong*, for instance, they referred to the game's protagonist as Mario, despite the lack of any similarity between Nintendo's overall-clad carpenter and the shirtless stickman seen on screen.[33] Arcade fans were clamoring to play their favorite games at home, even if they got cut-rate or imitation products. PC-oriented magazines catered to the tastes of amateur programmers, providing pages of type-it-yourself source code for clones of popular arcade titles. Despite its shortcomings, home play was an understandable salve to the arcade's relentless quarter drain.

Imitators proliferated in the arcades as well, often unabashedly lifting a popular game's screen layouts, gameplay, and characters. The most egregious cases were outright theft. Disreputable manufacturers affixed a new marquee to the arcade cabinet without bothering to alter the internal hardware, spawning the likes of *Crazy Kong, Konkey Kong, Congorilla, Donkey King,* and a plethora of other tragic name variations.[34] Nintendo pursued these bootlegs and clones with litigious fervor in an effort to curb piracy and economic losses.[35] Despite Nintendo lawyer Howard Lincoln's efforts in litigating thirty-five copyright infringement cases and confiscating thousands of counterfeit circuit boards, Nintendo estimated they lost nearly $100 million to *Donkey Kong* copycats.[36]

Meanwhile, Nintendo was keen to meet legitimate demand for *Donkey Kong* with an official console port. Home versions of popular arcade titles provided new revenue sources, prolonged a videogame's life for years, and helped publicize the company brand. Nintendo, guided by Yamauchi, had ambitions for worldwide success, so they licensed the arcade ape to nearly every viable (and sometimes non-viable) platform of the day, from Amstrad CPC to ZX Spectrum.

The clear powerhouse among home console ports was Nintendo's first licensee, Coleco.[37] The ColecoVision's pack-in version of *Donkey Kong* was lauded by press and consumers alike for its arcade fidelity, despite its decreased palette, altered sound and sprites, and missing "cement factory" stage. The game bolstered sales of Coleco's fledgling console, challenging Atari's multi-year reign of the home market. The ColecoVision was technologically superior to the aging Atari VCS, and the accuracy of Coleco's arcade ports drove that point home visually and sonically. The ColecoVision soon became the arcade purist's console of choice.

Coleco's exclusive license with Nintendo lasted for six months, allowing them to sell half a million consoles. Once exclusivity lapsed, Coleco shifted roles from first-party to third-party development,[38] aiming to dip their toes in both ends of the profit pool, producing ports for hardware rivals Atari and Mattel while continuing production of the ColecoVision. Both competitors' machines were ill-equipped for *Donkey Kong*'s specifications. The Atari VCS port delivered a version of the ape that looked more like a giant gingerbread man tossing chocolate chip cookies than Jumpman's fearsome, barrel-chucking antagonist. The Mattel Intellivision port was less visually offensive, but still bare-bones: Kong, for one, remained a brown monochrome mess. The Atari 7800 version fared best, due to its more capable hardware, but Jumpman's running and jumping sound effects were gratingly brittle compared to the original. In the end, the platform did not matter to Coleco. If they sold cartridges for Atari or Mattel, they earned a cut; if consumers opted for the superior arcade facsimile, they would buy a ColecoVision.[39] Coleco benefited either way.

Orientation

As the wide spectrum of quality attests, *Donkey Kong* was a challenging console port. Like *Pac-Man* and many other Japanese cabinets, it ran on the Zilog Z80,[40] clocked at a whopping 3 MHz, nearly tripling the processing power of console contemporaries Intellivision or Atari VCS. The newer ColecoVision fared better partly due to a shared architecture, as it ran on a slightly faster version of the Z80. However, ports did not automatically benefit from similar CPUs or enhanced processing speeds. A host of hardware differences, from input mechanisms to available video RAM, had significant "behind-the-scenes" consequences that impacted the final visual results.

One such difference was *Donkey Kong*'s monitor. Arcade displays in the early 1980s were not off-the-shelf consumer televisions. Most cabinets of *Kong*'s era were stocked with screens from Electrohome (model G07) or Wells-Gardner (models K4600, K4900, and K7000), typically 19" or 25" color raster scans.[41] Nintendo sensibly chose a Japanese supplier, so *Donkey Kong* and its kin were outfitted with the Sanyo 20EZ.[42] Resolution- and frequency-wise, arcade monitors were identical to home sets. The key difference was the video signal. Most home televisions had, at best, a composite input. True to its name, the composite signal merged the monochrome (i.e., black and white) and color information into a single stream, significantly lowering the bandwidth necessary to convey the signal.

However, bandwidth savings were offset by a loss in quality. TV cameras output color information in three separate streams: red, green, and blue. Ideally, a monitor would accept and reproduce these streams individually. Once combined, they could no longer be cleanly separated again. As a result, composite signals produced display errors like *dot crawl*, where checked patterns of color artifacts noticeably creep along the border of two color bands. Arcade monitors, in contrast, were RGB (or Red Green Blue) and thus kept the individual color streams separate and intact. Compared to home televisions, arcade monitors looked sharper and more vivid, with fewer image imperfections.

Kong's display, to accommodate Jumpman's vertical ascent, was also taller than it was wide. No custom hardware was necessary for such an orientation—horizontal displays were simply rotated on their side, while the arcade hardware handled the appropriate graphical flip. This "trick" was more evident in cocktail arcade cabinets designed for seated play. Two or more players sat on opposing sides of the cabinet, looking down at the monitor. For each player's turn, the screen would reorient to their perspective. Typically the orientation was set in advance by an arcade operator or technician. For *Donkey Kong*, a jumper switch on the CPU could set "upright" or "table" orientation (along with the number of lives, score level, and number of coins per play).[43]

The vertical 3:4 aspect ratio was common in arcade games, but a significant hurdle for console ports. Videogame consoles, unlike arcade cabinets and some PCs, did not include their own monitors.[44] Fortunately, most game players had a convenient solution on hand: their television. By 1980, over seventy-five million U.S. households owned a television, nearly 98% of the total population; half of these households owned more than one.[45] Japanese households reported similar statistics.[46] This provided great flexibility for display choices, as nearly every household had a screen suitable for videogames. Market saturation clearly benefited console manufacturers, as they did not have to factor a monitor into manufacturing costs. Of course, one tradeoff was the fixed orientation. Home televisions were designed for broadcast television, not arcade games, so they conformed to the industry-standard 4:3 aspect ratio. For *Donkey Kong*, this meant either compressing vertical platforms or eliminating them altogether. The ColecoVision port, for instance, had only five girders in stage 1 (not counting Pauline's platform), in comparison to the arcade's six.

Donkey Kong's graphics were similarly difficult to duplicate on a console, due both to the default size of its graphical tiles and the memory available to store them. The visual elements that comprised the screen were split between two tile types—sprite and character—that occupied distinct locations in memory, a clear precursor to the PPU's pattern tables. And as discussed in chapter 1, sprites were typically assigned to objects that moved: Jumpman, barrels, bouncing jacks, Pauline, and Kong himself. Character tiles, on the other hand, customarily comprised any static background elements: girders, ladders, letters, numbers, and the GUI.

Donkey Kong had the memory capacity to store 128 16x16-pixel sprites and 256 8x8-pixel character tiles. Though both tile sets cover equal areas, subdividing them differently had clear design advantages. Since character tiles were used to draw the game's architecture, smaller dimensions allowed the designers to sculpt more granular variations in size and structure. As we will see shortly, the tile permutations necessary to construct the girders' angled planes consumed a significant amount of character space. Slimming girders to fit within an 8x8-pixel mosaic saved memory and increased the variety of background elements.

Building personable cartoon objects, however, was challenging in such a narrow frame. Increasing the sprite tile size fourfold provided a wider palette for character variety. Nearly every moving object in *Donkey Kong*—barrels, fireballs, cement pies—fits within a 16x16-pixel perimeter. Even Jumpman's impressive range of animations—jumping, running, climbing, falling, dying—is blocked within single sprites. Pauline and Kong are the obvious exceptions. Pauline is taller than Jumpman, so her head and shoulders require an additional sprite to accommodate her height. Kong, as the titular antagonist who is meant to dwarf the other characters, occupies six sprite slots—his head alone is larger than Jumpman's entire body.

Donkey Kong's chunky sprites also provided a significant programming advantage for object movement. In tile-based graphics systems, one tile is often not adequate to represent an entire object. Objects are thus built out of multiple tiles that move in unison. Moving a single-tile object is straightforward—simply update the tile's x- and y-coordinates to the desired screen position. Multi-tile objects require careful software coordination to assure that all tiles move as a single unit, or *metatile*.

Character animation compounds the complexity. Certain tiles in an object may need to update while others remain static. In Jumpman's case, each frame of his walk animation occupies a single sprite, so the animation routine can cycle through single tiles with minimal programming overhead. Animating Donkey Kong's massive frame is trickier. At times, his body will rotate, requiring all of his tiles to change. However, when he faces the player and stomps his feet, portions of his body remain fixed, while others move. Using larger sprites required fewer multi-tile updates, simplifying *Donkey Kong*'s sprite animations and object movements.

The Ape in the Background

Nintendo's first cartridge hardware was the Nintendo ROM, or NROM. The initial spate of NROM games, such as *Donkey Kong* (1983), *Mario Bros.* (1983), *Door Door* (1984), and *Nuts & Milk* (1984), had austere interiors. At least initially, Famicom PCBs had only two unlabeled "glob-tops" onboard.[47] This low-cost method of semiconductor production bonded and protected the PRG-/CHR-ROM ICs and their connections with a coating of black resin epoxy.

Despite its unassuming appearance, the HVC-NROM-128 that housed Famicom *Donkey Kong* was a good match for its arcade progenitor. Though it only used half of NROM's available PRG-ROM capacity (16KB), it still doubled the program space available in arcade *Donkey Kong*. Tile-wise, NROM's 8KB of CHR-ROM matched the arcade's sprite and character outlay, although 16x16-pixel sprites were not an option. Nintendo wisely struck a compromise by providing both 8x8- and 8x16-pixel tile options, but the developers chose the former option for the Famicom port. And while the 2A03 could not match the arcade's Z80 processing speed, the Famicom's specs were a far cry from the VCS's five movable objects or even the ColecoVision's 8KB of total cartridge ROM. It is clear that the Famicom was engineered not only to port *Donkey Kong*, but to surpass any competitors' prior efforts.

Nonetheless, a few key platform differences made an arcade-accurate port impossible. For one, there are fundamental aspect ratio differences between platforms. The arcade monitor's vertical resolution is 224x256 pixels, while the Famicom's visible NTSC resolution, accounting for overscan, is the exact inverse.[48] Note that in this regard the Famicom's PPU has a clear advantage over the ColecoVision's VDP. The latter outputs 256x192 pixels, constraining its vertical proportions even more significantly than the Famicom's. While the Coleco port omits the construction site's top girder and moves Kong and Pauline to the right side of the screen, the Famicom port maintains the arcade girder count by subtly compressing the space between platforms (figure 2.2). This is most evident in the reduced gaps between broken ladders and the increased clutter toward the top of the screen, where the score, life, stage, and bonus indicators squeeze obtrusively into the playfield. Spatially, the arrangement makes better sense for the game's vertical narrative, since Donkey Kong can carry Pauline directly off-screen, rather than into the scoreboard. However, to save on tiles, the Famicom port eschews any animated sequences. Once Mario reaches the top girder, gameplay freezes, a fanfare plays, and the game cuts directly to the next stage.

2.2 The title screen (left) and construction site stage (right) from NES *Donkey Kong*. (Source: NES-101 capture)

As expected, stage 1 in Famicom *Donkey Kong* is composed almost entirely of background tiles, since the girders, ladders, Kong's barrel supply, the blue oil can, and the score display remain largely static throughout gameplay. The largest moving element is Donkey Kong himself. He occupies a 48x32-pixel area, or twenty-four total tiles. But that total only accounts for one position; when Kong moves, new tiles must come into play. As a result, over half of one pattern table's tiles are devoted to drawing Donkey Kong (figure 2.3).

Though he can pivot and stomp, Donkey Kong is not built of sprites, a crucial platform-level distinction that fundamentally alters the Famicom port's fidelity to its source. *Donkey Kong*'s arcade hardware could handle up to sixteen sprites on a scanline, and with their 16x16-pixel area, it was possible to accommodate Kong and other moving objects without risk of exceeding that count. The Famicom PPU, however, can only display eight sprites on a single scanline. To circumvent this limit, programmers shuffled sprite priorities in OAM frame to frame, causing sprites to visually flicker but preventing any one sprite from disappearing completely. If a player's character was, for example, built from multiple sprites (as is usually the case), portions of that character's body might appear and reappear as it passed a particular horizontal vector shared by other sprite-based objects.

If Kong were built of sprites, there would be situations where he (six tiles wide), multiple barrels (two tiles wide), and even Jumpman (two tiles wide) might simultaneously occupy the same horizontal plane, causing one or more objects to flicker out of existence. If that object happened to be Jumpman, it would not only be aesthetically unappealing, but would distract from *Donkey Kong*'s precision jumping demands.[49] Moreover, a flickering Kong would have been visually unacceptable for Nintendo's marquee port. Nintendo chose not to compromise on the port's visual integrity and instead constructed Kong from background tiles.

Not that Famicom *Kong* is flicker-free. There are circumstances where the game's multiple moving objects align horizontally, but they are rare. Players focused on the action likely never notice the split-second flickers. In this respect, *Donkey Kong*'s vertical gameplay design is ideal for translation to the Famicom, since elements that travel horizontally, like barrels or fireballs, are sequestered into discrete "bands," i.e., each stage's platforms. Since the arcade hardware permitted double the sprites per scanline, the game design did not have to be as stringent about the quantity of cascading objects. Subsequently, the original version feels a bit more frantic and fast-paced than the console port, since more sprites can crowd each platform.

Compare *Donkey Kong* to another of Nintendo's early arcade ports, *Balloon Fight*. The game is similar to Williams Electronics' 1982 arcade game *Joust*, though the latter's ostrich-riding knights are replaced with men suspended by balloons who flap their hands to gain altitude. The goal in *Balloon Fight* is to pop your competitors' balloons by colliding into them at a slightly higher elevation. Collide face-to-face and you and your rival will bump off one another harmlessly; collide slightly lower and your rival will pop your balloons. Like *Donkey Kong*, *Balloon Fight* is vertically oriented (the original arcade version also scrolled vertically, though the Famicom port does not), but the floating mechanic creates wider variations in sprite movement. Players and enemies can move along vertical, horizontal, and diagonal axes, space often shared with both static and dynamic environmental obstacles. *Donkey Kong* has more of a "gravitational pull," where most objects (besides Jumpman) are flowing toward the bottom of the screen. In *Balloon Fight*, the balloon men can flap their hands to actively fight gravity. Consequently, there is much less control over how many objects will appear on a single scanline simultaneously. As a result, *Balloon Fight* exhibits significant flicker, as sprites float about the screen erratically.

Sprite conflicts also help explain Pauline's revised placement. In the arcade version, Pauline is captive atop the highest platform, a horizontal girder parallel to Kong's line of sight. There, she cries "Help!" while waving her arms and waddling back and forth in anticipation of Mario's arrival. On the Famicom, Pauline is relocated to a new horizontal girder aligned with Kong's torso. This placement puts Mario's damsel awkwardly close to the ape, but it also clears space for the score indicators and keeps her out of the horizontal vector of barrel movement. From a narrative perspective, it also allows Mario to reach the uppermost platform without spatially "reuniting" with Pauline, since their girders are not attached. Arcade Kong snatches Pauline from her girder and carries her upward. The console version defers Mario's victory and makes a more sensible transition to the following stage, turning a hardware-necessitated concession into a narrative device.

Versatile Girders

With Kong occupying a majority of the background pattern table, how did *Donkey Kong*'s programmers allocate the remaining space? Primarily to letters, numbers, and girders. The first two should not be surprising, since each letter and number requires its own tile. Reserving tiles for ten numerals, twenty-six characters, and assorted punctuation and decoration (e.g., the brackets surrounding the BONUS text) quickly absorbs pattern memory. But why so many girders? If we look closely at the stage 1 screenshot in figure 2.2, we can see that each platform is composed of the same 8x8-pixel girder segment, positioned one after another in a row. And if that's the case, shouldn't the programmers only need one pattern tile in CHR-ROM to draw the entire structure?

As explained in chapter 1, there is an important difference in the way sprites and background tiles are placed on the screen. Each sprite has manipulable x- and y-coordinates that allow the programmer to place them with pixel precision, while background tiles are "locked" to the 32x30 name table grid. As a result, Jumpman can run along angled girders with relative ease, since his position can be shifted a single pixel at a time. But the girders themselves pose greater difficulties. Due to the 8-sprite-per-scanline limit, the girders are too wide to be built with sprites. But as background tiles, there is no way to shift them pixel-by-pixel to create the construction site's graded slopes.

Consequently, the incline comes at a cost: each pixel shift in the girders' angular ascent requires a separate tile. Inspecting *Kong*'s pattern table data reveals twenty-eight individual background tiles necessary to build the construction site, including those girders that have ladder attachments (figure 2.3).

While wasteful from a memory perspective, the incremental tile arrangement is true to both the look and process of arcade *Donkey Kong*, which renders and stores its girder tiles in an identical fashion. The difference is that arcade *Kong*'s girder slopes are more drastic. Vertical pixel

2.3 *Donkey Kong*'s background pattern table viewed in tile-editing software YY-CHR (detail). Note the number of tile variations necessary to draw Kong and the angled girders.

increments occur every sixteen pixels, so one beam may have up to thirteen individual segments. The Famicom port's decreased vertical space cannot support such steep inclines, so its middle girders are nine segments long, with each segment measuring four tiles across. Straight platforms were a necessary concession for some ports, but flattening *Donkey Kong*'s girders not only does aesthetic disservice to the arcade game, it breaks the stage's risk/reward structure: taller ladders make Jumpman more susceptible to falling barrels, but they provide a quicker route to the top.[50] Changing the angles changes the game.

With the majority of background tiles accounted for, there was little space left for decorative flourishes like custom title screen letterforms. To make use of the tiles at hand, *Donkey Kong*'s programmers used a single tile—the platform graphic from the rivets stage—to spell out "DONKEY KONG" in large letters on the title screen (figure 2.2).[51] Using background tiles as letterforms was not solely an aesthetic decision. In most tile-based graphics architectures like the Famicom's, there are no system-level character sets or pre-fab fonts. Every element seen onscreen is sourced from the sprite and background tiles, so adapting the rivet tiles for use in the title saves valuable ROM space.

Both arcade and Famicom versions of *Donkey Kong* include a full alphanumeric set: twenty-six letters, digits from zero to nine, and a few special characters. It is evident that Nintendo borrowed directly from the arcade's character set for the home version, since the alphanumerics are nearly pixel-for-pixel identical. Only a few are subtly modified (e.g., the arcade's "W" has angled strokes rather than vertical stems). Lifting an entire alphanumeric set makes sense for an arcade-accurate *Donkey Kong* port, but only if the port adopts their purpose: the scoreboard. Many contemporary *Donkey Kong* reviews mentioned various ports' lack of the cement factory or elevator stages, but few mentioned the lack of the arcade's high score screen. During its attract cycle, *Donkey Kong* shows the title screen, the high-score table, then demonstration play.[52] The order is significant. Imagine a skilled player who returns to the arcade on a regular basis to check up on her competition. She is not interested in a gameplay demo since she has played the game many times. She wants to see the leader board first. *Kong* ranks the five highest players with rank, score, and most importantly, a three-character name. The user-editable "NAME" column justifies the ROM space devoted to the full (English) alphabet. It is a limited palette for competitive expression, but it serves the purpose of allowing a skilled player to leave her signature.[53]

Famicom *Donkey Kong*, in contrast, adopts the full alphanumeric set without a real need to do so. The cartridge maintains the player's current score and the overall high score, but both revert to defaults when the system powers down. In fact, the high score is wiped from RAM even on a soft reset. Beyond the score displayed along the upper portion of the screen during demo and game play, there is no high score leader board, no rankings, nor any meaningful score persistence. Unless a player left the machine running continuously as in an arcade (an unlikely scenario for home play), the scores reset. Players could not enter their initials, so the hi-score lacked any competitive attribution. If Nintendo had eliminated the tiles for letters that never appear onscreen,[54] they could have liberated nine slots of pattern table memory, which coupled with the thirty-odd tiles of unused space in the sprite pattern table, might have allowed them to restore a few of the port's deleted animations.

Missing Pies

While interstitial animations were arguably supplemental to *Kong*'s core gameplay, the port's most significant cut was an entire stage—the so-called "pie factory," nicknamed after the cement trays that roll along multiple tiers of shifting conveyor belts. In arcade *Donkey Kong*, the pie factory was stage 2, directly following the construction site.[55] It was also the most visually and programmatically sophisticated of the four stages, since belts shifted direction, ladders raised and lowered, and obstacles and enemies spawned from multiple locations. Even Kong glided left and right as the belts turned—a necessary visual cue since the belts themselves did not animate (though their end caps did rotate).

Conveyor movement was likely the biggest barrier to stage 2's inclusion. Since Kong was a sprite in the arcade version, dragging him along the belts was a matter of simple coordinate updates. For home platforms with smaller sprites or harsher sprite-per-scanline restrictions, porting this behavior was challenging. The Atari 800 port included the pie factory, but left Kong stationary. The DOS and Apple II ports scrolled Kong appropriately, but allowed his tiles to merge with the ladders as he passed by. Between the two Commodore 64 ports, only Atari's featured a sliding Kong,[56] but he stood motionless as the conveyor carried him to and fro. On the Famicom, shifting Kong's position via background tiles would require either expending large numbers of tiles to increment his body within the name table grid, much like the girder inclines, or a sophisticated mid-screen scrolling effect that is practically impossible without added cartridge hardware.

Despite these programming challenges, there is a code-level clue that Nintendo at least considered including the pie factory. Famicom *Donkey Kong* reserves an address in RAM ($53) to hold the current stage variable, which may contain three valid values—1, 3, or 4—that correspond to the construction site, elevator, and rivets stages, respectively. Value 2 is conspicuously absent. With an emulator, it is possible to manually "poke" stage 2 during gameplay, creating a glitchy hybrid of game elements from all three stages: barrels fall, a duplicate Kong (with improper palette) is on the center of the top platform, and Mario can plummet through invisible elevators. Though no graphical evidence remains from the excised pie factory stage, the mismatched behaviors and reserved slot in RAM indicate the programmers at least experimented with its inclusion.

In 2010, Nintendo officially rereleased Famicom *Donkey Kong* preloaded on the PAL Wii as part of the 25th anniversary of *Super Mario Bros.*[57] The updated ROM (i.e., game image) ran on the Wii's Virtual Console via emulation with a few minor visual differences from the NES/Famicom version, among them a revised title screen that read "©1983–2010 NINTENDO" instead of "©1981 NINTENDO CO., LTD."[58] But most surprising in the Wii rerelease was the return of the pie factory in its proper position at stage 2. The update also reinstated a few interstitial animations—once Mario reaches the top of each platform in the first three stages, Donkey Kong grabs Pauline and carries her up the ladder. However, none of the opening cinematics or stoner favorite "How High Can You Get?" screens were included. Similarly, Kong's tiles remained unaffected by the shifting conveyor belts on his platform—though the programmers cleverly chose not to animate the end caps, opting for a diegetic mechanical solution to a technical limitation.

But how were Nintendo's retroactive additions possible? After a few industrious hackers at Lost Levels managed to extract the Wii's *Donkey Kong* ROM and examine its contents,[59] they found that the ROM no longer fit the NROM profile—rather, it was updated to the more spacious CNROM mapper (chapter 6), allowing for 32KB of bank-switchable PRG- and CHR-ROM, which in turn provided ample space for additional stage logic and animation tiles. Disassembly of the revised ROM revealed that much of the source code was identical to the 1983 release, with a few rather slapdash patches to shoehorn stage 2 into the existing game structure. (Accordingly, poking "2" into the current stage variable in the 2010 revision now produces expected glitched behaviors, e.g., barrels moving like cement pies.) Based on the disassembly's structure, Lost Levels forum members conjectured that Nintendo hacked their own ROM image rather than digging up the original source code.[60]

The pie factory's inclusion also makes the Famicom's per-scanline sprite limits glaringly obvious. Since the cement trays convey along flat horizontal planes, there is considerable flicker when multiple trays share the same platform. Barring the other technical reasons Nintendo may have chosen to drop the cement factory, the rampant flickering likely helped ease the decision of which stage to omit. All things equal, it made sense to drop the stage that suffered the most glaring visual drawbacks.

Binary Kill

Donkey Kong received one other notable amendment during the porting process: its infamous kill screen. Due to a programming oversight in *Donkey Kong*'s code, arcade play cannot progress past level 22 (in-game, each *level* equals one cycle of multiple *stages*). The BONUS timer, which serves as the countdown clock for each stage, is calculated by multiplying the current level number by ten then adding forty.[61] Once the player reaches level 22, the calculated result exceeds the maximum value of a single byte, $FF (or 255). Rather than catching the byte overflow and adjusting accordingly, the value wraps around to zero and loads the BONUS with inadequate time to finish the stage. After a few seconds of play, Jumpman halts, spins, and dies. *Donkey Kong*'s kill screen earned widespread attention thanks to the 2007 film *King of Kong*, since the programming bug set a hard limit on high scores. Unlike many arcade games, competitors cannot play *Donkey Kong* until they are too tired to continue or the score counter resets. Besting the world record requires careful strategy to maximize the score before the kill screen occurs.

Though arcade and Famicom *Donkey Kong* do not share the same source code, the latter remarkably "ports" the kill screen. The difference is that the Famicom version delays its appearance for far longer.[62] In addition to the current stage variable, the game also stores a separate variable in RAM for the current level. Each time the player completes the three-stage cycle (girders, elevators, rivets), the level variable increments. (Internally, the level variable initializes to 0, but displays onscreen as L1.) The BONUS counter can only be one of four values—5000, 6000, 7000, or 8000—corresponding to current level values 0, 1, 2, and 3. To determine the BONUS counter (in reality, its first two digits, since the second two are always zero), decimal value 4 is subtracted from the current level variable. If the result is negative, a code branch occurs and the leading digits are fetched from data stored in a small lookup table. Any positive result (as well as zero) ignores the fetch and loads the BONUS with its maximum value. Ideally, any level beyond the third should yield a BONUS of 8000.

The subtraction check functions properly until the level variable reaches $84 (or 132). Subtracting $04 from this value yields $80. Though it appears the result should pass the positive check, it does not, due to a quirk of binary math. A single byte can represent either unsigned values 0 to 255 or signed values −127 to 127. The latter choice is called *two's complement* and relies on a special binary bit flag to determine the appropriate sign. Two's complement reserves the leftmost bit of a byte to indicate either positive (0) or negative (1) numbers. When *Donkey Kong*'s BONUS check yields $80, whose binary form is %1000000, the CPU may evaluate the number as either 128 or −128. Since the programmers did not include a check for the negative flag, the CPU reads a two's complement value, causing the code to branch improperly and fetch the wrong leading digits for the BONUS timer (04). With only 400 time units allotted, Jumpman cannot reach the top of the stage. Consequently, level 133 (internally, 132) is Famicom *Donkey Kong*'s kill screen.

It is likely the two's complement edge case was not a pressing concern for *Donkey Kong*'s programmers. Few people have the skill or patience to endure the 300-plus stages buffering the player from Mario's binary-induced death spin. In fact, the programmers appear to have accommodated fewer than ten level iterations. The subroutine that fetches the background tile to display for the current level has no safeguard to cap its incrementing beyond numeral 9. Even if it did, the screen layout does not provide the adequate space to display double-digit values in the level bracket. And since the numeral tiles are stored at the beginning of the background pattern table, the code uses an index value to seek the appropriate digit to display on screen.[63] Venturing beyond level 9 first causes the graphic index to cycle through the alphabet tiles, then the sequential array of background graphics. Far before they made it to the kill screen, the finest *Donkey Kong* players would have noticed peculiar tile fragments in the level display—a section of barrel or a bit of Kong's body—indicating that they were in dangerous, uncharted territory.

Beyond Jumpman

Few home consoles were capable of porting *Donkey Kong* accurately. Dedicated hardware was impossible to match with an all-purpose machine, but Nintendo's console and cartridges were valiant efforts. While NROM's base outlay of PRG-ROM and CHR-ROM bested the arcade giant, the latter's larger sprite size and impressive sixteen sprite-per-scanline limit forced Nintendo to make a pattern table concession that snowballed into cutting tiles, animations, and ultimately an entire stage.

Nonetheless, the NROM board served the technical needs of Nintendo's opening salvo of games, supporting excellent arcade conversions that would stabilize the Famicom's launch, prove its hardware mettle, and attract the attention of third-party developers. Moreover, *Donkey Kong*'s dual appearance in arcades and on the Family Computer bookended a rapid corporate transformation. In two years, Nintendo evolved from eclectic Japanese toymakers to global players in the videogame industry. And they did so by deftly navigating a series of challenging ports—geographically, culturally, and technologically.

The Family Computer was designed with *Donkey Kong* in mind, but it was engineered with affordances that looked beyond *Donkey Kong* toward new styles of play. None of Nintendo's three Famicom launch titles required scrolling, for instance, but Ricoh and R&D2 designed a PPU capable of panning across name tables with ease. By all accounts, Nintendo was not looking to capitalize solely on their arcade successes; they were looking ahead to the possibilities of future game experiences. There was more in store for Jumpman.

Overall, if anybody can bring video games back, Nintendo, with its new fourth-generation game system, will be the one.

— Edward Semrad, *Milwaukee Journal*, Oct. 5, 1985

I only want three things for Christmas, this year. I'm getting older so I don't want any toys. I want a ten to nineteen inch color television, a jean acid washed, insulated jacket and last but not least the Nintendo Entertainment System.

— Andrea Way, *Evening News: Letters to Santa*, Dec. 24, 1987

Today, the debut of a videogame console is a worldwide media event. Years prior to its appearance, the rumor mills churn over leaked details from microchip vendors, overseas assembly lines, and game developers tapped to receive advance development kits. Hardware prototypes are revealed during industry showcases like E3, Gamescom, or the Tokyo Game Show. Technical specs are scrutinized and compared. Preview builds of "next generation" software are unveiled to showcase the superior capabilities of the new machine. Excitement and anticipation build until the console's launch date, a term borrowed from the maiden voyages of nautical craft. Hyperbolic perhaps, but an apt comparison— these multi-million dollar experiments in cutting edge technology are jettisoned into the treacherous waters of free markets to either sink or sail.

In the early 1980s, there was no such mania. Videogame consoles rarely had publicized launch dates. Their manufacturers introduced them to department and toy stores like any other new product, typically testing the waters in select target markets before moving on to a nationwide—not worldwide—rollout. A simultaneous global launch was both financially risky and a significant manufacturing and distribution challenge. This is still true today. While the "Big 3" publishers—Sony, Nintendo, Microsoft—manage to launch their home consoles "worldwide," the adjective typically describes Japan, Western Europe, and the United States. India, Asia, Australia, South America, and other parts of the world receive new consoles on a staggered schedule, often years after their initial launch date. Portable systems and videogame software tend to follow traditional distribution models, launching in their native market first, then disseminating across the globe. The difference between staggered launches of the 1980s and the 2010s is timing. While American consumers may wait six months to receive the latest iteration of Nintendo's DS handheld, they had to wait years for the Famicom to reach Western shores. And in reality, there were few waiting for it at all. Save for a handful of the most devoted videogame importers or games journalists, nobody outside Japan had ever heard of the Family Computer.

When the Famicom did arrive as the Nintendo Entertainment System, or NES, it looked radically different than its elder sibling. A subdued monochromatic box replaced the colorful red and white plastic toy. It was no longer a family computer, but an austere "entertainment system," meant to sit inauspiciously among one's VCR, stereo system, and cable box. The Famicom's colorful cartridges—now stark gray "Game Paks"—no longer protruded from the top of the console, but slid discreetly into the front of the system. The console's packaging floated the system and its peripherals against a gradient of deep blue melding into a star field (not unlike the backdrop of *Radar Scope*) and marketed its contents with assertive adjectives: "Control Deck," "Deluxe Set," "Action Set," "Power Set," "Super Set," and "Challenge Set." It was all serious, futuristic business—a strategy calculated over months to introduce Nintendo's domestic console to the world at large.

American Crash

It took a remarkable mixture of talent, timing, and tenacity to bring the NES to life. By all industry accounts, Nintendo was heading toward a massive failure far beyond the scale of a few thousand unsold *Radar Scope* cabinets. In 1983, when the Famicom debuted in Japan, the U.S.

videogame market was tumbling toward disaster, threatening to wither away just as it had begun to bloom.

The so-called "videogame crash" of 1983 is well-trodden in surveys of videogame history.[1] A complex series of economic, industrial, and cultural factors coalesced into the systematic collapse of the industry's major players. But prior to the crash, the industry was booming. In 1981, arcade revenues exceeded $4 billion—*Pac-Man* alone accounted for $150 million.[2] By 1983, home videogame sales, then dominated by Atari's eighty percent market share, contributed an additional $3 billion, a more than sixfold increase from revenues in 1981.[3]

Atari's explosive success became part of their downfall. With millions of consoles in American homes, the Atari VCS was the target platform for first-rate, second-rate, and cut-rate software alike. Beyond its in-house development teams, Atari had little control over the quality of software that reached its console. The flood of mediocre games surged so steadily that it became difficult for consumers to differentiate quality from shovelware. When Atari bet big on licensed properties like *Pac-Man* and *E.T.*, then shirked on the time allotted for programmers to produce quality code, the situation worsened.[4] Retailers slashed prices on poor or overprinted games, creating a race to the bottom for software prices that made it difficult for quality games to stay profitable.

Supply-side troubles, again prompted by the videogame boom, led to unwieldy product lead times and increased competition among console manufacturers. Chip shortages compelled toy companies to hedge their inventories, forcing excess product into the retail channel. Videogame hardware crowded warehouses and store shelves. As more competitors followed the gold rush, advertising budgets skyrocketed.[5] The growing personal computer market exacerbated these effects, as those manufacturers were now sourcing the same components for their systems while competing for the same consumer dollars. PC encroachment likewise spurred videogame manufacturers hoping to capture part of the emerging market to produce ill-considered hybrids, like the Coleco Adam, that failed to distinguish themselves as either capable computers or videogame systems.

Cultural differences between external management and freewheeling Silicon Valley programmers were also coming to the fore. Development cycles were compressed to capitalize on the boom, while game designers were given little or no credit for their work. Videogame companies were acquired by large media and communications conglomerates. In a symbolic move, Nolan Bushnell, Atari's founder and a figurehead for the early videogame industry, left two years after Warner acquired his company. As videogames became big business, the atmosphere of fun, creativity, and innovation gave way to profit margins, corporate infrastructure, and market demands.

Likewise, public perception of videogames was faltering. As children and teens spent increasingly more time in arcades or in front of TV screens, parents and legislators became concerned for their moral fortitude. Surely the barrage of twitchy, fast-paced graphics and violent gameplay was causing long-term harm. As Donovan recounts in his survey of videogame history, even the U.S. Surgeon General Dr. Everett Koop weighed in: "Everything is 'zap the enemy,' there's nothing constructive."[6] Arcades began to face tighter restrictions, even outright bans. All the pieces came tumbling down, as Kline et al. explain in *Digital Play*:

> The reckoning was brutal. What began as a general slow-down in demand careened over the brink into a vertiginous crash that all but wiped out the industry in North America. Time Warner/Atari sales of two billion dollars in 1982 dropped forty percent the following year and the division lost $539 million. The crisis worsened because companies had leveraged capital in anticipation of constantly escalating sales. By 1984 revenues had dropped to less than half of what they had been two years before.[7]

Several promising U.S. consoles and companies were caught in the ensuing death spin. The ColecoVision, despite its early success as the lead console for arcade ports, was swept into the dustbin. GCE/Milton Bradley's innovative Vectrex console, featuring a built-in vector display, was abandoned before it had a chance to find an audience. Even Atari's 7800, a marked improvement over the VCS that rivaled the Famicom's graphic capabilities, drowned in the wake of the crash.

Journalists speculated that the console videogame craze was giving way to a PC-centric future as computers reached price parity with videogame hardware. In 1983, the *New York Times* reported that, "For $75 to $200, consumers can buy a basic computer that can play games—although without some of the advanced graphics available on video game machines—and can also serve some educational functions and figure the family finances. Computer makers are betting that consumers will sacrifice better game-playing for more serious pursuits."[8] In the United States, the future for dedicated videogame consoles seemed bleak in the face of cheaper, all-purpose machines.

With the U.S. videogame industry in steep decline, Nintendo knew that they would not be able to export their Family Computer without significant alterations. Toy retailers were fleeing at the slightest whiff of a new videogame console. They had learned a calamitous lesson with Atari that they were not keen to repeat. Nintendo's success would require a radical rethinking of the Famicom's design, more consistent with the trends of the U.S. PC, toy, and consumer electronics industries than the tastes of Japanese children.

Nintendo's first attempt at the American Famicom, dubbed the Advanced Video System (AVS), debuted at the January 1985 Winter Consumer Electronics Show (WCES) in Las Vegas.[9] The AVS was an inspired sample of 1980s futurist industrial design, prompted by Nintendo of America's request that designer Lance Barr make the U.S. version of the console "high-tech sleek yet accessible,"[10] more computer than toy. Ironically, his initial concepts were far more "family computer" than the Famicom ever turned out to be.

An early concept sketch of the AVS depicted a black unit with a sloped trapezoidal shape, wider in the front than back, with controllers docked along its upper edge, separated from the remainder of the system by a narrow track of ridged black plastic.[11] Barr axed Nintendo's patented plus controller for a square plate with red arrows indicating the four cardinal directions, but revived the Famicom's ill-fated square buttons.[12] And like the Famicom, only the leftmost player one joypad included Select and Start buttons, though they were stacked vertically, aligned to the immediate right of the directional pad rather than the center of the joypad.

Interestingly, two keyboards dominated the console's face. The first had alphanumeric characters set flush with the surface but scalloped slightly to accommodate typing. Below were two rows of additional keys arranged like a piano keyboard, covering nearly two octaves and a half. The "sharps" were labeled numerically from one to twelve, allowing them to pull double-duty as standard PC function keys (labeled F1 to F12). A red Nintendo logo emblazoned the left corner of the system, a stark emblem on an otherwise monochromatic console. Overall, the concept was dark, sleek, and angular, ironically reminiscent of the MSX PCs popular in Japan.

Though Barr's initial concept sketch was never realized, the final AVS prototype shown at WCES carried over several of its design cues, albeit in an exploded view. Barr scrapped the integrated system in favor of a modular design: three main components—control deck, keyboard, and tape deck—were meant to stack together symmetrically and, Voltron-like, form the complete Video System. The concept sketch for this version of the AVS revealed a mildly enhanced palette of white, gray, and black, with red accents—the same palette used for the final NES hardware.

But like the previous concept, the keyboard was still the largest component, meant to supply the base for the tape and control decks,[13] whose combined widths matched its footprint. The text in the AVS concept drawing labeled the top components as the "Tape storage subsystem" and the "Video game subsystem." These labels reflected Nintendo's shifted focus in the American market—the videogame component was now a subsystem of a complete computational device, rather than the central unit. It was a computer that also played videogames, rather than a console with optional PC features. Likewise, the tape deck was meant to be one part of a larger ecosystem of ambitious peripherals, including a standalone musical keyboard, a futuristic update of the Famicom light gun, and an arcade-style joystick. Barr also planned to obviate the nested controllers— and cords altogether—with infrared.

Barr purposely designed the AVS prototype to "look more like a sleek stereo system rather than an electronic toy,"[14] integrating easily with similar components in a home entertainment system. When not in use, the console's bevy of wireless peripherals and modules could be stowed discreetly. Nonetheless, the potential buyers at WCES were not impressed by the AVS prototype.[15] The design was both too evocative of a PC and too complex for a toy, a worst-of-both-worlds scenario that failed to please either potential market. As Sheff explains, "No one cared about the remote control, and they hated the keyboard—a turnoff to kids, industry executive believed (parents were irrelevant). The AVS had all the problems not only of the video-game business but of computers too. No one would touch it."[16]

Barr simplified the design. The tape deck, keyboard, and joystick disappeared. The infrared was nixed for cost and reliability reasons, so cords returned.[17] A number of new concept sketches appeared, each maintaining the simple palette, but experimenting with all manner of surface shapes, controller storage solutions, and hardware switches. But ultimately, the flattened control deck design prevailed.

Based on all extant documentation, blueprints, sketches, and prototypes of the Nintendo Entertainment System, it appeared as though the final console would have a "top-loading" cartridge slot like the Famicom. A pre-release promotional photograph sent to U.S. journalists in 1985 (figure 3.1) showed the slimmer AVS style control deck, a wired AVS light

3.1 An early NES promotional image featuring the prototype AVS. (Source: Marty Goldberg, personal collection)

gun, wired versions of the prototype controllers, a new robot peripheral, and an unlabeled game (*Duck Hunt* appears onscreen) that matched the dimensions of a Famicom cartridge.[18] It was not until late in the design process that Barr would once again have to rethink the console's form to accommodate one final—but major—revision.

Zero Insertion Force

In most cartridge-based consoles prior to the NES, videogames were inserted vertically, typically by slotting the cartridge into an exposed port that contained a card edge connector. Atari, Magnavox, Coleco, and Sega had all used similar loading mechanisms in their consoles.[19] Nintendo did the same with the Famicom and looked to follow suit for the AVS. But convention had a cost—a cartridge protruding from the top of an appliance was unequivocally a videogame console and Nintendo was adamant about positioning their new video system as something different. At the eleventh hour, Nintendo devised an alternative that literally hid the cartridge from view.

Nintendo engineer Masayuki Yukawa invented a novel "low insertion force connector"—essentially a spring-loaded cartridge bay—to guide cartridges toward the internal card edge connector, now mounted horizontally. Users flipped the hatch on the front of the NES, held the

cartridge by its ridged grip, eased it into the console until they met resistance, then pushed it down into the hollow recess of the machine. If loaded properly, the tray locked into place.

The mechanism was unlike any prior console design and handily kept the cartridge out of sight.[20] But the cart's atypical travel and orientation warranted additional redesigns. As Barr explained, the pivoting tray required a roomier console interior "designed around the movement of the game," as well as a lengthier cartridge shell: "Many of the features remained, such as the two-tone color, left and right side cuts, and overall 'boxy' look, but the proportions changed significantly to accommodate the new edge connector."[21]

Nintendo's U.S. patent for the front-loading design claimed that their "zero insertion force" (ZIF) mechanism solved a number of problems: it protected the circuit board from "spurious radiation," it minimized "the abrasion of the connecting electrodes of the circuit board of the memory cartridge," and required less force for a small child to operate. But Nintendo's mechanical solution to a market problem ultimately spawned more problems than it solved. The ZIF's spring mechanism and pivoting tray introduced more moving parts, which in turn introduced a greater potential for mechanical breakdown. The delicate spring mechanisms either gave way over time or enabled too much contact between the cartridge PCB and NES motherboard. The 72-pin connector that coupled with the game pak's exposed ROM would bend or corrode over time, leading to either the NES's infamous blinking screens or a mess of garbled graphics (indicating a poor connection between the CPU/PPU and cartridge ROM).

An inherent design flaw of all edge connecting game cartridges exacerbated the issue.[22] The exposed edge of the PCB was more susceptible to dirt, moisture, and all manner of unforeseen abrasions a child could invent. Nintendo aimed to preempt mishandling by including coated vinyl dust covers to store games, similar to slip covers used to protect VHS tapes, vinyl records, or Nintendo's own Famicom disk cards. Though Famicom owners experienced their own errors due to dirty or corroded contacts, the top-loader design and swiveled plastic cover made them less prevalent. Tellingly, Famicom games were never sold with vinyl sleeves.

NES owners invented ad hoc solutions to "fix" the machine as it gradually became less reliable: blowing into cartridges, sliding the cart in at strange angles, wiggling the cart inside the tray, or simply giving the console a few well-placed smacks like a malfunctioning CRT. Ironically, every cart had a cautionary warning sticker affixed to its back that read, "DO NOT CLEAN WITH BENZENE, THINNER, ALCOHOL OR OTHER SUCH SOLVENTS." It was a reasonable advisory for children, but an alcohol-soaked cotton swab was far better at cleaning dirty contacts than blowing along the exposed PCB edge. Nintendo even used the flaw as a market opportunity, patenting and selling authorized cleaning kits—essentially a custom alcohol-soaked cotton swab—and opening official service outlets throughout the United States. Even today, a vibrant aftermarket of 72-pin edge connector replacements has arisen to repair the inevitable effects of the ZIF mechanism.

Nintendo's miscalculated engineering unwittingly became part of the NES's folklore. Blowing along the exposed edge of the cart (which does more harm than good) has become part of the *lingua franca* of the Nintendo Entertainment System.[23] But as we will see in the next section, it was not only the ZIF that caused consoles to go haywire—another NES-exclusive revision would further contribute to the millions of blinking screens.

10NES Racket

In 1986, the Famicom received a disk drive peripheral that supported expanded ROM space, cheap rewriteable media, and the ability to save game progress without unwieldy passwords. The Family Computer Disk System (FDS) included numerous anti-piracy measures, both physical and digital, that users, hackers, and pirates summarily circumvented. As a result, Nintendo eventually dropped support for the FDS and opted to develop cartridge-based augmentations that quickly surpassed the benefits of disk-based media (chapters 5 & 6).

A U.S. patent for a disk-based peripheral indicates that Nintendo considered exporting the FDS to the United States.[24] Presumably, the add-on would have connected to the NES via its expansion port, located on the bottom of the console beneath a snap-on plastic cover. The 48-pin port had lines for audio I/O, joypad reading, and CPU interface, among other functions,[25] so it would have been capable of supporting an FDS-like device, along with many other peripherals, much like the Famicom's own expansion port. However, by the time the patent was awarded, the Family Computer Disk System was already on the decline. The U.S. FDS never came to fruition and the expansion port remained unused for the duration of the console's lifespan.[26]

Nintendo's regional piracy problems were not limited to disks. Though significantly more costly for pirates and hackers, cartridges could be dumped and copied. Manufacturers of bootleg cartridges thrived (and continue to thrive) in markets located outside Nintendo's primary North America/Europe/Japan triumvirate. Russia, for instance, never received an official Nintendo Famicom release. Instead, the Dendy, a Chinese-produced "Famiclone" system distributed by Russian company Steepler, arose to meet market demand, sustaining a vibrant ecosystem of pirate hardware, software, television shows, magazines, and even an official mascot—the Dendy elephant—throughout the 1990s.[27] Architecturally, the Dendy was a peculiar hybrid, similar to a PAL NES, albeit with a faster clock speed (1.77MHz) and a truncated VBLANK period.[28] Its exterior case and cartridges, however, resembled the Famicom's, though it lacked the trademark red accents.[29]

Because of this Pandora's box of hardware and software bootlegs afforded by Famicom's lack of copyright protection, Nintendo aimed to preempt all threats of piracy, importing, and unlicensed software with the NES redesign. Their solution was the Checking Integrated Circuit (CIC), or lockout chip, a custom IC borne inside every NES console and game pak.[30]

The CIC was a 4-bit microcontroller with its own registers, instruction set, and ROM.[31] When players inserted game paks into the NES, each respective lockout chip executed a special handshake algorithm, known internally as 10NES. Both cart and console contained identical CICs, but they performed different roles based on how they were wired to one another. Among the CIC's sixteen-point pinout, there was one pin apiece devoted to data input, output, and a lock/key setting.[32] Console and cart chips could both send and receive data from one another when their I/O pins were wired to the other's opposing pins, but the former chip served as the "lock" while the latter functioned as the "key." The lock was wired to a capacitor whose output was used as a random seed to pick from among sixteen possible encryption streams. The lock relayed the stream selection to the key, then both had to output that stream while monitoring the input from one another to ensure a match. If a conflict occurred, the lock triggered a system reset, which also reset the CIC communication. Consequently, if a player inserted an unauthorized (i.e., keyless) cart, the reset cycle would repeat indefinitely.

With the CIC and 10NES, Nintendo implemented an early form of digital rights management (DRM), a hardware/software encryption mechanism meant to deter unauthorized access to their proprietary hardware. Of course, under the auspices of consumer and copyright protection, they had also barred unauthorized developers from producing NES software. Furthermore, thanks to the CIC's potential for malfunction, Nintendo had engineered another means for the NES to break down.

In a study of the CIC's influence on the establishment and evolution of DRM, O'Donnell argues that, "The 10NES chip in the NES...shifted user and consumer understandings of and expectations for videogames in ways that differ from music, movies, and other forms of emerging digital media technologies."[33] He adds, "In nearly all respects, DRM was birthed by the videogame industry with very little media user and consumer resistance."[34] While it is true that the CIC forcibly revamped the videogame industry's licensing structure and served as a model for future copyright protection mechanisms, it is questionable how much "consumer understandings" were altered, especially by implicating them as passive participants in a copyright sea change. CICs were housed in cart and console interiors. Few customers had any idea that the lockout chips existed. The only artifact of their operation was system failure. To the end user, the cycling resets triggered by a failed CIC handshake was identical to those caused by a bent or corroded ZIF mechanism. There were no error messages or user prompts indicating whether the game, hardware, or user was at fault.

Beyond thwarting bootleggers (and legitimate users), the CIC ensured a competitive advantage by enforcing Nintendo's strict licensing practices. In order to avoid their industry predecessors' fates in the U.S. videogame crash, Nintendo erected legal and hardware barriers to protect the integrity of their software catalog. Only sanctioned licensees could produce cartridges for the NES and said licensees were subject to stringent rules governing both the manufacture and content of their videogames. Developers were unaccustomed to such strict control after the software free-for-all of the late 1970s and early 1980s. European developers in particular balked at the restrictions, in most cases refusing to be cowed into compliance and instead focusing their efforts on the burgeoning PC market.[35] U.S. developers had no such luxury, as the NES quickly came to represent the videogame industry in toto. Nintendo's early wager on the NES paid off; they filled the vacuum of the post-crash market and seized control mercilessly, lording over vendors, retailers, and developers alike.[36]

Exclusive manufacturing rights ensured Nintendo's supply control, but it also exposed them to supply-side risks. An industry-wide chip shortage in 1988 impacted not only Nintendo's first-party game supply, but all of their subsidiary licensees.[37] *Zelda II*'s American release, for instance, was delayed for months, while third-parties suffered worse, with delays of a year or more. Some publishers claimed that Nintendo was purposefully throttling the supply chain to artificially inflate demand.[38] A CES report from the October 1988 issue of *Electronic Game Player* conveyed the growing sense of dissatisfaction surrounding Nintendo's licensing practices:

> Since they claim they have only limited quantities of the necessary chips, they are allocating only a small percentage of the third-party licensees' original orders (thus, if SNK originally ordered 500,000 copies of *Iron Tank*, they're provided with possibly as few as 50,000 copies). This is already causing tremendous supply and demand problems (take *Double Dragon* for instance), since you won't be able to find copies of the games for months after their first production.[39]

Sega and Atari saw this as an opportunity to capitalize on developer dissatisfaction. *Electronic Game Player* further reported that both companies "approached several third-party manufacturers in an attempt to persuade them to their machines."

CES '88 was not Atari's first attempt to undermine Nintendo. In 1986, displeased by Nintendo's licensing demands, Atari employees worked in earnest to reverse engineer the lockout chip. They first attempted to intercept and decode the communication between cart and console CICs, but that proved too difficult. They then decapped the chip, chemically peeling apart the silicon substrate to study its underlying physical structure. According to subsequent court accounts, Atari's engineers failed to crack the code in either effort.[40] In December 1987, Atari grudgingly agreed to Nintendo's licensing arrangement and produced three sanctioned game paks: *Pac-Man, Gauntlet,* and *R.B.I. Baseball.* However, by early 1988, Atari's lawyers resorted to social engineering to break Nintendo's code, as the U.S. Court of Appeals' decision explained:

> Atari's attorney applied to the Copyright Office for a reproduction of the 10NES program. The application stated that Atari was a defendant in an infringement action and needed a copy of the program for that litigation. Atari falsely alleged that it was a present defendant in a case in the Northern District of California. Atari assured the "Library of Congress that the requested copy [would] be used only in connection with the specified litigation."[41]

At the time, the threat of litigation was a lie, but Atari had the bravado to make it true. They sued Nintendo under antitrust law in December 1988, citing unfair monopolistic practices. Meanwhile, Atari's engineers had successfully produced the Rabbit chip, a microprocessor that mimicked the 10NES key.[42] Nintendo countersued in 1989, claiming breach of contract and patent and trademark infringement, petitioning the district court of appeals to halt further production of Tengen cartridges. Nintendo prevailed; the courts ruled that Nintendo designed an "original program" and that 10NES contained "protectable expression" subject to copyright law. [43]

Other unlicensed cartridge developers devised inventive means to outwit 10NES without resorting to Atari's subterfuge. Dan Lawton, a programmer for Color Dreams, managed to stun the CIC temporarily with a −5V surge as the NES booted.[44] Consequently, Color Dreams carts, housed in distinctive powder blue cases, included a DC voltage pump mounted on the PCB to permit their games to run unhindered. American Game Cartridges (AGC), American Video Entertainment (AVE), Camerica, Bit Corporation, Active Enterprises, and Bunch Games (a low-price subsidiary of Color Dreams) employed similar mechanisms in their cartridges.

Australian company Home Entertainment Suppliers (HES) ported many of the aforementioned companies' unlicensed titles for play on the Australian NES. Contrary to the common usage of the word, HES "ports" did not involve software conversion from one hardware architecture to another. Instead, HES transplanted game ROMs into new cartridge enclosures, swapping the CIC stun for a bizarre "piggyback" case design. In lieu of shocking the lockout into submission, players could attach a licensed NES game pak to the piggyback cart, using the former as a pass-through device that could deliver the necessary encrypted handshake. The kludgy workaround actually solved a new problem facing unlicensed developers. Once Nintendo got wind of the voltage spike technique, they released NES revisions that defeated the CIC stun, once again rendering unlicensed games unplayable. The piggyback cart's Trojan horse solution obviated the need to defeat the CIC at all.

The debacles surrounding the ZIF and the CIC eventually led Nintendo to discard both when the Nintendo Entertainment System model NES-001 was revamped as the NES-101 in 1993. Nintendo shrunk the console considerably—thanks to a "new" top-loading card edge connector—discarded the CIC (along with region lock), dropped the RCA composite out, and excised the expansion port. As Barr recounted:

> The redesigned NES did not use the "zero force" connector, but instead relied on a direct insert connector. Form following function, the new connector placed the game 90 degrees to the main PCB and eliminated much of the bulk needed for the old electronics and connector. The redesign was made several years after the original, which was designed in 1984. The boxy look was out and I thought it was time for a more sleek and inviting look.

As a portent of future regional console unity, the NES-101 also brought the NES and Famicom into design parity. A similarly-revised Family Computer, the AV Famicom, was identical to the NES-101 save for its flattened top (to accommodate the FDS RAM Adapter Cartridge), 60-pin edge connector, 15-pin expansion port, and higher-quality composite A/V output.

Though the NES/Famicom redesign was a compact, reliable machine, it came too late in the console's lifespan. By 1993, the Super Famicom/Nintendo was already three years old in Japan and two years old in the United States. And though the NES-101's exterior drew cues from its younger, more capable successor, inside it was still the same old chips from 1983.

Operating Buddy

The Nintendo Entertainment System Deluxe Set, Nintendo's first NES retail bundle, was the culmination of many months' work of design refinement and marketing strategy. The sizable box included the NES control deck, RF switch, AC adapter, a host of instruction manuals and warranty cards, two controllers, the Zapper light gun, and the Robotic Operating Buddy (or R.O.B.).[45] Two bundled games, *Gyromite* and *Duck Hunt*, served to showcase the Deluxe Set's peripherals, but R.O.B. was the clear centerpiece.

The robotic toy was the bait that finally caught the industry's interest. When Nintendo introduced R.O.B. to the NES family, the toy industry saw a glimmer of potential. An all-new console was a non-starter post-crash, but a robotic playing buddy could divert consumer attention from the NES's core purpose. And in light of Nintendo's long and successful past as a toy-making company, R.O.B. made perfect sense in the NES lineup. Unsurprisingly, Yokoi, the veteran toymaker, and his team in R&D1 helmed the project, delivering a remarkable marriage of mechanical design and novel console interface that would appeal to consumers and retailers alike.

Nintendo marketing aggressively worked the robot angle—their early promotional materials made R.O.B. the center of attention. NOA's first in-store point-of-purchase displays were oversized R.O.B. replicas, whose illuminated torsos bore the full lineup of NES software. At Nintendo of America's New York launch party, "silver-plated R.O.B.s were strewn around the room as showpieces," with another oversized robot serving as the sculptural centerpiece.[46] The first televised NES commercial featured R.O.B. emerging from an egg, marking "the birth of the incredible Nintendo Entertainment System."[47] The picture of R.O.B. in a 1985 Macy's ad for the NES dwarfed both the system and its games.[48] The headline copy, "VIDEO ROBOTS," was set larger than any other text on the page, including the name of the console (figure 3.3).

Likewise, R.O.B.'s purple-backlit head, glowing red LED and vacant-lensed eyes occupied the majority of the Deluxe Set box. On the back, the requisite posed tableau of a family crowded around a TV, transfixed by *Duck Hunt*, featured R.O.B. staring idly back at the viewer. The text on the back promised "The first truly interactive home video game system," thanks to its futuristic pair of peripherals:

> No other video system features R.O.B.—the wireless video robot who plays games right along with you. Or the Zapper, the amazing light-sensing gun that puts sharp-shooting accuracy right in the palm of your hand. This extraordinary pair of video partners interacts with you and the screen, allowing you "hands on" video action.

How these peripherals trumped other consoles' "interactivity" is unclear—nearly every prior console had its host of unique and bizarre accessories—but R.O.B. did watch the television screen alongside its human players. In fact, the robot fulfilled the promise of Barr's abandoned wireless

3.3 Excerpt from the NES Macy's ad featured in the *New York Times*, November 17, 1985.

peripherals in a unique, if roundabout manner. R.O.B. was wireless, but
not due to embedded infrared or any other proprietary wireless protocol.
Instead, R.O.B. received its commands from the television via a sequence
of carefully timed flashes it detected with photosensitive lenses (i.e., its
eyes). However, its only means to relay commands back to the console was
through the same interface as the player—the controller. So R.O.B. did
play alongside the user as advertised, albeit in a strange circuit connecting
human, console, software, and television.

R.O.B.'s body comprised a plastic hexagonal base with a central post
supporting its torso (with two attached arms) and head. The robot's movements were coordinated by a series of battery-powered motors and gears.
Six notches along the "spine" allowed R.O.B.'s entire torso to ratchet up
and down. The central post could also rotate to align R.O.B. with five of
the base's six sides (the torso could not twist completely backward). The
same five sides were notched to accommodate accessories included with

the game software. Attached to its torso were two articulating arms that could open or close. Detachable hands allowed R.O.B. to grip accessories like gyroscopes or stackable blocks. No matter how the robot twisted, its head remained fixed, since it required a solid line of sight with the television. One could also angle R.O.B.'s head up or down if its base was not on the same level surface as the television. To ensure proper signal reception, supported games provided a calibration step to test R.O.B.'s vision. If the television picture was too bright, R.O.B. could malfunction, so a special filter was included to fit over its photosensors.

Gyromite was one of only two NES game paks that R.O.B. could play. (Since Nintendo sold the console in myriad hardware/software configurations after its initial launch, a standalone version of *Gyromite* came in an oversized box that included R.O.B.'s accessories.)[49] A special armature used to hold *Gyromite*'s namesake gyroscopes clipped into the two accessory notches on R.O.B.'s right-hand side. The front and front-left notches supported another armature meant to hold a joypad plugged into the second controller port. Along this armature were two mechanical levers that terminated in small circular "platforms," one red and one blue. When weight (i.e., a gyroscope) was placed on the platform, the lever would mechanically depress either the A or B button on the second controller.

The rear-left accessory notch held a motorized spinner. Using the included pincer hands, R.O.B. could grasp the gyroscopes and place them inside the spinner, where they would rotate rapidly around their fixed post. R.O.B. could then drop the spinning gyroscopes on the circular platforms. There they could spin in place and keep the buttons held down for a short time, until they spun down and toppled. If the player was agile enough, they could instruct R.O.B. to drop both gyroscopes in turn, allowing the A and B buttons to activate simultaneously.

Gyromite's gameplay involved guiding a balding, lab coat-clad character named Professor Hector (Player 2 controlled Professor Vector) over a series of multi-tiered platforms blocked by blue and red cylindrical columns and a number of roaming birdlike foes called Smicks. The player had limited interaction with Hector—the professor could move horizontally across platforms, move vertically along ropes, and pick up turnips to drop and distract his adversaries. If Hector collected the bundles of dynamite scattered throughout the stage before the allotted time expired, the round completed and the next stage began. However, the red and blue columns served as gates blocking Hector's progress. The only way to raise and lower gates was to instruct Hector to issue commands to R.O.B., his robot companion.

In many NES games, pressing Start paused the game. In *Gyromite*, Start triggered a ready state, indicated visually by the screen's background changing from black to blue (what the manual calls "Robot transmission mode"). Hector then faced the player and cupped his hands as if holding a joystick, a visual cue indicating that he was looking "outside" the frame of the television screen. At this point, R.O.B. was now drawn into the diegetic space of the videogame as a participant. The player/Hector could then issue commands: Pressing up or down on the D-pad ratcheted R.O.B.'s torso up or down two notches, left or right rotated the central post, and B or A respectively closed and opened R.O.B.'s hands. Using these simple commands in various combinations allowed R.O.B. to interact with its accessories and, ultimately, the second controller. In order to lower a blue column, for instance, the player had to enter a string of button presses to make R.O.B. do the following:

A) rotate to the proper position above a gyroscope

B) lower the hands into position near the gyroscope post

C) grasp the gyroscope

D) raise and rotate to the proper position above the motorized spinner

E) place the gyroscope into the spinner and allow it to fully oscillate

F) lift and rotate the gyroscope into position above the blue circular platform

G) lower the gyroscope onto the platform

H) release the gyroscope

This entire robotic retinue performed a single mechanical function: pressing the A button on the second controller.

Green Screen

More interesting than R.O.B.'s laborious choreography was the means through which it received instructions. Whenever the player/Hector issued a command during "transmission mode," the screen would noticeably flicker between black and green. The flash was not meant for human eyes; R.O.B.'s optical lenses were synced to the refresh rhythm of the cathode ray television, so it perceived a sequence of optically-encoded "bits" meant to trigger the appropriate movement.[50]

Commands were encoded in two sequential, binary "data packets." The first was a "ready" signal, indicating that R.O.B. should anticipate further instructions. In *Gyromite*, the on and off bits of a message were represented by the screen color: off was black and on was green.[51] For each bit of the issued command, the screen flooded with a single frame of color. Using an emulator, one can slow down the flashes in order to read the color sequences that correspond to each command. The ready packet was three frames of black, one frame of green, then a final black frame, a binary message encoded as %00010. Directly after, an 8-bit 'instruction' packet requested one of R.O.B.'s handful of mechanical commands. For example, the eight-frame sequence green, black, green, green, green, green, green, black (%10111110) instructed R.O.B. to close its hands, while %11101110 opened them.

Gyromite's programmers employed two simple but efficient techniques to display R.O.B.'s optical commands onscreen. First, to accomplish the screen flashes, they flood-filled all onscreen tiles with green and black. Rather than manually shuffling sprites offscreen or substituting blank background tiles, *Gyromite's* programmers simply updated all four entries of all eight palettes to a single color. In other words, during the screen flashes, all the tiles are still in place—they are merely painted a uniform color to render them invisible.

Second, the programmers used a unique PPU feature called sprite 0 to accurately time the frame-length flashes. Sprite 0 is a special, high-priority tile, so named because it occupies the first—or zero—position in sprite OAM. When an opaque pixel of a background tile overlaps an opaque pixel of sprite 0, a special collision flag is raised. In fact, it is the only built-in collision detection that the PPU offers. Programmers conventionally used sprite 0 to execute mid-screen scrolling splits (chapter 4). In *Gyromite's* main play mode, for example, the screen is divided into two sections: a narrow status bar that contains the player's score and timer, and the lower play area. At the beginning of a round, when the game reveals the stage's entire two-screen layout, the upper status bar remains stationary while the play area scrolls horizontally underneath.

The NES has no hardware capability to split scrolling points at an arbitrary scanline—such an effect must be properly timed and executed in software. Sprite 0 marks the boundary between two sections and signals the CPU that the boundary point has been "hit." Once that boundary is known, the PPU's scroll registers can then be manipulated, creating a region of name table tiles that can scroll independently of those above the boundary. Scores of Famicom/NES games use this technique to divide the screen into two distinct regions: status bar and scrolling playfield.

Disabling *Gyromite's* background tiles in an emulator during gameplay reveals a lone pixel hovering near the top of the screen. That graphical point is the opaque portion of sprite o used to trip the status flag. As soon as the PPU encounters that pixel and notices that it is nestled behind an opaque portion of a background tile, a sprite o hit is fired.

In many Famicom and NES games that use sprite o in this way, you can use an emulator to hunt for a conspicuous tile or pixel that marks the scrolling boundary line (figure 3.4). In *Tecmo Bowl*, it's a single white pixel like *Gyromite's*; in *Ninja Gaiden*, a slender pink line; in *Excitebike*, a black block; in *The Legend of Zelda*, a bomb;[52] and in *Super Mario Bros.*, the bottom sliver of a coin (chapter 4). In all cases, it is a graphical artifact meant to be hidden from player view, a signal only the PPU is meant to see.

While R.O.B. was an innovative feat of optical, electrical, and mechanical engineering, its ponderous motorized movements limited its gameplay practicality. R.O.B. was too slow to control any videogame that might require fast reflexes or quick timing. It is telling that one mode of play in *Gyromite* involved raising and lowering gates while an automated Professor Hector literally sleepwalked through the stage. Players discovered that it was less time consuming simply to take control of the second gamepad themselves (or have a friend play R.O.B.'s part) and circumvent R.O.B.'s involvement altogether.

The robot was an impressive showpiece that served Nintendo's purposes, but it wasn't particularly fun. As Nintendo employee Gail Tilden recalled, "That thing was definitely like watching grass grow...It was so slow, and to try and stand there and sales-pitch it in person and try to make it exciting; you had to have the eyes lined up just right or it wouldn't receive the flashes. It was kind of a challenge."[53] Nonetheless, the robot helped divert attention, at least temporarily, from the NES's gaming core and instead focus consumers on a novel gadget. Once players discovered that the NES was an enjoyable console based on the merit of its games alone, R.O.B. was quickly forgotten. After its initial two games, the operating buddy was no longer allowed to play.[54]

"AFTER THE EYES FLASH..."

The Deluxe Set's light gun peripheral fared better than R.O.B. throughout the NES's lifespan. The Zapper was one of the few hardware add-ons that emerged relatively unscathed from the console's AVS-to-NES metamorphosis, but its legacy reached further into Nintendo's past than the Famicom, Game & Watch, or even videogames. Photo-electric shooting ranges, hosted in converted bowling alleys, were popular in Japan prior to the *Space Invaders*-fueled arcade explosion, and Nintendo had their own successful "Laser Clay Ranges."[55] For home play, Yokoi had created

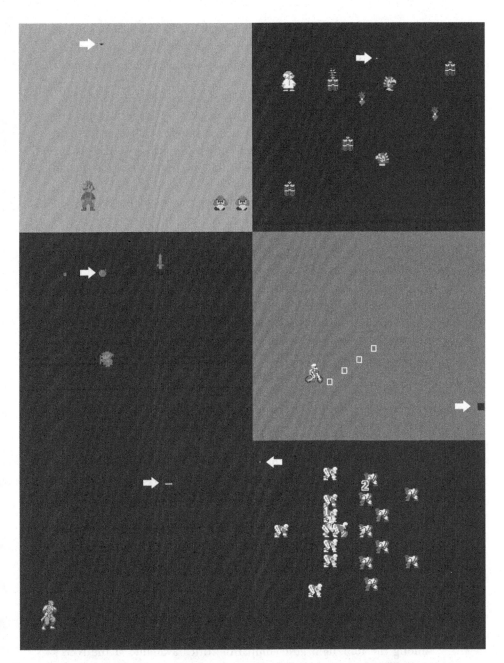

3.4 Annotated screenshots of six games with their background tiles disabled, permitting a better view of the sprite 0 flags used to divide status bars from scrolling playfields. Clockwise from upper left: *Super Mario Bros.*, *Gyromite*, *Excitebike*, *Tecmo Bowl*, *Ninja Gaiden*, *The Legend of Zelda*. (Emulator: FCEUX 2.1.5)

toy target games like *Custom Gunman Target* (1976), *Custom Lion Target* (1976), and the remarkable electro-mechanical target game called *Kousenjuu Duck Hunt* (1976), which used a projector to cast flying ducks on a wall.[56]

Following these early models, in 1984 the Famicom received its own light gun (ガン) peripheral, fashioned after a classic Western six shooter, that attached to the console's 15-pin expansion port. And since the light gun already had respectable software support in Japan (billed as the "Video Shooting Series"), it was a logical choice to port to the NES, though not without a few important translations.

Nintendo was rightfully concerned that American parents would find a realistic revolver unacceptable for children. As a result, Lance Barr prototyped a more futuristic gun design to match the AVS' palette and form factor. Though the initial model folded into a wand and used infra-red like the original prototype gamepads, the final retail light gun nixed these capabilities in favor of a more economical and ergonomic design—a cabled, non-collapsible laser gun painted gray and white. The NES Zapper's new aesthetic conformed well to toy trends in the mid-1980s, sharing retail space with a host of other gun-shaped toys like Lazer Tag, Photon, and the sundry *Star Wars* accessories that stocked department store shelves. And while the Zapper successfully skirted any anti-gun outrage, Nintendo did eventually have to make one further alteration. In compliance with a U.S. federal regulation requiring "toy, look-alike, and imitation firearms" to be either translucent or painted in bright pastels, Nintendo opted to repaint their Zapper barrel and handle blaze orange.[57]

While the Zapper was not as mechanically sophisticated as R.O.B.—its sole moving part was a red, spring-loaded trigger that sounded a resonant metallic *clang* when squeezed—the photodiode housed in its barrel functioned similarly to the robot's eye lenses. The light gun did not rely on a sequence of coded flashes, but it did require the same frame-accurate light/dark discrepancies that drove the robot's movements. And unlike R.O.B. (or the Famicom Gun), the Zapper connected to the NES's standard joystick ports. In fact, two Zapper status bits were located in the same internal joypad registers ($4016 and $4017) used to poll for controller input: one bit recorded whether the Zapper trigger was pulled or released, while another monitored whether light was detected.[58]

Among the four light gun-compatible titles available at the NES's launch,[59] *Wild Gunman* (1985) best illustrated both the hardware mechanics underlying the light gun's function and Nintendo's continued eagerness to repurpose early game concepts for new platforms. In its introductory mode (Game A), a large outlaw moseyed into a nondescript desert landscape punctuated by cacti, tufts of foliage, scattered fossils, and a distant red mesa. Once the outlaw reached center screen, he paused, yelled "FIRE!!", and his eyes flashed like jewels. A timer then started, and the player was meant to fire before it reached the designated time limit.

The gameplay scenario mimicked a Western duel, though with less fatal results. Pull too early and you triggered a "FOUL!"; pull too late and the screen blinked in shades of red, presumably indicating a survivable wound, since you were permitted to draw again. Precision gunplay was not necessary. Game A required that the player simply pull the trigger while the Zapper barrel pointed at any portion of the television screen. Shoot the cactus or the sky if you liked—you would still register a successful hit.

Wild Gunman's name, Wild West dueling scenario, and flashing eyes were all callbacks to Nintendo's innovative light gun game from 1974, a Yokoi-designed hybrid of toy hardware, photosensors, and film projection. As the International Arcade Museum describes, "The game has an image projection system that uses a 16mm film showing an outlaw gunslinger appearing in an alley and the player has to draw his or her gun and shoot that outlaw before the outlaw draws his gun and shoots."[60] When the game began, a pre-recorded narrator announced the instructions, repeated in truncated form onscreen: "AFTER THE EYES FLASH... SHOOT!" Players wore a belt to holster a six-shooter that was wired to the game's cabinet. Inside there were two projectors used to branch between film reels depending upon whether the player drew and fired in time. Like its NES successor, the arcade version of *Wild Gunman* relied solely on speed rather than accuracy. Aiming at any part of the screen registered a hit.

Keen-eyed gunslingers who spent time with the NES update of *Wild Gunman* might also have noticed that, similar to *Gyromite's* transmission mode, the screen flashed briefly when they pulled the trigger. And as expected, this flash contained the visual information necessary to communicate with the Zapper. Inside the gun barrel was a small photodiode, a light-sensitive transistor that converted light into electrical signals. Via the controller port, the converted signal fed into the joystick registers described above. To poll for successful shots, Game A first flashed a full frame of black, then white. If the Zapper detected the white target, its light sensor bit triggered, and the game logic registered a hit.

But there was also a sly bit of built-in signal translation that took place to prevent false positives—i.e., player cheating. Pointing the gun at a lightbulb, fluorescent overhead, or any other ambient light source resulted in a lost gunfight. In short, the Zapper would not signal a hit unless its photodiode detected light from the television. To ensure that the target was located onscreen, Nintendo's Satoru Okada engineered a unique electrical filter that rejected any frequency content that did not match the television's horizontal oscillation frequency.[61] If the light source was the proper frequency, the light sensor bit recorded a hit.

The Zapper's reliance on the oscillation of the CRT's sweeping horizontal blank precludes its use on modern televisions. *NESDev* community member Damian Yerrick, who coded an extensive Zapper test/demonstration program called *Zap Ruder*, explains why this is so:

> The Zapper and similar light guns have the photodiode connected to a 15.7 kHz resonator to detect whether light is actually coming from adjacent scanlines of a CRT's raster scan and not a light bulb. The trouble is that LCD TVs don't have that 15.7 kHz flicker. The only sort of Zapper game that works on an NES connected to a modern TV is one that uses the trigger and not the photodiode.[62]

In other words, a chasm of perception divides human sensors (eyes) and electro-mechanical sensors (photodiode). Besides the sharper, higher-resolution display of a modern LCD, we still see television the same way—whether with liquid crystal or electron gun, our eyes are consistently and sufficiently fooled to perceive believable moving images. But the Zapper's photodiode, trained to the rhythms of the CRT, is rendered blind.

Black Boxes

Early NES games had a uniform packaging style. Keeping in line with the outer space backdrop of the console's packaging, the first seventeen NES launch titles (and a subsequent thirteen post-launch titles) arrived in boxes printed front-to-back in black, dotted with small glimmering stars. The upper half of the box front displayed a sample of the game's graphics, zoomed to a scale that showcased their flat pixellated topographies. And nowhere on the box could one find the words "video game."

Nintendo was purposefully foregrounding the NES's graphics capabilities in direct response to the marketing tactics of earlier competitors. Atari's beautifully-painted box covers, for instance, were speculative leaps of fancy that relied on strong imaginations to link them with the chunky graphics seen in-game. Nintendo could not risk such a disconnect during their tenuous launch. Gail Tilden, NOA's VP of Brand Management, felt that, "There was an over-promise in the games that had been introduced prior…The consumer might see some beautiful fantasy graphics on the front, or a photographic image of people playing tennis, and then it was really just some enhanced version of *Pong*."[63] The idea was to advertise exactly what the hardware could deliver.

The black boxes represented Nintendo's concentrated focus on an unambiguous, unified, and regulated product line. Nintendo stamped each game with a "seal of quality" assuring consumers that all software met the company's approval standards. The stream of mediocre unlicensed games that clogged the U.S. market in 1983 would find no quarter on this new Entertainment System. In reality, the seal was more marketing gimmick than quality guarantee. A more accurate moniker would have been "seal of control," the final symbolic mark of Nintendo's licensing practices. The seal did not fend off bad games, but it did guarantee that Nintendo had had their hand in sculpting the game's content to conform to the corporate image.

Beyond the graphic illustration, the sole differentiator between black box titles was Nintendo's own sub-classification system. Nintendo created seven series headings grouped by genre and peripheral: Action, Arcade, Light Gun, Programmable, Sports, Education, and Robot. As expected, the Action, Arcade, and Sports series were stocked with familiar Famicom titles. The Arcade series—*Donkey Kong*, *Donkey Kong Jr.*, *Donkey Kong 3*, *Mario Bros.*, and *Popeye*—were further distinguished by a metallic silver band beneath their title text with "The Original!" printed in script above and "Arcade Classics Series" printed in bold blue text below, showcasing Nintendo's marquee titles. The promise of arcade-quality console ports, absent since the ColecoVision's demise, was now a reality. The oddball Programmable series (*Excitebike*, *Wrecking Crew*, *Mach Rider*) showcased games with built-in level editors, albeit with no means to save in-game creations.[64] The Education series, represented solely by *Donkey Kong Jr. Math*, was clearly meant to placate parents' fears about bringing videogames into the home.

Though they aimed to distance themselves from Atari in the name of honesty, Nintendo was not above cover embellishment. Most of the character graphics were given comic book motion lines to make the artwork more dynamic: the ball bounced from left to right in *Pinball*, the skier zoomed into frame in *Slalom*, and barrels whooshed from Donkey Kong's hand. Most cover graphics also ignored the PPU's capabilities, tilting sprites at diagonals, bumping up palette counts, and adding sub-pixel details. Nintendo also cleverly swapped Jumpman for Mario on the *Donkey Kong* cover, leveraging the more marketable platforming plumber to sell their arcade classic. The recasting made marketing sense, but misrepresented the cart's actual CHR-ROM contents. Nintendo certainly scaled back the fantasy of earlier Atari fare, but the artwork was not a one-to-one representation of the product within.

There were also differences between NES and Famicom boxes, due in part to the size of the cartridges within. As discussed in chapter 1, Famicom carts were designed to resemble audio cassettes. The Sony Walkman was wildly popular in Japan in the early 1980s, and it made marketing sense to evoke a visual resemblance between cassettes and videogames. However, as cartridge hardware expanded to accommodate additional ICs, batteries, and the like, Famicom cartridge shapes began to diversify. This happened as early as 1984, when the *Family BASIC* cartridge's extended WRAM and battery switch required a taller PCB and cartridge enclosure.[65] Famicom cartridges likewise came in a kaleidoscope of colors and shells, whose designs were apparently left to the discretion of the licensee. The only consistency in Famicom design comparable to the black boxes were the fourteen Famicom cartridges manufactured between July 1983 and October 1984 that featured the "pulse line" graphic—named after its resemblance to the output of an electrocardiogram—in lieu of game graphics or illustrations.[66]

As the NES became entrenched in the U.S. market, Nintendo relaxed its uniform marketing aesthetic. The final few titles to use the black box style weren't even black. *Metroid* and *Kid Icarus* adopted the pixelated illustrations and overall graphic design, but shipped in silver boxes. *Ice Hockey* was grouped into the Sports Series but had a solid blue box with the photograph of a hockey player in place of the usual pixels. Nintendo gradually abandoned the uniformity of their first-party titles, maintaining no consistent house style beyond the prominent Nintendo logo. Likewise, the Series moniker was unceremoniously discontinued with the black boxes.

Some third-party developers adopted Nintendo's packaging aesthetic to establish their own brand identity. Bandai, one of the first Japanese licensees to release games in the U.S., hewed closest to the black box aesthetic. Their boxes featured a black-to-gray gradient background, a Nintendo-style diagonal marquee, and an actual screenshot in place of Nintendo's augmented pixel art. They also overlaid a cartoon illustration of the game's lead character and invented their own series categories. *Chubby Cherub* (1986), *Ninja Kid* (1986), and *M.U.S.C.L.E.* (1986), for example, were part of Bandai's short-lived "Character Action Series."

Other licensees developed house styles that strayed from Nintendo's black box brand. Konami adopted silver boxes with vibrant cartoon illustrations of in-game action dominating the cover, reviving the Atari artwork tradition that Nintendo initially abandoned.[67] Early titles by Capcom, like *Trojan* and *Mega Man*, featured a gradient blue background with floating neon wireframe grids, while their later boxes (e.g., *Duck Tales*, *Mega Man 2*, *Gold Medal Challenge '92*) shifted to a solid purple backdrop. Other third-parties followed suit: Jaleco opted for white boxes, unlicensed manufacturer Tengen chose gold, and Tecmo titles had a simple red band across the box bottom.

While packaging styles shifted to better differentiate their developers and distributors, cartridge manufacture was kept under strict control. Nintendo was the sole gatekeeper to their console. Submitting to their licensing terms meant relinquishing unprecedented control over production, release schedule, content, and quantity.[68] Worse still, developers had to pay upfront for the privilege, as Donovan explains:

> Licensees had to pay Nintendo to manufacture their game cartridges so even if the game sold badly Nintendo made a profit. Nintendo also took a cut of every NES game sold, dictated when the game could be released, told licensees how many games they could release every year, and got to decide whether a game was good enough to be released.[69]

The same company that had supplicated itself to U.S. toy retailers now had unprecedented power over their own corporate image, from content to hardware. As Nintendo steamrolled the competition, the situation worsened for developers, now caught in a double bind. Producing a videogame hit meant tapping into the massive NES audience, but obtaining a license meant bending to Nintendo's will. Nintendo further stifled their competitors' efforts by demanding all games developed for the NES be exclusives. Atari, NEC, and Sega were hard-pressed to find developers willing to risk their licensee status by porting their NES titles to competing platforms.

Color Dreams

Alongside the controller and the console's monochromatic palette, the distinctive shape and color of the NES game pak is one of the platform's most enduring cultural icons.

NES game paks measured approximately 12cm x 13.3cm x 1.6cm, though they were not symmetrical rectangular solids. The cartridge bottom was notched by several millimeters on either side so it would seat properly in the console, but its plastic enclosure also protected the narrow

PCB pin edge that protruded from the cartridge interior. A recessed area near the top left edge of the cartridge fit the forefinger and thumb, a welcome aid for inserting and removing the cartridge from the ZIF mechanism. Ridges were molded into both sides of this recessed area and extended vertically along the front of the cartridge, providing both a convenient gripping surface and a subtle aesthetic flourish echoing the striped ridges of the NES. Unlike most top-loading cartridges, which could be grasped with the entire hand or levered out with an eject mechanism, game paks were built to be pinched, pushed, and pulled.

To differentiate games, Nintendo affixed a rectangular sticker to the cart front, each featuring a reproduction of the game's box artwork. The upper lip of the sticker, displaying the game's title, folded around the top of the cartridge. This served two purposes: the title was visible both when the pak was inserted into the console and when it was stacked with other games (a common way to store games, since most boxes were discarded). And thanks to the ridged grip described above, the sticker was positioned slightly right of center, providing the cartridge face a striking asymmetrical design. Finally, a small embossed triangle below the bottom left edge of the sticker indicated the proper way to insert the game pak into the console.

Game paks were roughly 1cm wider than Famicom carts due to twelve additional pins lining the PCB edge.[70] But they were also nearly double a standard Famicom cart's height thanks to the ZIF mechanism. The pak had to be long enough to reach the internal card edge connector without also losing one's game (or fingers) within the chassis. Though most cart interiors were largely empty space, the taller shells did have one side benefit: they could accommodate cartridge hardware expansions. Later Koei titles like *Gemfire* (1992), for instance, that used the MMC5 mapper (chapter 6), a battery, and added RAM, needed additional interior clearance to fit their extended PCBs.[71]

Beyond the obvious mechanical reasons, Nintendo's industrial designers appear to have chosen the cart's dimensions based on a popular consumer electronics format: the VHS tape. If the NES console was meant to integrate discreetly with similarly boxy home entertainment equipment, the games would need to do the same. Of course, extending the game pak even further to mimic a VHS tape would have made them both absurdly tall and far too large to fit in the console. Instead of adding more empty space to the game pak, Nintendo extended the packaging height. Consequently, all NES games had styrofoam risers nested at the bottom of their boxes to prop up the cartridges. Though a touch shorter and thinner than VHS sleeves, NES boxes fit comfortably alongside a movie library or video rental display.[72]

Several early NES titles shared a hidden bond with their Famicom siblings that was not obvious from their exterior appearance: they smuggled Famicom boards with Nintendo-manufactured adapters built in. Cracking open early NES conversions like *Excitebike* often revealed a 60-pin Famicom glob top protruding from a black plastic housing labeled NES-JOINT-01, an in-house Famicom-to-NES converter. The NES-JOINT not only did the proper pin conversion to make the game NES-compatible, it also added the CIC lockout chip, effectively piggybacking copyright protection onto the Famicom board. If one dismantled the adapter from the cartridge and pulled out the *Excitebike* PCB, the NES-JOINT functioned as a makeshift converter for any Famicom PCB. Aftermarket Famicom-to-NES convertors, like the Honey Bee Family Adapter, were eventually sold as standalone products, but Nintendo added their own covert solution in order to speed the manufacture of carts for the U.S. market.

The earliest NES carts were also fastened at five points with flat-head screws, meaning they could be easily disassembled with a standard screwdriver. However, once Nintendo discontinued using the NES-JOINT, they also replaced the five slotted screws with three 3.8 mm security screws (by removing two interior posts) that required a special bit to remove. To compensate for the removal of the upper two screws, the flat cartridge top was replaced by two interlocking plastic prongs used to secure the cart's halves in place.[73]

Nintendo had several reasons to limit access to the cartridge's interior. First, they could prevent children from opening and potentially damaging the delicate PCBs. Second, they could deter pranksters or thieves from swapping PCBs between cartridge shells, a potential problem for videogame rental stores. Third, they could bolster their nascent service industry. As the popularity of the NES skyrocketed in the States, official Nintendo Service Centers popped up nationwide. Locking down access to the cartridge ensured that consumers would bring their service dollars to authorized technicians rather than fixing problems themselves.

Nintendo received a U.S. patent for their distinctive cartridge design,[74] legally solidifying their resolute gray shells as the de facto look for tens of millions of NES games. Beyond a few exceptions, like the gold *Legend of Zelda* and *The Adventure of Link* game paks, the rest of the world never experienced the Famicom's kaleidoscopic spectrum of game cassettes.[75] And while Nintendo ultimately failed to curb unlicensed game production, they did protect their industrial design. Though unlicensed companies' box designs could pass easily for a "real" Nintendo game (minus the seal of quality),[76] they had to alter their cartridge shells to avoid infringement. This resulted in a number of cartridge redesigns that creatively avoided Nintendo's industrial design while still enabling the cart to seat properly within the console. Tengen produced a svelte black cartridge with symmetrical ridged notches built into the lower half of its prominent angled lip. While aesthetically distinctive, the lack of finger holds on either side made the cart difficult to remove. American developer Color Dreams, who later transformed to the Christian-centric software house Wisdom Tree, designed a curved gripping surface and attention-grabbing powder blue cases (which they later replaced with black). Camerica opted for metallic gold and silver carts, while AGCI simply chose an alternate shade of gray to complement its starkly minimal exterior. Today, the colorful banner of the unlicensed game pak is carried on by the fan community. Homebrew manufacturer and distributor Retrozone, for example, produces carts in several translucent hues—green, blue, red, and clear[77]—finally introducing a touch of Famicom color to the reserved NES palette.

Devil World

Nintendo's control over NES cartridges extended beyond manufacture and distribution; they had the final say on content as well. Agreeing to be a licensee meant that Nintendo could amend any game-related materials, from commercials to graphics, that they felt might be objectionable to their audience. Among Nintendo's content guidelines were rules governing in-game portrayals of religious iconography, sex, nudity, racial stereotypes, controlled substances, profanity, violence, and politically incendiary content.[78] According to former NOA Product Analyst/Specialist Phil Sandhop, these rules were clearly documented and uniform for all publishers—"Everyone had a copy of the policy and it was the same for all games"—including Nintendo. "We maintained an even hand with our games as well as the third parties," Sandhop recalled.[79]

Indeed, Nintendo's content guidelines were not reserved solely for licensees. Many of their own games were either modified for Western audiences or withheld from certain regions altogether. One conspicuous example is デビルワールド, or *Devil World*, released for Famicom in 1984. Co-designed by Shigeru Miyamoto and Takashi Tezuka prior to *Super Mario Bros.*, the game was an amusing marriage of *Pac-Man*-style gameplay and Christian iconography. The player controlled a small, fire-breathing dragon named Tamagon, who was confined within a shifting maze administered by a winged blue demon named Devil. Tamagon collected crosses, Bibles, and white dots while avoiding either being crushed by scrolling pillars or colliding into wandering pink cyclopean creatures. Despite its Christian allusions, *Devil World* was likely not a work of deliberate blasphemy—Tamagon and his foes were colorful cartoon sprites and the titular Devil perched at the top of the screen was clad in red boots and underwear. Nonetheless, Nintendo chose not to release the game in the United States based on its potential to offend conservative parents. Europe, however, received a PAL conversion with no alterations in 1988.

Even Nintendo's star franchises were subject to drastic revisions. Based on the monumental success of *Super Mario Bros.* in Japan and abroad, Nintendo sensibly followed up with a sequel. *Super Mario Bros. 2*, a Family Computer Disk System exclusive, expanded the gameplay of its predecessor without significant graphical alterations. Instead, the design team ratcheted up the difficulty and introduced a number of devious gameplay changes: Mario and Luigi had noticeable differences in running and jumping ability; power-up blocks could yield harmful poisonous mushrooms; gusting winds made jumps more treacherous; and vaulting the flagpole was specifically programmed into the engine, albeit to punish players by warping them to earlier levels. Directors Miyamoto and Tezuka worked directly against many of the conventions established in *Super Mario Bros.*, creating a far more challenging game. As a result, the disk's booklet and sleeve featured a gold ribbon that read, "For Super Players," meant to warn away those who had not mastered the first game.[80]

Nintendo of America deemed the game unsuitable for American audiences due to both its difficulty and its close visual resemblance to its predecessor. Nintendo chose an alternate Famicom Disk System game, *Yume Kōjō: Doki Doki Panic* (1987), to take *Super Mario Bros. 2*'s place. *Doki Doki*, directed by Kensuke Tanabe, had actually begun as the prototype for a possible *Super Mario Bros.* sequel, but both he and Miyamoto were dissatisfied with the early results. *Super Mario Bros.*'s horizontal gameplay was shifted to a vertical orientation and designed around co-operative platforming, but early prototypes did not prove to be much fun.[81] Tanabe and Miyamoto decided to shelve the project.

The abandoned prototype was eventually revived for a cross-promotional videogame designed to coincide with Fuji Television's 1987 Yume Kōjō festival. The festival mascots starred as the four lead characters in the game, now set in an *Arabian Nights*-inspired dream world. Miyamoto and Tanabe worked in earnest to infuse *Doki Doki* with more *Super Mario*

Bros. -inspired elements, like horizontal scrolling, warp zones, and hidden power-ups. As a result, *Doki Doki's* gameplay evolved into a sensible substitute for the American sequel to *Super Mario Bros.* The FDS disk was cross-ported to an NES cartridge and received a graphical overhaul, replacing the Yume Kōjō mascots with Mario, Luigi, Peach, and Toad, along with other visual and audio tweaks meant to bring the game further in line with the Mario universe.[82]

Despite Sandhop's earnest insistence, Nintendo's guideline enforcement was frequently inconsistent, even arbitrary. This was especially true in the case of modifications made to Western-developed PC titles that were ported to the NES. American developer Jon Van Caneghem's first-person RPG *Might & Magic* was originally released for the Apple II in 1986. Due to its popularity, it was ported to a range of PCs and consoles, including both the Famicom and the NES as *Might & Magic: Secret of the Inner Sanctum* (in 1990 and 1992 respectively). The Famicom/NES ports received graphical upgrades, additional dialogue, and new locations, puzzles, and enemies. However, in its transition from American PC game to Famicom port and back again as an NES cartridge, *Might & Magic* underwent a number of Nintendo-mandated content revisions, including the erasure of small halos above the angels' heads on the Wheel of Luck, the deletion of a plaque adorned with a minotaur head (reminiscent of a Satanic goat's head), and the revision of all in-game instances of "devil" to "incubus."[83] Other objectionable content apparently eluded Nintendo's testers. The female Water Elemental and Medusa sprites, for example, appear topless, with the latter fully exposed.[84]

Translations

As with any emergent media, the rising popularity of videogames attracted the attention of franchises from film, television, and a host of other media and products that hoped to cash in. Thus the NES library received a glut of licensed properties, including cartoons (*The Little Mermaid, The Simpsons: Bart vs. The World, Tiny Toon Adventures*), toys (*Teenage Mutant Ninja Turtles, Micro Machines*), sports (*Major League Baseball, NFL, Michael Andretti's World GP*), television game shows (*American Gladiators, Jeopardy!, Fun House*), movies (*Robocop, Total Recall, Mad Max, Darkman*), and even food (*M.C. Kids, Spot, Yo! Noid*).[85] The Famicom saw the same influx of cross-media ventures, though understandably they were drawn from commercial and pop culture sources familiar to Japanese audiences, including anime/manga series like *Dragon Ball, Akira, Captain Tsubasa, Tetsuwan Atom*, and *Crayon Shin-chan*.

Although Japanese comics, cartoons, and animated films were gaining fans in the 1980s (chapter 2), Famicom publishers did not expect American children (or their parents) to accept these unfamiliar or otherwise "weird" foreign characters. When Japanese media properties did cross over, they were largely revamped for NES release. In *Power-Up*, Kohler writes:

> Some major graphical alterations happen when the game in question is based on an anime series, and the game publisher would rather that Americans didn't know that. So the famous manga character, a strange duck-like ghost, in Bandai's Famicom game *Obake no Q-Taro* was changed to a curly-haired angel for the game's US release as *Chubby Cherub*. The hero of *Gegege no Kitaro*, a Famicom game based on an anime about a strange little boy who hunts ghosts, was changed to a ninja and the game was released in the US as *Ninja Kid*, stripped of its anime roots.[86]

Another notable example was *Kamen no Ninja: Akakage*, a 1988 Famicom game based on the anime series *Akakage*. The TV show, set in feudal Japan, starred the titular ninja wearing a distinctive red mask shaped like a bird's spread wings. In 1990, Capcom released the FDS game *Kamen no Ninja: Hanamaru*, itself a cartoonish adaption of the *Akakage* series starring a child-like version of the protagonist. Based on their source material, neither game was suitable for U.S. release, so Capcom undertook a substantial localization of the latter title. The result was *Yo! Noid*, a NES cart starring the Noid, a commercial mascot used to market Domino's pizza in the 1980s.

Yo! Noid's localization was an impressive, wholesale graphical update. Not only did Capcom replace Hanamaru with the Noid, but the natural landscapes—islands, arctic tundra, etc.—were redrawn to resemble urban locales reminiscent of New York City. However, the underlying structure of the levels remained unchanged, even when that structure made little logical sense. An island level in *Kamen*, for instance, became a pier-side cityscape in *Noid*, but the patterns of platforms and the distinctive vertical bobbing motion of the level were identical in both versions. In *Kamen*, Hanamaru's primary attack was a mechanical bird perched on his shoulder that he would send out to dispatch foes. Capcom swapped the bird for a yo-yo, an object that could feasibly replicate the avian swooping attack, but made little sense in the Noid's repertoire. Similarly, the card game used to resolve boss confrontations in *Kamen* was converted into a pizza-eating contest.

Though not all developers could afford such drastic updates, Famicom games routinely had their cover artwork altered for worldwide release.[87] The wide-eyed cartoon characters typical in Japanese anime and manga were swapped for characters inspired by Western comic book, sci-fi, and fantasy traditions. For instance, the cover of *Argos no Senshi: Hachamecha Daishingeki* portrayed the cartoonish hero Senshi, who would not look out of place in an *Astro Boy* episode, wielding the Diskarmor, a shield/ boomerang hybrid that closely resembled Captain America's trademark weapon. The English localization changed the title and Senshi's name to *Rygar*, updated the character artwork to resemble a He-Man knock-off, and dropped the Diskarmor's potentially copyright-infringing look. But beyond those updates, little else was changed for the NES version.[88]

Even in cases where Nintendo's guidelines benefited cultural sensitivity, their application was inconsistent. Capcom's unique "jump-less" platformer *Bionic Commando*, featuring a protagonist with an extendable robotic arm that allowed him to swing across platforms and grapple objects, was first released for the Famicom as *Hitler's Resurrection: Top Secret* (1988). The game's primary antagonists were soldiers of the Imperial Army, a neo-Nazi regime led by General Wiseman. The Famicom cover art portrayed the hero Raddo (ラッド) swinging into the fray while riddling an enemy soldier with bullets. Looming large in the horizon was an oversized Hitler who, true to the title, was resurrected for the game's concluding boss fight. In-game locations were littered with Nazi regalia—swastikas adorned flags, podiums, dossiers, and architectural facades—while a cutscene featuring Wiseman showed him raising his left fist in the manner of the Nazi *heil* salute.

Nintendo rightfully decided that the game's scenario and imagery would be distasteful outside Japan—or outright banned in Germany, where allusions to Nazism were strictly regulated according to *Strafgesetzbuch*.[89] The resulting localization was comically inadequate. Prior to U.S. and European release, Capcom changed all swastika graphics to eagles (still vaguely reminiscent of Third Reich propaganda), renamed the Nazis as "Badds," updated Wiseman to Generalissimo Killt, and provided Hitler the pseudonym "Master D."[90] Hitler's in-game character sprites, however, remained unaltered, a significant detail in light of the game's concluding sequence. As Master D attempts to flee in a helicopter, Raddo swings from above and launches a missile into the cockpit. Master D then yells "AH…!" as a four-frame animation shows his head graphically disintegrating into fragments of blood and flesh.

Judging by the makeshift translations and roughly four-month turn-around time between Famicom and U.S. release, Capcom likely did the best they could to revise the game's content. Much like Famicom *Donkey Kong*'s kill screen, few players were likely to see this gory sequence, since *Bionic Commando* was a challenging game. Substituting a non-violent finale would have meant either overhauling the game's pattern tables or excising the sequence from the source code altogether, a diversion of time and resources that were already dedicated to translating the game's text and supporting documentation.[91]

From its uncertain launch to its market peak, the Family Computer's conversion from a Japanese to an international console was fraught with translation problems, from exploding Hitlers to dodgy instruction manuals to ill-advised industrial design. Nintendo's calculated effort to preempt their domestic piracy problems led to a machine burdened with an effective but flawed lockout chip. The market pressure to conform the console's exterior to the expectations of a U.S. videogame industry reticent to risk investment in an unproven console led to a novel but faulty spring-loaded cartridge mechanism. The desire to protect both consumers from objectionable content and their own console from the fate of its predecessors led Nintendo to implement draconian content regulations and licensing policies that frustrated developers and hampered Nintendo's reach in the European market.

And yet the Nintendo Entertainment System persevered and prevailed, reviving a U.S. console market on the brink of disappearance. Millions of Nintendo players absorbed the console's errors and flaws into the lexicon of videogame culture. Players remember the *Metal Gear* guard's exclamation "I FEEL ASLEEP" or Error's existential phrase not as unforgivable flaws, but as playful, ridiculous, and even mysterious expressions of a specific era of videogame history. T-shirts portraying an NES game pak with the caption "Blow Me" encapsulate, albeit tastelessly, a shared cultural lore. "I AM ERROR" is as much a personification of Nintendo's 8-bit console as it is a mistranslated line of dialogue from one of its games.

I don't think anyone at Nintendo ever thought we would be able to pack so much value into a cartridge with a ROM of that capacity, or that we would sell so many worldwide.

— Masayuki Uemura, *Iwata Asks, Volume 2: NES & Mario*

Of course you know about Worlds 1–1 through 8–4 in Super Mario Bros., but did you know that there is a World −1 as well?

— Agent 826, *Nintendo Power*, 1988

スーパーマリオブラザーズ, or *Super Mario Bros.* (hereafter *SMB*), is a side-scrolling platformer released for the Famicom on September 13, 1985. Although Shigeru Miyamoto is often credited singularly for its creation, he worked alongside a small team of programmers, designers, and composers over a period of several months to bring the game to life:[1] Takashi Tezuka, the game's co-designer, had worked with Miyamoto on the dot-eating maze game *Devil World*; Koji Kondo, who composed the game's inspired soundtrack, was also a *Devil World* alum; and Toshihiko Nakago, the game's lead programmer, had worked on Famicom ports of several Nintendo arcade properties, including *Donkey Kong* and *Donkey Kong Jr.* The Miyamoto/Tezuka/Nakago/Kondo team would collaborate for many years on a number of Nintendo's most famous Famicom titles, including *The Legend of Zelda* for the FDS (chapter 5), which they developed concurrently with *SMB*.

Genre firsts are notoriously difficult to pin down. *SMB* was not the first platformer, nor even the first from Nintendo, as we see elements of the genre in *Donkey Kong*'s multi-level play. The "platform"—or "platformer"—label describes the various obstacles that the player's character must run across, vault, or climb as they make their way to a specified goal.[2] In *Donkey Kong*, the platforms are girders that Mario must traverse to reach the top of the stage. Though *Donkey Kong* ostensibly took place at a construction site, the limitations of its arcade hardware dictated that the girders hung inexplicably in space, bound only to the ladders that connected them. In *SMB*, the platforms are arrangements of various bricks and blocks that comprise the architecture of the world. Here, the fantasy setting precluded any need to explain why these blocks floated in mid-air. They were simply there for Mario, Luigi, and their foes to clamber across.

The original arcade *Mario Bros.* was one of the first Nintendo video-games to offer a theme and variation on *Donkey Kong*'s seminal *mechanics*—a shorthand gaming term loosely describing both the range of available character actions and their haptic feel. The object was no longer to reach the top quickly, but to defeat the myriad turtles, crabs, flies, and icicles that spilled from enormous green sewer pipes. The critters emerged from the top of the screen, dropped down to platforms suspended at multiple levels below, then crawled into pipes at either side of the screen to repeat the cycle. Mario (and brother Luigi) could eliminate their foes only by bumping platforms from below. This would flip the enemy and leave them helpless for a short amount of time. Mario then had to jump on the plat-form and touch the incapacitated foe to boot them from the screen. Mario's range of motion was not significantly enhanced from *Donkey Kong*, but the transformation of jumping from a simple evasive tactic to an offensive strategy would have a huge impact on *SMB*'s gameplay. *Mario Bros.* also introduced a number of franchise mainstays: the subterranean setting, Mario's job change from carpenter to plumber, green pipes, bumpable terrain, Mario's sibling Luigi, green and red turtles,[3] collectible coins, Mario's skidding stops, the POW block, and even fireballs (though they chased Mario, rather than serving as an offensive tool).

SMB inherited the platformer conventions of *Donkey Kong*, *Mario Bros.*, and other early Nintendo games and exploded them beyond the borders of the single screen. Again, *SMB* was not the first game to do so.[4] On the arcade front, games like *Defender* (1981), *Xevious* (1982), and *Moon Patrol* (1982) all featured backdrops that scrolled smoothly along either horizontal or vertical axes. In *Moon Patrol*, your agile lunar craft could even jump obstacles. Of course, these games were all firmly embedded in the sci-fi genre popular at the time, so their looped or infinite scrolling often reflected the vastness of outer space. Rock-Ola's little-known *Jump Bug* (1981), featuring a hopping red automobile, and Namco's *Pac-Land* (1984) were also early predecessors of *SMB* that involved running and jumping across a scrolling plane.

The Atari VCS had its share of scrolling games, but few that could rightfully be called platformers. *Pitfall!* (1982) is the closest to form, featuring both a world that extended to the left and right of the visible screen and a memorable character, Pitfall Harry, who could leap barrels, swing on vines, and shuffle across alligator heads. However, instead of scrolling, *Pitfall*'s screens progressed one at a time, triggered by Harry crossing the screen's border on either side. *Mountain King* (1983), while visually rudimentary, copped the familiar "levels-and-ladders" gameplay style of *Donkey Kong*, but added continuous four-way scrolling—an impressive programming feat for the VCS.

With so many able predecessors, why and how did *SMB* succeed so tremendously? What is it about the game that entertained tens of millions of videogame players and drove the world to Mario mania? To modern eyes, *Super Mario Bros.*'s pop cultural familiarity and gameplay simplicity perhaps obscures the sophistication of its inner processes. In twenty-odd thousand lines of assembly code, burnt to mask ROMs and housed in plastic cartridges, Nintendo inaugurated a new era of console videogames. And despite the tens of millions who have played it, few have taken the time to lay its code and cartridge bare to examine how and why it works.

This chapter delves into the game's source in order to analyze how code and platform coordinated to shape the Famicom's seminal platformer, the game that would become the archetype for thousands of clones, homages, and play-alikes. *SMB* is the consummate demonstration of the Famicom's strengths and limitations, a tiled world of plumber-sized pipes and expansive blue skies built around the platform's distinctive hardware affordances. The technical terms introduced in chapter 1 are explored in greater depth, using *SMB*'s engine to illustrate practical implementations of scrolling, metatiles, data compression, attribute tables, mirroring, sprite 0 splits, and assembly language programming. If *Donkey Kong* was the game the Famicom was *engineered* for, a minimum set of hardware specs necessary to feasibly reproduce the arcade hit, *Super Mario Bros.* was the game the Famicom was *designed* for, pushing those specs to their technological and creative limits.

Ironically, as a game that was a spiritual sequel to *Mario Bros.* and that would quickly receive its own arcade port, *SMB* served as an important bridge title between the rapidly disappearing age of arcade play and a new era of games designed specifically for the home. *SMB* had a simple narrative with a clear endpoint that became an objective in and of itself. Mario could complete his quest in a way that Jumpman never could. More importantly, Mario's Mushroom Kingdom, dense with secrets, permeable borders, and non-linear warping, encouraged players to spend hours combing through its brickwork structure. With *SMB*, Nintendo was coming home.

Kinoko Kingdom

Super Mario Bros.'s scenario is dead simple, albeit bizarre. A malevolent turtle king named Bowser has captured the Princess Toadstool and secreted her into a castle. Meanwhile the peaceful residents of the Kinoko (or Mushroom) Kingdom (キノコ王国) have fallen under Bowser's sorcery and have subsequently been transformed into "rocks, bricks, and horsetail plants."[5] It is the Mario Brothers' task to rescue the Princess from Bowser and restore peace to the Kingdom.

The damsel in distress trope has countless precedents in literature, film, and videogames,[6] but the locale and residents of the Mushroom Kingdom are, like *Donkey Kong*, a unique amalgam of Eastern and Western influences. But *SMB* is arguably weirder than its arcade forebear. Miyamoto and team steeped the game's design in influences from Japanese manga, folklore, geography, and cuisine, meanwhile infusing the brew with anachronistic Western ingredients. Yet despite its hybrid origins, *SMB* required no localization for its in-game content. The minor bits of text and dialogue were already in English in the Famicom original. The real translation work went into the game's supporting texts, namely the manual, box, and artwork.

This is particularly evident in the original Japanese names of Mario's enemies. Bowser, for instance, is an English-exclusive name. In Japanese, he is called 大魔王クッパ, akin to "Great Demon King Koopa,"[7] a name that clearly would not have passed NOA's strict guidelines on religious imagery (chapter 3), but does allude to King Koopa's resemblance to the demons of Japanese art history, both in ancient scrolls and mid-century anime.[8] Miyamoto, who drew the original box art for the game, modeled Koopa's design after the Ox King from the 1960 Toei animated feature *Alakazam the Great*.[9] Thus the artwork presents Koopa in a form far more bovine than reptilian, bearing little resemblance to his in-game sprite—a discrepancy later pointed out by Tezuka and amended by, ironically, former Toei artist Yoichi Kotabe.[10]

Additionally, the クッパ (*kuppa*) portion of Bowser's Japanese name contains a cultural reference that would be lost to Western audiences, since it is the Japanese name for a Korean soup dish.[11] Miyamoto, apparently designing while hungry, picked this name in favor of two other Korean dishes: ユッケ (*yukke*) and ビビンバ (*bibinba*). Similarly, Princess Toadstool was originally Princess Peach (ピーチ姫) and the small brown Kuribo (クリボー), or "chestnut people" were inspired by shittake mushrooms.[12] In English, they translated to the culturally questionable "Goomba," a term that might better stereotype Mario and Luigi than ambulatory fungi.

Several enemies are named after the Japanese onomatopoeia that describe their behavior: the "Pakkun Flowers" (パックンフラワー) are named after the *paku* sound made when eating (also the original derivation of Pac-Man's name); the fish are called "Puku-Puku" (プクプク), a sound that denotes swelling up; and the flying turtles are called "Pata-Pata" (パタパタ) to describe their flapping wings.[13] Other names are culled directly from Japanese folk tales: "Jugemu" (ジュゲム), the cloud-bound turtle who rains spiny eggs on Mario in World 4–1, is borrowed from a Japanese *rakugo* (a form of theatrical monologue) wherein two parents cannot decide on the name of their child. When advised by a priest on several possible names, the father remains indecisive and thus chooses all of them. The comically long string of names begins with Jugemu. Likewise, the name of the eggs that Jugemu throws, "Paipo" (パイポ), is borrowed from the same tale.

The Mushroom Kingdom's cloud motif derived from the same source material as *Alakazam the Great*, namely *Journey to the West*, a 16th-century Chinese novel.[14] *Journey*'s primary protagonist, Sun Wukong (the Monkey King), possesses numerous magical powers, including the ability to jump across and ride upon clouds, transform into other living creatures or inanimate objects, and alter his size. Considering Miyamoto's familiarity with *Alakazam* and the Monkey King tale, it is no surprise that Wukong's fantastic feats found their way into Mario's repertoire, not only in *SMB*, but in future games in the series.[15]

The unlikely flora, fauna, and even the name of the Mushroom Kingdom drew directly from the creators' cultural landscapes. As Miymoto explained:

> Since the game's set in a magical kingdom, I made the required power-up item a mushroom because you see people in folk tales wandering into forests and eating mushrooms all the time. That, in

turn, led to us calling the in-game world the "Mushroom Kingdom," and the rest of the basic plot setup sprang from there.[16]

Tezuka contributed the concept of enormous sprouting vines, cribbed from the *Jack and the Beanstalk* fairy tale, that led to landscapes of over-grown mushroom caps and traversable clouds.[17] The trademark green pipes first seen in *Mario Bros.* were inspired by the ubiquitous "waste ground with pipes" found in manga.[18] Miyamoto thought oversized pipes could sensibly transport Mario and Luigi through the gameworld. The curved hills punctuating the backdrop of the Kinoko Kingdom were call-backs to the hills of rural Sonobe, where Miyamoto spent his childhood.[19] And thanks to the concurrent development of *SMB* and *The Legend of Zelda*, a few objects, like the spinning fire bars, were plucked from the latter for use in the former—yet another example of Nintendo adapting and repur-posing its own creative work.

Amid this menagerie of noisy foes, ambling food, and fairy tale allu-sions, we once again find Mario and Luigi, the sibling pair of Italian plumbers. Clad in workaday caps, overalls, and mustaches, they make for unlikely foils to Kinoko's psychedelic fantasy world. It is hard to imagine middle-aged plumbers starring in any contemporary big budget video game save Nintendo's own, as they would likely suffer the judgment of online forums and internal focus testing. Not that Nintendo didn't have the market in mind—according to Tezuka, the game was not designed from the outset to include the unlikely heroes. However, after he discov-ered continuing strong sales of the Famicom's *Mario Bros.* port a year after its release, he and Miyamoto decided that the Mario Brothers should be the stars of their new game.[20]

As we saw with *Donkey Kong*, the exaggerated cartoon figures of Japanese manga and animation suited the limited tile mosaics of 8-bit platforms like the Family Computer. Realism was never the Famicom's strong suit; Princess Peach's mangled sprite in *SMB* is unfortunate proof. And offering a grab bag of cultural and popular quotations, both Eastern and Western, certainly lent force to *SMB*'s universal appeal. It had a touch of familiarity that connected with children and adults across the world, despite its surrealistic tenor. As Miyamoto said:

When we make our games we try to make things that are not focused on one market or one particular culture or one particular people, and where there are some difficulties in that, I really think it does free us up in a different way to just make what we want and hope that univer-sal appeal will branch across all cultures.[21]

Tens of millions of copies of *Super Mario Bros.* later, it is clear that Miyamoto, Nakago, Kondo, and Tezuka accomplished their goal.

In the end, the look and profession of the characters or the narrative cohesion of the story are all mere set dressing for the game's core conceits: running, jumping, stomping, swimming, bumping, bashing, skidding, kicking, and climbing. It made the most sense to import the characters' physical abilities above all other attributes. Abstracted away from the Kinoko Kingdom, these activities defined the model for a genre that would sustain the Famicom, its hardware successors, and a duo of athletic plumbers, for decades. And at the heart of the platformer was a platform custom-engineered to render colorful worlds of scrolling blocks.

A World of Attributes

In chapter 1, we saw that a single name table contains 32x30 tiles. Simply storing a single screen's worth of data as a sequential list of tile IDs—each requiring one byte—would require 960 bytes of ROM. Dividing NROM's max capacity (40KB) by this value would provide enough space to store forty-one screens—assuming we leave no memory for graphics, sound, or code. But *SMB* has far more than forty-one screens. In fact, it has eight worlds containing four areas each—a total of thirty-two individual levels—each of which comprises dozens of screens. Within those levels, there are myriad terrain types, ranging from cracked stonework to smiling billows. Mario travels over ground, underground, among clouds, and underwater. He climbs vines, descends pipes, skirts whirlpools, grabs flagpoles, and navigates lava-filled mazes. So how is it possible to cram so much data into the modest NROM, to build a world in only forty kilobytes?

The answer is twofold: metatiles and compression. A metatile is an aggregate of two or more tiles treated as a single computational object. Mario is a metatile, as are Koopa Troopas, as are coin blocks, as are clouds, as are pipes, and so on. All Famicom games use metatiles of some fashion, and many use meta-metatiles, aggregate objects comprised of metatiles which are themselves composed of smaller tiles. Limiting objects to an 8x8-pixel area would quickly impose debilitating restrictions on graphical complexity.

Metatiles have important computational advantages for data storage and manipulation. First, metatiles simplify tile updates. Moving a single Mario "object" is simpler than updating four individual tile coordinates. Of course, a metatile's constituent patterns do not congeal automatically; custom software must control such aggregations. But well-planned game engines do not create individual subroutines to handle every metatile object. Such an approach would bloat source code beyond a manageable scale. Instead, object handling is grouped according to type, i.e., a "player object handler" can perform the backend calculations and tile coordination necessary to move Mario and Luigi metatiles, while an "enemy object handler" can perform similar functions for their foes.

Second, breaking the game world into larger repeatable chunks and spooling them out in varied combinations permits larger and more diverse levels. With careful tile and level design, developers can mask the terrain's underlying patterns. Repetition of a handful of building blocks can even contribute to the overall style and coherence of the game environment. *SMB*, for instance, employs palette swaps to great effect to introduce variation in otherwise identical bricks and tiles. Simply swapping brown for blue gives *SMB*'s overworld and underworld stages distinct visual styles, despite using identical pattern tiles.

In a scrolling engine such as *SMB*'s, compression takes on additional importance. The PPU does not have sufficient VRAM to store more than two name tables worth of tiles. Prior to the release of *Excitebike, Spartan X*, and similar scrolling games, few Famicom titles demanded more than two contiguous screens—if they scrolled at all. Once scrolling became the norm, programmers had to devise efficient methods to update name tables offscreen, just beyond the screen's perimeter, without breaking the continuity of the game world. With sufficiently lengthy levels, updating uncompressed name table tiles became both processor- and memory-intensive. Metatile compression served to alleviate both problems by grouping associated tiles into larger data structures that could be stored and unpacked efficiently.

More sophisticated multi-directional scrollers like *Blaster Master* pack metatiles *within* metatiles to produce even larger aggregate objects. Game-specific tools like snarfblam's *Blaster Master* level editor ReMaster help illustrate the game's meta-metatile structure visually, allowing us to see its objects from an "engine-level" view. In figure 4.1, a portion of the game's first overhead stage appears on the left with black borders dividing its individual screens. On the right, the game's "structures" (meta-metatiles) are arranged in a grid display. Note how every screen on the left is composed of structures from the right.

The downside of an engine using such structures is that they restrict the granularity of a level's design. The stone arrangements that appear multiple times throughout the stage, for instance, cannot be edited at the individual stone level—the level designer may only choose from structures that contain stones in pre-ordained arrangements, then "paint" patterns

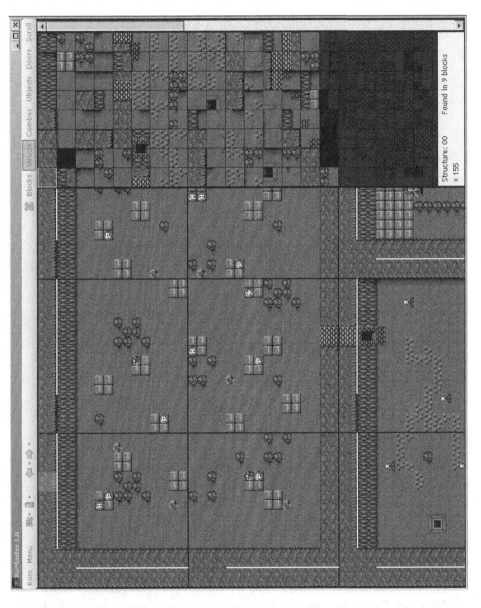

4.1 The *Blaster Master* level editor ReMaster reveals the game's underlying meta-metatile structure. (Source: ReMaster 1.0)

using those structures. The upside is that aggregate structures save significant programming overhead, since they can be packed and unpacked in ROM as needed, saving hundreds or thousands of bytes.

Metatile structures are equally advantageous for the PPU attribute table architecture. Again, attribute tables are the 64-byte areas immediately following each of the PPU's four name tables. Each byte contributes palette data to a 32x32-pixel area of the name table, which is then further subdivided into four 16x16-pixel areas. These sub-areas receive two bits from the attribute table, meaning that any 2x2-tile area of background tiles is limited to a single four-color palette. In-game objects larger than those dimensions must either share the same palette or exhibit abrupt clashes along the attribute table's seams.

Consequently, *SMB*'s entire world is carefully structured around attribute table boundaries so no unsightly clashes arise. The smallest background objects—bricks, terrain, ? blocks, coins—are all one 16x16-pixel metatile in size. Kinoko Kingdom abounds with sharp right angles, best exhibited by the massive stair-step structures that conclude each non-castle level. And these shapes are perfectly suited to the platformer genre. Various heights and widths of rectangular blocks make excellent obstacles for running, jumping, and climbing.

Single Engine

A videogame engine is its code core. It functions like a software CPU, coordinating the processes that drive the game: preparing which graphics to render onscreen, handling physics, defining objects and their collisions, switching major game states, etc. Today's industry standard engines, like Epic's Unreal Engine or Crytek's CryEngine, are designed to abstract these functions into modular APIs adaptable to myriad videogame genres, from first-person shooters to real-time strategy. Such solutions are popular among publishers and developers because building a custom engine from scratch demands massive investments in time and resources. Licensing a capable middleware solution can speed up videogame development substantially. Reusing and adapting an existing engine, especially for a familiar game type, is often more time- and cost-effective than recoding the wheel.

Famicom game engines were much less flexible. Memory limitations meant that engines were catered to the needs of a single game or a series of similar games. Adapting the turn-based role-playing engine of *Final Fantasy* to a platformer like *Mega Man* would be, at best, a painful test of programmer patience—but more likely impossible without massive code modifications. Nonetheless, Famicom-era engines still strove toward abstraction and modularity. Like the metatiles described above, efficient engines were designed to group objects and processes into like types to avoid redundancy. It is far better to design a physics routine that handles multiple objects than to apply the same basic rules individually to fifteen similar enemies. In other words, the engine should not care if the object is a Koopa or a Goomba—they both fall into a pit and die identically. *SMB*'s engine is designed with an elegance and sophistication that belies its modest ROM footprint. Nagako and his co-programmers used a multi-layered, back-to-front approach that parses objects in surprising ways, contrary to how both player and processor perceive the final visual results.

SMB's engine renders levels according to three related processes, each handling its own range of objects. The first of these, what I will call "set decoration," is an "automatic" algorithm that unrolls the level based on a set of initial conditions. The second is the area object data, primarily the platforms—bricks, pipes, power-up blocks—that Mario bashes, vaults, and bumps. The third is the enemy object data, governing the number and position of enemies blocking Mario's path.[22] Keep in mind that each of these processes is primarily handling background tiles (enemy sprites are a clear exception), meaning that any "layers" we speak of are merely programmer-constructed abstractions. The Famicom's PPU can only ever render a single layer of background tiles. Sprites may be above and behind background tiles based upon their priority, but even this aspect of depth is an abstraction. Placing a sprite in front of another tile simply means that the PPU renders that object's pixels rather than another's. A television only has one plane of pixels; there are no pixels hidden behind other pixels.

Also keep in mind that the term object is not used in its conventional programming sense. Objects in modern object-oriented programming (OOP) languages like Objective-C or Java are data structures consisting of *properties* with associated *procedures* (i.e., methods) that can manipulate those properties. Individual objects are actually instances of a common *class*, an abstracted construct used to prototype all objects of a given type. To use a common programming analogy, we could define a "Car" class that includes some basic properties, like wheels, color, and body type. Until we create a particular instance of that class, we are not describing any car in particular, merely an abstract model. Likewise, we might define a number of methods to query, update, or manipulate our class properties. For instance, a "PaintJob" method could change the color of our car, the "FlatTire" method could subtract a wheel, and so on. One of OOP's key benefits is modularity. It is far easier to instance thousands of different cars for a traffic simulator, for instance, than to create new data constructs for each individual car.

6502 assembly language is not object-oriented. It contains no classes nor even pre-built data structures. Data is moved to and from registers, where it can be added, subtracted, compared, or bitwise operated. Assembly source executes from top to bottom until an interrupt fires. Once the interrupt is handled, it returns to the sequence and continues. The code's only modularity derives from simple jump commands and branches that can detour the program counter to alternate memory locations. As such, I use the term object loosely to describe groups of tiles handled as a single entity, or, in rarer cases that I explain below, a behavior or event that triggers at a specific location onscreen. With that in mind, let's look at each of the engine's processes in turn.

The set decoration is itself divided into three successive computational layers, what doppelganger's *Super Mario Bros.* disassembly labels "background scenery," "foreground scenery," and "terrain."[23] Background scenery is the dominant backdrop of each level, comprising the Kinoko Kingdom's weather, flora, and architecture. These are the hills, clouds, bushes, trees, and fences that give the Kingdom its distinctive character and break up the monotony of the saturated blue and black skies. There are sixteen individual 1x3-metatile (16x48-pixel) background blocks, or meta-metatiles, used to construct three different forty-eight metatile-wide background patterns. The first of these the player encounters is the hills, clouds, and bushes motif seen in World 1–1, 4–1, 6–1, and 6–2 (figure 4.2). Next is the clouds motif, used as the backdrop for any stage that appears to be suspended in midair: 1–3, 2–3, 3–3, 4–3,

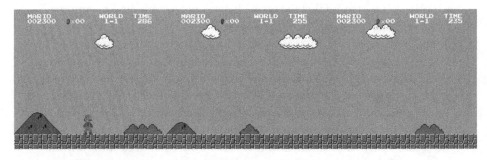

4.2 The hills, clouds, and bushes motif, one of three forty-eight metatile-wide "background scenery" patterns rendered by the *Super Mario Bros.* engine. If Mario jumps the flagpole in World 1-1, this pattern will repeat indefinitely, until the timer runs out. (Emulator: FCEUX 2.1.5)

5–3, 6–3, and 7–3. The final motif of clouds, trees, and fences appears in 2–1, 3–1, 3–2, 5–1, 5–2, 7–1, 8–1, 8–2, and 8–3. Any remaining levels have either solid black (underground, castles, nighttime cloud bonus level, coin rooms) or solid blue (daytime cloud bonus area, underwater) backgrounds with no constituent background scenery.

Using either the Game Genie peripheral (chapter 6) or an emulator that supports cheats, it is possible to view uninterrupted patterns of background scenery. The "Moon Gravity" Game Genie code, for example, allows Mario to vault above the top of the screen, easily clearing level-ending flagpoles. While such a stunt is possible without cheat devices, it is difficult to execute. And those who succeed are often disappointed to find that there is no hidden world or warp zone, merely infinitely scrolling terrain. Even the Game Genie manuals warns, "If you're playing to complete the game rather than just explore it, don't jump over the flagpoles—or else you'll get 'stuck' and have to reset."[24]

Getting stuck is not a glitch or error—it is simply the engine performing its job as intended. The background scenery rendering is automatic in the sense that it does not rely on a predetermined level length. The engine works like a loom, unspooling the selected forty-eight metatile pattern until a flagpole object triggers the level's conclusion. When the player skips the flagpole (figure 4.2), the background scenery repeats as intended, exposing the engine's underlying process and pattern. Also note that each meta-metatile component of background scenery is "vertically exclusive"—i.e., each hill, bush, cloud, fence, or tree never overlaps another's vertical plane.

Foreground scenery is rarer, comprising only three repeated tile columns: the dark blue water that floods 2–2, 7–2, and a portion of 8–4; the lower water/lava columns used in castle pits or below bridges (e.g., 3–1); and the high brick walls that appear only in 8–3. Foreground scenery's appearance is largely determined by the area object list header, as we will see below.

The final set decoration component, terrain, describes long stretches of horizontal tiles. The most common use of terrain is for Mario's runway, but it also describes stretches of tiles along the ceiling and, in some cases, mid-screen runs as well. (While the term terrain may seem inappropriate to use for ceiling tiles, remember that Mario is often able to run "out of bounds.") Terrain rendering comes in sixteen combinations of top, middle, and bottom thickness, depending on the level's needs, ranging from no terrain to a screen-filling solid. Terrain unspools at the specified height until a special "hole object" overwrites it or an "area change object" alters its thickness or position.

Though the three parts of the set decoration are all tile members of the single name table plane, the game engine assigns each layer a different rendering priority, much like the PPU handles sprites in the OAM queue: terrain on top, foreground scenery below it, and background scenery further back. Again, there are no hidden foreground tiles lurking behind the terrain—those tiles with highest priority are simply the ones that the PPU ultimately renders. The routine that handles the set decoration starts with the background scenery first, then checks to make sure no foreground scenery needs to be rendered, and finally checks if there is any terrain to render. So, for instance, if there are no high walls or ground to be drawn, a rounded green hill can emerge. A quick visual check of level 8–3 confirms this process: the high wall obscures the lower clouds, trees, and fences, which in turn are occluded by Mario's two metatile-high runway of cracked stone.

Perceptive players may notice that the terrain is the only portion of the set decoration that Mario and his enemies can collide with. The clouds, hills, trees, and walls are mere ornament, part of an endless tapestry in front of which objects play. In other words, the terrain is the background's background. Though this pseudo-layering is hard to conceptualize in a flat 2D plane, contemporary game designers have provided a glimpse of how Kinoko Kingdom might look when tilted into perspective. Morgan O'Brien's PC game *Super Mario Bros. 2.5-D* (2006), for instance, adds depth to *SMB*'s familiar scenery and characters. Keyboard commands shift the camera's perspective on the Mushroom Kingdom as if it were pressed into the shallow glass frame of an ant farm. Though its background priorities are different than *SMB*'s actual engine, *Super Mario Bros. 2.5-D* adopts the same layered perspective, allowing certain elements to advance and recede in depth. Traversable elements like blocks, pipes, and terrain are given volume (z-axis depth) so Mario can climb and run across them. Sprites, clouds, and bushes, however, remain paper thin.[25]

Oriented Objects

If the set decoration comprises *SMB*'s "background background," what constitutes its "foreground background"? Two remaining layers: area objects and enemy objects. These layers constitute the "real" substance of the Mushroom Kingdom: the stompable Buzzy Beetles, the unpredictable jumping springs, and the bumpable, bashable bricks. And equally important, they constitute what players would call the level design, the intentional arrangement of objects meant to teach, guide, and challenge the player's skills. In short, the blue skies and spotted hills may provide

1–1 with a cheerful backdrop, but it is the specific sequence of blocks, pits, Koopas, and pipes that have made the level iconic.

Several hundred bytes of *SMB*'s PRG-ROM are dedicated to area object data, which encodes each specific level sequence into compact byte blocks. World 1–1, for example, is encoded as follows:

```
;level 1-1
L_GroundArea6:
        .db $50, $21
        .db $07, $81, $47, $24, $57, $00, $63, $01, $77, $01
        .db $c9, $71, $68, $f2, $e7, $73, $97, $fb, $06, $83
        .db $5c, $01, $d7, $22, $e7, $00, $03, $a7, $6c, $02
        .db $b3, $22, $e3, $01, $e7, $07, $47, $a0, $57, $06
        .db $a7, $01, $d3, $00, $d7, $01, $07, $81, $67, $20
        .db $93, $22, $03, $a3, $1c, $61, $17, $21, $6f, $33
        .db $c7, $63, $d8, $62, $e9, $61, $fa, $60, $4f, $b3
        .db $87, $63, $9c, $01, $b7, $63, $c8, $62, $d9, $61
        .db $ea, $60, $39, $f1, $87, $21, $a7, $01, $b7, $20
        .db $39, $f1, $5f, $38, $6d, $c1, $af, $26
        .db $fd²⁶
```

This 101-byte string describes the level's sequential placement of objects, from the first coin block to the final castle facade. The byte sequence must adhere to a strict format so the engine can funnel objects to their appropriate rendering routines. In general, the area object data describes the meta-metatiles used to draw rows of bricks, vertical pipes, and staircases. However, as we will see below, it can also handle a few single-metatile objects, as well as a few special "objects" that serve more as level attributes than physical obstacles.

Each of *SMB*'s non-repeating levels, underground coin rooms, warp zones, transition screens, and bonus areas share the same area object format.[27] Data ranges in size from the 9-byte interstitial screen used to shuttle Mario from overworld to underground/underwater levels, to the massive 163-byte block that defines subterranean World 1–2, which has one of the densest arrangements of breakable blocks. Its closest competitor is the 161-byte World 4–2, also set underground. Unsurprisingly, considering their byte expenditure, these are the only two subterranean levels in the game.

The basic structure of area object data is simple: the first two bytes encode the header, the final byte (always $fd) is a string terminator that signals the end of the data, and all the bytes in-between are handled as pairs—the first byte encodes the object's screen coordinates and the second byte selects the metatile and its attributes. The complexity of the format lies in its extreme economy. Nearly every byte in the block encodes multiple flags, values, and controls within its bits.

The header defines the level's initial conditions. Two bits of the first byte, for instance, set the timer for 400, 300, or 200 ticks. Another two bits set Mario's and Luigi's initial vertical position. On most levels, they begin on the ground, but in levels following the interstitial animation that shows them entering a pipe, they drop from the top of the screen. Miyamoto thought it was important that the characters' spatial transitions made logical sense—inasmuch as plumbers traveling through human-sized pipes can be logical:

> I thought it was strange how Mario was already standing there underground when that level begins. Why is Mario, who just passed in front of a castle, standing underground? I couldn't fit in a sequence showing him falling underground, so I decided to have him just plop down from the top of the screen, and—surprisingly—that was just fine.[28]

The second byte controls values related to the set decoration, including the terrain height combinations, background and background scenery colors (e.g., nighttime with green hills), and what doppelganger calls the "area style," which can affect both the terrain tile type or its palette.

The meat of the data lies in the chain of byte pairs sandwiched between the header and the terminating byte. Again, the first byte of each pair denotes the object's position. Each half of the byte, commonly called a *nybble*,[29] is assigned to the screen's x- and y- coordinates. However, these positions are not the pixel-based coordinates the PPU uses to increment the scroll register or position sprites onscreen. Instead, *SMB*'s engine assigns a special grid of metatile rows and columns based on name table-sized "pages." Each page is divided into sixteen metatile-wide (i.e., 16-pixel) columns, numbered $0 to $F, and twelve metatile-wide rows, numbered $0 to $B (figure 4.3).

Note that the columns span the entire width of the page, but the rows do not encompass its total height. As we will see later, the top two rows of metatiles are reserved for the non-scrolling segment of the screen used to display status information. While Mario and a few other sprites may occupy this screen region, area objects are *never* permitted above the dividing line. Similarly, the bottom row $B marks the threshold between the object area and terrain. Any coordinate bytes beyond row $B have a special function that do not require a vertical coordinate.

To illustrate how the engine's decoding process works, let's take a look at the first seven byte pairs (after the header) from World 1–1:

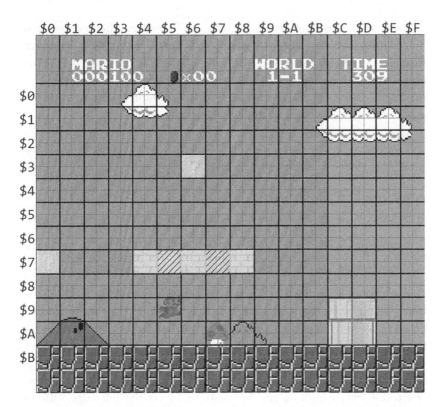

4.3 An annotated "page" of World 1–1's area object data. Striped areas indicate objects drawn "atop" other objects. (Emulator: Macifom 0.16)

BYTE PAIR	COL,ROW	OBJ BINARY	DESCRIPTION
$07, $81	0,7	10000001	{P} [sm.] ? block (coin)
$47, $24	4,7	00100100	[lg.] row of bricks (length 4)
$57, $00	5,7	00000000	[sm.] ? block (power-up)
$63, $01	6,3	00000001	[sm.] ? block (coin)
$77, $01	7,7	00000001	[sm.] ? block (coin)
$C9, $71	C,9	01110001	[lg.] vertical pipe (height 2)
$68, $f2	6,8	11110010	{P} [lg.] vert. pipe (height 3)

I have expanded the hex block into a tabular format to better clarify the data encoding. The first column lists the original byte pair. Column two divides the upper and lower nybbles into comma-delimited coordinates; column first, then row. The third column expands the second byte into its binary value, which is necessary to parse the data compressed within. The final column lists a short description of the area object, notated in a custom shorthand.

The first byte pair above describes an object at metatile column $0, row $7. Using the annotated grid in figure 4.3, we can match the object data with its corresponding onscreen object. We see that the first question block lands precisely where we expect. Of course, without the reference image, we would not know which object occupies that position. To find the object type, we must look at the second byte, which, at this point, is an inscrutable series of binary digits. To disclose their contents, we break down each byte according to the following scheme:[30]

```
PsssMMMM
||||||||
||||++++- 'Modifier' bits contingent upon value of 'selection' bits.
||||      Designates 'small' obj. type or 'large' obj. attributes
||||      (i.e., obj. height/width or whether a pipe is usable).
||||
|+++----- 0: If d4-d6 set to 0, d3-d0 select 'small' objects
|            with no height or width (e.g., ? blocks).
|            1-7: Use value to select 'large object' type.
|
+-------- 'Page select' flag
```

To readers unaccustomed to this type of notation, I have grouped related bits by letter labels that designate their function. Each digit place is numbered from 0 to 7 in reverse order, meaning that digit 7 (d7) is on the far left and digit 0 (d0) is on the far right.

Notice in figure 4.3 that while the first object's coordinate position is column $0, row $7, Mario is not currently on World 1–1's opening screen. When the level begins, Mario is positioned near the left edge with an entire screen's worth of empty terrain to the right. Yet there is no area object data until the first ? block. This is due to *SMB*'s aforementioned set decoration process, which unspools the background unimpeded until it is issued a command to alter its course. Notice that d7 of the first area byte is binary 1. This position is a flag that indicates a "page select." Anytime d7 is set, a new page is "turned" (in the object description, I denote this with {P}). Since our first object has its page select flag set, the engine knows to auto-generate an entire name table's worth of set decoration before the first object is rendered.

This clever bit of engine organization allowed *SMB*'s programmers to store object coordinates in a single byte, making them page-relative rather than area-relative. In other words, if the engine saw the entirety of level 1–1 as a single chunk, its column coordinates would extend far beyond the sixteen metatiles of a single screen. The horizontal coordinate would then exceed the capacity of a single nybble and require an additional byte to encode. Multiply that single byte addition by every y-coordinate of every object in the area data and *SMB*'s PRG-ROM size would quickly balloon beyond NROM's limit, resulting in cuts to the number and diversity of levels. Dividing each level into pages compressed object data considerably.

The remaining byte tell the engine which object to render. The "selection" bits (d4-d6) act as controls: if all three digits are zero, the engine selects a "small" object based on the value stored in the "modifier" bits (d0-d3); if any digit is non-zero, the three bits store the selection value of a "large" object and the "modifier" bits store that object's attributes. Small objects are those that require no height or width value—they always have a fixed size. This includes all types of ? blocks (power-up, coins, hidden coin blocks), bricks (power-up, vine, star, coins, 1-up), hidden 1-up blocks, underwater exit pipes, empty blocks, and the jumping board. Large objects are those that may vary in height or width, including vertical pipes (usable or not), rows or columns of bricks, rows or columns of solid blocks, rows of coins, and what doppelganger calls the AreaStyleObject (i.e., grass platform ledges, mushroom cap ledges, and the Bullet Bill cannon).

Our object's second byte reads %10000001. Following the page select bit (d7), the three selection bits (d4–6) read %000, signaling a small object. Reading right to left, the modifier nybble %0001 selects object 1. In *SMB*, objects are grouped by type in lookup tables located directly after the area rendering subroutine.[31] The value stored in the modifier digits acts as an offset within each individual lookup table to choose the appropriate object. The small objects table is listed below:

```
;small objects (rows $00-$0b or 00-11, d6-d4 all clear)
        .dw QuestionBlock        ;power-up
        .dw QuestionBlock        ;coin
        .dw QuestionBlock        ;hidden, coin
        .dw Hidden1UpBlock       ;hidden, 1-up
        .dw BrickWithItem        ;brick, power-up
        .dw BrickWithItem        ;brick, vine
        .dw BrickWithItem        ;brick, star
        .dw BrickWithCoins       ;brick, coins
        .dw BrickWithItem        ;brick, 1-up
        .dw WaterPipe
        .dw EmptyBlock
        .dw Jumpspring
```

Starting our count from zero, we see that object 1 in the lookup table is the ? block containing a coin, exactly as we see on screen. Properly unpacked, two bytes of data tell us which object will be rendered, what size that object will be, where it will be positioned on the current page, and on which page it is located—remarkably economical for sixteen bits.

Let's look at the next byte pair in the area object list. The first byte, $47, indicates that the object is located at column $4, row $7. The second byte, $24, is equivalent to binary value %00100100. D7 is not set, so the object will render on the current page. This time, however, the selection bits have the value %010, indicating both the type of object (large) and its offset in the large object lookup table (2). Consulting the source, we see that large object 2 is RowOfBricks. And since the object type is large, the modifier bits will designate the Row's attributes. Attributes vary according to the item type. The modifier bits for the RowOfBricks object sensibly designate the width of the row. If it were the ColumnOfBricks, those bits would designate its height; likewise for the VerticalPipe. (However, VerticalPipe has one additional attribute—if d3 is set, it is usable, meaning that Mario can enter the pipe to descend to a bonus coin room.) The modifier digits for the current RowOfBricks have the value %0100, or 4. Remembering to count from zero, we know that the row will be five bricks wide. And comparing the data from the byte pair to figure 4.3, we see that there is a brick row starting at column $4, row $7 spanning right five metatiles to end at column $8.

The remaining byte pairs expand similarly. The next five object bytes expand to binary values %00000000, %00000001, %00000001, %01110001, and %11110010. The first four objects have d7 values of 0, so they too will remain on the current page. The first three have 0s in their selection bits, so they will be small objects. According to the modifier bits, the first of these will be object 0 (? block with power-up) and the second two will be, once again, object 1 (? block with coin). However, notice the placement: the first and third ? block are both on row $7, positioned at column $5 and $7 respectively—directly on top of the previous five-brick row. Since there are no background layers, the engine simply renders the most recent object in the queue. In other words, if our area data list included three objects with coordinates $2, $6, listed in the following order—empty block, coin block, star block—only the star block would be rendered. Once again, this is an efficient rendering technique. Drawing the five-block row with two interspersed item blocks only takes six bytes with the current layering method. Drawing five individual blocks one after another would require ten bytes.

Following the three small ? blocks, there is an object with its selection bits set to %111. In the source lookup table, that value corresponds to the large object VerticalPipe. Since the pipe is vertical, its modifier bits describe its height and whether it is usable. The value %0001 corresponds to a height of two metatiles (including the pipe's lip), while the 0 in d3 denotes a non-usable pipe.

Notice that, despite accounting for all six area objects in figure 4.3, there is a still a final byte pair remaining. However, its expanded binary value %11110010 shows the page select set in d7, so the resulting object (a 3-metatile high vertical pipe) should render on the following page. Sure enough, if one plays beyond the screen pictured, the next object Mario encounters will be a slightly taller vertical pipe.

Spring in the Air

Working through a few level objects helps us appreciate both the sophistication and efficiency of *SMB*'s data compression. The paging metaphor breaks each level into manageable units that relativize the metatile coordinate system, while the individual bits of the object byte form an interlocked system of controls and modifiers that can choose from a large selection of construction elements, each with its own distinct attributes. However, there is one last area object type left to explore.

As noted above, when an object's row value exceeds $B, it is classified as a special object. Further into level 1–1, for instance, we find the byte pair $9c, $01. The first byte indicates that the object's page position is column $9, row $C. Row $C is not a screen coordinate, but a group of special objects (with corresponding lookup table) that includes pits, pits with water, rope pulleys, high and low ? block rows, and bridges. Expanding the second byte to %00000001 indicates that the object will be a two-metatile wide pit. While a hole might seem like a banal special object, it actually performs two unique functions: it signals the terrain tiles to stop rendering for a specified length, and it permits player and enemy objects to plummet offscreen.

SMB's trademark staircases are special objects selected with row $F. Like pits, they require a starting column and a run length. Once those initial conditions are set, a subroutine renders the staircase starting at one metatile high and incrementing one step up until the specified width is reached. The staircase leading to the flagpole in World 1–1, for example, has a modifier nybble value of %1000, indicating that it has a length of nine metatiles (as always, count from 0). However, the staircase subroutine only renders objects left to right. The pair of "pyramid" staircases seen near the end of 1–1 are drawn with special staircase objects for their ascenders and individual solid block columns for their descenders.

Other special objects trigger engine behaviors rather than graphical elements. In row $D, for instance, there are two object types that doppelganger labels AreaFrenzy and ScrollLock. The former handles levels such as 2–3, wherein enemy Cheep-Cheeps spawn continuously beneath Mario as he runs across suspended bridges, or level 5–3, wherein Bullet Bills fire at Mario from unseen cannons beyond the screen's right edge.

The ScrollLock is more self-explanatory. Certain game areas, such as warp zone area, momentarily wrest scrolling control from the player, locking screen movement to a fixed rate.

A final special object is notable due to *SMB*'s close affinity to *The Legend of Zelda*. The "loop command" occurs only in castle levels like World 4–4, wherein Mario's path splits into an upper and lower level. If the player chooses the lower path, the same sequence of screens will loop indefinitely. The upper path, however, breaks the loop and permits Mario to move forward to a three-tiered path, which contains another looping sequence. In 7–4, the spatial maze is more complex. The double- and triple-tiered paths require multiple branches (e.g., upper, bottom, middle, upper) to pass successfully.[32] In code, the loop function involves checking Mario's y-coordinate position and footing (he must be on solid ground) against a prescribed area coordinate. If either condition fails, the current page is reset and the appropriate area data is re-rendered. Notably, *SMB*'s spatial loops are the only circumstances that allow Mario to return to portions of the level that have already scrolled offscreen—though, appropriately, he may only do so by continuing to the right.

At this point in our analysis, the engine has populated the set decoration and area objects, but the level is still devoid of Mario's enemies. Fortunately, enemy object data closely models the area object format. The complete byte block for level 1–1 reads as follows:

```
;level 1-1
E_GroundArea6:
      .db $1e, $c2, $00, $6b, $06, $8b, $86, $63, $b7, $0f, $05
      .db $03, $06, $23, $06, $4b, $b7, $bb, $00, $5b, $b7
      .db $fb, $37, $3b, $b7, $0f, $0b, $1b, $37
      .db $ff
```

Enemy object data occupies far less space than area objects since levels are more populated with bricks, blocks, and staircases than with Koopas and Goombas. While enemy data blocks lack any opening header bytes (which would be redundant), they do still require a terminating byte, $FF, to signal the data's conclusion.

The remaining bytes use the same position/object pairs as the area data, with a few notable variations: First, enemy objects have valid page row values up to and including $0D. The remaining unused rows—$0E and $0F—are once again reserved for special objects. (Objects in row $0E are the sole exception to the byte pair rule; their function requires a third byte, explained below.) Second, enemy object types are not sorted by size. Digits d0-d5 in the object byte reference a single lookup list, so decoding objects based on selection bits is not necessary. Third, enemy object positions vary from area object positions. For the latter, for example, a position of $3, $6 denotes that the metatile's position will be in the 16x16-pixel area described by the intersection of the specified row and column planes. For enemy objects, the row denotes the horizontal position upon which the object stands.

To illustrate these differences, we will once again excerpt the opening portion of the byte block and expand it into tabular form:

```
BYTES       COL,ROW  OBJ BINARY  DESCRIPTION
$1E, $C2    1,E      n/a         Area change (address offset: $C2)
$00         n/a      00000000    Area change 'check'/page #
$6B, $06    6,B      00000110    Goomba
$8B, $86    8,B      10000110    {P} Goomba
$63, $B7    6,3      10110111    {P} Goomba pair
$0F, $05    0,F      00000101    Page control
```

The first byte triplet is a special case. Doppelganger labels enemy objects in row $0E as "area change objects," which function when Mario enters a pipe, climbs a vine, or falls into a pit in a bonus cloud section. Consequently, the second byte is an address offset used to designate which area Mario will end up in when such an event occurs. The lower nybble (d0-d3) of the third byte tells the engine which page of the designated area Mario should begin on when he arrives in the new area. The upper nybble (d4-d7) of the third byte, however, is used as a check for the area change object. If Mario's current world does not match the world stored in the third byte, the area object change will not take effect. In the data above, the current world must be 0, so World 1–1 passes muster. When Mario enters the one usable pipe in the level, he descends to the underground coin room. In general, the world check permits the reuse of enemy object data in multiple levels, ensuring that the pipes and vines of a given level operate properly.

The next three byte pairs are more conventional. The first byte denotes page coordinates, while the second byte denotes the enemy type along with two additional condition flags. Digit d7 of byte two continues to signal the page advance flag. D6, however, is the "secondary hard mode" flag. If a player successfully completes *SMB* and chooses to begin again without resetting, enemy quantities and types are changed to make subsequent plays more difficult. If the hard mode flag is not set, the enemy object is not rendered. The remaining six bits (d0-d5) are used to select the enemy type. In the table above, the first three objects are a single Goomba (%000110), another single Goomba, and a Goomba pair (%110111), each on separate pages.

Note the position bytes for these three objects. The first two Goombas are positioned vertically on top of row $0B, which coincides with the top of the terrain. In other words, the engine spawns them on the ground, like Mario. But other objects have more peculiar origins. When Mario encounters the first Goomba pair, they are pacing back and forth between two adjacent pipes. Based on their position, we might reasonably infer that they began on the ground like the previous two. But according to their coordinates in the table above, they spawn a few metatiles from the top of the screen. That is, they originate in mid-air and drop into position between the two pipes, a process that is never seen by the player. The only way to check this behavior, besides parsing the object data, is to replace the enemy object with a type that is unaffected by gravity. In figure 4.4, a simple hex edit replaces the double Goomba object with an immobile jumping board, so we can freeze the object midair, revealing its point of origin.

As we saw in our discussions of R.O.B. and the Zapper in chapter 3, the ways that hardware "perceives" the game onscreen is often incongruent with or even counterintuitive to player perception. The same applies to software—not only in relation to the player, but also to the hardware itself. The player, for instance, sees a single screen of graphics at a time. Beyond artistic tricks that simulate depth in tile-based graphics, the

4.4 With the aid of a hex editor, World 1–1's double Goomba object byte is replaced with a jumping board in order to reveal its peculiar mid-air origin. (Emulator: Macifom 0.16)

overall image is two-dimensional and flat. We already know that internally the Famicom differentiates between two types of tiles—background and sprite—that follow different positioning, palette, and priority rules. For the PPU, sensibly, the name table describes a single flat plane of background tiles. The *Super Mario Bros.* engine, however, differentiates further, assigning software priorities to background tiles that do not exist in hardware. In other words, the PPU can only ever see a flat name table, while the engine can split that name table into multiple layers. Player, engine, and processor all view the Kinoko Kingdom from radically different vantages.

Vertical Mirror

Players returning to *Super Mario Bros.* nearly three decades after its debut may quickly notice that the game scrolls exclusively along a single vector. Short of dying (or the special loop command), once a column of name table has passed beyond the left screen edge, Mario can never return to that space.

Subsequent games in the *Super Mario* series permitted movement in either direction.[33] The NES version of *Super Mario Bros. 2* included vertical and horizontal areas with bi-directional scrolling, albeit limited to one direction at a time. *Super Mario Bros. 3* upped the scrolling ante: Mario (and Luigi) could run, jump, swim, and fly along any axis. The added diagonal trajectory supported a new gameplay mechanic—the raccoon suit—that allowed Mario to fly for short periods of time once he had gained sufficient speed on a stretch of unimpeded runway. However, both successors benefited from the TSROM/MMC3 mapper, an internal hardware addition that expanded the cartridge ROM considerably (chapter 6). In the case of *Super Mario Bros. 3*, the mapper upgrade multiplied the PRG capacity eightfold, the CHR capacity sixteenfold, and added 8KB of RAM.

SMB's play style demands a modest memory overhead to maintain onscreen and offscreen objects. Since Mario can break blocks, bump out their contents, and collect coins, those objects' status must be stored until Mario scrolls past them. Likewise, to maintain the illusion of a world that extends beyond the current screen, moving enemies or ricocheting shells should pass into and out of frame believably. But such actions must take place within feasible boundaries. If Mario could bash a hundred brick metatiles scattered throughout a level then backtrack to those screens, the engine would have to manage a hefty ledger of objects in RAM to ensure that broken blocks stayed broken (as in *Super Mario Bros. 3*). Likewise, a skittering shell cannot be tracked as it glides across an entire level. In short, NROM cannot sacrifice the memory necessary to track objects for their entire lifespan.

To compensate, the *SMB* engine maintains a narrow "sliding window" wherein all objects are permitted to "exist." Once an object passes beyond that window, whether through their own volition or as a result of the screen scrolling past them, the engine "forgets" them. They are summarily dropped from memory and no longer exist as active objects. The sliding window contains two full screens of decoded metatiles (32x13) that shift right as the screen scrolls. As the player moves, the camera is positioned in the direct center of the window, leaving an eight-metatile "buffer" on either side of the gameplay screen.

The buffers provision a plausible range of motion for enemies that travel offscreen. If a kicked Koopa shell or a shambling Goomba move out of frame but then collide with a pipe or enemy within the buffer, they will react accordingly. If the enemy wanders beyond the buffer, it disappears permanently.

SMB's U.S. instruction manual makes special note of the peculiarities of the sliding window:

> Because the screen moves from left to right, there are enemies off the edge of the screen that can't be seen. You can't kill enemies you can't see by sending a [shell] off the screen after them. Why not? Maybe they jump over the enemy when Mario isn't looking! Strangely enough, however, if a kicked [shell] bumps into a [pipe] off the screen, it comes ricocheting back at Mario. If you hear the sound of a ricochet, jump right away so you'll be ready when it comes flying back onto the screen.[34]

Grasping the engine's frame of perception makes it clear that it is not simply that the player cannot see enemies—they do not yet exist. And as silly as it sounds for unseen enemies to jump shells, we have seen from the enemy object data examples that objects sometimes spawn in unexpected locations, often above a hurtling shell. Similarly, there are instances when Mario can kick and follow a shell, which clears enemies in his path. If the shell moves beyond the screen's right edge but stays within the sliding window, enemies can sometimes spawn between Mario and the ricocheting shell, meaning that the enemy object data has not rendered until after the shell has passed the object's coordinates.

Literal edge cases such as these illustrate the engine's weird perimeters. Along the window's right border, the engine is busy preparing objects prior to their screen entrance. They do not pop into existence fully

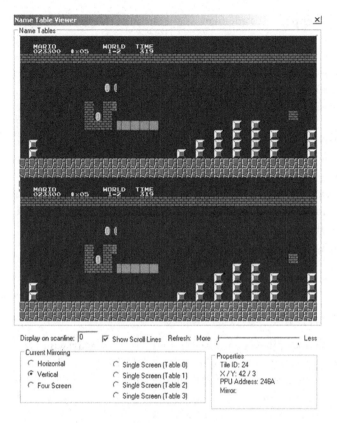

4.5 The customary 2x2 arrangement of name tables exhibiting vertical mirroring. (Emulator: FCEUX 2.1.5)

formed, but must be assembled according to the rendering rules outlined in the previous section. As you will recall from chapter 1, the Famicom's scrolling capabilities take advantage of the name tables' mirrored layout. Since *SMB* is soldered for vertical mirroring, its name tables may be arranged in the 2x2 arrangement seen in figure 4.5.

Though name tables are listed sequentially in the PPU's memory map, arranging them in a 2x2 matrix makes visual sense of the mirroring setting. The upper two name tables are duplicated along the x-axis, while the lower two name tables mirror their contents exactly. Vertical mirroring is suited for horizontal scrolling because the engine can track along two contiguous name tables solely by updating the scroll register's x-coordinate.

The challenge for games that scroll beyond two screens is wrapping seamlessly from one name table to the next. In *SMB*, the sliding window's eight-metatile buffer provides adequate space ahead of the current player screen to decode the set decoration, area objects, and enemy objects, render them onscreen, and have them ready just prior to the player's arrival. Each time Mario advances two metatiles onscreen, a two-metatile wide column of world is drawn at the right edge of the sliding window, while another column of equal width is erased from its left edge. The rendering engine acts like a more reliable version of the animator's hand in the famous Daffy Duck short, "Duck Amuck," vigilantly tracking Mario's advance along the screen, drawing in scenery before he arrives lest the whole scrolling facade be revealed.

Mirroring is also used in its conventional sense to reduce the pattern tiles necessary to draw objects. In doppleganger's disassembly, for instance, the following table lists the sprite indices that comprise power-up metatiles:

```
PowerUpGfxTable:
        .db $76, $77, $78, $79 ;regular mushroom
        .db $d6, $d6, $d9, $d9 ;fire flower
        .db $8d, $8d, $e4, $e4 ;star
        .db $76, $77, $78, $79 ;1-up mushroom
```

Each power-up metatile is composed of four 8x8 sprites drawn in the following order: upper left, upper right, bottom left, bottom right. Each byte value above references a tile index from the sprite pattern table. The regular mushroom, for example, is stored in four sequential bytes between $76 and $79 (all easily locatable in FCEUX's PPU Viewer).

An economical use of palette swaps and sprite mirroring reduces the number of constituent pattern table tiles by half. Notice that both mushrooms use the same sprites (with different colors) while the fire flower's and star's left and right halves are simply mirror images across the metatiles' y-axes. Coins, Podoboos, Piranha Plants, Bloopers, Spiny eggs, empty power-up blocks, drawbridge axes, stomped Goombas, fireworks, empty shells, jumping boards, the Mushroom Retainer, and even portions of Mario's body are composed of mirrored tiles. Top to bottom, Kinoko Kingdom is flush with symmetry.

The design benefit from using mirrored metatiles was that it freed pattern memory for additional objects. As Nakago and Tezuka recount, the designers strove to save space whenever possible:

Nakago: Even with mushrooms and flowers, we'd be looking to limit the bytes we used, so we'd draw half of the object then flip it around to display it.
Iwata: That's why these objects are all symmetrical.

Nakago: That's true of the stars too. They're symmetrical. There was the advantage that you could get an object that was double the size using only half the bytes.

Iwata: So all of these things were ways of limiting the number of bytes you were using.

Tezuka: That's right. We came up with all kinds of objects, all the time trying to limit the bytes we were using.[35]

As the designers acknowledge, the platform's affordances were structuring the world and its objects with an underlying symmetry, from the macro—large repeated patterns of metatiles that shaped the rhythm of hills, fences, and clouds—to the micro—flowers and stars constructed from mirrored halves.

Exergue

In the previous chapter, we discussed a special tile in Object Attribute Memory called sprite 0. Famicom programmers commonly used sprite 0 to time special raster effects, like splitting the screen at a designated scanline to provide the player with a static status bar that would not perpetually scroll offscreen.

Despite its position of honor in OAM, sprite 0 is rarely conspicuous. When the PPU renders objects, sprites with a lower position in OAM have higher screen priority. When objects overlap, the PPU must use a number of rules to decide which object's pixels will be drawn and thus appear "on top." If all sixty-four sprites were stacked onscreen in an 8x8 pixel pile, sprite 0 would always appear to be above the rest. However, sprite 0 does not have to sit atop background tiles in order to fire properly. Like any other sprite, sprite 0s priority bit can be set to be either in front of (0) or behind (1) background tiles. Most programmers wished to hide sprite 0, so they limited its size to one or a few pixels and tucked it discreetly behind background tiles.

SMB uses sprite 0 to demarcate the upper four tile rows of non-scrolling status information seen at the top of the screen (e.g., in figure 4.4). Reading left to right, we see the current player (Mario or Luigi) and score; the current stock of coins (0–99); the current world and level (e.g., 3–1); and the remaining time. *SMB*'s sprite 0 has a novel shape compared to most games; it mimics the bottom sliver of the coin tile that records Mario's current stash. Onscreen, it is placed directly behind the status bar coin whose shape it imitates (figure 3.4). *SMB*'s sprite 0 placement coupled with the game engine's porous upper screen boundary reveals an interesting quirk of the PPU's rendering process. Sprite 0 has two potentially contradictory priority attributes: its OAM position means it appears above all other sprites, while its OAM priority bit places it behind background tiles. So what happens when a sprite with the inverse attributes—lower OAM priority, but higher background priority—passes in front of the coin that hides sprite 0?

In most cases, the overlap never happens. Few sprites in *SMB* are permitted to breach the invisible border marked by sprite 0—even those that are airborne, like cloud-riding Lakitu. Mario is the obvious exception. He can scale tall brick structures and jump beyond the top of the screen, clipping his head out of view. In certain levels, Mario could cross the screen's upper threshold, allowing the player free reign to run in front of the status bar. Mario's ability to break through this diegetic wall, obfuscating data meant for the player's eyes, added to the game's mystique. Players felt as if they were violating the rules by running along the upper border, despite this being a necessary technique to discover *SMB*'s hidden warp zones.

Mario's spatial transgressions provide a simple method to reveal sprite 0's hiding place without the need to disable background tiles in an emulator. In World 1–2, it is possible to position Mario above the upper brick border and nudge his leg into position over the coin icon, causing the PPU to render an odd "triple overlay" effect.[36] While the majority of the coin background tile is positioned properly behind Mario's sprite, the lower portion of the coin rests in front of his boot. But if you look closely, you can see that the coin sliver is painted orange, the color of the background tile, even though the visible tile is sprite 0, which should be painted blue (figure 4.6).

The layer confusion between boot, coin, and sprite 0 demonstrates several competing priorities at play: sprite 0 has priority over all other sprites, but its individual sprite priority attribute places it behind any background tile; Mario's constituent sprites have priority above background tiles, but below sprite 0. When the PPU evaluates the scanline with overlapping tiles, it must "decide" which pixels to display on top. We would expect Mario to trump all other tiles, since he has priority over the background and the background has priority over sprite 0. But sprite 0's OAM position creates a strange compromise: the shape of sprite 0 sits atop Mario's leg, but the pixels are painted like the background tile. So sprite 0 is paradoxically both above Mario's sprite and behind the background tile. To the trained eye, that slight crescent of pixels marks the invisible line beyond which Mario's world is permitted to scroll.

4.6 The PPU's tile priority rules reveal sprite 0's location without disabling background tile visibility. (Emulator: FCEUX 2.1.5)

Status Bar

Though many games used sprite 0 splits to sequester scrolling from non-scrolling regions, it was not always necessary. Depending on the quantity of information necessary to convey, it was often simpler to use stationary sprites to compose status icons. But as always, the PPU's sprite limits applied—sixty-four total onscreen simultaneously and eight on a single horizontal scanline—setting hard limits on the shape and density of information displayed.

Contra's horizontal status bar, for example, is minimal compared to *SMB*'s. *Contra* uses the upper region of the screen solely to track player one and player two's current life count, marked with blue and red ribbon sprites, each drawn with a single 8x16-pixel tile. If both players manage to net extra lives during play (or input the Konami code), the onscreen display will max out at four ribbons each, i.e., the horizontal sprite maximum. During the game's attract loop (or if one player loses all of their lives during 2-player play), the status bar reads "GAME OVER," the first word stacked above the second in order to observe the eight-sprite limit.

Contra's restrained status bar is possible because the programmers included an independent interstitial screen displaying the players' total lives count, score, and current stage name, eliminating the need to keep such information visible onscreen. Nonetheless, *Contra*'s raised platforms, vertically scrolling level ("Waterfall"), and main protagonists' superhuman jumping talents all pose problems for the status bar. Enemy, player, and projectile sprites frequently pass through the ribbons' horizontal plane, creating noticeable flicker.

Contra's gameplay, especially with two simultaneous players, generates vast numbers of sprites—primarily bullets—onscreen, all vying for rendering priority. Accordingly, Konami's programmers designed the game engine to constantly cycle the OAM positions of all onscreen sprites. If one watches the sprite slots in the Nintendulator emulator during gameplay, the sprites appear to cascade in waves across OAM in a hypnotic rhythm, adding and subtracting sprites from the flow as they move into and out of frame. In other words, the programmers conceded a constant flow of sprite flicker in exchange for an overwhelming amount of onscreen action. And no single sprite element is given special treatment—player sprites disappear as frequently as Spreader shrapnel. The end result is an impressive screen density, despite the incessant flicker.

Mega Man shares *Contra*'s sprite-based status bar, but chooses an inverse orientation. Depending on the player's game progress, up to three status elements will be onscreen simultaneously: Mega Man's life bar, equipped weapon energy, and score.[37] Since the life and weapon energy bar are several sprites long, they are displayed vertically. At seven tiles high, this arrangement prevents the horizontal flicker problem present in *Contra*, but permanently limits the horizontal sprite density of nearly one quarter of the screen's vertical resolution. When the energy bar appears beside the life bar, sprite density is even further constrained. The tile row that displays the player's score, positioned directly above the life bar, suffers far worse. The score uses seven tile-sized digits, so any sprite object with a width greater than two tiles that passes through its plane triggers flicker.

Mega Man's engine uses an OAM cycling scheme similar to *Contra*'s. When sprites are active onscreen, their OAM positions are continuously swapped. However, unlike *Contra*'s cascade effect, *Mega Man*'s sprites are shifted around OAM in logical groups. For instance, during a section of the Fireman stage where columns of fire rise from the floor, the sprites are arranged in OAM in the following order (assuming Mega Man is stationary and the game is paused): sprite o (positioned offscreen); seven score display tiles; seven life bar tiles; seven weapon energy tiles; ten Mega Man tiles; sixteen tiles used to draw fire column one; and sixteen tiles used to draw fire column two. When OAM is cycled in the next frame, the arrangement changes to the following: sprite o; fire column two; fire column one; Mega Man; score display; life bar; and weapon energy. In other words, the sprites are cycled as metatiles and shuffled according to a scheme that assures no screen element will disappear for multiple consecutive frames. In this configuration, the score display metatile always has priority above the life and energy bars, but the arrangement does not matter in-game—their fixed positions ensure that their respective horizontal planes never intersect.

The OAM cycling routine creates odd circumstances where sprites will disappear even when the scanline limit has not been exceeded. If, for example, Mega Man fires three bullets while the fire columns are raised, portions of the right column will disappear. This is clearly not a scanline overflow but an overflow of available sprites, i.e., the fire columns are given lowest priority when the onscreen sprite count exceeds sixty-four. Consequently, the game engine moves the three trailing sprites of column two's metatile out of the OAM queue on odd frames to make room for Mega Man's Power Buster bullets, which for obvious hit detection purposes must always remain onscreen.

Like *Contra*, *Mega Man*'s mixture of vertical and horizontal level design creates numerous occasions where sprite limitations are violated. In figure 4.7, we can see a number of sprite priority trade-offs that take place during one gameplay sequence. At far left, Mega Man extends his arm to fire three bullets while another enemy bullet intersects the same plane. To compensate, tiles from both the life bar and Mega Man's head disappear. In the middle frame, a tile of Mega Man's torso erases as it passes the score tiles. And finally, at far right, Mega Man once again sacrifices his body to the score sprites. However, if we advanced another frame of game time, the priorities would swap in each screen capture, reviving some tiles while erasing others.

Mega Man's sprite-based status bars work because other necessary status cues (e.g., number of lives, available weapons) are either tucked away in a sub-screen or communicated diegetically. For instance, Mega Man's current equipped weapon does not require a status bar prompt—instead, his suit palette swaps to a new color to indicate the change. If additional status elements were moved into the normal gameplay screen, there would be barely any sprites left over to display enemies or items.

It is a testament to the games' quality that *Contra* and *Mega Man* became so popular in spite of their obvious technical concessions. In both games, there are few screens that do not suffer from significant flicker. An overabundance of onscreen objects, often subject to individual CPU-intensive collision checks, frequently overwhelms both game engines and causes noticeable slowdown.[38] Yet both games are still widely hailed as two of the NES's finest software showcases.

Though both *Contra* and *Mega Man* benefited from more advanced mappers than *SMB* (chapter 6), the former's choice of sprite-based toolbars were not affordances of better cartridge hardware. Both the sprite 0/background tile and sprite-based approach had advantages and drawbacks. For *SMB*, employing sprite 0 meant sacrificing a large portion of the upper playfield to static status information that, in some cases, could

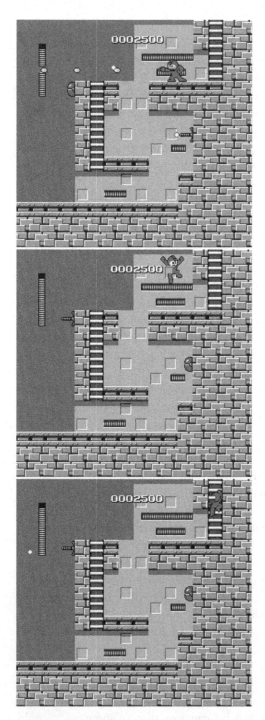

4.7 Multiple screenshots from *Mega Man*'s Cut Man stage demonstrate OAM cycling priorities at work, alternately deleting portions of Mega Man's body, the life counter, and enemy fire. (Emulator: Macifom 0.16)

be covered by the player's sprite. But the use of background tiles eliminated any potential sprite flicker. For *Contra* and *Mega Man*, the gains in screen real estate required a sacrifice of sprite fidelity—a certain threshold of flicker was allowable as long as it did not significantly inhibit gameplay. It also meant adapting the game engines to account for constant shuffling of sprite OAM. Decisions like the size, orientation, and information density of status elements at first appear to be dictated more by the videogame designer's whims, but at the platform level, they are decisions hewn closely to hardware and software constraints, even woven into the structure and design of the game engine itself.

Camera Lakitu

In videogame parlance, "camera control" is associated with 3D polygonal gaming. Extruding the flat, tile-based worlds of 2D videogames along the z-axis created new design problems. Representing a player avatar within a space that adheres to perspectival rules demands consideration of both how that avatar is positioned and from what vantage point that avatar is seen. If, for instance, the camera is positioned low to the ground, angled up, and tight on the avatar, it will crowd the majority of the screen, obscuring terrain, obstacles, and enemies. This setup might work for NPC conversations in an RPG, but function poorly in a flight simulator. If the camera is elevated to a position directly above the avatar's head, the player now has a bird's eye view of their surroundings—ideal for gameplay that demands a wide scope of the playfield (e.g., sports or real-time strategy) but poor for precise platforming or an intricate fighting game.

As videogame designers grappled with this problem during the first generation of 3D consoles and PCs, they experimented with a variety of solutions. In 3D platformers like *Super Mario 64*, camera control was both automated and player-controlled.[39] In most cases, Mario's spatial proximity to terrain or other objects dictated the camera position. Sliding down an icy path, for instance, would trigger a high angled view, while dialogue segments would swing the camera behind Mario's shoulder so the player could see with whom he was conversing. In egregious cases of camera misbehavior, the player's perspective might be trapped behind a block of in-game architecture, completely obscuring their view of Mario.

Super Mario 64's designers gave the player limited camera control via the Nintendo 64 controller's four C buttons. At the time, the 3D camera and its sometimes unpredictable behavior were so novel they had to be explained by a diegetic device. In-game, the Lakitu Bros., the

Spinies-chucking Koopas who menace Mario from the clouds in *Super Mario Bros.*, track Mario's movements with cameras slung from fishing poles. The camera is thus anthropomorphized and mobilized, creating at least a plausible explanation for why it might sometimes have "a mind of its own." This device is introduced early in the game when one of the Lakitu Bros. descends from the sky and tells the player about their journalistic enterprise: "Mario has just arrived on the scene, and we'll be filming the action live as he enters the castle and pursues the missing Power Stars." We never see more than one brother talking with Mario, presumably because the other has to film the conversation.

Three dimensions added new challenges to camera positioning, but this was not a novel phenomenon, even in the 2D era. Viewpoint is a concern for any video game, from *Pong* to *Gears of War*, and often establishes not only the player's position in the game world, but the genre as well (e.g., first-person shooters). Camera position was less complex in single-screen games common to the arcade era, since game designers rarely had to shift perspective from screen to screen or grant the player camera control. However, the introduction of 2D scrolling made camera position more complex, since new data was streaming into the player's view at variable rates. The camera had to be close enough for the player to recognize and interact with objects onscreen, but distant enough to permit the player to react to new objects as they entered the frame. Scrolling direction played a crucial part in this decision. If the player moved left to right, it made sense to allow a larger buffer on the right side than the left, so the player might better anticipate and react. Likewise for vertical scrolling space shooters: the player's spaceship was placed along the bottom of the screen so there was ample room for enemies to stream in from above. Multi-axis scrolling increased the complexity further. If the player could move in any of four cardinal directions, where should the player's avatar be placed on the screen and how distant should the camera be from that position?

Although *SMB* scrolls along a single, non-reversible vector, its engine handles camera movement in subtle ways. At the opening of each outdoors level, Mario stands 40 pixels to the right of the screen's left boundary.[40] The position is not arbitrary—the designers are cueing the player to run forward toward the stretch of unobstructed runway set against an inviting backdrop of open blue skies.[41] Mario's metatile likewise faces right to further signal the player's prescribed path.

Once the player moves, the scrolling almost immediately kicks in and Mario's position appears to lock near center screen. If the player maintains a steady running pace, the world moves in lockstep, only halting

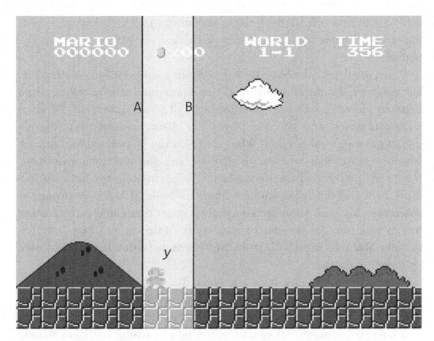

4.8 The two scrolling thresholds designated in *Super Mario Bros.*'s game engine. Boundary A occurs at player x-position $50 (80 pixels), while boundary B occurs at player x-position $70 (112 pixels). Region *y* is the engine's "momentum field." (Emulator: OpenEmu 1.0.2)

when the player chooses to slow their progress—perhaps to vault a platform, bump a block, or squat into a pipe. The camera is fluid and responsive, always permitting the player ample time to adjust to enemies or obstacles as they appear. But Mario's locked position slightly left of center gently suggests that the player should continue moving right.

To achieve the camera's flexible pace, the game engine employs two distinct scrolling thresholds (figure 4.8). The first boundary (A) is 80 pixels (5 metatiles) from the left edge of the screen. As soon as the leftmost pixel of Mario's metatile passes that invisible line, scrolling commences. The second boundary (B) is 112 pixels (7 metatiles) from the left edge of the screen. The 32-pixel region between boundary A and B serves as a "momentum field" (*y*) wherein Mario accelerates toward his maximum sprinting velocity and gradually "locks" into his rightmost position.

If the player walks forward tentatively, Mario will remain in this field until the player either stops to reverse direction or accelerates to running (holding right) or sprinting (holding right + B) speed. Boundary

B functions as a soft limit: if Mario accelerates to a high enough speed, his x-coordinates can sometimes drift several pixels right of the boundary.[42]

This may seem like bog-standard scrolling behavior for a platformer, but consider the implications of the complex interactions taking place between player input, sprite positioning, and scroll movement. Between x-coordinates 0 and 80, the player has direct control over Mario's metatile, as we would expect. When we press the D-pad and buttons, we sensibly intuit that we are directly moving the character onscreen. However, once Mario passes boundary A, we begin to control both Mario's movement and the scroll amount simultaneously. If Mario continues to accelerate, his x-position updates slightly faster than the scroll, allowing him to lock into position near boundary B. At this point, if we continue to move Mario forward without halting his momentum, his x-coordinate no longer updates.

Our control has now been transferred almost fully to directing the scroll—or the "camera," if we wish to adopt the familiar metaphor. (The sole exception is jumping, since pressing A still grants us control of Mario's y-coordinate.) Of course, stopping or turning left immediately wrests Mario's horizontal position back into our hands, but from the game engine's perspective, our input orchestrates a series of fluid hand-offs between sprite and scroll control. This process is wholly opaque to us and, frankly, counterintuitive to our common phenomenologies of interactivity. We think *SMB* plays well because we have total control over Mario's movements—his jumps, ducks, and frictional slides feel responsive and fluid. But this is a perceptual illusion. Sometimes we do move the man, but other times we move the world. And sometimes we move both.

Mario x Crown

Kinoko Kingdom is full of secrets—many intentional, many not. As early as World 1–1, *Super Mario Bros.*'s designers left clues to a world literally hidden beneath the surface. Pressing down on a particular pipe shuttled Mario to a subterranean room filled with coins. And the short runway prior to Mario's first pit jump concealed a reward revealed only by a miscalculated jump—an invisible 1-up block. Once players stumbled across those first precious secrets, the whole Kingdom took on a mysterious air. What other surprises had the developers hidden away?

Players picked apart *Super Mario Bros.*'s intricacies with fervor. In Japan, Tokuma Shoten's *Super Mario Bros.: The Complete Strategy Guide* was a surprise bestseller, topping the non-manga book sales charts in 1985 and 1986.[43] Futami Shobo's *Super Mario Bros. Secret Tricks Collection* held the number 10 and 3 spots in the same two years.[44] Strategy guides provided players exhaustive maps of the game's hidden power-ups, warp zones, beanstalks, and bonus coin levels. They outlined scoring strategies, shortcuts through stages, and tricks to stockpile lives. A Koopa descending the staircase at the end of 3–1, for example, could be stomped in such a way that the player could hop endlessly on its shell as it ricocheted against the wall, multiplying point values until it started generating extra lives. But the trick had an underlying programmatic consequence—overly greedy players who amassed too many lives found that their next death resulted in a game over.[45] And the results of that action first tipped off players to a world of secrets that might be beyond the purview of tips and tricks books.

The first indication that the "greed penalty" was unintended appears during the black interstitial screen that displays the player's current world and their accumulated lives. Once Mario has more than nine lives, the counter begins to display strange characters. In figure 4.9, Mario has $39 (58) lives, represented in-game by the "crown" graphic and a right triangle.

The crown hieroglyph is an intentional artifact used to indicate the tens place. Mario team expected some players to amass more than nine lives, but they did not build in any checks to prevent the graphical errors triggered when the player exceeded nineteen. Like the Level indicator in Famicom *Donkey Kong* (chapter 2), *SMB*'s lives display uses an offset to fetch the appropriate tile for the ones position, based on the current number of lives. 0 through 9 display in sequence, as expected; when the player accrues ten lives, a crown marks the tens place and the 0–9 cycle starts again. Once twenty lives are earned, an "A" curiously appears in the ones position.

In the background pattern table, 0–9 occupy the first ten tiles slots, then A-Z, followed by a number of solid colored tiles, symbols, and then the game's remaining background elements. Once the numbers have cycled from 1 to 9, then work through 0–9 a second time, the display routine begins fetching tiles beyond the numbers. The triangle seen in figure 4.9 represents 58 lives ($39 is decimal 57, but $00 lives is 1 onscreen, so we add one to the actual value). The graphic is actually the slope of a hillside which appears blue because it is using the numeral tile's attribute assignment.

But why does death trigger a game over when the player accumulates too many lives from the shell-hopping trick? The answer is identical to the programming flaw that triggers the kill screen in Famicom *Donkey*

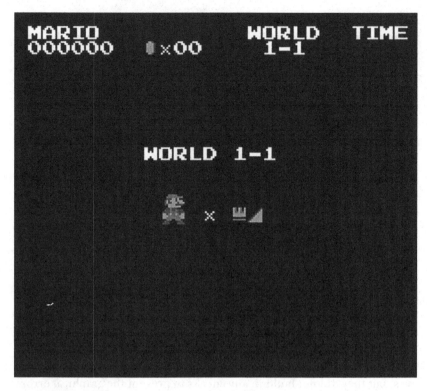

4.9 Accumulating more than nine lives in *Super Mario Bros.* causes unintended CHR-ROM tiles to seep into the lives counter. (Emulator: Macifom 0.16)

Kong (chapter 2). The memory location that stores Mario's lives, located in RAM at $075A, is a single byte long. Once that byte reaches values exceeding $7F (or 127), the sign bit becomes 1. Without a proper check, the game interprets values $80 (128) and higher as negative lives. When that occurs, Mario is considered to be on his last life, so the next death triggers game over.[46]

The 3–1 trick illustrates the careful balance struck between programmer intent and player expectation. The Mario team concluded that most players would not exceed 127 lives and therefore it was not worth the bytes to build in proper checks to create an upper bound for 1-up accumulation. When players discovered the means to push the system's boundaries, both beneficial (lots of lives) and non-beneficial (potential death) results surfaced. Miyamoto and team knew about the 3–1 trick prior to the game's release, but they decided to leave it in because it was fun. And they likely knew that it contained its own checks and balances, rewarding players who wanted a reasonable amount of extra plays, but penalizing those who went overboard.

Minus World

SMB also had glitches that the team never predicted. The so-called "minus world" is the most famous of these. Reaching the minus world requires skillful maneuvers that few players can reproduce, lending to its mythological allure. Near the end of world 1–2, where Mario enters the pipe to return to the surface, it is possible to jump in such a way that Mario's body can glide through the brick boundary separating the pipe from the warp zone area. Once Mario ejects into the warp zone—and if the player is careful not to trigger the scroll lock—Mario can enter the first pipe before the standard "Welcome to Warp Zone!" text appears onscreen. When the interstitial screen appears, the current level is listed as "World −1."

The level that follows is less mysterious than its name, since it is merely a duplicate of World 7–2 that loops endlessly. Mario can proceed left to right as normal, but once he reaches the exit pipe, he is cruelly deposited at the level start with no recourse but to while his time and lives away.

Nintendo officially corroborated the existence of the minus world in the third issue of *Nintendo Power*, describing it as "an endless water world from which no one has ever escaped."[47] The bare bones explanation gave players little indication of exactly how Mario might glide through solid brick ("After many tries, Mario may be able to go through the wall"), but the photographic proof settled the question of whether it was possible. The minus world fell in line with the numerous other secrets hidden throughout the Mushroom Kingdom, fueling rumors that the designers had tucked away secret levels for only the most skilled players to find. But the minus world is not designed—there is no area object data set aside for the looping water level (beyond that intended for 7–2), nor any other bonus levels beyond the conventional thirty-two. There simply was not enough leftover ROM space to tuck away extraneous secret levels. Instead, the minus world is a result of the serendipitous coupling of flexible engine design and collision detection shortcomings.

As we have seen, beyond sprite 0's simple hit detection, the Famicom has no hardware provisions for checking collisions between tiles. Collision detection must be handled exclusively in software. However, checking every point around a given metatile against all valid collision points of all other onscreen objects is far too computationally costly for the 6502 to handle in a single frame. Instead, programmers created bounding boxes around objects to check and compare only a handful of collision boundaries. In *SMB*, Mario has two points, one for each foot, that check whether he collides with the floor. The drawback to simple boundary boxes is that they are porous. If collision points on two objects happen to pass by one another without a proper collision, character objects can pass through otherwise "solid objects" like bricks or pipes.

SMB, like many other games of its era, includes an ejection routine to compensate for holes in boundary checks. If, for instance, the horizontal position of Mario's right foot is determined to be inside a block while he is moving right, the engine will eject Mario in the opposite direction, forcibly pushing his metatile out of the wall. This works for most common cases, but it is not a failsafe method. Part of the minus world trick relies on Mario gaming the collision ejection routine by jumping in a crouched position while facing left. If the player can then collide with the brick wall at an exact metatile boundary, quickly pressing left causes Mario to eject *right*, forcing him through the wall tiles until he emerges from the bricks on the other side. Doing so finds Mario in the warp zone earlier than expected and fails to properly trigger the scroll lock.

Mario's faulty collision shortcut is only the first key to triggering the minus world. When Mario arrives early, the engine has improperly loaded the warp zone data for world 5–1 (which is normally found in 4–2). However, that warp zone contains only one pipe. Since the warp zone in 1–2 has three pipes, the far left and right pipes are set to warp to the nonexistent World 36–1. The reason why erroneous data is loaded in the warp zone area is too complex to discuss here, but where the pipe sends Mario is a result of the world number variable being set by an arbitrary data byte. As doppelganger explains, the world level is improperly set to $01:

When the value 36/$24 is used as the world number, this code uses the number $24 as the offset, and gets the number $33, which tells it to look exactly $33 bytes past the start of where the area address offsets, which happens to have the byte value $01. The problem is that the look-up table it uses to find the addresses to its level and enemy data is only 36, or $24 bytes long, and $33 bytes past the starting byte is actually outside of the area offset lookup table, which puts it in the enemy data address table. The value $01, which is equivalent to world 2-2/7-2, is actually retrieved from data it's not supposed to access![48]

In short, when Mario ducks down a pipe that rightfully should not be there, the engine seeks the current level to load in a data area beyond its intended lookup boundary.

SMB's use of metatile-encoding to store its level layouts combined with 6502 assembly's byte-based mnemonics means that level data can be loaded from arbitrary locations in PRG-ROM. Consider the following short code snippet:

```
LDA #$00
STA $0775
```

As discussed in chapter 1, each line of assembly has two parts: the instruction and a value/memory location. The code above loads the accumulator with the value $00, then stores that value at memory location $0775. However, the alphabetical characters mean nothing to the CPU. Prior to execution, the above code must be assembled—i.e., translated—into a raw byte stream that the 2A03 can understand. Since each three-letter mnemonic has a single byte equivalent, when the above code snippet is assembled, it reads:

```
A9 00
8D 75 07
```

Again, the text mnemonics are for the programmer's benefit; they make the code more legible. The CPU simply reads bytes. And whether the CPU interprets a byte as instruction or data depends on the context. In the snippet above, those bytes are meant to load a value and store it at the specified address. However, if the program executed a subroutine that jumped to the code above and read the five bytes as music data the assembled bytes would not perform the same load and store instructions. Instead, A9 to 07 would be treated as five byte values meant to be relayed to the music engine.

This agnosticism toward data and instructions is precisely why *SMB*'s engine can "generate" level layouts beyond the thirty-two that the Mario team designed. When the subroutine that fetches metatiles for a given level is manipulated to point toward an arbitrary location in PRG-ROM, either by accident or through player intervention, the engine can read instruction bytes as area object data. When glitches occur, that flexibility is also its curse.

In the Famicom Disk System port of *SMB*, for example, entering a minus world pipe does not lead to the same endless water level. The results are far more bizarre. Mario begins above ground in a mushroom cap level completely submerged in water. Floating Princess sprites and gray Bowsers populate the landscape, which is colored in the green and pink hues of an underwater stage. Stranger still, World −1 ends with a modified staircase and a flagpole rather than an endless loop. Players may actually proceed further into the minus world, to −2 and −3. The conclusion of the latter world leads Mario to an empty Bowser bridge and a congratulatory message, though no Princess appears. The game then resets to the title screen and permits level selection, as if the player had completed the game.

The discrepancy between minus worlds lies in the code layout. Data on cartridge and disk are arranged according to different specifications. PRG- and CHR-ROM on cartridges are stored in separate ICs while disks store their data serially, along with the various headers and gaps the Disk Player requires to read that data properly (chapter 5). As a result, the offset fed to the warp pipe in 1–2 will land on a different byte, pointing to an alternate byte block for the engine to interpret as area and enemy object data. So players beware: when traversing the minus world, the medium matters.

Mario World

Super Mario Bros. was Nintendo's breakout console hit, spawning one of the most popular and influential videogame franchises of all time and spurring Nintendo's acceptance in the U.S. videogame market—in fact, saving that market from imminent collapse. *Super Mario Bros.* helped make the company's name synonymous with videogames. In the U.S., "playing Nintendo" replaced "playing Atari" as the linguistic metonym for playing any videogame, not just software exclusive to Nintendo's console. *Super Mario Bros.* also entrenched the platformer as the NES genre *par excellence*, spawning a chain of look- and play-alikes that continue even today.

So to return again to the chapter's opening question, what made *Super Mario Bros.* such a standout hit, adored both in Japan and abroad? For one, Kinoko Kingdom was a vivid, surrealist world composed of a strange mélange of Eastern and Western influences. The striking blue skies alone were a marked departure from the black void that served as the backdrop for videogames of all genres. But Mario's strange world had a predictable internal logic, despite its surreal setting—pipes took you underground, beanstalks led to clouds, and large castles were as imposing on the inside as they appeared from the outside.

Meanwhile, the means provided to the player to explore this world— Mario and Luigi—had a fantastic feel. They could walk and run, with realistic acceleration that affected the distance and trajectory of their jumps. Hard stops were supplanted by realistic skidding turns. The all-or-nothing static arc of Mario's jump in *Donkey Kong* and *Mario Bros.* was replaced with flexible "air control," the ability to coax the character's movements after pressing the jump button. Thus players could weave Mario's body through narrow passages, around blocks, and under enemies—all in mid-air.

These same skills were required to uncover the game's secrets. The myriad pipes and blocks were enticements to explore, symbolized famously by the blocks stamped with gleaming question marks. Mario shrank, grew, and gained fantastic powers like a modern-day fairy tale character—albeit one sporting overalls and a mustache. Some pipes were plugged, but others led to underground passages or level-skipping warp zones.

But Kinoko Kingdom's arrangement was not arbitrary. Miyamoto's team worked hard to lead the player through their cartoon world, teaching them skills via play, absent any in-game text or tutorial. *SMB*'s was a world meant for extended sessions and repeated play—a true console game.

In combination, these traits cohered into one of those most beloved and influential videogames of all time. And each of these elements, in turn, was sculpted by the Famicom platform. The level structure, the blocks, the colors, the physics, the music—all conformed to the architectures of the 2A03, the 2C02, the NROM, the Famicom controller, and the CRT television. The platform founded the platformer.

スキナミチヲユケ / *TAKE ANY ROAD YOU WANT*

— *The Hyrule Fantasy / The Legend of Zelda*

There is no better book, no better mirror, than the landscape itself.

— Takeshi Yamagishi, "Landscape and the Human Being"

A blank yellow cartridge hovers above a faceted metallic vista, its planar surface stretching into an infinite gradient of purple and black. The cartridge rotates lengthwise and vanishes in a beam of radiance as a yellow diskette takes it place, now held aloft by slender fingers. "The gaming world is about to change from cartridges to disk cards!"' an announcer exclaims. Disembodied hands reach into frame to demonstrate the connections necessary to join the Famicom to its new shoebox-shaped companion. "Dramatically better games will be at your fingertips!" the announcer continues, as a green-clad elf plunges his sword into an enormous unicorn dragon.[1]

So went the auspicious television debut of Nintendo's 1986 disk drive peripheral, the Family Computer Disk System (FDS), and *The Hyrule Fantasy* | ゼルダの伝説, better known in the West as *The Legend of Zelda*. Promising "three times the power" of standard cartridges, Nintendo's disks were set to change the console's future. PCs had benefited from the expansive, inexpensive, and rewriteable storage medium for many years, but for home consoles, disks were uncharted territory. The Disk System would be Nintendo's first attempt to extend the Famicom's storage potential and answer competitors who were introducing newer, faster machines.

Nintendo's concurrent development of *Super Mario Bros.* and *The Legend of Zelda* signaled an important bellwether in their hardware future. With the former game, Nintendo had reached a paradoxical zenith—Mario's adventures raised the bar for console platforming, but at the same time packed NROM's memory to capacity. Mario had reached his final castle with nowhere left to run. Yet *The Legend of Zelda* promised a new platform future bolstered by disk capacity and random-access memory, augmenting the Famicom's processing and graphical power to expand game worlds and multiply the characters within. The FDS primed Nintendo's new elven hero for a quest unlike any console players had seen before. But Nintendo's commercial was only half right: the gaming world was about to change thanks to disk cards, but the format shift was a brief material detour on the way to an alternate hardware future.

"PLEASE SET DISK CARD"

Nintendo's Family Computer Disk System shipped February 21, 1986 for ¥15,000 (roughly $80 in 1986), besting the launch price of its base unit. The rectangular drive fit neatly underneath the Famicom and matched the console's distinctive palette (figure 5.1).

The FDS body was maroon with a black face, white lettering, and a small yellow eject button. It received power either from an included AC adapter or, alternatively, six C batteries—in case the outlet was already full from the Famicom's and TV's wall warts. The drive attached to the console via a cabled RAM adapter that slotted into the Famicom's card edge connector like a game cartridge. True to its name, the adapter provided 32KB of DRAM (Dynamic RAM, manufactured by Sharp) for PRG code, 8KB of SRAM (Save RAM) for CHR data (mapped directly to the PPU's address space), and an application-specific integrated circuit (or ASIC) called the 2C33.[2] The custom IC stored the FDS system BIOS,[3] coordinated I/O with the Famicom, and drove an additional audio channel (chapter 7). Disks loaded in the front of the unit and a small red LED indicated when read/writes were in progress.

Diskettes were ideal for videogames. They were less expensive to manufacture than cartridges, (re)writable, and had more storage space for data and graphics. Following their standard practice of repurposing existing technology for new products, Nintendo partnered with Mitsumi to manufacture modified versions of their proprietary Quick Disk format.

5.1 A Famicom sitting atop the Family Computer Disk System peripheral. The black RAM adapter is attached to the Famicom's cartridge slot. (Source: Evan Amos, Wikimedia Commons)

Mitsumi disks were smaller than standard 3.5" floppies: their inner magnetic disk measured 2.8" and they were housed in either 3"x3" or 3"x4" plastic shells. Data densities varied according to OEM customer specifications, but Nintendo's double-sided "disk cards," as they rebranded them, held approximately 64KB on either side.[4] Though Quick Disks were used in some obscure 8-bit computers, stand-alone word processors, and a few MIDI sequencers and synthesizers, Nintendo would be the widest adopter of the format.

Beyond cosmetic differences, Quick Disks' underlying physical structure and data access were functionally different from conventional disks.[5] Standard floppies used a *random access* technique to fetch and write data. The surface of their flexible magnetic disks were traced with a series of concentric tracks. Each track was further subdivided into individual, fixed-length sectors (standard 3.5" disk sectors, for instance, were always

4KB). When a program requested data for writing or retrieval, the disk drive's spindle motor rotated the disk and a secondary stepper motor moved the read/write head to the appropriate sector. Thanks to the disk's discrete segmented design, the read/write head could dip into the magnetic disk at any point along its surface, making data access fast and efficient.

Alternatively, a Quick Disk used *sequential access* to write and retrieve data. Its magnetic surface was visually similar to a standard floppy, but the series of tiny tracks circling the disk's circumference traced a single spiral leading to the disk's center, like the grooves of a vinyl record. While the disk spun, the read/write head moved like a phonograph stylus from the outer to the inner edge of the disk. Once it reached the end, it had to reset to the outer edge before it began another scan. Whether the requested data was stored along the outer edge or near the center spindle, the head had to follow the spiral track from start to finish each scan. As a result, sequential access was much slower than random access—it took nearly six seconds to scan a Famicom disk. Players accustomed to instant-on cartridges were introduced to a novel console phenomenon: loading screens. And the vinyl analogy extended further—since Quick Disks were double-sided, players now found themselves flipping disks during gameplay.

Quick Disks, like all floppy disks, were more delicate than cartridges. Cartridge shells protected the majority of the circuit board, exposing only the "card edge" that connected to the console. Famicom and NES shells alike were designed not to open for an obvious practical reason: when one's customers are primarily children, physical safeguards are necessary to curb rough handling or accidental damage. Most Famicom carts were secured with interior plastic clips that made them nearly impossible to pry apart without fracturing the exterior shell. NES carts were primarily fastened with three 3.8mm security screws that required a special bit to loosen (chapter 3). Famicom disk cards also had a rigid plastic shell, but the magnetic disk remained exposed via a narrow vertical window. Embossed icons warned against touching the disk or placing it near magnets, but there were no physical safeguards to prevent such mishandling. Nintendo omitted the metal shutters common to 3.25" floppies in favor of a more economical solution: retail disk games were stored in wax paper sleeves, slotted into a hinged plastic case (like a miniature CD jewel case or MiniDisc shell), then sticker-sealed, along with the game's manual, inside a flexible plastic box.

Quick Disks were chosen for their ability both to save in-game data and to write new games onto existing disks. Nintendo implemented a forward-thinking sales and distribution model for what videogame marketers now call DLC, or downloadable content. Customers could bring disks to merchants that installed Nintendo kiosks and have store employees copy new software to their existing disks for less than the cost of a new game. Blank disks cost about ¥2000 (~$12), a considerable discount from the average ¥5000 (~$30) cartridge. Moreover, rewriting an existing disk with a new game cost a mere ¥500 (~$3.25).[6]

The kiosk model also allowed Nintendo to administer early versions of "online" play. Special contests were held for selected titles like *Golf Japan Course* and *Grand Prix F1 Race*. Disk System owners could purchase special (shuttered) blue disk cards,[7] earn a high score at home, then bring their disks back to the store. Retailers uploaded the player's score to a central database via Nintendo's Disk Fax kiosk. At the conclusion of the competition, top players were rewarded with prizes, including stationery sets, VHS tapes, trophies, and special gold "prize card" disks.[8]

NINJENDO

The flip side to easy disk copying was software piracy. Nintendo foresaw the risk and purposefully chose the Quick Disk format with piracy prevention in mind. Beyond their distinctive colored shells and smaller size, disk cards were embossed with "NINTENDO" along both sides of their graspable bottom edge. The recessed logo was not mere ornamentation; like the slimmer disk profile and atypical file access, the feature was meant to deter unauthorized disk duplication. The FDS drive had a screw-mounted plate affixed to the inner lip of the disk bay that held the raised counterpart of the disk lettering. Disk cards without the proper recessed edge failed to physically clear the drive bay, preventing the game from loading. In effect, this was the mechanical sibling of the CIC lockout chip embedded in all Nintendo Entertainment System consoles and game paks (chapter 3).

Nintendo's U.S. patent for the abandoned version of an NES Disk System claimed that using non-proprietary disks would encourage illegal reproduction of their software, flood the market with low-cost copies, economically damage Nintendo and its suppliers, and confuse consumers about which games were authentic. Nintendo devised a material solution to a software problem, ensuring that "the data recording device can be authenticated by its structure or form."[9] This is similar to tactics used in the early PC gaming industry, where special code wheels or text keys hidden in printed manuals served as physical deterrents to software piracy. Nintendo went a step further, carving their copyright protection directly into the media.

Predictably, their anti-piracy precautions failed to thwart software theft. Workarounds emerged almost immediately following the peripheral's launch. Unlicensed disk manufacturers simply mimicked the recessed NINTENDO letters with slight spelling variations: NINFENDO, NINJENDO, or the witty INTEND, with N and O replaced with empty squares.[10] Similar letterforms and bare indentations cleared the drive's logo protuberance as easily as Nintendo's sanctioned cavities. And since the variations did not technically violate Nintendo's corporate trademark, they could be marketed openly. Hackers also devised a number of disk modifications to enable cross-media copying. Clipping metal brackets to the disk cards, for example, extended their profile so they would fit standard floppy drives.

Nintendo retaliated with their own modifications. For those pirates who had managed to turn the Disk System itself into a disk copier, Nintendo released a FDS revision with an onboard Drive Controller Chip that prevented the drive from rewriting a disk's entire contents. Fan site Famicom World also discovered a secondary circuit added to later Disk System models that incorporated yet another layer of copy protection. Though as they demonstrated on their site, disabling the protection involved little technical knowledge beyond basic soldering skills.[11] On the hardware front, Nintendo was fighting a losing battle.

Nintendo also tried to mitigate piracy through software. Disk cards included a number of built-in error checks, some stemming from the peculiarities of their proprietary format. Unlike the uniform sectors of standard disks, Quick Disks stored data in "blocks" of varying length.[12] Due to this dynamic structure, data blocks had to be labeled and formatted in a specific way. Prior to each block, there were "gaps" of data padding (i.e., zeros) to compensate for mechanical variance in the time it took for the disk drive head to return to the outer edge of the disk and signal a "ready" state to the RAM adapter. Additionally, since the ready signal relied on a mechanical switch within the disk mechanism, it often triggered early, so the RAM adapter was programmed to ignore roughly the first twenty-six thousand bits read from disk. Once the RAM adapter was ready to accept valid data, it waited until the gap terminated with a single byte flag ($80) to indicate the start of a new block.[13] The next data byte, called the block ID, designated the format and length of data to follow. The length specification byte was crucial, since there were no other means to signal when the file's data had ended. Following the actual file data, there was a 2-byte *cyclic redundancy check*, or CRC. Finally, there had to be another small data gap (approximately 975 bits wide) prior to the start of any subsequent block. The repeated gap, start byte, block ID, data, CRC pattern structured the entire disk.

A block ID was expected to be one of four values: $01, $02, $03, or $04. Blocks 01 and 02 were specially formatted headers required for the disk to function properly after boot-up, so they had to appear at the start of either disk side. Block 01 contained fifty-five bytes of metadata including the total number of disks, the current side number, the game's name and version, and the disk's manufacturing date.[14] Most critical were the first fifteen bytes of the block indicating the block ID ($01) and an ASCI-encoded string that read *NINTENDO-HVC*.[15] The text served as a software copyright mechanism; if the BIOS could not find the string, the disk aborted loading.

Block 02 contained just two bytes: its own block number ($02) and the total number of blocks on disk. Oddly, the number stored here did not have to match the actual number of blocks present on disk; the BIOS simply ignored any blocks beyond the number provided. Developers capitalized on this behavior to implement custom copyright mechanisms. Konami included a checksum algorithm in アルマナの奇跡 (*The Miracle of Almana*) to verify the contents of each file on disk. Editing a single byte in any file, as illegal disk writers commonly did, would send the game into an infinite reset loop.

Other mechanisms embedded messages to potential pirates when a checksum failed. These were generally good-natured, aiming to steer pirates toward the proper path. Nintendo's *Doki Doki Panic*, for instance, stated, "SORRY...PLEASE USE OFFICIAL DISK WRITER SHOP" when users attempted to illegally copy the game. Nasir Gebelli, programmer of Square's とびだせ大作戦 (*3-D WorldRunner*), inserted a personal plea to dissuade illegal copiers:

I WOULD LIKE TO THANK YOU FOR YOUR INTEREST IN MY GAME> UNFORTUNATELY YOU WILL NOT BE ABLE TO PLAY THIS ILLEGAL COPY. BUT THE GOOD NEWS IS THAT YOU CAN PURCHASE THIS GAME FROM YOUR COMPUTER STORE SINCERELY, N A S I R[16]

The ubiquity of these in-game warnings showed that Nintendo and third-party developers alike knew their games were being copied and were working in earnest to stop software theft.

But these code-based checks and balances were just as susceptible to circumvention as the hardware itself. Hacker International, one of the most prolific publishers for the Disk System, despite their lack of a license, released several variations of their Disk Hacker utility, which broke the software copyright protection, allowing users to copy games on the FDS without the need for hardware modifications.[17] They also used their own technology to produce games, like a *hentai* parody of popular RPG *Dragon Quest*, called *BODYCONQUEST I: Girls Exposed*.[18] Players found their quest rewarded them not with treasure, but with pixelated erotica.

Adventure Mario

Launch title *The Hyrule Fantasy* | ゼルダの伝説 (hereafter *Zelda*) was the FDS's showcase game, but it was not initially specced for the peripheral.[19] Due to the game's expected technical requirements, the development team began work on the VS. UniSystem, one of Nintendo's two arcade platforms based on the Famicom architecture.[20]

Nintendo's arcade hits had raised them to worldwide prominence, but their console's breakout success reversed standard porting procedures. *Duck Hunt*, *Excitebike*, *Ice Climber*, *Clu Clu Land*, and *Super Mario Bros.* began as Famicom cartridges that were later ported to arcades, typically with tweaks to augment their difficulty, alter graphics, and add in competitive play—the trademark of the "VS." moniker.[21] The industry was shifting, and Nintendo was pushing the Famicom as the lead console without abandoning the lucrative arcade market. This was especially important in Japan, where arcades remained a viable platform. In the United States, however, the shift in focus from arcades to home play initiated the former's gradual decline toward obsolescence.

UniSystem PPUs were largely identical to the Famicom PPU, minimizing the turnaround time to port console games to arcades. Additional registers handled arcade-specific functions: detecting quarter drops, acknowledging credits for either player, flagging DIP switch toggles, and so on.[22] The most significant divergence was color. Famicom and UniSystem did not share the same palette entries, so games required color value adjustments to display properly on the arcade PPU. Moreover, there were multiple PPU variations used in UniSystem cabinets (with the model number format RP2C0X), each with distinct palette data that served as a novel form of visual copyright enforcement. Pirate ROMs would play, but the in-game colors would be wildly inaccurate without the matching picture processor.[23]

Early in production, Miyamoto's team shifted *Zelda*'s development to the Disk System. Again, *Zelda* was developed alongside *Super Mario Bros.* and shared the same core team—Miyamoto, Tezuka, Nakago, and Kondo—along with credited programmers Yasunari Soejima and I. Marui.[24] Game concepts, programming techniques, and graphical assets flowed between the two games: the spinning "firebars" originally designed for *Zelda* later moved to *SMB*'s castle levels;[25] both Ganon and Bowser shared the "Great Demon King" title in the original Japanese manuals; both included spatial mazes that required a designated movement pattern to unlock; both featured a "second quest" with revamped difficulty; both were inspired by Japanese geography and folklore; both had distinct overworld and subterranean levels; both used the same palette cycle (and color values) to animate flashing items (e.g., coins, ? blocks, the Triforce seen on the title screen); and so on. Early on, Mario was even slated to star in both titles, as design documents reference *Zelda*'s early prototype as "Adventure Mario."[26]

As development progressed, the team realized that the plumber's platforming skill set was inappropriate for an adventure, so the "Mario" portion of the title fell away. Mario's trademark abilities were running and jumping; Link, *Zelda*'s eventual protagonist, could do neither. He relied on the staple items of fantasy adventuring: swords, shields, wands, maps, and keys. And similar to the player characters of tabletop role-playing games, Link gained better gear, amassed treasure, and discovered new items as the player progressed. The simple small/big/fiery progression of *SMB* was replaced with a richer, more deliberate character upgrade path.

Zelda is an adventure game centered on Link's quest to gather eight golden triangles (the Triforce) so he may rescue Princess Zelda from the clutches of Ganon, a fearsome porcine beast who has brought blight upon the land of Hyrule. The game world is split into two primary sections: the "overworld"—comprising Hyrule's trees, mountains, and waterways—and the dungeons hidden beneath. Dungeons test the player's combat skills, spatial navigation, and puzzle-solving abilities. Link must procure keys, bomb walls, clear enemies, and uncover secret passages to progress to each dungeon's boss. Dungeon layouts and boss locations are obscured until the player either enters a new room or discovers each level's map and compass. As Link completes dungeons, he collects Triforce fragments, gains health reserves ("heart containers"), upgrades his weapons and armor, and obtains items that help him defeat foes and unlock later levels. The boomerang, for instance, can stun foes momentarily or track across the screen to snag unreachable items. The candle can illuminate darkened rooms, harm enemies, or burn down trees to uncover hidden items or stairwells. Link also encounters helpful non-player characters (NPCs) dispersed throughout Hyrule's caves and dungeons: merchants sell ammo replenishments, fairies restore health, and wizened mystics offer cryptic clues.

Zelda's overarching gameplay theme is exploration and discovery, a proper foil to *Super Mario Bros.*'s timer-constrained platforming. Hyrule's scope and depth demand a larger time commitment than touring Kinoko Kingdom. Even the speediest run-through of the former takes more than a half hour, while the latter takes less than a fifth of that time. Of course, those are world record times—players new to *Zelda* in 1986 spent hours plumbing its dungeons. And as with *SMB*, specialized guidebooks cropped up to satisfy player demands to uncover its secrets. Hyrule was a world to be scoured, not sprinted. Players could travel many routes to reach the same goal, since only a few areas of the world were blocked from the outset. Once Link obtained a few items, the entire game world opened up. Dungeons could be played out of sequence or skipped altogether. The most skillful players could even forgo the sword—the weapon Link receives at the game's outset—for the majority of the game.

Miyamoto has cited two influential videogame precedents for *Zelda*'s play style: *Black Onyx* and *Ultima*.[27] The former, released for the NEC PC-8801 in 1984 (and later ported to the MSX and Famicom), was a landmark in Japanese gaming history. *Black Onyx* developer and American expat Henk Rogers, a devotee of *Lord of the Rings* and *Dungeons & Dragons*, introduced party-based, fantasy dungeon crawling to Japanese audiences, paving the way for Japanese RPG breakouts *Final Fantasy* and *Dragon Quest*.[28] The *Ultima* series, also Western-developed, first reached Japan in 1985,[29] the same year *Zelda*'s development began. Like *Black Onyx*, *Ultima II* revolved around first-person dungeon crawling, but also featured an impressive tiled overworld map that linked the game's underground labyrinths—a clear precursor to Hyrule. *Ultima*'s innovative time-traveling mechanic was also part of *Zelda*'s initial design. In a 2012 interview, Miyamoto revealed that the player was meant to travel between Hyrule's past and future, and the hero would act as the "link" between them. Weirder still, the Triforce pieces were meant to be microchips.[30] Though they ultimately settled on the fantasy setting, Miyamoto and team would revisit the time-linking concept in future *Zelda* titles.

It's a Secret to Everybody

One of *Zelda*'s overt but unacknowledged influences was the Japanese arcade game ドルアーガの塔, or *Tower of Druaga*. Published by Namco in 1984, *Druaga* followed the hero Gilgamesh as he ascended sixty floors of the titular locale to rescue the priestess Ki from the demon Druaga. Players viewed the tower interiors from an overhead perspective, but the individual character and enemy tiles appeared in profile. Each tower floor was the width of three screens, which players could scroll to either side to explore. Like a fantasy Pac-Man (with whom *Druaga* shared its arcade hardware), Gil navigated around and through labyrinthine walls in search of equipment, treasure, and a key to unlock the door to the next level.

A large contributor to *Druaga*'s legacy was its opaque difficulty. Each of the levels' hidden treasures were revealed according to stipulations that ran the gamut from benign (kill a Blue Knight on level 3), to luck-based (walk over a particular floor tile three times), to spatial (pass by each of the screen's four corners), to metagame (press the 1P Start button), and even to the inexplicably arcane (press the joystick right seven times, left once, and right another seven times).[31] The game provided no clues for how a player might surface the treasures, despite the fact that missing some items made it impossible to complete the game. Arcade players had to decipher *Druaga*'s secrets through luck, perseverance, and community. Sharing individual breakthroughs was the only means to progress collectively.

The same cryptic spirit informed *Zelda*'s design, which had its own share of hidden rooms, ability-boosting treasures, and puzzling spatial mazes.[32] Link could pass through invisible walls, summon a teleporting whirlwind with a magic flute, trigger doors by clearing a room's enemies, discover healing fairies in tucked-away lakes, and slide large blocks aside to access hidden stairwells. Similarly, *Zelda*'s nine dungeon entrances were tucked away in hard-to-find locations, with only vague clues provided to guide the player. Nearly every screen had a secret to uncover.

Initially *Zelda* had no overworld. Like *Druaga*, it was exclusively a "dungeon crawl," but included an interesting cooperative function catered to the FDS's new storage format. Miyamoto explained *Zelda*'s initial prototype in *Hyrule Historia*:

> The first thing I thought about was a game that made use of the Disk System's function of rewriting data so that two players could each create their own dungeons and make the other player solve them. We actually created such a game, and when I played it, I felt it was very fun playing in the dungeons themselves. So we put together a game with a series of dungeons underneath mountains distributed around Death Mountain for a single player to solve them. But we also wanted it to feature a world above, so we added forests and lakes, and so Hyrule Field took form gradually.[33]

Though *Zelda* is known as a "top-down" adventure game, players viewed Hyrule Field from a hodgepodge of conflicting angles, with the viewpoint skewed considerably to aid the player's perspective. Link and much of the landscape elements looked as if they were plucked from a side-scrolling platformer, since they appeared in profile, while other enemies (e.g., Gleeok, Octorok, Patra) and terrain (e.g., bridges, lakes) adhered to an overhead perspective. Dungeon interiors were stranger still, as the walls sloped inward toward an apparent vanishing point, aiding the player's view of central doorways. Oddest of all were the gray basement levels used to hide special items. Perhaps owing to their close affinity to *SMB*'s castle levels, these rooms were viewed from a platformer-style side view.

Hybrid perspectives notwithstanding, *Zelda*'s most interesting spatial innovation was its screen-to-screen movement. Earlier adventure games, including the groundbreaking VCS forebear *Adventure* (1979), allowed player movement in any cardinal direction. However, most predecessors used immediate spatial cuts between screens rather than multi-directional scrolling.[34] *Zelda* split the difference: Link could not scroll seamlessly from screen to screen as Mario did, but he could push forward in any direction. When Link reached a screen edge, his travel temporarily halted as the engine hoisted his body in place, scrolled the next screen into view, then dropped him at the opposite edge. The net effect resembled a smoothly panning slideshow.

Though future adventure and role-playing games would implement seamless multi-directional scrolling (chapter 6), *Zelda*'s slideshow technique struck a clever compromise between the single-screen movement of earlier arcade and console games and the single-vector scrolling of the emerging platformer genre. Furthermore, the slideshow pace suited *Zelda*'s adventuring premise. Link was not meant to speed quickly through levels in pursuit of a time-restricted goal; he was meant to wander the landscape and unearth its secrets.

In light of their concurrent development, it is remarkable how stark the gameplay differences between *Zelda* and *Super Mario Bros.* were. Consider each game's opening play screen: Mario stood near the left edge, head in profile, facing the open runway before him. His posture and position beckoned the player to run right. Link faced away from the player near center screen presented with four unmarked paths: north, east, west, and a mountainside punctured by a dark cave. His posture and position beckoned the player to choose a path and explore.

Their respective title screens provided similar cues. In *Super Mario Bros.*, the title banner was integrated into World 1–1's landscape. After pausing for a few seconds to await player input, demonstration play began (in silence). As Mario moved, the title banner scrolled offscreen as if it inhabited the same diegetic space as the Koopas and coin blocks. Mario hopped a few pipes and stomped a few enemies to teach the player how to platform. Unlike *SMB*, *Zelda*'s title had no traditional attract loop. Instead, the game's name was wreathed in garland floating above an idyllic waterfall, set against Kondo's famous opening theme. Left idle, the scene faded as the game's backstory scrolled into view. *Zelda* paid no allegiance to the tropes of arcade play. There was no demonstration mode, no character introduction, and no glimpse of the world to come.

Over and Underworld

Super Mario Bros.'s engine was built for athletic platforming. As we saw in chapter 4, metatile elements like pipes, blocks, and pits could be positioned and arranged in various lengths and widths atop a looping backdrop of repeated scenery. The engine's flexibility mirrored the game's design process. In a 2011 interview, Nakago explained how he had to make painstaking daily tweaks to level object data based on the prior night's playtesting,[35] indicating that level design was an iterative process of experimentation and refinement. Levels could be expanded and contracted at will, obstacles rearranged, enemies multiplied, world orders shuffled—all in service of creating a series of varied, enjoyable courses for players to run.

Such an engine was ideal for a side-scrolling platformer whose levels, while visually and thematically consistent, did not have to cohere into a holistic world. *Zelda* required a different approach, as the Hyrule overworld had to make sense as a unified space. From screen to screen, the paths of Hyrule's rivers, mountains, forests, and shorelines connected realistically to form a landscape larger than any single screen could contain. Level design folded into world design, since individual screens had to nest carefully within a larger structure; editing any single element rippled outward to the larger whole. Miyamoto's pre-production sketches of Hyrule indicate that, unlike *SMB*'s levels, much of the overworld's structure was designed in advance of its translation into code. From prototype to final form, *Zelda*'s design was a process of refinement rather than iteration.

Zelda's engine design reflects these fundamental structural differences in design philosophy. Unlike *SMB*'s manipulable object data, *Zelda*'s overworld and dungeons are comprised of roughly 140 "pre-fab" vertical strips laid in sequences of either sixteen (overworld) or twelve (dungeon) columns to create several dozen reusable screen layouts. Layouts are divided into overworld and dungeon types, since each has its own strip height—eleven and seven metatiles, respectively.[36] And since *Zelda*, unlike

SMB, uses 8x16-pixel tiles, it only takes two sprite or background tiles stacked side-by-side to form a 16x16-pixel metatile unit. But within each strip, individual objects, such as trees or mountain metatiles, cannot be moved or sized at will—the column is *Zelda*'s "atomic unit" of layout design.

Zelda's graphics engine is a remarkably complex and compact system that allowed the programmers to condense the top-level meta-structure of Hyrule's 128 overworld screens into a slim 2KB, a mere three percent of the disk card's single-side capacity. Each overworld screen is defined by sixteen ID bytes, one for each of its columnar units. Four bits of the column ID index a pointer table that may reference up to ten graphical strips, while the remaining four bits designate which of those strips will be selected from a separate "byte stream" of metatile data.[37] These bytes are then parsed by the rendering engine, as they contain flags to indicate the start of a column, the metatile to be drawn, and a flag indicating whether that metatile will be doubled.[38] Instead of a scrolling tapestry upon which objects are arranged, *Zelda*'s engine is a series of nested Russian dolls containing tiles within metatiles within columns within screens within a world.

As a result of its underlying programmatic structures, *Zelda*'s overworld and dungeon layouts exhibit the same thrifty symmetries seen in *SMB*. In figure 5.2, a typical overworld screen is broken down into its columnar elements. Identical strips are annotated with matching overlays (e.g., the seven lightest strips all contain two trees at the bottom edge) to highlight their repetition. Notice that, among the sixteen columns, only six are unique. And within those columns, there are only five unique background metatiles: empty terrain, a tree, the mountain interior, and two opposing mountain edges. Yet the net visual effect is a complex maze of trees bordered by an impenetrable southern forest, a narrow mountain pass to the west, a wide exit to the east, and several narrow exit channels to the north.

Players who navigate Hyrule's overworld can quickly grok its larger structure thanks to the mini-map in the upper left side of the status bar. A green rectangle notates Link's position within a larger gray rectangle that maps, in minimal form, Hyrule's quadrilateral geometry. Internally, the 128 rectangular screens that comprise the overworld are stored in two contiguous 8x8-screen matrices, matching the programmatic map to its representational map.

What players likely miss is that *Zelda*'s underground lairs adhere to a similar pattern. Internally the nine dungeons are arranged to fill four additional 8x8-screen matrices—twice the area of Hyrule's overworld—

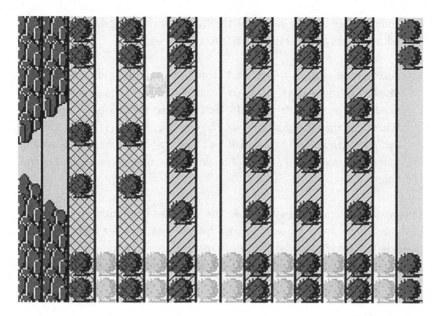

5.2 A truncated screenshot of *The Legend of Zelda* annotated to show the repetition of vertical metatile strips. (Emulator: Macifom 0.16)

with each matrix holding between one and three dungeons. Dungeons 2, 3, and 6, for example, fit into a single matrix, while the 57-screen final dungeon occupies an entire matrix on its own. In *Zelda*'s instruction manual, the dungeons have anthropomorphized names, such as Moon, Eagle, or Lizard, but these are creative justifications to explain away their jigsaw layouts, which interlock like a non-standard pentomino puzzle.[39] The outstretched "wing" of the Eagle level, for instance, comprises the negative space that shapes the "head" and "body" of the adjoining Lizard level. So unlike the overworld, the dungeons' programmatic structure shares no spatial relationship to their in-game arrangement. While conjoined in code, they remain geographically unmoored beneath Hyrule's surface.

Zelda famously includes a separate "second quest" with rearranged dungeon layouts whose entrances are hidden in alternate overworld locations. Despite their revised shapes, the second quest dungeons still fit—albeit in different arrangements—within four linked matrices. In addition to four new pentomino-esque shapes, the dungeons now form each letter of "ZELDA," a nod to both the game's captive princess and the shortcut method used to unlock the second quest.[40] According to Nakago and Tezuka, the second quest resulted from over-exuberant design efficiency. Once Tezuka sketched the final interlocking design, he presented it to Nakago for translation into code:

> Tezuka-san said, "I did it!" and brought this to me. I created the data exactly in line with it, but then Tezuka-san made a mistake and only used half of the data. I said, "Tezuka-san, there's only half here. Where did the other half go?" and he was like, "What?! Oops, I messed up." But Miyamoto-san said it was fine just like that. So, using the half of the memory that was left over, we decided to create the Second Quest.[41]

This was a radical departure from the extreme economizing necessary in *Super Mario Bros.*, whose "second quest" was a series of bit flags in the existing area object data rather than a full-scale reorganization of the game's maps. *Zelda*'s second quest did not simply exchange a few enemy types—it doubled the world.

Random Access

Thoughtful map compression certainly helped Miyamoto's team craft Hyrule into a much larger world than those seen in prior Famicom games, but the engine's construction did not directly arise from Quick Disks' newfound affordances. The medium more directly affected Hyrule's enemy population and a number of background processes that subtly influenced *Zelda*'s play experience.

To the Famicom, the RAM adapter looked like a standard cartridge. Its 32KB/8KB program/character split matched the basic NROM profile. But the RAM housed within meant that their respective contents were not fixed. Unlike ROM, whose "read-only" contents were burnt to chips and sealed forever, RAM allowed "random access," permitting data to be read from disk and written to RAM at any time. While the FDS could not circumvent the hard limit of the CPU's and PPU's respective addressing spaces, it could move code and tiles into their "view" as needed. A pattern table could only ever contain 256 tiles, but each tile could be written and rewritten again and again.

Zelda harnessed rewriteable memory to make the landscapes and dungeons of Hyrule feel as if each contained its own indigenous species. Its manual split enemy species by their location—these are "the nasty characters Link bumps into in the Overworld," it said, listing Tektites, Leevers, Peahats, and several other creatures found exclusively above ground. The underworld, in turn, had over twenty unique minions and bosses, many of which were exclusive to a handful of dungeons. Overworld and underworld felt distinct.

But variety came at a cost. Compared to the near-instantaneous screen transitions familiar on cartridge games, Link's passage between areas felt monumentally slow. Plunging into each dungeon's entrance did not trigger the same slideshow that carried Link screen to screen. Instead, two black "curtains" closed from the edges of the screen as the engine cut to darkness. Due to the disk drive's serial access method, several seconds elapsed as new tile and map data streamed from disk to RAM adapter. Monitoring FCEUX's PPU Viewer during the dungeon transition reveals that nearly half the tiles of each pattern table update to accommodate the new characters, topography, and interface elements (figure 5.3).

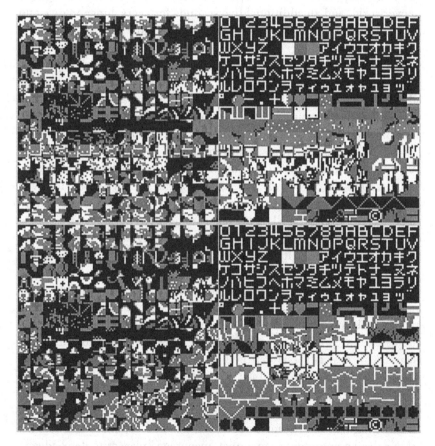

5.3 FDS *Zelda*'s pattern table contents in the overworld (top) and in the first dungeon (bottom). The majority of tiles from each table's lower half are swapped during the transition. (Emulator: FCEUX 2.1.5)

What's remarkable is that *Zelda*'s designers structured the game's patterns so that no loading was required within environments. Every tile that comprised the overworld's menagerie of terrains, NPCs, villains, items, and text fit within 8KB of CHR memory. Link could comb the entire overworld and never face a load screen, and the same was true for each dungeon. Only major transitions—overworld to underworld, title screen to opening screen—required the player to wait.

To *Zelda*'s credit, disk loads were front-loaded and thoughtfully paced. A brief blackout curtain bookending Link's dungeon explorations at least had a plausible sense of in-game realism (or at least theatrical style). Nonetheless, the occasional loads did add up: ten seconds elapsed from disk boot to title screen, another five from title screen to name entry (accompanied by a disk eject/flip), another five from name entry to overworld, and an additional five seconds for every dungeon dive and overworld return. The FDS struck a devil's bargain with players, trading data for time.

Indeed, future FDS games would prove far more wearisome to players' patience than *Zelda*'s occasional blackouts. Bothtec's 1987 side-scrolling adventure game レリクス暗黒要塞 *(Relics: Dark Fortress)* required a disk flip and nearly fifteen seconds of loading between title screen and gameplay. But the initial wait was a mere portent of future delays. Each of *Relics*'s frequent screen transitions required a five-second load. Accidentally falling off a ladder you had just climbed, a common occurrence due to the game's stodgy controls, necessitated a ten-second round trip as you plummeted to the screen below then clambered your way back to where you'd began. Stranger still, *Relics*'s gameplay often halted mid-scroll as the player hit unseen, apparently arbitrary, loading thresholds.

The primary culprits behind *Relics*'s frequent loading was its use of large (and admittedly impressive) multi-sprite characters coupled with poor map planning. Bothtec's designers inexplicably used tile swapping to animate nearly all of the player's movements, introducing a minuscule but noticeable lag between input and animation as the adapter accessed disk data. Likewise, any time the player advanced to a region with new adversaries, their patterns had to load into memory, requiring a separate disk load to fetch the necessary tiles. Unlike *Zelda*, whose objects were carefully arranged to never exceed an area's CHR-ROM allotment, *Relics* dropped in elaborate, sprite-heavy characters at every turn. In combination, *Relics*'s disk dependencies formed *Zelda*'s design antipode, a game that encouraged players to deny adventure, forgo exploration, and pray they never faced another dreaded loading screen.

Another important benefit of disk cards was their flexible mirroring. Besides *Zelda*, two of Nintendo's early disk games—メトロイド *(Metroid)* and 光神話 パルテナの鏡 (aka *Kid Icarus*)—allowed scrolling in four directions. *Metroid* in particular is known for its long vertical shafts connected by corridors that protagonist Samus Aran accesses via shootable bubble doors. *Metroid*'s gameplay design is structured much like *Zelda*'s, although oriented more toward action and platforming than trawling dungeons. As Samus, players explored the hostile planet Zebes, collecting weapon and suit upgrades to unlock new areas, traverse hidden corridors, and combat bosses. The ability to backtrack and move along both horizontal and vertical planes was crucial to *Metroid*'s "open world" structure, but the game's scrolling vectors were mutually exclusive. In short, Zebes' bubble doors masked an underlying mirroring flip.

In NROM cartridges, a game's mirroring setting was hardwired—physically soldered in place on the PCB. Developers had to choose their mirroring arrangement in advance and design the game's scrolling engine accordingly. The FDS, in contrast, had a hardware register ($4025) that could toggle between vertical and horizontal mirroring at any time. In *Metroid*, pushing Samus through a bubble door that served as the "joint" between horizontal and vertical corridors triggered a mirroring toggle, allowing name tables to "arrange" in a configuration more conducive to that corridor's scrolling vector.[42] *Kid Icarus* used the same technique to swap between its sequestered horizontal and vertical areas. In both cases, the Disk System's hardware capabilities were subtly structuring level design.

Software-configurable mirroring proved equally meaningful to *Zelda*'s design. Multi-directional scrolling stitched Hyrule's screens into a unified overworld rather than a series of disconnected playfields. But *Zelda*'s overhead view and dungeon layouts demanded better continuity than even *Metroid*'s corridors provided. Link needed access to all cardinal directions at any juncture. What is surprising is how *Zelda*'s programmers managed mirroring to make his passage appear seamless.

As discussed in previous chapters, the PPU has access to four name tables, two of which are mirrored duplicates.[43] In the FCEUX emulator, the Name Table Viewer arranges name table data spatially to better visualize the PPU's internal mirroring settings, positioning each name table as follows:

```
[ NT0 ][ NT1 ]
[ NT2 ][ NT3 ]
```

When gameplay begins, *Zelda* uses the FDS's default horizontal mirroring, meaning that NT0/NT1 and NT2/NT3 contain mirrored data. In this configuration, the engine is "primed" for vertical scrolling. The opening screen begins in NT0 with Link positioned to head north, east, or west. If we push Link north, we expect the engine to first fill NT2 with the upcoming screen then advance the scroll register upward until its contents fully occupy the gameplay window.

The actual process is far stranger. Gameplay in *Zelda* almost always takes place in NT0 due to a series of imperceptible swaps that occur at the beginning and end of each screen transition. Traveling north from the opening screen backfills NT2/3 with a copy of the contents of NT0/1.[44] Once complete, the scroll register immediately shifts fully to NT2/3, then pushes upward into NT0/1, this time updating its data row-by-row with the upcoming screen. In figure 5.4, you can see four steps of this process, from the opening screen to the resulting push upward, with the horizontal line marking the scroll's current position. Counterintuitively, the net result of this name table dance is that Link both begins and ends his passage in NT0.

Horizontal movement is even more curious. If we direct Link eastward from the opening screen, NT2/3 once again begin to backfill, though this time with the contents of the upcoming screen. Once complete, the engine then toggles vertical mirroring to force an immediate "rearrangement" of the contents of all four name tables.[45] Comparing frames two and three in figure 5.5, you can see that the mirroring switch appears to displace each screen counterclockwise like a sliding block puzzle. The scroll register then pushes right to pan the gameplay window over the contents of NT1/3. As the scroll presses on, the eastern screen is also drawn behind its boundary in the NT0/NT2 region. Once the transition is complete, the program toggles back to horizontal mirroring and the scroll is reset to NT0. For all the manic background shifting and sliding, Link once again ends up where he started.

The irony of Link's travel from screen to screen is that the game engine's processes are antithetical to *Zelda*'s gameplay design. For a game whose structure encourages exploration and freedom of movement, at the platform level, Link's mobility is surprisingly constrained. He pushes against the borders of the world, only to be forcibly picked up and scooted to the opposite side while backdrops shift and shuttle beneath his feet. In this light, the spatial puzzle of the Lost Woods is the perfect visual metaphor for the engine's scrolling routine: Link appears to travel, but only ever arrives at the location whence he began.

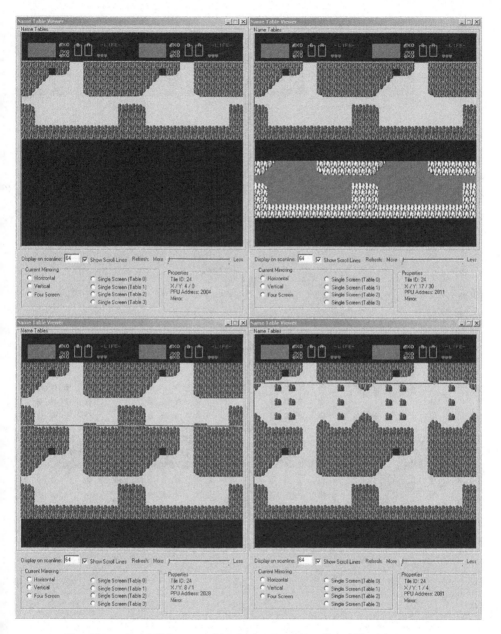

5.4 Four "frames" of *Zelda*'s name tables during vertical scrolling. (Emulator: FCEUX 2.1.5)

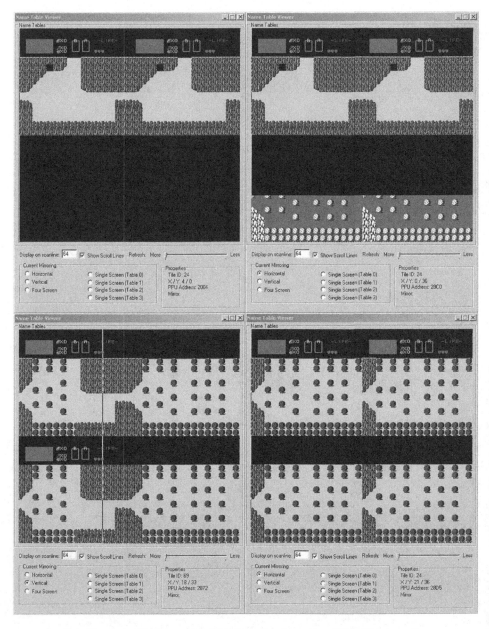

5.5 Four "frames" of *Zelda*'s name tables during horizontal scrolling. (Emulator: FCEUX 2.1.5)

Hold RESET

Due to mounting piracy problems and the development of expanded cartridge hardware (chapter 6), Nintendo abandoned plans for exporting the FDS outside Japan. Nintendo did not, however, wish to abandon the crop of lucrative first-party software that they had developed for the platform, so they began cross-porting several disk titles to NES game paks. Aside from the FDS's exclusive sound channel (channel 7), Nintendo's engineers devised replacements for the peripheral's augmentations (and consequently eliminated loading times). But supplanting one of the disk format's key features—save games—posed a challenging design problem.

Many of Nintendo's first-party disk games were designed around multi-session play and relied upon the peripheral's ability to store the player's progress so they could resume at a later time. In the FDS versions of *Metroid*, *Kid Icarus*, and *Zelda*, for instance, players had a choice of three file slots wherein they could save not only one game, but multiple concurrent games. In households with several children or in instances where someone might lend their disk to a friend, this lowered the risk of losing one's progress.

Without a disk, how could programmers replicate these save files? Some opted not to. Cartridge ports of both *Metroid* and *Kid Icarus* lost save files in favor of password systems.[46] And these passwords were not only lengthy—twenty-four characters—they also required manual selection from sixty-four individual letters, numbers, and punctuation marks. Thus retrieving one's progress depended not only on accurately transcribing the password, but also replicating it onscreen each time one wanted to play. Konami's port of *Castlevania* nixed saving altogether, transforming a challenging but fair action-adventure disk into a mercilessly difficult game pak.

Zelda did not suffer the same fate. Nintendo decided to maintain the disk version's triplicate file slots, even replicating their layout for the cartridge port (figure 5.6). To do so, Nintendo added two new components to the game pak: an 8KB SRAM chip stored any variables necessary to reinstate a player's progress, and an attached 3V CR2032 "coin" battery, common in watches and calculators, provided the necessary voltage to prevent SRAM's volatile contents from dissipating. In *Zelda*'s U.S. manual, Nintendo highlighted the data's longevity, along with a special proviso: "The battery is used to retain the player's data for five years. However, depending on the conditions under which the Game Pak is kept (such as exposure to high temperatures, etc.), the life of the battery may be shortened."[47]

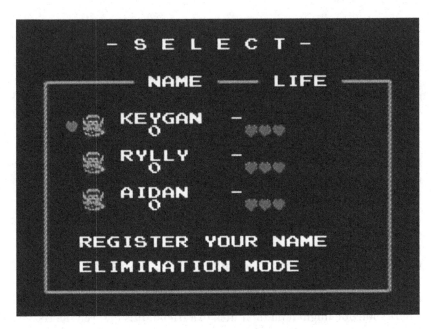

5.6 The *Legend of Zelda* cartridge mimicked the save slot layout of the FDS version, but used battery-backed SRAM to save game data. (Source: NES-001 capture)

Typical of Nintendo's hardware woes, the save system surfaced a new problem: power cycling the console created small voltage spikes that risked scrambling the contents of SRAM, eradicating any save data. The initial run of *Zelda* game paks included a warning sticker affixed to the cartridge back: "The Game Pak contains batteries. It may be damaged if: 1) Game Pak is removed or inserted with the power ON, or 2) the power switch is turned rapidly ON and OFF." Nintendo aimed to do due diligence, but there was no in-game warning, and the likelihood that children read such notices carefully (or at all) prior to playing was slim. Furthermore, not all power cycling was due to player negligence. Over time, the combined effects of the fragile ZIF connector, bent pins, a temperamental CIC, and dirty cartridge contacts could trigger their own series of harmful resets. As consoles aged, the likelihood of save corruption increased.

Power spikes occurred because of a board-level voltage mismatch. While a cartridge was in the console, SRAM was connected to both the 3V coin battery and the console's 5V power line. From the player's perspective, powering the console down appeared instantaneous, when in reality there was a gradual downward slope in voltage supply.[48] Once that voltage slipped beyond a certain threshold, the CPU could no longer be expected to behave reliably—it could, for instance, attempt to write garbage data to arbitrary locations in memory. For games without SRAM, this was not a problem. Each time a game reset, either from a cold boot or a soft reset, instructions in PRG-ROM initialized all relevant memory locations to a known state. In most games, RAM was cleared, the PPU was allowed to stabilize, decimal mode was disabled, and so on. When SRAM was present, the battery picked up the slack once the console's voltage dropped below the safety threshold, ensuring that the memory had a consistent power supply while the console's power was off. However, the battery offered no insurance against the CPU's erratic behavior during power down. One errant data write to SRAM could corrupt a save file irreparably.

In response, Nintendo devised a stopgap: holding RESET while powering the console down would return the program to a known state and maintain that state during the voltage drop-off. In *Zelda* cartridge revisions, Nintendo included a supplementary warning on the cart label, in red text, as well as new cautionary instructions inside the manual.[49] More importantly, Nintendo added an in-game warning. When Link lost his final heart, the player was asked to either CONTINUE, SAVE, or QUIT, followed by a new text block that urged players to, "HOLD IN RESET BUTTON AS YOU TURN POWER OFF." Many perplexed NES players thought this button sequence was required to save their data, but it was simply a means to ensure its integrity.

Following *Zelda*'s lead, future battery-backed titles incorporated some variation of the "Hold RESET" text whenever the player was required to save. Similarly, instruction manuals provided their own copious warnings. In the emergent console role-playing game (RPG) genre, this created a conflict between a game's narrative aims and its obdurate materiality. Story-centered games like *Final Fantasy*, *Dragon Warrior*, *Ultima: Exodus*, or *The Bard's Tale* were attempting to shake off the vestiges of their arcade roots. High scores, demonstration modes, and frequent player death were giving way to more sophisticated narrative structures, influences from cinema, and multi-session gameplay. But the irruption of the warning text amid in-game dialog felt anachronistic, as when the innkeeper in *Final Fantasy* said, "Welcome...Stay, to save your data," then added, "Don't forget, if you leave your game, Hold RESET while you turn POWER off!!" *Dragon Warrior* attempted to weave the save warning into the game's diegesis: "Let me teach to thee the Spell of Restoration! Thou shouldst write this down and keep it." But if developers made the save reference too esoteric, it ran the risk of being ignored. As a result, NPCs often slipped in a brief line of non-diegetic commentary to directly address the player rather than the player's character.

Nintendo did not rely solely on reeducating players' save habits. Later MMC1 revisions had capacitance barriers to regulate the console's voltage flow and the ability to temporarily disable SRAM so its contents were protected from voltage spikes. Though these measures greatly decreased the chances of any erratic overwrites, the "Hold RESET" warning reinforced good player habits and, like other unintended errors, soon slipped into the vernacular of NES folklore.

Hakoniwa no Famicom

Thanks to both his affable personality and his unprecedented string of celebrated videogame hits, designer Shigeru Miyamoto became Nintendo's public persona. Today, he still leads some segment of Nintendo's high-profile E3 trade show presentations, typically beaming through a demonstration of the latest iteration of the franchises he helped create. In 2004, he strode onstage to uproarious applause, brandishing Link's sword and shield as he introduced the Nintendo Wii's first *Zelda* installment, *Twilight Princess*. In an industry where most creators work in anonymity, Miyamoto's recognition among Western videogame fans is remarkable.

Like many vaunted designers, Miyamoto's personal background is now braided into the works he creates. For his part, Miyamoto tends not to self-mythologize. Autobiographical accounts of his childhood and education have been modest and consistent over the years. As many interviews recount, his extracurricular interests—music, manga, gardening, pet ownership—directly inspire the videogames he oversees. As a child, for instance, Miyamoto was fond of exploring the surrounding woods and caves near his home in Sonobe, a small village northwest of Kyoto.[50] Sheff's account in *Game Over* is still one of the most eloquent:

> Investigating hillsides and creek beds and small canyons, Miyamoto once discovered the opening of a cave. He returned to it several times before he worked up the courage to go in. Lugging a homemade lantern, he went deep inside until he came to a small hole that led to another cave. Breathing deeply, his heart pounding, he climbed through. He never forgot the exhilaration he felt at this discovery.[51]

A patina of fairy tale storytelling certainly enriches such accounts, but it is safe to assume that Miyamoto's childhood sense of wonder, danger, and discovery in his immediate natural environment served as an inspiration for Link's dungeon-diving adventures.

While it seems like a symptomatically modern impulse to materialize one's childhood memories of hillsides, rivers, and forests according to the discrete logic of binary data, we find familiar analogs in the practice of gardening. Both the monumental sculpted vistas of Versailles and the modest potted plant are denatured and domesticated to varying extents, albeit according to drastic differences in budget and aesthetic taste.

Throughout their careers, Miyamoto and Tezuka have repeatedly used the same analogy in their own work, comparing Kinoko and Hyrule to "miniature gardens" wherein their virtual and human actors play. In 1998, Miyamoto told *Nintendo Online Magazine* that, "Instead of thinking of it as making a game, think of it as nurturing a miniature garden called Hyrule."[52] Again, in a 2004 interview, he told *CVG* that, since Famicom *Zelda*, "I have been making much of the ambience that players feel, as if they had actually visited and explored a miniature garden called Hyrule that can be placed in your desk drawer."[53] And in a 2002 interview, Miyamoto said of Kinoko and Hyrule: "Both games are the same in how you play around in the environment. Both have areas similar to miniature gardens, and in both games you search for solutions."[54]

Journalists and critics pass this off as an aesthetic metaphor, akin to Brian Wilson's famous remark that the Beach Boys' seminal album *Pet Sounds* was like a "pocket symphony," or as a literal description of the greenery depicted in their games. Neither interpretation is invalid, but they do miss a subtle cultural point rooted deeper than mere metaphor.

"Miniature garden" is a translation of the Japanese kanji 箱庭, or *hakoniwa*, which Miaymoto and Tezuka use as shorthand to describe the condensed natural motifs seen in both games—trees, hillsides, caves, lakes—as well as the players' ability to explore them. Typically, *hakoniwa* are small boxes filled with sand and populated with stones, plants, and scale architecture, often mirroring their surrounding landscapes. Miniature gardens simultaneously abstract and concretize the natural landscape into a handful of representative elements: a stone is a mountain, a small plant is a tree, and so on. The *hakoniwa* tames and enfolds the exterior world into an object ready for aesthetic contemplation.

In *The Compact Culture*, Lee argues that refinement and reduction are the hallmarks of Japanese aesthetic design, exhibited consistently across all manner of production: poetry, folding fans, living spaces, food, and, more recently, electronics. As a result, Japanese industry is not obsessed, as Western culture is, with invention, but innovation: "While Americans may have dreamed of inventing the computer," he writes, "Japanese dreamed of shrinking it down and putting it in everyone's home,"[55] a characterization consistent with Nintendo's stated aims for the Family

Computer (chapter 1). The same impulse to condense a mountain into a single stone drives the desire to pack tens of thousands of circuits into a single IC.

In gardening, Lee writes, the Japanese wield a metaphorical "rope" that they use to draw in distant landscapes, a natural equivalent to the manufacturing processes that miniaturize transistors into tighter and tighter spaces. Gardening is the large-scale integration of meadows, mountains, and forests:

> [T]he Japanese, using their unique imagination and their skill at reducing what is found in nature, would pull with their metaphorical rope mountains and sea into their tiny gardens. But before one can pull the vastness of nature into the narrow confines of a garden, one must first contract it, make it smaller.[56]

Nature collapsed into *hakoniwa* does not function as metonym; the miniature substitutes for nature, and betters it by harmonizing disorder into refined aesthetic form.

Miyamoto and Tezuka's *hakoniwa* metaphor is particularly poignant in light of Japan's modern environmental practices. In his otherwise glowing 1996 profile of Nintendo, Katayama notes with a tinge of nostalgic remorse that Japanese children no longer have access to the natural playgrounds familiar to Miyamoto in his childhood. But he later adds with apparent optimism that the virtual worlds found in videogames may offer a solution to Japan's ecological problems:

> In the good old days, Japanese children had fields and meadows they could run around in, but nowhere in our cities today will you find such places. As a consequence of development, our children can no longer roam freely. Nor is it just children who have been robbed of their play spaces. Adults have lost them too... It is no longer a simple matter for people to "play" with nature, and the more distant and farther removed it becomes, the more need there is for new "natural environments." Game machines and their computer chips give immediate access to unlimited "meadows," a new "nature."[57]

Through technology, Nintendo manages to capture the outdoors for a generation unable to do so in real life. But the subtext, optimistic or not, is a palpable sense of loss.

The cultural and ecological toll that Katayama references is likely unfamiliar to Western audiences. Among the most persistent stereotypes of the Japanese is that they have an inborn harmony with nature. But Western sentiment also oscillates between two contradictory extremes: a xenophobia, incubated after World War II, of a culture intent on economic conquest through technological superiority; and a fascination with an idyllic, conformist culture in perfect union with nature. The Japanese are somehow simultaneously the bastions of bonsai trees, HDTV, bento boxes, the Walkman, haiku, high-speed cellular networks, geishas, and the Nintendo Wii.

Alex Kerr, an American native who moved to Japan as a young child, dispels the romanticized naturalist discourse surrounding Japanese culture and surveys the costs of Japan's relentless pursuit of modernization since the 1950s. In *Dogs and Demons*, he draws out the traditional roots of Japan's relationship to nature and contrasts them with the reality of modernization projects run rampant:

> But those who live or travel here see the reality: the native forest cover has been clear-cut and replaced by industrial cedar, rivers are dammed and the seashore lined with cement, hills have been leveled to provide gravel fill for bays and harbors, mountains are honeycombed with destructive and useless roads, and rural villages have been submerged in a sea of industrial waste.[58]

Kerr offers a devastating indictment of Japan's modern ecological practices, but one rooted in a love for his home and countryside, a landscape he has seen worn away by the unbridled advance of ossified bureaucracy. Public works projects like building monuments or shoring up riverbanks with concrete exist solely to feed bureaucratic demands, regardless of their environmental ramifications. Kerr writes, "The emphasis on shared responsibility and obedience leads to a situation in which nobody is in charge, with the result that once it is set on a certain course, Japan will not stop."[59] Modernization never ceases—it reproduces itself in perpetuity.[60]

The Japanese people's relationship to nature is not myth. Harmony with nature is part of their history, culture, and aesthetic purpose. But that harmony has been mythologized to the point that the representation overrides reality. Kerr argues that this split has created a difficult cultural tension, especially for artists:

> The gap between Japan's traditional image of itself and the modern reality has riven the nation's present-day culture. Artists must make a hard choice: try to re-create a vanished world of bamboo, thatched houses, and temples (but in a cultural context in which sterility rules

and all these things have become irrelevant) or go with the times, giving in to dead, flat industrial surfaces. Cut off from the latest trends in Asia or the West, designers find it hard to conceive of natural materials used successfully in a modern way, or of modern designs that blend happily into a natural context. This unresolved cultural conflict is a secret subtext to art and architecture in Japan today.[61]

What better resolution of natural and modern impulses is there than the Famicom's virtual *hakoniwa*? Nature tamed and tidied along a raster grid. Rivers and caves etched in silicon. Undying forests uniform in their perfection.

Kerr is not alone in his criticism, nor are his observations new. Writing in *Science* in 1974, Watanabe reiterated the conventional wisdom surrounding American and Japanese conceptions of nature. While the former's view of nature is as "an object of man's investigation or exploitation for human benefit," the latter's is as "an object not of his mastery, but of his appreciation...even his best companion."[62] But Watanabe also highlights a tension in Japanese values between historical self-identity and the reality of modernization. The result, he argues, is that the Japanese paradoxically "merged with nature, forgetting themselves and even forgetting the dreadful destruction constantly inflicted upon nature and themselves."[63] He closes with a sober admonition: "The urgent task before the Japanese people is, therefore, that they fully realize man's responsibility for nature, unite this realization with their traditional closeness to nature, and endeavor to overcome the current environmental crisis."[64] By Kerr's account, that realization never came.[65]

There is a troubling paradox underlying Miyamoto's and Tezuka's desire to capture the wonder of exploration in caves, the pleasures of gardening, or the meditation of a walk within the confines of a videogame. On the surface, they are simply aiming to create an enchanting world for their players, one that adheres to its own fantastic verisimilitude. Hyrule and Kinoko Kingdom are meant to live and breathe while the player visits. But there is also an endemic cultural malaise embedded beneath these virtual worlds, one too often forgotten when we focus myopically on the graphics onscreen or the deftly crafted console resting beside our televisions.

A platform study is as much about an object's external relationships to other bodies as it is about the internal relationships between mask ROM and CPU registers. The Family Computer is a real material thing, part of a complex network of social, ecological, and cultural actors, both human and non-human. Though many appear to strive to be, a videogame is never merely a benign object of entertainment. Games like *The Legend of Zelda* have a massive influence on popular culture, inspiring new generations of children, artists, and designers alike, but their worlds often reflect subtle, often hidden, values about the cultures from which they arise. There is a bed of melancholy underlying *Zelda*'s garden in a drawer, a virtual abundance meant to placate a real ecological loss.

Platform studies ostensibly aims at the "root" of computational production, the substrate of plastic and silicon that drives computation, graphics, and sound. In fact, Montfort and Bogost reinforce the archeological metaphor in their "five-level" categorization of digital media analysis. "Platform" rests below "code," which rests beneath "form/function," and so on through "interface" and "reception/operation."[66] The authors emphasize that all levels are enveloped by "culture and context," so that a platform "is not an alien machine, but a cultural artifact that is shaped by values and forces and which expresses views about the world." But the layered structure implies a vertical configuration wherein platforms provide the base, as well as the temporal precedence, for all subsequent layers. In their schema, a computer's architecture is necessarily prior to its code or interface.

But platform studies must also consider what comes prior to the platform, what Mark Sample calls the "pre-platform." He asks, "What refuse—discarded, forgotten, overlooked, or dismissed people, places, things, and events—precede the making of the platform and design of the code and execution of the game?"[67] In other words, it is worthwhile to step back and evaluate the human and ecological "platforms" that fuel and feed the development of our consoles and computers. Where is silicon sourced? Who mines the rare earths? Who solders ICs to PCBs? How are obsolete platforms disposed of? And do videogames ever mirror these concerns? *Super Mario Bros.* is as much about dismantling Mario's landscape as it is about running and jumping. Kinoko's hills are paved with brickwork, punctuated by man-sized drainage pipes that Miyamoto derived from the "wasteground with pipes" he saw on his office commute.[68] *Zelda* has a similar subtext of ecological destruction—in search of dungeons and treasures, Link bombs the mountainsides and burns away the few living trees remaining in Hyrule. Of course, we can push these readings too far; after all, the Famicom's fantasy worlds are not designed to make logical sense or adhere to the limitations of the real world. But consciously or not, videogame worlds reflect our fantasies and fears, our desire for power and our powerlessness. Perhaps Miyamoto and Tezuka built a garden that reflected a world they knew. Or perhaps they built a garden they wished their world could be.

Disk Trouble

Most players who grew up with the NES likely never knew about the Family Computer Disk System or that landmark games like the *Legend of Zelda* started on a disk card rather than a cartridge. Whether the Disk System would have succeeded abroad is open to speculation. The PC industry was certainly better established outside Japan, so disks might have made a compelling argument for transitioning PC players over to the Nintendo console—especially in Europe.

Then again, if the dismal history of console peripherals has taught the videogame industry any lessons, it is that the Disk System was more likely to flop than not. Consumer acceptance notwithstanding, the FDS and its disks were plagued by mechanical and design defects: its proprietary drive belts were flimsy and prone to break; the shutterless disk cards were exposed to dirt and damage; when errors occurred, the onscreen messages were difficult to interpret; strong magnets could erase game data; and frequent loads kept players waiting.

Yet despite its hardware troubles and the plague of piracy, the Disk System was not a failure in Japan; by some accounts, the peripheral sold nearly 4.5 million units.[69] Nintendo and third parties alike supported the add-on with software for several years. Among the more than two hundred titles released were the console debuts of *The Legend of Zelda*, *Zelda II*, *Kid Icarus*, *Ice Hockey*, and *Metroid*, alongside enhanced ports of Famicom titles like *Vs. Excitebike* and lesser-known Japanese exclusives like the influential text adventure *Famicom Tantei Club*. In fact, the disk originals are arguably the definitive versions of the games, thanks to their richer soundtracks and robust save systems.[70]

Though Nintendo filed a successful U.S. patent for the FDS, they ultimately abandoned plans for American release, opting to solve memory limitations and copyright circumvention with upgraded cartridge hardware. Moreover, Nintendo's first taste of disk piracy likely soured them on rewritable media for years to come. In later hardware generations, when competitors Sony, Sega, and NEC had all moved on to CD-, then DVD-based media, Nintendo clung to costly cartridges. Even the Game-Cube, Nintendo's first console to support optical media, used smaller proprietary disks in lieu of DVDs, echoing their earlier predilection for the Quick Disk.

In the end, the Disk System's impact was felt as much in its absence as in its presence. If not for Nintendo's losing battle against disk piracy, the CIC lockout chip may have never been a part of every NES cartridge and console. Without the pins added to game pak PCBs, their physical form might have taken a different shape. Without the lock-and-key mechanism of the CIC, far fewer consoles may have failed to boot games when the connections degraded. And with a viable companion in tow, the NES's neglected expansion port might have expanded the horizons for future peripherals, audio channels, or data connections. Had the FDS made its way abroad, the NES might have been a wholly different machine.

To understand Bank Switching, picture a game program as one page in a storybook. The first thing you'll notice is that you can only write so much on a single page. A one page story might be okay, but if you want to expand the story, you'll need to add more pages. It's the same with games.

- "Why Your Game Paks Never Forget," *Nintendo Power*, 1991

Fight bosses so big they can't fit on one screen.

- *Low G Man* box text, 1990

Since the late 1970s, when the first era of dedicated ball-and-paddle games gave way to cartridge-based consoles, the consumer electronics press has grouped videogames' historical timeline into discrete generations.[1] Early on, generations were defined by their processor architectures—16-bit supplanted 8-bit, 32-bit supplanted 16-bit, and so on—until raw horsepower no longer had the same technological cachet. At that point, generations left their binary posturing behind in favor of less quantitative distinctions, whether they were about media formats (e.g., DVD vs. CD), industrial design (e.g., "slim" models), add-on services (e.g., embedded apps), or merely a nod to established tradition (e.g., the "five-year cycle").

The succession of "next generation" hardware traces back to the early era of PCs, arcade machines, mainframe computers, and even military innovations. But the generational metaphor has had a particularly forceful influence on the trajectory of videogame history since its beginning. For one, it helps construct competitive narratives between hardware peers, a model perfected during the so-called "console wars" waged between Nintendo and Sega in the early 1990s and played out in each subsequent generation by two or more of the industry's dominant manufacturers. Beyond the fans who earnestly pledge allegiance to their favorite brand, the usual winners are not consumers, but the corporations who reap the economic benefits of increased public exposure and marketing attention.

The generational metaphor likewise reinforces a culture of obsolescence that relies, as Slade argues in *Made to Break*, on technological, psychological, and planned obsolescence to "stimulate repetitive consumption"[2]—especially in advanced industrialized nations like the United States, the United Kingdom, and Japan. When new consoles launch, consumers are urged to pack up their outdated hardware so the "next gen" may assume its rightful place in the current gen. Publishers follow suit by shifting development schedules to the new machines. Absent software support, the "last generation" platforms wither and die.

More perniciously, the generational metaphor does categorical boundary work, not only crowning the winners and losers of a given generation, but nominating which platforms do or do not get to participate in said generation. And without fail, the winner is always the console—never a PC, handheld, or arcade platform—that secures the biggest market share. As stable platforms with defined launch and discontinuation dates, console lifespans are easy to align, their processors are easy to compare, and their market impacts are easy to quantify. Secondary or periphery platforms that fail to fit the mold are either footnoted in or excluded from the generational timeline. Console revisions (Sega Genesis 3), regional exclusives (Epoch Cassette Vision), niche platforms (Casio Loopy), hybrids (Famicom Titler), clones (Yobo FC Twin), emulators (MAME), add-ons (Sega CD), handhelds (WonderSwan), enhancements (GameShark), toys (Tiger Electronic), and market failures (Philips CD-i) struggle to find a home in canonical generations.[3] Likewise for PCs, whose generic, upgradeable architectures and operating systems can span multiple generations, often leading the technological vanguard (e.g., "gaming PCs") and obstinately defending the rearguard (e.g., Windows XP's continued corporate presence) simultaneously.

Similarly ignored or abandoned in the generational timeline are the regions that do not receive consoles within their initial launch window—or fail to receive officially licensed consoles altogether. The NES's debut in Europe, for instance, trailed the U.S. by a year. Parts of Western Europe,

New Zealand, and Australia received the NES a year later still. South America, Africa, Russia, and large swaths of Asia were passed over completely. Those nations instead relied on gray market imports or clones that nonetheless sustained vibrant software ecosystems decades or more past a console's official debut. The generational metaphor is meant to have a global scope, but only the entrenched players of late capitalism perpetuate the bloodline.

It is not that generations are useless, impractical, or inherently flawed. Categories do help us make sense of technological history and, for better or worse, the videogame industry has internalized the generational metaphor into its operating logic, even, as is Sony's style, numbering consoles to clarify and reinforce the line of succession. However, we must be mindful that aggregating the prized progeny of each generation is merely one lens through which we may view videogame history. Indeed, when we pay attention to the worldwide scope of platform adoption, the ebb and flow of life cycles through cloning and emulation, the communities that sustain hardware hacking and software modifications, and the vernacular histories of computing that resist simple linear definitions, we find that generational metaphors collapse.[4]

Despite being the lynchpin of videogames' "third generation," the Famicom's own hardware and software history resists simple generational categorization. How does the FDS fit into the Famicom's timeline, especially since it was never sold outside Japan and its birth and death took place within its host console's lifespan? How do we compare the simple, arcade-inspired gameplay of *Son Son* (1986) or *Baltron* (1986) to sophisticated, late-era Famicom games like *Lagrange Point* (1991) or *Kirby's Adventure* (1993)? These games neither look, sound, nor play the same and, to the untrained eye, appear to belong to different eras. And how does cartridge hardware that fundamentally alters the way a platform looks and sounds shape that platform's perimeters? At what technological event horizon is a Famicom no longer a Famicom?

In this chapter, we will look at a number of expansions the Famicom experienced throughout its lifespan, especially as it responded to encroaching competition. In some cases, this meant hardware expansion, building on the lessons learned from the Disk System or defending against the encroachment of third-party cheat devices. In other cases, this meant expansions of genre or visual style catalyzed by influences from the bustling personal computer industry. The most significant expansion would emerge from the console role-playing game, a genre that would dominate Japan's gaming consciousness for more than a decade, and one that would first find mainstream domestic success on the Family Computer.

Prior to the Famicom's debut, the Japanese console ecology was largely populated by a slew of *Pong* and *Breakout* clones (including Nintendo's successful Color TV Game series), poorly-received (and poorly-localized) Western imports like the Atari 2800, and a few "Made in Japan" machines like the Bandai Super Vision 8000 (1979), the Epoch Cassette Vision (1981), and Nichibutsu's My Vision (1983). Though none of these systems ignited the console market, there was still a thriving tradition of home videogame play among Japanese personal computer (*pasokon*) owners.

PCs faced severe growing pains in Japan due to linguistic and technological barriers. Detailed Japanese ideograms were difficult to render on low-resolution monitors and the language's vast syllabaries proved challenging to adapt to a standard keyboard interface. Nonetheless, a domestic PC industry blossomed and thrived as displays and interfaces improved, introducing millions of Japanese players to their first taste of videogames outside the arcades.[5] NEC, who later introduced the Famicom competitor PC-Engine/TurboGrafx-16 (1987), dominated the market from the late 1970s through the 1990s, beginning with their PC-8000 (1979), PC-6000 (1981), PC-8800 (1981), and PC-9800 (1982) series. Domestic competitors Fujitsu and Sharp followed with their own popular offerings, like the former's FM series (1981) and the latter's X series (1982), alongside comparable machine from Tomy, Toshiba, and the MSX line.

PC ports proved important to the Famicom's success, as key developers like HAL Laboratory, Falcom, and Square—alongside popular software titles like *Metal Gear*, *Nobunaga no Yabou*, and *Ys*—first cut their teeth on *pasokon* platforms before their Family Computer debuts.[6] PCs affordances were markedly different—Japanese platforms were generally Z80-based (chapter 1), had more RAM and ROM to spare, and used disks, cassettes, or hard drives to store media—and software trends followed suit. Role-playing, strategy, and text adventures, all demanding greater time commitments and memory resources than the average arcade fare, fit comfortably in the domestic PC space.

But the Famicom's unprecedented success demanded attention from PC developers. While NEC would sell nearly twenty million PCs across its entire product line, spanning two decades, Nintendo matched that figure in a shorter time with a single platform—then tripled sales abroad. The sea change in the home videogame market was moving toward consoles, and PC developers were guiding their software to follow the tide. As influences passed from *pasokon* to Famicom, the platform's expressive horizons expanded.

One of the first titles to bridge the PC/Famicom divide hailed from peculiar origins. Yasuhiro Fukushima was an ambitious entrepreneur who had tried his hand at several different career paths in the late 1970s. His first profitable venture was a publishing company catering to the real estate industry, but an earlier stint as a Toshiba sales representative had turned him onto the potential of the budding PC software industry. He decided to merge both interests. In 1982, Fukushima rebranded his publishing company Enix—a portmanteau of "ENIAC," one of the first computers ever developed, and "phoenix," denoting the company's software-centric rebirth.[7]

Enix was a publisher in the truest sense. Fukushima initially had no in-house programmers, designers, or engineers, so he devised a clever gimmick to kickstart Enix's software lineup. Enix's "First Game Hobby Program Contest" promised an impressive ¥1 million (~$5000) grand prize to the best software submissions.[8] Thanks to their aggressive publicizing to magazines, electronics shops, and hobbyist clubs, (as well as a promise that the prize was, in fact, genuine), Enix corralled nearly three hundred entries.[9]

The contest allowed Enix to debut with an impressive software catalog. In February 1983, after some outsourced programming cleanup, Enix published thirteen winning titles on every viable Japanese PC platform, including the NEC PC-6001, PC-8801, Fujitsu FM-8, FM-7, and Sharp X1.[10] The eclectic library of shooters, puzzle, card, sports, action, and adult games was immediately successful, so Enix kept up their harried publishing pace. Thanks to a second programming contest, they added thirteen additional titles to their roster in October 1983. Within a year, Enix held five positions in the top ten best-selling PC software category—including the top three spots—and netted ¥300 million in profits.[11]

Among the first winners' pool were two standout designers. Precocious programmer Koichi Nakamura, still in high school when he entered the contest, submitted ドアドア (*Door Door*), an arcade-inspired ladder and platform game fusing elements of *Pac-Man*, *BurgerTime*, and *Donkey Kong*. The game starred the egg-shaped, baseball cap-wearing Chun, who evaded his pursuing aliens by leading them through—then closing them behind—a series of sliding doors. A charming bit of broken English on the introductory screen summed up *Door Door*'s objective: "HOW MANY ALIENS CAN YOU SHUT UP?" *Door Door* sold well on PC and Chun became the namesake for Nakamura's development company, CHUNSoft, which he founded in 1984.

The other promising winner, Yuji Horii, worked as a computer games journalist at weekly manga magazine *Shonen Jump*. While less accomplished as a programmer than Nakamura, Horii's entry, ラブマッチテニス (*Love Match Tennis*), was a colorful, albeit rudimentary, tennis simulation.[12] Horii's real strengths were his writing abilities and industry partnerships. While at *Jump*, for instance, he befriended artist Akira Toriyama, the creator of wildly popular manga serials *Dr. Slump* and *Dragon Ball*, who would become a key future collaborator.

Carpeting the PC field with software proved to be a successful business strategy, but Fukushima had his sights set beyond the diaspora of home computer platforms. After securing a publishing license from Nintendo, Fukushima shifted his contract programmers' focus to porting Enix's catalog from PC to Famicom. By 1984, Nintendo had sold over one million consoles, creating a far larger target market than any single Japanese PC platform could offer. More importantly, the Famicom offered comparable specs at an unbeatable price, retailing at one-sixth the cost of its nearest PC competitor. Nakamura's *Door Door* (1985) became Enix's first Famicom cartridge and proved immediately lucrative: while *Door Door* sold 80,000 copies across multiple PC platforms, the port sold nearly 200,000 copies on the Famicom.[13]

More importantly, the porting initiative brought Nakamura and Horii together for the first time, a matchup that would prove monumental for both Enix's continued growth and the future of Japanese videogames. The duo first collaborated on a Famicom conversion of one of Horii's most innovative PC titles. 1985's ポートピア連続殺人事件, or *The Portopia Serial Murder Case*, was not only the first showcase of Horii's writing talents, but also the first Famicom graphical adventure game.[14]

Port Utopia

In the U.S., graphical adventures were part of a long tradition of adventure games that originated on the mainframe computers that first populated universities, businesses, and government facilities. Since these machines had limited (if any) graphical capabilities, the earliest adventure games described their worlds with words. Player interaction in these "text adventures" involved inputting short command strings—usually in verb/noun pairs like "GO NORTH" or "GET LAMP"—to explore, resolve encounters, and solve puzzles. As technology progressed, adventure games migrated from campus mainframes to personal computers and added graphical enhancements to help illustrate the text descriptions. The popularization of the mouse as an input device led to direct interaction with onscreen objects, spawning the point-and-click adventure subgenre.[15]

Due to their roots in literal wordplay, text adventures were radically different than most arcade and console games. With no limitations based on graphical acuity, designers had greater leeway with world-building, dialogue, and narrative. While a simple plot directive like "Save the princess!" could support any number of platformers, richer fictions were necessary for videogames that relied more on the mind than the eye.

Portopia's scenario was unlike any prior Famicom game. Players assumed the role of Boss, a detective investigating the apparent suicide of Kouzou Yamakawa, the president of "loan shark company" Yamakin Loans. Players viewed the investigation from Boss' perspective, accompanied by his assistant detective, Yasu. Players moved from location to location questioning suspects and searching for clues. Each screen featured a single vignette in the upper left corner depicting the current location: the exterior of a house, a seaside vista, a crime scene, a downtown club, etc. The text below provided supplementary descriptions, dialogue with Yasu and other NPCs, and prompts for player actions.

6.1 In *Portopia*, gameplay consists of the main window, dialogue text, and a list of commands. The main window displays storybook-style illustrations of locations around Kobe, Japan, the site of the PORTOPIA '81 expo. (Source: PowerPak, NES-001 capture)

In the PC original, players had to input commands via keyboard. To better accommodate the Famicom controller, Horii and Nakamura simplified player input to a few preset action words like "Move" or "Arrest" that the player could select from an onscreen menu.[16] Though the vignettes were devoid of animation, certain commands would trigger tool icons to appear onscreen so the player could more directly interact, albeit in a limited manner, with the scene. The magnifying glass, for instance, helped the player inspect the scene, while the hammer could strike objects—or suspects, if the player opted to play the bad cop. Beyond the blinking cursor, the only moving elements on the screen were the text descriptions, which were drawn onscreen character by character like a police teletype.

Portopia, like Enix, was a portmanteau of two English words: "port" and "utopia." Horii borrowed the neologism from Japan's World's Fair exhibition site located on Kobe's Port Island.[17] Portopia was part of a fifteen-year "land reclamation project" that involved shuttling three billion cubic feet of soil from the Kobe mountains then enclosing it within a concrete breakwater.[18] Upon completion, Port Island was the world's largest artificial island, hosting PORTOPIA '81 for nearly seven months between May and September 1981. The Japanese "Cultural City on the Sea" was meant to symbolize Japan's renewed effort to open their cultural borders to an international audience. Millions of tourists visited Portopia, but the locale's reproduction in digital form is emblematic of Japan's true cultural expansion in the 1980s—videogames.[19]

Mirroring its namesake event, Horii set *Portopia* in Kobe. The player's investigations led Boss to many real-world landmarks, like the Port Island dock in Kobe harbor (figure 6.1). This was atypical for a videogame at the time—even an adventure game. Like RPGs, Western adventure games drew heavily from the traditions of *Dungeons & Dragons* and fantasy literature. As their names indicate, iconic games like *Colossal Caves* and *Hunt the Wumpus* revolved around exploring subterranean spaces and battling fantastic monsters. Graphical limitations made it simpler to depict fantasy and cartoon scenarios, but *Portopia*'s restrained scope and atypical drawing technique made the realistic setting possible.

Portopia used an NROM board like *Super Mario Bros.*, but its gameplay style was the antithesis of Nintendo's platformer, featuring no scrolling, physics, soundtrack, scoreboard, player avatars, or levels. Horii intended the game to play like an interactive crime novel with the player starring as the lead detective. Progression was based on the successful navigation of the story, not the blocks, pipes, or turtles that appeared onscreen. As such, most of the game's sprites and background

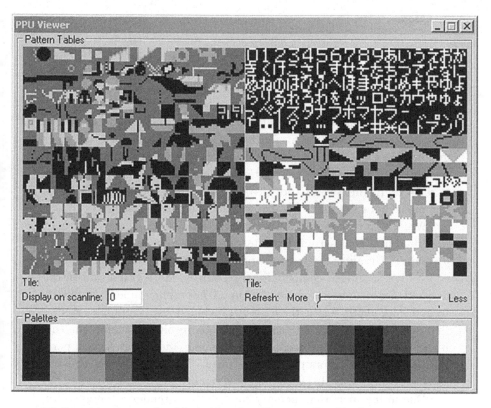

6.2 *Portopia*'s unconventional "primitives-based" pattern tiles. (Emulator: FCEUX 2.1.5)

tiles were enlisted to draw the game's locations. To achieve a sufficient level of graphical diversity between vignettes while still adhering to the bounds of 8K of CHR-ROM, Nakamura stocked *Portopia*'s pattern tables with simple geometric primitives: curves, squares, triangles, lines, etc. (figure 6.2).

All Famicom games used stretches of repeated tiles to build larger structures, but these tiles tended to represent "single-use" elements from the game world. The brick tile in *Super Mario Bros.* was used hundreds of times, but whether blue or brown, it was only ever a brick. In *Portopia*, a simple bisected rectangle could serve multiple purposes—the edge of a door, the side of a house, a horizon line—depending on its color and orientation. Even the game's human cast was assembled from various arrangements of modular body parts. *Portopia*'s simple geometric landscapes and bright colors conveyed a pleasing picture book aesthetic that fit its pulp narrative style.

Text Mode

Nakamura's unconventional approach to graphics programming stemmed from *Portopia*'s platform history. PCs in the early 1980s typically offered two exclusive display modes: text or graphics. In text mode, only a limited set of character glyphs—letters, numbers, and a few symbols—could be displayed onscreen. These were stored in memory as individual character tiles. Characters were the display's fundamental atomic unit; the programmer had no access to individual pixels. Therefore, resolutions were measured in the number of characters that could fit the height and width of the screen. The NEC PC-6001 (1981), for instance, had a single 32x16 text mode, enough room to display 512 characters edge to edge.

While characters were well suited to word processing or file navigation, building games from fixed text elements limited their graphical diversity.[20] Graphics modes, in contrast, gave programmers pixel-level control but sacrificed computational resources. More graphical control demanded more memory, dependent upon the graphics mode's granularity and color depth. Again, the PC-6001 included several graphics modes that decreased the available color palette as resolution increased. The highest, 256x192, was exclusively monochrome; the lowest, 64x48, permitted up to nine colors per display "pixel." Game developers struck a constant compromise between graphical fidelity and palette diversity.

Due to the increased memory consumption, rendering in graphics mode was also more processor-intensive. The NEC PC versions of *Portopia* used the majority of the screen to display the current location vignette. Screen elements were outlined line-by-line, then color-filled row-by-row. Complex locations depicting multiple buildings receding into the horizon, like the opening street scene, took thirty seconds or more to render on the PC-6601 (1985), which ran in a 4-color 320x200 graphics mode. Despite being four years older, the PC-6001 could render the same scene in half the time, since it ran in the lower resolution (128x192) 2-color mode. In either case, players spent much of their play time waiting for the scenery to render.[21]

Portopia's primitives-based pattern tables worked as a smart compromise between the graphics modes of early PCs and the Famicom's tile-based architecture. But the compromise only worked because of the game's slow-paced genre—with limited animated elements, the distinctions between sprites and background tiles were not as ironclad. Only a few tiles were dedicated to moving objects, so Nakamura was free to use the remainder of CHR-ROM to store Japanese glyphs and background primitives.

Due to the Famicom's dedicated PPU, Nakamura's port gained immediate improvements over its PC predecessors. Vignettes rendered immediately, so players could focus on advancing the storyline instead of watching the processor laboriously draw each scene. Removing the platform-enforced time inflation made the game shorter, so Horii and Nakamura added new content: another character, several locations, and a somewhat anachronistic homage to *Wizardry* in the form of an underground, first-person "dungeon." In the dungeon, the main window displayed a simple geometric maze that the player could navigate using the D-pad instead of menu commands, making it the only section of the game where the player gained direct control over Boss' movements. But instead of running through a dungeon in search of treasure, the detectives hunted for evidence. It was a contemporary Japanese update to the fantasy dungeon crawl.

Portopia was such a departure from standard console fare that it required supplementary assistance to ease players into its gameplay style. The manual included a dramatized story summary, introductions to the major characters, a detailed breakdown of text commands and items, and a generalized strategy for how to begin Boss's investigation. There was also an extensive "Portopia Q & A" section that read like a FAQ from a modern strategy guide. The first entry addressed the lack of a save function:

Q: I've played for more than two hours, but I was unable to solve the mystery. I've decided to come back to the game tomorrow, so I turned off the power switch on my Famicom. The next day, can I play from where I left off?
A: When you turn off the power, the memory that keeps track of how far along in the story you have progressed is erased.[22]

Losing progress was customary for action or arcade games, especially on consoles, but restarting a plot-driven game was likely jarring to players accustomed to PC adventures. To curb complaints, the Q&A reassured players that subsequent restarts would progress much faster since they already knew what to do. Nonetheless, the manual encouraged note-taking, providing a categorized "Investigation Notes" section directly following the Q&A.

Nonetheless, the manual's concluding "Notice to Owners" included Enix's last ditch effort to assuage any fears that the game might be "broken" if the player was unable to progress:

ROM cartridges are not defective unless the game display appears obviously garbled. If you cannot solve the mystery, you are not leading the investigation correctly. At times during your investigation, an item that you have taken may not appear in your items list, may not be available for examination, or may not be available to show to people. This is because it is not necessary to solve the game and thus was programmed in this manner. This is not a defect in the ROM cartridge or in the program...The mystery is solvable; please do not give up, and good luck![23]

Apparently players adapted to the learning curve, as *Portopia* sold 700,000 copies. It also proved to be massively influential to the Japanese adventure genre. *Portopia* clones proliferated on the Famicom, much like the platformer boom that began after Nintendo's debut of *Super Mario Bros.* Over time, the graphical adventures inspired by Horii's groundbreaking game narrowed into a genre that would soon flourish in Japan: the visual novel.

Despite its success in Japan, *Portopia* was never ported to the NES. For one, its content was mature for a videogame: the plot centered around a series of murders, the investigation took players to adult locales like a strip club and hostess bar, and several vignettes depicted crime scenes, like the silhouette of a man who had hanged himself from a tree. Such scenes would have never met Nintendo's strict content approval outside of Japan without a substantial overhaul. Furthermore, the game's scenario was steeped in Japanese culture. Few U.S. children would have recognized landmarks in Kobe, much less the reference to the PORTOPIA '81 Expo. Certain clues were triggered by dialing familiar Japanese phone numbers, which followed a different format than U.S. numbers. Even within Japan, the Famicom version received a few noticeable content alterations. The PC-6601 port opened with the sound of gunfire and three "bullet holes"—actually asterisks—puncturing the screen, followed by a wailing police siren. For the Famicom conversion, the siren remained, but the gunshots were removed. Finally, one of the PC vignettes depicting the chalk outline of the murder victim had a noticeable bloodstain near the victim's head. The Famicom port kept the chalk outline but omitted the blood.[24]

The other presiding factor limiting translation was technological. According to the documentation to DvD's *Portopia* fan translation, only two of the NROM binary's 40,960 bytes were unused. In other words, Enix faced the same capacity barrier as the *Super Mario Bros.* team, but due to different circumstances: *SMB* was packed with objects while *Portopia* was packed with text. Translating Horii's script to English would have required compromising textual edits—or expanded memory, as DvD explains in their translation notes: "Because English text uses roughly twice as many characters to say the same thing in Japanese, and the original game used MTE compression on the Japanese text, we needed to expand the size of the ROM file to fit in the text."[25] Though non-trivial from a programming standpoint, ROM expansion for play in an emulator costs nothing, since no physical ROM must be manufactured. In 1985, however, expanding NROM was not yet possible. Considering its PC heritage, *Portopia* was an ideal candidate for the Disk System, but at the time the peripheral was still unknown outside of Nintendo R&D. Had Enix embraced the Disk System early on, the peripheral's fate might have taken a different course.

Weighing the cultural, economic, and technological factors, a *Portopia* translation was likely not worth the risk, effort, or expense. A handful of adventure videogames found their way to the NES—notably *Shadowgate*, *Deja Vu*, and *Uninvited*—but they were spurious outsiders, not beacons of a burgeoning console adventure trend. In America, adventure games were a PC genre—and one quickly fading in popularity. In Japan, *Portopia* triggered a videogame phenomenon, but one that was localized. Ironically, Nakamura and Horii's follow-up homage to the PC role-playing game would follow the same trajectory.

New Maps

As both *Super Mario Bros.* and *Portopia* demonstrated—though through vastly different means—NROM could only stretch so far. And as *Zelda* demonstrated on the Disk System, cramming more background and sprite tiles into a game could make an immediate visual impact. Hyrule felt appreciably bigger than Kinoko Kingdom or Kobe's Port Island, but its magnitude came at the price of a kludgy peripheral and a proprietary medium. There had to be a better way, some means to axe the plastic and cabling and sneak hardware in unseen.

The solution arrived via cartridges. Within four months of the Disk System's launch, Capcom released 魔界村 (*Makaimura*), known in the U.S. as *Ghosts 'n Goblins*.[26] Today, most players remember the arcade port for its Satanic themes and equally devilish difficulty, but the cartridge interior concealed its own sinister portent of the Disk System's future. Besides its black shell, *Makaimura* looked identical to any other Famicom cart, but inside, the circuit board was etched with two unfamiliar labels—"HVC-UNROM-01" and "CHR RAM"—and had an extended PCB shoulder that held two new integrated circuits. These inauspicious logic components were not only significant enough to warrant a new board name, they also marked a new era for the Famicom and its games.

UNROM was one of the first *discrete logic* boards released for the Famicom.[27] Discrete logic chips contained one or more logic gates that performed the Boolean functions necessary for a memory management technique known as *bank switching*. Bank switching allowed the 2A03 to "see" more data by shuffling identically-sized banks in and out of its address space. UNROM divided the 32KB CPU address space into two segments: one 16KB bank remained fixed, while the second segment could swap between seven additional 16KB banks. In sum, *Makaimura* could access an impressive 128KB of PRG-ROM.

Due to their cartographic enhancement capabilities, the components that administered bank switching (and other advanced logic) were commonly called "mappers." But why were banks necessary? Why not include a single 128KB chip instead of segmenting memory into discrete areas? For one, NROM's ROM thresholds were not arbitrary, but governed by physical, computational, and economic considerations. Nintendo's standard mask ROM had twenty-eight pins, of which fifteen were dedicated address lines (numbered A0 through A14) that relayed communications between CPU and cartridge.[28] Each line was assigned to one bit of the largest possible address the CPU could access, totaling 2^{15} addressable memory locations in cartridge ROM—or 32KB. Adding a single address line would have doubled capacity to 64KB, but it also would have required a new IC design, which in turn would have raised the overall cost per cartridge. Uemura and team calculated their costs to cater to *Donkey Kong*, not a future era of memory-hungry games.

UNROM's second immediate benefit was its CHR-RAM.[29] While functionally identical to the FDS RAM adapter's 8KB of pattern RAM, mapper-based CHR-RAM could swap tiles at a much faster rate than the Quick Disk's serial loading logjam could provide. We can witness this benefit firsthand in *Makaimura*'s character animations. The player avatar Sir Arthur had two gameplay states: at full strength, he wore a suit of armor; after a single enemy strike, he was reduced to his underwear. In the sprite pattern table, the armored and disrobed tiles shared identical positions, though not simultaneously. When Arthur collided with an enemy, a small segment of tiles in CHR-RAM updated with underwear sprites, allowing two distinct animation cycles to occupy the same pattern table indices, overwriting one another as needed. The switchover was fast and seamless.

UNROM worked out great for Capcom and *Makaimura*, but why did Nintendo bother building mappers when they had already "solved" the

ROM cap with Quick Disks? They did so partly to keep pace with industry trends. Third-party developers like Jaleco and Konami were already experimenting with their own discrete logic boards so they could better port their advanced arcade and PC titles to the Famicom.[30] Nintendo stepped in soon after, providing their own "official" solutions via UNROM and CNROM, but the discrete logic components they used were low-cost, off-the-shelf parts sourced from the world's major hardware vendors, some of whom were competitors. *Makaimura*'s multiple board revisions alone contained chips from NEC, Sharp, Toshiba, Panasonic, Texas Instruments, and GoldStar.[31]

Yamauchi, never one to miss a competitive advantage, assigned R&D3—headed by Genyo Takeda—to develop Nintendo's own mapper technology,[32] even while Yokoi's R&D1 worked on the Disk System and its suite of first-party titles. By doing so, Nintendo could maintain strict licensing control over their products, even at the chip level. And while it might have seemed counterproductive for Nintendo to have supported two independent divisions working on competing formats,[33] Yamauchi felt that internal competition would keep the teams focused and motivated.

The fruit of R&D3's labor was a chip that Nintendo could call their own. True to form, in 1987 Nintendo filed a U.S. patent for R&D3's "multi-memory controller," or MMC, which provided capabilities similar to discrete logic circuits but in a consolidated—and proprietary—package.[34] Nintendo's in-house mappers would become the predominant mapper technology for Famicom carts and the only mappers available to worldwide developers, since the latter had to defer manufacturing control to their parent licensor. In the end, this proved detrimental to the NES's hardware variety, since many of the Famicom's third-party mappers would provide some of the most interesting console upgrades, especially for audio (chapter 7).

Whether discrete logic or MMC, the number and size of a mapper's banks—especially PRG-ROM—had meaningful consequences to a game's design. For bank switching to work, either one bank had to remain fixed so function-critical code was always accessible, or that function-critical code had to be duplicated across multiple banks at identical addresses.[35] All-at-once bank switching required careful code planning to ensure that data was in the right place at the right time. If, for instance, the engine was busy reading sound data for music playback and that data's bank swapped, the engine might read in arbitrary data as music and produce unexpected sounds. In more critical cases—like a bank switch that triggered during a subroutine call that resulted in the program counter returning to an unexpected address—the game might crash.

CHR-ROM banking posed no risk of program failure, but it did afford interesting visual effects, especially if mappers allowed partial pattern table banking. Some, like Nintendo's MMC3 and Sunsoft's FME-7, could bank as little as 1KB (64 tiles) at a time, making bank-switched animation feasible.[36] Games with granular banking soon enlivened their backgrounds with swaying flora, blinking signs, churning water, and spinning machinery. *Super Mario Bros. 3* (MMC3) banked 2KB segments of CHR-ROM, reserving half of its background pattern table for animation duties, like the dancing greenery on the World 1 overworld map, airship propellers, rotating coins, and the question marks sliding across block faces. Sunsoft's *Batman: Return of the Joker* (FME-7) used smaller 1KB banks to fake parallax scrolling effects like the rolling storm clouds crowning the sky in stage 1–1. Mappers like CNROM, in contrast, could only bank the entire 8KB of CHR-ROM at once, so tile substitutions were primarily reserved for major character or area changes.

A residual effect of bank switching and CHR-RAM was a general loosening of byte accounting. NROM developers suddenly faced with multiple times the program and character memory were more prone to leave behind, unintentionally or not, vestigial code and graphics that did not make it into the final game.[37] Remnants of unused test levels, in-game text, character animations, items, enemies, debug menus, developer credits, stage music, and Easter eggs were scattered throughout Famicom games that suddenly had space to waste.[38] Mappers rapidly expanded the visual (and archival) complexity of Famicom games. There were quantifiably more characters, animations, and special effects onscreen. Bouncing fauna and rotating fans made backgrounds appear livelier. Complex parallax movement, now possible with artful tile management, kept the Famicom apace with platforms with more advanced graphical processors. Mappers also extended the Famicom's in-game maps, providing the memory to build out worlds far larger than Hyrule's overworld and underworld combined.

Role-Playing

As the brief "dungeon" portion of the *Portopia* console port made clear, the Enix team were fans of Western role-playing games. As PC enthusiasts, both Horii and Nakamura had had first-hand play experience with *Ultima* and *Wizardry*.[39] They wanted to replicate the experience on consoles, but their small-scale graphical adventure had already pushed the NROM to capacity.

Nintendo's discrete logic mappers arrived just in time, and Enix was one of the first third-party developers to capitalize on their benefits. CNROM was not a huge step up from NROM—PRG-ROM still maxed at 32KB—but the 32KB of bankable CHR-ROM was a fourfold boost in pattern table memory that significantly expanded (both in number and size) the available cast of in-game creatures, a hardware benefit that would prove crucial to their new game's manga-inspired graphical style.

But tile counts had not been Enix's sole concern prior to embarking on their next project. They also worried that role-playing games might be too complex for first-time players who were accustomed to console and arcade fare. *Portopia* proved that a text- and narrative-heavy game was both economically and technologically feasible on the Famicom, but the team would need a new approach to fuse the storytelling of adventure games to the strategy and scope of the Western RPG.

Ultima and *Wizardry* were landmarks of the computer role-playing genre, but they drew influences from the gameplay traditions of "pen and paper" (or "tabletop") RPGs like *Dungeons & Dragons* and their war game predecessors. Computers were ideal for handling the computational minutiae driving character creation, combat resolution, experience tracking, and the other calculations players typically did by hand. But tabletop RPGs were not simply statistical exercises; role-playing was equally grounded in open-ended storytelling and player choice, gameplay aspects that were (and continue to be) much more difficult to simulate with computers.

Dungeons & Dragons was also a social gaming experience shared by a multi-member adventuring party, so players' roles were divided according to broad fantasy archetypes—magic-users, fighters, thieves, clerics—to provide a better division of labor for role-playing. While the Dungeon Master (DM) controlled the panoply of non-player characters (NPCs) and monsters, each player typically controlled a single adventurer. In the absence of online or LAN play, early PC RPGs mimicked the tabletop model as best they could, condensing role-playing's social elements into calculated interactions between player and computer—the former controlled one or more adventurers while the latter took over the DM's duties.[40]

Enix's new role-playing project, ドラゴンクエスト (*Dragon Quest*) honed character creation to its essence.[41] The first and only customization necessary prior to play was your character's name. *D&D*'s six standard ability scores—strength, dexterity, intelligence, wisdom, constitution, and charisma—compressed to two: strength and agility. Leveling followed a simple linear track based on experience points gained from defeating monsters in battle. The adventuring party was pared to one "classless" hero who could handle both melee and magical attacks. Accordingly, combat was simplified to a single melee command and a modest spell system. Your hero could battle only one monster at a time, narrated textually through a series of turns that relied on simple strategy rather than reflex. Enix wagered that minimizing customization options would both respect the console's affordances and make the game accessible to RPG novices, especially children.

Character naming was a recent addition to Famicom games. Miyamoto thought it was important to give players the option to name their character in *The Legend of Zelda* to better emphasize the relationship between the player and their onscreen avatar.[42] "Link" was a placeholder name meant to denote that tie, but the player's input had no real significance beyond the label of their save file. In *Dragon Quest*, your name became part of the story—NPCs and battle narration alike hailed you by your chosen name. Enix even considered character naming significant enough to use as a marketing angle: "The main character is you yourself. When you start the game and enter your name, the King and the townspeople will call you by that name."[43] Naming made your role-playing experience unique.

Narrative novelties aside, names had a programmatic function, serving as input data for your character's statistical progression. Nakamura programmed an algorithm to parse the name's first four characters and use them to select one of sixteen initial character "builds."[44] The variance in strength, agility, HP (hit points), and MP (magic power) were not especially wide, but the difference between a strength of 3 or 6 could make a big difference in player survival during the game's early encounters. More importantly, each of the sixteen starting builds funneled to one of four "growth tracks," determining how your stats would advance for the remainder of the game. Some tracks simply skewed characters more toward strength vs. magic or vice-versa, while others were deliberately stunted. Certain unlucky player names generated characters that were quantitatively worse than others. In a real procedural sense, your name guided your destiny.

Walkabout

After name selection, *Dragon Quest*'s play began in the audience of King Lars, who presided over the throne room of Radatome (ラダトーム) Castle.[45] Lars spoke a brief monologue, informing you that you were a descendent of the Hero Loto, who was once given a Ball of Light that could seal away monsters. However, the evil Dragon King (りゅうおう) had stolen the Ball and subsequently unleashed the repressed hordes upon the land of Alefgard. The King beseeched you to defeat the Dragon King and return the ancient relic to his protection.

Once you cleared the throne room and ventured outside the castle, the perspective shifted abruptly. Inside Radatome, the architecture and NPCs were scaled roughly according to "real-world" proportions. The castle interior had multiple floors and rooms wherein the residents went about their business. Though condensed and viewed from a cutaway perspective, the walls were meant to convincingly represent the castle's scale. Outside, your viewpoint changed to a tiled overworld view that the U.S. instruction manual called "walkabout mode." Though your character remained the same size, locations and terrain were compressed to miniature pictorial indices. Radatome, once a vast castle, was now merely a 16x16-pixel icon.[46]

Most contemporary videogame players have assimilated the visual language of varying spatial perspectives, but in the 1980s, and especially for younger audiences, such counterintuitive shifts required additional instruction. Nintendo of America spent several months priming American children for the introduction of the *Dragon Quest* localization in the pages of *Nintendo Power*. A twelve-page spread in the July/August 1989 issue included screen captures of the player's character outside the town with the following captions: "Towns appear small from outside their protective walls, but this is an illusion…Actually, the towns are large."[47] In the same way that early cinema-goers had to learn that cuts could traverse space and time, early game players had to learn that their character did not grow to colossal size outside the city's walls.

Once acclimated to the walkabout illusion, you likely spied the Demon's Isle, an inaccessible landmass bordered by ocean, swamps, and craggy mountains located due south of Radatome. As you would eventually learn, the Isle housed the site of the game's final confrontation, the Castle of the Dragon King. Showcasing the game's ultimate objective early on was an inspired use of aspirational design and a direct counterpoint to *Zelda's* exploratory model. In *Dragon Quest*, there was no ambiguity about the end goal—the player simply had to learn how to reach it.

As Horii explained in a recent interview, players unfamiliar with RPGs needed clear signposts to guide them:

> Other role-playing games back then had the players go wherever they pleased, but with *Dragon Quest* we dared to make scenarios starting

out the character with various linear objectives. Once the players had achieved a series of clear-cut objectives, gradually building up the character's strength, they could eventually venture out on their own with more freedom.[48]

"Gradually building up" is an accurate phrase. Progressing in *Dragon Quest* required a lot of time spent in battle. Grinding, as the process is more commonly known, involves the prolonged repetition of enemy encounters (usually in a limited portion of the game world) in order to accumulate experience, treasure, and equipment. Though its name is not complimentary, players are split about its value. Those who appreciate grinding tend to acknowledge its basis in fantasy verisimilitude. New adventurers do not begin as all-powerful heroes; they have to dedicate hours to slaying monsters before they are ready to face more powerful foes. Experience points, while clearly an abstraction, are an attempt to quantify the qualitative process of practice, knowledge, and training. Detractors, on the other hand, characterize grinding as wasted hours spent at work when they should be at play.

One of grinding's underlying problems is its partial translation of a system adopted from tabletop role-playing. In *Dungeons & Dragons*, at least ideally, leveling flows naturally from storytelling. Ostensibly the party should be killing monsters for an overarching purpose that advances the narrative. If they happen to stumble into an encounter that is beyond their level, the (benevolent) DM adjusts the difficulty on the fly. Video-game grinding extracts the procedural aspect of leveling—its raw statistical component—from its narrative structure. Especially in early RPGs, leveling takes place in a suspended temporal state where the plot, no matter how urgent or dire, is put on hold until the player fulfills their leveling quotas. In a tabletop campaign, delaying one's quest may seal the world's fate; in *Dragon Quest*, the delay is necessary to adequately prepare for the Dragon King.

Indeed, grinding was mandatory in *Dragon Quest*. Though Lars gave you gold to start your adventure, it was not enough to purchase adequate equipment, even among the game's early selections. Instead, you had to choose weapons, armor, and supplies strategically, weighing cost against power and defense. However, Horii and Nakamura structured the game so players would not grow frustrated early on. Advancing to the second level only required seven experience points. Granting that you followed the King's advice and bought supplies, even the most incompetent players could struggle through the handful of monsters necessary to reach level two. The designers hoped that early advancement would spur the player onward.

Command?

Adventurous players soon found that they could not stray far from Radatome. Exploring the overworld map was risky. Threats did not roam openly as they did in adventure games. Any step could trigger a random encounter, as wandering monsters remained cloaked by statistical probability. And even the weakest enemies could deplete your hero's health after a few turns. Until he leveled up, you kept him on a short leash.

Dragon Quest's random encounters derived from *Wizardry*, whose own system traced back once again to tabletop role-playing games. Early editions of *Dungeons & Dragons* in particular encouraged the random generation of monsters, treasure, and even dungeon layouts. Dice rolling was a key role-playing mechanic, emphasizing the dangerous nature of the party's environs; when exploring a hostile dungeon, one could be attacked at any moment.

To temper fortune's fates, encounters in *Dungeons & Dragons* were scaled according to the party's level and location. The 1983 *Dungeon Masters Rulebook* explained how dungeons could be "any number of levels deep" and that, "in general, the deeper you explore in a dungeon, the more dangerous it becomes."[49] Wandering monsters gave dungeons an organic, lived-in feel that helped sell the campaign's realism. Handing the role of DM over to the CPU meant that wandering monsters no longer spawned from physical dice rolls. The RPG internalized algorithmically the ubiquitous danger of the overworld. Threat avoidance was no longer a matter of reflex, but subject to a hidden calculus governed by code.

Dragon Quest likewise used algorithmic processes to both deliver encounters at an acceptable frequency and ensure that players were not unfairly overwhelmed. To both ends, the developers divided Alefgard's world map into an 8x8 grid with each cell assigned one of fourteen different enemy zones scaled in difficulty according to the types of enemies within.[50] Each zone could contain between two and five enemy types. Zone 0, for instance, encompassed Radatome's immediate vicinity. Here, the player could only encounter the blue or red Slimes, the weakest enemies in the game. In contrast, in zone 12, which surrounds the Dragon King's castle, the player could encounter some of the game's toughest foes, like Demon Knights and Starwyverns.

The overworld zones gated wandering monsters according to their toughness, sculpting a programmatic architecture beneath Alefgard's hills, plains, and deserts. Zones spiraled out from Radatome in increasing difficulty, and the designers developed clever signposts to direct players along optimal paths. The U.S. instruction manual warned players to "Beware of bridges! When you cross a bridge you'll arrive at an area where stronger monsters live."[51] This was sage advice—the developers placed bridges near zone borderlines, so players crossing them experienced a meaningful computational difference in enemy strength when they reached the other side. Other geographical cues, like mountain ranges or narrow rivers, were designed to funnel the player through smooth gradations of encounter types so they did not unexpectedly wander into regions beyond their abilities.

Players could encounter creatures at every step. While the types of enemies encountered were dictated by the player's current zone, the chance of an encounter was based on the current terrain type, no matter which zone the player was in. Plains tiles were the least populated; players faced roughly a 1:24 chance of a random encounter.[52] Hill and desert tiles, however, had a 1:8 chance of an encounter—the highest in the game. The only exception to the rule was zone 0. So as not to overwhelm beginner players, there was an additional probability check that made it less likely to trigger an encounter there. In other words, the math reinforced the narrative—you were statistically safer within Radatome's immediate radius.

Once an encounter triggered, battle information occupied four subwindows layered atop the overworld map. The central window depicted your current enemy in a small framed landscape reminiscent of *Portopia*'s vignettes. And like the former game, you confronted your enemies in first-person view, as the enemy window conveniently obscured your hero's walkabout sprite. The leftmost window displayed your name and level (レベル), along with a list of English abbreviations for your current stats: HP, MP, G(old), and E(xperience). The top command (コマンド) window listed four possible actions—Fight (たたかう), Spell (じゅもん), Escape (にげる), and Tool (どうぐ)—again echoing *Portopia*'s menu-driven interaction. As the battle proceeded, the bottom window provided play-by-play text for all player and enemy actions.

The first two lines displayed during most players' first random encounter have since become famous among role-playing fans:

スライムが　あらわれた！
コマンド？[53]

6.3 Based on *Dragon Quest*'s probability algorithm for random encounters, the Slime is statistically the most likely first combat encounter. (Source: Powerpak NES-001 capture)

In English, the text reads, "Slime appeared! Command?" True to the text, the creature in the center window resembled a small blue dollop of gelatin with wide saucer eyes and a red grin, the first hint of *Dragon Quest*'s manga influences (figure 6.3).[54]

Like most RPGs influenced by *Dungeons & Dragons*, battles proceeded in turns. The player struck, enemy damage resolved, the enemy retaliated, player damage resolved, the player cast a spell, spell effects resolved, and so on until the encounter completed, as a result of either death or fleeing. Since your hero was never visible during battle and the enemies never moved, action took place through descriptive text, a minimal presentation style clearly indebted to early graphical adventures.

Dragon Quest is often criticized in the West for its tedious menu-driven gameplay. Since your hero sprite could only face forward, engaging in conversation not only required selecting a talk command, but also a cardinal speaking direction. Changing castle or dungeon levels similarly required positioning your hero above a stairway tile, pressing A to select the menu, then choosing STAIRS from the available options. Searching for items and picking up treasure were equally labor-intensive. In subsequent RPGs like *Final Fantasy*, one could simply walk over stairs to use them or press A to speak to an NPC, reserving menus for shopping, combat, or status updates.

While antiquated compared to subsequent RPGs, *Dragon Quest*'s menu system was a clear successor to the text parsers of PC adventure and role-playing games. For Horii and Nakamura, eliminating the need for a keyboard in favor of a simple list was a convenience. In *Wizardry*, one had to memorize spells from the instruction book and type them each time they were cast.[55] In *Dragon Quest*, you selected spells from a list. In this sense, *Dragon Quest* was a stopgap between the PC and console RPG traditions—it streamlined the selection process of the former without fully embracing the "direct" interaction afforded by the latter.

Not that *Dragon Quest* did not offer its own genre refinements. When you inevitably stumbled into a battle you were not yet prepared for, death was far more forgiving than in prior PC RPGs. Defeat cost you half your gold and a scolding from Lars, but you kept your experience and equipment. At worst you had to trudge across the map to resume your quest minus some cash in pocket. *Wizardry*, in comparison, was far crueler. Dead party members had to be carried through the maze until they were either revived by magic or transported to the temple for resurrection. Total party death meant rolling a new adventurer group to return to the maze and hunt for the fallen dead. Hours of progress could be lost, often thanks to antagonistic game design.[56]

Dragon Quest's most antagonistic moment came in its final encounter. When you finally reached the Dragon King, he offered you a choice. In exchange for your allegiance, he promised you "half of the world." The nobler choice, as expected, infuriated the Dragon King, triggering a final battle. The partnership was a ruse, of course—if you accepted his offer, the Dragon King revealed that your half of the world was the "World of Darkness." He then recited a Spell of Restoration (i.e., password)—echoing King Lars's incantation identically—that returned you to the beginning of the game with no gold, experience, or equipment. Making the selfish choice yielded a fitting punishment—you had to begin the game anew.

Walkabout mode surfaced new technical challenges for the Famicom's scrolling hardware. In prior chapters, we discussed games that either scrolled exclusively along a single vector (*Super Mario Bros.*), limited scrolling to one axis at a time (*Kid Icarus*, *Metroid*), or implemented controlled multi-directional scrolling with careful name table and mirroring updates (*The Legend of Zelda*). A few outliers faked multi-directional scrolling using clever level design. *Devil World*, for instance, was soldered for horizontal mirroring but duplicated its symmetrical playfield across name tables (minus the upper/lower status bars). The game's truncated viewport and natural screen wrapping made the playfield appear as if it scrolled infinitely in any direction.

Dragon Quest, in contrast, implements true multi-directional scrolling.[57] Your hero may walk freely in any cardinal direction, and the overworld map neither wraps along edges nor limits transitions to an auto-scrolling slideshow. The only borders are geographical.

Dragon Quest's CNROM board has hardwired vertical mirroring, so scrolling along the horizontal plane works similar to a platformer. Columnar updates occur just beyond the screen's perimeter as the player advances east or west. At any point in walkabout mode, there is a full name table's worth of map space buffering your character's position. Figure 6.4 is a snapshot of FCEUX's name table viewer during an encounter. The largest shaded rectangle outlines the player's viewport.

The lighter column on the right, overlaid with crosshatching, is outside the player's view, but is pre-buffered in case they push further east. Beyond that narrow band lie the metatile columns furthest west from the player's current location, since the name tables are currently wrapped across name table borders. In other words, if the player heads west after the battle concludes, there is nearly a full name table's worth of rendered map ready to receive them. If they head east, there is only a single metatile column.

The black line bisecting the upper and lower halves designates the mirroring boundary. Notice that if the player heads north or south, there are no tile buffers awaiting their arrival—the mirroring structure precludes any advance preparations because data beyond either edge wraps to the opposite side. Thus if *Dragon Quest* had no means to scroll vertically, venturing beyond the southern hills would find the player walking across the bottom border and emerging at the top of the screen in the plains bordering the northern edge.

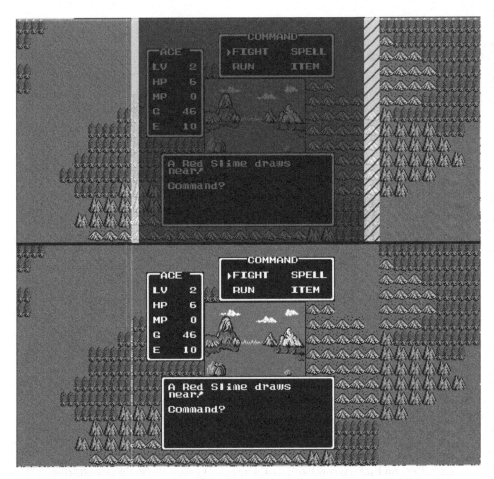

6.4 An annotated screen capture of *Dragon Warrior*'s name table arrangement during combat. (Emulator: FCEUX 2.1.5)

Clearly, looping in this manner would spoil Alefgard's cartographic realism, so tile rows must be moved into place one-by-one as the player advances north or south. Though there is adequate time during VBLANK to update a tile row, a more troublesome architectural problem arises. Like Kinoko Kingdom, Alefgard and its constituent towns, castles, and dungeons can not squeeze into 32KB of ROM without efficient data packing, so *Dragon Quest* stores its map data in compressed metatiles measuring 16x16 pixels square, a size that perfectly aligns with attribute table borders. However, the PPU's mirroring structure combined with four-way scrolling does not provide an adequate buffer to hide attribute updates as new columns or rows are moved into place. For east–west movement, this isn't an issue, since color mismatches can be hidden beyond the border in the name table buffer. For north–south movement, there is no place for the errors to hide.

In *Dragon Quest*, attribute mismatches happen in plain sight along the upper and lower screen edges. While pushing south beyond Radatome, you can clearly see an 8-pixel high strip of lake tiles that appear orange and green instead of blue and white; conjoining mountainsides are frocked in identical hues. In both instances, the proper row updates have loaded, but the screen has not yet scrolled far enough for the tiles' accompanying attribute data to update. The mountains and sea are orange and green because they are currently assigned to the forest/plains palette, residual information from the screen's topmost metatile row. Scrolling "against the mirror" does not provide an adequate buffer zone to hide the attribute borders.

Attribute errors provide a shorthand visual clue to a game's mirroring setting, since the errors will match the mirror's edge. *Contra*, for example, predominantly scrolls horizontally, but on its vertical waterfall level, we see attribute clashes along the upper edge. As expected, its UNROM board uses vertical mirroring. *Super Mario Bros. 3*, oddly enough, uses horizontal mirroring despite Mario's two screens of limited flying height,[58] so attribute errors appear along the left and right borders of the screen. Likewise for *Zelda II* and *Teenage Mutant Ninja Turtles*, whose four-way scrolling overworlds were both set to horizontal mirroring.

Most developers, Nintendo included, either allowed attribute errors to show or relied on CRT overscan to "naturally" hide unsightly borders. Others developers were more proactive. *Alfred Chicken*, published by Mindscape in 1994, used two hardware techniques to mask attribute errors. First, the black border visible on the rightmost edge of the screen was actually a column of 8x16-pixel black sprites that covered the attribute seam. (To ensure that sprite overflows would never cause the border to flicker, the sprite column occupied the first fifteen slots of OAM.) Second, the leftmost black border used the hardware clipping mask, the same technique that prevented sprites from wrapping unrealistically around screen borders in single-screen arcade games (chapter 1). In combination, the sprite stack and clipping mask allowed *Alfred Chicken*'s screens to scroll in four directions, clash-free.[59]

Dragon Quest likewise used the clipping mask—the leftmost narrow column overlay in figure 6.4—but to different ends. As you walked right, sprites (e.g., NPCs) had to scroll convincingly off the left hand of the screen rather than disappearing in halves. While *Dragon Quest*'s gameplay style was a far cry from *Mario Bros.*, the clipping mask served the same function in both games. And as an added benefit, the mask widened the lefthand buffer area for metatile updates.

Whether developer oversight or necessary evil, attribute seams were visual evidence of a console expanding beyond its initial design parameters. Few arcade or console videogames of the early 1980s scrolled in four directions. The Famicom's mirrored name table design indicates that Uemura's team planned ahead for scrolling along a single vertical or horizontal plane, but not both in combination. To compensate, developers had to invent software solutions to solve a rigid hardware constraint.

Save by Haiku

Dragon Quest had a number of advantages in the Japanese market that prior RPGs could not match. First, thanks to Horii's publishing connections, Enix secured the popular manga artist Akira Toriyama to illustrate the in-game enemies and supplementary artwork.[60] Toriyama's massively popular *Dr. Slump* and *Dragon Ball* serials appeared in *Shonen Jump*, one of Japan's most widely circulated manga publications. Though Toriyama's style was difficult to convey in *Dragon Quest*'s condensed overworld, the first-person battle screens provided the perfect frame to showcase larger character portraits.

Toriyama's style better catered to Japanese tastes, especially manga fans, than the Western fantasy traditions drawn from *Dungeons & Dragons* and *Lord of the Rings*. The colorful characters were also a far cry from the wireframe stick figures of *Wizardry* and *Ultima*. They had a mischievous comic quality uncommon in RPGs—*D&D*'s gelatinous cube was far less menacing, and much more relatable, as the wide-eyed, grinning slime. Tellingly, in lieu of screenshots, Toriyama's artwork dominated *Dragon Quest*'s box cover and print advertising. Enix promoted the game based on the strength of its illustrative design alone.

Dragon Quest's second rather serendipitous personnel score was Koichi Sugiyama, an established composer for film and television (and a videogame enthusiast) who caught the publisher's attention with a mail-in customer questionnaire for Enix's 1985 PC-88 *shogi* title 森田和郎の 将棋 *(Kazuo Morita Shogi)*. As Sugiyama recounts, "Whoever received the note recognized my name and gave me a phone call asking if I could compose some music for them. I said yes, and that was how I began making game music."[61]

Though unassuming on the 2A03, *Dragon Quest*'s eight themes had a strong compositional backbone informed by Sugiyama's Western classical music influence. Videogames had had a tradition of using classical themes in their soundtracks (since they were public domain and thus cheaper than hiring someone to write songs),[62] but composing new "classical" work was less common. Though orchestral grandeur was tough to convey with the Famicom's three tonal channels, Sugiyama's rousing title screen overture and the regal yet melancholy theme used as a backdrop to King Lars' opening monologue were certainly closer to Bach or Vivaldi than Kondo or Tanaka.[63]

Another key element driving *Dragon Quest*'s cultural character was its script. Horii was a writer by trade and he invested *Dragon Quest* with a Japanese idiom steeped in the hip irreverence of the manga he admired. The tone was a perfect match for Toriyama's artwork and a novelty for a sword and sorcery game. While *Dragon Quest*'s "lone hero rescuing a princess and slaying a menacing evil" plot was bog standard fantasy fare, the game's style lived and breathed through its NPCs, whose dialogue was frequently irreverent, weird, or tongue-in-cheek. The back of *Dragon Quest*'s box touted over 100 NPCs to encounter, and Horii made sure they were truly characters, not just information retainers strung along the path to each quest objective.

One of *Dragon Quest*'s most infamous conversations hailed from a woman in the town of Rimuldar:

```
*　おいで　ぼうや。
ぱふぱふしてほしいなら
50ゴールドよ。
```

Literally translated, she offers to sell the player a "puff-puff" for 50 gold. The service was not as scandalous as its translation implies—essentially the player was paying her to jiggle her breasts.[64] A vendor in Melkido proposed a more reputable, if no less puzzling, request to exchange her "*Portopia* for your *Dragon Quest*." Horii likewise peppered the game with self-referential shoutouts, like listing Nakamura's first name, Koichi (こういち), as the player name for back-of-the-box screenshots and including his own name in a special password.

Since *Dragon Quest* CNROM profile lacked battery-backed SRAM, it had no means to save data. To ease the pain of a multi-line password system, Horii implemented a literal poetic device. Save strings were twenty characters long, but subdivided into four lines of five, seven, five, and three characters apiece—a haiku-like structure that was "familiar to all Japanese and easier to type."[65] For example, a password that advanced the player to Level 10, along with a healthy stock of gold, equipment, and items read as follows:

ふるいけや　かわずとびこむ
みずのおと　ばしや

The password was a hiragana rendition of one of the most famous haiku in Japanese history, penned by 17th-century poet Matsuo Basho. The verse is notoriously difficult to translate to English, but a fair transcription reads something like: "An old pond / frog leaping / water sound." Other passwords were less literary but equally straightforward to remember, including in-jokes, references to the game's characters, callouts to the developers' friends, and a list of Japanese cities.[66]

Character Sets

Readers familiar with Japanese will likely notice that *Dragon Quest*'s script is written entirely in hiragana and katakana. While, as we will see below, there is a strong technical reason to do so, the syllabary-based script also made *Dragon Quest* more accessible to younger players. Japanese schoolchildren (and non-Japanese students) learn hiragana first, prior to mastering the kanji. Its syllables comprise the entirety of the Japanese language, so any complex character can be broken down into its constituent phonetic elements. As a result, Japanese can be written entirely in hiragana if necessary, a trait that both Japanese primary school texts and *Dragon Quest* share.

The katakana syllabary mirrors hiragana's phonetic elements but is generally used for non-Japanese loan words—like "computer" (コンピューター) and "coffee" (コーヒー)—or special textual emphasis akin to italics in English. This second use is especially prevalent in manga, where writers use katakana extensively for sound effects and onomatopoeia. In English, we have plenty of *whooshes*, *blams*, and *zaps* to embellish comic book actions, but manga has a vast nuanced language devoted to the textual/auditory description of moods, bodily functions, motions, sensations, and natural phenomena.[67]

Horii drew on this rich reserve to add idiomatic flavor to the game's magic spells. *Dungeons & Dragons*, itself inspired by pulp fantasy literature, canonized a fantasy vocabulary that PC RPGs commonly borrowed. Regardless of the game, magic-users and clerics could cast variations of

Light, Cure, Shield, Magic Missile, and the like. Horii copied the spell effects, but invented his own half-nonsense, half-onomatopoeic language to describe them.[68] When players cast ギラ (gira), ホイミ (hoimi), or ラリホー (rarihō), they were not choosing from familiar Japanese words but from names meant to evoke the action or effect of the spell. In English, an equivalent might be a sleep spell called "ZZZZZZ" or a wind spell called "whoooosh." Japanese players versed in manga glommed immediately to Horii's linguistic style. Importing the tropes of a familiar medium helped break down any barriers that might keep players from understanding *Dragon Quest*'s unfamiliar genre.

Rendering Japanese posed a formidable problem in both the growth of Japan's domestic PC market and in the translation of software across regions. Though many Japanese videogames included English text in part because of its cool exotic appeal,[69] there were also meaningful platform constraints that hindered Japanese's appearance onscreen. The Famicom, for one, had far too little CHR-ROM space, regardless of mapper, to store even a fraction of the kanji character set. Even narrowing the field to the roughly two to three thousand characters in common use was implausible. Instead, most developers opted to use the hiragana syllabary, often interspersed with a few select kanji or katakana. This decreased memory expenditure considerably, since the full hiragana syllabary includes only forty-six characters. Even accounting for hiragana's particles and diacritics, the memory tradeoff was far more palatable.

Moreover, while the English alphabet contains only twenty-six letters, the Japanese syllabary is mostly built from compound phonic elements, so words tend to be more compact than in English. Take *Dragon Quest*'s primary antagonist as a simple example: whether one chooses "Dragon King" or "Dragonlord," the English translations are several characters longer than the original five-character hiragana りゅうおう. Indeed, no monster name in *Dragon Quest* is longer than seven characters (e.g., しにがみのきし), while many of the English translations are ten or more (e.g., Armored Knight). Propagate such modest savings throughout the entirety of the game's text and one begins to amass significant memory savings.

Dragon Quest slimmed its tile syllabary further by separating common characters from their diacritics. へ, べ, and ぺ, for instance, all share the same base radical, though their pronunciations vary (*he, be,* and *pe*, respectively). Instead of storing a character for each of the three syllables, separate characters were created for the radical (へ), the *dakuten* marker (゛), and *handakuten* marker (゜). Doing so eliminated around thirty redundant tiles in CHR-ROM.[70]

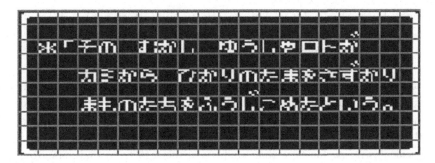

6.5 An enlarged screenshot from an emulator VRAM Viewer shows the name table distribution of hiragana characters in *Dragon Quest*'s dialogue box. Note that diacritics occupy their own tiles in separate rows above the primary characters. (Emulator: NO$NES v1.0)

This separation also explains why diacritics appear to float above the text they modify. As you can see in figure 6.5, dialogue is spaced with empty name table rows between each line. When diacritics are necessary, they are placed in the empty row above the relevant letter. English, of course, does not require diacritics, so text in the localized port is spaced much tighter, eliminating individual line spacing in favor of sentence spacing. Here, the compromise between linguistic and platform limitations generated two distinct graphical results.

For Japanese text, the upfront loss in CHR-ROM paid off later in PRG-ROM savings; whether the technical tradeoff was worthwhile depended on the game. *Super Mario Bros.*'s few lines of text made more sense to display in English, since including a full hiragana character set would have meant sacrificing a number of architectural background elements with no real benefit to gameplay (and certainly less universal appeal). In *Dragon Quest*, the opposite was true, as Horii explained: "Because *Dragon Quest*, when it first came out, graphically it was more symbols, the attractiveness of the game had more to do with the wording and the dialogue."[71] Dialogue, not graphical detail, was the game's centerpiece, so the added text tiles were worth the memory cost.

In their design focus, Nintendo's and Enix's directors make for interesting foils. Miyamoto has always taken the path of mechanical purity, pruning his miniature gardens of elements not directly related to play. In a conversation between him and Horii, Miyamoto stated his aims plainly: "The stories of Mario and Zelda titles have always been supplemental to the actual gameplay. Action games only have stories attached to make the experience more interesting."[72] To wit: How did

Mario's movements feel? How well was the world constructed for his abilities? What tools best fit Link's adventure? Were the dungeons fun to find and explore? Horii, in contrast, billed himself as an author, aiming to bring a deeper literary touch to his games. He wanted to translate the depth of PC role-playing games to the console without sacrificing plot, character, or world. Throughout their decades of design, Miyamoto has always been the mischievous toymaker and Horii the playful wordsmith.

Spell of Restoration

Dragon Quest's combination of accessibility, literary flourish, manga-inspired artwork, classically informed composition, and native Japanese character struck a nerve with the Famicom audience. It was not a runaway success like *Super Mario Bros.*, but it sold one million copies within the first six months of its May 1986 release, eventually selling 1.5 million.[73] For Nintendo, it was enough to invest in the game's potential success abroad. But a videogame so imbued with Japanese idiom and whose genre relied so heavily on text would prove far more challenging to localize than *Super Mario Bros.* or *The Legend of Zelda*.

The first complication was the name. *DragonQuest* was already trademarked to a tabletop RPG owned, ironically, by *Dungeons & Dragons* publisher TSR,[74] so Enix amended the title to *Dragon Warrior*. The second more substantial overhaul was the language. It was already a steep technological challenge to fit a revised alphabet and script in ROM, but Horii's idiosyncratic literary style was equally difficult to adapt to English. The localization team instead chose to adhere to *Dragon Quest*'s Western fantasy roots, adopting elevated Elizabethan English, replete with thees and thous. Though the localization was particularly well executed, especially compared to its contemporaries, the script, pared of Horii's quirks, lost all of its playful character and felt anachronistic in light of Toriyama's lively character designs.

Nonetheless, Enix put considerable effort into the technical translation. All character sprites were expanded to allow them to move in any direction. Beyond the aesthetic improvement of no longer "crab-walking" across Alefgard, the change eliminated the need to specify speaking direction in the command window. Enix also added corner tiles for the shoreline, so water curved more naturally around terrain edges. Finally, *Dragon Warrior*'s mapper upgrade from CNROM to MMC1 allowed the developers to scrap the poetic password system, trading Basho for batteries.

While Toriyama's art was a strong selling point in Japan, his name carried little cultural cache in the States. Consequently, all of the game's packaging, manuals, and marketing materials were updated with westernized fantasy artwork. While exceptionally crafted, these localizations did not exude the same charm as Toriyama's creations. Both boxes depicted the same scene—a warrior facing a dragon with a castle framed in the distance—but the NES version received a more dramatic, painterly cover, with the hero's face obscured, in favor of the sharp lines and squat figures of the original.

Initially, Nintendo tried to position *Dragon Warrior* as a spiritual successor to *The Legend of Zelda*. In the Winter 1987 issue of *Nintendo Fun Club News*, the newsletter precursor to *Nintendo Power*, a sneak peek of *Dragon Warrior* promised that it was "as challenging as *The Legend of Zelda*!" and, "If you liked the interactive video challenge of *The Legend of Zelda*, you'll love *Dragon Warrior*."[75] Although the newsletter circulated over a year after the game's Famicom debut, the screenshots clearly depicted *Dragon Quest* pre-localization: sprites were unchanged, characters only faced forward, and the shoreline tiles remained hard-edged. Furthermore, all proper names of characters and locations still referred to the Japanese originals. Apparently even the cartridge hardware was not yet settled, since the feature mentioned visiting the King to retrieve the "Mantra of Resurrection," i.e., a password.

Closer to the game's August 1989 release, Nintendo initiated a months-long marketing push in *Nintendo Power*. *Dragon Warrior*, billed as "Nintendo's own long-awaited role-playing adventure," first appeared in the Previews section of the May/June 1989 issue. Clearly foretelling the game's fate stateside, its Power Meter scores—*Nintendo Power*'s editorial review metric—ranked lower than the other four games previewed in the same issue, namely *Mega Man 2*, *Faxanadu*, *Uncle Fester's Quest*, and *Clash at Demonhead*. The following issue had a lengthy *Dragon Warrior* feature but gave the coveted cover spot to Capcom's *Mega Man 2*. Nonetheless, for months after the game's release, *Nintendo Power* devoted dozens of pages to the game in hopes of generating a hit.[76]

Since Nintendo employees had full control over the magazine's content, a game's editorial coverage was an important barometer for how a game was regarded internally. And though *Nintendo Power*'s articles often verged on advertorial, editors Gail Tilden and Howard Phillips tried to steer players clear of low quality games. As Tilden remarked in a 2012 interview, "we still had a concern that people would buy games that they didn't enjoy, and if a family made too many poor purchasing decisions, purchasing products that weren't terrific, then they would walk away from being involved with the NES."[77] In light of Nintendo's push to make *Dragon Warrior* a hit, its placement behind lead stories on *Mega Man 2* and *Faxanadu* did not speak well of *Nintendo Power*'s editorial opinion.[78]

Thy Hit Decreased

Apparently undaunted by internal peer review, Nintendo optimistically manufactured a massive stock of *Dragon Warrior* game paks. But their eagerness to circumvent retail supply problems overshot consumer demand. The gap in release between its Japanese and American debuts made *Dragon Warrior* appear retrograde in comparison to other RPGs. And it was. Famicom players were already enjoying several *Dragon Quest* sequels, games that expanded the formula of the original by adding multi-member parties, battles against multiple enemies, non-linear narratives, and customizable character classes. An early preview in *EGM* reflected the game's Western reception: "Nintendo's highly touted Dragon Warrior (Dragon Quest) isn't that special at all. Go play Ultima from FCI and you'll practically get the same game!"[79] *Dragon Quest*'s linear grind seemed out of fashion, ironically even in comparison to the games that had influenced it.

    Dragon Warrior did not simply suffer from a lack of inspiration—partly it failed because a console RPG market did not yet exist. But Arakawa was confident Nintendo could create one. *Nintendo Power* spent months priming its readers with gameplay previews, backstory, screen shots, and promises that *Dragon Warrior* would redefine console games for every possible demographic:

> The introduction of Dragon Warrior represents more than just the release of a new game. It marks the beginning of a new and different direction for NES games. A few other RPGs have preceded this release, but none comes close to being part of as monumental a game series as Dragon Warrior. In Japan, this is the game that launched three sequels, and is unmatched in popularity. By devoting a larger percentage of Game Pak memory to game depth, game play has evolved into a much more complex and rewarding adventure. In addition, mere finger-speed and sweat are no match for the challenges which lie in wait for every player. Now more than ever before, an era of deductive reasoning is challenging us all to excel—young and old, male and female. Your NES is coming of age.[80]

But *Dragon Warrior* did not prove to be the landmark title Arakawa and Nintendo desired. No measure of lofty rhetoric could overshadow the fact that by 1989, the game was outdated and outmatched compared to its peers. Though they shared the same mapper profile, *Mega Man II* outclassed the aging RPG in graphics, gameplay, and sound. Sophisticated platformers—not Japanese RPGs—marked the NES's coming of age. But it wasn't that RPGs were anathema to American tastes. Square's competing RPG *Final Fantasy* proved that a Japanese RPG could be successful, especially with *Nintendo Power* backing its cause. *Dragon Warrior* had simply lost its unique spirit through time and translation.

Less than a decade after the late-to-market *Radar Scope* cabinets sat unsold in a warehouse, Nintendo once again faced an oversupply of a dated game Americans simply did not want. And once again, they spun their failure into a success. In a clever marketing move, Nintendo offered *Dragon Warrior* for free to new and renewed subscribers of the fledgling *Nintendo Power*. They brought Enix's RPG to market by force, flooding American homes with free copies of the game. By Nintendo's account, the stunt brought in nearly half a million new subscribers and introduced *Dragon Warrior* to its hard-won American audience.[81]

Big Boss

While the *Dragon Quest* team expanded the scope of role-playing and storytelling in console games, other developers used the new capabilities of discrete logic and ASIC mappers to create visual special effects that were previously impossible on the Famicom.

Boss fights are a staple of videogame design. As their honorary title indicates, bosses are higher-ranking enemy combatants that challenge the player's accumulated skills, typically blocking access to later stages until defeated. Though prototypical forms existed in the arcade era—the concluding round of Amstar Electronics' *Phoenix* (1980), for instance, pitted the player's starship against an enormous mothership, and Williams Electronics' *Sinistar* (1982) featured a fearsome, skull-faced spaceship that used a special digital audio chip to verbally taunt the player—the cyclic nature of arcade gameplay typically did not map well to the sense of progression and finality gained from boss fights. Even in *Donkey Kong*, Jumpman never directly battled the ape, opting instead to decouple the girders beneath his feet; once complete, the level loop would begin anew. In most early arcade games, if there was a boss, it was not the game's culmination, but a checkpoint along the path to higher difficulties.

Super Mario Bros. once again embodied the median point between arcade and console forms. The Great Demon King Koopa was the game's singular boss who appeared at the end of each world. Though the Koopa Kings seen prior to World 8–4 were cast as impostors hiding lesser enemies, they used the same sprites and featured only minor pattern variations—namely, spewing fewer flame and hammer projectiles. Once 8–4 was complete, Mario's quest concluded with a congratulatory message from Princess Peach and her encouragement to continue playing at a higher skill level. In short, players could tackle the game in two ways: continue the cycle and compete for higher scores—a gameplay holdover from its arcade roots—or take satisfaction that they had beaten Koopa, the final boss, and thus the game.

As Famicom games grew in sophistication, the size and complexity of boss fights evolved in kind. At the platform level, bosses sorted into two general types: sprite- and background-based. The former were more mobile, but OAM limitations set an upper limit on their size, lest their bodies devolve into a flickering mess. Konami's 1986 FDS title *Akumajō Dracula* (aka *Castlevania*) drew from a menagerie of film and literary sources to stock its boss rooms with enormous sprite-based adversaries for Simon Belmont to slay, but the crowd of moving bodies and projectiles resulted in significant sprite flickering.

In contrast, bosses built from background tiles could fill the screen, but were limited to a few (or no) moving parts. Konami's 1988 port of *Contra* featured monstrous architectural boss creatures, but they were largely static background tiles embellished with sprite appendages or projectiles to add movement. The H. R. Giger-inspired, xeno-mechanical creature waiting atop Stage 3's waterfall, for instance, had no moving elements beyond its gaping maw and two writhing arms, whose complex gesticulations and impressive size caused considerable CPU slowdown and OAM cycling.

The *Mega Man* series struck a compromise between sprite- and background-based foes. The level-ending robot masters, typically comparable to Mega Man's size, were built from sprites, as was made clear from the frequent OAM cycling that occurred when combat ensued. But once the players cleared the robot masters, Mega Man could assail Dr. Wily's castle, a multi-stage gauntlet populated by several screen-size bosses that moved around the screen with startling agility.

In the first Dr. Wily stage of *Mega Man 2*, for example, Mega Man must ascend the face of Wily's hideout, which stretches seven screens tall. Upon reaching its apex, Mega Man proceeds right through a corridor that opens into a cavernous interior. The muted blue backdrop of the evening sky transitions to a stark black void festooned with green cabling. The walkway ends abruptly, forcing Mega Man to jump across two suspended platforms. The second of these leads to a series of precarious 16x16-pixel blocks, first arranged in a brief sinusoidal pattern, then extending in a straight line toward the right edge of the screen.

Navigating the Mega Man-width blocks is difficult enough considering their irregular height and spacing, but the platforming difficulty is quickly compounded by the sudden appearance of the enormous Mecha Dragon, the end level boss who rises from the darkness below. Mecha takes chase on the lefthand side of the screen as Mega Man hops along the hanging blocks (figure 6.6). If the player loses pace, Mecha destroys the robotic hero with a single touch.

Both the single-block platforms and Mecha's appearance mark fascinating behind-the-scenes structural transitions. The first cue is a scroll change. For the majority of the level, scrolling is player-controlled, split between distinct horizontal and vertical sections. Once Mega Man crosses the gap between the fifth and sixth hanging platform, however, there's a noticeable hitch as the engine switches to automatic scrolling. However, the new fixed scroll rate is an illusion coordinated by a clever graphical trick. The third hanging block that Mega Man crosses is actually the final metatile drawn from the background pattern table. Once the scroll index passes the third block, both name tables are cleared to blank tiles. The remaining blocks onscreen are no longer background tiles, but sprites that track across the screen at a fixed rate, maintaining the "autoscroll" illusion.[82] The visible hitch signals the engine's transition from hardware scrolling to simulated sprite scrolling.

The static black background sets the stage for Mecha's appearance. Once Mega Man lands on the eighth hanging block, a stack of green sprites appear from the bottom of the screen, a bit of visual flair animating Mecha warping into place behind Mega Man. A few frames later, with Mecha's name table tiles in place, the background palettes flip on and the robotic dragon appears. As Mecha takes chase, Mega Man must hop nimbly from block to block until scrolling ceases and the final confrontation takes place.

Mecha is surprisingly well-animated considering its size. The dragon bobs up and down as it pursues Mega Man, then makes a series of vertical and horizontal attack movements during combat. Portions of its body also animate—namely the hinged jawline, tiny flapping wings, and the lower portion of the tail. The wings and jaw in particular cross the sprite-heavy rows near the upper region of the screen, where they frequently coincide with the status bars, floating platforms, and Mega Man, triggering noticeable OAM cycling. Though sprites handle the Mecha's individual appendage kinematics, scrolling updates govern its body position. Tracking the "camera" over the static name table achieves two effects: it simulates Mecha's attack movements without needing to update any tiles and permits the smooth movement of a large non-sprite object. The flat black background and sprite platforms are necessary to sell the effect. If there were any other decorative elements in the background, they would scroll along with Mecha's body and break the illusion.

Sizable moving enemies set against a solid black background evolved into a Famicom convention (figure 6.6). Any time players reached a level's finale and the background suddenly transitioned to black, they could expect that a massive boss was about to appear. Genres and settings that naturally afforded black backgrounds, like space shooters or underground lairs, made natural fits for such encounters—though most any game could shoehorn them in by suddenly fading to black.

6.6 Massive bosses set against a black backdrop became a recurrent design motif in mid- and late-era Famicom/NES games. Pictured clockwise from upper left: *Mega Man 2*, *Salamander*, *METAFIGHT*, *Isolated Warrior*. (Source: NES-001 PowerPak capture)

Konami's 1987 space-shooter *Salamander* (aka *Life Force*) almost exclusively portrayed its boss menagerie of weird one-eyed brains, floating skulls, and flying dragons using background tiles. As the player's ship approached the end of a level, the existing terrain would either abruptly end or dissolve from view using an elegant tile animation. Sunsoft's 1988 Famicom cart 超惑星戦記 *METAFIGHT* (aka *Blaster Master*) fused vehicle-based platforming segments with overhead *Zelda*-style subterranean levels. Each of the latter areas culminated, like *Salamander*, in a room whose background evaporated to make way for the boss to appear. NTVIC's axonometric shooter *Isolated Warrior* peppered its boss battles with impressive mid-screen raster effects that could stretch creatures across the screen. And finally, Nintendo's *Super Mario Bros. 3* showcased an innovative hybrid form—Koopa's multi-screen airships—where the level itself became the boss (which, in turn, contained its own boss room). The same concessions applied; the ships had to sail against a monochrome sky so scrolling changes could make them appear to bob up and down.

Part of the impulse to create screen-filling bosses stemmed from platform competition. As new consoles, arcade hardware, and PCs entered the market with better specs, Famicom developers aimed to match the former's graphical capabilities, often by using the PPU in unconventional ways. British game designers Ste and John Pickford, for instance, cut their teeth on European PCs like the ZX Spectrum and Amstrad CPC. When they began work on *Ironsword: Wizards & Warriors II* and *Solar Jetman: Hunt for the Golden Warship*, both released in 1989, the NES was far outclassed graphically by contemporary PCs. Ste was designing most of the graphics in Deluxe Paint (DPaint),[83] an Amiga graphics editor, then conforming those designs to the NES's PPU which was, he wrote, "designed for scrolling video games, not static, detailed images."[84]

Highly detailed static images were a common sight during PC loading screens, a phenomenon unknown to cartridge-based systems. Ste's background in designing loading artwork shifted to the NES's elaborate title/attract screens (an arcade holdover) and screen-sized bosses. During *Ironsword*'s design, Ste explains:

I think we were obsessed with trying to make impossibly large creatures when we were designing this game, as loads of the bosses and sub-bosses were made using either all the sprites available, or using the background as part of the creature instead of just sprites. The Dragon King's body is made of characters and is part of the background. Only his head and neck actually moves, and only that is made of sprites. It's also fairly vertical so that it doesn't fall foul of the NES limit of only eight hardware sprites on any horizontal line. I thought this was dead clever at the time.[85]

Much of the artwork that arose from European NES developers was strikingly detailed compared to that of Japanese and American developers. *Solar Jetman*, for example, had painterly interstitials that were commonplace in Amiga games, but rare for the NES.

Clearly the influx of competitor platforms in the late 1980s and early 1990s pushed developers to wring unconventional tricks from an aging platform. From Donkey Kong's construction from background tiles to Dr. Wily's devious contraptions to the Pickford's adaptations of PC practices, programmers continually used the Famicom's sprite and background pattern tables against type in an effort to mimic newer, more advanced platforms.

Game Genie

Nintendo was not the sole arbiter of their console's hardware extensions. All manner of rapid-fire joysticks, head-mounted and voice-activated controllers, inflatable boxing opponents, 3D glasses, drawing pads, and even exercise bike attachments came to market in hopes of extending the console's capabilities and cashing in on Nintendo's market dominance. Most of these were ill-advised gimmicks with little software support—like Brøderbund's majestically awful U-Force infrared motion controller—posing no threat to Nintendo's console integrity. But one accessory managed to raise Nintendo's ire to the point of litigation.

Codemasters' Game Genie was a cartridge extension that bridged between the NES and its game paks. Booting the device dropped players in a custom BIOS (the "Code Screen")—three rows of blanks wherein players could enter up to three codes before booting their game pak. Game Genie publisher Galoob also included a sizable *Programming Manual and Codebook* with codes for over two hundred games. Each title had a small, lighthearted blurb describing its gameplay and a few recommended code combinations. The number of codes were generally weighted toward popularity—a title like *Wheel of Fortune* had only four listings, while *Super Mario Bros. 3* had thirty-eight.

Most codes granted standard gameplay buffs: extra lives, additional ammo, larger treasure stores, infinite continues, etc. Others created handicaps—starting with a single life, less fuel, limited continues—to challenge more experienced players. The most interesting codes tinkered with game engine parameters governing physics, drop rates, or enemy behaviors. Such tweaks allowed players to "sequence break" portions of the game, access otherwise inaccessible areas, or simply crash the game. Most of the entries for *Super Mario Bros.*, for instance, bestowed Mario and Luigi with extraordinary jumping abilities or introduced "moon gravity," both of which allowed them to jump over most of the stage's obstacles, including the flagpole. Some codes improved play, like the *Donkey Kong Classics* entry that retrofitted Mario with "air control," overriding his fixed-arc jumps. Others created weird or quirky effects, like the *Mega Man 2* code that made Mega Man appear to moonwalk backward or the *Archon* codes that granted players unrestricted movement across the chessboard.[86]

The published codes were not the sole corpus of cheats. Codemasters designed the Game Genie with expansion in mind. The back of the codebook included an order form for quarterly "Code Update issues," which provided subscribers codes for new games and updates for older titles. The codebook also included a three-page "Video Game Home Programming" section with tips for modifying codes. Though players could type in letters at random, Codemasters recommended simple two-letter substitutions to generate variations of working codes. Regardless of method, the point was to dive in and experiment, as the codebook reassured players, "Remember, programming is an art that requires lots of patient, trial-and-error experimenting! The techniques will not work on all codes, but keep trying until you discover a code that works."[87] Though using the Game Genie was not programming in the conventional sense, the software interface did provide a straightforward means to indirectly manipulate the game's ROM without fear of damaging the cartridge or console. Codemasters reminded users multiple times that any errant codes could always be fixed with a reset: "If a code you program interrupts the game or causes an undesired effect, just turn off the power and turn it on again, and then program different codes to play."[88]

The Game Genie hardware was a gold shell roughly half the length of a standard NES cartridge. Its lower end had a protruding card edge connector to attach to cartridges, while the opposite end had its own recessed 72-pin PCB meant to slot into the console. A flexible plastic guide extended from the bottom and fit the length of the attached cart. The guide had a molded plastic grip that served three purposes: halting the appendage's insertion at the proper depth, "catching" the console's lid (which had to remain open while the Game Genie was inside), and giving the player a handle that could remove the cartridge without leaving the Game Genie lodged inside the NES. The end result was a less cumbersome version of the unlicensed HES piggyback carts used to circumvent the NES's CIC (chapter 3).

However, the protruding design worsened the flaws of the NES-001's ZIF mechanism. The Game Genie's connecting end was slightly larger than a standard game pak, so it required greater force to insert and remove, and the rather low-tech plastic guide was not a reliable means of ensuring that players did not insert the Game Genie further than recommended. Even when properly seated, the game pak hung beyond the console's lip. With prolonged abuse, the NES's pin connectors would warp and bend; distended pins created poorer contacts with cartridges; poorer contacts led to blinking screens. And since the console's door could not close while the Game Genie was in use, its interior was more susceptible to dust, moisture, and other debris. The peripheral's sole physical benefit was eliminating the need to seat cartridges, saving wear and tear on the ZIF's spring mechanism.

With the hardware fitted properly and a game inserted, players powered on the NES as they normally would. The peripheral's physical position allowed it first dibs at program execution, so players were booted directly into the Game Genie's custom BIOS. The interface had a chunky pixel look reminiscent of an Atari VCS port of Hangman. However, the throwback aesthetic was a space-saving measure. Codemasters drew all of the interface elements with sixteen tiles and seven colors (one of which cycled to produce a rainbow strobing effect). Most of the graphics were background tiles—only the pointer hand, "swirling star" cursor, and the animated tiles used to float or explode letters were sprites—though both background and sprite tiles drew from the same pattern pool.

Each tile's 8x8-pixel matrix was split into four quadrants, creating "meta-pixels" that effectively reduced tile resolutions from sixty-four pixels to four. All onscreen BIOS graphics were then drawn using the sixteen variations of filled and unfilled meta-pixels (figure 6.7).

The result was an innovative subversion of the Famicom's tile-based graphic system. Instead of rendering unique tiles for each graphical element, Codemasters created a generic set of pattern tiles with which

6.7 This annotated excerpt from the Game Genie ROM's pattern table shows the sixteen sprite/background tiles used to draw the Game Genie's user interface. (Emulator: FCEUX 2.1.5)

to build all of their onscreen objects, much like Nakamura had done in *Portopia*. Such memory savings were necessary because the Game Genie only had 4KB of PRG-ROM, a mere quarter of even the most basic NROM boards. Simplifying the GUI served to minimize the memory devoted to visual elements, freeing up space for code logic.

Like its enclosing hardware, the Game Genie software was parasitic—it operated on the host system, but intercepted data flow between cartridge and console. The Game Genie could watch for reads in program memory ($8000-$FFFF) for up to three addresses, intercept the intended value, then substitute new data in its place. This form of code manipulation was similar in function to the PEEK and POKE commands (used to read and set the contents of memory, respectively) popular among hobbyist PC programmers in the 1970s and 80s. However, Codemasters purposefully obfuscated their interception algorithm to prevent easy reverse engineering by players and market competitors alike.

The Game Genie's cryptography worked by coding hexadecimal values to letters then rearranging their sequence. There were sixteen letters available on the Game Genie screen, one for each hexadecimal digit, arranged in two rows of eight: A, E, P, O, Z, X, L, U and G, K, I, S, T, V, Y, N. Players could enter up to three codes per game, each either six or eight letters long (though some effects required multi-line codes). Six-letter codes devoted four bytes to the desired 16-bit address and two bytes to the data value. Eight-letter codes used their additional two bytes for a comparison check value that served as a simple work-around for bank switching.[89] If the proper bank was in place, then the comparison value would match the value at that address; only then could the new data value be returned. If an unexpected bank was in place, the comparison would fail and the Game Genie would return the expected value in PRG-ROM. In most cases, the comparison worked, but there was no failsafe—the check would not work properly if identical values for separate variables were stored in the same address in multiple banks.

To illustrate a simple example, the *Super Mario Bros.* code AATOZA reduces Mario and Luigi's initial life count to 1. As seen in row 2 of the table below, the code letters translate to the hexadecimal string $006920. And since the Game Genie code-parsing algorithm shifts individual bits, we will expand the individual hex digits to binary:[90]

A	A	T	O	Z	A
0	0	6	9	2	0
0000	0000	0110	1001	0010	0000
1678	H234	+IJK	LABC	DMNO	5EFG

The *bolded* binary digits comprise the data value the code intends to pass to an address. Beneath each digit is a numeral between 1 and 8, indicating the order in which the data value is reassembled. The example above is simple to reconstruct: %00000000, or $00. The remaining digits comprise the code's desired address, this time labeled in order from character A to O. The final bit, labeled with the + sign, is a flag indicating the length of the code—0 for six characters and 1 for eight. Note that this leaves us with a 15-bit address. Since addresses map between $8000 and $FFFF, the high bit is always assumed to be 1.[91] Thus our final address is $1001 0000 0110 1010 = $906A. Consulting the *Super Mario Bros.* disassembly, we find the value read from that address is #$02 = 2, which is subsequently stored in RAM at $075A and $0761, the locations of both players' default starting lives.[92] In *SMB*, the life count displayed is one higher than the stored variable, so substituting the Game Genie value #$00 = 0 at that location sets the default lives to 1, as advertised.

Galoob's peripheral was an instant hit, soliciting 550,000 orders following its 1990 announcement. But Galoob clearly understood Nintendo's penchant to litigate any hardware that circumvented their licensing structure, as they sought a preemptive "declaratory judgment that its Game Genie did not violate any of Nintendo's property rights"[93] and an "injunction prohibiting Nintendo from interfering with the marketing of the Game Genie," including modifying the NES.[94] Nintendo retaliated with their own injunction against the Game Genie's sale, citing copyright infringement. Nintendo successfully delayed the Game Genie's debut for over a year but ultimately lost the case. Galoob's lawyers argued that the peripheral did not create infringing derivative works, but "adaptations" that were covered under fair use.[95] As recompense, Galoob was awarded a $15 million bond paid by Nintendo to make up for lost sales during the preliminary injunction. When Nintendo later appealed the payout, Galoob triumphed again. The Game Genie hit U.S. shelves in August 1991, posting one million sales by the end of the year and eventually selling as many as 6.5 million units worldwide.[96]

No POKEs

Codemasters had another hardware trick up their sleeve, but this time aimed at manipulating software costs rather than software cheats. In November 1992, Codemasters partner publisher Camerica released the Aladdin Deck Enhancer, a black plastic cartridge that housed swappable "Compact Cartridges." The Enhancer was shaped similarly to a conventional NES game pak with a trapezoidal portion of its lower half missing.

Codemasters devised a novel approach to game manufacture and distribution that would leverage the Nintendo's split ROM architecture (chapter 1): the Enhancer contained a custom CIC override, mapper, and 8KB of CHR-RAM for shared use across multiple games, while individual Compact Cartridges contained a single 256KB PRG-ROM IC soldered to a slim PCB. Customers could purchase inexpensive Compact Cartridges separately, then slide them into the Enhancer to form a complete game pak.

The back of the Enhancer's box boasted its "64K memory upgrade for better graphics, bigger games!" alongside Camerica's prediction that, "Aladdin is the future in console game play." Exactly how this 64K was an upgrade and in relation to what was unclear. Detaching the CHR-RAM and mapper from the PRG-ROM made great economic sense, but neither mapper nor RAM provided any benefit not found in conventional game paks. Tellingly, the Aladdin's sole six Compact Cartridges were later released as standard carts, albeit in Camerica's distinctive gold cartridges.[97]

The Deck Enhancer's quick demise was based more on circumstance than confusing hardware promises or lackluster software. Both *Dizzy the Adventurer* and *Fantastic Adventures of Dizzy* were quality adventure games drawn from a series that had proven successful on European PC platforms. *Micro Machines* was likewise one of the NES's finest top-down racing games. But Camerica folded just before Aladdin's debut, forcing Codemasters to assume North American distribution responsibilities at the zero hour. Worse still, by late 1992, the NES had already been replaced by the Super Nintendo, rendering any game pak innovations largely moot. Ultimately, the Aladdin and its games saw limited release—a good idea birthed too late in the console life cycle.

It is no surprise that Aladdin and the Game Genie arose from a European developer. Since the videogame industry was born and raised in the United States, most videogame histories focus heavily on that region, despite the fact that the European videogame industry followed its own trajectory, showing a markedly larger interest in PCs than dedicated consoles.[98] The 1983 crash, in particular, is often given an implicit worldwide scope, when in reality it primarily derailed the U.S. videogame industry. Japan's PC market was isolated but thriving—led by native manufacturers NEC, Fujitsu, and Sharp—and the Famicom, of course, would debut the same year that the crash began. In Europe, consoles had not become as entrenched as they had in the U.S. Instead, true to the *New York Times*'s prediction quoted in chapter 4, PCs were becoming the videogame machines of choice.

In England there was intense competition in the low-cost PC market, spearheaded by Clive Sinclair's eponymous 1980 PC, the Sinclair ZX80, which cost just £99.95 fully assembled.[99] Its low cost put computers into the hands of those who could not afford the pricier Commodore PET or Apple II—or even dedicated videogame consoles. As videogame historian Donovan writes, "The success of the ZX80 marked the moment when affordable home computing became a reality in Britain."[100] A cottage industry of game programmers and basement businesses grew up around the budget machine, selling their games on cassette (the cheaper alternative to floppy disks) via mail-order and local computer shops. The Sinclair symbolized the DIY programming equivalent of three chords and a guitar in punk rock—for £99.95, you could be a videogame rockstar. The PC was a tool for creative expression that closed console architectures could not replicate.

Throughout the 1980s, improvements to the Sinclair line, like the popular ZX Spectrum (1982), thrived alongside the Commodore 64, Amstrad CPC, Oric-1, and the government-funded BBC Micro. These and similar low-cost alternatives disseminated beyond Britain into France, Spain, Germany, and Australia.[101] Platform-specific publications like *Zzap!64* and *The Micro User* formed to support the major PC formats, and their writers and subscribers largely viewed dedicated videogame consoles as ossified, retrograde technology. Game cartridges, which cost upward of £60, struggled to compete with cassettes priced at £1.99 (regardless of the latter format's abysmal loading times). Furthermore, PCs cultivated an active subculture of software piracy, trading, and modification.

In the 1987 debut issue of UK magazine *The Games Machine*, just a few months prior to the NES's first British Christmas season, the editors provided an overview of the Famicom from a decidedly PC-centric perspective: "As the Nintendo doesn't have keyboard facilities, POKEs cannot be entered to modify games. To compensate, hidden cheat modes abound..."[102] From the European perspective, Nintendo's console was a walled garden. Such restrictions were unfamiliar to a computing culture reared on the open architecture of PCs. The only barrier to entry in the Spectrum market was hardware ownership and some programming chops; Nintendo, meanwhile, exacted licensing agreements and total control over manufacture, marketing, and content. The games reflected opposing philosophies—Nintendo was the platform for family-friendly play; PCs offered that and every other imaginable genre.

Furthermore, by 1987, the NES's aging 6502 struggled to keep pace with modern PCs, a fact exacerbated by Nintendo's lack of retail experience outside Japan and the U.S. They first partnered with Mattel, granting them distribution rights in the UK, Italy, and Australia, but the toy company fumbled spectacularly, angering important UK retail partners by announcing deals before they were secured.[103] In 1988, Nintendo spun off Nintendo Entertainment Systems International (NESI) in hopes of correcting their distribution misstep, but "in the absence of any sales and distribution infrastructure and little UK marketing expertise, sales continued to falter at less than 600 hardware units per month."[104] In subsequent years, Nintendo passed marketing and distribution duties to Serif (marketers for *Trivial Pursuit* and *Pictionary*), then Bandai (the toy company behind Teenage Mutant Ninja/Hero Turtles as well as Famicom development veterans), before once again grabbing the reins in 1995.[105]

The NES eventually found minor success in European markets, thanks to the appeal of its first-party software catalog and licensed retail bundles,[106] but that success paled in comparison to Nintendo's near-monopolistic command of the U.S. and Japanese markets. Nintendo's late regional expansions found them floundering in territories indifferent to dedicated consoles and the software cultures they signified.

Extended Attributes

Throughout the Famicom's life span, Nintendo produced several ASIC mappers, which grew in capability and specialty, allowing the Famicom to break many of its own hardware rules. MMCs not only administered bank switching, but eventually implemented scanline counters (to replace sprite 0's screen-splitting function), onboard PPU-RAM, and additional sound channels (chapter 7).

Nintendo named its chips in sequence, from MMC1 (April 1987) to MMC6 (December 1990).[107] Higher sequence numbers did not necessarily indicate better features, increased adoption by developers, or discontinued manufacture of previous mappers. Nor did ASIC mappers obsolete discrete logic boards. Price considerations and per-game memory requirements dictated a developer's choice of mapper.[108] MMC1's and MMC3's balance of cost and capabilities made them the most popular ASIC choices, accounting for roughly 13% and 33% of Famicom and NES mappers, respectively.[109] Other mappers saw limited use or offered slight variations on previous models. MMC2 was used in a single game—*Mike Tyson's Punch-Out!!*—while the similar MMC4 mapper appeared in fewer than five.

Nintendo's penultimate ASIC mapper, MMC5, was its most powerful. The usual answer to lagging hardware was a peripheral add-on, but the MMC5 was a console upgrade housed in a cartridge. Beyond the increased cartridge size (which applied only to Famicom carts—NES game paks already had the adequate height), the hardware augmentation was imperceptible. The games magically looked and sounded better.

The MMC5's flagship feature was an additional 1KB of multi-purpose onboard memory called Extended RAM, or ExRAM. ExRAM had a control register ($5104) that allowed the programmer to select from several modes. In one mode, ExRAM served as a third, supplementary name table which, used in concert with MMC5's flexible mirroring options, allowed previously impossible name table arrangements. The diagram below shows one such configuration using the console's standard name tables (A and B) in a "diagonal" configuration, augmented by the additional ExRAM name table (X):

```
[ A ][ B ]
[ X ][ A ]
```

With three name tables on hand, games could theoretically scroll both vertically or horizontally with a full screen's worth of graphics "buffered" on either side, eliminating attribute glitches without relying on sprite columns, clipping masks, or other workaround solutions.

ExRAM also provided an extended attribute mode that bypassed the PPU's attribute tables in favor of the data held in ExRAM, which at 1KB capacity could provide a byte-for-byte palette-to-name table match. In other words, each 8x8-pixel background tile could have an individual palette assignment rather than sharing its color data with three other tiles. *Just Breed*, a Famicom-exclusive RPG published by Enix in 1992, used MMC5's extended attribute mode to paint vivid backgrounds that rivaled those seen in early Super Famicom titles. The in-town architecture boasted conical spires and spherical vegetation that blended seamlessly into the surrounding backgrounds. Shadows cast realistically from the edges of buildings. Even intricate shorelines cut convincingly between ocean and grassland without abrupt attribute clashes.

Another novel addition was support for a vertical screen split. MMC5 could monitor the PPU's current background tile fetch on a given scanline and trigger a name table split at a specified tile position. HAL's 1990 space shooter 宇宙警備隊SDF was the only game to use the feature, and even then it reserved the vertical split for a brief opening attract sequence. Figure 6.8 shows the split screen in use. The gridded region with the ship

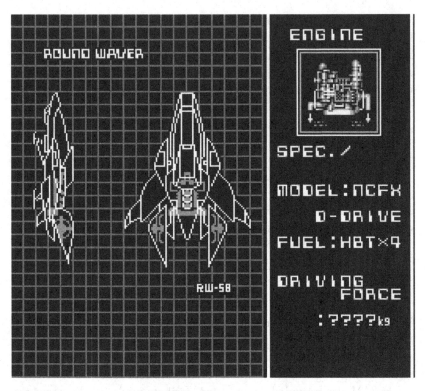

6.8 The attract mode from 宇宙警備隊SDF is the only commercial example of MMC5's vertical split screen function. (Emulator: Nestopia v1.40)

schematic uses a standard VRAM name table, while the rightmost bordered region is filled with contents of the ExRAM name table. Once each ship part's specs are displayed, the rightmost region scrolls in the next entry from the bottom of the screen.

The effect required quite a bit of technological wizardry for minimal visual payoff, especially in light of the vertical split's limitations. The split region could only contain the contents of ExRAM and, dependent on the side selected, could only display the corresponding region of the name table's contents. Though the opposing side could scroll normally, there was no horizontal scroll control over the split region. Consequently, any vertical scrolling in the split region would behave as if vertically mirrored, i.e., wrapping at the top or bottom.[110] If there were any useful gameplay applications of the vertical screen split, *SDF*'s brief use of the feature does not give us any indication of its potential.

MMC5 also had several less exotic features. The board could address PRG-ROM/RAM and CHR-ROM capacities up to a staggering 1,024KB

(1MB). The flexibility of banking options was equally impressive—both PRG and CHR supported four independent banking modes with bank sizes between 8KB and 64KB for the former and 1KB and 8KB for the latter.[111] In 8x16 sprite mode MMC5's CHR-ROM register setup also permitted games to access 12KB of CHR-ROM. Separate 8KB and 4KB register access allowed programmers to reference 512 sprites and 256 background tiles simultaneously without bank switching.[112]

Despite its litany of features, few MMC5 games were manufactured.[113] The chip's limited adoption was a function of chronology and cost. MMC5 did not appear until late in the Famicom's lifespan and it was expensive compared to other capable mappers. Unless the game was a sure hit or otherwise demanded MMC5's capabilities, the added cost was not worth the investment, especially if alternative mappers sufficed. For the purposes of most games, MMC3 and MMC1 offered all the features developers needed. And if they wanted advanced scrolling, better attribute control, and increased name table space, it made more sense to switch development to the superior Super Famicom.

Those developers that did opt for the advanced IC only used a fraction of its feature set, primarily taking advantage of its extraordinary ROM capacities. Koei used the MMC5 more than any other publisher, porting their popular historical strategy games from PC platforms to the Famicom and NES. However, games like *Gemfire*, *Uncharted Waters*, and *Bandit Kings of Ancient China* largely used the chip's expanded memory capacity to process in-game statistics and AI decision-making. While *Gemfire*'s box touted its "newest technology for better graphics and game play," "64K RAM with battery backup," and "4 Megabit Cartridge," the in-game results were underwhelming. Koei games had minimal animation, static backgrounds, and a handful of gameplay screens—visually, they could not stack up against an MMC3-based action game like *Super C*.

Nonetheless, showcase MMC5 titles like *Just Breed* demonstrated how far the Famicom had developed in its almost decade-long run in the console videogame market. They were closer in kin to Super Famicom titles than *Donkey Kong* or *Door Door*. *Just Breed*'s gameplay and Koei's simulations were adapting elements from 16-bit RPGs and PC strategy games rather than their own 8-bit predecessors. Influences from the "next generation" were folding back in on the prior generation. The console's late-generation titles remind us that the Famicom did not exist in a technological vacuum—PCs, handhelds, arcades, and successor consoles were pushing developers to expand the Famicom's repertoire into genres it was never designed to manage. And developers were often producing games for multiple platforms simultaneously, so they had to devise techniques to perform similar effects across drastically different architectures.

Though the MMC5 marked the technical peak of Nintendo's Famicom ASIC engineering, third-party manufacturers continue to push mapper technology forward. Even today, manufacturers of new Famicom titles continue to devise mappers to accommodate curious conversions of unlicensed properties and massive multi-carts that shove ten or more games into a single PCB.[114] Chinese manufacturers in particular have engineered mappers to accommodate unlicensed cross-generational conversions of videogames like *Aladdin*, *Street Fighter II*, *Sonic the Hedgehog*, and *Final Fantasy VII*. Though they often bear little resemblance to the originals—*Final Fantasy VII* used 3D polygonal graphics that tile-based systems obviously cannot replicate—they are nonetheless impressive engineering feats, often supporting ROM capacities of several megabytes (and befuddling emulator authors who aim to support such wild hardware variations). And while Nintendo does not sanction such activities, the efforts of piracy continue to support an ecosystem that thrives in regions of the world where Famicom clones offer an economically feasible alternative to expensive modern consoles. Thirty years on, the limits of a console meant to play *Donkey Kong* continue to expand beyond what Nintendo ever could have envisioned for their Family Computer.

I don't use a keyboard or any instruments... It gives you a more open mind, I would say. You're thinking along the lines of the computer and not along the lines of a keyboard or whatever instrument you would use.

— Timothy Follin, *The Making of* Solstice *for NES*, 1990

I programmed the computer and the computer generated the sounds... I was not playing, but somehow, music was coming out.

— Koji Kondo, *Electronic Gaming Monthly* interview, 2005

In August 2013, European net label bitpuritans released *2A03 Puritans*, a compilation of songs composed, true to its title, exclusively with the Famicom's Audio Processing Unit (APU).[1] While the album sounds like a lost archive of NES soundtracks, the range of styles and techniques on display belie its vintage trappings. TQ-Jam's "Milky Fields" begins with a breezy melody reminiscent of a Sunsoft platformer, but midway through shifts to a four-on-the-floor dance beat that sounds distinctly twenty-first century. Likewise, KungFuFurby's sprawling, eleven-minute "Null and Void," while technically feasible on the console, dwarfs the length of any extant NES track. And while *2A03 Puritans* is available in modern formats such as MP3 and FLAC, bitpuritans also provide links to NSFs—a lightweight, community-created format for 2A03 playback—along with the original source files for playback in FamiTracker, a modern composition tool for creating 2A03 music.

While *2A03 Puritans* may sound anachronistic to many contemporary listeners, for several decades *chiptunes*—the popular term used to describe music that targets a specific, usually vintage, sound processor—have sustained a thriving community devoted to making new music for old machines. And while not all chiptune artists ascribe to bitpuritans' Protestant ethic, many do pride themselves on an authentic reproduction of the 2A03's sonic character.[2] But why do electronic musicians who have an almost limitless range of samples, synthesizers, and software at their disposal turn to a thirty year-old processor engineered to generate three simple waveforms, noise, and gritty one-bit samples?

To answer this question, we will take a close look at the APU's design, capabilities, and sound characteristics, along with the hardware designers who tried early on to supplement its simple voices. Accompanying the mapper-based extensions introduced in the previous chapter were audio augmentations that radically altered the Famicom's sound capabilities, but unlike the MMC3 or UNROM, none of these hardware upgrades appeared in cartridges outside Japan. In fact, much of the Famicom's sonic history would be lost without the active efforts of artists devoted to fashioning a videogame platform into a musical instrument.

Crystal Heartbeat

As noted briefly in chapter 1, part of the console's computational core—the 2A03—is an integrated audio processing unit. The APU is a versatile instrument that generates every sputtering engine in *R.C. Pro-Am*, every whip crack in *Castlevania*, every machine gun report in *Contra*, and every percussive shuffle in *Super Mario Bros.* Yet it contains no elements of traditional instruments—no embouchure holes, felt hammers, mylar heads, or horsetail bows. Circuitry does not vibrate to produce sound. Electronic musicians do not pluck traces on a silicon wafer. Bits do not shift air. So how can a processor sing?

The answer is synthesis, the prototypes of which developed in the early twentieth century but reached widespread audiences in the 1960s, when avant-garde composers and pop musicians alike began to incorporate the sounds of electrical circuits—via synthesizers—into their performances. By the 1980s, the synthesizer was ubiquitous in popular music, though not just in the new wave of artists with artfully sculpted hair preening for MTV. The sounds of synthesizers had been a mainstay of videogames since their inception, orchestrating the lockstep march of aliens in *Space Invaders*, the bowing girders in *Donkey Kong*, and the ghost-gobbling chomps in *Pac-Man.* The heritage of sound born in arcades carried on to consoles as well.

The 2A03's sound generator is commonly called a *pseudo* Audio Processing Unit (pAPU) since it lives alongside the 6502 in a single die.[3] Architecturally it is part of the CPU, but programmatically it is treated as a discrete entity—like the PPU, it has its own reserved control registers that may be issued instructions independent of other processes. Composing with the APU is not like composing on a piano. It cannot be played with a keyboard; it has no inherent understanding of notes, scales, or tempo. Instead, composing is identical to programming: audio data is encoded, stored, and interpreted in the same format as code, byte by byte in hexadecimal numerals.

Though most synthesizers are associated with piano keyboards, that connection is a result of cultural, social, and marketing forces, not an inherent technological trait. Synthesis describes the method of sound construction, not an interface or performance style.[4] The first synthesizers had no traditional controllers. A synthesizer's individual modules—oscillators, filters, envelopes—could be patched in various configurations to generate, shape, and modulate sound waves. Playing a modular synthesizer more resembled patching a phone call than strumming a guitar. However, as more traditional (e.g., pop, rock, and jazz) musicians became interested in synthesizers, the demand for more predictable, user-friendly interfaces arose. The piano keyboard mapped well to the pitch relationships desired by musicians who wished to keep their temperamental electronic instruments in tune with an ensemble. For experimental musicians who saw synthesizers as an escape from the confines of traditional melodic structures and playing habits, the keyboard was a regressive addition.[5]

The first synthesizers were also analog instruments. Their discrete electrical components—capacitors, resistors, transistors, etc.—generated continuous variations in voltage that modeled, or were analogous to, the variations in air pressure that produce sound. Such synthesizers included one or more voltage-controlled oscillators (VCOs) to produce predictable voltage fluctuations over time. If the fluctuations cycled at a frequency audible to human ears, once amplified and passed through a material surface, like the cone of a speaker, oscillators made sound.

Analog sound synthesis's genesis from electrical components caused unique usability problems. Temperature and moisture changes could wreak havoc on their circuitry, causing, at best, tuning fluctuations, and at worst, total hardware failure. Digital synthesis promised to smooth the inconsistencies of analog synthesizers by regulating output according to discrete mathematical values. Digitally controlled oscillators (DCOs) replaced continuous voltage signals with a stream of digitally encoded amplitudes, chopped and coded into numeric data. The more slices a processor could make per unit of time, the closer the digital signal modeled the analog source. Via a digital-to-analog converter (DAC), those values were translated back to electrical signals that could then be routed to an amplifier.

The APU, like the majority of console audio hardware, is a digital synthesizer, but its close union with the CPU makes it different than dedicated programmable sound generators (PSGs) found in similar platforms, even those that share a 6502 microprocessor. The Commodore 64's SID chip, for instance, can be stripped from the PC and used as a standalone instrument,[6] which Swedish manufacturer Elektron proved in the late 1990s with the SidStation module, a hardware synthesizer with a SID core that was controllable via MIDI, rotary dials, and a numeric keyboard—no PC required.

There are no such means to extract the Famicom APU from the 2A03. Every tone it generates is synced to the CPU, which in turn is clocked to a crystal oscillator, a vibrating piezoelectric element that generates a precise frequency—21.477272 MHz for the NTSC Famicom/NES and 26.601712 MHz in the PAL NES. To derive each system's CPU clock rate, those frequencies are then divided by either 12 (1.789773 MHz) or 16 (1.662607 MHz) respectively.[7] Though additional dividers slice the system clock into smaller subdivisions and route them to various hardware counters, the Famicom's crystal core is the console's baseline frequency, its central driving heartbeat.[8]

While it is largely free from the stability issues of early analog synthesizers, the APU's union with an 8-bit microprocessor introduces its own peculiarities. In chapter 1, we saw that the difference between NTSC and PAL clock speeds were based on the discrepancy in television refresh rates. Games that relied on precise VBLANK timing (e.g., *Battletoads*) would behave erratically or crash when played on an NES from a mismatched region. Since audio likewise relied on the CPU clock, porting an 60Hz NTSC game to the 50Hz PAL standard without proper sound engine compensation played back the game's music and sound effects at 5/6 the intended speed. Many of Nintendo's early PAL releases, *Donkey Kong* among them, suffered from this problem. Conversely, playing a proper PAL port of a game on an NTSC system (e.g., Tecmo's 1988 title *Shadow Warriors*, the PAL version of *Ninja Gaiden*) would speed up audio in the inverse proportion.

Though musicians endlessly debate the merits of analog vs. digital synthesis, there is no objective metric by which one can say that either produces "better" sounds. Each contributes its own timbre, and even the lowest-quality digital encoding can generate sonic material that composers find musically interesting. For some, the Famicom's five channels would be far too restrictive for serious composition. But for a generation of skilled artists, the 2A03 became a rich platform for creative musical expression.

As a single component in an already complex package, it is remarkable that the Famicom received the five channels it did. Consoles in the 1980s routinely had three or fewer voices at their disposal. The Atari VCS's TIA, for example, which handled both sound and graphics, had only two audio channels, each of which was severely limited in its waveform types and pitch range.[9] The Texas Instruments SN76489, used in the ColecoVision and Sega's SG-1000, a Famicom competitor, had four voices: three square wave generators and a noise channel. In terms of audio capabilities, the Famicom outclassed its peers. Based on its range of voices and hardware effects, the APU was more comparable to a PC PSG than any contemporary console synthesizer.

Sound Shapes

Sounds are described visually by their *waveforms*, the repeating patterns that arise when variations in a signal's intensity (air pressure, voltage, etc.) are plotted over time. In synthesis, these are named according to their general shape—triangle, sine, sawtooth, etc. A signal's *frequency* describes the number of times this pattern repeats per second (measured in Hertz), while its *amplitude* describes the intensity of change. Conventionally, waveforms are graphed with times along the x-axis and amplitude along the y-axis.[10]

Though the APU has five dedicated hardware channels for sound, only three generate waveforms. The first two are nearly-identical pulse waves,[11] named as such because their amplitudes "pulse" on and off with little or no slope in between, creating a visual cadence of rectangles arranged one after the other. Pure pulse waves sound crisp and bright, reminiscent of a clarinet or a distorted electric guitar. Due to their sonic character, they typically take the lead melodic role in Famicom music. When you are humming along to the main themes of *The Legend of Zelda*, *Mega Man*, or *Contra*, you are likely mimicking the pulses.

The third channel is a triangle wave, which in contrast to the pulses, tends to sound mellow, smooth, and muted, like a flute or bowed double bass. Due to an internal hardware difference, the triangle channel covers a wider frequency range than the pulses, meaning that it can stretch to both lower and (much) higher pitches, from near-subsonic bass to ear-piercing squeals.[12] Additionally, unlike the pulse or noise channels, which each have their own 4-bit (16-step) volume control, the triangle has no volume envelope—it is either on or off. In combination, these traits made the triangle channel ideal for bass. And indeed, in most Famicom soundtracks, the triangle handles the low end.

The fourth channel, a pseudo-random noise generator, is unique among its APU peers. By definition, noise is meant to be purely random, meaning that its waveforms exhibit no repeating cyclic pattern and that its frequency content is distributed evenly across the entire spectrum. Translated to musical terms, noise has no pitch. Composers cannot use it to construct melodies or chords because it cannot be tuned. In common parlance, noise is unwanted sound, so why include it as part of synthesizer? Because noise is non-melodic but not non-musical. By carefully sculpting its volume, duration, and playback speed, composers can extract all manner of percussive and special effects, from multi-part drum kits to fiery explosions.

Each channel has its own set of register-level controls, allowing composers to craft the APU's raw waveforms into expressive instruments that can better mimic a range of physical instruments and playing techniques (or craft wholly alien tones). The simplest of these is the *length counter*, which controls the duration of a channel's sound. Notes may be held for variable intervals according to a simple automatic countdown timer, allowing composers to construct meaningful tempo relationships (e.g., whole, half, sixteenth notes) between instruments. In short, the length counter provides a straightforward means to control rhythm.

Excluding the triangle, each channel has a dedicated hardware *envelope*, or a series of values that describe a signal's shape over time, to control it volume. Compared to contemporary synthesizers, the APU's two envelopes are rudimentary: one outputs a single constant volume and the other produces a simple loopable decay.[13] The former is straightforward—set a volume and forget it. The latter is slightly more nuanced, as the channel's volume starts at a specific value then decreases linearly until it reaches zero. While simple in function, the decay envelope helps APU channels mimic instruments that naturally decline in volume over time, like a guitar or piano, instead of shifting jarringly from peak amplitude to silence. Nintendo used the hardware decay in many of their early Famicom soundtracks. *Clu Clu Land*, *Mahjong*, *Donkey Kong*, *Ice Climber*, *Donkey Kong Jr.*, and *Devil World* all set decays on both pulses, usually at staggered lengths, to create gentle volume slopes at the end of each note. When percussive tracks were present (a rarity in 1983), Nintendo's composers used combinations of short and long decays on the noise channel to simulate closed and open hi-hats.

The pulse channels have two special hardware features that no other channel shares. The first is a variable *duty cycle* ratio that can switch between four values: 12.5%, 25%, 50%, and 75%.[14] The percentages describe the proportion of time the waveform spends in its positive versus negative amplitude position in a single period.[15] Altering a pulse wave's duty cycle is a simple way to change its *timbre*, or tone color, without changing its frequency. Narrower duty cycles produce hollow, reedy tones; wider ratios sound thicker in comparison.

In addition to giving each pulse channel three distinct tones to choose from, duty cycles can also be swapped at any time, even mid-note. Duty cycle *modulation*—essentially the rapid variation of pulse width ratios—is one of the APU's (and chiptunes') trademark sounds, mimicking expressive musical effects like the onset of a bandpass filter or the rapid transient of a percussive attack.[16] Moreover, triggering rapid modulations during a single tone creates a distinctive fluttering or warbling effect that can fake arpeggiated runs (i.e., notes in a chord played individually in quick succession) without actually changing the frequency.[17] Konami and subsidiary Data East used this trick to great effect in several of its soundtracks, such as *Bad Dudes* and *Cobra Command*.

The pulses' second hardware feature is a sweep unit. Triggering the effect causes the channel's wavelength to "sweep" up or down at a given rate. Depending on the rate and direction, the audible result is similar to sliding one's finger across the neck of a violin, causing the string's pitch to glide smoothly between notes. Though this same effect is possible by manually updating a pulse's frequency, the sweep unit provides a quicker automatic means to do so. While sweeps have limited musical use beyond rapid note bends, the sweep is particularly useful for generating sound effects like character jumps, sirens, or gunfire.

Human ears perceive changes in frequency as pitch variation. When a pianist moves from left to right on a piano, they are playing notes of increasingly higher frequency, starting at 27.5Hz (pitch A0) and ascending to 4.186kHz (pitch C8). However, piano keys do not represent all possible frequencies between those bounds. To prevent the instrument from being infinitely wide, keys are tuned to specific frequency ratios. Those that sound pleasing to our ears are based on centuries of convention, our cultural heritage, and personal preference. Traditional Indian music uses pitch intervals that may sound unconventional or "out of tune" to North American ears; likewise for African, Asiatic, and other regional musics. Tuning is a function of culture.

One strength of synthesizers is their ability to be that theoretical infinitely wide piano, representing not only the conventional frequency relationships of acoustic instruments, but all frequencies in between. Translating music across cultures is difficult or impossible when indigenous instruments are based on different pitch relationships. How does one replicate the elegant bends of the silk-stringed Japanese koto using a fretted, steel-string acoustic guitar or the shifting frets and resonant gourd of an Indian sitar? While the 2A03's trio of waveforms cannot replicate the individual timbres of these instruments, its frequency output is limited by neither construction nor culture, making it equally adept at replicating Asian, Western, and many other regional musics. Though Famicom/NES soundtracks leaned heavily on Western genres—especially rock and classical—such choices were based more on the composer's taste, the project's budget, and the APU's tonal qualities than any inherent frequency limitations. So unlike language or differences in cultural norms (chapter 3), music was rarely a barrier to a game's international release.

ROM DMC

The 2A03's fifth and final channel cannot synthesize waveforms or noise. Instead it provides a rudimentary means to output samples.

Sampling in its earliest sense was a manual process. Disc jockeys could prolong choice instrumental breaks by reversing a vinyl record's position beneath the phonograph's tone arm, thereby repeating short "samples" of the original song.[18] DJs judged the position and duration of musical phrases according to sight, sound, and touch, using the record's physical grooves and the turntable's fixed speed to locate and repeat samples with exceptional precision. DJs were among the first "analog" samplers in the same way that "computers" first described people—not machines—who performed computations.

In the 1980s, instrument manufacturers E-mu Systems, Korg, Roland, Akai, and Ensoniq introduced a range of affordable hardware samplers that could digitally encode audio snippets to disk. In prior years, two sampler models—the Fairlight CMI and the Synclavier—dominated the (admittedly tiny) market, but both were bulky and costly, relegating them largely to studio or institutional use. Though their cheaper successors were less technologically advanced, more musicians had access to them, and they were small enough to use in live performance. With digital samplers, DJs and non-DJs alike had ready access to loopable digital copies of drum breaks, horn stabs, and vocal phrases—or any other recorded sound—freed from the manual dexterity necessary to manipulate turntables. The sampler could augment a DJ's technique or replace it altogether.

It is here that two meanings of sampling often conflate. A sample is both a segment of prerecorded sound reused in a different musical context—like the short loop of Leon Haywood's "I Want'a Do Something Freaky To You" used to form the backing track of Dr. Dre's "Nuthin' But A 'G' Thang"—and the fundamental unit of all digital audio. Converting an analog waveform into a digital waveform requires translating a continuous signal into a format a microprocessor can understand—discrete numeric data. An analog-to-digital converter (ADC) takes thousands of snapshots—or samples—of a waveform over time. When the samples are reassembled and played back in sequence, they produce a digital representation of the analog signal. Though confusing, it is accurate to say that samples are constructed from samples.

The Famicom is not a sampler like the Ensoniq Mirage or the E-mu Systems SP 1200. It has no means to record audio directly nor store it internally. Instead, samples are either recorded in advance, encoded and stored as binary data in ROM, or output directly by the DMC. So while the 2A03's sampling channel is far less capable than a dedicated hardware sampler, it did provide game developers a modest means of incorporating sounds that were impossible to generate via the pulse, triangle, or noise channels. And considering that the Famicom debuted prior to most commercially available samplers, it is remarkable that it had sample-playback capabilities at all.

Technically, the APU's fifth voice is a 1-bit delta modulation channel, or DMC, designed to encode and playback digitized samples. DMC sampling differs from standard digital audio capture that uses pulse-code modulation (PCM), wherein each sample point of an incoming signal is recorded independently as a sequence of variable amplitude values, or pulses. Delta modulation, in contrast, is *differential*: if the current input signal amplitude is higher than the previous sample, the output is raised by a fixed delta value; if it is lower, the output subtracts the delta value.[19] Since the encoder only needs to store whether the comparison is higher (1) or lower (0), a single bit suffices.

Delta modulation is ideal for systems with limited memory, but 1-bit sampling introduces encoding errors that audibly distort the source audio. If the source signal's amplitude shifts suddenly, for instance, it takes several samples for delta modulation to "catch up," since its slope can only shift one delta value per sample. This *slope overload distortion* alters the shape of the digital output and introduces noise. In contrast, when the source signal remains static, delta modulation cannot accurately record whether each successive amplitude is higher or lower, since there is no change. To compensate, it fluctuates above and below the static signal, introducing a distortion called *granular noise*.[20] Ideal analog input sources with amplitude slopes that transition gradually and consistently rarely exist, so any DMC playback on the Famicom sounds noisier, grittier, and more distorted than its source.

The Famicom DMC provides two sample playback methods. The first and more common technique uses direct memory access (DMA) for "automatic" playback. To initiate sample playback, composers set the sample's starting address, its length, and desired playback frequency. Once the channel is enabled, the DMC's *memory reader* fills an 8-bit *sample buffer*, which the *output unit* then empties until the counter register reaches zero.[21] Based on the status of a loop bit, once the sample buffer empties, playback either stops or loops. *Mike Tyson's Punch-Out!!* uses short DMC loops to simulate two crowd cheering noises, one heard during the title screen and the other during pivotal fight events, such as the beginning of a round or after knockouts.[22]

DMA playback simplifies the use of samples, but also limits their flexibility. Beyond setting the loop control, composers can only alter the sample's playback frequency (by decreasing a 4-bit *rate index* value), effectively lowering the pitch of any DMC sample.[23] Early samplers and synthesizers used a similar method to get more mileage out of their limited sampling memory. One might record a sample of a piano's C note at each octave, then decrease each sample's frequency at fixed intervals to fill in the missing keys. While this technique conserved memory, it also created unnatural encoding artifacts. Decreasing the frequency of a sample also increased its length, so a C sample that was 1.2 seconds long might increase to twice that length when dropped an octave, creating a noticeable slurring effect, like dropping the speed of a 45 rpm record to 33 1/3. Likewise, slowing the sample could highlight unwanted harmonics or DAC interpolation errors.

Further compounding its playback limitations, the DMC's sixteen rate index steps are not "well-tempered," i.e., aligned to a useful musical scale. In other words, the DMC can generate sixteen approximate pitch relationships, listed here from highest to lowest frequencies: C11, G10, E10, C10, A9, G9, F9, D9, C9, B8, A8, G8, F8, E8, D8, C8.[24] Assuming a base note of C it is possible to construct a reasonable major scale, but the lack of accidentals and the patchwork inclusion of notes spanning several octaves makes DMC-based melodic composition challenging.[25] Furthermore, none of the notes have precise intonation, especially in the higher registers. E10, for instance, is sharp by 17 cents, rendering it audibly out of tune. To compensate for DMC tuning quirks, developers often sampled multiple notes for an instrument, then raised or lowered their frequencies to fill the necessary scale range.

Though automatic playback makes DMC usage simpler, the alternative direct load method, which can write raw PCM data directly to the DAC, offers greater sample control and potentially higher quality.[26] Freed from the rate index control, custom 7-bit samples can have arbitrary lengths, provided the composer has adequate ROM space to store the sample data. However, this technique requires such a high volume of data throughput and processing attention that any usable musical phrase or voice sample typically required halting game logic entirely to wait for playback.

Games that used the direct load method generally relegated PCM playback to static title screens (e.g., *Bart vs. the Space Mutants*) or altered gameplay to accommodate the brief pauses required to play samples. *Sesame Street: Big Bird's Hide and Speak* used a complex pseudo-phonetic sample system to construct its impressive vocabulary, all spoken by Big Bird's real voice actor, Caroll Spinney. While Big Bird speaks, playfield graphics remain static, save for a simple beak animation that sneaks in sprite updates between speech samples.[27] In Will Harvey's NES port of his PC title *The Immortal*, enemy growls and groans were streamed as PCM data during one-on-one battle scenes. In the game's first encounter, for example, there is a noticeable pause when your wizard strikes down his goblin foe, evincing a brief death cry. The pause artfully transforms a necessary hardware halt into a dramatic delay, timed precisely before the killing blow.

Vox Apparatus

Regardless of method, DMC samples required copious ROM space, so most developers used them like hip-hop producers used early hardware samplers: for percussion. Drums hits were ideal for sampling because they were brief—typically a second or less—and did not need to be pitched to make them musically useful. Building even the simplest piano melody, for instance, required samples for each note. If a composer chose instead to downsample a single piano key, they faced the tuning and distortion problems described above. Konami's Hidenori Maezawa, whose soundtrack credits include *Gradius*, *Teenage Mutant Ninja Turtles*, *Contra*, and *Super C*, explained the APU's significant sampling limitations in a 2009 interview:

For sampling, the resolution of the sound was very low—it sounded cheap. Normally, when you sample, your software will interpolate the whole scale. With the Famicom, though, we had to sample every single note. But of course, doing that eats up memory space. So really, it was terribly limited—I had to decide which notes we were going to use, and which ones I should sample. It was all very complicated and difficult.[28]

Despite his misgivings, Maezawa used the DMC extensively in both *Contra* titles. By offloading the kick and snare sounds to the DMC, he allowed the noise channel to focus on a single drum component (e.g., hi-hats), augmenting the percussion's realism, since both channels could play simultaneously. Sampled drums also freed up the noise channel for sound effects without sacrificing percussion altogether.

A few developers reconciled with the DMC's quirks and used it for melodic samples. Sunsoft titles *Batman: Return of the Joker*, *Journey to Silius*, *Gremlins 2*, *Gimmick*, and *Super Spy Hunter* all had DMC bass lines that sounded deeper and more realistic than the triangle bass.[29] However, Sunsoft's composers had to use multiple bass samples—namely A#, B, C, C#, and D—to compensate for the pitch table's frequency gaps.[30] Despite the better frequency coverage, Sunsoft bass lines still suffered from distortion and tuning problems. Several of composer Naoki Kodaka's bass tracks for *Gremlins 2* pedaled on a single note in two octaves, highlighting subtle mismatches in pitch. Slight dissonances notwithstanding, the DMC bass became a trademark Sunsoft sound and freed Kodaka to use the triangle and noise channels to create a well-rounded drum kit, complete with tuned toms.

Though less common than percussive samples, developers also used the DMC to encode voice. Synthesized speech emerged in electronic toys, pinball machines, and videogames in the late 1970s and early 1980s, initially as a hardware audio gimmick meant to entice potential players. Taito's *Galaxian* derivative *Stratovox* (1980) inaugurated the arcade speech era, featuring a crude 8-bit DAC that output four sampled phrases, each equally impossible to discern. A slew of more articulate titles followed, such as *Berzerk* (1980) and *Gorf* (1981), which were both notable for using speech synthesis to simulate machine sentience. Players approaching *Berzerk* heard it proclaim, "Coins detected in pocket" during its attract mode, while *Gorf* was more direct in its intentions: "I devour coins."

The craze for arcade speech and talking toys like the *Speak & Spell* soon spread to the console market. Mattel engineered the Intellivoice Voice

Synthesis Module as an add-on for the Intellivision in 1982, but the kludgy, expensive peripheral failed to drum up developer or consumer enthusiasm.[31] Nintendo made the wiser decision to include a general-purpose sampling channel that could handle speech, instruments, or any other sound. They wagered that any speech synthesis required beyond the DMC's capabilities was better suited to supplementary cartridge hardware, not a separate peripheral.[32]

Speech samples had limited use in-game, so they were often reserved for special occasions like title screens or stage completions.[33] Sports games were well-suited to speech samples, providing an added touch of verisimilitude to referees or announcers. Konami used them frequently for their sports titles. *Double Dribble*, for example, announced its name during the title screen and had the referee say "Free throw" when a player suffered a foul.[34] Hockey game *Blades of Steel* had a similar title introduction and a number of voiced samples for passing, face offs, fights, and player falls. In other games, they were a simple technological showcase. Natsume's *S.C.A.T.*, for instance, had a remarkably eloquent introduction, wherein the DMC narrated the player's mission—"You must destroy them. The Earth is counting on you!! Good luck!" Rare's *High Speed*, a digital reproduction of the classic Williams pinball machine, was one of the only games to use the DMC's low fidelity for thematic effect, as its voice samples simulated police CB dispatches.

The Wind or the Drums

With only five channels at the 2A03's disposal, sound prioritization was a necessity. Moreover, each channel was monophonic, meaning that only one note could play at a time. If Mega Man's buster shot and the lower voice of composer Manami Matsumae's Cutman melody fired simultaneously on the same pulse channel, a programmatic decision had to be made about which was heard. There was no hardware trick that automated such tasks—the game's sound engine had to be designed to prioritize one sound over another, dependent on what the developers deemed to be the most important audio information for a given frame.

Famicom games generally foregrounded sound effects over music, since without audible feedback for jumps, menu selection, weapon reports, and item pickups, their worlds felt sonically hollow. Sound effects also provided an immediate feedback mechanism for player input, especially when visual cues were hidden or unavailable. When the player directed Mario to kick a Koopa shell into a Goomba, for instance, the engine responded visually by removing the Goomba sprite from the screen and aurally by triggering a brief pulse wave effect. Once the player understood the audio-visual correlation, the game could then introduce situations where the visual referent was absent. When a Goomba walked offscreen, the engine continued to "see" its location (chapter 4) even though the player could not. However, since kicking a shell offscreen could still kill the Goomba, an audio cue could communicate that the collision took place.

Games that devoted all five channels to their soundtrack had to allow for dynamic exclusions when sound effects were triggered, muting any music that might normally occupy that channel. Attentive composers constructed their music to allow for brief dropouts, like Kondo's harmonized staccatos from the *Super Mario Bros.*'s World 1–1 music. There the pulses and triangle channel played in rhythmic unison throughout the entire song, so masking individual voices did not significantly damage the melody. Similarly, the brief note durations offered adequate space for sound effects to nestle in between.

During gameplay, pulse channel one handled Mario's jump, bumping blocks, the pause jingle, descending pipes, raising the flag, tossing fireballs, and stomping enemies. Pulse channel two voiced coin collection, Mario's power-up transformations, and the end-of-level score counter. When any sound effects triggered, they immediately superseded the music. In most cases, the combined brevity of the sound effect and Kondo's doubled melody lines made the dropout unnoticeable. However, there were occasions where sound effects could erase the pulse melodies entirely. When Mario jumped repeatedly beneath a multi-coin block, the interplay between jump (pulse one), coin collection (pulse two), and block bumping (pulse one) reduced the soundtrack to its bass line (triangle) and percussion (noise). Fortunately, the cacophony of coin collection helped mask the halved orchestration.

The nuances of channel exclusions are often difficult to hear because the engine is handling sound at the frame level, where prioritization shifts can happen in fractions of a second. Many sound effects may be only a few dozen frames long, so briefly muting a melody to make a coin chime is likely to go unnoticed. But when sound effects sustain for extended lengths, musical gaps become noticeable.

The FDS version of *Super Mario Bros. 2* added a gameplay mechanic that, assuming you could survive the game's steep difficulty, made it easy to hear sound prioritization at work. Starting in World 5–1, Mario encountered levels with gusting wind, indicated visually by a flurry of green leaves. For the few seconds it appeared, the wind altered Mario's jumping trajectories, and its ebbing intensity was matched in the noise channel by a burst of static that swelled and decayed. Since both wind and drums lived on the same channel, the duration of the former's effect masked the percussion completely.

The Legend of Zelda provided an even simpler means to hear APU priorities at work. During dungeon levels, Kondo's score used three voices: the triangle created the vibrato bass while the pulses cleverly intertwined in alternating two-note sequences to form the melody line. As in *Super Mario Bros.*, both pulses contributed significantly to sound effects: pulse one covered the "typewriter" text effect, enemy strikes, and item counter increments, while pulse two handled enemy death and item collection. But pulse one changed priorities when a special status condition arose: once Link's health dropped to a single heart container, half of the dungeon melody halted to sound a persistent beeping tone—Link's fairy tale EKG. The swap was most noticeable during screen transitions. When Link passed beneath a threshold and the next screen scrolled into place, the engine temporarily reverted pulse one back to the melody until the transition was complete.

Today we do not have to rely solely on hardware-native examples to hear channel exclusions at work. Most modern emulators include APU mixers that allow users to mute or solo individual channels. Such tools are indispensable for understanding which channels handle which roles and how the sound engine prioritizes effects and music.

In the opening level of *Contra*, if we isolate the first pulse channel, we notice that the lead melody begins to play as soon as our combatant drops into view. However, any time we fire our weapon, gunfire replaces the music. As we proceed right, the first few enemies come into view. If we shoot them, their death explosions silence the gunfire; likewise for firing at heavier enemies (which produces a high-pitched *ping*) or picking up weapon power-ups. When our character jumps, we notice that a small pulse *tick* sounds when he hits the ground, yet firing while landing supersedes the effect. And finally, the abrasive buzz heard when our character dies masks music, jumping, and gunfire—in fact, it supersedes every other sound effect but the pause chime.

Silencing all but the triangle channel creates a wholly different sonic landscape. Its only duty is the bass line, so it plays throughout the level with no interruptions. The second pulse is equally single-minded, carrying the lead melody and nothing else. The noise channel has an interesting complementary role, rattling off the track's hi-hats when it is not busy augmenting the first pulse's gunfire, explosions, landings, and death tolls. Since *Contra* is a Konami game, we might guess that drum duties are primarily handled by the DMC. Soloing that channel verifies our hypothesis.

Isolating APU channels in this way helps us understand how developers approached sound engine design. In *Contra*, three channels—pulse two, triangle, and DMC—are devoted exclusively to the music. This is a sensible division of labor, distilling the game's soundtrack to a rock 'n' roll-style "power trio"—lead, bass, and drums—while pulse one and noise team up to handle the sound effects. And any time they are unoccupied with their primary job, they fill in the musical gaps. No matter what combination of gameplay elements arises, neither the soundtrack nor sound effects will fully disappear. Both are critical to the game's holistic sonic presentation.

Sound effect priority likewise teaches us which auditory information the developers deemed most valuable. Status alerts like pausing, dying, and collecting weapon upgrades get top billing. This makes good design sense, since the first two signal game-altering states that the engine must immediately convey to the player, and the third is an important audio corollary to a visual cue—the player's weapon becomes more powerful when they run over a pickup. Consequently, the pickup sound interrupts gunfire to indicate the change. Henceforth we associate the sound with artillery improvements, even if our visual focus is elsewhere. Explosion, gunfire, and small ornamental effects like player footfall have lower priority. They augment the graphical spectacle but do not convey critical gameplay information. Through sound, *Contra* is teaching the player how they should prioritize visual information by shifting sonic information into and out of their auditory field. In the absence of sound, a significant portion of the game's communicative structure is lost.

Sonic Racing

In absence of an audible example, the best means to summarize the 2A03's practical sonic application is to step carefully through a short example, paying attention to the relationship between voices, their use as both tonal components and sound effects, and a few arrangement tricks that best demonstrate each channel's versatility. To do so, we will look at one of the Famicom's earliest sound experiments.

Excitebike (1984), a brainchild of Nintendo R&D1, arrived soon after the Famicom's launch and later became a member of the NES's 1985 launch catalog. Players competed in side-scrolling motocross time trials—either solo or against CPU-controlled racers—on one of five tracks. Racing in front of an endless horizon of fans, players dodged hazards, wrecked opposing racers, and vaulted massive ramps while trying to avoid both overheating and devastating somersault crashes.

Like other arcade-inspired titles of its time, *Excitebike* had a minimal soundtrack. Nintendo's Akito Nakatsuka composed only three tunes, each under ten seconds long, to play during the game's title, track selection, and awards ceremony screens. In the title song, noise, triangle, and pulses perform their customary musical roles. The dual pulses take the melodic lead, harmonizing in pitch and duration throughout the song. However, if we listen closely, we find that their timbres are not identical. By isolating each pulse channel and recording its waveform (figure 7.1), it is clear that each has a different duty cycle ratio—pulse one uses 12.5%, giving it a thinner, buzzier quality, while pulse two uses 50%, producing a fuller, rounder sound.

Perceptive listeners might also notice that each note of pulse one's melody bends upward in pitch, an effect that is especially prominent at the end of each measure, when the lead holds for an additional eighth note while it slides more than an octave past its root. Nakatsuka achieved this unconventionally warbling lead by using the hardware sweep unit, a trademark style that he would later perfect in *Zelda II* and *Mike Tyson's Punch-Out!!*

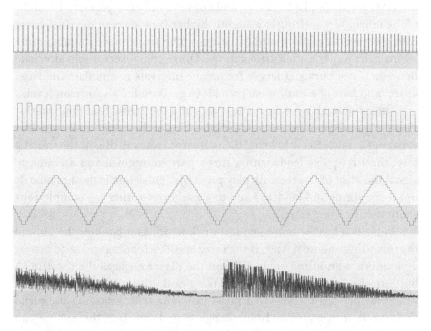

7.1. Representative in-game selections from each of *Excitebike*'s four active sound channels. Top to bottom: pulse one, pulse two, triangle, noise. (Source: Nestopia v1.4.1 output to Sound Studio 3.5)

The remaining two channels play supporting roles. The triangle predominantly pedals on bass note pairs until the two-measure finale, when it lends its harmony to the pulse melody. Meanwhile, the noise channel has the simplest role. Using short bursts of noise, Nakatsuka mimics a snare drum, accenting the beats on two and four to better highlight the syncopations of the melodic voices. Like the bass, the percussion breaks cadence at the end, matching the melodic rhythm until closing with an elegant snare roll.

Though difficult to hear without examining the track in a dedicated NES sound format (NSF) player, the concluding roll uses two different "frequencies" of noise (figure 7.1). While the noise channel has its own frequency control like the pulses, the composer may only select from one of sixteen preset values. To produce noise, the channel relies on a continuous pseudo-random number generator (RNG) that outputs a repeating 32,767-bit sequence. Triggering the noise channel taps into that stream *in situ*, meaning that two "identical" noise notes are statistically unlikely to be the same.

However, the noise is not truly random, because its underlying bit sequence is finite and looped. Thus altering the channel's frequency alters the RNG stream's playback rate and consequently the perceived "pitch" of the noise.[35] By shifting to a slightly higher frequency in the final drum roll, Nakatsuka creates a subtle distinction between snare sounds, mimicking a drummer's stick articulations. Other composers would alternate between noise bursts at larger frequency intervals to simulate the bass, snare, and hats of a traditional trap kit (e.g., *Duck Tales*'s Amazon level).

Once the track selection tune ceases and the racers find their marks, there is no in-game music. Instead, the APU orchestrates an impressive variety of sound effects to bring the motocross track to life. At the starting line, the first pulse leads with a three-part countdown and a chime to signal the start of the race. As play proceeds, pulse one is used primarily to accent jumps and landings and to signal overheating/lap completions (both use the same tone).

Pulse two has far more textural work to do, as it handles the bulk of the throttling engine noises. If the racer is still, a looping trill at 50% duty cycle mimics an idling engine. When the player engages the throttle (A button), the pulse arpeggiates quickly upward until it reaches top speed, where it once again levels to a rapid two-note trill. Engaging the turbo (B button) triggers an audible change to indicate that the engine can overheat—now in a 12.5% duty cycle, the engine sounds much shriller. At peak speed, just before the engine overheats, the turbo pulse holds on a single note.

The triangle acts as a support for pulse two. During engine idles, the triangle does not trill, but harmonizes a single note in a lower register, adding a cycling low frequency rumble. During acceleration, the triangle uses the same arpeggiated sweep to signal increasing speed, but again forgoes the concluding trill in lieu of a single cycling note. Lacking any duty cycle switch, the triangle makes no audible change between normal throttle and turbo, but it does provide an accompaniment to pulse two's overheating pitch.

The curious part of the triangle throttling is that it is audibly softer than the triangle in the intro and track selection song. But knowing that there is no triangle envelope (i.e., volume) control, how is this possible? At the output stage, the four waveform channels are sub-mixed into two groups: pulses are sent to output pin 1, while the remaining three are sent to pin 2. Summing in this manner has a circuit-level effect that creates volume output interactions among members of the second group.[36] The result is that changing parameters on the DMC can affect the noise and triangle channels, sometimes in creatively useful ways. Feeding the maximum value ($7F) to the DMC's 7-bit PCM control register, for instance, decreases both the noise and triangle's volume by nearly fifty percent. If the DMC is otherwise unused in a track, manipulating its register can provide coarse volume control. Several of Nintendo's earliest titles, including *Ice Climber* and *Clu Clu Land*, use this oblique envelope to step down the triangle's output. *Excitebike* uses the same technique to literally throttle the triangle's engine—no surprise, since Nakatsuka composed all three games.

We might expect noise to pull a lot of weight in a game whose sound design focuses primarily on engine effects, but the noise channel has surprisingly little input. A brief burst punctuates lane changes and loops when the bike skids out of bounds, but noise's primarily role is to Foley bike crashes. If the racer mistimes a jump, the bike propels through several uncontrolled somersaults, ultimately flinging its rider to the side of the course. The crowd then roars as the player taps buttons furiously, prodding the racer to remount their bike and continue the race. The noise channel orchestrates the initial crash by cycling rapidly between five of the lowest noise frequencies ($A-$E), rhythmically decaying the volume to emulate the bike's circular tumbling pattern. The crowd, in contrast, is voiced by a single low-frequency ($E) noise loop, sculpted into waves with a volume envelope that begins low, rises to a peak, recedes, rises to a second peak, then fades to zero.

Excitebike is certainly not the pinnacle of 2A03 sound design, nor even a full exhibition of the APU's features, but it is a remarkable display of the chip's versatility and range. Nakatsuka not only crafted three memorable tunes from a barebones palette, but he reconfigured those voices to create multi-layered sound effects that both sold the realism of the race and instructed players through clear audio cues. Jumps sounded lively, the bike accelerated through multiple sonic stages, and racers could monitor their engine temperature audibly without constantly consulting the onscreen gauge. Beyond those utilitarian features, Nakatsuka demonstrated some of the APU's less obvious hardware tricks, using sweeps for music and manipulating the DMC to affect the triangle's volume—all merely a year after the Famicom's debut. Innovative composers like Nakatsuka, who were early on establishing the possibilities of the APU's five channels, presaged a generation of musicians and sound designers who would drive those basic sounds into previously unheard territories.

Making Waves

Though NES owners were able to play many FDS cross-ports thanks to cartridge mappers, few ever heard the difference made by one of the Disk System's lost features: an additional sound channel. Unlike the NES, the Famicom included a sound-in pin on the card edge connector that permitted external sound to combine with the APU's internal channels.[37] Though developers would later embed audio hardware in cartridges, the FDS was the first peripheral to contribute a new voice to the 2A03's stock ensemble.

The Disk System did not replicate either of the APU's waveforms. Instead, it used a rudimentary form of single-cycle wave synthesis that allowed composers to "draw" custom waveforms of any geometry using a series of sixty-four amplitude steps, each ranging in value between 0 and 63.[38] Sawtooth, sine, and other more exotic shapes were now at the composer's disposal. And since the wave's geometry was stored in RAM, the program could write and rewrite waveforms as needed. The only limitation was that the wave channel could not be written to and produce sound simultaneously.

Despite its inability to multi-task, the wave channel still proved multi-talented. In *Zelda*'s original disk release, Kondo used three different FDS wave shapes in the opening theme, sculpting a unique timbre for each section of the song. Examining a visual plot of the wave data for each "instrument" (figure 7.2) illustrates how *Zelda*'s FDS waveforms were neither pulses nor triangles.[39] But the proof was in the sound: Tone 1 had a clamped nasal timbre, Tone 2 shimmered like tubular bells, and Tone 3

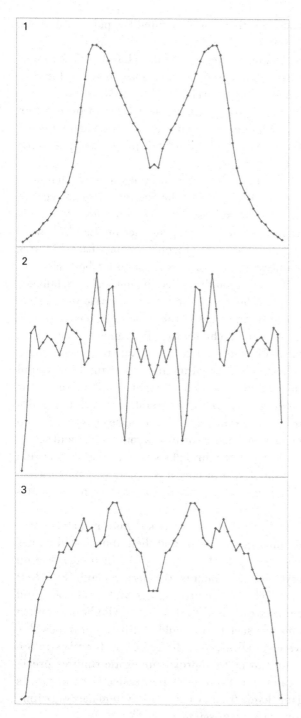

7.2 Reconstructions of the three FDS wave data "instruments" heard in the opening theme from *Zelda*'s original disk release.

had a clear, piercing character that complemented the pulse lead. None of these sounds were possible on the 2A03.

The smartest aspect of *Zelda*'s opening theme is how Kondo arranged the song with voice switching in mind. Minor pauses between the FDS melodies provide adequate time to write enable RAM (silencing the channel), load new wave data, then write protect RAM in preparation to play the next note. Kondo demonstrated that the FDS channel could output multiple waveforms in a single song with proper compositional planning.

Developer SEDIC built an entire game around the wave channel's switching capability. Despite being one of the Famicom's most creative aural and visual experiments, the side-scrolling shooter *Otocky* (1987) is little known outside Japan because of its dependence on the FDS's wave channel. Instead of firing bullets, your anthropomorphic spaceship fires red spheres that snap and return like a yo-yo, useful for both clearing enemies and snatching items. As you fly, collecting musical note bubbles fills a bar of eighth notes at the bottom of the screen. Stages loop continuously until the note meter fills and triggers the stage's end boss.

Bubbles with the letter A or B change the "instrument" that corresponds to those buttons. Pressing A fires your spheres, triggering a musical tone that matches both the rhythm and key of the background soundtrack. Furthermore, firing in each of eight possible directions triggers a different pitch. Button B fires several area effect missiles that produce a percussive rattle sourced from the noise channel. As you play, you build the game's soundtrack according to your instrument selection and firing patterns. No two playthroughs sound the same. So while *Otocky* poses as a cartoon shooter, at its core it is a generative music game presaging titles like *Rez*, *Lumines*, and *Bit.Trip Runner* by more than a decade.[40]

The FDS wave channel voices all of *Otocky*'s A-button instruments. Each level has new instruments to collect, and their abbreviated names are listed in the screen's lower status bar (figure 7.3). The tonal selection is diverse, including keyboard instruments like electric piano (EPIANO) and clavichord (CLAVI), orchestral mainstays like viola and oboe, and even indigenous Japanese instruments like the *mokkin* xylophone. Limited to the APU's basic waveforms, such tones would be difficult or impossible to mimic, but the wave channel handles the game's rich orchestration with aplomb, shaping waveforms to approximate exotic timbres previously unheard on the Famicom. Even more impressive is how *Otocky*'s instrument-switching mechanic transforms a Disk System hardware limitation into an innovative gameplay system.

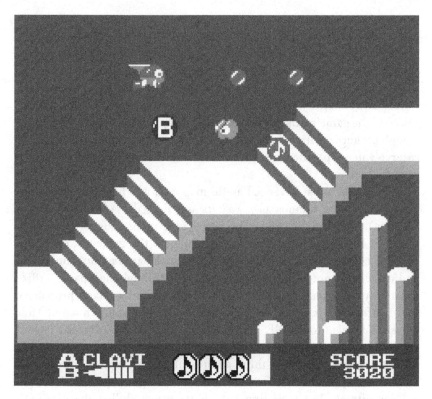

7.3 *Otocky*'s generative soundtrack relied on the Disk System's additional audio channel. (Emulator: FCEUX 2.1.5)

No other FDS games were structured around the peripheral's audio channel like *Otocky*. Other developers used the wave channel as a simple embellishment, an extra voice to either add texture to soundtracks, as Kondo did, or more often to concoct novel sound effects, as composer Hirokazu Tanaka did for *Metroid*'s weapons and creatures. The FDS's wave synthesis was ideal for such extraterrestrial sounds, but outside of first-party titles, few developers explored the wave channel's creative range. Mid-song waveform switching was a rarity—most disk composers simply set a single waveform shape and used it for the entirety of the game's soundtrack.

The wave channel lived and died with the Disk System, so the peripheral's gradual decline in Japan and aborted launch abroad silenced it for good. As with bank switching, CHR-RAM, and game saves, the way forward for augmented Famicom audio was via cartridges. But surprisingly, it would not be Nintendo, but their third-party partners, who would outfit mappers with increasingly sophisticated audio circuits.

The Konami Virtual ROM Controller VI (or VRC6), developed in part by *Super C* composer Hidenori Maezawa,[41] upped the ante from the FDS's solo voice, adding three additional sound channels: two pulses and a sawtooth wave.[42] The benefits were obvious: Konami's composers could thicken the sound of the game's existing soundtrack by duplicating voices, form more complex chords without sacrificing other compositional elements, or reserve voices specifically for music without the need to divert them to sound effects.

VRC6, like most advanced audio mappers, was heard in only a few games. Its most famous use was its debut: 悪魔城伝説 (*Akumajou Densetsu*), released in 1989. The cart had a monstrous 256KB/128KB outlay of PRG-/CHR-ROM, in part to support the game's twenty-plus original compositions. Composers Hidenori Maezawa, Jun Funahashi, and Yukie Morimoto put both 2A03 and VRC6 through their paces, utilizing nearly every sound channel in concert to construct a dark, propulsive score influenced equally by rock and classical music.[43] Konami later ported *Akumajou* to the NES as an MMC5 cart, but the console's lack of external audio access precluded the VRC6's added channels, despite MMC5's native support of three additional audio channels (two pulses and a PCM). Konami did a fantastic job translating the spirit of the original soundtrack, but forfeiting half of its voices dulled the original's dynamism.

Despite VRC6's use in only three Famicom games, Konami developed a second audio-enhancing mapper called VRCVII (or VRC7). Although named as if it were a technical successor, VRC7 was actually a scaled-down derivative of the Yamaha YM2413, a chip that offered six channels of frequency modulation (FM) synthesis.

FM synthesis traveled a long road from invention to market saturation. Stanford researcher (and accomplished musician) John Chowning first developed the algorithms driving FM in 1967, then spent several years refining and expanding their practical application in sound. In 1973, Stanford licensed the patents to Yamaha, who then worked with Chowning for nearly a decade before releasing their first commercial FM synthesizer, the GS1, in 1981. By combining two or more *operators* (Yamaha's branded term for a sine wave combined with an envelope generator),[44] FM could produce waveforms with complex overtones unlike any previously heard in analog synthesis. In its basic form, a *modulator* operator, acting as a control signal, was routed to a *carrier* operator in various frequency and amplitude ratios. While similar in concept to a traditional LFO (low-frequency oscillator), FM differed by allowing the frequency of the modulator to remain in the audible range, which, in combination with the carrier signal, produced a new, harmonically complex waveform.[45]

Though frequency modulation was possible with analog oscillators, the rapid advancement of DCOs in the 1980s made the complex mathematics behind FM easier to reproduce and manipulate. At its most inharmonic, FM produced uniquely "digital" sounds, often crystalline and exotic, but it was equally adept at representing timbres unachievable with earlier analog and digital synthesizers, particularly bells, xylophones, acoustic guitars, electric pianos. When Yamaha's 1981 advertisement for GS1 proclaimed, "THE FM STANDS FOR THE FUTURE OF MUSIC," it was remarkably prescient—FM's expressive novelty led it to become the dominant voice of pop music in the 1980s.[46]

FM had an equal impact on the videogame industry.[47] Arcade, PC, and console developers began embedding Yamaha's tech in their platforms, introducing game players both to new alien soundscapes and more realistic renditions of traditional instruments. The eight-voice, four-operator Yamaha 2151 (OPM) chip, originally manufactured for use in dedicated synthesizers, was first heard in Atari's *Marble Madness* (1984), but spread to dozens of other arcade titles, including Sega's *Outrun* (1986), Taito's *Double Dragon* (1987), and Capcom's *Street Fighter II* (1991). In the console market, manufacturers either released peripherals that upgraded the sound of existing machines, like the Sega Mark III's FM Sound Unit, or used FM chips as companion sound processors for newer consoles, as in Sega's 16-bit Mega Drive. PCs adopted both approaches. Some systems were upgradeable via cartridges, as in the MSX-Audio standard, or via sounds cards, like Creative Technology's original Sound Blaster and the AdLib Music Synthesizer Card. Other systems, particularly Japanese PCs, had FM built-in, like the NEC PC-8801mkII SR and the Sharp X68000 series.

While FM exploded the sonic possibilities of synthesis, it was notoriously difficult to program. The frequency relationships between carrier and modulator could create harsh dissonances if not set in the proper proportions, and the complex math driving waveform interactions was inscrutable to most musicians.[48] FM did not encourage the same "turn some knobs and see what happens" philosophy prevalent in earlier analog synthesizers. These difficulties, combined with the cramped LCD displays of early FM synths that stymied detailed sound programming, had the potential to dissuade new buyers. Consequently, a distinct shift in synthesizer marketing took place, prioritizing easy access to manufacturer-supplied sounds above DIY experimentation.[49]

The Yamaha DX-7, introduced in 1983 and still one of the best-selling synthesizers of all time, was popular in part for its user-friendly presets. Its manual touted that it was "delivered ready to play, loaded with 32 beautifully voiced, useful, factory preset sounds," assuring users that, "You don't have to program a thing...unless you want to."[50] Musicians had a library of usable patches pre-programmed into the synthesizer's memory, leaving the complex math to Yamaha's in-house sound designers.[51] While the early history of analog synthesizers was marked by musicians' willingness—by necessity, since there were no presets—to program their sounds, the era of digital synthesizers evolved into one of factory presets. The synthesizer with the largest program library and the simplest user interface stood out in the marketplace.

Following the industry preset trend, VRC7 had fifteen built-in instrument patches along with one user-editable instrument. While composers could define any number of instruments to occupy the user slot, only one user patch could play at a time. However, they had eight registers to define their custom instrument's sonic characteristics (e.g., ADSR, tremolo, vibrato) along side three registers to set the chosen instrument, pitch, and dynamics for each voice.[52] Despite VRC7's capabilities being on par with PC sound cards, Konami only released one game that used FM synthesis, sci-fi RPG *Lagrange Point* (1991), which with its host of funky basses, sparkling chimes, tinny brass, and pizzicato strings, undoubtedly contains one of the richest soundtracks of any Famicom game, rivaling the FM-driven compositions of the Sega Mega Drive. The icy, brooding soundtrack sounded unlike anything else on the Famicom, providing the perfect match for *Lagrange Point*'s far-future deep space setting. But the VRC7 suffered the same fate as the MMC5—it simply arrived too late for the aging Famicom. FM ultimately did stand for the future of music, but one that would arrive in the next generation of consoles.

Gimmicks

Though Namco was best known for their arcade titles, they, like so many other third-party publishers in the 1980s, wished to tap into the lucrative Famicom market. Under their rebranded console publishing division Namcot, the company developed Famicom ports of many of their arcade games and became one of Nintendo's first third-party licensees to manufacture their own cartridges (in Japan). By 1986, Namcot were producing custom circuitry for carts like *Mappy-Land* and *Family Circuit*, eventually culminating in the NAMCOT-163 (or N163), a custom mapper that provided not only an IRQ counter and bankswitching capabilities but dedicated audio hardware as well.

Compared to other mappers the N163 had the richest polyphony, supporting up to eight channels of single-cycle wave synthesis.[53] But unlike Nintendo's similar FDS channel, the N163 could produce wave shapes of variable size—between four and two hundred fifty-six steps in length.[54] However, the N163's higher channel count came at a cost. Since all eight channels clocked serially rather than simultaneously, increasing the channel count required more processing time to cycle between channels. At the highest channel counts, the switching rate actually shifted into the audible range, causing the mapper to emit a high-pitched whine. Reducing the number of enabled channels sacrificed voices but improved audio quality.[55]

At nine games, Namco's N163 was the best-supported audio extension besides Nintendo's FDS wave channel. But due to its serial clocking design, only two games—*King of Kings* and *Erika to Satoru no Yume Bouken*—used the full channel count.[56] Namco's remaining N163 games used only half of the available voices, striking a fair compromise between compositional complexity and tonal fidelity.

Following Namco and Konami's leads, Sunsoft took a crack at their own custom audio mapper designed for a criminally overlooked platformer called *Gimmick!*, released in January 1992. True to the game's name, Sunsoft's mapper would follow the third-party trend and appear in only one cartridge, but the game and its soundtrack were so lovingly and artfully polished that *Gimmick!* would become one of the Famicom's true swan songs.[57]

Gimmick! programmer Tomomi Sakai recruited Sunsoft's top talent to design the game, but he looked outside the company to find the right composer. Prior to development, he had heard and admired Masashi Kageyama's soundtrack-in-progress for NEC PC-Engine title *Out Live*, but knew the transition from the PC-Engine's six programmable wavetable channels to the Famicom's APU would be a compositional challenge. As Sakai recalled in a 2011 interview, "I knew I wouldn't have to worry about the music quality if Kageyama was going to be our composer, but I had to do something about the fact that there weren't enough sound channels. That's when I decided our game would have a built-in sound expansion."[58]

The result was the Sunsoft-5B mapper. Like Konami's VRC7, the 5B was a modification of another popular chip—the General Instruments AY-3-8910—found in a number of consoles and PCs, including the Intellivision, Vectrex, Amstrad CPC, and the Sinclair ZX Spectrum. Its additions were modest compared to Konami's and Namcot's mappers, augmenting the APU with three basic pulse channels, a noise generator, and an envelope generator (with ten selectable shapes), though neither of the latter two features were used for *Gimmick!*'s soundtrack.

While the trio of pulses was not technologically stunning, they provided the voices Kageyama needed to create music on par with his PC-Engine compositions. In a 2011 interview he said, "I was forced to think about music as though it were a puzzle. You can't create an awesome-sounding chord without using all 4 channels."[59] With the 5B and APU in unison—and not counting Sunsoft's trademark DMC bass—Kageyama had six melodic channels to work with:

> I wanted to break the existing Famicom channels. My goal was to take what people generally considered to be the sound of the Famicom, and kick it up a notch. The game served as a testing ground, an environment in which I was able to pursue the question of whether or not I would be able to create awesome music using only a small number of channels.[60]

Kageyama certainly put his APU/5B duo through its paces. *Gimmick!*, one of the few Famicom soundtracks to have titled songs, bounces across genres like Gimmick on his stars. At times ebullient ("Good Weather"), funky ("Aporia"), sinister ("Paradox"), melancholy ("Sophia"), and poppy ("Strange Memories of Death"), Kageyama composed a seminal Famicom soundtrack that sounded as if it was meant for a platform from another era of gaming.[61]

Gimmick!'s late release created distribution headaches, as retail vendors were moving on from the Famicom to focus on its successor. Sakai recounts, "At the time, most dealers wouldn't partner with us to distribute *Gimmick!* When we exhibited it at places like the Tokyo Toy Show, people would come up and ask, 'Is this game for the Super Famicom?' When they learned it was the Famicom, they'd lose interest and walk away. And there I was, thinking I'd get a good response for making a next-gen game on the original Famicom!"

Sunsoft's custom hardware likewise ensured difficulties for a worldwide release. Ultimately, *Gimmick!* was only released in one other region, Scandinavia (PAL-B), as *Mr. Gimmick* in May 1993. Of course, as an NES game pak, the game received a mapper downgrade to Sunsoft's FME-7, identical to the 5B minus the audio channels. As with most NES porting casualties, *Gimmick!*'s exceptional gameplay survived, but its distinctive voice was lost.

In the modern console era, augmenting audio quality through hardware is a strange notion. Today's machines are more playback devices than proper synthesizers. Composers create music as they would for an album or film score, pack the resulting tracks into the necessary format, and hand them off to the development team. Technical progress has given composers limitless options for videogame music, but it has also flattened the distinctions between consoles. The output of the Game Boy, NES, and Commodore 64 are now subsumed under the chiptune moniker, but the sonic character of those machines are far more unique than those of the Xbox 360, PlayStation 3, or Nintendo Wii. Games ported across those platforms will exhibit visual differences, but their soundtracks will remain the same. There is no "sound" of the Xbox 360 any more than there is a "sound" of an Onkyo CD player. And the thought of augmenting either's audio capabilities with special discs is absurd.

What we have gained in audio fidelity, we have also lost in audio diversity. Today, if you hear a videogame with a chiptune soundtrack, it is not because its native audio channels are churning out pulses, triangles, and noise natively. Rather, the composer has made an aesthetic choice, not a hardware choice.

.NSF

How do we listen to 2A03 music free from the conflicts of sound effects, in-game timers, or prescribed level lengths? Initially, this required help from the games' developers, who would include "sound tests" within ROM to permit arcade technicians to test audio components without playing the game. As their name implies, most sound tests were meant for diagnostics only. Like debug modes or infinite lives tricks, the sound test was a special reward awaiting players who could suss out the special codes or arcane series of button inputs necessary to unlock them.[62] But only a handful of Famicom and NES games included accessible sound tests. As a result, access to a game's soundtrack was contingent upon a player's skill. If you could not play (or cheat) your way to Dr. Wily's stage in *Mega Man*, you would never hear that stage's theme music.

The 2A03's integrated design makes song extraction a tricky process. One cannot simply excavate the APU and feed it data separate from the CPU. And since audio data is identical to game code, locating music amid other data requires knowledge of the game's code structure. Ripping audio is also not as trivial as inserting a disc and pressing an import button. Even with the necessary tools, the ripped data does little good without the means to play it back. A string of bytes with no software context are about as useful as a CD with no CD player. The fact that most games have custom sound engines compounds the problem. Imagine if every AAC file purchased from Apple required its own version of iTunes to play.

In the late 1990s, NES hardware hacker Kevin Horton developed a 2A03 playback device he named the HardNES. Horton's Frankenstein breadboard included a field-programmable gate array (FPGA) for program logic, external RAM, a socketed PlayStation memory card reader, audio amplifier, an EPROM for control code, and, of course, an NES CPU.[63] During playback, an external display output song metadata and displayed a basic graphic equalizer. Though the HardNES was a hobbyist project never meant for commercial production, its design has had a longstanding impact on the NES community, but more for its playback format than its hardware profile.

In order for the HardNES to play NES tracks, Horton not only had to rip the relevant data from game paks, but also package that data in a format the hardware could understand. The result, the Nintendo Entertainment System Music (NESM) file, contained the audio data, the game's sound engine, and a header describing the file's contents and memory structure. Today, NESM is better known by its file extension .NSF, or NES Sound Format, and it is still the dominant format for encoding, distributing, and playing back 2A03 music.

An NSF file requires a prepended 128-byte header, eight times the length of the iNES header used to format ROM data ripped from a cartridge (chapter 8). Though it might seem strange that the header used to describe an entire game is shorter than that used to encode its audio data, the majority of the space is filled by three 32-byte strings used to store the name of the game, songs, artists, and copyright holders, much like the ID3 metadata container used to tag MP3s. The remainder of the header is more utilitarian, noting the number of tracks, region encoding, any audio expansion hardware, etc. An NSF file differs from an MP3 in that it contains the *entirety* of a game's soundtrack (and sometimes sound effects), functioning more as a specially formatted playlist than a codec for wrapping individual audio files. The closest analogy is the .M3U playlist file that commonly accompanies digital albums.

Horton designed the NESM specification to be simple and expandable. And it was—provided you had the ripped data to prepend it to. Horton provided the wrapper, but it was up to the fan community to fill it with music. Doing so proved challenging because NES song data is not carefully cataloged in ROM or arranged according to standardized rules. Each sound engine might position its data differently according to the needs of the game, memory limitations, programming style, and so on. Excavating the desired data can be tedious work. The ripper must understand the intricacies of the APU, 6502 assembly, and the basics of program flow. Equipped with the proper toolset, NSF ripping is a process of informed detective work.

To start, knowledge of the Famicom memory map and mapper behavior helps parse the search into logical structures. For instance, in cartridge-based games, all program code is mapped to the 32KB of addresses between $8000-$FFFF. This is a hard architectural limit, regardless of the mapper or banking structure. If you are searching for audio in an NROM game, there are only 32,768 possible bytes to sift through. Mappers complicate matters by swapping in new banks of code depending on the game's current operations, but most do so in chunks of either 8KB or 16KB. Subdividing the code into discrete sections simplifies the hunt.

In some cases, one can make assumptions about data layouts based on the game's developer, since companies would often reuse sound engines or follow predictable code organization patterns. Chris Covell's early NSF ripping guide has one such example: "Let's just say that the best-case scenario is many Capcom and Sunsoft games. They have their music code at $8000-$BFFF, their INIT routine is at $8003, and the PLAY routine is at $8000. Couldn't be simpler."[64] In the Famicom era, when development cycles were measured in months, code reuse made a lot of economic sense, especially when multiple concurrent games might share the same programmer. At Capcom, for instance, Yoshihiro Sakaguchi developed the audio engine for many of their Famicom titles between 1985 and 1992, including *Ghosts'n Goblins*, *Gun.Smoke*, and the *Mega Man* series.[65] Likewise for Naohisa Morota, Sunsoft's resident sound programmer, who developed their audio engine, the Sunsoft DMC bass, and the 5B mapper used in *Gimmick!*[66] Understanding the company's development heritage further simplifies the searching process.

Once the proper data is located, the ripper specifies three key 16-bit addresses: the audio data location, the entry address of the audio initialization routine, and the entry address of the audio playback routine. These addresses vary from game to game. Some developers spread audio data across multiple banks, making it trickier to compile a complete playlist. Furthermore, songs are often not arranged in the order they are heard during gameplay. Purists might prefer their NSF tracklist to match the data's arrangement in code, but most rippers opt to rearrange the final NSF according to the songs' in-game sequence. DMC samples (or direct PCM writes) pose additional problems, since samples may be located in a different part of memory than their accompanying song and may need to be manually moved. Other games might use unconventional (or simply poor) programming techniques to run their audio engines. In short, there is no one-size-fits-all solution. Each game demands its own ripping strategy.[67]

One fortunate collateral effect of the community effort to rip every existing Famicom and NES game was the discovery of unused tracks. As discussed in chapter 6, the extended memory capacities afforded by disk cards and hardware mappers led developers to leave behind vestigial bits of code, unused routines, scrapped enemy designs, programmer comments, hidden messages, and even song data. Some tracks were accessible in sound tests, but never heard in-game, like *Gimmick!*'s fantastic "Strange Memories of Death." Games could also lose song data during localization, where music might be dropped due to a feature deletion (e.g., the name entry music used in the FDS version of *Castlevania*),[68] or due to gameplay structure (e.g., the final eight seconds of a *Gremlins 2* track were never heard because its accompanying cutscene ended before the song's completion).[69]

The final part of the NSF equation is the player—the software that can interpret the NSF format and play it back. Based on the target platform, an "NSF player" can describe many different types of software. Some players, like Horton's original HardNES, run "natively" on the 2A03 but require custom hardware/software to interpret NSF files, coordinate memory access, run graphical displays, and so on. Players that run on modern PCs provide an emulation layer so the original data runs on a virtual implementation of the APU. Depending on their emulation accuracy, software players may not replicate APU hardware intricacies like sampling frequencies, mapper audio channels, or PAL timing differences.

Many early players ran within other digital audio software, like the popular NotSo Fatso and Nosefart plug-ins for WinAmp. Newer players run as standalone software, each with its own set of features. Brad Smith's (aka rainwarrior) Windows application NSFPlay supports extended audio hardware and includes, among other debugging tools, an excellent visualization tool that maps notes to piano keys as they play in real time.[70] Richard Bannister's Mac application Audio Overload, in contrast, supports multiple platforms besides the NES and opts for an output waveform display in lieu of a keyboard. Other NSF players hybridize the chronology of videogame history, like Mr. SID's NESsivE ATtaCK, which plays back 2A03 audio on the Commodore 64.

Besides its closer fidelity to the source, the NSF has a clear size advantage versus uncompressed audio formats like WAV and AIFF or even the lossy compression of an MP3. An online NSF archive of over 1400 soundtracks, representing nearly every commercial Famicom, NES, and FDS game produced, fills a mere 30MB, less than the size of most albums encoded in MP3. In the late 1990s, when high-speed Internet was still at a premium and consumer hard drives were still measured in megabytes, the compact NSF format made it much simpler to distribute videogame soundtracks among the fan community. This same trait would contribute to the explosion of NES ROM trading discussed in the next chapter.

Tracking

In conventional digital audio software, time is plotted horizontally. Audio and MIDI data, represented by rectangular blocks, are arranged one after another to play in linear sequence. Blocks stacked vertically belong to different tracks, which are commonly reserved for a single instrument—guitar, snare, vocal—or group of instruments—a string ensemble—so the engineer can exercise maximum control over their volume, stereo position, effects, etc. Blocks stacked vertically can play simultaneously, but only one sound may play if two blocks overlap horizontally. In other words, only one sound may play per track at any given time position.

Digital sequencers are so named for their visual arrangement of sound blocks. To sequence a song is to put its constituent audio blocks in the musician's desired order. But despite their digital medium, sequencers remain closely wed to the recording studio's analog past. Many interface elements are skeuomorphs of the tape machine and its transport controls, the mixing console, rack-mounted effects units, keyboards, and other equipment found in real world studios. In the early years of digital recording, virtual reconstructions of familiar hardware helped ease engineers' transition from magnetic reels to disk drives.

But not all digital composition tools ape their analog predecessors. Among the chiptune community, specialized music software called *trackers* are generally preferred to commercial sequencers because their function and design better reflect their targeted platforms. To the untrained eye, the tracker GUI resembles a complex spreadsheet more than a musical tool. There are no staves or notes, nor blocks of audio data, merely columns and rows of letters, numbers, and symbols. Most user interaction occurs via keyboard shortcuts rather than mouse input. Some trackers lack even the most common digital audio interface elements, like play or stop buttons. Their closest analog equivalents are piano rolls, the perforated paper used to automate player pianos in the early twentieth century.

In 1987, programmer Karsten Obarski released the first tracker program, The Ultimate SoundTracker, for the Commodore Amiga.[71] The

POSITION	0000 +| -|	PATTERN	USE PRESET	U
PATTERN	0000 +| -|	PLAY	SAVE SONG	S
LENGHT	0001 +| -|	STOP	LOAD SONG	L
PRESET	0001 +| -|	EDIT	LOAD SAMPLE	L
SOUND	0001 +| -|			
LENGHT	0000 +| -|	THE ULTIMATE		
VOLUME	0000 +| -|	SOUNDTRACKER		
REPEAT	0000 +| -|			
REPLEN	0000 +| -|	1987 by Karsten Obarski V1.21 PAL		

SONGNAME: _
SAMPLENAME: _

00   Melody   Accompany   Bass   Percussions

7.4 The Ultimate Soundtracker for Commodore Amiga. (Emulator: FS-UAE)

upper half of the screen displayed the myriad rows of controls dedicated to playback and file management, while the lower half was divided into five columns, the first showing the song's current position and the remaining four listing SoundTracker's quartet of supported instruments: Melody, Accompany, Bass, and Percussions (figure 7.4). The lower columns were bisected by a horizontal bar that highlighted the play position and any notes currently playing on each track. As a song played, data streamed bottom to top, with the current notes passing through the center row like mileage on a car speedometer.

SoundTracker displayed notes, effects, and parameters as alphanumeric data within each instrument column, subdivided by note name and octave on the left and a four-character control parameter on the right. Pitch, duration, volume, and effects (e.g., portamento, arpeggio, modulation) were all controlled via these two sub-columns.[72]

Conventional sequencers not only proceeded left to right, but also moved unilaterally. Looping was possible for single demarcated segments, but it was not possible to, for instance, script the playback head to loop a two-bar phrase four times, play the following eight bars, return to the beginning sixteen bars of a song, then skip ahead twenty-four bars to the song's finale. SoundTracker, in contrast, constructed songs from patterns—a sequence of sixty-four rows—that could play back in any order and loop as needed. Looping not only reflected the programmatic structure of game logic but also fit the repetitive structure of in-game play. Game composers could not, for instance, reliably predict how long a player might take to complete a given level. Breaking songs into small, modular loops not only saved memory, but gave programmers the flexibility to repeat sections of music for as long as gameplay demanded.[73]

SoundTracker's four-track layout visually mirrored its platform's sound architecture. Amiga's Paula chip could output four simultaneous 8-bit PCM channels, grouped in pairs for left and right stereo playback.[74] But rather than synthesizing waveforms internally, SoundTracker was fully sample-based; Obarski supplied the tracker with fifteen preset instruments sampled from his Yamaha DX21 FM synthesizer.[75] Though this limited SoundTracker's sonic palette, packaging the samples with the program made it simpler to share songs among users. Obarski devised the module (or MOD) format to store both the sequence information and instruments in a single file. Packaging this data in tandem made the MOD file a "hybrid between pure sample data files such as WAV…and pure sequencing information files like MIDI."[76] Its simplicity and portability led the format to become one of SoundTracker's (and the Amiga's) most lasting legacies.

The SoundTracker disk also included a "playroutine" that exported a song's source for use in demos, intros, and videogames. In the early history of videogame sound, programmers regularly played the role of composer due to the lack of native compositional tools. Musicians who knew assembly and were comfortable composing manually in hexadecimal were rare. Tools like SoundTracker provided a middle ground between code and composition. The tracker mirrored its underlying platform but spoke the language of musicians. Melody channels, instruments, and C#4 made better sense than bit shifting, length counters, and indirect addressing. SoundTracker's playroutine enabled musicians to write in a more user-friendly environment, then hand their work off to the programmer for easy translation to code.

Unfortunately, SoundTracker's innovations and ease of use ultimately assured its demise. Within months of its commercial release, hackers disassembled the program source, expanded its functionality, and redistributed it for free as TJC SoundTracker II. Copies and clones spread rapidly among the PC demo scene, curbing the original's commercial success but ensuring the proliferation of its graphical layout, step-sequencing functions, and file structure.[77]

SoundTracker's close relationship to the Amiga architecture inspired the tracker format's translation to other platforms. Michel Iwaniec's (aka Bananmos) NerdTracker 2, released for MS-DOS in 1998, was one of the first trackers programmed to emulate the 2A03.[78] Though NT2 expanded

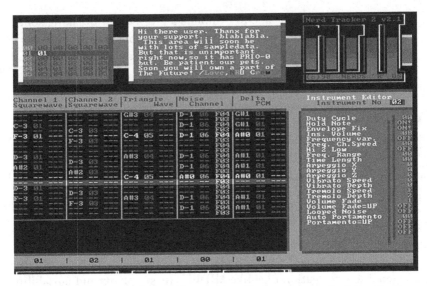

7.5 NerdTracker 2 for MS-DOS (SDL port pictured) adapted the tracker layout for the Famicom's five hardware channels. Here the tracker is playing Memblers' arrangement of the *Gradius* level 1 music.

SoundTracker's columnar count to five (each labeled to match the Famicom's corresponding channels), provided a robust instrument editor, and rearranged the GUI, the program's basic functionality was clearly indebted to Ultimate SoundTracker and its progeny (figure 7.5).

Two key differences were that NT2 did not run natively on the console nor did it use samples of Famicom waveforms. Instead, NT2 emulated the Famicom's APU on a contemporary platform, aiming to maintain as much fidelity as possible to the source processor while adopting the modern amenities of a GUI.

NT2 was a boon for APU-based music. Not only did it free composers from writing sound engines and composing in hexadecimal, the tracker could output track data in NSF for easy distribution and listening on software players. For composing purists, NT2 files could also export data for use on a real console, similar to SoundTracker's playroutine. However, NT2 files were not suited for use as a full-blown sound engine, since they left no means to include sound effects. NerdTracker projects better catered to standalone musical projects.

SoundTracker's platform-native tracking legacy has come full circle for the 2A03. Composer Neil Baldwin, who wrote standout soundtracks for NES game paks like *Magician* and *James Bond Jr.* in the early 1990s, now develops homebrew audio tools and instruments that he distributes for free online. His NTRQ tracker runs natively on the NES and replicates much of the visual style and function of trackers originating in the Amiga era. What NTRQ sacrifices in user control—one must navigate its interface using the NES gamepad—it gains in accuracy. Musicians can track directly on the 2A03 with no intervening emulation layer.

In subsequent years, more accurate PC trackers have replaced Nerd-Tracker within the chiptune community. The open source FamiTracker for Windows is currently one of the most accurate, feature-laden, and widely used 2A03 trackers.[79] While it adopts the same look and feel of previous trackers, FamiTracker focuses solely on the Famicom APU and its associated audio mappers. As of 2014, it supports the five APU channels, FDS audio, MMC5, VRC6/7, and N163. Additional tools like rainwarrior's NSF Importer now make it possible to translate NSFs into FamiTracker data, allowing musicians to dissect, rearrange, and remix the music of the Famicom era.

It may seem odd that musicians around the world are now creating tracks on a thirty year-old Japanese computer using software that owes its heritage to a European programming scene from the late 1980s, but as we have seen in previous chapters, the Famicom is frequently the site of these intersecting cultural and creative histories, absorbing the influence of unlike platforms to extend and expand its own expressive output.

Chiptunes

The concurrent developments of Famicom emulation, the NSF standard, and APU tracking software has unlocked the 2A03's potential as a musical instrument divorced from the context of videogames. In the 1980s, when composition for videogames became a job in its own right, the men and women who made music for consoles and PCs were not part of a named subgenre of electronic music. Furthermore, it is ironic that few of these composers thought of themselves as electronic musicians. In most cases, they were trying to replicate conventional popular genres—whether rock, rap, classical, or jazz—with the buzzing beeping oscillators of a microprocessor. But as years passed, more musicians began choosing compositional platforms based on aesthetic preferences rather than market preferences.

Chiptunes developed around musicians' desire to explore the creative dimensions of obsolete chips, whether the 2A03, SID, Paula, POKEY, or any other number of outdated synthesis platforms. The 2A03 has had a prominent role in this scene in part due to its versatile range of voices and unique audio expansion hardware. The Famicom's original composers proved that nearly any genre was possible with two pulses, a triangle, noise, and a simple sampler, and today's chiptune musicians have wrung more from five channels than Nintendo's engineers likely thought possible. But the 2A03's prominence within chiptune music is also a consequence of the Famicom's market dominance, especially in the United States, where tens of millions of players became accustomed to its sonic signatures.

As all genres tend to do as they age, chiptunes now describes a broad range of approaches to composition. Platform purists continue to use only the stock or extended mapper voices that were available in commercial cartridges. Others use emulation to explore impossible combinations of audio hardware, using the MMC5, VRC7, and N163 in a single track, for example. Bands like Anamanaguchi or the Depreciation Guild use the Famicom as the centerpiece of a traditional rock ensemble, layering guitars, drums, and vocals atop the 2A03's chirps and squeals. Other artists use chiptunes as a stylistic reference, evocative of a particular genre or era of videogames, regardless of whether any actual chips were involved.[80] Synthesizers are chosen according to their affinity to the 2A03's sound without necessarily adhering to its architectural limitations. Though the lauded 2012 soundtrack for *Fez* is categorized as "8-bit" and "chiptune," for instance, artist Disasterpeace did not use NES hardware, opting instead to compose with software synths that evoke its distinctive timbres.[81]

For those musicians still attracted to the 2A03, why choose such harsh, arbitrary restrictions when the options for synthesis are now virtually limitless? Driscoll and Diaz's astute history of chiptunes elicits a number of answers from its artists, ranging from cost to technological curiosity, alongside a detailed analysis of the genre that "draws on the interrelated histories of home computing, video gaming, bulletin board systems (BBS) and Internet communications, and electronic music."[82] The authors ultimately argue that a more performative, even incantatory, fusion of nostalgia and cultural memory drives chiptune music:

> Contemporary chiptune artists wield their repurposed gaming hardware in a ritual attempt to activate the personal attachments that many young people have formed with these objects. Artists whose compositions might fall into other genres distinguish themselves from performers who use a laptop or a sampler by deploying familiar but seemingly childish pieces of technology in a highly visible and surprising way.[83]

Nostalgia is certainly a powerful motivating factor. Driscoll and Diaz rightly wonder whether chiptunes will die with the generation that grew up with them, as 2A03 music is evocative not only of its own technological underpinnings, but of a specific era of videogames. Listeners with an affinity for that era do not solely hear the chiptune artist—they hear pleasing echoes of *Super Mario Bros.*, *The Legend of Zelda*, and *Mega Man.* Through chiptunes, their personal aural histories are reenacted in endless variations.

Nintendo understands this better than anyone. The Famicom's legacy is perpetuated as much through its music and sound effects as it is through its characters and graphical style. The APU's influence resurfaces yearly in modern sequels to Nintendo's Famicom hits. Collecting coins in *Super Mario 3D World* (2013) still triggers a jingle nearly identical to the pulse wave heard in *Super Mario Bros.*, despite the nearly three decades that separate them. As platforms change and sound processors refresh, the 2A03's sonic legacy is perpetually born anew.

But nostalgia cannot account for all chiptune artists, especially as new musicians, who were too young to experience the Famicom or NES firsthand, join their ranks. Paradoxically, in the limitless field of contemporary electronic music, constraints become liberating. Artist nullsleep, one of the chiptunes scene's stalwarts, describes the appeal:

> Chip music has kept me interested for over 10 years now because I feel like there is still a lot left to explore. I'm very interested in the themes of appropriation and limitation, which are important aspects of this form of music... I like the idea of taking these old video game consoles and repurposing them as cheap synthesizers and sequencers—totally subverting their original commercial intent. The fact that this early generation of hardware was quite technically limited also has its appeal. I think that working within those limitations can actually help focus and foster creativity.[84]

In the same way that an 8x8-pixel tile can distill an animated character to its essential qualities, five channels of limited flexibility can establish rigid parameters for creative exploration.

Nullsleep also acknowledges a subversive quality to chiptunes, a resistance to the dominant rhetoric of technological progress and generational strata that drives videogame history. Markets may declare a platform obsolete, a generation over, a chip outdated, but artists can reclaim the market's trash as new creative treasures. In part, chiptunes' thriving culture expresses platform studies' latent optimism. The Famicom has been abandoned commercially, replaced by decades of processor improvements, but its function as a creative tool remains undiminished. The study of obsolete consoles is often fueled by misguided nostalgia, but the desire to probe the boundaries of computer hardware is not limited to childhood fascination or a self-conscious quotation of the "retro." The Famicom is not exhausted. Neither is the Amiga, nor the PC Jr., nor the PC-8801, nor *Pong*. We have not yet begun to understand these machines. They are complex, living objects. No amount of reverse engineering can master them. Decades past their death, they continue to speak, think, and sing.

SIM-U-LATE *vt*: to pretend, feign.
EM-U-LATE *vt*: to equal.

— *Hewlett-Packard Journal*, October 1980

Emulators herald the end of the era of the proprietary video game console because they render such dedicated gaming boxes technically superfluous. Emulation programs improve, PC hardware technology advances relentlessly—and the notion that games must be played on the console hardware for which they were developed is becoming as antiquated as an old Atari game system.

— Howard Wen, *Salon.com*, 1999

Since the early 1990s a subgenre of play called *speedruns* has tested the limits of videogame skill, performance, and technical mastery. The aim of the speedrun is to play a game as quickly as possible, by any means possible, short of cheating, passwords, or other "non-diegetic" exploits. Games that might take an average player tens of hours are reduced to an hour or less. Notoriously challenging NES games like *Contra* or *Ninja Gaiden* are completed in mere minutes.[1]

In 2003, speedrunner Morimoto posted a virtuosic eleven-minute run of *Super Mario Bros. 3*,[2] executing a flawless demonstration of Mario's platforming prowess. And he did so with style—during the airship portions of the game, where the scroll speed is fixed, Morimoto danced around the screen effortlessly, weaving through cannon fire, shifting platforms, and spinning wrenches. Viewers marveled at Morimoto's skill. The run seemed too good to be true. And it was—Morimoto had used the Famtasia NES emulator to seamlessly splice small segments of gameplay into a masterfully scripted performance.[3]

The discussion surrounding the "falsity" of Morimoto's run publicized an emerging split within the speedrun community: the purists on one hand and those assembling *tool-assisted speedruns* (or TAS) on the other. Though the "tool-assisted" moniker, like "speedrun," originated among *Doom*'s high-level players, it quickly flourished in console emulation communities, describing any run that leveraged the features of an emulator to complete games in the fastest possible time.[4] With newfound software assistance, the TAS opened up exciting possibilities for speed improvement. One of the first websites to host such performances, TAS-Videos, describes the practice succinctly in their site header: "Tool-assisted game movies. When human skills are just not enough."

Compare their motto to that of the long-standing "unassisted" speedrun community site, Speed Demos Archive (SDA): "Playing through games quickly, skillfully, and legitimately." SDA does not allow the use of emulators, primarily due to their ability to slow games to individual frames, manipulate input piecemeal, and replay performance segments at normal speeds. They also cite technological consistency as a competitive flaw, since "most emulators and virtualization programs have minor inaccuracies in timing and slowdown that prevent accurate comparisons between runs."[5] Unassisted speedruns are akin to rigorous athletic or musical performances, structured around exhaustive practice, minor tweaks to form and execution, and subtle aesthetic flourishes. Competitors will undergo intensive practice regimes, playing games hours a day for months or years to work up a record speedrun. Improving the world-record run for popular contested titles is like Olympic competition in the 100m dash—a game of tenths of seconds. The fastest *Super Mario Bros.* run, for instance, has improved by thirteen seconds between 2004 and 2014.[6] For SDA, these acute thresholds of performance require standards to ensure fairness for all competitors.

The TAS, in contrast, is less about the perfection of physical performance and reflex than it is about entertainment and technical virtuosity, propelled by meticulous observation, code study, and trial and error. Games are run and rerun between thousands of manual save states until the runner discovers the optimal time-saving sequence of key presses. Code and hardware are scrutinized to reveal any exploits, glitches, or programmer errata that might improve the assembled run. Often physically impossible key presses (e.g., up and down simultaneously) or "luck manipulation"—understanding the underlying algorithms that manifest as "random" events, like beneficial item drops—produce speed gains achievable solely beyond the realm of human skill. Performance times are no longer measured in human scale but in microprocessor scale, down to the individual rendering frame, and runners adjust their language to reflect the difference (e.g., "I saved a few frames with this run"). TASVideos encourages moviemakers: "Probe the game. Try, observe, and learn how it calculates things, and use the data to your advantage. Remember, it is only a computer program, and computer programs are predictable."[7] At this level, there is an unparalleled intimacy of play between human and machine. Together, tool and flesh choreograph an elegant mastery of code.

TASVideos acknowledge the accuracy concerns underlying SDA's prohibition of emulators by restricting their movies to an approved list of emulators. As of 2014, the site recommends BizHawk, an emulator that focuses on "core accuracy and power user tools while still being an easy-to-use emulator for casual gaming."[8] A TAS is about the mastery and manipulation of a game's rules, not the exploitation of an emulator or a deliberate alteration of the game's source code. Traditional and tool-assisted runs are similar in this regard: glitches are acceptable since they exist within the game's designed rule set (whether explicitly intended by the game's programmers or not), but cheat codes are generally verboten. An equivalent board game analogy for *Monopoly* would be using a consensual house rule like stacking fine money in a central pot vs. photocopying your own bills to slip into your personal cash supply. Ethical regulations like these date back to the original *Doom* speed demos, which allowed external tools like slow motion or segmented recording, but not the in-game "godmode."[9] In practice, it is a rather fine-grained distinction. According to SDA:

> Using glitches is simply trying to use whatever is within the rules of the game to your advantage. When you use a cheat device or outside alteration, then you're breaking the game's rules. As for cheat codes and debug codes, they differ from glitches in being intentionally programmed, so they are naturally outside the rules of the game as defined by the designers.[10]

Compare this to TAS's more flexible policy:

> If the key sequence is mentioned in the manual as a normal means of playing, it is (usually) allowed. Additionally, continues used in arcade

games bought through the use of coins is considered similar to a cheat code, as it provides advantage to the player, and goes against the typical concept of a TAS. These rules are not strict, but are motivated by the same concept as the guideline that says you should play on the hardest difficulty.[11]

The guideline referenced above emphasizes entertainment, an important distinction between traditional and tool-assisted speedruns. The TAS is meant to be compelling to watch. Even if a game is popular or challenging, a rote execution of skill might be boring for the viewer. Though speed is the preeminent concern, it may be sacrificed in exchange for entertainment. The governing guideline is to keep it interesting. And "guideline" is the operative word, since all of TASVideo's suggestions for producing entertaining movies are cordoned to their own section, separate from the more stringent rules. For SDA, speed is king and that overarching mandate is stated clearly in their rules: "We only publish the fastest runs submitted to us. Players are expected to use every method at their disposal, including glitches, to minimize time; side issues such as entertainment are secondary."[12]

The speedrun has now gained widespread recognition among gaming communities, so much so that speedruns are often built into videogames as supplementary challenges. This runs the gamut from big-budget, big-studio releases like *Grand Theft Auto IV*, which includes an achievement for completing all story missions under thirty hours, to independent titles like *Braid*, which includes an achievement called "Speed Run" for completing the game in less than 45 minutes. There were precedents for speedy play before "speedrun" was coined—*Metroid*'s best ending was only unlocked by completing the game under an hour—but it is now established as a legitimate means of play external to any in-game reward. A side benefit of mainstream attention has been a renewed interest in legacy games and an accompanying rise in the accuracy and features of emulators for myriad systems. Emulation is now a major part of how many people play games, whether they know it or not. Commercial ventures like Nintendo's Virtual Console hosts emulated versions of several hundred vintage games for play on their Wii and DS consoles. Curated collections of arcade games like *Midway Arcade Treasures* use an emulation layer to package games for playback on modern consoles. Those willing to delve into legal gray areas can find torrents of every NES, SNES, and N64 game bundled alongside their respective emulators or simply visit a site that allows them to play vintage games through an in-browser emulator.

But despite emulation's ubiquity, few have explored its history, nor its relationship to how we interpret platforms. So before we delve further into emulation's role in present-day play, we need to rewind several decades to the birth of emulation and uncover its early influences on our contemporary understanding of the term and its uses.

The Conversion Problem

In the 1950s, IBM was in a transitional period. Rapid developments in tube and transistor technologies were antiquating their electro-mechanical punched-card machines, then widely used for military, business, and scientific applications. But obsolescence was born from within: IBM was cannibalizing the "old-fashioned" data processing industry they'd helped create with a new, modern successor: the computer industry.

IBM's growth in the 1940s and 50s was overwhelming. Their initial line of vacuum tube computers were so popular and technology was moving so fast that they were continually churning out hardware revisions to keep in pace with both market demand and engineering breakthroughs. Unrelenting innovation was great for new buyers, but it left existing customers in the lurch.[13] Early computers were custom-configured to both their price segments (e.g., high-, mid-, low-cost) and their industry-specific applications (e.g., military, business, scientific), with no system of standardization in place to transition between old and new machines. As IBM stretched out to wider markets, product diversity became unwieldy, while existing customers found it difficult to upgrade to better computers absent any compatibility solution. Imagine spending hundreds of thousands of dollars on a custom-configured computer, adapting your business to its unique idiosyncrasies and resource demands—including new staff to program, run, and maintain it—then repeating that process from scratch when a newer model came along. What would compel you to upgrade? Or worse, compel you *not* to switch to a competitor's product? IBM knew this was a serious challenge to their long-term growth.[14] They had to cater to the conflicting demands of established customers on one hand and rapid innovation on the other.

By the early 1960s, IBM had reorganized internally to reflect its diverging interests: its punched-card and early vacuum tube machines were cordoned into the General Products Division (GPD), while its more recent (and future) computers fell within the Data Systems Division (DSD). Though there was frequent cross-pollination of engineers between divisions, each was responsible for its own profit quotas. Naturally, rivalries formed around competing ideologies: the GPD reflected IBM's heritage, along with the bulk of its profits, while the DSD represented its uncertain future—a future meant to obsolete and replace the products of the GPD. As new or revised products were introduced independently in each division, internal schisms increased, with no clear solution to the diversification problem.

In late 1961, IBM established a task force dubbed SPREAD (Systems Programming, Research, Engineering, And Development) to stem inter-divisional conflict and propose a new, ambitious goal for their corporate future. Members of both divisions were tapped to outline a plan for a company-wide, unified line of computers. The market was shifting and IBM had to adapt or otherwise lose their competitive edge. Adaptation meant a more flexible, unified computer architecture, as Pugh et al. explain:

> With each processor a member of a graded, compatible line, proces-sor capabilities could not cater to a particular application class. A looming question was whether the observed differences between business and scientific applications truly demanded differing pro-cessor instruction sets for cost-effective performance. Contemporary products...while still manifesting either a business or scientific emphasis, were tending to blur some of the distinctions evident in earlier products. Customers increasingly seemed inclined to serve both an accounting office and an engineering department with a single computer facility.[15]

SPREAD's work was prescient. They tackled not only the pressing eco-nomic realities of IBM's long-term growth, but a number of fundamental computational problems that we now take for granted, from the use of a stack architecture to the bit length necessary to encode characters for a full alphanumeric set (they wisely chose eight bits versus six). In the end, SPREAD drafted a proposal that outlined their recommendations for IBM's New Product Line (NPL) alongside its potential strengths and weaknesses.[16]

IBM introduced the resulting product family, the System/360, in 1964. True to the foresight of the SPREAD group, a large part of the NPL's eventual success (and long-term legacy) was program compatibility across all System/360 models.[17] Of course, compatibility was only useful for cus-tomers once they had bought into the new product family. SPREAD's report advised about a serious complication, the so-called "conversion problem," a need to translate programs from old machines to the newer, now radically different, architecture. Conversion was time-consuming, costly, and error-prone, and it had to be done without grinding their customers' businesses to a halt. Customers that now relied on computers for their day-to-day data processing could not cease operations while a new system was put in place. Likewise, it was not reasonable to expect customers to jettison the sizable investments they had already made in programs and programming costs.

The conversion problem was not new. Its specter had haunted IBM's engineers for several years prior to System/360s introduction, with no real comprehensive solution. One avenue was semi-automatic conversion, wherein software would perform an instruction-by-instruction translation from the old architecture to the new, which would then be pruned and edited by a human programmer. This turned out to be optimistic vaporware—no one had actually built such a program. And beyond the challenges of devising and implementing it, the number of personnel hours necessary to provide support and documentation were quickly deemed impractical.

Simulation was another avenue. The process was essentially mimetic—the simulator machine stored a program that mirrored both the functions and components of the simulated machine:

> The first processor's memory contained not only the simulator program but also areas used to represent registers and memory of the other. The area representing the other processor's memory was initially loaded with the application program. Then one of the simulator's subroutines would fetch an instruction from simulated memory, analyze the instruction, load simulated registers, and then branch to another subroutine designed to simulate execution of the given instructions.[18]

Though simulation was a proven conversion technique, it was unreasonably slow. Simulation was not a one-to-one translation, but one-to-many. The simulation program not only allotted resources to imitate the target's memory area, but also stored the simulation program itself. Executing a single instruction on the simulated machine resulted in multiple instructions running on the simulator (the "fetch, analyze, load, branch" steps quoted above). Any multiplication of necessary instructions meant a subsequent increase in execution time. Simulating computers with similar architectures could mitigate instruction proliferation, but even in the best case scenario, simulated programs ran forty times slower.[19] In the early 1960s, the net effect of simulation's performance hit was measured in minutes rather than microseconds.

In summer 1963, IBM engineers Stuart Tucker and Larry Moss devised a novel solution to the conversion problem. A late addition to the NPL spec granted its hardware some excess space in the control store, a high-speed area of read-only memory dedicated to running microcode. Microcode is different from the source code we typically associate with programming, typically the domain of high-level languages like C++, Perl, or Java. The term microcode was given its prefix due to its close relationship to the microprocessor, at a scale of intimacy beyond even low-level languages like assembly. The control store was devised in the early 1950s as a means to implement circuit-level control of the CPU—logic gates, voltage fluctuations, etc.—in a more flexible and programmable memory store. Writing routines in the control store was called microprogramming—similar to programming, but at a more fundamental level.[20]

Tucker and Moss used the NPL's expanded control store to implement several dozen microprogrammed instructions customized for conversion. Their microcode, running in conjunction with a simulator and a few specialized circuits, decreased conversion speeds dramatically. So dramatically, in fact, that their emulation was practically indistinguishable from a program running on the original machine, save for the fact that it often ran *faster* on the new host. The engineering team's efforts effectively updated a legacy program's performance to levels beyond its native hardware. The novelty of reversing the conversion problem was not lost on Tucker and Moss:

> [They] deemed the new combination of software, microcode, and hardware sufficiently different from a conventional simulator to merit a new name. [Moss] suggested emulator, a word whose root goes beyond the notion of imitate to embrace "equal" or "excel." An emulator came to consist of two entities, a software part and a processor part (the latter being microprograms and special circuits) called the compatibility feature.[21]

Tucker published his and Moss's work in the 1965 article, "Emulation of Large Systems."[22] There he outlined previous attempts at conversion, from simulation and translation (i.e., automatic conversion) to reprogramming (what we would now call porting). And each, in turn, was dismissed for its inefficiencies. Emulation turned out to be the best solution to the conversion problem primarily because it cherry-picked the best bits of prior failures. Simulation, for instance, was used as a hardware "diagnostic" step, highlighting any trouble spots that might hamper performance. Those wrinkles were ironed out manually, with specialized microcode or hard-wired "transistor logic." In other words, there were elements of automated machine analysis and human revision working in unison at all levels, from circuits to the control store to programmed software.

Four points are important to emphasize in the early history of emulation: first, the original conception of an emulator was a hybrid solution, involving both software and hardware, that harnessed the advantages of previous unsuccessful strategies; second, emulation differed from simulation by exceeding the simulated source; third, IBM devised emulation for use in its own hardware, not its competitors' machines; and fourth, emulation was not devised in the PC era. Emulation developed concurrently with the computer industry, in the era of "large systems," and was essential for its continued growth.

Machines That Do Not (Yet) Exist

Today, in the context of videogames, we think of emulators as software-based solutions. Nestopia or Nintendulator do not require custom-soldered transistors or special graphics cards to emulate NES games. They run alongside other applications, like word processors or web browsers, but load ROM images rather than text or HTML files. Likewise, emulators are not constrained to a particular operating system, nor even PCs. NES emulators run on nearly every operating system since the mid-1990s, from MS-DOS to Linux, and most consoles, from Sony's PSP to Nintendo's own Virtual Console on the Wii.

Conceptually, software emulation is as old as the original "hybrid" solution. Tucker hinted at the possibility of pure microcode emulation only a few paragraphs after he coined the term, writing, "Although all the functions could be handled with only microprogramming, a significant speed advantage is gained by adding some transistor logic."[23] The primary obstructions for IBM's engineers were logjams in processing speed. Until CPUs became faster, dedicated transistors would prove more capable.

After a few years, Moore's Law transformed theory into reality. In 1969, computer scientist Robert Rosin published an article on emulation that divested the term's definition of any reliance on supplementary hardware:

> [W]e use the term "emulator" to describe a complete set of microprograms which, when embedded in a control store, define a machine. We shall call a machine which is realized by an emulator a "virtual

machine" and the machine which supports microprograms a "host machine."[24]

Rosin's conceptual divergence had two key implications. First, it reframed emulation as a theoretical and practical concern outside the scope of a single corporation. Rosin's footnote to the quote above specifically mentions Tucker's earlier paper but points out that the latter's definition is "reflected in the products of the IBM Corporation," while "several other manufacturers appear to use the term as defined in the present paper." Rosin was an academic rather than an IBM employee, so his research was not geared specifically to the success of a product line. Second, it abstracted the native platform from its roots in circuits and registers to a machine defined solely in code. Though emulation in the late 1960s was still in the realm of microcode rather than high-level languages, the conceptual break was already taking place.

As "virtual machines," emulators could take on all the connotations of the term: idealized, practical, imitative, "close enough." Even immaterial. A virtual machine was an abstracted machine; hardware could be represented in code prior to its physical instantiation. In practical terms, a programmer could configure, test, and modify a computer that had not yet been built. In 1978, Marsland and Demco published an article on the PDP-11's (a microcomputer popular for educational, scientific, and business use) potential as a "universal" emulator that could support multiple architectures. Besides the obvious advantage of running programs from several legacy mainframes on a single host, they listed a number of other appropriate cases for the use of emulation. Among them:

(1) The configuration of the target machine is too small for software development. During such development the emulator could provide extra assistance in the form of better debugging aids, larger virtual machine, and access to the host's peripherals.
(2) The target machine does not (yet) exist.[25]

These two use cases are particularly pertinent to the development of videogame hardware, especially in the Famicom era.

When new consoles are in development, they begin as a set of specifications, usually built to suit a specific software profile. In Nintendo's case, they aimed to build a console capable of playing *Donkey Kong* (chapter 1). As the realities of cost, speed, and industrial design came to the fore, concessions had to be made: the Z80 core was swapped for a 6502, controllers were connected directly to the board, the keyboard peripheral was dropped, and so on. Meanwhile, software had to be developed while the hardware design was still in progress. Otherwise, no games would have been available for console launch. Early photos of the Famicom prototype show bare metal chassis, one each for the CPU and PPU, slotted with large circuit boards. But this is not the hardware Teiser and his fellow Atari executives saw during their visit, since Nintendo "had only just received their 1st pass silicon (with some bugs) and were not able to show us a fully assembled and working prototype."[26] Instead, early versions of *Donkey Kong Jr.* and *Popeye* were demoed "on their TTL emulator." In other words, Famicom emulation preceded the Famicom console.

Consistent with Marsland and Demco's first case for emulation, the memory constraints of consoles necessitated software development on virtual systems. Today, most consumer PC software is developed on the same hardware that runs it. Mac developers use Macs to develop software that will run on other Macs. Likewise for Windows or Linux developers.[27] Console development requires a different strategy. Typically, development studios license "dev kits," specialized hardware whose architecture, in concept, mimics the Tucker-style emulator. But consoles of the 1980s rarely had an operating system, firmware, or BIOS.[28] Thus console videogames could not be developed on the consoles that played them.

Early Famicom games, for example, were developed by Nintendo on the NEC PC-8001,[29] a popular, Z80-based Japanese PC launched in 1979. Later in the Famicom's life-cycle, separate systems were used to create a game's assets. Photos from a 1989 Japanese educational text show Nintendo employees working on level layouts, graphics, and code for *Super Mario Bros. 3.*[30] The graphics designers used Fujitsu FM R-50s, a DOS-based business PC released in 1987. The programmers were relegated to more antiquated fare: the HP 64000 Logic Development System, first introduced in 1980.[31] The HP mainframe allowed up to six developers to work on a shared network without the constraints of conventional time-sharing systems—each work terminal had its own processor and memory. The HP also included an "emulator pod" with a socket to host interchangeable target processors, including the 6502. Programmers could write, debug, and even download their code to physical ROM, since each terminal had a "PROM personality interface unit," a friendly marketing name for a built-in ROM burner.[32] They could then socket the ROM into a cartridge and test their code on a Famicom. Again, emulators like the HP 64000 were not simply replicating, but also augmenting their target platforms. Not equal, but better—a relationship that persists into the modern era of console emulation.

Console Emulation

In the home videogame market, the conversion problem took a different cast. In the early 1980s, most manufacturers had only introduced a single cartridge-based console. As Fairchild and Atari discovered early on, it was cheaper to mass-produce individual ROMs in plastic cases than to manufacture the games and their hardware in a single package. The transition from single-purpose to cartridge-based consoles, meant to ease both manufacturing costs and consumer investment, developed into a conversion problem known by another name: backward compatibility.

The backward compatibility problem arises during the technological shifts that take place as consoles are retired in favor of new machines. How might console manufacturers encourage consumers, some of whom had invested a lot of money in building up a software library for the current console, to upgrade to a newer system? And should they help ease the transition by developing some hardware or software means to play their back catalog on new consoles?

For many console generational shifts, the answer to the second question has been no. Manufacturers presume that consumers buy new consoles to play new games. Those who wish to play older games must keep obsolete consoles operational. Nintendo in particular has taken this approach numerous times: the Super Famicom could not play Famicom games, the Nintendo 64 could not play Super Famicom games, and the GameCube could not play N64 games. Prior to the Wii, Nintendo's compatibility exceptions were either in the portable domain (e.g., the original DS played GBA software) or in odd lateral hardware support, such as the Super Game Boy, a peripheral that not only supported Game Boy games on the Super Nintendo, but added limited colorization, sound, and two-player functionality.

Part of the reason for lack of backward compatibility was the early consoles' limited processing capabilities. Though the Super Famicom's 5A22 microprocessor was nearly twice the 2A03 CPU's speed, it still could not fully emulate the NES. Similarly, the Super Game Boy only managed backward compatibility via piggybacked hardware—the full Game Boy CPU was housed in its cartridge adapter. And Nintendo was not the first to adopt this strategy for cross-console compatibility. The 1983 version of the VCS successor, the Atari 5200, was revised for compatibility with the CX-55 VCS Cartridge Adapter, an unwieldy bit of kit that allowed 2600 games to play on the newer console. The CX-55 was a reactionary move on Atari's part, in response to competitors Coleco and Mattel releasing their own 2600-compatible hardware, the Expansion Module No. 1 and the

Intellivision System Changer. In a 1983 Mattel catalog, Atari owners were reassured that they could "finally upgrade to Intellivision, without leaving all their Atari 2600 cartridges behind."[33] Providing backward compatibility for one's rivals was a litigiously risky move, one rarely repeated in console videogame history without preemptive licensing agreements.[34]

The Sega Genesis supported compatibility for Master System games with the Power Base Converter. Unlike Atari or Nintendo, Sega benefited from the foresight to embed the Master System's Z80 and sound processor into the Genesis itself. Similarities in the two consoles' VDPs allowed the newer system's chip to stand-in for the elder system's graphics processor. As a result, the Power Base served primarily as a pass-through device to rectify the cartridge mismatch between Master System games and the Genesis cartridge slot—the heavy lifting was done onboard.

Many of these examples straddle the line between Tucker-style emulation and so-called "clone" systems. Often the host console did not shoulder any of the emulation weight, but acted as the I/O and video processor for a parasitic platform. The Intellivision certainly could not bear the processing burden of emulating the VCS, so its System Changer included a 6507 replica built from "off-the-shelf" components, at least according to Mattel's counterclaim to Atari's threat of litigation.

Contemporary consoles are powerful enough to emulate their ancestry in software alone, though they still leverage hardware solutions for certain cases. Nintendo's Virtual Console on the Wii offered an assortment of NES, Super Nintendo, and N64 titles as well as offerings from prior rivals Sega and NEC. GameCube support, however, was handled similarly to the Power Base. Initial versions of the PlayStation 3 offered hardware-level support for the PlayStation 1 and 2 library, but later ousted the latter in favor of software emulation—a decision advertised as cost-related but certainly motivated by the bevy of HD "remasters" of PS2 software that soon followed.

Microsoft's Xbox 360 was one of the rare consoles to opt completely for software emulation. Microsoft rolled out this support incrementally, picking and choosing backward compatibility based on the most popular and/or demanded Xbox titles, eventually supporting several hundred games. Their Xbox Live Arcade (XBLA) service has also seen a diverse set of emulated ports spanning console and arcade generations from the Atari VCS to the Sega Dreamcast. Most notably, the abandoned Game Room service, a downloadable simulacra of a personalized arcade (including virtual quarters for purchase), emulated a host of VCS, Intellivision, and arcade titles. Though contemporary emulation offerings appear to mimic the cross-compatibility tactic of the Expansion Module or System Changer, note that all of these services emulate competitors who are no longer active in hardware manufacturing. Sega and Atari are fair game for virtual consoles, but you will not find a first-party Nintendo property on a Sony console.

Split Format

The aim of console emulation is simple: to allow users to play game software from a given platform with the closest approximation to the original experience as possible. In all cases, perfect accuracy is the driving design goal, but in practice, perfect emulation is nearly impossible to achieve. Emulation is not solely a matter of replicating the target console's CPU, but also any additional co-processors, I/O devices, lower level instruction sets, and so on. In the Famicom's case, that means the CPU, PPU, APU, controllers, light gun, and any number of peripherals, from the FDS to the Game Genie. Each of these core and ancillary components are necessary for complete and accurate emulation.

For the needs of most players, low-overhead emulators that play most popular games with reasonable accuracy are fine. Small glitches or color inconsistencies are acceptable to (or go unnoticed by) most players, so long as the overall look and feel of the original game are intact. For the TAS community, there are more stringent requirements that most players would never notice, like cycle-accurate CPU timing and frame-level control. But higher accuracy comes with a concomitant increase in processor demands, especially if the emulation is purely software-based. Emulation is a constant balancing act between speed, allegiance to the source hardware, compatibility, and providing useful tools for the players.

Until the 1990s, emulating a console on a personal computer was not viable; most PCs did not have the necessary processing power to accurately model another platform. As a computational device, the NES had only one mandate: execute the game code. Every bit of RAM, every byte of storage, every spare clock cycle was rallied for the sole purpose of getting the game on the screen. PCs, in contrast, were multi-modal Renaissance machines meant to run games alongside spreadsheets, documents, email, and web browsers. All processes were obliged to share from a single pool of resources. This discrepancy in purpose meant that consumer PCs were typically a generation or two behind the curve in console emulation.

Equally daunting for accurate console emulation was the lack of adequate technical documentation. Access to such documents was reserved for official licensees and protected legally, as Nintendo held copyrights over the form and function of their console. Circumventing the licensing track required outright theft or tedious reverse engineering. Even if unlicensed developers could obtain the official Famicom documentation, they still faced a steep language barrier. While some developers enlisted the aid of translators, others opted to trudge through the guts of the NES to figure it out themselves.

The latter tactic was the strategy of most emulation developers. The NES's operation had to be sussed out through study and experimentation, so the early NES emulation scene benefited from a concerted community effort. Many developers shared their meticulous research, homespun documentation, and source code with one another. But many of these coders, being young or otherwise shrouded by online anonymity, were brash, competitive, or outright malicious. Competing emulators were mocked online; ethical debates arose between freeware, shareware, and commercial software advocates; prominent coders left the emulation scene in anger and frustration; and source code was copied and even stolen from unprotected hard drives. Emulation development appears less contentious now, as robust NES documentation is freely available online, but in the nascent years of NES emulator development, there was a fragile balance struck between enmity and community.

The first Famicom emulators appeared as early as 1996.[35] Developer Nobuaki Andou programmed the first publicly-released software, a Japanese shareware program called PasoFamicom (or PasoFami).[36] Though it is still in active development (and now emulates a number of other consoles), PasoFami failed to gain the widespread popularity of subsequent emulators due to its language barrier, cost, and complex file structure for game images. PasoFami required a special "split format" for Famicom games, consisting of four separate files: .PRM (header file), .PRG (data), .CHR (data), and .NAM (game title). Though unwieldy for users, the multiple data components more accurately mirrored cartridge hardware and separated supplemental header and title information from the game's contents.

PasoFami also required a registration fee of ¥3000 (~$30). The unregistered version ran for one minute, then halted the game and flashed a pop-up window asking for registration. In response to PasoFami's linguistic and monetary barriers, hackers produced patches and cracks to translate the GUI into English and circumvent the "nag message." Threads on the comp.emulators.misc discussion board frequently labeled it "crippleware," due to its prohibitive timer lockdown. One commenter justified his own and others' software piracy based on the inconveniences of cost and translation:

There's a difference between shareware and crippleware, and Paso-Fami is definitely the latter. And, besides, it's in Japanese. We can hardly be expected to evaluate a crippled Japanese program in America. THAT'S why you see the cracks, THAT'S why you see the translations. Shareware is software you evaluate before you buy. The demos of PasoFami don't provide NEARLY enough to evaluate the product. Also, by pirating in the US market, we are not affecting the Japanese market, which is what the emulator was aimed at. So who are we hurting by our rampant piracy of PasoFami in the US? Certainly not Noubbaki, as we'd never have stuck with it at ALL if it weren't for the cracks and translations. It cost him no sales, and was a form of free advertising.[37]

The worldwide "advertising" was effective—English-language sites hosting PasoFami commonly included the crack download alongside the retail binary. In retaliation to the rampant piracy, Andou began setting code traps in the source of his official releases, meant to spring when the emulator was patched or otherwise tampered with. He likewise focused exclusively on the Japanese emulation market, requesting that PasoFami be removed from all sites besides his own. But by the time Andou had rejected non-Japanese "evaluators," several new emulators were appearing, eventually pushing PasoFami to the periphery of the emulation community's attention.

The Birth of .NES

By fall of 1996, there were at least six new NES emulators either in development or publicly available: Marat Fayzullin's iNES, Alex Krasivsky's LandyNES, Mr. Snazz's VeNES, YoSHi and Riff's qNES, TaNdRuM's dNESe, and Paul Robson's NESA.[38] iNES, despite its $35 registration fee, emerged as the early leader.

In the early 1990s, Krasivsky (aka Landy) was working on a Nintendo emulator for MS-DOS that he planned to call interNES, or iNES for short. Early on, Fayzullin stepped in to assist in the development, then, when Landy "lost interest in the project," he carried on with iNES on his own.[39] In the documentation accompanying an early version of interNES, Fayzullin cited his collaborator's contributions several times: "The original code was written by Alex Krasivsky from Moscow. I added missing CPU commands, wrote screen drivers, and did some thorough hacking to make the emulator run about 85% of games."[40] Due to alleged interpersonal issues with Fayzullin, Landy retired from the iNES project and shifted his attention to his own emulator, LandyNES.

Fayzullin's iNES arrived at an advantageous time, since the emulation community was looking for a simpler, English-native alternative to Paso-Fami. iNES proved to be stable, functional, and well-documented. Fayzullin was one of the first developers to assemble and share technical details of the NES that he, Landy, Robson, YoSHi, and others in the emulation community had discovered through testing and experimentation. Fayzullin's compiled "Nintendo Entertainment System Architecture" is a fascinating snapshot of the state of knowledge about the console in late 1996.[41] In particular, mapper and sound emulation were uncharted territory. Fayzullin provided scant documentation for the four most common mapper types and noted, "There are several other mappers, some of them very sophisticated. INES partially supports them, but as this support either doesn't work correctly, or the mappers are uncommon (such as 100-in-1 cartridge mapper), I don't cover them here." The "Sound" section simply read, "To be written"—fitting, since early Windows builds of iNES had poor sound emulation.

As of 2014, iNES is still in active development, but its popularity has waned in comparison to its contemporary competitors. However, its legacy is still alive in the .NES file extension. Apart from being an emulator, iNES was also a standard format for encoding the data ripped from NES cartridges. Early on, as NES emulators became more popular, the desire to stock one's hard drive with a full catalog of NES games intensified. However, stripping a NES cartridge's data was not as simple as ripping a CD or transferring photos from a flash drive; there was no cartridge slot in the computer that one could plug a game into for quick transfer. "Dumping" a cart's contents, as it was called, required a hardware cartridge copier to transfer the data. (Early on, the iNES homepage provided the schematics for such a device.) The resulting binary dump was called a ROM image, or simply ROM—"Read Only Memory"—the portion of a cart's memory that could be read from but not written to. Though this shorthand was something of a misnomer, since a cart could also contain RAM or the image could be derived from a Famicom disk, the name stuck. ROMs were and are the stock-in-trade of the emulation community.

Of course, raw binary images were not enough. Once dumped, the data then had to be formatted into a file that the emulator could understand. Since NES carts contained a variety of augmentative hardware (chapters 6 & 7), emulators could not rely on a one-size-fits-all configuration. To compensate, Fayzullin devised a straightforward sixteen-byte string to append to the images providing crucial hardware descriptions of the dumped cart, such as the mapper type and the cart's mirroring setting. Once concatenated, the header and the image were known as a .NES file, ready for play in the iNES emulator.

Though .NES was developed in conjunction with the for-pay iNES, it was by no means proprietary to its host emulator. Other developers built in iNES support to accommodate the influx of .NES files circulating online in lieu of developing multiple competing formats. Paul Robson, developer of the open-source DOS emulator NESA (and later TNES), explained that he chose the format due to its quick adoption and ease of use:

> Most of the ROMs were already in that format and it was documented properly. It was the only sensible choice because of the different mappers—you couldn't just have a binary dump of the ROMs, you had to have some form of system for saying how it was wired up. There's umpteen "mappers" for the NES.[42]

Progress in the NES emulation scene moved extraordinarily fast. Developers had to quickly glom to a sensible standard or otherwise see their emulator fizzle into obscurity. Fayzullin had first-mover advantage, coupled with a simple, open format for describing ROMs. Fayzullin's gracious attitude toward sharing technical information (and reciprocal sharing back to him) meant that the entire emulation community benefited from the iNES format. The snowball effect intensified as subsequent emulators adopted .NES because previous emulators had done so.

The .NES file improved on the PasoFami split format in several ways. It was a single, unified file with a commonsense extension. Users did not have to understand the underlying cartridge architecture that informed the .PRG and .CHR extensions or why they required a header to function properly in an emulator. Semantically, it also made sense to the average computer user that an NES emulator would run .NES files. With the introduction of the iNES format, it became much easier for NES emulation to spread. The hunt to collect "NES ROMZ" ensued, prompting a grassroots network of ROM-hosting sites to appear online. Especially in non-Japanese countries, where PasoFami was near inscrutable, users shifted their attention to iNES. As its popularity grew, so did the need to support .NES files.

Dirty Headers

A new conversion problem arose between competing emulator formats. iNES did not support PasoFami's split images, so users had to develop utilities to translate .PRM to .NES. Initially, Fayzullin posted command line instructions for assembling .NES files manually:

```
1. Create a 16-byte header:
   "N""E""S"$1A$xx$01$01$00$00$00$00$00$00$00$00$00
                   ^^^
                   this byte is either $01 for 16kB games or
                   $02 for 32kB games

   and call it, let us say, mario.hdr

2. Do

   cat mario.hdr mario.prg mario.chr > mario.nes

   You have the .NES file now.⁴³
```

Ambitious users could also strip the raw .PRG and .CHR segments from their PasoFami files, use a hex editor to append the appropriate iNES header, and assemble a functional .NES ROM. By the late 1990s, all-in-one utilities like Matt Conte's cajoNES ("the only NES ROM tool with balls") automated the process, permitting conversion to and from the PasoFami format, as well as another emerging Japanese format, .FAM.⁴⁴

Enabling the conversion of PasoFami and other incompatible formats to iNES was not simply a means of besting competing emulators. Many of the games available in .PRM, .FAM, or .DKA (Famicom Disk format) were Japanese-exclusive Famicom games. For the majority of Western NES players, emulation was their first avenue to experience a substantial portion of the Nintendo catalog. Importing games posed a series of challenges: differing cart shapes and sizes required either the purchase of a Famicom or 72-pin/60-pin converter; language barriers cordoned off many Japanese-heavy titles; and the time and cost involved in shipping titles across the Pacific dissuaded all the but the most persistent or wealthy Famicom fans.

Emulation mitigated all of these challenges. Cartridge pinouts were not a problem for ROM images and language barriers would soon be surmounted through ROM hacking efforts. Shipping cost and distance were eliminated by online distribution. The sole physical barrier was getting the Famicom cart dumped and formatted, but this only had to be done once. Of course, this did not solve the problem of Western players gaining access to Famicom carts in order to dump them—it merely amplified the importance of leveraging the work that had already been done by the emulation community. A treasure trove of Famicom games lay locked behind their emulator formats. Conversion tools like cajoNES were the key.

The critical portion of the iNES format is its header, the first sixteen bytes of the .NES file that describe the contents and arrangement of the data to follow. Bytes 0–3 are always the same: $4E, $45, $53, and $1A. These hexadecimal values are the ASCII encodings of the letters "NES" followed by the ASCII SUB control character, meant to denote an EOF (end-of-file).[45] (So even as the .NES format lives on in modern operating systems, it still bears a permanent trace of its MS-DOS heritage.) Byte 4 describes the size of the cartridge's PRG-ROM split into 16K banks, while byte 5 describes the size of CHR-ROM split into 8K banks. Bytes 6 and 7 are flags whose individual bits denote a number of cartridge features, including the mirroring type, the presence of a special "trainer,"[46] and whether battery-backed SRAM is present. Most importantly, the last four significant bits of bytes 6 and 7 contain, respectively, the lower and upper nybble of the mapper number.

Mapper numbers are a classification system Fayzullin implemented to answer the need for a standardized system to organize and collate the manifold in-cart circuitry used in licensed, unlicensed, pirate, or otherwise bootlegged carts. Emulation as an archival effort aims to support all Famicom/NES/Dendy/clone/pirate/homebrew cartridges available worldwide, not just those sanctioned by Nintendo. Since Fayzullin chose to reserve a single byte for the mapper number, there are only 256 available mapper slots. In the 1990s, this was thought to be sufficient to cover all possible mappers, but the continuing global life of Nintendo's 8-bit console, especially in the bootleg markets of Asia, South America, and Eastern Europe, has led to the continued proliferation of unique mapper hardware.

The original iNES mapper specification organized the numbers by similar board types and function. Fayzullin's numbering did not follow mapper development chronologically nor adhere to a master list provided by Nintendo (since there was none). Thus, for example, MMC3 (mapper #4) and MMC5 (#5) appear sequentially before MMC2 (#9) and MMC4 (#10). Likewise, variations within single board profiles, e.g., various flavors of CxROM or MMC3, are problematically represented by a single number. The underlying logic behind the numbering choices appears to be based on abundance—the most common PCB types were assigned the lowest numbers. According to the NesCartDB, iNES mappers #0–4 (NROM, MMC1, CNROM, UNROM, MMC3) comprise nearly 80% of the most commonly used PCBs. Other choices were more functional: Mapper 0 makes sense for NROM, since it came first (and is technically not a mapper at all). Today, as new mappers are developed or discovered, numbers are assigned by their availability.

In the early iNES specification, header bytes 7 through 15 were ignored—or more accurately reserved for future implementation. Ignoring byte 7 meant that initially only four bits were allotted for mapper numbers, resulting in an exponential loss of available mapper slots, from 256 down to 16. Until those bytes were needed (and supported by emulators), proper headers were supposed to pad the remaining bytes with os. However, since emulators at the time ignored this portion of the header, the space ended up as a dumping ground for self-promotional graffiti.

One of the more infamous cases was the nine-byte string $44,$69,$ 73,$6B,$44,$75,$64,$65,$21, whose ASCII translation read "DISK-DUDE!" This header signature was a residual artifact of using the NES Image utility, a ROM format converter released in 1996 by Australian programmer John Pappas, aka DiskDude. NES Image was one of the first conversion utilities available at a time when many PasoFami users were switching to iNES. Dumping new ROMs or sourcing .NES versions was either resource intensive or time-consuming, so users made the obvious choice of using NES Image to translate their existing ROM stockpiles. The tool's popularity sent thousands of DiskDude-branded ROMs into the wild.

As emulators evolved and began using the reserved iNES bytes, DiskDude's self-aggrandizing gesture began to gain infamy, though not in the manner he probably hoped for: DiskDude ROMs were breaking emulator support. With unexpected data in the reserved header bytes, the "dirty ROMs" failed to load properly due to a mapper mismatch. This prompted a wave of new ROM utilities designed to scrub dirty headers. DiskDude ROMs continually frustrated emulation developers working toward a standardized iNES format and more accurate emulation.[47] If a user's ROMs failed to work in a given emulator, they were more likely to blame the emulator than the ROM, especially if it had worked in the past. Supporting legacy ROM formats became a new conversion problem within the emulation community. Emulator authors had to decide whether to include checksums, header fixes, or other workarounds to accommodate dirty ROMs, or to summarily reject them in favor of accuracy and standardization.[48]

To his credit, Pappas' utility was not the only header corruptor. The "aster" signature ($61,$73,$74,$65,$72), named after a utility of the same name, appeared frequently, along with "DisNi," "MJR," and other ASCII remnants. By version 3.34, NES Image no longer injected its author's name, a welcome modification that unfortunately, even in 1997, arrived too late. In the utility's documentation, Pappas wrote, with mock incredulity:

[Version 3.34] removed any extra "junk" (?) in the .NES format header. In previous versions, the version number of NES Image, or the word "DiskDude!" was present: I have seen many Nintendo ROM Images with this information within the header...great to see people actually used this utility!

His enthusiasm will be long-lived. Despite the emulation community's efforts to whitewash dirty ROMs, they continue to be an infinite-headed hydra. The rampant circulation of ROMs in the 1990s ensured that Disk-Dude multiplied beyond any manageable scale. If just one ROM hosting site used NES Image, their corrupted ROMs could have reached potential thousands of downloaders, each of whom could trade, copy, or host those files for other users, who could pass them along in turn, and so on in perpetuity. Even today, torrent packs of every imaginable NES and Famicom ROM are littered with DiskDude's header junk.

Though dirty ROMs continue to be a bane to emulator authors, their persistence is a boon to researchers. They create an embedded archive of a file's geneaology, an ASCII trace of its circulation within a community of programmers and programs. Without such evidence, these minor histories would be lost.[49]

The Severed Hand

Bloodlust Software, founded by Icer Addis (aka Sardu) and Ethan Petty, posted the first public release of their new NES emulator on April 3, 1997. News of NESticle v0.2—released as freeware—quickly circulated online. Its unique portmanteau, anatomical icon, and laissez-faire documentation initially did not inspire much confidence in its quality. Even Bloodlust's bundled README.TXT called the emulator "essentially the product of 2 weeks of boredom and a smattering of effort."[50] But the juvenile overtones belied the emulator's speedy interior and easy-to-use feature set. Bloodlust had leveraged a number of breakthroughs within the NES development community to build a sleek emulator that could run handily on 486 and Pentium PCs.[51]

NESticle v0.2 was spartan compared to today's NES emulators, but it had a visual charm that helped differentiate it from its contemporaries. The GUI was colorful and easy to use, wrapping its chunky windows in vibrant shades of blue accented with gray, green, and white (a look strangely similar to Windows XP's default "Luna" theme, which debuted four years later). Consistent with Bloodlust's house style, they replaced the mouse pointer with a severed left hand extending its pointer finger,

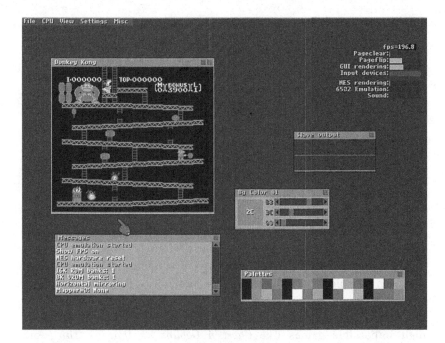

8.1 NESticle vo.2 running a *Donkey Kong* ROM with several sub-windows open.

terminating in a bloody stump (figure 8.1). In subsequent versions, the stump dripped animated blood.

Taste notwithstanding, NESticle featured several useful utilities beyond playing NES ROMs. Via the "View" pulldown menu, users could access visual representations of the NES's internal parts and processes, including the pattern tables, name tables, palettes, and waveform output. For many NES players, this was their first exposure to the platform's technical underpinnings. Viewing the pattern table, one could see the ROM's entire graphics set, arranged into contiguous background and sprite sections. Clicking either section allowed users to cycle between available palettes in order to better identify specific tiles. More remarkable was the palette view, which allowed users to isolate and edit palette entries in real time. Want to make Donkey Kong pink instead of brown? Locate his associated background palette and adjust the three RGB sliders. The "Messages" view outlined NESticle's various processes as well as details about the currently loaded .NES file. Selecting "Get ROM info" displayed the ROM's outlay of PRG and CHR memory (or ROM and VROM, as NESticle labeled them), mirroring, and mapper number.

NESticle also implemented simple systems for both saving one's game and taking screenshots. Keying F5 or F7 would respectively save and load the current emulation state, independent of the game's in-game saving mechanism (or lack thereof). True to its name, the save state captured a "vertical slice" of the NES's internal state at a given frame. This included the contents of RAM, status register flags, stack contents, program counter location, patterns, name tables, attributes, mirroring setting, and so on.[52] The resulting file was saved as the ROM's name with an .STA extension (e.g., BalloonFight.sta) in the NESticle directory. Loading a save state reversed the process, injecting the emulator with a set of parameters to reinstate the virtual NES (and its accompanying ROM). Similarly, F9 captured a .PCX (a DOS image format) snapshot of the current screen and saved it alongside the ROM file.

Both features had instant appeal. Born-digital screenshots obviated the need to set up a camera to capture a game's graphics or record a high score. Players accustomed to the limited or non-existent save systems implemented in NES games were suddenly able to save and reload as they pleased. Difficult games could now be broken into smaller segments—levels, screens, or a handful of key presses—if a player so desired. It was now possible for many more players to tackle nigh impossible games like *Ghosts'n Goblins* or *Dragon's Lair*. And more significantly, since save states were stored separately from the ROM file, they could be shared and swapped online and on floppy disk, provided the receiving player had NESticle and the matching ROM on their computer. Popular emulation sites like Zophar's Domain served as repositories for downloadable save states,[53] especially those stacked with a host of in-game power-ups or positioned at the conclusion of a final boss battle, allowing the user to easily view the game's ending. NESticle's feature bred a new form of assisted play—either cheating or player advantage, depending on your perspective—that would later evolve into the tool-assisted speedrun. Save states were the first step along that path.

Although many save states were captured legitimately by skilled or patient players, they could also be opened and modified with a hex editor. Players with enough time and patience, coupled with some elementary knowledge of the NES hardware and the ROM image's memory layout, could isolate variables that determined the player's in-game attributes. This was particularly useful for maxing out lives and collectibles or equipping RPG avatars with enough gold, equipment, and experience to breeze through battles. Sliver X's guide to state hacking *The Legend of Zelda*'s item inventory highlights the mix of technical knowledge, experimentation, and blind luck that was involved:

The way this works is that there aren't individual bytes representing each item. All of them are represented by 01, with the exception of the 2nd potion, White and Magic swords, the Silver Arrow, the Red Candle, Triforce, and the Red Ring...Another thing to note is that items you can have multiple numbers of, such as bombs, keys, and Rupees can be represented by numbers up to their maximum limit of 255, which is FF...A few instances of weird shit can happen if you change a byte to something out of its range, like changing the sword byte to 04 or the Potion to 05. Try messing around with some crap, you might get some cool results.[54]

Cottage communities grew up around the creation, hacking, and distribution of NESticle .STA files. For the most popular titles, hackers took it one step further and programmed game-specific editors. These custom programs allowed players to edit NESticle's save states in a more user-friendly environment than the bare numeric fields of a hex editor.[55]

NESticle also had its share of technical drawbacks. For one, version 0.2 supported only four mappers (0–4). This covered a large swath of the NES and Famicom library, but excluded several "greatest hits," like *Castlevania III* (iNES 005/MMC5), *Battletoads* (iNES 007/AOROM), *Cobra Triangle* (iNES 007/ANROM), *Mike Tyson's Punch-Out!!* (iNES 009/MMC2), and the entire *Wizards & Warriors* series (iNES 007/AxROM).

Due to the sparse documentation of the NES's APU, NESticle's audio implementation was also severely underdeveloped. Bloodlust's README. txt recommended simply turning the sound off if users found it irritating.[56] And while NESticle's palettes were not as jarring as the soundtrack, they were wildly inaccurate compared to the NES's typical composite output. More importantly, mid-screen raster effects, used for status bar splits or palette swaps, were not properly understood at the time, so games that relied on carefully-timed PPU updates either did not work or exhibited noticeable glitches. Bloodlust attributed this to the shortcomings of the NES:

> There are still some bugs with games that utilize split screens. In my opinion, the NES method of split screening is utterly horrible. Lots of games rely on CPU speed to tell when to split the screen, others use a dumb hitflag, and others use IRQs. Games that switch pattern tables halfway through the frame were a bitch. Adjusting the HBlank/ Vblank length under Settings/NesTiming may fix some split screen quirks.

Whether Sardu's assessment is true or not, today's emulator authors tend to withhold judgment of Nintendo's engineering prowess and instead implement the console's architecture as accurately as possible.

Despite its shortcomings, NESticle development progressed quickly. Within two months of its debut, NESticle introduced online play (for Windows users), recording and saving audio output, and the ability to record and playback gameplay movies.[57] This latter feature was the logical extension of the .STA format. NESticle movie files (.NSM) recorded the emulator's current state as a standard .STA along with any subsequent player inputs detected until the user selected "Movie/Stop."[58] The resulting file was the combined record of a machine's initial state and a player's frame-by-frame performance.

Once Bloodlust introduced the .NSM format, sites featuring archives of NESticle movies proliferated. For the first time, NES players could witness extended game performances remotely. Prior to emulation, that type of telepresence was only available via television broadcasts or VHS direct-feed captures of gameplay, usually sold by game magazines to demonstrate tactics and tricks for a handful of games. But large-scale VHS production and distribution was impractical for most hobbyist players.

Even digital video distribution faced steep technological barriers. In the mid-1990s, hosting or viewing video online was rare. The necessary infrastructure of Internet bandwidth, PC processing power, and consumer-grade digitization software was not yet in place. Even downloading video was resource-intensive—few modems could shuttle data more than a few kilobits per second, nor could most hard drives accommodate massive video files. But describing a "movie" as a sequence of key presses mitigated the limitations of bandwidth and storage. NESticle movies were modestly sized, even by late-1990s standards, consuming approximately 432KB per hour. As long as the viewer had the proper emulator, ROM, and .NSM file, they could replay a lengthy gameplay movie at native resolution on their computer screen.

Hacks and Patches

The user modifications NESticle afforded were a new phenomenon for console owners. Few had the resources or know-how to dump, edit, and burn custom EPROMs. A handful of NES games like *Excitebike* and *Wrecking Crew* featured built-in level editors, but such tools were uncommon, edits were temporary, and there were no means to share creations with other players. Hardware cheat devices like the Game Genie only permitted users to tweak existing game parameters, and without knowledge of the peripheral's underlying code generation algorithm, players were typing codes blindly in hopes of surfacing novel results.

Emulation eliminated the hardware barrier from the modification equation. Suddenly players had the ability not only to play NES games, but also to edit, reconfigure, and remix them—a practice commonly known as "ROM hacking." *Super Mario Bros.*'s popularity made it an early and frequent target for player revision,[59] and NROM's lack of bankswitching made it trivial to pick out and edit individual tile patterns in CHR-ROM. Most alterations were simple visual tweaks, such as writing one's name in Kinoko's clouds, editing Mario's hair color, or "upgrading" the sprite and background tiles to resemble those from later games in the series. Modders also outfitted Mario in a range of outlandish—and frequently offensive—costumes and accessories, including a clown wig, wheelchair, Nazi regalia, an Afro, drug paraphernalia, and even a Ku Klux Klan hood. Intentionally or not, ROM hacks were intermingled with clean dumps of *Super Mario Bros.*, so unsuspecting downloaders might be surprised to find a ninja in Mario's place when they launched their .NES file. Eventually, as these variations spread online, it was a challenge to find a *Super Mario Bros.* ROM that had not been altered in some way.

ROM hacks likewise introduced strange cross-fertilizations of game worlds, a digital fan fiction that combined characters and scenarios from different games: Link's sprite appeared in *Super Mario Bros.*, Mario made cameos in *Metroid* (and every other conceivable game), Pauline replaced Jumpman as *Donkey Kong*'s protagonist, and *Galaga*'s armada of spaceships transformed into beer cans and bottles. Other hacks were less innocuous—overtly racist, violent, and homophobic versions of popular games cropped up in equal measure. With few barriers to expressive creation, the best and worst traits of online culture were on display.

The ease of modding existing games encouraged budding artists and level designers who might not otherwise have had access to programming tools. Mario's thirty-two original levels were reimagined and rearranged to the point that they resembled homegrown versions of the Japanese *Super Mario Bros. 2*, meant to offer new challenges to players who had mastered Mario's first adventure. Fan-remixed versions of *The Legend of Zelda* scrambled the dungeons and power-ups, much like Nintendo's own Second Quest. But all of these hacks were executed within the original ROM's parameters. Without altering the source code, any edits were still governed by the game's mapper and engine. No ROM hack, for example, could allow the *Super Mario Bros.* engine to scroll left. Elementary modifications could not bypass code-level constraints.

As ROM hacking evolved, modders pushed beyond rearrangement and remixing to tool-assisted reprogramming. IKA's top-to-bottom hack of *Rockman 2*, *Rockman No Constancy* (2007), constructed all-new level layouts, increased the game's difficulty, modified weapon and boss behaviors, altered tile patterns, and rescored the soundtrack.[60] GameMakr24's *Zelda Challenge: Outlands* (2001) gave *The Legend of Zelda* a similar treatment—every aspect of the original was changed, from the storyline to the NPC dialogue.[61] DahrkDaiz's *Mario Adventure* (2004) delved into *Super Mario Bros. 3*'s engine, adding save features, new enemy types and behaviors, random weather effects, and more.[62] This so-called "assembly hacking" required in-depth technical knowledge of the NES hardware coupled with the advanced capabilities of modern emulators, spawning fresh games from obsolete engines.

An equally important ROM hacking innovation was the translation patch, a supplementary file that could rewrite a ROM's contents (and often expand its mapper profile) to translate the in-game text from one language to another. Again, NES emulation's rapid online dissemination granted players access to games that were otherwise unavailable short of importing Japanese or European consoles and cartridges. ROM distribution eliminated economic and geographic barriers, but language still barred access to foreign titles, especially Japanese-intensive graphical adventure and RPGs. However, ROM hacking gave players access to a game's tile and program data, which in turn made fan translations possible. Players began to take localization into their own hands.

But custom translations were not as simple as swapping a few tiles, especially between languages whose grammars and character sets were drastically different (chapter 6). A single kanji ideograph, for instance, might require one or more words in English translation. This mismatch led to condensations of dialogue or menu items that ranged from artful to nonsensical—the "I AM ERROR" problem born anew, though this time as a result of limited memory rather than faulty translation. Many text-heavy RPGs like *Final Fantasy II* used compression to pack dialogue into fewer bytes, so merely locating the text in memory proved challenging, much less decrypting the techniques used to store it.

Building on the techniques they learned while disassembling commercial games, translation groups developed their own compression tricks to sneak more data into a game ROM. The documentation accompanying Demiforce's 1998 translation of *Final Fantasy II* detailed one such process:

Another technique is one of DTE (Dual Tile Encoding). DTE method was cracked on 1/16/98, meshed by the combined talents of Landy, Alex W. Jackson, and Dark Force. What it means is we took advantage of a coding technique Square uses in its japanese for the "chon chon" marks. Since there are two tiles used in chon chon characters, we took the subordinate tile and placed it after the dominant character, allowing us to display two characters with just one byte call in the ROM. When first implemented, we had about 1000 extra bytes to work with (!!!), so ever since then there's been a lot more leniency concerning detail and story length.[63]

Hobbyist translation efforts such as these, which could take months or years to complete, expanded the diversity of accessible Famicom software and exposed non-Japanese audiences to games that were previously unplayable. They also foregrounded the platform's mediating effects on a game's expressive content, an underlying layer of material translation necessary to adapt Japanese to English and cartridge to ROM.

The explosion of user-friendly emulators like NESticle helped catalyze the cultural cross-fertilization between Asian, European, and American nations presaged in the decade prior by arcade games, science fiction, comics, and animation (chapter 2). Non-Japanese players had access to a less mediated version of Japanese culture, since the Famicom-exclusive games now available as .NES files were never meant for audiences outside of Japan. Dumping ROMs directly from their Japanese sources circumvented Nintendo's corporate control over game content and distribution. Forbidden games like *Devil World*, Miyamoto's only title that never made its way to the U.S. (chapter 3), were playable by fans for the first time.

Beyond the obvious Famicom exclusives, players began to notice discrepancies in games that were released in multiple regions. Famicom Disk System originals had richer soundtracks and robust save systems. Discrepancies in cartridge hardware often hamstrung U.S. releases of Famicom titles, as in *Contra*, whose Japanese version featured animated backgrounds and interstitial cutscenes. VS. System and PlayChoice-10 varieties of familiar titles began to appear alongside their console versions. PAL exclusives joined the ranks of the NTSC catalog. Dumps of bootleg and pirate carts introduced regional variations previously unknown outside Russia, China, and Taiwan.

Developers answered the onslaught of multiplying ROMs—many of which were of questionable quality and origin—with a standardized classification system. Utilities like GoodNES, part of a larger GoodTools software suite, audited a user's ROM catalog against a verified database and labeled them according to region, variation, and quality. (ROM auditing utilities could also properly rename files and scrub dirty headers.) Distributed ROM packs often contained a text guide to help players decipher the trail of symbols and letters that now followed file names (e.g., "Metroid (E) [!].nes"). PsychophobiA's "GoodCodes.txt," for instance, covered the GoodTools hieroglyphs used for Genesis, SNES, Game Boy, and NES ROMs. Country codes were typically single capital letters in parentheses: (J) for Japan, (U) for USA, (E) for Europe, and so on. Bracketed codes indicated variations such as hacks [h], bad dumps [b], pirates [p], translations [T], or, ideally, verified good dumps [!]. Players now had a shorthand reference, written directly to the file name, to help them sort the thirty variations of *Metroid* on their hard drive.

But how did "bad dumps" originate and circulate in the first place? Errors that occurred during image transfer, hacking, zipping, or uploading files introduced data corruption to the cartridge's raw binary stream. Unwitting players would then download, copy, and share those files, polluting the pool of good dumps with bad. Nonetheless, if a ROM was particularly rare, it might be the only dump available until a cleaner source surfaced, and semi-working ROMS were better than no ROM at all. Furthermore, once utilities like GoodNES appeared, it was simple to scan one's library and highlight offending files. If a user chose not to discard the corrupted ROM (or simply didn't understand the [b] designator), its further dissemination would at least be flagged for future downloaders. Even amidst the grey legalities of ROM dumping, hacking, and distribution, rules arose to ensure the pedigree of one's virtual collection.

Text Movies

NESticle was not the first NES emulator, but it introduced or popularized a number of now standard augmentations like save states, simple tile editing, and movie recording. Above and beyond those early innovations, contemporary NES emulators now offer near-IDE levels of code manipulation. FCEUX, for example, features a built-in hex editor, inline assembler, debugger, and PPU viewer.[64] Modern emulators not only play games, but dissect and disclose their processes, allowing users to watch the game engine access and write registers, populate pattern tables, manipulate RAM, and more. It is like going to a movie theater and watching the film run from Final Cut on a seat-mounted laptop that allows you to tweak the speed, angles, and edits to your liking.

Though the film metaphor seems like an apt fit for the tool-assisted speedrun, since the outcome of its performance is commonly called a "movie," that label does not accurately describe either its process or result. NESticle .NSMs were save states with twice-per-frame key presses appended. The underlying content was not visual, but a chain of bytes meant to trigger response from an emulator loaded with the appropriate ROM. The .NSM was more akin to a macro or script than what we would commonly call a video. Likewise, tool-assisted runs are not spliced sections of normal gameplay, but meticulously assembled frames of player input, closer in function to animation and choreography than filmmaking. In a practice called "re-recording," players drop the game's playback speed significantly and cycle through small segments of gameplay—bookended by save states—altering variables until they generate an optimized run.[65] Once that segment is satisfactorily complete, they create a new save state and the process continues.

In FCEUX, a movie is a specially formatted plain ASCII text file saved with the extension .FM2.[66] The .FM2's ASCII format is advantageous since it is human-readable. Once one is familiar with .FM2's syntax, it is easy to decode the system of key presses and edit them like a spreadsheet. Like the ROMs they enact, movie files contain a short header followed by a data stream. The header is a chain of key-value pairs used to describe the emulator version, the type of input device used, the frame length of the movie, runner comments, and so on. The header for Nick Mong's (aka mmbossman) TAS of *Arumana no Kiseki*, for example, reads as follows:

```
version 3
emuVersion 20100
rerecordCount 13078
palFlag 0
romFilename Arumana no Kiseki
romChecksum base64:hjO8JpyaAlI9rmzVvydgCA==
guid F91714F1-7905-8548-6B40-C4600750A645
fourscore 0
port0 1
port1 1
port2 0
comment author mmbossman⁶⁷
```

The checksums, ids, and version numbers are meant to ensure the TAS's exact replication on a user's system. Without the properly calibrated setup, a movie will not play back accurately.[68]

The data section following the header is called the input log. Each frame of the movie is given its own line, bookended by pipe ("|") characters. Following the first pipe is the input port value (e.g., "0" for joypad 1), another pipe, then eight "bits" representing the possible joypad presses for that frame. The text block below is a four-frame excerpt from Mong's TAS:

```
|0|R..U....|........||
|0|R..U..B.|........||
|0|R..U....|........||
|0|R..U...A|........||
```

Line/frame 1 represents the D-pad's right (R) and up (U) keys pressed *simultaneously*. Frame 2's input continues to hold right and up while also pressing B. The final two frames release B then press A. Note that the preceding text block describes only 1/15 of a second. The full TAS input log of a NES speedrun, which is typically under twenty minutes in real-time playback, can run tens of thousands of lines long.

A finished movie reads as a frame-by-frame list of inputs in sequential order, an editable input recipe for perfect play. Conceivably, with superhuman skill and memorization, a player could replicate this list on real hardware. In practice such play is impossible, since speedruns often rely on mutually exclusive key presses (e.g., left and right simultaneously) in a single frame, a feat humanly and mechanically implausible. Mashing left and right on the D-pad requires at least two fingers and a fair bit of force—a task much too convoluted to execute in 1/60 of a second, much less in a series of similarly deft key presses.

These strange inputs, in turn, trigger conditions that the game's programmers did not account for. When object interaction in a game engine expects to execute branch statements based on binary inputs—if the player presses up, move up, otherwise, move down—"overloading" the system with unforeseen input can create unexpected behaviors. A sprite's coordinates, for instance, might suddenly update by several pixels more than intended, bypassing the collision detection check that was meant to prevent the sprite from passing through a solid wall. Holding up and down simultaneously while riding elevators in *Zelda II*, for example, allows the player to warp vertically through dungeon levels.[69] Input glitches like these are the holy grail of TAS assemblers, allowing them to short-circuit large segments of gameplay in the name of faster completion.

What motivates this type of play? Can we still label it "play" as such? And what do the limits of play teach us about the limits of platforms? James Newman provides a number of answers to the first question in his discussion of "superplay."[70] First, there are the goals common to video-games, non-digital games, sports, and many types of unstructured play: creative expression, competition, socializing, self-improvement, community-building, and public recognition. Another process at work, and a proclivity of digital media like videogames, is the mastery and manipulation of an underlying procedural system—"playing" and "gaming" in the sense of bending or breaking rules to gain an advantage.

Newman explains that "this system of rules and boundaries is not fixed but rather is permeable and in a state of flux as it is interrogated, operated on, and played with. Moreover, the system may behave in an unpredictable manner unintended by the game designers due to imperfections in the code or unanticipated emergent contingencies."[71] In this interplay, Newman concludes, "both player as performer and game system should be considered agents in the process of gameplay."

Rule-breaking is certainly enticing to TAS assemblers. There is a transgressive aspect of playing a game "wrong," while in the process, playing it better than any human could. The perceived rigidity of computational platforms—slaves to the stark microcosm of algorithms and binary digits—loosens as we witness the odd spectacle of a violated game space. The game engine behaves erratically when fed unexpected inputs. Algorithms run awry. Binary says "and" instead of "either/or." This is why the TAS movie, in its text form, is eventually recorded as a movie proper that can be posted online and shared with others. The TAS community's emphasis on entertainment value insists that a run must be seen.

TAS text movies archive encounters between source code and input code. Over time, as a platform is better understood, one might reasonably assume that the human player's role will eventually disappear, that a computer might learn to play the emulator and ROM with limited external assistance. TAS assemblers are already building external tools to automate some aspects of the TAS-building process. Adelikat's TAS of *Gradius*, for instance, uses a "macro editor patch" for FCEU that allows him to program complex input strings, resulting in the ship flying in a number of predefined patterns:

> To create this run, I used a "macro-editor." With this editor, I can create a series of button presses and put them together into a single command. This allows me to push one button to initiate very complex movement patterns. Writing my name "adelikat" for instance was a large programmed macro...I simply had to find a frame to start it that didn't result in the ship being destroyed.[72]

As the TAS evolves, tools are encroaching into play itself.

Choreographic Play

N. Katherine Hayles coined the term "dynamic heterarchy" to describe a "multi-tiered system in which feedback and feedforward loops tie the system together through continuing interactions," whose tiers "continuously inform and mutually determine each other."[73] She develops the term to describe our encounters with various electronic texts, but reminds us that these heterarchies can be biological as well, like the complex "system" formed between mother and fetus.

The adjective "tool-assisted" indicates a dynamic heterarchy between player and emulator that operates in the execution of a speedrun. The player initializes the system through input, making an onscreen character run, jump, or shoot. The system then reacts procedurally—an adversary appears, the character's body makes contact with an object, a timer ticks down. Based upon this feedback, the player then adjusts their subsequent input—or, more crucially, revises prior inputs by resetting the system to a known state in order to either perfect their input or evaluate an alternate system response. In real time (e.g., the traditional speedrun), this trade of actions and reactions is linear and unpredictable. A player cannot retroactively adjust their input stream beyond the typical looped structure of play, death, and re-play, while the range of system reactions are too numerous or complex to react to with normal human reflexes.

By leveraging the assistance of the emulation tool, the execution of the underlying computational processes becomes legible. A player witnesses the machinations that take place in a single frame or cycle. At this fine-grained level of perception, fissures arise: the sparse boundaries of objects permit elisions of solids and bodies; a system expecting only single inputs per frame reroutes to unexpected junctures when this expectation is overloaded; the bare clockwork of computation becomes predictable, even manipulable. Tool-assisted speedrunners have even coined a clever oxymoron—"luck manipulation"—to describe their ability to coax a game's pseudo-random processes toward predictability, like avoiding enemy encounters in *Dragon Warrior* or triggering favorable item drops in *Mega Man 3*.[74]

Even experienced video game players are left bewildered by a number of the most extreme tool-assisted runs. The content of a glitched performance borders on illegibility as fragments of displaced tiles rearrange into 8-bit cubist collages, bizarre visual references to what was once a playable game.[75] Other TASs are comical in their brevity. The run for Genesis title *King's Bounty* completes the lengthy turn-based strategy game in under ten seconds—and most of that time is spent loading the screen. In a 2009 feature on "insanely thrilling" tool-assisted speedruns, videogame journalist John Teti describes a *Rockman* run that uses bugs and exploits "to such a degree that the action is distorted and barely recognizable, almost like an avant-garde film."[76] Teti is alluding to the systematic breakdown of spatial and temporal boundaries that violate viewers' expectations of continuity, coherent objects, and even legible behavior of the underlying procedural system. In everyday computer use, the glitch or bug are phenomena to be avoided. The TAS elevates and foregrounds error as a means to mastery.

What happens at the limits of the tool-assisted speedrun, when all possible avenues for gains in speed and glitch manipulation are exhausted? One possibility is the emergence of a TAS that is meant to be visually interesting or aesthetically pleasing for its own sake, regardless of whether speed is sacrificed in the process. Practices such as these, which hover at the fringe of many disciplines, including dance, animation, performance, video, and sport, I call *choreographic play*.

Adelikat's *Gradius* TAS is a prime example of the form. Since *Gradius* is a side-scrolling shoot-'em-up, it seems an odd choice for a speedrun, as most of its gameplay speed is fixed. Scrolling progresses at a constant rate regardless of player action. Barring death or pre-scripted action sequences, the player is meant to arrive at the end of a stage on schedule. Only the boss fights that occur at the end of each stage grant any leeway in the final run time. Accordingly, Adelikat's description under the "Overall Aim" heading in his author's notes emphasizes both speed and beauty:

> The goal is to take a game with this kind of speed potential and push it to the limit. This allows me to create a run where the on screen animation becomes a visual pattern resulting in the less & less importance on the game itself. The run transcends the usual gaming logic and becomes a sort of abstract art. The run becomes something unique and emphasizes the potential for TASes to truly be considered art.[77]

I am less concerned with the artistic merits of the TAS than their careful marriage of speed, form, and motion. Using the spaceship to paint geometric patterns or the author's name emphasizes the subjective element of the TAS while still leveraging the automated assistance of non-human tools. The underlying aesthetic dimension of play—a trait we appreciate in sport, musical improvisation, and videogames alike—points to a new direction in emulation-assisted play that is not focused squarely on raw speed or entertainment.

Baxter's mesmerizing TAS of *Arkanoid* has similar aims.[78] He chooses to skip the time-saving Laser power-up, which can obliterate blocks by shooting them with the paddle, in favor of the 3-ball power-up, which releases two additional balls on the screen. The result is a hypnotic high-speed juggling act that is as compelling sonically as it is visually. The geometric arrangements of kaleidoscopic bricks emanate erratic melodies as they struggle to keep apace of the ricocheting balls. Similarly, Baxter and AngerFist's collaborative multi-screen TAS of *Mega Man 3, 4, 5,* and *6*—played simultaneously by the same sequence of inputs—coalesces into a manic cacophony of sound and image, more John Cage than Keiji Inafune.[79] In all cases, the weird creative artifact that is a TAS exposes the strange limitations of medium specificity that exist at the borderlines of all media. A completed TAS is called a movie, but it is not. Instead it is, all at once, a text file, a performance, a dance, an animation, a procedural event, sport, entertainment, a social act, an ethics, an archive, and yet still a videogame.

The vitriol initially surrounding Morimoto's *Super Mario Bros. 3* TAS implied that the human element was somehow slipping away, that automata would eventually surpass the efforts of flesh and blood. An artificial intelligence system could conceivably find the best routes, manipulate luck in beneficial ways, and minimize the key presses necessary to complete a game. Certainly some of the scripting tools now available to automate play lean toward that outcome. But we should be wary to rely solely on the end result of the TAS process. The final "movie" is a human impossibility, but using it as an example of eliminating human intervention ignores hundreds of laborious hours invested into perfecting a run. Moreover, as long as games are differentiated at the engine level, there can be no reliable means to algorithmically generate speedruns for a wide swath of games. The engine driving *Ninja Gaiden* is fundamentally different than the one driving *The Legend of Zelda*. Their object handling, collision detection, sound routines, bankswitching, and compression algorithms make it impossible to write a generic TAS-generator that could compete with the most meticulous human assemblers. Stranger still, the efforts of the TAS community now influence the traditional speedrunners. The latter study the techniques of the former to learn new strategies, adapt their play styles, become more mechanistic and precise in their play. Humans emulate emulators. New and unforeseen heterarchies arise.

Afterword: Famicom Remix

This isn't a compilation…

- Nintendo's official NES Remix *website*

In December 2013, Nintendo simultaneously announced and released *Famicom Remix*, known as *NES Remix* outside Japan, for download on the Wii U eShop. *Famicom Remix* compiles sixteen first-party titles, from *Super Mario Bros.* to *Urban Champion*, representing Nintendo's early console history. Though most of these games were available for download previously as standalone Virtual Console titles, *Famicom Remix* introduces, true to its name, a series of escalating gameplay variations that recasts each game as a host for dozens of mini-games, similar to Nintendo's popular *WarioWare* series.

Players must first complete a number of trivial exercises meant to acclimate them to each game's mechanics. An introductory challenge series in *Zelda*, for instance, requires the player to 1) enter the cave in the opening screen and grab the sword, 2) clear a screen of Octoroks, 3) revive life from a fairy, 4) purchase an item from the shop, and 5) find and enter the first dungeon. The sum of these actions takes approximately forty-five seconds. Successfully completing challenges awards stars and points that unlock new challenges, new games, and special remix levels.

In the standard challenge mode, games are presented in their original format. Beyond some sprite scaling to bring the PPU's native resolution up to modern standards, a border to pad out the 4:3 resolution to 16:9, and the *Remix* HUD, no in-game embellishments are added. *Ice Climber* looks and plays like the original, for better or worse. However, *Famicom Remix*'s namesake mode introduces odd variations of the games' core mechanics, enhanced graphical effects, and mixtures of characters and settings. In one remix series, the player must guide Link through a Death Mountain screen while its pixels gradually abstract into blocky mosaics, then seconds later use Link to complete *Donkey Kong*'s opening girders scene—without the benefit of Jumpman's jump. Similar challenges require players to speedrun *Super Mario Bros.* stages, collect the bonus coins in *Mario Bros.* with a duplicate Mario sprite, finish an *Excitebike* track with only a spotlight to guide them, and navigate a *Donkey Kong Jr.* level while the background tiles blink on and off.

Famicom Remix 2 quickly followed in April 2014, reaching further into Nintendo's first-party catalog with twelve additional games, ranging from their most famous sequels, like *Super Mario Bros. 3* and *The Adventure of Link*, to their final Famicom release ワリオの森 *(Wario's Woods)*. The sequence of challenges and unlocks are largely similar, though the individual tasks feel more developed, since the range of titles are no longer predominantly single-screen arcade fare. The sophisticated open-world adventuring of *Metroid* generates a richer series of challenges than, say, *Pinball* or *Wrecking Crew*. Genre subtleties notwithstanding, it is clear from the sequel's rapid development time that Nintendo found a successful, iterable formula.

In the U.S., critical reception to the series has been mixed.[1] The initial excitement of playing recontextualized NES classics quickly evaporates in the face of the menial gameplay labor required to unlock the game's more inventive remix levels. It is a sentiment best expressed in Kyle Orland's *Ars Technica* review, which calls the collection "more evocative than transformative," banking on Nintendo's "vast troves of nostalgia" to ultimately produce another franchise rehash—"recycled and chopped up classics dressed up in a new form."[2]

The critical malaise is partly attributable to a mismatch between Nintendo's intended audience and the demographics of games journalism. Seasoned players who have spent decades with Nintendo's catalog find directives like "jump a barrel" rote, but to new or younger players, the grammar of nostalgia—and its accompanying haptic reflexes—is not so ingrained. Nintendo's own gender-specific marketing indicates as much: "All those games our dads played passionately back in the day have been reborn!"[3] This is not a game designed for the dads (and hopefully moms) to relive their Famicom halcyon days. It is a game meant to introduce a new generation to Nintendo's legacy.

Orland's deeper complaints stem from a misunderstanding of *Famicom Remix*'s technological underpinnings. Series director and programmer Koichi Hayashida stressed in a 2014 interview that he wanted the games to be "true to the spirit of the originals," including Famicom quirks like OAM cycling and gameplay slowdown,[4] and several textual and technical details indicate that *Remix* is, in fact, running on a sophisticated emulation core rather than ground-up rebuilds of each game. For one, the development turnaround indicates that Hayashida's team is not creating custom replicas of dozens of Famicom games (as Capcom did for faux-retro releases *Mega Man 9* and *Mega Man 10*). While their engines are simplistic by modern standards, accurately modeling the look and feel of games as disparate as *Metroid* and *Ice Hockey* in only four months would be impossible. Building *Remix*'s engine around a single emulation core that can play and manipulate multiple ROM images is far more feasible.

There are also platform-specific clues that emulation drives the *Remix* series. In *Super Mario Bros. 3*, attribute glitches are clearly visible along the screen's border, sprites cycle accurately when the scanline limit is exceeded, and power-ups spawn properly behind blocks.[5] In *The Legend of Zelda*, APU channel priorities and the noticeable sound engine hiccup while scrolling dungeon screens are identical to those found in the original. In remix stages, when background tiles vanish to add an extra challenge, only tiles from the sprite pattern table remain. In *Donkey Kong Jr.*, Jumpman and Donkey Kong disappear, since they are composed of background tiles. Replicating these arcane platform behaviors to such exacting detail would be possible in a custom engine, but not in *Remix*'s limited development time.

As the Game Genie proved decades ago, manipulating memory registers to create alternate physics or life counts is a straightforward process, even on hardware. With emulation, altering game attributes is far simpler. *Famicom Remix*'s introductory challenges likely use a variety of save states to place the player at predetermined points. *Remix*'s engine can then watch for specific changes in memory—did Link collect the sword?—to trigger a challenge's success or failure. HUD cues like the circles and arrows that instruct players during challenges have no effect on gameplay, so they can simply be painted atop the emulation window.

The remix stages prove trickier to assess since they clearly violate the PPU's capabilities. Game protagonists swap, objects have depth and shading, backgrounds are painted with smooth gradients, tiles expand to many times their original size, and sprites duplicate without any apparent processor impact. But as we saw in the previous chapter, *Famicom Remix* is duplicating, albeit in a polished commercial package, the work ROM hackers and emulator authors have produced for decades. Link has been playable in *Donkey Kong* since NESticle made it simple for any user to draw over in-game pattern tiles. Sharable save states and hex editing have made it trivial to play a game from any point with any outlay of stats and equipment you might desire. Blinking a game's background tiles into and out of existence is a clever gameplay challenge, but the effect only requires a one-bit PPU register toggle. Even *Remix*'s advanced graphical tricks have corollaries in the emulation scene. Procyon Loto's FCE3D, for instance, is a fork of the FCEUX emulator that incorporates voxel rendering, extruding the PPU's tiles into 3D space.

But emulation can only extend so far. One can poke and prod at the ROM's memory, augment the PPU's rendering routines, isolate audio channels, or simulate NTSC artifacts, but one can not fundamentally alter the game's engine without extensive reprogramming. Assembly hacks like *Rockman No Constancy* require deeper technical engagement than emulation alteration. To produce such a drastic gameplay overhaul, one must delve into the source and alter code. So when Orland levels his strongest complaint against *NES Remix*, it belies a misunderstanding of the platforms at work:

> The most frustratingly intriguing bit of *NES Remix* is found in a couple of microgames that throw *Legend of Zelda* hero Link into levels from *Donkey Kong*, showing Nintendo's willingness to actually mix together its disparate game worlds in some interesting ways. Unfortunately, Link can't even use his trademark sword in these levels, functionally transforming him into just a version of Mario that can't jump. It's kind of incredible that Nintendo didn't take the concept of mix-and-match characters and environments further, especially when indie fan games like *ROM Check Fail* have already done so with aplomb.[6]

Regarding *Donkey Kong*'s inclusion of a jumpless, swordless Link, Orland adds: "What's the point?"

The point is that the remix Orland desires is impossible without a platform-level redesign of *Donkey Kong*'s mechanics. It is simple to re-skin Jumpman with Link's sprite and disable the jump button—these all fall within *Donkey Kong*'s engine parameters. But introducing a mechanic that does not exist would require injecting new assembly routines, a meticulous and time-consuming task not worth the effort for a twenty-second mini-game.[7] One does not simply mix the *Legend of Zelda* and *Donkey Kong* engines and expect a gameplay hybrid to arise. Games like *ROM Check Fail* that scrape the graphical and audio assets from classic games and reconfigure them in chimeric form do so superficially. Spending time with Mario's controls in *Super Mario Bros.* then swapping to *ROM Check Fail* makes it clear that the engines are not the same. ActionScript and assembly bear different fruit.

Famicom Remix, in a single digital object, encapsulates the multiple themes driving this book's purpose. The divergent regional titles are a nod to an era in Nintendo's history when translation was a mediating factor in their potential success abroad. Worldwide release of a game called *Famicom Remix*, its title redolent in gold and maroon, would stir some Nintendo diehards, but the majority of videogame players who still have no idea what a Famicom is or was would pass it over as a Japanese oddity. But *NES Remix*, its title emblazoned atop the familiar shape and palette of an NES controller, has a far bigger impact on audiences outside Japan.

Subtler translations are at work in the selection and presentation of *Remix*'s titles. In Japan, Nintendo respects their own platform chronology and offers the original FDS versions of *Ice Hockey*, *The Legend of Zelda*, *Zelda II*, *Kid Icarus*, and *Metroid*, complete with emulation of the peripheral's additional sound channel. *NES Remix* swaps appropriately to their respective NROM and MMC1 cartridge ports minus the bonus audio. Likewise, *NES Remix* receives two versions of *Super Mario Bros. 2*—the NES "original" and the so-called "Lost Levels"—while *Famicom Remix* contains FDS *Super Mario Bros. 2* and *Super Mario USA*.

From a platform studies perspective, *Famicom Remix*'s gameplay quality or the resulting review metrics are its least interesting characteristics. More fascinating is the game's reabsorption of the Famicom's platform history after its commercial demise. Speedruns, save states, and ROM hacks are all residuals of emulation development, the output of a community that has existed largely among amateur programmers and Nintendo hobbyists, often at the periphery of legality. Nintendo is not simply re-presenting their own legacy, but directly competing with the emulation ecosystem that has thrived for decades, generating their own Famicom hacks and remixes. Nintendo is redefining its platform in its own emulated image. But they are also expanding the notion of what the Famicom platform is and can be.

Nintendo adopts the trendy musical lingo of the "remix" and "mash-up" to market the *Remix* series, but the culture of reappropriation, revision, and recycling evinced by these terms has been a prevalent part of Nintendo's design philosophy since at least the 1970s, when Gunpei

Yokoi began adapting proven concepts from his toy designs to electronic and computer games. With Nintendo's future uncertain in the face of competitors who are more adept in mobile gaming, app ecosystems, online infrastructures, and third-party recruitment, critics are quick to attack Nintendo's rigorous adherence to proven franchises and formulas.

That assessment holds a grain of truth. The whimsical animation used to show progress during a Virtual Console download often feels like a metaphor for Nintendo's design strategy—Mario runs left to right in an infinite loop, collecting coins, while the player waits eagerly, hoping something will change. But the criticism also ignores Nintendo's history of patient iteration, often conjuring the phoenix of success from the ashes of failure. *Radar Scope* yields *Donkey Kong*. The LCD calculator yields the Game & Watch. The Game & Watch yields the D-pad and the Nintendo DS. The Virtual Boy yields the 3DS. And on and on. The Wii U may be a bust—it is too soon to tell—but it is certain that its creative spark will live on in a future design.

Among hobbyist programmers, the Famicom and NES's futures are bright. Thanks to the convergence of increasingly accurate emulators, robust development tools, and crowd-sourced documentation, the homebrew community has begun to produce games that rival commercial NES titles. Sivak's *Battle Kid* series, miau's *Super Bat Puncher* demo, Rachel Simone Weil's *Track + Feel II*, Damian Yerrick's *Thwaite*, Gradual Games' *Nomolos*, shiru and pinwizz's *Zooming Secretary*, Adolfsson and Eriksson's *Driar*, and thefox's *Streemerz* are all standout examples. Hundreds of other programmers, hardware hackers, artists, designers, and musicians continue to use the Famicom as a platform for creative expression, independent of Nintendo's commercial concerns.

When we try to comprehend the entirety of a platform's uses, its expressive range, its variation in hardware and software, its persistence and improvement through emulation, we find that its reach is strangely liminal. What is the Nintendo Family Computer platform? Is it a collection of ICs, PCBs, card edge connectors, and silicon traces assembled in a plastic frame? If so, then what is the NES, the Sharp Twin Famicom, the Mattel PAL NES, the Dendy? Is the platform merely an abstraction of hardware that can play Famicom and NES games? If so, then we have suddenly expanded the field to all manner of Famiclones and emulators, from the homebrewed RetroZone PowerPak to NESticle to *Animal Crossing*'s unlockable NES games to *Famicom Remix*.

In light of these blurred boundaries, it is clear that a platform is an evolving negotiation between static and dynamic forms. A finalized configuration of hardware and software must be settled upon as a basis for creating digital objects, but that configuration is susceptible to translation, transposition, modification, revision, expansion, and emulation. A platform is therefore more convention than console, more abstraction than assembled product. And how strange that platform studies, an approach so rooted in material objects, should lose grasp of its borders at the moment when they feel closest at hand.

Appendix A: Famicom/NES Bibliographic Descriptions

Platform studies owes much to the discipline of bibliography, which provides systematic descriptions of manuscripts, books, codices, pamphlets, rolls, and other printed matter. Bibliography is itself split into manifold sub-disciplines, each with its own corpus of study, technical language, and process.[1] Readers are likely most familiar with *enumerative* (or reference) bibliography, the list of works, print and otherwise, found at the end of this and other books. In its utilitarian form, the enumerative bibliography is meant to provide readers with enough information to locate the sources mentioned in the text.

Other branches of bibliography analyze printed matter for evidence of their production. *Codicology*, for instance, narrows its study to the codex as a material form, distinct from papyrus rolls (*papyrology*) or various legal documents (*diplomatics*). Similarly, *analytical* bibliography studies printed books as "products of a particular manufacturing or technical process."[2] In other words, the content of the book is not the focus. Rather, the bibliographer examines the work as a specific material artifact comprising ink, paper, binding, printer's marks, and so on. Two books with identical authors, chapters, and words may in fact be wholly distinct physical objects. The related discipline of *descriptive* bibliography widens the analytic net to describe all features of a particular book, whether they are related to the print process or not. Stray marks, bookplates, page counts, and missing leaves all fall within the descriptive purview.

To claim that videogame bibliography demands a closer allegiance to the practices listed above assumes that a unified practice called "videogame bibliography" even exists. At their best, videogame citations adhere to the barest enumerative models. Even in those texts that most seriously grapple with electronic artifacts as objects that exhibit physical properties worthy of description, such as Kirschenbaum's *Mechanisms* or Montfort and Bogost's *Racing the Beam*, videogames are still afforded scant bibliographic information. Their treatments within the text are generally better. Kirschenbaum, for instance, devotes an entire chapter to a "forensic investigation" of the Apple II game *Mystery House*, but the comprehensive work done in that chapter is supported by the following bibliographic entry:

Williams, Roberts and Ken Williams. *Mystery House*. Los Angeles: Sierra On-Line, 1980, 1987. Available online at ftp://ftp.apple .asimov.net/pub/apple_II/images/games/adventure/.[3]

Kirschenbaum's citation uses a familiar enumerative model, but in a study so intimately concerned with the material substrate of disks and drives, what does this tell us about the object itself? What is the disk size and file format? What do the multiple dates denote? Are they the release dates of the original disk or the disk image available for download? Kirschenbaum mentions the APPLEWIN emulator as a means to play Apple II disk images, but was that the emulator he used to investigate *Mystery House*? And should we not differentiate between emulated and non-emulated media?

One problem facing videogame bibliography is the medium's relative youthfulness. Commercial videogames have only been with us since the 1970s. Generations of consoles and games still litter yard sales, attics, pawnshops, and thrift stores. Our familiarity with and access to videogames is taken for granted, since many of us are old enough to recall first-hand experience with the entire history of videogames—a claim that cannot be made by scholars of other media. There is an implicit assumption that we all know what a *Super Mario Bros.* cartridge looks like, so why bother with thorough descriptions?

Consider the following citations for *Super Mario Bros.* culled from a number of scholarly texts on videogames. In Newman, all references to the game are listed with title alone—no dates, authors, or bibliographic citations. In contrast, traditional printed texts, films, and even websites merit standard enumerative listings.[4] The game fares the same in Kline— no date, attribution, or citation.[5] In Wolf, we see a slight improvement, complete with media-specific distinctions to indicate that both a videogame and a film share the same title: "*Super Mario Bros.* (game, 1985; film,

1995)."[6] In Montfort and Bogost, we have the following: "Nintendo. *Super Mario Bros.* Nintendo Entertainment System. Designed by Shigeru Miyamoto. 1985."[7] In Bogost's *How to Do Things with Videogames*, we find a terser version: "*Super Mario Bros.* Nintendo Entertainment System. Developed and published by Nintendo, 1985."[8] In both cases, we see the acknowledgment of a console, credits for a developer/publisher, and a release date. Bateman is a notable outlier, tipping his hat to materiality, despite a minor factual inaccuracy: "Nintendo EAD (1983). *Super Mario Bros.* [Cartridge], Nintendo Entertainment System, Kyoto, Nintendo Co., Ltd."[9]

Compare these citations to bibliographic descriptions found among fan communities. BootGod's NES Cart Database lists *fourteen* individual entries that include "Super Mario Bros." in the title. These range from the original Famicom release to the German RevA multi-cart *Super Mario Bros./Tetris/Nintendo World Cup*. Each entry include copious technical details, part listings, scans of carts and boards, manufacturer information, revisions, chip labels, and more. The NintendoAge game search, which pays closer attention to variations in cart labels, box art, and related miscellany, lists more than two dozen entries for *Super Mario Bros.* The rabbit hole runs deeper when we consider arcade versions, ports, tabletop toys, ROM hacks, and the hundreds of extant pirate cartridges featuring *Super Mario Bros.* that circulate worldwide.

Are these variations important? Consider a hypothetical foil from the print world:

Tolstoy, Leo. *War and Peace.* 1869.

Would this citation be sufficient for a scholarly article? Am I citing the original Russian? If not, who were the translators? Is the French translated inline or in footnotes? Is the text based on the original manuscript, the printed version, a later revision, etc.? I use this example as an extreme case, but the above citation style is the shorthand we see used time and again for videogames, if we see any at all.

Worse yet is the conflation of emulated and physical videogame artifacts. Chapter 8 has hopefully divested readers of the notion that ROMs are identical to cartridges. Emulation serves admirable aims in preservation, archiving, scholarship, convenience, and accessibility, but it is never perfect. In *The Medium of Video Games*, an early example of videogame scholarship, Wolf provides a prescient warning for scholars relying on emulation:

For researchers trying to track down hard-to-find games, emulators can sometimes give a good idea what certain early games were like. However, not all emulators give exact renditions of the games they are emulating; graphics may not appear at their original ratios, and the experience of watching a computer screen is often quite different from that of a television screen, or better still, a period television of the sort on which the games would have been played. Emulators can be of use in video game research, but users should beware of the differences and get firsthand experience whenever possible.[10]

Even the lowly 6502, an ancient slab of silicon compared to today's microprocessors, is an almost infinitely complex bit of hardware, subject to manufacturing bugs, temperature fluctuations, corrosion, and programmer exploitation. And this is only one component of a complex console, a machine that continues to yield surprises unknown to programmers and engineers of the Famicom era. And while ROMs may reproduce identical *visual* results when played alongside physical cartridges, we know that they often carry along unseen textual artifacts of their history, circulation, and distribution. None of these aspects should be ignored when we take bibliographic account of our digital objects.

Montfort, following the work of Clara Fernandez-Vara, proposes that emulators count as "editions" (or "printings") of a computer.[11] This approach leans in the right direction, but there is an assumed hierarchical and chronological organization that belies the reality of emulated systems. As he says, "The first edition would be the original piece of hardware," but the "original" is often not a given. In many cases, for both hardware and software, emulation precedes the physical platform. Even in the Famicom era, game software often ran on an emulation terminal before it was burnt to an EPROM for hardware testing. In such cases, the physical object is rightly the edition of a prior emulated form.

Though I list specific works and authors above, the point is not to pick on this or that scholar. The point is to raise the bar for the minimum acceptable quality of bibliographic information. Quality descriptive bibliography is hard work. It is, on its own, a platform studies problem that warrants careful attention to the types of descriptions available for any given computational object. In other words, rich bibliographic records necessarily require a baseline technical understanding of the objects they describe. This is true for analog and digital media alike. If I do not understand the form and function of the Famicom's various mappers, for instance, I may not comprehend their importance to a game's descriptive listing. Likewise, the bibliographic description that suits a Famicom cartridge will not necessarily suit a ColecoVision cartridge, TurboGrafx-16 HuCard, Xbox Live Arcade download, or PlayStation 3 Blu-Ray disk. There is not a generic enumerative style that will apply to all videogames across all platforms.

This presents a problem for videogame texts with a wide scope. As a Famicom scholar, I may possess the terminology to describe that platform's media but meanwhile lack the platform-specific knowledge to properly cite a PlayStation 2 game. My listings for the latter will suffer as a result. And *I AM ERROR* inevitably fails on this account. Chapter 2 alone lists dozens of arcade games, most with their own peculiar hardware architectures. Granting each its due description poses a sizable research challenge. One solution is to build up a body of platform-specific descriptions that others may use as a model for their own research, in the same way that codices or contracts have their own unique languages and methodologies. Once a workable model forms, it may disseminate to the scholarly community for adoption and, more importantly, refinement. But such shared knowledge will take time and work.

I AM ERROR aims to be an example of good form, both in theory and practice, within its narrow scope of platform history. Outlined below are two models for bibliographic records of Famicom/NES artifacts, both physical and digital. The first is a proposed enumerative form I adopt for all Famicom/NES cartridges and disks cited in the book. The second enumerative model describes ROMs meant for play in a compatible emulator. Since ROMs are a different digital object than the hardware they describe, they deserve a separate entry. Again, I have adopted this model throughout the book, making sure to notate when a game is played on authentic hardware or on an emulator, especially when screenshots are provided.

The proposed listings are models, not canon. In my examples, I borrow extensively from the bibliographic tradition. Over time, these conventions may prove inadequate. But until videogame bibliography develops its own voice, it must speak with borrowed tongues.

Listing 1: Enumerative type for citing Famicom, NES, and compatible cartridges and disks.

Format:

Title. Platform (media), TV format [Region]. Catalog ID (Form, Revision). PCB Class [Mapper | ROM1 size/type | ROM2 size/type | ... | Lockout model | Mirroring]. Developer {Credits}: Publisher, Release date.

Videogame authorship poses problems for citation, especially games hailing from the early years of the medium. The standard enumerative model that lists author first is often stymied by the absence of a single author (since games are usually designed by teams of tens to hundreds) or any credits at all. As such, listing the game title first is preferable. Games are commonly known by their title rather than by their designers, so this aids readers consulting citations. It also groups similar titles across divergent platforms. Comparing the myriad ports of *Donkey Kong* is far simpler when they are listed sequentially.

The choice of how and where to list the game's creative team is up to the discretion of the bibliographer. One choice is to treat the videogame as an "edited volume," using the creative lead/director as the "editor." This does not solve the auteur-centric problem inherited from cinema, wherein the director takes top billing above all other collaborators, but it does serve the practical purpose of narrowing down dozens or hundreds of contributors to a short list. I opt to list known contributors in braces next to the developer credit. This may be omitted for editorial purposes or if the contributors are unknown. There are no perfect solutions to videogame attribution, only those that suit the text at hand.

The title should be as accurate as possible. Japanese titles in particular pose problems for Famicom citations (in English) since the labels often display Japanese titles, English titles, or a mixture of both. When possible, list the most prominent title first, along with the alternate title in parentheses. When the title is a translation not seen on the actual cart, indicate it as such.

Next list the platform and media type. Famicom games come as carts or disks and should be labeled as such. Pin sizes further differentiate Famicom (or pirate) carts from NES game paks. Pin sizes may be truncated to "72-p. cart" or "60-p. cart" if preferred. The TV format and region follows, indicating the cart's proper playback and country of origin.

Catalog IDs designate Nintendo's internal cataloguing scheme, though many third-party licensees adopted similar nomenclature. Within parentheses, one can list further details about the cartridge form factor (e.g., 3- or 5-screw, prototype, test cart) and any relevant revision information (e.g., bug fixes or scrubbed content were often shipped as separate revisions).

The PCB class and subsequent cartridge hardware descriptions can vary in length according to the complexity of the mapper and the underlying ICs. When applicable, the mapper should be listed first, followed by

ROM types and capacities, lockout chip (or circumvention hardware), batteries, SRAM, and sound chips. The last element in this field will designate the cart's mirroring setting (e.g., "V" for vertical, "H" for horizontal, "MC" for mapper-controlled).

The final line lists the development house, any known contributors, publisher, and release date. Many FC/NES games do not a have known release dates. Sometimes we know the specific day, other times merely the year. Use the most accurate date possible.

Family Computer Disk System games require a slightly different format. The media type is double-sided QuickDisk, which may be truncated to "d.s. QD" if preferred. Unlike cartridges, FDS disks only have a single capacity, so it is not technically necessary to list the number each time. However, for the sake of consistency, I have chosen to do so in the examples below. Also note the number of disks when known and, if applicable, the disk side(s) the game occupies.

Examples:

> *Castlevania III: Dracula's Curse.* Nintendo Entertainment System (72-pin cartridge), PAL-B [Germany]. NES-VN-FRG (3-screw, DAS). NES-ELROM [MMC5 | 256KB PRG | 128KB CHR | CIC 3195A | MC]. Palcom: Konami, Sept. 1990.

> メトロイド (trans. *Metroid*). Family Computer Disk System (double-sided QuickDisk), NTSC [JP]. FMC-MET. Disk (one) [8KB PRG-ROM | 32KB PRG-RAM | 8KB CHR-RAM | MC]. Nintendo R&D1/Intelligent Systems: Nintendo, 6 Aug. 1986.

> スーパーマリオブラザーズ (trans. *Super Mario Bros.*). Family Computer (60-pin cartridge), NTSC-J [JP]. HVC-SM. HVC-NROM-256 [32KB PRG | 8KB CHR | V]. Nintendo {Kondo, Koji; Miyamoto, Shigeru; Nakago, Toshihiko; Tezuka, Takashi}: Nintendo, 13 Sept. 1985.

> *Super Mario Bros.* Nintendo Entertainment System (72-pin cartridge), NTSC [US]. NES-SM-USA (3-screw, REV-A). NES-NROM-256 [32KB PRG | 8KB CHR | CIC 3193 | V]. Nintendo {Kondo, Koji; Miyamoto, Shigeru; Nakago, Toshihiko; Tezuka, Takashi}: Nintendo, Oct. 1985.

> *U-Force Power Games.* Nintendo Entertainment System (72-pin cartridge), NTSC [US]. <Unknown> (3-screw, prototype). NES-GNROM [32KB PRG UV EPROM | 32KB CHR UV EPROM | CIC 6113B1 | V]. TOSE Software: Broderbund, 1990 (unreleased).

Listing 2: Enumerative type for citing Famicom, NES, and compatible ROMs/patches/save states used in emulation.

Format:

Original cartridge/disk title [Type]. Author. "Filename and extension." File size. Mapper format: Mapper number. [File header in byte format]. Date modified. Emulator. <Download source>

Though originally derived from a dump of a physical cartridge, a ROM intended for play on an emulator is a fundamentally different object than its progenitor. ICs that are separate in a physical cart are combined into a single binary data stream and appended with a header to describe their contents. The underlying data may be identical, but its form and configuration are significantly altered. As such, the ROM file demands a separate enumerative format.

The original cartridge or disk title is listed first, as above. A small bracketed designator indicates the format (ROM, IPS patch, save state, etc.), followed by the name of the file(s), including extension(s).[12] Of course, since files may be renamed at the user's discretion, such titles may vary considerably. However, ROM files' names and contents have proven surprisingly resilient, contrary to the perceived "ephemerality" of digital artifacts. Likewise, homebrew utilities for naming ROMs according to prevailing community standards have ironed out many of the inconsistencies that arise from user intervention, file transfer, hacking, and so on. Certain ROM hacks, demos, or homebrew programs may have a known author. In such cases, the author may be listed prior to the file name.

Next list the file size followed by the mapper format and mapper number. In combination, these details can indicate whether a given ROM has been altered from its initial mapper configuration in order, for example, to add additional capabilities, increase ROM space, play on a specific emulator, and so on. The mapper number indicates a specified cartridge hardware configuration and emulator compatibility. Not all emulators support all mappers. In most cases, the mapper format will be iNES or iNES 2.0, since those are the reigning standards. However, alternatives did and do exist (e.g., PasoFami), so they should be specified.

All valid .NES files will include a 16-byte header. If the format is a ROM, the header should be listed in full. For iNES headers, grouping bytes into four groups of four is recommended for better readability. Bytes do not need to be labeled with hexadecimal notation (e.g., "$") unless it aids readability. It is also acceptable, based on the bibliographer's preference, to list the ASCII equivalents to the byte-encoding. For non-iNES formats, a comparable header description should be included.

Next list the ROM's last date modified field (*not* the user's last access, as used in website citations) and, if applicable, the emulator(s) used for analysis. For patches, hacks, or save states, the release date may be available and would be preferable to the modified date (though they are typically identical). Since emulators vary widely in accuracy, the emulator listing provides the reader with information about how the author viewed the particular file. If NESticle is listed rather than Nintendulator, for instance, the reader will know that the file's raster effects, sound, or palettes may have been emulated improperly.

Finally, if known, the file's download source may also be listed in angled brackets. Standard URL format is desirable.

Examples:

Casino Kid 2 [ROM]. "Casino Kid 2 (U).nes" (131KB). iNES: 2. [4E45531A 08002000 00000000 00000000]. 18 Oct. 2002. Macifom v0.16.

The Legend of Zelda [ROM]. Elric. "Quest of Zelda V0.15 (Zelda Hack).nes" (131KB). iNES: 1. [4E45531A 08001200 00000000 00000000]. 7 Jan. 2003. Nestopia v1.4.1.

Isolated Warrior [ROM]. "Isolated Warrior.nes" (262KB). iNES: 4. [4E45531A 08104000 00000000 004D4A52]. 19 March 2000. RockNES v5.08.

Super Mario Bros. [ROM]. "Mario's Adventure (SMB1 Hack).nes" (41KB). [4E45531A 02010544 69736B44 75646521]. 16 Jan. 2003. Macifom v0.16.

Super Mario Bros. [IPS patch]. acmlm. "StrMBro1.ips" (aka *Strange Mario Bros. 1*) (12KB). [50415443 4800000B 00054E49 322E3100]. 20 May 2000. FCEUX v2.1.5. <http://www.romhacking.net/hacks/14/>

Super Mario Bros. 2 [ROM]. "Super Mario Bros 2 (U) (PRG 0).nes" (262KB). iNES: 4. [4E45531A 08104100 00000000 00000000]. 29 Jan. 1995. FCEUX v2.1.5.

Appendix B: Glossary

1oNES: The lock-and-key "handshake" software that runs on the NES's Checking Integrated Circuit (CIC).

2A03: Shorthand for RP2A03G, the IC package that contains both the Famicom's modified 6502 CPU and custom APU.

2A07: Shorthand for RP2A07G, the PAL version of the 2A03, which features a modified memory divider ratio and adjusted PCM audio playback rates.

6502: Shorthand for the MOS Technology 6502 8-bit microprocessor. The Famicom's 2A03 package features a Ricoh-manufactured revision of this popular chip lacking decimal mode. Many popular computing platforms in the 1970s and 80s used the 6502, including the Apple II, Commodore 64, and Atari 800XL.

Accumulator: A special 8-bit register of the 6502 used to store data for the purposes of arithmetic and/or logical operations.

Address: The location of a data word in memory.

Advanced Video System (AVS): An early prototype of the Nintendo Entertainment System designed by Lance Barr and shown at the 1985 Winter Consumer Electronic Show. Its modular design included a control deck, cassette tape storage, QWERTY keyboard, infrared controllers, joystick, light gun, and a musical keyboard.

Application-specific Integrated Circuit (ASIC): An integrated circuit designed and manufactured for a specific, often proprietary, purpose. Nintendo's custom memory management controllers (e.g., MMC1) are ASICs.

Assembly Language: A low-level programming language corresponding closely to its host CPU architecture.

Attribute Table: A 64-byte array located at the end of the Famicom's four name tables that designates the palette entry used for each 16x16-pixel (i.e., 2x2-tile) region of the background.

Audio Processing Unit (APU): The Famicom's programmable sound generator, which has five dedicated channels: triangle, noise, two pulses, and delta modulation.

Bank Switching: A technique used to extend the usable memory addressable by a microprocessor. In the Famicom, mappers could swap banks of ROM into the CPU's address space when values were written to a designated hardware register.

Binary: A base 2 number system that represents all numbers as combinations of either 0 or 1. For instance, decimal 9 is %1001 in binary. Binary values in the book are prefixed with "%."

Bit: Shorthand for "binary digit," the fundamental unit of information that a computer can compute, abstracting the two physical states of any bistable element, e.g., the "on" or "off" state of a semiconductor gate.

Bit Depth: In digital audio, the "vertical resolution" of sample data, i.e., the number of bits used to encode a sample's amplitude.

Bit Flag: A single bit used to indicate the occurrence of a specific "event," e.g., a carry overflow resulting from binary addition.

Black Box Games: The first game paks released for the U.S. Nintendo Entertainment System that shared a uniform packaging style, most prominently the black star field background and exaggerated pixel graphics. Some collectors extend the designation to include a few non-standard exceptions, such as the "silver box" releases of *Kid Icarus* and *Metroid*.

Byte: An eight-bit unit of data, typically represented as either eight binary digits (%01011101) or two hexadecimal digits ($5D).

Card edge connector: The "top-loading" style of cartridge connector that was the industry standard prior to the NES's "front-loading" zero insertion force (ZIF) connector.

Cathode Ray Tube (CRT): A highly pressurized tube containing a barium-coated cathode that, when heated, emits negatively charged electrons. CRT is also shorthand for a television or monitor that contains such a tube.

Character Internal RAM (CIRAM): The 2KB portion of VRAM that stores the Famicom's name and attribute tables.

Character ROM/RAM (CHR-ROM/CHR-RAM): The cartridge IC that contains the pattern data used to draw sprites and background tiles onscreen. CHR-RAM is supplied pattern data during program execution.

Checking Integrated Circuit (CIC): A hardware microcontroller included in all Nintendo Entertainment System consoles and game paks. When a pak is inserted, both lockout chips execute the 10NES "handshake" software to ensure that the pak is valid, i.e., manufactured by Nintendo under their licensing terms.

Chiptunes: A genre of electronic music produced using synthesizers sourced from vintage arcade, console, or PC microprocessors—i.e., "chips."

Crystal Oscillator (Xtal): A vibrating piezoelectric crystal that provides a precise clocking frequency for a microprocessor's CPU.

Delta Modulation (DM): A 1-bit, differential pulse-code modulation (DPCM) technique used to sample audio data. Instead of encoding the sample amplitude data, DM encodes the current sample's difference—either positive (1) or negative (0)—from the previous sample.

Delta Modulation Channel (DMC): An APU channel that can playback prerecorded samples or stream raw PCM data.

Dendy: The unauthorized Russian Famiclone system originally marketed and sold by Steepler.

Digital/Directional Pad (D-Pad): The patented cross-shaped directional input device first devised by Nintendo engineer Gunpei Yokoi for the portable Game & Watch LCD systems. The joystick alternative became the *de facto* standard for game controllers after the NES's release, continuing until the advent of 3D gaming. Also commonly called the "cross pad" or "plus pad."

Emulator: Originally a hybrid hardware/software solution meant to mimic (and often augment) a target platform, specifically for the purposes of supporting legacy software. In contemporary videogame parlance, an emulator is software designed to play games from older console, PC, or arcade platforms on a more modern machine.

Erasable Programmable Read-Only Memory (EPROM): A ROM whose contents can be erased (typically by exposing it to sustained ultraviolet light) and rewritten.

Famiclone: A hardware clone of the Nintendo Famicom, typically associated with the unauthorized sale and distribution of pirate software. Since Nintendo's NES hardware patents have expired, Famiclones are no longer illegal to manufacture. Thus third-party NES-compatible consoles are sold in videogame stores or used as a hardware baseline for affordable computing in developing nations.

Famicom: See **Family Computer.**

Family Computer Disk System (FDS): The disk drive add-on to the Family Computer originally intended to make up for the shortcomings of cartridge mask ROMs. The proprietary "disk cards" initially had higher capacities, permitted game saves, and were cheaper to manufacture. Due to piracy and the development of more capable cartridge mappers, Nintendo discontinued the peripheral.

Family Computer: Nintendo's first cartridge-based videogame console released in Japan in July 1983 and commonly known by its portmanteau, Famicom. It is significantly smaller than its international counterpart, the NES, and is distinguished by its white and red color scheme, top-loading cartridge slot, and hardwired controllers.

First-party: A videogame developer who is also the platform owner/manufacturer. Nintendo was the sole Famicom/NES first-party developer. Also see **Second-party** and **Third-party**.

Game Pak: The marketing term devised by Nintendo of America's Gail Tilden to describe NES cartridges.

Glitch abuse: A practice in the speedrun community that exploits programming errors, bugs, or other in-game errata to grant the player a competitive edge.

Glob Top: A low-cost method of semiconductor production that bonds and protects the IC and its connections with a thick coating of black epoxy resin. Many early, unlicensed, and pirate Famicom carts use this technique to bond cartridge ROM to the PCB.

Hexadecimal: A base 16 numbering system commonly used in assembly language programming. Values 0–9 are numbered as in the decimal system, but 10–15 use the characters A-F. Each digit of a hexadecimal value represents four bits. Hexadecimal values and addresses in the book are prefixed with the "$" character. In other sources, a trailing "h" may also be used (e.g., $3Co = 3Coh).

Hex Editor: Software that represents a game's raw binary data file as hexadecimal-encoded bytes for the purposes of editing, hacking, or analysis.

Homebrew: A term adopted from the home beer brewing community to describe videogames and software tools created by amateur or nonprofessional programmers.

Horizontal Blank (HBLANK): In Famicom programming, the HBLANK is the interval of time between when the scanning electron gun reaches the edge of the screen and when it resets to the opposite edge to resume scanline rendering.

interNES (iNES): An early shareware NES emulator, released in 1995, as well as the community-adopted standard header appended to NES ROMs to indicate mapper number, PRG-ROM banks, mirroring, etc.

Kill Screen: An impassable final screen in otherwise "infinite" arcade-style games, usually resulting from programmer oversight, limitations of 8-bit architectures, and prolonged expert play.

Large Scale Integration (LSI): An integrated circuit containing roughly between one thousand and tens of thousands of logic gates/transistors.

Light Gun: A videogame peripheral that employs a light-sensing circuit housed inside a gun barrel to simulate target shooting on a television monitor.

Launch Title(s): The software available on the same day that a new videogame platform is released.

Localization: The process of modifying a game's content for release in a foreign market. In the simplest cases, localization strictly involves translation (e.g., Japanese to English menus, text, dialogue, etc.). In sophisticated examples, cultural allusions that might be misunderstood (or found offensive) are either updated to references relevant to the target audience or excised altogether.

Lockout Chip: See **Checking Integrated Circuit (CIC)**.

Mapper: Additional cartridge hardware that permits the Famicom to perform tasks that were not possible with the base hardware, such as bank switching or scanline counting.

Mask ROM: A cost-efficient form of read-only memory named after the "masking" technique used during fabrication.

Memory Management Controller (MMC): The official published name for Nintendo's ASIC mappers. Nintendo's original patents described it as the "multi-memory controller."

Memory Map: A tabular representation of a microprocessor's addressable memory and each segment's associated function and/or contents.

Metatile: A graphical and computational object composed of multiple sprites and/or background tiles, typically used to build characters larger than a platform's default sprite size and/or to locate and compress larger groups of graphical elements.

Mirroring: Duplicating a memory area across multiple addresses in a memory map.

Name Table: A 960-byte region in PPU memory used to store pattern tile indices designating the arrangement of the 32x30-tile background. The PPU has addresses for four name tables, but sufficient memory to store only two. Consequently, two name tables are mirrored.

.NES: iNES-compatible file extension for dumped cartridge data, including the contents of CHR- and PRG-ROM along with a prepended header.

NES-001: The original model of the NES, commonly called the "front-loader" or "toaster," characterized by its boxy industrial design and greyscale color scheme. The NES-001 included the ZIF cartridge loader, both composite and RF outputs, an expansion port, and the CIC lockout chip.

NES-101: The 1993 redesign of the NES, commonly called the "top-loader," that removed the NES-001's ZIF connector, lockout chip, expansion port, composite output, and front-loading cartridge slot in favor of a more robust card edge connector and a chassis style more akin to its successor console, the Super Nintendo.

Nintendo Entertainment System (NES): The "localized" version of the Family Computer released by Nintendo in the United States in 1985 (and elsewhere in subsequent years). Commonly pronounced "Ness" or "N-E-S."

Noise: A signal with no discernible periodicity whose energy is distributed across the entire frequency spectrum.

Non-Maskable Interrupt (NMI): An interrupt handler generated by the 2A03 that signals the start of the VBLANK period.

.NSF: The "NES Sound Format," a popular malapropism for the Nintendo Entertainment System Music (NESM) format, originally developed by Kevin Horton for the HardNES, a hardware NES music player. Like the .NES standard, .NSF includes both dumped cartridge data and a prepended header.

Nybble: Four bits, or half of a byte.

Object Attribute Memory (OAM): A 256-byte segment of (independent) PPU memory that stores attributes for the Famicom's sixty-four available onscreen sprites.

OAM Cycling: A technical term describing onscreen sprite flicker. When sprites exceed the Famicom's eight-per-scanline limit, programmers cycle the contents of OAM to prevent a given object from disappearing completely.

Overscan: A variable image area around the four edges of a television screen or monitor that may not reliably be seen by the viewer. Famicom/NES graphics in the overscan area may be cropped, depending on the display.

Pattern Table: The first 8KB of the PPU's VRAM. Each pattern table is 4K and contains either 256 background or sprite tiles.

Printed Circuit Board (PCB): The material substrate used to support and connect electronic components. Its conductive pathways are typically etched from laminated copper sheets.

Picture Processing Unit (PPU): The common name for the Famicom's custom Ricoh RP2C02G-0 graphics processor. The PPU handles all aspects of rendering the Famicom's video signal.

Pixel: Shorthand for "picture element," the smallest graphical unit of a pattern tile.

Platformer: A videogame genre that involves a character running across, jumping, climbing on, or otherwise surmounting multi-tiered obstacles or terrain, i.e., platforms.

Program Counter (PC): A 16-bit register that contains the address of the next instruction to be executed by the CPU.

Program ROM/RAM (PRG-ROM/PRG-RAM): The cartridge ROM directly addressed by the CPU. It contains the program's source code and data.

Pulse-code Modulation (PCM): A method of representing a continuous audio signal as discrete digital data. PCM quality is governed by the digital converter's sampling rate and bit depth.

Random Access Memory (RAM): A form of computer data storage that may be both read from and written to.

Read-Only Memory (ROM): A form of computer data storage that may only be read from.

Register: A CPU memory storage location. In the 6502, registers are eight bits wide.

ROM: The colloquial term for data dumped from cartridges for play on emulators. NES ROMs typically include the contents of CHR- and PRG-ROM and an appended header.

ROM Hack: A videogame ROM that has been altered from its original commercial release. Often these are simple graphic replacements or enhancements, but they can also include significant revisions to level designs, enemy behaviors, physics, in-game items, narrative, dialogue, and so on.

Robot Operating Buddy (R.O.B.): An optically controlled robot peripheral included both in the original NES Deluxe Set and as a stand-alone accessory. Although heavily emphasized during the NES's initial promotion and marketing, only two software titles supported it. A Famicom version was also released.

Run Length Encoding (RLE): A simple form of compression commonly used in the 8-bit era to eliminate the redundancy of multiple repeated tiles. Instead of listing each tile in sequence, a tile's reference is provided, followed by its "run length" (i.e., how many times it is repeated), and a final terminating byte.

Sample: In audio, a sample is discrete digital representation of a continuous signal. In musical practice, a sample is a short—often looped—section of previously recorded musical material.

Sampling Rate: In digital audio, the number of samples encoded per second, commonly measured in kilohertz (kHz). CD-quality audio has a sampling rate of 44,100 samples per second, or 44.1kHz.

Scanline: A single line, or row, of the raster scanning pattern traced by the CRT's electron gun.

Scrolling: The simulation of movement through a virtual space that is larger than that contained in a single television frame.

Second-party: A videogame developer who is either partly owned or funded by the platform manufacturer to produce games exclusive to that platform. Intelligent Systems, for example, who worked on titles such as *Wild Gunman*, *Duck Hunt*, and *Metroid*, comprised members from both Nintendo R&D1 and Nintendo partner Iwasaki Electronics. Also see **First-party** and **Third-party**.

Speedrun: A competitive gameplay practice that aims to complete a game as quickly as possible, without the assistance of cheats, hacks, or computer tools. In some cases, emulators may be used, but they are not required. A special variation called segmented speedruns permits stitching together multiple runs to form a single, master speedrun. Traditional, or "single-segment," speedruns are performed in one continuous session.

Sprite: A pattern table object that may be moved independently from other objects. The term may also designate a group of related tiles—e.g., the Mario "sprite"—though technically such examples are metasprites. The Famicom has two selectable sprite sizes: 8x8 or 8x16 pixels.

Sprite 0: The first entry (position 0) in sprite OAM, commonly used to time mid-screen scrolling changes.

Third-party: A videogame developer licensed to produce games for another company's platform. Konami, Enix, and Namco, for instance, were third-party developers who produced games both for the Famicom and competing platforms. Also see **First-party** and **Second-party**.

Tile: An 8x8- or 8x16-pixel area of graphics data.

Tool-Assisted Speedrun (TAS): A speedrun that is performed on and assisted by an emulator and its associated enhancements (i.e., tools), such as save states, re-recording, frame-by-frame advance, scripting macros, etc.

Tracker: Music sequencing software that uses a vertical display based around columnar monophonic tracks, each typically designating a hardware channel from the source platform.

Vertical Blank (VBLANK): In Famicom programming, VBLANK measures the interval of time between when the electron gun completes its raster scanning pattern and when it resets to the screen's upper corner to recommence scanning. In some contexts, VBLANK may also describe the *distance* traveled during that time, typically measured in scanlines. VBLANK varies according to the refresh rate of the television.

Video RAM (VRAM): In Famicom parlance, VRAM describes the memory allotted to both the PPU's name tables and palettes (CIRAM), as well as the CHR-ROM/RAM on the cartridge. In some technical documents, CIRAM and VRAM are synonymous.

Waveform: A visual representation of sound's variation in air pressure (i.e., amplitude) over time. Waveforms are commonly named according to their approximate geometric shape, e.g., square wave, triangle wave, sawtooth, etc.

Word: A two-byte unit of data. This is the common length of an address used in Famicom/NES programming (e.g., $2001). Note that word length varies according to the processor architecture.

Z80: Shorthand for the popular, low-cost Zilog Z80 8-bit microprocessor, introduced in 1976. Numerous consoles, consumer electronics, and arcade boards used the Z80, including the Nintendo Game Boy, Sega Master System, ColecoVision, *Pac-Man*, *Donkey Kong*, Texas Instruments TI-81 calculator, and the Roland Jupiter-8 synthesizer.

Zapper: See **Light Gun.**

Zero Insertion Force (ZIF) connector: Nintendo's patented, VCR-style cartridge loading mechanism used in the NES. Though novel, it proved to be more susceptible to corrosion, debris, and wear after long-term use. Nintendo eventually released an updated console, the NES-101, that returned to the more traditional card edge connector.

Zero Page: The memory addresses located at the start of a CPU's memory map, beginning with a leading zero. In 8-bit architectures, addressing zero page memory takes fewer processor cycles, so it is used to store data that requires frequent access.

Notes

Chapter 0

1. Tanner, "Adventure of Link - Retranslation."
2. To cite a recent example, *ZeldaDungeon.net* ran a short piece titled, "I Am...Not Error?" The comments are illuminating.
3. Mandelin, "A Look at the Metroid Series' Varia Suit."
4. For example, Kazuhisa Hashimoto, who worked for Konami in the Famicom era, said in an interview, "It was normal for a NES game to be designed in 4–6 months by a team of 4 people. This practice didn't really change until the Super Nintendo era." See Tanner, "Konami: The Nintendo Era."
5. Derrida, "Letter to a Japanese Friend," 275.
6. Sandifer, "Am Error."
7. When referring to the platform as a whole, I have opted to use Famicom as the shorthand for the Family Computer, the NES, and their multiple revisions. When I refer to the NES specifically, I mean to reference its regional model exclusively.
8. Donovan, *Replay: The History of Video Games.*
9. Sheff, *Game Over.*
10. Chaplin and Ruby, *Smartbomb.*
11. Provenzo, *Video Kids: Making Sense of Nintendo.*
12. Ryan, *Super Mario: How Nintendo Conquered America.*
13. Montfort, "Continuous Paper: The Early Materiality and Workings of Electronic Literature."
14. Kirschenbaum, *Mechanisms.*
15. See Chaplin and Ruby, *Smartbomb*; Dillon, *The Golden Age of Video Games*; Donovan, *Replay*; Gamespite, *GameSpite Quarterly 5*; Goldberg, *All Your Base Are Belong To Us*; Herman, *Phoenix*; Kent, *The Ultimate History of Videogames*; Kline et al., *Digital Play*; Kohler, *Power-Up*; Ryan, *Super Mario*; Sellers, *Arcade Fever*; and Sheff, *Game Over.*

Chapter 1

1.	Masaharu (trans. Tanner), "Part 6 - Making the Famicom a Reality."
2.	Katayama, *Japanese Business into the 21st Century*, 169.
3.	Sheff, *Game Over*, 29.
4.	Masaharu (trans. Tanner), "Part 6 - Making the Famicom a Reality."
5.	GAMECOM and Famicom have obvious similarities in English. However, in Japanese the former is rendered in four characters ガメコム pronounced *gamekomu* (gah-may-ko-mu). To maintain the English-style pronunciation of "GAME-COM," Nintendo would have opted for the five-character ゲームコム, pronounced *geemukomu* (gay-mu-ko-mu). My thanks to Aria Tanner for pointing out the subtleties of the Japanese pronunciations.
6.	Masaharu (trans. Tanner), "Part 8 – Synonymous With the Domestic Game Console."
7.	The Famicom name is actually trademarked by Nintendo's longtime hardware partner Sharp. See Masaharu (trans. Tanner), "Part 8 – Synonymous With the Domestic Game Console."
8.	Katayama, *Japanese Business into the 21st Century*, 166.
9.	Sheff reports Yamauchi's admonition to stave off competition for "at least one year" (*Game Over*, 29), while Uemura says three. See Nintendo of America Inc., "Iwata Asks - Volume 2: NES & Mario," 1.
10.	Sheff, *Game Over*, 30.
11.	Masaharu (trans. Tanner), "Part 7 - Deciding on the Specs."
12.	Dillon, *The Golden Age of Video Games*, 38.
13.	Despite Yamauchi's decision, Sharp and Nintendo continued to work in close partnership for many years. Sharp, for instance, manufactured the officially licensed Family Computer / Family Computer Disk System all-in-one console called the Sharp Twin Famicom.
14.	Nintendo of America Inc., "Iwata Asks - Volume 2: NES & Mario," Section 1.
15.	See Masaharu (trans. Tanner), "Part 7 - Deciding on the Specs" and Aoyama and Izushi, "Hardware Gimmick or Cultural Innovation? Technological, Cultural, and Social Foundations of the Japanese Video Game Industry," 431.
16.	Nintendo of America Inc., "Iwata Asks - Volume 2: NES & Mario," Section 2.
17.	Sheff, *Game Over*, 32. Yamauchi later contested this figure to the Japanese press.
18.	Nintendo of America Inc., "Iwata Asks - Volume 2: NES & Mario," Section 2.
19.	Masaharu (trans. Tanner), "Part 7 - Deciding on the Specs."
20.	Masaharu (trans. Tanner), "Part 8 - Synonymous With the Domestic Game Console."
21.	See O-Young, *The Compact Culture*, 24.
22.	Teiser, "Atari - Nintendo 1983 Deal."
23.	Ibid.
24.	W., Dan et al. "Exclusive Interview with Donkey Kong Creator Shigeru Miyamoto."
25.	This design conceit would appear again in Lance Barr's design of the Nintendo Entertainment System (chapter 3).
26.	Masaharu (trans. Tanner), "Part 8 - Synonymous With the Domestic Game Console."

27. The reset and power switches have explanatory stickers. The left one reads, in Japanese, "When removing a cartridge, please be sure that the system is off," and the right, "Pressing the reset switch will cause the score you've obtained to be deleted." The internal eject mechanism, a wide plastic bar with two protruding arms, is attached to the interior of the console's upper cover. The mechanism has a thin metal bracket that attaches to the red slider used to hoist cartridges out of the system. When the player pushes the slider, the metal bracket, itself attached to a small spring, rolls the mechanism along its angled arms until they collide with the cartridge. With a slight bit of pressure, the arms pop the cartridge off the card edge connector. Since the slider is spring-loaded, once the player releases pressure, it moves back to its initial position. It is a handy mechanism, but largely for show. Players could also grip the cartridge and pull it out manually, but Nintendo R&D1's lead engineer Gunpei Yokoi thought the eject lever added a nice toy-like feel, delighting children: "Even when they weren't playing games, they could entertain themselves by clattering around." Masaharu (trans. Tanner), "Part 8 - Synonymous With the Domestic Game Console."

28. C.f., Hosokawa, "The Walkman Effect."

29. Nintendo only missed the mark by a few millimeters: Famicom carts measure 11cm x 7cm x 1.7cm in comparison to the 10.9cm x 6.9cm x 1.7cm dimensions of a cassette case.

30. The expansion port also has an instructional sticker: "Please don't touch the terminals using fingers or metal objects. This will cause failures."

31. Sheff, *Game Over*, 33.

32. A 1987 profile of the Famicom noted that Nomura Securities "announced plans to develop a system allowing investors to use their *famikons* to read market information and to buy and sell stocks at home." See Kodansha Ltd., *Best of Japan*, 182.

33. There are several accounts of how and why Nintendo settled on the Family Computer's trademark color scheme. The red, for instance, has roots in Japanese culture, where historically color could indicate social rank and hierarchy. 小豆色 (or azuki-iro) is a deep red derived from a bean used in many Japanese dishes and treats.

In 2010, ITmedia reported that Nintendo chose azuki red for reasons unrelated to cultural allusions. Like the hardwired cords, white and azuki red were simply the least expensive options for colored plastic. However, a Nikkei Electronics retrospective profile of the Family Computer's development reports that President Yamauchi picked the colors from an advertisement. While commuting with Uemura, the president pointed toward a billboard for DX Antenna and said, "That's a good color." Despite the apocryphal tone of the account, the similarities between DX Antenna's package design and the Famicom's color scheme are striking. Even the DX logo's diagonal stripe is reminiscent of the "pulse line" design used on many early Famicom cartridges.

Uemura later refuted both accounts, stating that the color was "simply an order from the president. He had this dark red scarf that he liked to wear a lot; it was just a color that he liked. For an executive like him, the external design is one of the easier ways to put his mark on the project, so to speak."

For more information, see Ashcraft, "Report: Why Does The Nintendo Famicom Have The Color Red?", Masaharu (trans. Tanner), "Part 8 - Synonymous With the Domestic Game Console," and Gifford, "Masayuki Uemura and the Family Computer project."

34. Many Nintendo products (and unofficial knockoffs) since 1983 feature the Family Computer color scheme, including a special Japan-exclusive edition of the Game Boy Advance SP, painted to mimic its elder console.

35. See "Magnavox Odyssey TV Commercial - February 1973," "Fairchild Channel F Commercial [1976]," and "Coleco Telstar 1976."

36. The wired controllers ran into the rear of the console, threaded across the length of its interior, and connected to the front of the motherboard. The connecting cable was short—roughly 75cm long, with an additional 20cm wound inside the Famicom—keeping players on a short leash. The wired design proved troublesome in practical use. Since players could not easily replace faulty controllers, they had to send their entire console to Nintendo for repair. On the motherboard, the expansion port and controller connections share the same edge, so Nintendo could have run the cords directly into the front of the Famicom. In fact, Nintendo initially considered detachable controllers, but ultimately axed them to cut costs. Masaharu (trans. Tanner), "Part 8 - Synonymous With the Domestic Game Console."

37. Katayama, *Japanese Business into the 21st Century*, 167–8.

38. Nintendo of America Inc., "Iwata Asks - Club Nintendo: Game & Watch," Section 2.

39. The dual-screen portable format would return twenty-five years later as the Nintendo DS handheld.

40. V., "Nintendo Ultra Hand (ウルトラ ハンド, 1966)."

41. For these and other Gunpei Yokoi gadgets, see V., "Label: Gunpei Yokoi."

42. Crigger, "Searching for Gunpei Yokoi."

43. Inoue, *Nintendo Magic*, 125.

44. Ibid., 123. Also see BOCTOK Co., Ltd., *Bit Generation 2000 "TV Games."*, 58–9.

45. Johnstone, *We Were Burning*, 58–9.

46. Inoue, *Nintendo Magic*, 123.

47. During Yokoi's career, he oversaw the *Donkey Kong* arcade conversion, the Virtual Boy, *Dr. Mario, Yoshi's Cookie, Duck Hunt*, and the Robotic Operating Buddy.

48. The exceptions either used the buttons for non-directional purposes, as in *Flagman* (1980), or for two-player simultaneous play, as in *Judge* (1980) and *Lion* (1981).

49. Masaharu (trans. Tanner), "Part 8 - Synonymous With the Domestic Game Console."

50. Ibid.

51. Ibid.

52. Two of the microphone's notable implementations come from the Family Computer Disk System versions of ゼルダの伝説 (aka *The Legend of Zelda*) and 光神話 パルテナの鏡 (aka *Kid Icarus*). In the former, players may yell into the microphone to defeat the large-eared Pols Voice; in the latter, the microphone is used to "bargain" for shop discounts.

53. "Famicom History Part 2: Japanese Famicom Slang 101," *Famicomblog*.

54. This same griefing technique is possible in the NES version as well. In fact, even though player 2 has their own Start button, pressing it does not pause the game.
55. Katayama, *Japanese Business into the 21st Century*, 165.
56. The TurboGrafx-16, for instance, despite being touted as a 16-bit system, still contained an 8-bit HuC6280 CPU. The 16-bit designator described its dual GPUs (and clearly sounded more impressive than a TurboGrafx-8).
57. Throughout the book, I follow programming convention and use a "%" prefix to indicate binary values.
58. See iFixit, "Nintendo Family Computer (Famicom) Teardown."
59. PAL systems contain the RP2A07G chip, which has minor (but important) timing differences.
60. As noted previously, the 6502's low-cost competitor, the Zilog Z80, shared the dominance of the 8-bit era. The Z80 powered the ColecoVision, Tandy/RadioShack TRS-80 Model I, Sega SG-1000, Sequential Circuits Prophet 5, Roland Jupiter-8, Amstrad CPC, MSX, and the Sega Master System, among other platforms.
61. In most Famicom game source code, one can find the assembly mnemonic CLD (CLear Decimal flag) in the system initialization routines. This disables the console's decimal mode, despite there being no need to do so. This "safeguard" is a vestigial holdover from coding practice on other 6502-based systems.
62. Bagnall, *On the Edge*, 155, 296–297.
63. Ibid., 467–8.
64. Gifford, "Tetris...forever."
65. Also see Quietust, "Chip Images."
66. Peddle, Charles et al., "Integrated circuit microprocessor with parallel binary adder having on-the-fly correction to provide decimal results."
67. "6502 DecimalMode," *visual6502.org*.
68. This explains why the decimal-related 6502 instructions (e.g., ADC, SBC) still set the proper Decimal flag when executed on the Famicom.
69. The truth is in the details, as the ColecoVision VDP's read-only status register functioned remarkably similar to the Famicom's PPU Status Register ($2002). Bit 7 of the VDP Interrupt Flag triggered "at the end of the raster scan of the last line of the active display," effectively marking the beginning of VBLANK. The same bit in $2002 monitored whether the PPU was currently in VBLANK or not. The VDP status register's bit 6 was the Fifth Sprite Flag (5S), signaling when five or more sprites were concurrent on a single scanline. Bits 0–4 then stored the sprite flag that triggered 5S. Bit 5 of $2002 also recorded sprite overflow, although the Famicom had a higher maximum (8) and kept no record of which sprite had exceeded the limit.

Finally, bit 5 of the VDP status register recorded the "Coincidence Flag," a catch-all collision detection that triggered if *any* two sprites onscreen shared an overlapping pixel. This limited functionality worked for only a small range of gameplay types where coincidence events were discrete. In cases where multiple collisions might happen simultaneously, its use was less practical.

The Famicom had a coincidence flag of a different sort, governed by the status of sprite 0, the first entry in Object Attribute Memory. When a non-transparent pixel of sprite o overlapped with a non-transparent pixel of a background tile, bit 6 of $2002 set. Like the VDP's limited collision detection, sprite o had little practical import for conventional object collisions, but proved useful for scanline timing and raster effects (chapter 4).

For more details on the ColecoVision VDP, see Texas Instruments, "TMS9918A/TMS9928A/TMS9929A Video Display Processors. (Microprocessor Series)."

70. Montfort and Bogost, *Racing the Beam*.

71. Cartridges may also contain PRG-RAM or CHR-RAM, both of which may be rewritten at runtime (chapter 6).

72. The address space of a CPU is similar to geographic addresses, though much more rigid and uniform. We use a combination of street numbers, city names, and zip codes to locate individual houses in a neighborhood. In CPU space, all houses are equal in size and numbered in sequence from zero to the maximum possible number the address bus can handle—in this case, $FFFF. In decimal notation, the number of available addresses between $0000 to $FFFF equals 65,536, which when divided by 1,024 equals 64. Alternatively, we can express the 16-bit address bus in base 2 nomenclature: 2^{16}= 65,536. If you are curious how 65,536 "rounds down" to 64KB, this is a convention of byte counting in computational contexts, reflecting the asymmetry of base-2 and base-10 numbering systems. 1KB equals 1,024 bytes rather than 1,000.

73. Technically, the 2KB of memory reserved for name and attribute tables are not internal to PPU, but are resident in Character Internal RAM (CIRAM). However, Color Generator RAM (CGRAM), which stores palette data, is internal to the PPU.

74. In Japan, the *Tennis/Super Mario Bros.* swap is known as the "undercover trick." For more details, see Mandelin, "Legends of Localization: Super Mario Bros." and Altice, "The Famicom Cart Swap Trick."

75. I performed the cart swap trick on a top-loading NES-101 rather than a Famicom. The trick is not possible on an unmodified NES-001 due to the CIC lockout mechanism (chapter 3).

76. Since palettes are mirrored, actual palette memory is wider than 32 bytes. See "PPU memory map," *NesDev Wiki*.

77. Certain hardware tricks, such as timed mid-screen palette swaps, can push past the twenty-five color limit.

78. See Korth, "Everynes: Everything about NES and Famicom" and *NesDev Wiki*, "PPU palettes."

79. The Famicom also has a few other hardware tricks that can increase (or decrease) its color range. Three bits in the PPU control register located at $2001 (PPUMASK) are known as the *color emphasis bits*. Setting each bit causes the entire palette to intensify in either red, green, or blue, while darkening the other colors. In general, programmers used color emphasis to create special lighting effects or subtle transitions between screens. Another bit in PPUMASK sets the Famicom PPU to grayscale mode. When the bit is set, all four lower bits of a palette color entry are treated as zero, effectively narrowing the range of colors to three: two identical whites, gray, and light gray. Thus the Famicom grayscale has only two gray values and no black. Furthermore, when a color emphasis bit is set while in grayscale mode, the overall tint still changes. For

more information, see Covell, "NES Technical/Emulation/Development FAQ [ver. 1.7]."

80. Palette value $0D is considered "blacker than black" since its voltage oscillations dip below NTSC's black level. Though uncommon, some televisions can misinterpret the color as a sync signal, causing the display to malfunction. See Korth, "Everynes" and Horton, "NES Video Voltage Levels." Despite the glitch potential, a few commercial games, such as *Immortal* and *The Three Stooges*, used $0D as their black value.

81. Montfort and Bogost, *Racing the Beam*.

82. McCallum, "Memory Prices (1957-2013)."

83. Later, the FDS and cartridge mappers would allow programmer control of mirroring (chapter 5), as well as new arrangements like one-screen mirroring, four-screen mirroring, and a few other exotic varieties (chapter 6).

84. Furthermore, Nintendo's decision to cut name table RAM by half would create other design concessions, since scrolling in multiple planes became much more challenging than exclusive vertical or horizontal scrolling (chapter 6).

85. Figure 4.3 in chapter 4 gives a better approximation of the attribute table borders, since a grid is overlaid atop the *Super Mario Bros.* screen to show how objects are placed.

86. The visible area may be slightly tighter, depending on the region. Overscan may clip up to sixteen total scanlines from the upper and lower borders of an NTSC CRT but only a single scanline from a PAL display. The discrepancy creates divergent programming concerns according to the region: for NTSC games, important player information such as status bars should not be placed too close to the edges, lest it be cropped by the television; for PAL games, any sprites that need to be temporarily hidden should be properly placed beyond the PPU's boundaries, not simply within the presumed overscan area. See "Overscan," *NesDev Wiki*.

87. Today, many emulators give players control over how much of the frame to reveal and in many cases default to full-frame presentation, making border clipping more noticeable. Setting Nestopia's "Trim Border Area" preference, for instance, makes sprite wraparound in *Mario Bros.* look more convincing.

88. See Watkinson, *Television Fundamentals*, 10–14.

89. See Herrick, *Television Theory and Servicing*, 355–88.

90. Watkinson, *Television Fundamentals*, 60.

91. See "Ferry-Porter law" in Roberts, *Dictionary of Audio, Radio and Video*, 86.

92. France also received the PAL NES, but it contained a unique internal PAL-to-RGB decoder that made it compatible with SECAM televisions. See alex, "Composite out of a french PAL NES."

93. See *NesDev Wiki*, "Clock Rate."

94. We only count to 15 in a base 16 system because computers traditionally start counting from 0 rather than 1.

Chapter 2

1. Masaharu (trans. Tanner), "Part 6 - Making the Famicom a Reality."

2. The game's name is often cited as *Radarscope*, though the arcade's title screen clearly displays "RADAR SCOPE," with a space. The error likely derives from

the marquee title, where the space between the two words is slender (but legible).

3. "Radar Scope (1980)," *The Arcade Flyer Archive.*

4. The *Radar Scope* flyer featured the game screen superimposed behind a first-person view of the player's hands manning the ship's gun turret. The text below read, "YOU ARE HERE." Additionally, one version of the arcade cabinet was a partially-enclosed "cockpit" type, meant for players to sit inside.

5. Ostermayer, *The Radar Scope Pages.*

6. See Kent, *The Ultimate History of Video Games*, 157.

7. Arakawa blamed part of *Radar Scope*'s failure on the shipping time from Osaka to New York. Soon after, Nintendo of America relocated to a 60,000 square foot office in Seattle, reducing the shipping time to one week. See Firestone, *Nintendo: The Company and Its Founders*, 52–3.

8. After *Donkey Kong*'s success, King Features was less reticent about a licensing deal. Nintendo later released *Popeye* as a Game & Watch handheld (1981), arcade title (1982), and Famicom launch game (1983).

9. "Gunpei Yokoi talks Donkey Kong in 'Gunpei Yokoi's House of Games,'" *The End of Deep Layer*. Note that Yokoi retcons Princess Peach, Mario's damsel in distress from *Super Mario Bros.*, into Pauline's place.

10. Ibid.

11. "A Dream Walking: Popeye The Sailor #14."

12. Kohler, *Power-Up*, 39.

13. Lacey, "Novelty Games - Cute is Crucial."

14. Bloom, *Video Invaders*, 181.

15. Kohler, *Power-Up*, 2 (emphasis in the original).

16. Napier, *From Impressionism to Anime*, 3.

17. Patten, *Watching Anime, Reading Manga*, 55–57.

18. An October 1977 bulletin for a C/FO meet-up features a fan-made illustration of intermingling American and Japanese cartoon characters. In the foreground, none other than Popeye grins and rests his hand on Astro Boy's shoulder. Patten, *Watching Anime, Reading Manga*, 58.

19. Patten, *Watching Anime, Reading Manga*, 22–43.

20. Levi, *Samurai from Outer Space*, 8.

21. Kohler, *Power-Up*, 11.

22. Ibid., 18, 24, 207, 11.

23. Levi, 19.

24. Patten, 58.

25. Ironically, Atari is a Japanese word that founder Nolan Bushnell lifted from the game Go.

26. The only source I've found that notes this cinematic allusion is Herz, *Joystick Nation.*

27. For detailed accounts of the Nintendo / Universal litigation, see Sheff, 116–127 and Kent, 210–218.

28. United States Court of Appeals. "746 F.2d 112: Universal City Studios, Inc., Plaintiff-appellant, v. Nintendo Co., Ltd., Nintendo of America, Inc., Defendants-appellees." Quote edited for clarity.

29. Sheff, 48–9.

30. Kent, 158.

31. Gross, "Nintendo seeks to trademark 'On like Donkey Kong.'"
32. The closest analogy we see to the platform opulence of yesteryear is in the mobile space, where several platform players compete (e.g., iOS, Android, Windows, Blackberry, Symbian, etc.).
33. Kean, *Crash* 1 (Feb. 1984): 51–2.
34. See the "Clones" section of *Wikipedia*, "*Donkey Kong* (video game)."
35. Oddly, Nintendo licensed *Donkey Kong* to Japanese corporation Falcon Inc., granting them rights to produce an official clone: "In September 1981, Nintendo Co., Ltd. entered into a licensing agreement in Japan with Falcon, Inc., another Japanese corporation. This agreement authorized Falcon to produce a game called *Crazy Kong* which was to be identical or similar to *Donkey Kong*. Nintendo Co., Ltd. supplied stickers to Falcon to attach to the printed circuit boards used in the *Crazy Kong* game. The stickers were printed in the English language and indicated that the *Crazy Kong* circuit board was manufactured under a license from Nintendo Co., Ltd. Falcon paid a royalty of 10,000 yen to Nintendo Co., Ltd. for each game manufactured by Falcon. The license agreement expressly limited the right of Falcon to sell or use the *Donkey Kong* game under the name *Crazy Kong* to the territories of Japan. It prohibited Falcon from importing or exporting these machines or any similar machine and from having any third party produce or sell any such machine. It also prohibited Falcon from importing or exporting *Donkey Kong* or *Crazy Kong* circuit boards into the United States or anywhere outside of Japan. The license agreement was terminated on January 29, 1982." See United States District Court, "Nintendo of America, Inc. v. Elcon Industries, Inc."
36. Sheff, 116–17.
37. Commodore missed the first-mover advantage on the Nintendo arcade license. CEO Jack Tramiel called a last-minute halt to the contract due to a competing agreement with Bally-Midway. See Bagnall, *On the Edge*, 218.
38. Kent, 209–210.
39. Atari eventually brought *Donkey Kong*'s development in-house, delivering ports for the Atari 400/800, as well as the XL and XE series. Atari engineer Landon Dyer was responsible for those superior adaptations.
40. Nintendo of America Inc., "Donkey Kong Operation Manual [Model No: TKG4-UP]," 17.
41. See Fromm, "Troubleshooting Flow Charts for Monitors."
42. Nintendo of America Inc., "Donkey Kong Operation Manual [Model No: TKG4-UP]," 22.
43. Ibid., 5.
44. There are exceptions, most notably the Vectrex, whose embedded (vertical) monitor was a necessity; as its name suggests, it used vector- rather than raster-based graphics. Handheld and portable consoles are the other obvious exceptions.
45. See Carter, Susan B., Scott S. Gartner, Michael R. Haines, et al., eds., "Radio and Television" in *Historical Statistics of the United States*, Table Dg117–130 and Television Bureau of Advertising, "TV Basics."
46. See Katayama, 165: "'By the late seventies, color televisions had already reached a 95 percent penetration rate in Japan…'"

47. If there was any manufacturer identification, it was often a utilitarian white stamp with the game's ID followed by a number (e.g., "DK 223583" for *Donkey Kong*).

48. See *NesDev Wiki*, "Overscan."

49. For many of Nintendo's early titles, there is a simple trick to determine which onscreen elements are sprites and which are background tiles: pause the game. A few seconds after pausing, all sprites will vanish, thanks to the programmers toggling a bit in the PPU's second control register ($2001) that masks, or hides, all sprites. Nintendo likely added this "feature" either to keep players from studying stage layouts (an impossibility in arcade *Donkey Kong*) or to indicate visually that the game was paused (rather than locked up due to a malfunction).

50. Parallel girders would also preclude Kong's introductory show of strength, as he stomps the girders into their angled positions. This seems like a negligible detail, but consider its narratological and instructional purposes: for unfamiliar players, Kong is quickly established as the foe, and a formidable one to boot.

51. The title screen letterforms have minor variations between platforms: the Famicom version has a wider "D," one shifted tile in the "K," a simpler "G," and thinner letters on the bottom row. The letters are also better proportioned in the port. Both lines are center-justified and "KONG" has symmetrical four-tile columns of space on either side. The arcade version has an extra tile column on the left and two tiles for a trademark (™) crowding the right gutter, along with Donkey Kong's sprite sneering menacingly below. The port drops the trademark, the upper hi-score display, and Kong himself—due both to disparities in vertical space and the need to list the range of selectable game modes for home play.

52. On power-up, the cycle is abbreviated: the hi-score table displays first, then demo play. After that first iteration, the game locks into the loop described.

53. Arcade *Donkey Kong*'s character set, scoreboard, and upper HUD are residual evidence of its conversion heritage. The typeface, unsurprisingly, is identical to *Radar Scope*'s. The upper HUD, save for its palette differences, also shares *Radar Scope*'s configuration, down to the character spacing between lines. Stranger still are the shared default values for the current 1UP ("003700") and HIGH SCORE ("007650"). In fact, all five default leader board entries, as well as the leader board screen itself, are identical in both games. It is likely that Nintendo used a common character set across several arcades games in order to save time during development, a practice befitting their long corporate tradition of reuse.

    Donkey Kong's ancestry is visible outside the screen as well. The first few thousand converted units have *Radar Scope*'s distinctive red side panels instead of the blue that was later used. The red *Kong* cabinets are consequently much rarer and command higher prices from collectors.

54. By my count, the following letters are unnecessary: F, H, K, Q, S, U, W, X and Z.

55. Due to *Donkey Kong*'s relative difficulty, many players mistakenly think the elevator level is stage 2, since the cement factory does not appear in the first or second level cycle in the American version.

56. This is unsurprising, since the C64 could support eight, massive 24x21-pixel sprites onscreen simultaneously. See "Chapter 6 - Sprite Graphics" in Commodore Computer, *Commodore 64 User's Guide*.

57. Kemps, "Europe gets exclusive 'perfect version' of NES Donkey Kong in its Mario 25th Anniversary Wiis."

58. Why the date amendment after nearly thirty years? We now know that Nintendo did not develop *Donkey Kong* in-house. Miyamoto designed under Yokoi's supervision, but the programming and circuit production subcontracted to Ikegami Tsushinki Co., Ltd. This partnership was largely unknown until Ikegami sued Nintendo over the right to *Donkey Kong*'s source code. By 1981, Nintendo had become heavily involved in their arcade design, though Ikegami still handled programming, development, and manufacture. Post–*Donkey Kong*, Nintendo no longer required Ikegami's partnership, as they had reverse engineered—and in some cases copied—its source for use in *Donkey Kong Jr.* Ikegami claimed copyright infringement and sued for damages. Though the outcome of the claim settlement was never released to the public, there is evidence of the partnership in *Donkey Kong*'s character data: a small, turquoise logo with the letters "ITC" set in the center—Ikegami's logo. The soured partnership also explained the minor modification to the Wii ROM's title screen. Since Nintendo could no longer claim copyright for the arcade original, they shifted their copyright date to the Famicom debut. For more information, see Game Developer Research Institute, "Company:Ikegami Tsushinki" and Rard, "The Battle of Donkey Kong."

59. ArnoldRimmer83, "Donkey Kong Original Edition."

60. Ibid.

61. Kulczycki, "Technical: What's with the Kill Screen?"

62. For a lengthier technical discussion of the kill screen port, see Altice, "Porting the Kill Screen."

63. The same behavior occurs in *Super Mario Bros.* when the total store of lives exceeds nineteen. See chapter 4.

Chapter 3

1. See Kline et al., *Digital Play*, 103–8; Kent, *The Ultimate History of Video Games*, 219–40; Donovan, *Replay*, 95–109.

2. See Williams, "A (Brief) Social History of Video Games," 3; Stern, "Unloading ROMs: illegal piracy, an unfair trick, or free competition?," 86; Hemnes, "The Adaptation of Copyright Law to Video Games," 171.

3. Williams, 3.

4. Bogost and Montfort, *Racing the Beam*, 76–9, 127.

5. Kline et al., 105.

6. Donovan, 95.

7. Kline et al., 105.

8. "Computer or Video Games," *nytimes.com*.

9. Kent, 286.

10. Sheff, *Game Over*, 160.

11. Documentation of many pre-NES prototypes is available at Nielson, "The Nintendo Entertainment System."

12. The initial run of Famicom joypads were manufactured with rubber, square-shaped action buttons. Nintendo soon discovered that, after prolonged use, avid players wore their buttons away. As a result, Nintendo quickly switched to sturdier circular buttons molded from plastic.

13. Since the keys were hidden in the concept drawing, it is unclear whether a keyboard was meant to slide out or simply unstack when needed. Based on the final prototype, the latter is likely true, though the stacking design was probably scrapped because the keys would be hard to type on if the keyboard component were flat.

14. Margetts and Ward, "Lance Barr Interview."

15. *Electronic Games Magazine* summed up the games industry response with a short feature in their March 1985 issue titled "Nintendo's Final Solution": "Nintendo has decided to distribute the AVS here, perhaps as early as this spring. Considering that the videogame market in America has virtually disappeared, this could be a miscalculation on Nintendo's part." From Bloom, ed., "Nintendo's Final Solution."

16. Sheff, 162.

17. As with most of their failed experiments, Nintendo would not abandon wireless peripherals, but repurpose the idea for later consoles. The most contemporary example is, of course, the wireless Wii remote.

18. Semrad, "New Nintendo system way ahead of the field."

19. The Fairchild Channel F and the Intellivision used card edge connectors, but their cartridges loaded horizontally, similar to 8-track cassettes.

20. It was so unlike other console designs that Nintendo received a patent for the mechanism. See Yukawa, "Front Loading Apparatus for a Memory Cartridge Utilized for a Data Processing Machine."

21. Margetts and Ward, "Lance Barr Interview."

22. Edwards, "No More Blinkies: Replacing the NES's 72-Pin Cartridge Connector."

23. Likewise, the NES's unofficial nickname—the "toaster"—derives from the ZIF's function: cartridges are both loaded into the NES horizontally like slices of bread into a toaster oven and locked into place with a spring-loaded catch like a conventional "top-loading" toaster. It is a confused metaphor, but one that has stuck.

24. Nakagawa, "Recordable Data Device Having Identification Symbols Formed Thereon and Cooperating Data Processing System Having Registering Symbols."

25. "NES expansion port pinout," *NesDev Wiki*.

26. While initial runs of the NES had an easily accessible expansion port, later revisions covered the port with a plastic hatch that had to be forcibly broken to access. With the introduction of the top-loading NES-101, Nintendo dropped the port altogether.

27. Pichugan, "Steepler начал продавать Dendy (Steepler starts sales of Dendy)." Also note that the Dendy is still commercially available in Russia to this day.

28. For the exact technical differences, see *NesDev Wiki*, "Clock rate."

29. Also see Altice, "Dendy: The Unofficial Official Famicom of Russia."

30. Thanks to its innovative marriage of hardware and software, Nintendo received two patents for their authentication systems in 1989. See Nakagawa, "External memory having an authenticating processor and method of operating same," and Nakagawa, "System for determining authenticity of an external memory used in an information processing apparatus."

31. Segher, "The weird and wonderful CIC."

32. See "CIC lockout chip" and "CIC lockout chip pinout," *NesDev Wiki*.

33. O'Donnell, "Production Protection to Copy(right) Protection," 54.
34. Ibid., 61. Note that O'Donnell conflates (or at least is unclear about) the lockout chip's program and its hardware. Throughout, he calls the CIC the "10NES chip." However, 10NES is the program that runs on the CIC, not the chip itself. The patent text he cites (55) refers to 10NES as distinct from the CIC, but O'Donnell never makes the distinction in his article.
35. Donovan, 174.
36. Associated Press, "Nintendo Charged With Monopolizing Market."
37. See Olmos, "Chip Shortage Strains Computer Makers" and Pollack, "Shortage of Memory Chips Has Industry Scrambling."
38. McGill, "The ultimate video game: Nintendo vs Atari."
39. "Chip Problems Strangle the Video Game Industry," *Electronic Game Player* 1.4 (Sept./Oct. 1988): 25.
40. United States Court of Appeals, "Atari Games Corp. v. Nintendo of America Inc."
41. Ibid.
42. Atari/Tengen programmer Ed Logg says that while Atari's lawyers did obtain the 10NES patents under false pretenses, the information was not used in the production of the Rabbit chip:

    Kevin Gifford: Yeah, *Game Over* painted Tengen as basically stealing the patents for the lockout chip.

    Ed Logg: The trouble was it was already done before we saw it. We had already done the Rabbit chip long before we had seen it. So it's already done, and we see this and we're like "Oh shit." (laughs)

    KG: So you know for a fact the Rabbit was 100% original?

    EL: Yeah. I walked into the lab and they were reverse engineering the chip, and I asked what they were doing and they said, "Don't ask." (laughs) So I know the company was doing it, and I knew the people involved doing it.

    KG: Was this a major undertaking, the engineering?

    EL: It was basically three people. And they were certainly looking at the chip, let's put it that way. I'm sure they did a lot more that I didn't see. Tweaking the signals, seeing what comes out, that kind of stuff. And I was working on the FC at the time. We had reverse engineered the Famicom and I was already developing on it.

    See Gifford, "Tetris...forever."
43. United States Court of Appeals, "Atari Games Corp. v. Nintendo of America Inc."
44. Valesh, "Nintendo, America!"
45. The Japanese version of R.O.B., released three months prior to the NES version, was called the Family Computer Robot and matched the Famicom's color scheme.
46. Cifaldi, "In Their Words: Remembering the Launch of the Nintendo Entertainment System."
47. "First Nintendo Commercial."
48. Nintendo of America, "VIDEO ROBOTS."
49. Due to R.O.B.'s early demise and minuscule software support, "big box" versions of *Gyromite* and *Stack-Up* (with included accessories) command high prices among collectors.

50. My thanks to Tursi and x87bliss at AtariAge for decoding R.O.B.'s behavior through careful reverse engineering and experimentation. See godslabrat, "Any interest in NES ROB homebrews?"

51. The precise color values are not critical, merely the contrast of light and dark. See ibid.

52. Only the NES port of *Zelda* uses sprite o for its screen split. The original disk version uses an IRQ scanline counter native to the Disk System.

53. Cifaldi, "In Their Words: Remembering the Launch of the Nintendo Entertainment System."

54. A further irony in light of Nintendo's initial marketing was R.O.B.'s platform agnosticism. Since the robot has no direct interface with the NES, it is possible to issue commands via any console that can replicate the proper sequence of screen flashes. Once R.O.B.'s flicker sequences were decoded, for instance, AtariAge community member Pioneer4x4 wrote a simple program to control the robot with an Atari VCS. See Pioneer4x4, "I got my Atari to control my Nintendo R.O.B. Robot!"

55. Light gun technology was actually Nintendo's first, inauspicious entry into the American videogame industry: "In 1971, Nintendo had—even before the marketing of the first home console in the United States—an alliance with the American pioneer Magnavox to develop and produce optoelectronic guns for the Odyssey (released in 1972), since it was similar to what Nintendo was able to offer in the Japanese toy market in 1970s." Picard, "The Foundation of *Geemu*: A Brief History of Early Japanese video games."

56. See V., Eric, "Nintendo Kousenjuu Duck Hunt (光線銃 ダックハント, 1976)."

57. Electronic Code of Federal Regulations, "PART 1150—MARKING OF TOY, LOOK-ALIKE AND IMITATION FIREARMS," §1150.3 - Approved markings.

58. Note that some early NES technical documents have the Zapper flags reversed (e.g., Chadwick, "Nintendo Entertainment System Documentation Version: 2.00").

59. The four NES light gun launch titles were *Duck Hunt, Gumshoe, Hogan's Alley*, and *Wild Gunman*.

60. "Wild Gunman (1974)," Internet Arcade Museum.

61. Okada received a U.S. patent for the technique. See Okada, "Video Target Control and Sensing Circuit for Photosensitive Gun."

62. "Question about coding for NES zapper," *NesDev*.

63. Cifaldi, "In Their Words: Remembering the Launch of the Nintendo Entertainment System."

64. The games included a SAVE option, but no on-cart memory to do so. The original cartridges used the optional Famicom Data Recorder to save levels. Though the peripheral was never released outside Japan, the menu options were never deleted in localization.

65. bootgod, "Family BASIC (Revision A1)."

66. See "Pulse Line Cartridges," *Famicom World*.

67. Feldman and Walters, "Konami Box Art."

68. However, Nintendo did have their favored licensees. Top-shelf developer Konami, for instance, were able to circumvent restrictions by creating a subsidiary company, Ultra Games. When Konami reached their yearly ceiling for game releases, they could then transfer publishing credit to Ultra.

69. Donovan, 168.
70. NES game paks had 72 pins, versus the Famicom's 60. Ten were wired to the NES's unused expansion port. The remaining two connected to the CIC.
71. See bootgod, "Gemfire."
72. Worldwide, box styles varied by region. In Great Britain, Canada, and France, Nintendo largely used the standard extended box design. The enhanced pixelated cover artwork was also identical. Minor variations included a line of text ("GAME OF") to prefix the title, along with the relevant regional translation. The French cover for *Hogan's Alley*, for instance, said, "GAME OF / JEU DE HOGAN'S ALLEY." The Seal of Quality was similarly duplicated and translated. In regions where Mattel distributed the NES, their corporate logo was affixed to the front cover near the Seal of Quality.

    In Spain, covers were altered more significantly. The pixelated artwork was replaced by the cartoon illustration style of the Famicom originals. The Nintendo logo, updated to the more modern red and white version, was moved to the lower left and subtitled "VERSION ESPAÑOLA." The series icon was deleted and replaced with a translated text version. For example, *Balloon Fight*, now in a silver box, had the text "SERIE ACCION" directly beneath the title.

    The greatest international divergence in box design came from the "short box" variants released in certain Asian and European markets. In these regions, Nintendo eliminated the styrofoam risers and shrunk the boxes to fit the actual height and width of the game paks.
73. As a result, the screw count and plastic surface along the pak's upper edge is a quick visual cue to approximate the game's production date (and has since become a variant sought by collectors).
74. Yukawa, "Cartridge for Game Machine."
75. There were a few notable variations of the NES game pak: the yellow test carts used in Nintendo's authorized service centers, black carts used in Famicom game kiosks in hotels, and the holy grail of NES collectors—the gold Nintendo World Championship cart awarded to contest winners.
76. Unlicensed distributors could not copy the Nintendo seal's text, but they could brand their own. HES boxes, for example, had their own circular serrated seal, appropriately free of any quality claims: "H.E.S. CARTRIDGE FOR NINTENDO. Use with a Nintendo cartridge. (Instruction enclosed)."
77. Among Retrozone's cartridge reproductions (viewable at retrousb.com) is the updated version of *Donkey Kong* with the "pie factory" level reinstated (Chapter 2).
78. McCullough, "Nintendo's Era of Censorship."
79. Wirth, "Spotlight: Earthbound."
80. W., "Interview with Shigeru Miyamoto Volumes 1 and 2."
81. Kohler, "The Secret History of Super Mario Bros. 2."
82. To disambiguate the U.S. and Japanese titles of the same name, the NES version of *Super Mario Bros. 2* was eventually ported back to the Famicom as *Super Mario USA* (1992).
83. "Might and Magic: Oddities, Theories, and Unused Content," *Flying Omelet*.
84. *Might & Magic* is a conspicuous example of double translation. Instead of porting the native English PC version directly to the NES, it was refracted through

both the Japanese language and Nintendo's content regulations before U.S. release.

85. For those who might miss the 1980s food references, the final three games featured characters representing McDonald's, 7-Up, and Domino's Pizza, respectively.

86. Kohler, *Power-Up*, 207.

87. See Fieldsted, "Category Archives: Cultural Anxiety."

88. *Rockman* is one of the most notorious examples of NES artwork localization. The lively anime-inspired Famicom box art closely matched the look of the in-game sprites. The U.S. version, titled *Mega Man*, was an artistic train wreck of disjointed perspectives, improbable anatomy, and questionable characterization that bore little resemblance to the game advertised. "Box art Mega Man" has since become part of NES lore, even resurfacing as a playable character in 2012 fighting game *Street Fighter X Tekken*.

89. See "Strafgesetzbuch section 86a," *Wikipedia*.

90. "The Bionic Commando Database," *The Almighty Guru*.

91. In the years since *Bionic Commando*'s release, Hitler's exploding head has metamorphosed from censorship oversight to NES cultural lore. The graphic animation continues to propagate, both as Internet meme (such as the J-Pop-infused web animation "OMG Hitler's Exploding on Bionic Commando!") and in videogame adaptation (it was faithfully "remastered" in the 2008 HD remake of the NES game, *Bionic Commando: Rearmed*). See "YTMD - OMG, Hitler's Exploding on Bionic Commando!" and "Bionic Commando Re-Armed: Exploding Hitler Head," poeTV.

Chapter 4

1. Miyamoto recalls that the team included seven or eight members. See W., "Interview with Shigeru Miyamoto Volumes 1 and 2."

2. In most cases, I will opt for the "platformer" name in an effort to distinguish the genre from a general computational platform.

3. In *Mario Bros.*, the turtles are called "Shellcreepers," while in future Mario games they are called "Koopa Troopas."

4. See "Platform game," *Wikipedia*.

5. See the "Manuals" section of MatoTree, "Legends of Localization: Super Mario Bros."

6. See Sarkeesian, "Damsel in Distress: Tropes vs Women in Video Games."

7. See "Names" in MatoTree, "Legends of Localization: Super Mario Bros."

8. See Papp, *Anime and its Roots in Early Japanese Monster Art*.

9. Nintendo of Europe GmbH, "Iwata Asks: Volume 8 - Flipnote Studio - An Animation Class."

10. Ibid.

11. W., et al., "Mario in Japan."

12. W., et al., "Super Mario Bros. - From Japanese to English."

13. See "Names" in MatoTree, "Legends of Localization: Super Mario Bros."

14. Nintendo of America Inc., "Iwata Asks - New Super Mario Bros.: Volume 2."

15. The mushroom-induced size change was originally attributed to *Alice in Wonderland* (Sheff, *Game Over*, 51; Kohler, *Power-Up*, 58), but Miyamoto has said that

there was no overt influence from the Lewis Carroll tale. See Nintendo of America Inc., "Iwata Asks - New Super Mario Bros.: Volume 1," Section 4.

16. Gifford, "Super Mario Bros.' 25th: Miyamoto Reveals All."

17. Nintendo of America Inc., "Iwata Asks - New Super Mario Bros: Volume 2," Section 6.

18. Nintendo of America Inc., "Iwata Asks - New Super Mario Bros: Volume 1," Section 3.

19. Chaplin and Ruby, *Smartbomb*, 66–9. The same childhood landscape would inspire the caves of Hyrule in *The Legend of Zelda*.

20. Nintendo of America Inc., "Iwata Asks - New Super Mario Bros: Volume 2," Section 5.

21. Snider, "Q&A: 'Mario' creator Shigeru Miyamoto."

22. "Area objects" and "enemy objects" are labels coined by doppelganger, not official source comments from Nagako, Miyamoto, or the rest of the *SMB* team.

23. Unless otherwise noted, terminology and source code excerpts from *Super Mario Bros.* are drawn from doppelganger, "SMBDIS.ASM - A Comprehensive Super Mario Bros. Disassembly." Specific code segments are cited with the line numbers from the disassembly. I also adopt many of doppelganger's naming conventions for objects, subroutines, variables, etc. to maintain consistency for readers.

24. Galoob, *Game Genie Programming Manual and Codebook*, 141.

25. Nintendo's own *Paper Mario* (2001) series adopted a similar visual style. The 2007 Wii sequel *Super Paper Mario* was ostensibly a 2D platformer with a literal 3D twist: the player could rotate the perspective along a vertical axis, permitting them to see hidden routes, retrieve power-ups, and pass obstacles that appear insurmountable in 2D.

26. doppelganger, "SMBDIS.ASM," line 4956–67.

27. Certain levels share identical area object data: 1–4/6–4, 1–3/5–3, 2–2/7–2, 2–4/5–4, and 2–3/7–3. However, their enemy object placement varies.

28. Nintendo of America Inc., "Iwata Asks - Volume 1: Shigesato Itoi Asks in Place of Iwata," Section 9.

29. See "Nibble," *Wikipedia*.

30. doppelganger, "SMB disassembly." Though the data tables and illustrations are mine, I am indebted to doppelganger's personal correspondence. He explained in exhaustive detail how the byte encoding worked.

31. doppelganger, "SMBDIS.ASM," line 3472–3529.

32. The *Legend of Zelda* has a similar spatial maze within the Lost Woods. Surrounding trees outline four conjoined paths that branch to each of four cardinal directions. If Link heads east, he returns to the prior screen. However, moving north, west, or south returns Link to the same screen in an apparent infinite loop. Like *SMB*'s castles, only a certain pattern of path choices (north, west, south, west) will lead Link out of the Lost Woods and into the adjoining Graveyard. Both games' mazes produce unmappable cartographies that can only be represented through movement vectors.

33. Excluding the FDS version of *Super Mario Bros. 2*, which used a nearly identical engine as the original.

34. Nintendo of America Inc., *Super Mario Bros. / Duck Hunt Instruction Booklet*, 19. Bracketed words are small illustrations in the original.

35. Nintendo of America Inc., "Iwata Asks - New Super Mario Bros: Volume 2," Section 6.

36. My thanks to Damian Yerrick for explaining the technical details (and providing the name) for this PPU rendering quirk.

37. Note that future iterations of *Mega Man* dropped score tracking.

38. Ironically, the console's shortcomings are now part of the *Mega Man* franchise's trademark style. In 2008's "retroboot" of the series, *Mega Man 9*, simulated sprite flicker and engine slowdown were selectable features via the game's "Legacy Mode." See Webster, *"Mega Man 9* to feature intentional, optional glitches."

39. The instruction manual explains the camera's shifting roles. In the "Camera Options" section, it reads, "One of the tricks of this game is to use the camera skillfully. You are not just the player, but the cinematographer, too!" A page later, in "Camera Operation Mode," it reads, "During the game, depending on the scene, the Camera Mode will automatically switch to the 'recommended' view." See Nintendo of America, *Super Mario 64 Instruction Booklet*, 20–1.

40. Note that this and subsequent coordinates describe the upper left pixel of the upper left sprite in Mario's metatile, a point located a few pixels to the left of his cap.

41. See Anthropy, "level design lesson: to the right, hold on tight."

42. Steve Swink provides an excellent but slightly "higher-level" take on Mario's physics and camera interaction in Swink, *Game Feel*, 206–220.

43. See BOCTOK Co., Ltd, *Bit Generation 2000 "TV Games,"* 89; Gifford, "Mario Mania I (1985-6)"; and Gifford, "More on Tokuma's Mario Guide."

44. Gifford, "Mario Mania I (1985-6)."

45. *Nintendo Power*'s inaugural issue outlines the 3–1 trick in the "Counselor's Corner" section. They tell players, "You may want to stop building lives at around 100. If you get too greedy, the program has a built-in 'Game Over.'" Nintendo of America, Inc., "Counselor's Corner - Super Mario Bros." *Nintendo Power* 1 (July/Aug. 1988): 52.

46. Also see Kaluszka, "How the Super Mario Bros. extra lives system works (I think)."

47. Nintendo of America, Inc., "Classified Information - Explore the mysterious minus world." *Nintendo Power* 3 (Nov./Dec. 1988): 55.

48. doppelganger, "the minus world explained v2.0." doppelganger's document, at over 4,000 words, is the most detailed description of the minus world behavior, based on his thorough disassembly of the *SMB* source.

Chapter 5

1. "Famicom Disc System CM (English)," Trans. Clyde Mandelin (aka matotree). Observant *Zelda* fans may note that the metallic surface featured in the commercial is patterned with Triforce shapes.

2. Taylor, "Famicom Disk System technical reference." Booting the FDS triggered a short fanfare as a large flashing banner emblazoned with the Nintendo scrolled into view from the top of the screen. If there was no disk loaded, the bottom of the logo read "PLEASE SET DISK CARD." Then, both Luigi and Mario (in their

original *Mario Bros.* attire) appeared in turn, competing to flip a light switch hanging from the bottom of the banner. It was a simple animation, but it showed that the RAM adapter itself had executable code onboard, functioning as a surrogate cartridge.

3. The ROM BIOS mapped directly to CPU memory space in an 8K block spanning $E000 to $FFFF.

4. Theoretically, an FDS disk card can hold 65,500 bytes per side, but a fraction of that available space is filled with zeroed "gaps" and 16-bit cyclic error-correcting codes (CRCs) bookending data blocks, as well as the disk's requisite header data. See *NesDev Wiki*, "Family Computer Disk System" for more details.

5. For a detailed history of the floppy disk's development, see Pugh, et al., 510–21.

6. See Sheff, 75 and McFerran, "Slipped Disk - The History of the Famicom Disk System."

7. The blue contest disks were much scarcer than yellow. Rarest of all were white prototype disks used internally for FDS development. See Famicom World, "Nintendo's Development Disks."

8. See Famicom World, "Holy Grails."

9. Taylor, "Famicom Disk System technical reference."

10. *Famicom Disk System*, "Disks."

11. *Famicom World*, "FDS Power Board Modifications."

12. Taylor, "Famicom Disk System technical reference." The distinction between blocks and files is unclear and inconsistent in much of the FDS documentation. I use block to designate a discrete section of related bytes, such as the header. A file is composed of several blocks, namely the header, data, and CRC.

13. The full byte was not necessary. The FDS only looked for a single bit flip from zero to one to indicate the end of a gap and the start of a new block. The FDS read disks in reverse bit order, so the binary value of $80 indicated a string of zeroes ending with a 1 (%10000000).

14. *NesDev Wiki*, "Famicom Disk System."

15. The 14-byte string is 2A 4E 49 4E 54 45 4E 44 4F 2D 48 56 43 2A, which can be read from the header of FDS ROMs in a hex editor.

16. *Famicom Disk System*, "Disk Copy."

17. Gifford, "Hacker International's head speaks."

18. DvD Translations, "ReadMe-DvD_Translations-BodyConQuest_I-Girls _Exposed-revA.txt."

19. The FDS's seven other launch games were largely cross-ports of Famicom sports cartridges like *Baseball* and *Tennis*.

20. Nintendo of America Inc., "Iwata Asks - New Super Mario Bros: Volume 2." Nintendo's two Famicom-based arcade platforms were the Vs. UniSystem and the PlayChoice-10.

21. There were third-party VS ports as well, such as *Vs. Castlevania*, *Vs. Goonies*, *Vs. Platoon*, *Vs. Gradius*, etc.

22. Korth, "Everynes: Everything about NES and Famicom."

23. "Nintendo Vs. Unisystem," *John's Arcade.*

24. Both the FDS and NES version of *The Legend of Zelda* contain staff credits, albeit in pseudonym form. However, the original prototype listed the contributors'

real names, with the exception of "Ten Ten" (Tezuka) and "Konchan" (Kondo). See *The Cutting Room Floor*, "Proto: The Legend of Zelda."

25. Nintendo of America Inc., "Iwata Asks - New Super Mario Bros: Volume 2."
26. "How 'Adventure Mario' became The Legend Of Zelda," *CVG*.
27. "Zelda no Video History of Zelda Documentary."
28. See Edge Staff, "THE MAKING OF...Japan's First RPG" and Parkin, "The Dragon Invasion."
29. Though *Ultima I* obviously preceded *Ultima II* in the West, the former did not receive a port to the PC-8801 until 1988. *Ultima II*, however, was ported to the PC-8801 and Fujitsu FM-77 (among other platforms) in 1985.
30. Sopalin, "Miyamoto, la Wii U et le secret de la Triforce."
31. Hamman, "The Tower of Druaga: Item Guide (v.1.11)."
32. *Zelda*'s creature and item menageries likewise shared a number of uncanny resemblances to *Druaga*'s sprites. Both had red/blue rings and candles, three levels of swords, red/blue elixirs, a blue wand, a spell book, shield-bearing knights, fidgeting slimes, teleporting wizards, and circular floating spirits. Viewed side by side, the two games' sprites are strikingly similar.
33. Unseen64staff, "The Legend Of Zelda [NES - Beta / Concept]." Also see Thorpe, *The Legend of Zelda: Hyrule Historia*, 2. Nintendo's internal development teams had experimented with player-constructed levels in earlier titles *Excitebike*, *Wrecking Crew*, and *Mach Rider*. Each game had a design mode that allowed players to place game objects within a level. Since all three were NROM cartridges, players had to save and load their designs to cassette via the Family Computer Data Recorder peripheral.
34. *Adventure* uses its spatial discontinuity to great effect, since many of its screens do not adhere to logical geometries. An eastern tunnel from one screen, for instance, can lead the player to the northern entrance of a non-adjacent screen.
35. Nintendo of America Inc., "Iwata Asks - New Super Mario Bros: Volume 2."
36. Dungeon screens are truncated by four metatiles because their bordering walls and doors are handled separately by the rendering engine.
37. My thanks to *NesDev* member snarfblam for describing and explaining *Zelda*'s metatile engine and compression technique. See *NesDev*, "Zelda FDS (and general disk-related questions)" for our discussion.
38. In addition, the data stream can describe multiple "overlapping" strips depending on where one enters it. See ibid.
39. Indeed, *Zelda*'s original design documents show that the team plotted the dungeon layouts as if solving a block puzzle. Tezuka pencilled two 16x8 grids on graph paper and shaded in each dungeon's layout with colored pencils. Miyamoto used the same technique to design Hyrule's overworld.
40. The second quest was meant to extend the life of the game and offer advanced players additional challenges. Players could unlock the second quest by either completing the game or entering "ZELDA" as their name in the player registration screen.
41. Nintendo of Europe GmbH, "Iwata Asks: Zelda Handheld History."
42. Name tables do not "move." Toggling mirroring simply updates which name table data is duplicated at which address.
43. Internally, the four name tables starting locations reside at the following PPU addresses: $2000, $2400, $2800, and $2C00.

44. Note that the status bar remains static throughout the engine's scrolling routine. This is achieved differently on different platforms: disk *Zelda* uses the FDS's scanline IRQ to time the screen split; cartridge *Zelda* uses sprite 0, whose bomb pattern mimics the counter in the status bar.

45. The reality is slightly more complex than setting bit 3 of $4025 to 0. $4025 is a disk control register that also handles a number of low-level disk drive functions, including turning the motor on and off. To ensure that updating mirroring settings does not conflict with the physical operation of the disk, the BIOS also provides several "pseudo-registers" to permit safe access to the mirroring status. During horizontal screen transitions, *Zelda* first updates $4025's pseudo-register, $00FA, then the actual register.

46. We can only speculate why Nintendo opted to cut battery saves from *Metroid* and *Kid Icarus*. Both boards looked identical to the *Zelda* MMC1 save for an auspicious blank spot on the upper left corner of the PCB labeled "Batt CR2032," clearly indicating where the battery would have been clipped. Both boards also included a superfluous 8KB of SRAM. Stranger still is an unused region of memory ($77FE-$782D) left in the *Metroid* source code that stored save data in the disk version but had no use with a password system in place (See "MetroidDefines" in Dirty McDingus, "*Metroid* Source Code Expanded."). Perhaps Nintendo decided the additional cost of the battery was not a worthwhile expenditure at the time. Perhaps the two games were riskier in the Western marketplace; *Zelda* had proven to be a massive hit in Japan, but an opaque sci-fi exploration game with a female protagonist and a Greek mythology-centered platformer were less of a sure bet.

47. Nintendo was hedging its bets, but it turns out they undersold the battery. Anecdotally, its shelf life has proven to be much longer, as many original *Zelda* carts still maintain their save data after twenty-five years (including the author's two personal copies).

48. See whicker's reply in "Static RAM in the SNES carts" (FistOfFury), *ZSNES Board*; *NesDev Wiki*, "MMC1"; and "Why DO you have to hold reset while turning power off?" (Protoman), *Famicom World*.

49. The instruction booklet warning also showed an updated screen shot displaying the new in-game warning. See Nintendo of America, Inc., *The Legend of Zelda Instruction Booklet*, 1987: 13–14.

50. Paumgarten, "Master of Play" and "Spelunking in Sonobe."

51. Sheff, 45.

52. "Nintendo Online Magazine Shigeru Miyamoto Interview - August, 1998," *ZeldaDungeon.net*.

53. Scott, "Miyamoto: 'I am lazy.'"

54. The original reads: 環境を遊ぶという意味ではどっちも一緒なんですよ。同じように箱庭のような場所があって、同じように解法を捜していくという。 Trans. Aria Tanner, personal correspondence.

55. Lee, *The Compact Culture*, 156.

56. Ibid., 75.

57. Katayama, 168.

58. Kerr, *Dogs and Demons*, 14.

59. Kerr, 232.

60. Smith echoes Kerr's sentiments in *Japan: A Reinterpretation*: "The construction state lies at the core of the postwar system. It helps to account for Tokyo's deranged pursuit of economic growth at any cost... And it is why we sometimes picture Japan as a machine with no one at the levers, a machine out of control." Smith, *Japan: A Reinterpretation*, 180.
61. Kerr, 35.
62. Watanabe, "The Conception of Nature in Japanese Culture," 187, 190.
63. Ibid., 192.
64. Ibid., 193.
65. Kerr also highlights the cultural tension at play between the image of "Japan as the land of the miniature" and the reality of "Japan's modern gigantism, the insistence on the biggest and the longest, the taste for the bombastic." Kerr, 228–35.
66. Bogost and Montfort, *Racing the Beam*, 146.
67. Sample, "What Comes before the Platform: The Refuse of Videogames."
68. Nintendo of America Inc., "Iwata Asks - New Super Mario Bros: Volume 1."
69. Sheff, 76.
70. The Disk System also spawned a notable hardware variation. Nintendo continued its longstanding partnership with Sharp and sanctioned the Sharp Twin Famicom (ツインファミコン), a hefty console hybrid that combined the Famicom and FDS into a single integrated enclosure. Sharp adopted many of its design cues from Nintendo's console: carts top-loaded, disk cards inserted in the front, hardwired controllers docked on the console (although along the back, rather than the sides), and a dedicated lever popped carts out of the system. However, a special sliding lock ensured that carts and disks could not play simultaneously, physically blocking disk card insertion when the other format was engaged in some models, and vice-versa in others. Along the unit's right side were two expansion ports: one was the standard 15-pin port used for connecting peripherals, while the other was, perplexingly, an interface that allowed a second Famicom to use the Twin's disk drive. The Twin also diverged in its palette, offering two hardware colors (each with its own later revision). Though one Twin variation came in red, its hue was softer than Famicom maroon. More importantly, the Twin upgraded the Famicom's visual output, providing a composite A/V port in addition to the stock RF connection.

Chapter 6

1. See Editorial & Business Headquarters, "Game Makers Plan Future." My thanks to Zach Whalen for this reference.
2. Slade, *Made to Break*, 5.
3. Also see Whalen, "Channel F for Forgotten."
4. See Weil, "No Bad Memories (Or, Video-game nostalgia and the academic and popular discourses that shape it)."
5. Picard, "The Foundation of *Geemu*: A Brief History of Early Japanese video games."
6. Ibid.
7. Smith, "Feature: What's in a Name?"
8. Iwamoto, *Japan on the Upswing*, 200.

9.   Ibid., 200.
10. "List of Enix home computer games," *Wikipedia*.
11. Iwamoto, 200.
12. Like Nakamura, Horii would eventually adopt his own company name, Armor Project.
13. "ドアドア," *Wikipedia Japan*.
14. Its NEC PC-6001 predecessor, released two years prior, was one of the first Japanese graphical adventure games. See "Early Japanese Adventures (1982–1986)" in "Adventure Game," *Wikipedia*.
15. For an overview of the adventure genre, see Wolf, *The Video Game Explosion*, pp. 81–90.
16. While Nintendo offered a keyboard attachment for the Famicom, they only supported it with two software titles, both versions of the programming cartridge *Family BASIC*.
17. For photos and news reports of Portopia '81, see Cotter, "Portopia '81."
18. "Japanese Flock to Exhibit Focusing on the Future," *nytimes.com*.
19. In light of Kerr's indictment of Japan's environmental policies (chapter 5), there is an added irony that Kobe's government would mine their natural resources to raise an artificial island out of the sea and enshrine it in concrete. See Kerr, 37.
20. Nonetheless there is a strong tradition of text mode games. Two of the most revered, even today, are *Rogue* and *Nethack*, both of which use the ASCII character set to represent their in-game "graphics."
21. The slow rendering times were likely a by-product of the game being programmed in BASIC.
22. Enix, Inc., "The Portopia Serial Murder Case Suspense Adventure Game Instruction Booklet (How to play)," Trans. harmony7.
23. Ibid.
24. Investigating the crime scene in an emulator reveals that the chalk outline is drawn with background tiles—with one exception: a single sprite is used to draw a portion of the victim's head. DvD Translations speculates that the sprite might be evidence of a coverup of the blood from the original game. The mystery remains unsolved.
25. DvD Translations, "ReadMe-DvD_Translations-The_Portopia_Serial_Murder _Case-revB2.txt."
26. European releases dropped the plural "Ghosts," so the title was *Ghost'n Goblins*.
27. Due to the spotty documentation of many Famicom and NES releases, a precise history of cartridge mappers is difficult to determine. *NesDev*'s "Cartridge and mappers' history" provides one of the best summaries, nominating Jaleco's *City Connection* (Sept. 1985) as the "first game to use hardware other than 2 ROMs." CNROM appears by April 1986, with UNROM following soon after in June 1986.
28. *NesDev Wiki*, "Mask ROM Pinout."
29. *NesDev Wiki*, "CHR ROM vs. CHR RAM."
30. *NesDev Wiki*, "Cartridge and mappers' history."
31. See the entry for "Makaimura" in bootgod, *NES Cart Database*.
32. Sheff, 42–3.

33. The Japanese technology industry has a complex history of competition and cooperation among corporations. See Anchordoguy, *Reprogramming Japan* and Johnstone, *We Were Burning*.

34. See Nakagawa, Katsuya and Yoshiaki Nakanishi, "Memory cartridge having a multi-memory controller with memory bank switching capabilities and data processing apparatus" and Nintendo of America, Inc., "Why Your Game Paks Never Forget," *Nintendo Power* 20 (Jan. 1991): 28–31. In the latter source, Nintendo reassigned the MMC acronym to "memory management controllers."

35. Most important to duplicate were the three interrupt vectors used to direct code after console reset, NMI, or IRQ. See *NesDev Wiki*, "Programming UNROM."

36. CHR-RAM animation functioned similarly to CHR-ROM, though its tile updates were more granular, since entire banks did not have to swap as a whole. Developer Rare were especially adept at this method, using CHR-RAM updates to animate the titular heroes from *Battletoads* and the player's boat in *Cobra Triangle*.

37. Not to say that NROM games could not contain unused code or graphics. Several, including *Donkey Kong* and *Super Mario Bros.*, have yielded artifacts, just not to the extent that later ROM-rich games have.

38. The wiki-driven site *The Cutting Room Floor* has become a valuable repository of these programming artifacts, exhaustively cataloguing the binary minutiae found by combing through cartridge ROM and disk dumps. Some of their more remarkable entries include the sixteen unused levels in *Super Mario Bros. 3*, a detailed list of the differences between *The Legend of Zelda*'s prototype disk versus its official release, and *Erika to Satoru no Yume Bouken* programmer Hidemushi's now-infamous hidden diatribe excoriating his co-workers' laziness, hygiene, and sexual behaviors.

39. Gifford, "The Road to Dragon Quest."

40. The *Wizardry* manual made this explicit: "After you have selected activities for all the characters...the computer will mediate the combat." Sir-Tech Software Inc., *Wizardry (Instruction Manual)*, 32.

41. *Wizardry* and *Ultima* were both single-player games, but in the former, one's party could be up to six members strong, each with their own name, race, class, ability scores, and equipment. *Ultima* had the same character customization options, but restricted the player to a party of one.

42. Both character naming and a single character class were traits first seen in *Black Onyx*. See Parkin, "The Dragon Invasion."

43. The original Japanese read: 主人公はあなた自身。ゲームスタート時にあなたの名前を入れると王様や町の人はその名前で話しかけてきます。Translated in Kuntz, "DRAGON QUEST Japanese Game Script and Mini Playing Guide v5.11."

44. Speirs, "Dragon Warrior: Names/Stats/Levels FAQ." Note that there is a small error in Speirs' growth track table. See ShinerCCC's comment in Optimus-PriNe, "Dragon Warrior Run."

45. ラダトーム has varying English translations online, but I have opted for Nintendo's "official" pre-release translation of "Radatome" found in the Winter '87 issue of *Nintendo Fun Club News*. However, the names would change for the U.S. localization two years later: Lars is Lorik, Loto is Erdrick, Radatome Castle is

Tantagel, and the Dragon King is known as the Dragonlord, who awaits your hero in Charlock Castle.

46. *Ultima* pioneered this use of an overworld view in computer RPGs, but again, the roots of that visual style traced to tabletop role-playing and beyond that to centuries of war games, where tokens or figurines would represent armies on a battle map. In *Dungeons & Dragons*, the compression and rarefaction of in-game spaces was common in transitions between towns and dungeons, where player miniatures were scaled to their environment, and a larger world map, commonly gridded with squares or hexagons to quantitatively abstract movements over great distances.

47. *Nintendo Power* 7 (July/Aug. 1989): 40 [photo caption].

48. "Iwata Asks: Dragon Quest IX - Part 1: The History of Dragon Quest."

49. Mentzer, *Dungeons & Dragons Dungeon Masters Rulebook*, 22.

50. Loogaroo1 provides a color-coded visual breakdown of the game's zones. See, Loogaroo1, "Dragon Warrior: Enemy Territory Map."

51. *Dragon Warrior Instruction Booklet*, 17.

52. Technically, each grassland tile had either a 1/32 or 1/16 encounter probability, based on the player's current coordinates. Programmatically, these tiles had a checkerboard pattern, so each step alternated the probability. See Ryan8bit, "Dragon Warrior (NES) Formulas v1.0" for more details.

53. Kuntz, "DRAGON QUEST Japanese Game Script and Mini Playing Guide v5.11."

54. Artist Akira Toriyama's Blue Slime has since become one of *Dragon Quest*'s most beloved and enduring characters, spawning his own plush merchandise and spin-off games.

55. The spell memorization system served at least two purposes: one, it helped curb software piracy, since players needed the instruction manual (or an outstanding memory) to successfully cast spells; and two, it was a technological nod to the "Vancian" system of magic used in *Dungeons & Dragons*, where spells were memorized each day and lost from memory when used.

56. The MALOR teleportation spell, for example, required room coordinates to cast. If the player mapped their surrounding incorrectly, they could teleport into a wall, instantly killing the entire party. Worse still, casting MALOR during combat teleported the party to a random location, increasing the odds that your party would be "lost forever" within the maze. See Sir-Tech Software Inc., *Wizardry (Instruction Manual)*, 46.

57. Technically, eight-way movement would count as "true" multi-directional scrolling. *Dragon Quest* limits movements to one metatile at a time in one of four cardinal directions. Diagonal movement requires a more complex scrolling engine that can update both rows and columns simultaneously.

58. This is likely a design decision based on where the attribute errors might be most distracting to players. Mario's newfound flying ability, the centerpiece of *Super Mario Bros. 3*, might have been dampened if flight was always correlated with strange color blocks in the skies.

59. Vic Tokai's *Clash at Demonhead* (1990) and Hudson Soft's *Felix the Cat* (1992) use the same sprite-stacking technique seen in *Alfred Chicken*. The key trait all three share is the use of 8x16-pixel sprites. Without the increased height, the righthand column would use twice as many sprites, sacrificing nearly half of OAM to a border, an unacceptable expenditure for most games.

60. *Dragon Quest* was not Enix's first collaboration with Toriyama. In 1984, they released Dr.スランプ バブル大作戦 for the PC-6001/6601, a shooter starring Toriyama's character Dr. Slump.

61. Gifford, "Dragon Quest Composer Reflects on 24 Years of Games."

62. Gibbons, "Bip, Bloop, Bach? Some Uses of Classical Music on the Nintendo Entertainment System."

63. Sugiyama framed his own work in those terms. By 1987, he had already released the *Dragon Quest I Symphonic Suite*, performed by the London Philharmonic, and was organizing a live performance for the Tokyo String Music Combination Playing Group, embellishing the looped chiptunes of the original with subtle variations in theme and texture. Sugiyama's transposition of videogame music to orchestras and CD soundtracks served as a prototype for contemporary videogame orchestral reviews like Play! and Video Games Live.

64. The translators cleverly ported the innuendo in the U.S. localization—the same woman sold tomatoes instead.

65. BOCTOK Co., Ltd., *Bit Generation 2000 "TV Games,"* 89.

66. Kuntz, "DRAGON QUEST Japanese Game Script and Mini Playing Guide v5.11."

67. In Japan these are known as 擬音語 (*giongo*) or 擬態語 (*gitaigo*), used to describe "sound effects" and "state words," respectively. See Kamermans, "The giongo/gitaigo dictionary."

68. BOCTOK Co., Ltd., *Bit Generation 2000 "TV Games,"* 92.

69. For English use in Japan, see Stanlaw, "'For Beautiful Human Life': The Use of English in Japan."

70. *Dragon Quest*'s economical hiragana storage also reflects an important affinity with its predecessor *Portopia*. Unsurprisingly, both games share nearly identical syllabary tiles. Nakamura made some minor pixel adjustments to a few characters like き and ふ, but these appear to be cosmetic enhancements to make the characters' tricky strokes more legible in an 8x8-pixel tile. Otherwise, the games' hiragana are pixel-perfect copies that even share corresponding pattern table IDs. And due to the radical/diacritic division described above, they also share the same dialogue spacing seen in figure 6.5. Considering *Dragon Quest*'s abbreviated development schedule—roughly three to five months—time-saving strategies like copying one's own CHR-ROM "handwriting" were crucial (Aoyama and Izushi, 432). Programmatically, matching tile references would have also made code reuse much simpler.

71. Carless, "Interview: *Dragon Quest* Creator Horii's Talks Evolving Appeal With *DQIX.*"

72. Tanner, "Discussion Between Miyamoto & Horii."

73. See Iwamoto, 201 and *vgchartz.com*.

74. TSR was not the original rights-holder. They acquired the *DragonQuest* trademark and copyright from SPI in 1983. See Wizards of the Coast, "The History of TSR."

75. Nintendo of America, Inc., *Nintendo Fun Club News* 1.4 (Winter 1987): 14.

76. The coverage included an 8-page leveling guide, a 36-page pull-out Tip Book, an extended backstory, and an odd 4-page text adventure version of the game along with a pull-out map.

77. Cifaldi, "Nintendo Power: Remembering America's Longest-Lasting Game Magazine."

78. *Dragon Warrior*'s months-long absence from the Players' or Dealers' Picks sections shows that two key audiences—players and retail buyers—had little interest in the game. There was also no exposure in the Counselor's Corner or Classified Information sections, where Nintendo of America's in-house counselor team doled out hints and responded to players' letters. *Dragon Warrior*'s first of only two appearances in those sections was notably odd: the Nov./Dec. '89 issue had a generic "Role Playing Games" question ("How do I defeat the most difficult enemies?") that gave general tips for RPG leveling. Though no specific game was mentioned—an anomaly for the magazine—the included screenshot was from *Dragon Warrior*. By spring 1990, *Dragon Warrior* would finally gain some traction among players, peaking at #7 in the Players' Picks.

79. Quartermann, "Gaming Gossip," *Electronic Gaming Monthly* 3 (Sept. 1989): 28.

80. Nintendo of America, Inc., *Nintendo Power* 6 (May/June 1989): 53.

81. Nintendo of America, Inc., *Nintendo Power* 50 (July 1993): 39.

82. Mega Man is also forcibly aligned to the sprite blocks if he does not land in their direct center.

83. Pickford, "Ironsword Eagle working."

84. Pickford, "Ironsword title screen working."

85. Pickford, "Ironsword Dragon King concept art."

86. Codemaster categorized their codes by type and labeled them with icons. The most interesting effects fell under the "Mystery/Weird/Special/Defies Categories" label. See Galoob, *Game Genie Programming Manual and Codebook*, 15.

87. Galoob, *Game Genie Programming Manual and Codebook*, 14.

88. Ibid., 12.

89. The Mighty Mike Master, "NES Game Genie Technical Notes."

90. I have adapted this decoding chart from Benzene, "NES Game Genie Code Format DOC v.0.71."

91. *NesDev*, "Docs on game genie hardware?"

92. Hughes, "'Super Mario Bros NES' R.Eng project," line 009069.

93. United States Court of Appeals, "16 F. 3d 1032 - Nintendo of America Inc v. Lewis Galoob Toys Inc."

94. United States District Court, "Lewis Galoob Toys, Inc. v. Nintendo of America, Inc."

95. Ibid.

96. Ibid. When Nintendo could not defend themselves through litigation, they responded through manufacturing. Just as they had made internal revisions to the Disk System to thwart piracy and to the NES to disrupt CIC circumventions, Nintendo subtly changed the NES's cartridge port on the top-loading NES-101. Since the Game Genie was customized for the NES's front-loading shape, the peripheral no longer fit. Galoob responded with a slim black adapter, mailed to customers for free, that restored compatibility. And of course Nintendo's retaliation had no impact on the thirty million plus consumers who owned the original console.

97. Pack-in title *Dizzy the Adventurer* is the sole exception; it was only released as a Compact Cartridge.

98. Donovan's *Replay* is a notable exception to the U.S.-centric model. He has several excellent sections on industry developments in France, England, Australia, and eastern Asia.

99. Donovan, 113.

100. Ibid., 113.

101. Ibid., 125–137.

102. *The Games Machine: Computer and Electronic Entertainment* 1 (Oct./Nov. 1987): 36.

103. Hayes and Dinsey, *Games War*, 89–90.

104. Ibid., 17.

105. Ibid., 18.

106. Regarding the successful NES/*Teenage Mutant Hero Turtles* bundle, Hayes and Dinsey write that the UK was "the first market in the world where a standard NES bundle was outsold by a unique market bundle." Hayes and Dinsey, 62.

107. Nintendo ASIC mappers took on the MMC "brand," so it has become customary to designate games that use ASIC mappers according to their IC name versus their board name. MMC3 actually describes several boards—e.g., TKSROM and TLSROM—each of which may have different bank numbers or capacities. A single MMC group may also encompass multiple boards revisions. MMC1, for instance, includes eighteen distinct boards, including SAROM, SGROM, SL1ROM, SNROM, and so on. When multiple boards share the same prefix, they are categorized by a single generic group name, such as SxROM or TxROM, where x designates a sub-type. Even NROM, which up to this point we have used as a single moniker to describe any cartridge without a mapper up to 40K in capacity, includes multiple boards manufactured for both the Famicom and the NES: HVC-HROM, HVC-RROM, HVC-SROM, NROM-128, and NROM-256. Though functionally identical, their board IDs differ.

108. Iz-Tavares and Chang, "Programming M.C. Kids [1992]."

109. According to bootgod's "Top 10 PCBs list," the various board variations of the MMC3 appear in roughly 17.4% of all NES paks, with MMC1 trailing closely at 15.9%. CNROM and UNROM follow with 4.3% and 2.4% respectively. The Famicom had a wider distribution of PCB types and thus a slightly different "leader board." MMC1's 8.1% leads MMC3's 4.9%, while NROM, UNROM, and CNROM round out the top five. See bootgod, "Top 10 PCBs & mappers," *NES Cart Database*.

110. *NesDev Wiki*, "iNES Mapper 005."

111. *NesDev Wiki*, "MMC5."

112. *NesDev Wiki*, "iNES Mapper 005."

113. bootgod's *NES Cart Database* lists only 23 MMC5 games, and many of those are multiple regional releases of the same title.

114. Bootlegs are notorious for over-exaggerating their cartridges' game capacities. Titles like *10,000-in-1* are common, even when the cartridge contains only a few dozen games.

Chapter 7

1. *2A03 Puritans* is available online at http://bitpuritans.bandcamp.com/album/ 2a03-puritans

2. Collaborators NO CARRIER and Alex Mauer, for instance, pushed authenticity to its practical extreme, releasing their 2007 albums *Vegavox* and *Color Caves* on playable NES cartridges. For an overview of NO CARRIER's programming work, see http://www.no-carrier.com. Alex Mauer's music is available at http:// alexmauer.bandcamp.com.

3. Throughout this chapter, I will refer to the APU and 2A03 interchangeably. Technically, the 2A03 is distinct from the PAL 2A07, but I only reference the former for the sake of convenience unless the NTSC/PAL timing differences are of special note.

4. See Pinch and Trocco, *Analog Days*, 58–62.

5. See *Analog Days*, 43–5.

6. The Skrasoft Dev Blog has a nice practical explanation of the difference: "With a sound chip like the POKEY or a SID, getting sound out is as simple as updating a few memory spaces directly. That is, put some signals on input pins, trigger a write, and repeat *ad nauseum*. With the 2A03, it is not so simple. Being a CPU, it only accepts program code. Also, as a CPU it expects certain timings. While a POKEY just needs to be given data when something changes, the 2A03 needs continuously generated program code. It never ceases to demand, lacking any sympathy or respect for its gracious host." See "2A03 Synth Status," *Skrasoft Dev Blog*.

7. *NesDev Wiki*, "CPU."

8. As a result, the APU is considered a *direct digital synthesizer*: "Direct digital synthesis (DDS) is a technique for using digital data processing blocks as a means to generate a frequency- and phase-tunable output signal referenced to a fixed-frequency precision clock source. In essence, the reference clock frequency is 'divided down' in a DDS architecture by the scaling factor set forth in a programmable binary tuning word." Analog Devices, Inc., *A Technical Tutorial on Digital Signal Synthesis*.

9. Slocum, "Atari 2600 Music And Sound Programming Guide."

10. Amplitude may be either positive or negative. At zero amplitude, air molecules are at their rest state. Amplitudes above zero indicate a compression of molecules, while negative values indicate a rarefaction. Perceptually, our ears interpret the intensity of pressure changes as loudness.

11. The sole difference between the pulse channels is a minor discrepancy in pulse 1's sweep unit. See *NesDev*, "APU Sweep" for technical details.

12. The pulse channels' 11-bit programmable timers are sent to identical duty cycle generators, so both produce frequencies between 54.6Hz and 12.4kHz. The triangle channel has its own 5-bit step generator, so it covers a wider frequency range, dipping as low as 27Hz, near the threshold of human hearing. See Taylor, "2A03 Technical Reference."

13. Famicom sound designers usually chose to implement their own software envelopes, which could be as flexible or rigid as they desired.

14. Though 25% and 75% are inversely proportional, they sound the same. Thus there are only three perceptually distinct duty cycle timbres for either pulse channel.

15. APU pulses are often referred to as square waves, but the former appellation is more technically accurate. While all square waves are pulses, the inverse is not true. A proper square wave has a 50% duty cycle, meaning its positive and negative pulses are symmetrical in width. But lengthening either side proportionally shortens the other, changing the pulse's shape and, more importantly, its tonal character.

16. Tumblr site *Retro Game Audio* has an excellent audio/video analysis of duty cycle modulation. See bucky (aka explod2A03), "NES Audio: Duty Cycle Modulation."

17. A related trick that sounds similar to duty cycle modulation was imported from the work of influential Commodore 64 composers like Rob Hubbard. The SID chip had fewer voices than the 2A03, though its impressive range of filters, selectable waveforms, and modulation effects gave it a unique character that had no direct equivalent on the Famicom. Yet with only three voices, C64 composers had difficulty constructing chords. Devoting one voice to lead, one to bass, and the last for percussion left no room for harmonization. To compensate, C64 composers used arpeggios played at rapid speeds on a single voice to simulate chords.

18. Dean, *The Drum*, 299–300.

19. Brown, Sanner, et al., "Delta Modulation."

20. National Programme on Technology Enhanced Learning, "Lecture - 3 Quantization, PCM and Delta Modulation."

21. See *NesDev Wiki*, "APU DMC."

22. Composer Akito Nakatsuka also uses DMC samples for Soda Popinski's and Bald Bull's taunting laughter, a sound later recycled for Ganon's laugh during *Zelda II*'s Game Over screen. In fact, there are numerous sound effect similarities between the two games, e.g., colliding with an enemy in the overworld in *Zelda II* and executing a Star Punch in *Punch-Out!!*.

23. Register $4010 reserves four bits for a rate index value between $0 and $F. The highest index $F produces a (NTSC) period of 33.14kHZ, though again the 1-bit delta modulation regulates the overall sound quality more than the period value. Each index value's corresponding frequency differs for PAL consoles. See *NesDev Wiki*, "APU DMC" for more details.

24. See *NesDev Wiki*, "APU DMC."

25. Keep in mind that the listed pitches only describe frequency *relationships*, not preset sample tunings. In other words, setting the rate index to G10 for a flute recorded playing an A# does not tune the base sample by a semitone automatically. Rather, one can only rely on the pitch table if the instrument's sampled pitch matches the rate index note.

26. The DMC address register ($4012) is 16-bits wide but has only ten significant bits. The two highest bits are hardwired to 1, and the programmer supplies the subsequent byte, limiting the DMC's starting address to values between $C000 and $FFC0. All DMC binary data must begin in this range.

27. *NesDev*, "Big Bird's Hide and Speak sample compression."

28. Parish, "An interview with Konami's Hidenori Maezawa."

29. bucky (aka explod2A03), "NES Audio: Sunsoft Bass and Melodic Samples."
30. Ibid.
31. Intellivision Productions, Inc., "Intellivoice."
32. Due to the Famicom's close relationship with the ColecoVision (chapter 1), it is notable that the Intellivoice project was nearly implemented in Coleco's console. Thanks to the Intellivoice flop, Mattel realized it was cheaper to include speech hardware in each cartridge rather than build an external module. Their engineers pitched the idea to Coleco along with a prototype demonstration, but due to the unfortunate timing of internal layoffs at Coleco, the "ColecoVoice" project never took off. A few years later, Nintendo would use the same in-cart strategy for their mappers, including those that supported additional audio channels. See Intellivision Productions, Inc., "M Network Colecovision."
33. For several examples, see Benvenutti, Diogo Andrei, "Nintendo 8 Bits Voice Samples (2A03)."
34. In some cases, sound designers faked speech by cleverly manipulating one of the waveform channels. In *Mike Tyson's Punch-Out!!*, for example, referee Mario announces rounds, gives counts, and announces knockouts, all using pitched square waves. By correlating these tones with an onscreen text bubble, the programmers made our ears hear words that were not really there.
35. The noise channel had a second mode that would radically abbreviate the RNG's output to only 93 bits, altering the channel's standard percussive timbre to a metallic buzz. Third-party developer Capcom in particular used it for sound effects in *Darkwing Duck* (e.g., dialog), *Mega Man 2* (e.g., Metal Blade weapon), and *Duck Tales* (e.g., entering mirrors). But they also used metallic noise for several musical tracks, including *Duck Tales'* traveling music, *Code Name: Viper's* third level, and *Mega Man 2's* Quick Man stage.
36. Taylor explains the interaction in technical detail: "These analog outputs require a negative current source, to attain linear symmetry on the various output voltage levels generated by the channel(s) (moreover, to get the sound to be audible). Instead of current sources, the NES uses external 100 ohm pull-down resistors. This results in the output waveforms having some linear asymmetry (i.e., as the desired output voltage increases on a linear scale, the actual outputted voltage increases less and less each step)." Taylor, "2A03 Technical Reference."
37. For the NES, Nintendo opted to move the audio input to the expansion port, which remained unused during the console's life cycle. See chapter 3.
38. The custom waveform had a 6-bit resolution. Additionally, a second 64-step waveform could be used to modulate the first, or fundamental, waveform.
39. Though almost certainly a coincidence, Tone 1 and 3 bear striking resemblances to the silhouettes of a Pols Voice and Keese, two of *Zelda's* enemy creatures.
40. *Otocky's* designer Toshio Iwai would continue to experiment with music-based videogames, culminating in his acclaimed sound toy *Electroplankton* (2005) for the Nintendo DS.
41. Parish, "An interview with Konami's Hidenori Maezawa."
42. Konami's VRC chips are labeled with roman numerals in-cart, but the homebrew/chiptune community refer to them by numeric values, i.e., VRC6 and VRC7. Notably, VRC6's sawtooth also brought the Famicom to waveform parity

with the Commodore's SID, though it still lacked the latter's distinctive filters and modulations.

43. None of *Akumajou Densetsu*'s tracks used the APU's triangle channel, presumably due to its lack of volume control. Instead, VRC6's sawtooth channel handled the bass parts.

44. Yamaha Corporation of America, *Yamaha DX7 Digital Programmable Algorithm Synthesizer Operation Manual*, 23.

45. Aikin, 72–3.

46. Retro Synth Ads, "Yamaha GS1 (GS-1) and GS2 (GS-2), Keyboard 1982."

47. For an overview of FM's hardware uptake in videogames, see Barnholt, "The Magic of FM Synth."

48. For a sense of the mathematical complexity underlying FM synthesis, see Schottstaedt, "An Introduction to FM."

49. Théberge, *Any Sound You Can Imagine*, 75–7.

50. Yamaha Corporation of America., *Yamaha DX7 Digital Programmable Algorithm Synthesizer Operation Manual*, ii.

51. Théberge, 89.

52. See *NesDev Wiki* "VRC7 audio" and Horton, "VRCVIII CHIP INFO" for technical descriptions of these parameters.

53. Due to some early ROM naming confusion, the N163 is often mislabeled as Namco 106.

54. According to the *NesDev Wiki*, "Namco 163 audio," the wave length is set according to the formula $(64 - L) * 4$, where L is the 6-bit value set in N163's sound RAM. As a result, all waveform lengths are multiples of 4.

55. *NesDev Wiki*, "Namco 163 audio."

56. Composer Hirohiko Takayama, who wrote both soundtracks in 1988, defined three instruments to populate his channels, but primarily used two: a simple, sixteen-step sine wave for melodies and a linear sawtooth for bass. The third instrument, a 32-step "descending sine wave," appeared in only one song.

57. Several of Jaleco's *Moero!! Pro* sports games included an NEC D7756C speech synthesis chip, but its specialized function makes it trickier to classify it as a "proper" audio mapper. The NES versions of these games (e.g., *Bases Loaded*, *Racket Attack*), as usual, omitted the speech chip.

58. Tanner, "Making Mr. Gimmick!"

59. Tanner, "The Music of Mr. Gimmick."

60. Ibid.

61. Kageyama, Masashi and Naoki Kodaka, *Rom Cassette Disc in SUNSOFT.*

62. Accessing *Galaxian*'s sound test, for example, requires players to, "reset the game 44 times, hold A + B on Controller 2, and reset again." See *The Cutting Room Floor*, "Galaxian (NES)."

63. Horton, "HardNES."

64. Covell, "NES Music Ripping Guide."

65. "Yoshihiro Sakaguchi," *Videogame Music Preservation Foundation.*

66. "Naohisa Morota," *Videogame Music Preservation Foundation*.

67. For an exhaustive guide to the eccentricities of Famicom audio engines, see Gil Galad, "NSF ripper guide."

68. *The Cutting Room Floor*, "Castlevania (NES)."

69. *The Cutting Room Floor*, "Gremlins 2 (NES)."
70. NSFPlay is available for download at http://rainwarrior.ca/projects/nsfplay/index.html
71. Maher, *The Future was Here*, 194.
72. BuZz et al., "Soundtracker History."
73. Collins, *Game Sound*, 27.
74. Maher, 36–7.
75. Dahlberg, "Interview with Karsten Obarski."
76. Reckhard, "FREQUENTLY ASKED QUESTIONS (FAQ) LIST FOR ALT.BINARIES.SOUNDS.MODS."
77. Matsuoka, "Tracker History Graphing Project."
78. There was no NerdTracker 1. Iwaniec says, "Naming it NT2 was just a bit of a half-joke: At the time NT2 was written, FastTracker2 was the first choice for making music in the nordic demoscene, while the people who had ever tried the original FastTracker were few and far apart. So I figured adding a '2' suffix to it would be more likely to give it instant fame..." See *NesDev*, "Tracker history" (noattack).
79. Trackers are not the only means to compose on the 2A03. Within the VGM (Video Game Music) scene—Japan's chiptunes equivalent—one of the most popular tracker alternatives is the Music Macro Language (MML), a powerful, compact method of 2A03 composition capable of fine-grained APU timbral and timing manipulations that are otherwise impossible with graphical trackers. An MML score is a plain text file that contains macros dedicated to low-level APU functions and a sequence body that describes each channel's notes, parameters, and effects during playback. MML files do not play natively; rather they are compiled and converted via software into NSF files. For more information, see Manbow-J, "MCKC: MML > MCK Converter Ver 0.14," Coox, "MML," and nullsleep, "MCK/MML BEGINNERS GUIDE."
80. To be clear, I make no judgments on musical quality based on an artist's chiptune "authenticity." There are wonderful tracks from the entire spectrum of artists, no matter their compositional technique.
81. Vreeland, Tweet to author.
82. Driscoll and Diaz, "Endless loop: A brief history of chiptunes," [1.5].
83. Ibid., [4.3].
84. Holmes, "The Top 10 Chiptune Artists."

Chapter 8

1. See Andersson, "Contra_1017 [Contra in 10:17]"and Carstensen, "NinjaGaiden_1232 [Ninja Gaiden in 12:32]."
2. "[HD] TAS: NES Super Mario Bros 3 (JPN) in 11:03.95 by Morimoto."
3. Morimoto, "NES Super Mario Bros. 3 (JPN) in 11:03.95."
4. Lowood, "High-performance play: The making of machinima."
5. "Rules," *Speed Demos Archive*.
6. "Super Mario Bros.," *Speed Demos Archive*.
7. "Guidelines," *TASVideos*.
8. "Bizhawk," *TASVideos*.

9.   "Tools-Assisted Speedruns - About," *Doomworld*.
10. "Rules," *Speed Demos Archive*.
11. "Movies Rules," *TASVideos*.
12. "Rules," *Speed Demos Archive*.
13. Cf., Kidder, *The Soul of a New Machine*, 42–3.
14. Pugh et al., *IBM's 360 and Early 370 Systems*, 111–35.
15. Ibid., 127.
16. Haanstra, John W., Bob O. Evans, et al., "Processor Products—Final Report of SPREAD Task Group, December 28, 1961."
17. With one exception: the smallest processor model, announced a few months after the initial System/360 line.
18. Pugh et al., 159.
19. Ibid.
20. Ibid., 131. Slade, *Made to Break*, 188.
21. Pugh et al., 161.
22. Tucker, "Emulation of Large Systems."
23. Ibid., 754.
24. Rosin, "Contemporary Concepts of Microprogramming and Emulation."
25. Marsland and Demco, "A Case Study of Computer Emulation," 113.
26. Teiser, "Atari - Nintendo 1983 Deal."
27. The contemporary exception is mobile development. Mobile devices are either too constrained for native development (e.g., early WAP systems) or vendors do not allow code to compile on their devices (e.g., Apple).
28. Mattel's Intellivision is a notable exception: it had a BIOS and a built-in character set—rarities in the early console era.
29. Masaharu (trans. Tanner), "Part 8 – Synonymous With the Domestic Game Console."
30. Covell, "The Stars of Famicom Games."
31. Dolan, *Hewlett-Packard Journal*.
32. Ibid., 4.
33. Intellivision Productions, Inc., "1983 Intellivision/M Network Catalog."
34. Today, differentiation is more important than generic compatibility. Microsoft and Sony invest millions of dollars in exclusives—games programmed for their console solely—in order to draw consumers away from rivals.
35. The official PasoFami site's hit counter has been active since 8/20/1996. Marat Fayzullin also notes on the active iNES site that his emulator was released in 1996, after PasoFami was already available. Kun, "Funny Fantasy," also provides download links to versions of PasoFami up to 2.7a, with a ROM pack dated from June 27, 1996.
36. Some sources will also refer to it as PASOWING, though this is a "translation error" related to the DOS filenames being set in caps. The Windows binary was labeled PasoWinG, as it required the "WinG" file to run properly.
37. Cochems, "Marcel de Kogel."
38. Nielson, "The Nintendo Entertainment System (NES) FAQ v.1.12."
39. Fayzullin, "iNES."
40. Fayzullin, "iNES.doc (v 0.6)."
41. Fayzullin, "Nintendo Entertainment System Architecture (version 1.4)."
42. Altice, "Interview: Paul Robson, programmer of the NESA emulator."

43. Roach, "comp.emulators.misc Frequently Asked Questions (FAQ) [3/3]."
44. Conte, "cajoNES version 0.99b."
45. "ASCII codes table - Format of standard characters," *ascii.cl.*
46. Trainers were a 512-byte code block originally used to hack games into a particular mapper. Trainers are deprecated and largely ignored by current emulators.
47. Dane, "Help with Nester."
48. Since emulators are largely developed by hobbyists and distributed for free, dirty ROM compatibility is left to the developer's discretion.
49. Another important trace is the "Date Modified" field common to Windows Explorer or OS X's Finder. ROMs freely available online are often unmodified versions of images that have been in circulation since their initial dump. When I downloaded the well-seeded "NESRen" torrent in March 2012, for instance, it contained hundreds of .nes files with "Date Modified" entries predating 2000.
50. Bloodlust Software, "NESticle Version 0.41 [README.TXT]."
51. According to Bloodlust's documentation, Sardu based his CPU code on Neil Bradley's m6502 emulation core, gleaned technical information from Fayzullin's NES.DOC, based the sound emulation on YoSHi's NESTECH.DOC, and supported the established iNES header format (with promises to later support PasoFami files).
52. goroh, "Nesticle(ver 0.42) stafile information."
53. And still does. See http://www.zophar.net/savestates/nesticle.html
54. Sliver X, "Hacking The Legend of Zelda NESticle save states."
55. The ZELDIT utility, for example, could edit a handful of *The Legend of Zelda's* overworld and underworld areas. The dungeon editor was notable for its visual presentation, as it revealed the tetromino-esque layout of the dungeons in memory (chapter 5). Players with no prior technical knowledge of the NES could learn visually how memory constraints dictated the in-game arrangement of tiles, items, and foes.
56. Bloodlust Software, "NESticle Version 0.41 [README.TXT]."
57. Bloodlust Software, "Official Bloodlust Software NESticle Page."
58. Since an .NSM was simply a state file with appended input data, the resulting file had built-in "backward compatibility," as Sardu noted: "Renaming zelda.nsm to zelda.sta will allow you to load the movie as a normal state file and play from the movie's beginning point." Bloodlust Software, "NESticle Version 0.41 [README.TXT]."
59. According to *NesCartDB*, *Super Mario Bros.* is the most commonly dumped ROM in all three regions (North America, Europe/Asia, and Japan). See bootgod, "Top 10 dumped games."
60. IKA, "Rockman No Constancy."
61. GameMakr24, "Zelda Challenge: Outlands."
62. DahrkDaiz, "Mario Adventure."
63. Demiforce, "Final Fantasy 2j English Patch [139readme.txt]."
64. "FCEUX," *Zophar's Domain*.
65. See adelikat, "How To make a Tool Assisted Speedrun."
66. adelikat, "FM2 Movie file format."

67. See Mong (aka mmbossman), "Submission #2486: mmbossman's FDS Arumana no Kiseki in 08:26.67."

68. A literal analog to this setup process is the calibration necessary in magnetic tape recording. Audio engineers who record analog must, for instance, carefully align, clean, and bias their tape machines in order for the recording to play back properly.

69. Kraft (aka Gigafrost), "Submission #690: Gigafrost's NES Zelda 2: The Adventure of Link 'glitched' in 06:16.93."

70. Newman, *Playing with Videogames*, 123–148.

71. Ibid., 124.

72. adelikat, "Submission #1324: adelikat's NES Gradius in 10:52.35."

73. Hayles, *Electronic Literature*, 45.

74. TASVideos, "Luck Manipulation."

75. For example, see T.M. (aka knbnitkr), "Submission #2836: knbnitkr's GB Makai Toushi SaGa in 01:47.17."

76. Teti, "As Fast as Impossible: 10 Insanely Thrilling Tool-Assisted Speedruns."

77. adelikat, "Submission #1324: adelikat's NES Gradius in 10:52.35."

78. W., Lennart (aka Baxter), "Submission #1693: Baxter's NES Arkanoid in 12:26.8."

79. W., Lennart (aka Baxter) and AngerFist, "NES Mega Man 3, 4, 5 & 6 (USA) in 39:06.92 by Baxter & AngerFist."

80. Players in the U.S. only knew *Final Fantasy II* and *III* as Super Nintendo games, since the series was renumbered for American release.

Afterword

1. Although Metacritic is a severely flawed metric for critical consensus, *NES Remix* and its sequel's respective 71 and 73 scores (as of May 2014) are appreciably lower than most first-party Nintendo releases starring Mario and Link.

2. Orland, "Review: NES Remix is more evocative than transformative."

3. Otero, "How Mario 3D World's Co-Director Gave NES Games a Second Life."

4. Ibid.

5. The latter behavior actually relies upon the "interaction between the sprite priority bit and the OAM index" described in chapter 4. Also see *NesDev Wiki*, "Tricky-to-emulate games."

6. Orland, "Review: NES Remix is more evocative than transformative."

7. Not that this process is without precedent: Nintendo did their own bit of assembly hacking, as described in chapter 2, to shoehorn the cement factory level into the 2010 rerelease of *Donkey Kong*.

Appendix A

1. Greetham, *Textual Scholarship: An Introduction*, 1–12.

2. Greetham, 7.

3. Kirschenbaum, *Mechanisms*, 277.

4. Newman, *Videogames*.

5. Kline et al., *Digital Play*, 177.

6.   Wolf, *The Medium of the Video Game*, 1.
7.   Montfort and Bogost, *Racing the Beam*, 165.
8.   Bogost, *How to Do Things with Videogames*, 177.
9.   Bateman, *Imaginary Games*, 295. Bateman mistakenly conflates the Famicom console release date (1983) with the cartridge release date (1985).
10.   Wolf, 186.
11.   Montfort, "Emulation as Game Facsimile (or Computer Edition?)."
12.   My thanks to Neal Wyatt for her helpful suggestions for the model structure.

Sources

Famicom / NES Cartridges, Disks, and ROMs

悪魔城伝説 (trans. *Akumajou Densetsu*). Family Computer (60-p. cart.), NTSC-J [JP]. KON-RC845 (black). KONAMI-VRC-6 [VRC6 | 256KB PRG | 128KB CHR | MC]. Konami: Konami, 22 Dec. 1989.

アルゴスの戦士 はちゃめちゃ大進撃 (trans. *Argos no Senshi: Hachamecha Daishingeki*). Family Computer (60-p. cart.), NTSC-J [JP]. TCF-AH (dark blue). HVC-UNROM [128KB PRG | 8KB CHR-RAM | V]. Tecmo: Tecmo, 17 Apr. 1987.

Arkanoid. Nintendo Entertainment System (72-p. cart.), NTSC [US]. NES-AR-USA (3-screw). NES-CNROM [32KB PRG | 16KB CHR | CIC 3193A | H]. Taito: Taito, Aug. 1987.

バルーンファイト | *Balloon Fight*. Family Computer (60-p. cart.), NTSC-J [JP]. HVC-BF (white). HVC-RROM [16KB PRG | 8KB CHR | H]. Nintendo: Nintendo, 22 Jan. 1985.

Balloon Fight. Nintendo Entertainment System (72-p. cart.), NTSC [US]. NES-BF-USA (5-screw). NES-NROM-128 [16KB PRG | 8KB CHR | CIC 3193A | H]. Nintendo: Nintendo, June 1986.

Balloon Fight. Nintendo Entertainment System (72-p. cart.), PAL-B [EUR]. NES-BF-EEC (3-screw). NES-NROM-128 [16KB PRG | 8KB CHR | CIC 3195A | H]. Nintendo: Nintendo, 12 Mar. 1987.

Battletoads. Nintendo Entertainment System (72-p. cart.), NTSC [US]. NES-8T-USA (3-screw). NES-AOROM [256KB PRG | 8KB CHR-RAM | CIC 6113 | MC]. Rare: Tradewest, June 1991.

Bionic Commando. Nintendo Entertainment System (72-p. cart.), NTSC [US]. NES-CM-USA (3-screw). NES-SGROM [MMC1B2 | 256KB PRG | 8KB CHR-RAM | CIC 6113B1 | MC]. Capcom: Capcom, Dec. 1988.

Blaster Master. Nintendo Entertainment System (72-p. cart.), NTSC [US]. NES-VM-USA (3-screw). NES-SLROM [MMC1B2 | 128KB PRG | 128KB CHR-RAM | CIC 6113B1 | MC]. Sunsoft: Sunsoft, Nov. 1988.

Castlevania. Nintendo Entertainment System (72-p. cart.), NTSC [US]. NES-CV-USA (3-screw). NES-UNROM [128KB PRG | 8KB CHR-RAM | CIC 6113 | V]. Konami: Konami, May 1987.

Castlevania III: Dracula's Curse. Nintendo Entertainment System (72-p. cart.), PAL-B [Germany]. NES-VN-FRG (3-screw, DAS). NES-ELROM [MMC5 | 256KB PRG | 128KB CHR | CIC 3195A | MC]. Palcom: Konami, Sept. 1990.

超惑星戦記　メタファイト (trans. *Chou Wakusei Senki: Metafight*). Family Computer (60-p. cart.), NTSC-J [JP]. TEC-MF (white). HVC-SLROM [MMC1A | 128KB PRG | 128KB CHR | MC]. Sunsoft: Sunsoft, 17 June 1988.

Cobra Triangle. Nintendo Entertainment System (72-p. cart.), NTSC [US]. NES-CU-USA (3-screw). NES-ANROM [128KB PRG | 8KB CHR-RAM | CIC 6113 | MC]. Rare: Nintendo, July 1989.

Contra. Nintendo Entertainment System (72-p. cart.), NTSC [US]. NES-CT-USA (3-screw). NES-UNROM [128KB PRG | 8KB CHR-RAM | CIC 6113A | V]. Konami: Konami, Feb. 1988.

Contra [ROM]. "Contra.nes" (131KB). iNES: 2. [4E45531A 08002100 00000000 00000000]. 19 March 2000. Nintendulator v0.975.

悪魔城ドラキュラ (trans. *Devil's Castle Dracula*). Family Computer Disk System (d.s. QuickDisk, yellow), NTSC-J [JP]. KDS-AKM. Disk (one) [8KB PRG-ROM | 32KB PRG-RAM | 8KB CHR-RAM | MC]. Konami: Konami, 26 Sept. 1986.

Devil World. Nintendo Entertainment System (72-p. cart.), PAL-B [EUR]. NES-DD-EEC (5-screw). NES-NROM-128 [16KB PRG | 8KB CHR | CIC 3195A | H]. Nintendo: Nintendo, 15 Jul. 1987.

Devil World [ROM]. "Devil World (E) [!].nes" (25KB). iNES: 0. [4E45531A 01010000 00000000 00000000]. 19 Jan. 2003. FCEUX v2.1.5, Macifom v0.16, PowerPak.

ドンキーコング | *Donkey Kong*. Family Computer (60-p. cart.), NTSC-J [JP]. HVC-DK (red). HVC-NROM-128 [16KB PRG | 8KB CHR | H]. Nintendo: Nintendo, 15 July 1983.

Donkey Kong [ROM]. "Donkey Kong.nes" (25KB). iNES: 0. [4E45531A 01010000 00000000 00000000]. 19 Mar. 2000. FCEUX v2.1.5, Macifom v0.16, NESticle v0.2, Nestopia v1.4.1, Nintendulator v0.975.

Donkey Kong [ROM]. "dkoe.nes" (66KB). iNES: 3. [4E45531A 02043000 00000000 00000000]. 29 Nov. 2010. FCEUX v2.1.5, Macifom v0.16, Nestopia v1.4.1. <http://xkeeper.net/private/pacman/> [Note: ROM originally appeared as a pre-installed download for the red Super Mario Bros. 25th Anniversary Wii, exclusive to Europe.]

Donkey Kong Classics. Nintendo Entertainment System (72-p. cart.), NTSC [US]. NES-DJ-USA (3-screw). NES-CNROM [32KB PRG | 16KB CHR | CIC 6113B1 | V]. Nintendo: Nintendo, Oct. 1988.

ドンキーコングJr. | *Donkey Kong Jr.* Family Computer (60-p. cart.), NTSC-J [JP]. HVC-JR (white). HVC-HROM [16KB PRG | 8KB CHR | V]. Nintendo: Nintendo, 15 July 1983.

Donkey Kong Jr. Math. Nintendo Entertainment System (72-p. cart.), NTSC [US]. NES-CA-USA (5-screw). NES-NROM-128 [16KB PRG | 8KB CHR | CIC 3193A | V]. Nintendo: Nintendo, Oct. 1985.

ドアドア | *Door Door*. Family Computer (60-p. cart.), NTSC-J [JP]. EFC-DR (black). HVC-NROM-128 [16KB PRG | 8KB CHR | H]. Chunsoft: Enix, 18 July 1985.

ドラゴンクエスト *(Dragon Quest)*. Family Computer (60-p. cart.), NTSC-J [JP]. EFC-DQ (black). HVC-CNROM [32KB PRG | 32KB CHR | V]. Chunsoft: Enix, 27 May 1986.

Dragon Warrior. Nintendo Entertainment System (72-p. cart.), NTSC [US]. NES-DQ-USA (3-screw). NES-SAROM [64KB PRG | 16KB CHR | 8KB WRAM | Bat. | CIC 6113 | MC]. Chunsoft: Nintendo, Aug. 1989.

えりかとさとるの夢冒険 *(Erika to Satoru no Yume Bouken)*. Family Computer (60-p. cart.), NTSC-J [JP]. NAM-YB-4900 (black). NAMCOT-163 [N163 | 128KB PRG | 128KB CHR | MC]. Atlus: Namco, 27 Sept. 1988.

Excitebike. Nintendo Entertainment System (72-p. cart.), NTSC [US]. NES-EB-USA (5-screw, NES-JOINT-01). NES-NROM-128 [16KB PRG | 8KB CHR | CIC 3193 | V]. Nintendo: Nintendo, Oct. 1985.

ファミリーベーシック | *Family BASIC*. Family Computer (60-p. cart.), NTSC-J [JP]. HVC-BS (extended cart., black, OFF/ON switch). HVC-FAMILYBASIC [16KB PRG (A) | 16KB PRG (B) | 8KB CHR | 2KB WRAM | Bat. | V]. Hudson Soft: Nintendo, 21 June 1984.

Final Fantasy. Nintendo Entertainment System (72-p. cart.), NTSC [US]. NES-FF-USA (3-screw). NES-SNROM [MMC1B2 | 256KB PRG | 8KB CHR-RAM | 8KB WRAM | Bat. CIC 6113B1 | MC]. Square: Nintendo, May 1990.

ギミック! *(Gimmick!)*. Family Computer (60-p. cart.), NTSC-J [JP]. SUN-GMK-6200 (black). SUNSOFT-5B [Sunsoft-5B | 256KB PRG | 128KB CHR | MC]. Sunsoft: Sunsoft, 31 Jan. 1992.

Gradius. Nintendo Entertainment System (72-p. cart.), NTSC [US]. NES-GR-USA (5-screw). NES-CNROM [32KB PRG | 32KB CHR | CIC 3193A | V]. Konami: Konami, Dec. 1986.

Gumshoe. Nintendo Entertainment System (72-p. cart.), NTSC [US]. NES-GS-USA (5-screw). NES-GNROM [128KB PRG | 32KB CHR | CIC 3193 | V]. Nintendo: Nintendo, June 1986.

Gyromite. Nintendo Entertainment System (72-p. cart.), NTSC [US]. NES-GY-USA (5-screw). NES-NROM-256 [32KB PRG | 8KB CHR | CIC 3193 | V]. Nintendo: Nintendo, Oct. 1985.

Gyromite [ROM]. "Gyromite (JUE).nes" (41KB). iNES: 0. [4E45531A 02010100 00000000 00000000]. 18 Oct. 2002. FCEUX v2.1.5, Macifom v0.16.

ヒットラーの復活 | *Top Secret*. (trans. *Hitler's Resurrection: Top Secret*) Family Computer (60-p. cart.), NTSC-J [JP]. CAP-HF (black). HVC-SNROM [MMC1 | 256KB PRG | 8KB CHR-RAM | 8KB WRAM | MC]. Capcom: Capcom, 20 July 1988.

Hogan's Alley. Nintendo Entertainment System (72-p. cart.), NTSC [US]. NES-HA-USA (5-screw). NES-NROM-128 [16KB PRG | 8KB CHR | CIC 3193 | V]. Nintendo: Nintendo, Oct. 1986.

The Hyrule Fantasy | ゼルダの伝説 (trans. *The Hyrule Fantasy: Legend of Zelda*). Family Computer Disk System (d.s. QuickDisk, yellow), NTSC-J [JP]. FMC-ZEL. Disk (one). Nintendo EAD: Nintendo, 21 Feb. 1986.

Ice Hockey. Nintendo Entertainment System (72-p. cart.), NTSC [US]. NES-HY-USA (3-screw). NES-NROM-256 [32KB PRG | 8KB CHR | CIC 6113 | V]. Pax Softnica: Nintendo, Mar. 1988.

Isolated Warrior. Nintendo Entertainment System (72-p. cart.), NTSC [US]. NES-W6-USA (3-screw). NES-TLROM [128KB PRG | 128KB CHR | CIC 6113B1 | MC]. NTVIC: KID, Feb. 1991.

ジャストブリード *(Just Breed)*. Family Computer (60-p. cart.), NTSC-J [JP]. EFC-I5 (white). HVC-EKROM [MMC5 | 512KB PRG | 256KB CHR | 8KB WRAM | Bat. | MC]. Random House: Enix, 7 Sept. 1990.

仮面の忍者 赤影 (trans. *Kamen no Ninja: Akakage*) Family Computer (60-p. cart.), NTSC-J [JP]. TDF-AK (light yellow). HVC-UNROM [128KB PRG | 8KB CHR-RAM | V]. Shouei System: Toei Animation, 20 May 1988.

Kid Icarus. Nintendo Entertainment System (72-p. cart.), NTSC [US]. NES-KI-USA (3-screw). NES-SNROM [MMC1 | 128KB PRG | 8KB CHR-RAM | 8KB WRAM | CIC 6113 | MC]. Nintendo: Nintendo, July 1987.

キング オブ キングス *(King of Kings)*. Family Computer (60-p. cart.), NTSC-J [JP]. NAM-KK-5900 (black). NAMCOT-163 [N163 | 128KB PRG | 128KB CHR | 8KB WRAM | Bat. | MC]. Atlus: Namco, 9 Dec. 1988.

ラグランジュポイント *(Lagrange Point)*. Family Computer (60-p. cart.), NTSC-J [JP]. KON-RC851 (black). KONAMI-VRC-7 [VRC7 | 512KB PRG | 8KB CHR-RAM | 8KB WRAM | Bat. | MC]. Konami: Konami, 26 Apr. 1991.

The Legend of Zelda. Nintendo Entertainment System (72-p. cart.), NTSC [US]. NES-ZL-USA (3-screw, gold). NES-SNROM [MMC1 | 128KB PRG | 8KB CHR-RAM | 8KB WRAM | Bat. | CIC 6113 | MC]. Nintendo: Nintendo, July 1987.

The Legend of Zelda 2 | リンクの冒険 (trans. *Link's Adventure*). Family Computer Disk System (d.s. QuickDisk, yellow), NTSC-J [JP]. FMC-LNK. Disk (one) [8KB PRG-ROM | 32KB PRG-RAM | 8KB CHR-RAM | MC]. Nintendo EAD: Nintendo, 14 Jan. 1987.

Life Force. Nintendo Entertainment System (72-p. cart.), NTSC [US]. NES-LF-USA (3-screw). KONAMI-UNROM [128KB PRG | 8KB CHR-RAM | CIC 6113A | V]. Konami: Konami, Aug. 1988.

光神話 パルテナの鏡 (trans. *Light Mythology: Palutena's Mirror*). Family Computer Disk System (d.s. QuickDisk, yellow), NTSC-J [JP]. FMC-PTM. Disk (one). Nintendo R&D1: Nintendo, 19 Dec. 1986.

Mach Rider. Nintendo Entertainment System (72-p. cart.), NTSC [US]. NES-MR-USA (5-screw). NES-NROM-256 [32KB PRG | 8KB CHR | CIC 3193A | V]. Nintendo: Nintendo, Oct. 1985.

Mega Man [ROM]. "Mega Man.nes" (131KB). iNES: 2. [4E45531A08002100 00000000 00000000]. 18 Oct. 2002. FCEUX v2.1.5, Macifom v0.16, Nintendulator v0.975.

Mega Man. Nintendo Entertainment System (72-p. cart.), NTSC [US]. NES-MN-USA (3-screw). NES-UNROM [128KB PRG | 8KB CHR-RAM | CIC 6113 | V]. Capcom: Capcom, Dec. 1987.

Mega Man 2. Nintendo Entertainment System (72-p. cart.), NTSC [US]. NES-XR-USA (3-screw). NES-SGROM [256KB PRG | 8KB CHR-RAM | CIC 6113 | MC]. Capcom: Capcom, June 1989.

メトロイド (trans. *Metroid*). Family Computer Disk System (d.s. QuickDisk, yellow), NTSC-J [JP]. FMC-MET. Disk (one). Nintendo R&D1/Intelligent Systems: Nintendo, 6 Aug. 1986.

Might and Magic (trans. マイト・アンド・マジック). Family Computer (60-p. cart.), NTSC-J [JP]. GAT-MP (white). HVC-TKROM [MMC3 | 256KB PRG | 256KB CHR | 8KB WRAM | Bat. | MC]. New World Computing {p. Gakken}: Gakken, 31 July 1990.

Might & Magic: Secret of the Inner Sanctum. Nintendo Entertainment System (72-p. cart.), NTSC [US]. NES-MP-USA (3-screw). NES-TKROM [MMC3 | 256KB

PRG | 256KB CHR | 8KB WRAM | Bat. | CIC 6113 | MC]. New World Computing (p. Gakken): Sammy, Aug. 1992.

Ninja Gaiden. Nintendo Entertainment System (72-p. cart.), NTSC [US]. NES-NG-USA (3-screw). NES-SLROM [MMC1 | 128KB PRG | 128KB CHR | CIC 6113 | MC]. Tecmo: Tecmo, Mar. 1989.

ナッツ&ミルク | *Nuts & Milk.* Family Computer (60-p. cart.), NTSC-J [JP]. HFC-NM (light blue). HVC-NROM-128 [16KB PRG | 8KB CHR | H]. Hudson Soft: Hudson Soft, 28 July 1984.

オトッキー *(Otocky).* Family Computer Disk System (d.s. QuickDisk, yellow), NTSC-J [JP]. ASC-OTO. Disk (one). SEDIC: ASCII, 27 March 1987.

Pac-Man. Nintendo Entertainment System (72-p. cart.), NTSC [US]. NES-PQ-USA (3-screw). NES-NROM-128 [16KB PRG | 8KB CHR | CIC 6113 | H]. Namco: Tengen, 1989.

Pac-Man. Nintendo Entertainment System (72-p. cart.), NTSC [US]. TGN-003-PM (unlic., Tengen shell, black). TENGEN-800003 [16KB PRG | 8KB CHR | CIC 337002 | H]. Namco: Tengen, 1989.

ポパイ | *Popeye.* Family Computer (60-p. cart.), NTSC-J [JP]. HVC-PP (green). HVC-NROM-128 [16KB PRG | 8KB CHR | H]. Nintendo: Nintendo, 15 July 1983.

ポートピア連続殺人事件 (trans. *The Portopia Serial Murder Case*). Family Computer (60-p. cart.), NTSC-J [JP]. EFC-PR (black). HVC-NROM-256 [32KB PRG | 8KB CHR | V]. Enix: Chunsoft, 29 Nov. 1985.

Pro Wrestling. Nintendo Entertainment System (72-p. cart.), NTSC [US]. NES-PW-USA (5-screw). NES-UNROM [128KB PRG | 8KB CHR-RAM | CIC 6113 | V]. Human Entertainment: Nintendo, Mar. 1987.

レリクス暗黒要塞 *(Relics: Ankoku Yousai).* Family Computer Disk System (d.s. QuickDisk, yellow), NTSC-J [JP]. BTC-RLC. Disk (one). Bothtec: Bothtec, 1987.

Rockman (trans. ロックマン). Family Computer (60-p. cart.), NTSC-J [JP]. CAP-RX (light blue). HVC-UNROM [128KB PRG | 8KB CHR-RAM | V]. Capcom: Capcom, 17 Dec. 1987.

Rygar. Nintendo Entertainment System (72-p. cart.), NTSC [US]. NES-RY-USA (3-screw). NES-UNROM [128KB PRG | 8KB CHR-RAM | CIC 6113 | V]. Tecmo: Tecmo, July 1987.

Snake Rattle N Roll. Nintendo Entertainment System (72-p. cart.), NTSC [US]. NES-RJ-USA (3-screw). NES-SEROM [32KB PRG | 32KB CHR | CIC 6113 | MC]. Rare: Nintendo, July 1990.

Solstice: The Quest for the Staff of Demnos. Nintendo Entertainment System (72-p. cart.), NTSC [US]. NES-LX-USA (3-screw). NES-ANROM [128KB PRG | 8KB CHR-RAM | CIC 6113 | MC]. Nintendo: Nintendo, Oct. 1985.

スパルタンX (trans. *Spartan X*). Family Computer (60-p. cart.), NTSC-J [JP]. NES-SM-USA (5-screw). HVC-SX (purple). HVC-NROM-256 [32KB PRG | 8KB CHR | V]. Irem: Nintendo, 21 June 1985.

Stack-Up. Nintendo Entertainment System (72-p. cart.), NTSC [US]. NES-BL-USA (5-screw, NES-JOINT-01). NES-NROM-256 [32KB PRG | 8KB CHR | CIC 3193 | H]. Nintendo: Nintendo, Oct. 1985.

Super C. Nintendo Entertainment System (72-p. cart.), NTSC [US]. NES-UE-USA (3-screw). KONAMI-TLROM [MMC3B | 128KB PRG | 128KB CHR | CIC 6113B1 | MC]. Konami: Konami, April 1990.

スーパーマリオブラザーズ (trans. *Super Mario Bros.*). Family Computer (60-p. cart.), NTSC-J [JP]. HVC-SM (yellow). HVC-NROM-256 [32KB PRG | 8KB CHR | V]. Nintendo EAD: Nintendo, 13 Sept. 1985.

Super Mario Bros. Nintendo Entertainment System (72-p. cart.), NTSC [US]. NES-SM-USA (5-screw). NES-NROM-256 [32KB PRG | 8KB CHR | CIC 3193 | V]. Nintendo EAD: Nintendo, Oct. 1985.

Super Mario Bros. [ROM]. "Super Mario Bros.nes" (41KB). iNES: 0. [4E45531A 02010100 00000000 00000000]. 10 Dec. 1999. FCEUX v2.1.5, Macifom v0.16, NESA v0.17, Nestopia v1.4.1, Nintendulator v0.975, RockNES v5.08.

Super Mario Bros. / Duck Hunt. Nintendo Entertainment System (72-p. cart.), NTSC [US]. NES-MH-USA (3-screw). NES-MHROM [64KB PRG | 16KB CHR | CIC 6113 | V]. Nintendo: Nintendo, Nov. 1988.

スーパーマリオブラザーズ2 (trans. *Super Mario Bros. 2*). Family Computer Disk System (d-s. QuickDisk, yellow), NTSC-J [JP]. FMC-SMB. Disk (one). Nintendo EAD: Nintendo, 3 May 1986.

Super Mario Bros. 2. Nintendo Entertainment System (72-p. cart.), NTSC [US]. NES-MW-USA (3-screw). NES-TSROM [MMC3 | 128KB PRG | 128KB CHR | 8KB WRAM | CIC 6113 | MC]. Nintendo: Nintendo, Oct. 1988.

Super Mario Bros. 3. Nintendo Entertainment System (72-p. cart.), NTSC [US]. NES-UM-USA (3-screw). NES-TSROM [MMC3 | 256KB PRG | 128KB CHR | 8KB WRAM | CIC 6113 | MC]. Nintendo: Nintendo, 12 Feb. 1990.

Super Mario Clouds [ROM]. BEIGE/Cory Arcangel. "SuperMarioClouds.nes" (40,976 bytes). iNES: 0. [4E45531A 02010100 00000000 00000000]. 18 Nov. 2002. Macifom v.0.16, FCEUX v2.1.5, Nintendulator v0.975. <http://web.archive.org/web/20021118090831/http://www.beigerecords.com/cory/21c/21c.html>

Super Mario Clouds v2k9 [ROM]. BEIGE/Cory Arcangel. "clouds.nes" (40,976 bytes). iNES: 0. [4E45531A 02010100 00000000 00000000]. 10 Dec. 2012. Macifom v.0.16, FCEUX v2.1.5. <https://github.com/coryarcangel/Super-Mario-Clouds/blob/master/clouds.nes>

スーパーマリオ | *Super Mario USA.* Family Computer (60-p. cart.), NTSC-J [JP]. HVC-MT (pink). HVC-TSROM [128KB PRG | 128KB CHR | 8KB WRAM | MC]. Nintendo: Nintendo, 14 Sept. 1992.

Tennis. Nintendo Entertainment System (72-p. cart.), NTSC [US]. NES-TE-USA (5-screw). NES-NROM-128 [16KB PRG | 8KB CHR | CIC 3193A | H]. Nintendo: Nintendo, 18 Oct. 1986.

宇宙警備隊SDF (*Uchuu Keibitai SDF*). Family Computer (60-p. cart.), NTSC-J [JP]. HAL-UI (black). HVC-ELROM [MMC5 | 128KB PRG | 128KB CHR | MC]. HAL Laboratory: HAL, 7 Sept. 1990.

Urban Champion. Nintendo Entertainment System (72-p. cart.), NTSC [US]. NES-UC-USA (5-screw). NES-NROM-128 [16KB PRG | 8KB CHR | CIC 3193A | V]. Nintendo: Nintendo, June 1986.

Volleyball. Nintendo Entertainment System (72-p. cart.), NTSC [US]. NES-VB-USA (5-screw). NES-NROM-256 [32KB PRG | 8KB CHR | CIC 3193 | V]. Pax Softnica: Nintendo, Mar. 1987.

Wild Gunman. Nintendo Entertainment System (72-p. cart.), NTSC [US]. NES-WG-USA (5-screw). NES-NROM-128 [16KB PRG | 8KB CHR | CIC 3193 | V]. Nintendo: Nintendo, Oct. 1985.

Wild Gunman [ROM]. "Wild Gunman.nes" (25KB). iNES: 0. [4E45531A 01010100 00000000 00000000]. 17 June 2000. FCEUX v2.1.5, Macifom v0.16.

Yo! Noid. Nintendo Entertainment System (72-p. cart.), NTSC [US]. NES-YC-USA (3-screw). NES-SLROM [MMC1 ⏐ 128KB PRG ⏐ 128KB CHR ⏐ CIC 6113 ⏐ MC]. Now Production: Capcom, Nov. 1990.

夢工場ドキドキパニック(trans. *Yume Kōjō: Doki Doki Panikku* or *Dream Factory: Heart-Pounding Panic*). Family Computer Disk System (d-s. QuickDisk, yellow), NTSC-J [JP]. FCG-DRM. Disk (one). Nintendo EAD: Nintendo, 10 July 1987.

Zelda II: The Adventure of Link. Nintendo Entertainment System (72-p. cart.), NTSC [US]. NES-AL-USA (3-screw, gold). NES-SKROM [MMC1 ⏐ 128KB PRG ⏐ 128KB CHR ⏐ 8KB WRAM ⏐ Bat. ⏐ CIC 6113 ⏐ MC]. Nintendo EAD: Nintendo, Dec. 1988.

Print and Online

"2A03 Synth Status." *Skrasoft Dev Blog*. 4 Oct. 2008. Web. 19 April 2013.

"6502DecimalMode." *visual6502.org*. 9 Sept. 2012. Web. 19 Feb. 2013.

"A Dream Walking: Popeye The Sailor #14." *YouTube*. Uploaded 16 Apr. 2011. Video. 4 July 2012.

adelikat. "FM2 Movie file format." *fceux.com*. 2009. Web. 13 July 2012. <http://www.fceux.com/web/FM2.html>

adelikat. "How To make a Tool Assisted Speedrun." *TASVideos*. 8 Apr. 2012. Web. 13 July 2012.

adelikat. "Submission #1324: adelikat's NES Gradius in 10:52.35." *TASVideos*. 27 Oct. 2006.

Aiken, Jim. 2004. *Power Tools for Synthesizer Programming*. San Francisco: Backbeat.

Albert, Ian. "Legend of Zelda Maps." *ian-albert.com*. Web. 22 June 2012.

Albert, Ian. "Super Mario Bros. Maps." *ian-albert.com*. Web. 22 June 2012.

Altice, Nathan. "Dendy: The Unofficial Official Famicom of Russia." *metopal.com*. Web. 15 June 2012.

Altice, Nathan. "The Famicom Cart Swap Trick." *metopal.com*. Web. 12 Sept. 2012.

Altice, Nathan. "Interview: Paul Robson, programmer of the NESA emulator." *metopal.com*. 6 Apr. 2012. Web.

Altice, Nathan. "Porting the Kill Screen." *metopal.com*. 24 Mar. 2012. Web.

Analog Devices, Inc. *A Technical Tutorial on Digital Signal Synthesis* [PDF]. *IEEE Long Island Section*. 1999. Web. 19 March 2013.

Anchordoguy, Marie. 2005. *Reprogramming Japan: The High Tech Crisis under Commu-nitarian Capitalism*. Ithaca: Cornell University Press.

Andersson, Freddy. "Contra_1017 [*Contra* in 10:17]." *Speed Demos Archive*. 19 May 2008. Video. <http://speeddemosarchive.com/Contra.html>

Anthropy, Anna (aka Auntie Pixelante). "level design lesson: to the right, hold on tight." *auntiepixelante.com*. 8 July 2009. Web. 25 April 2013.

Aoyama, Yuko, and Hiro Izushi. 2003. Hardware Gimmick or Cultural Innovation? Technological, Cultural, and Social Foundations of the Japanese Video Game Industry. *Research Policy* 32 (3): 423–444.

ArnoldRimmer83. "Donkey Kong Original Edition." *Lost Levels*. 18 Nov. 2010. Web. <http://forums.lostlevels.org/viewtopic.php?t=2460>

"ASCII codes table - Format of standard characters." *ascii.cl*. 2009. Web.

Ashcraft, Brian. 2008. *Arcade Mania: The Turbo-charged World of Japan's Game Centers*. Tokyo: Kodansha.

Ashcraft, Brian. "Report: Why Does The Nintendo Famicom Have The Color Red?" *Kotaku*. 11 Oct. 2010. Web. 12 June 2012.

Assénat, Raphaël. "Modding a NES to run Unisystem VS arcade games." *raphnet.net*. 7 Mar. 2011. Web. <http://raphnet.net/electronique/nes_vs/nes_vs_en.php>

Associated Press. "Nintendo Charged With Monopolizing Market." *Schenectady Gazette*. 8 Dec. 1989. Web.

Associated Press. "Nintendo revived sagging video game market." *Daily News*. 4 Aug. 1989. Web.

Bagnall, Brian. 2006. *On the Edge: The Spectacular Rise and Fall of Commodore*. Winnipeg: Variant.

Barnholt, Ray. "The Magic of FM Synth." *1up.com*. 25 June 2012. Web.

Barton, Matt. 2008. *Dungeons and Desktops: The History of Computer Role-Playing Games*. Wellesley: A K Peters.

Basto, Luis. "CP/M Emulators for DOS." *retroarchive.org*. Feb. 1993. Web. 12 Mar. 2012.

Bateman, Chris. 2011. *Imaginary Games*. Winchester, UK: Zero Books.

Benvenutti, Diogo Andrei. "Nintendo 8 Bits Voice Samples (2A03)." *YouTube*. Uploaded 22 July 2010.

Benzene. "NES Game Genie Code Format DOC v.0.71." *NesDev*. 10 July 1997. Web. 11 April 2013.

Bieniek, Chris. "ARTICLE 33—NINTENDO CES BROCHURE (1989)." *video-game-ephemera.com*. 2011. Web. 9 April 2013.

"*Bionic Commando* (Nintendo Entertainment System)." *Wikipedia*. 3 May 2012. Web. 9 May 2012.

"The *Bionic Commando* Database." *The Almighty Guru*. 16 Mar. 2012. Web. 9 May 2012.

"Bionic Commando Re-Armed: Exploding Hitler Head." *poeTV*. Uploaded 16 Aug. 2008. Video. 4 July 2012.

Bloodlust Software. "Official Bloodlust Software NESticle Page." *zophar.net*. Web. <http://bloodlust.zophar.net/NESticle/nes.html>

Bloodlust Software. "NESticle Version 0.41 [README.TXT]." *cd.textfiles.com*. 26 Aug. 1997. Web. <http://cd.textfiles.com/230/EMULATOR/NINTENDO/NESTICLE/README.TXT>

Bloom, Steve. 1982. *Video Invaders*. New York: Arco.

Bloom, Steve. 1985. "Nintendo's Final Solution." *Electronic Games Magazine* 3 (3): 8.

BOCTOK Co. 2000. *Ltd. Bit Generation 2000 "TV Games."*. Kobe: Kobe Fashion Museum.

Bogost, Ian. 2011. *How to Do Things with Videogames*. Minneapolis: University of Minnesota Press.

bootgod. *NES Cart Database*. Web. <http://bootgod.dyndns.org:7777/>

bootgod. "Family BASIC (Revision A1)." *NES Cart Database*. 30 July 2009. Web.

bootgod. "Gemfire." *NES Cart Database*. 17 Sept. 2006. Web.

bootgod. "Top 10 dumped games." *NES Cart Database*. Web. 4 July 2012. <http://bootgod.dyndns.org:7777/stats.php?page=4>

bootgod. "Top 10 PCBs & mappers." *NES Cart Database*. Web. 8 Nov. 2012. <http://bootgod.dyndns.org:7777/stats.php?page=6>

Brandon, Alexander. "Shooting from the Hip: An Interview with Hip Tanaka." *Gamasutra*. 25 Sept. 2002. Web. 30 Jan. 2013.

Brend, Mark. 2005. *Strange Sounds: Offbeat Instruments and Sonic Experiments in Pop*. San Francisco: Backbeat.

Brown, Christa, and Kurt Sanner, et al. "Delta Modulation." *ADDA: CD Data Conversion*. 17 Nov. 1999. Web. 16 April 2013. <http://www.clear.rice.edu/elec301/Projects99/adda/dmod.html>

bucky (aka explod2A03). "NES Audio: Duty Cycle Modulation." *Retro Game Audio*. 11 March 2012. Web. 11 April 2013.

bucky (aka explod2A03). "NES Audio: Sunsoft Bass and Melodic Samples." *YouTube*. Uploaded 16 March 2012.

BuZz et al. "Soundtracker History." *exotica.org.uk*. 8 July 2013. Web. 4 May 2014.

Calderon, Anthony. "The Nintendo Development Structure." *N-Sider*. 25 July 2005. Web. 8 May 2012.

Carless, Simon. "Interview: *Dragon Quest* Creator Horii's Talks Evolving Appeal With *DQIX*." *Game Set Watch*. 18 July 2010. Web. 10 April 2013.

Carstensen, Kevin. "NinjaGaiden_1232 [*Ninja Gaiden* in 12:32]." *Speed Demos Archive*. 1 Aug. 2011. Video. <http://speeddemosarchive.com/NinjaGaiden.html>

Carter, Susan B., Scott S. Gartner, Michael R. Haines, et al. eds. 2006. "Radio and Television." *Historical Statistics of the United States*. New York: Cambridge University Press.

Celius. "NTSC NES Square/Triangle Wave Note Values." Web. 26 Feb. 2013.

Celius. "PAL NES Square/Triangle Wave Note Values." Web. 26 Feb. 2013.

Ceruzzi, Paul E. 1999. *A History of Modern Computing*. Cambridge: MIT Press.

Chadwick, Jeremy (aka JDC/koitsu/YoSHi). "Nintendo Entertainment System Documentation v0.40." *GameFAQs*. Web.

Chadwick, Jeremy. "Nintendo Entertainment System Documentation [rev. 1.00]." Web. <http://tuxnes.sourceforge.net/nestech100.txt>

Chadwick, Jeremy. "Nintendo Entertainment System Documentation Version: 2.00." *NesDev*. 9 Oct. 1999. Web. 4 July 2012.

Chadwick, Jeremy. "YoSHi Leaves." *Archaic Ruins*. 5 Apr. 1997. Web. 16 Mar. 2012.

Chaplin, Heather, and Aaron Ruby. 2005. *Smartbomb*. New York: Algonquin.

Chatfield, Tom. 2010. *Fun Inc*. London: Virgin.

Chaudry, Gaby. *Gaby's Homepage for CP/M and Computer History*. Web. 12 Mar. 2012.

"Chip Problems Strangle the Video Game Industry." 1988. *Electronic Game Player* 1 (4): 25.

Cifaldi, Frank. 2010. "In Their Words: Remembering the Launch of the Nintendo Entertainment System." *1up.com*: 21 Oct. 2010. Web.

Cifaldi, Frank. "Nintendo Power: Remembering America's Longest-Lasting Game Magazine." *Gamasutra*. 11 Dec. 2012. Web.

Cifaldi, Frank. "Sad But True: We Can't Prove When Super Mario Bros. Came Out." *Gamasutra*. 28 Mar. 2012. Web.

Clan of the Gray Wolf. "NES Zapper - The Way Games Work." *YouTube*. Uploaded 4 Sept. 2011. Video. 4 July 2012.

Cochems, Chuck. "Marcel de Kogel." *comp.emulators.misc*. 3 Feb. 1997. Web. 4 July 2012. <https://groups.google.com/group/comp.emulators.misc/browse_frm/thread/26d83661f989725/599eb2a5531c6804?tvc=1&q=pasofami#599eb2a5531c6804>

"Coleco Telstar 1976." *YouTube*. Uploaded 12 July 2009. Video. 4 July 2012.

Collins, Karen. 2008. *Game Sound: An Introduction to the History, Theory, and Practice of Video Game Music and Sound Design*. Cambridge: MIT Press.

Commodore Computer. 1982. *Commodore 64 User's Guide*. Indianapolis: Howard W. Sams & Co., Inc.

"Computer or Video Games." *nytimes.com*. 28 April 1983. Web.

Conte, Matt. "cajoNES version 0.2." *Snakeyes Gaming Corp*. 20 July 1997. Web. 23 Mar. 2012. <http://www.snakeyes.org/util/files/cajones.txt>

Conte, Matt. "cajoNES version 0.99b." *cd.textfiles.com*. 1997. Web. <http://cd.textfiles.com/230/EMULATOR/NINTENDO/DOSTOOLS/CAJONES/CAJONES.TXT>

Coox, Jerry. "MML." *woolyss.com*. 27 April 2010. Web.

Cotter, Bill. "Portopia '81." *World's Fair Photos*. Web. 1 Nov. 2012.

Covell, Chris. "The Famicom Titler." *I want my RGB: Chris Covell RGB Project*. Web. 12 June 2012.

Covell, Chris. "NES Music Ripping Guide. [Version 1.4]" *NesDev Wiki*. 30 May 2000. Web. 1 April 2013.

Covell, Chris. "NES Technical/Emulation/Development FAQ [ver. 1.7]." 28 July 2008. Web.

Covell, Chris. "The Stars of Famicom Games." *ChrisCovell's Homepage*. Web. 29 Feb. 2012. <http://www.chrismcovell.com/secret/weekly/Stars_of_the_Family_Computer.html>

Crigger, Lara. "Searching for Gunpei Yokoi." *The Escapist*. 6 Mar. 2007. Web.

Crockford, Douglas. 1993. "The Untold Story of Maniac Mansion." *Wired*. 1.04. Web. 28 Feb. 2012.

Crockford, Douglas. "The Expurgation of Maniac Mansion for the Nintendo Entertainment System." *crockford.com*. Web. 10 May 2012.

CSG Imagesoft Inc. *The Making of Solstice*. 1990. Available online as "The Making of Solstice for NES." *YouTube*. Uploaded 1 May 2010. Video. <http://www.youtube.com/watch?v=894_PNqBkx4>

The Cutting Room Floor. "Castlevania (NES)." *tcrf.net*. 7 Jan. 2013. Web. 1 May 2013.

The Cutting Room Floor. "Galaxian (NES)." *tcrf.net*. 7 Jan. 2013. Web. 1 May 2013.

The Cutting Room Floor. "Gremlins 2 (NES)." *tcrf.net*. 5 Apr. 2013. Web. 1 May 2013.

The Cutting Room Floor. "Proto: The Legend of Zelda." *tcrf.net*. 21 Feb. 2013. Web. 9 April 2013.

D'Angelo, Henry. 1981. *Microcomputer Structures*. BYTE Publications.

Dahlberg, Mattias. "Interview with Karsten Obarski." *bitfellas.org*. 5 June 2007. Web.

Daiker, Brandon. "Mysterious curiosities of the Famicom Disk System." *N-Sider*. 8 July 2011. Web.

Dane. "Help with Nester." *Acmlm's board*. 27 Apr. 2005. Web. <http://acmlm.kafuka.org/archive2/thread.php?id=11813>

DahrkDaiz. "Mario Adventure." *ROMhacking.net*. 1 Jan. 2004. Web.

Dean, Matt. 2012. *The Drum: A History*. Lanham: Scarecrow.

Demiforce. "Final Fantasy 2j English Patch [139readme.txt]." *romhacking.net*. 18 Aug. 1998. Web. 13 July 2012.

Derrida, Jacques. 1991. "Letter to a Japanese Friend" in *A Derrida Reader: Between the Blinds*. Peggy Kamuf, ed. New York: Columbia University Press.

Digital Press. "Nintendo NES Manuals." *Digitpress.com*. 3 Mar. 2011. Web. 26 Apr. 2012. <http://www.digitpress.com/library/manuals/nes/index.html>

Dillon, Roberto. 2011. *The Golden Age of Video Games: The Birth Of A Multibillon Dollar Industry*. Boca Raton: A K Peters.

Dinsdale, Alfred. 1971. *First Principles of Television*. New York: Arno.

Dirty McDingus. "Metroid Source Code Expanded." *ROMhacking.net*. 27 Sept. 2010. Web. 10 April 2013.

Disch. "FDS Sound." *NesDev*. 14 July 2004. Web.

Disch. "NES Mapper List." *ROMhacking.net*. 7 Nov. 2007. Web. 11 April 2013.

Diskin, Patrick. *Nintendo Entertainment System Documentation* (version 1.0). Aug. 2004. Web. 27 Apr. 2012.

Dolan, Richard P., ed. *Hewlett-Packard Journal* 31 Oct. 1980.

"Donkey Kong 3." *The Arcade Flyer Archive*. 12 Aug. 2002.

"Donkey Wrong." *Snopes.com*. 13 May 2011. Web. 28 Mar. 2012.

Donnelly, James B., Gordon A. Greenley, and Milo E. Muterspaugh. 1980. "Emulators for Microprocessor System Development." *Hewlett-Packard Journal* 31 (10): 13–20.

Donovan, Tristan. 2010. *Replay: The History of Video Games*. East Sussex: Yellow Ant.

doppelganger. "SMB disassembly." Private message to author. 14 June 2012.

doppelganger. "the minus world explained v2.0." *romhacking.net*. 19 Mar. 2007. Web.

doppelganger. "SMBDIS.ASM - A Comprehensive Super Mario Bros. Disassembly." *romhacking.net*. 19 Mar. 2007. Web.

"Dragon Quest." *Dragon Quest Wikia*. Web. 20 Oct. 2012.

Driscoll, Kevin, and Joshua Diaz. 2009. *Endless loop: A brief history of chiptunes*. vol. 2. Transformative Works and Cultures. Web

DvD Translations. "ReadMe-DvD_Translations-BodyConQuest_I-Girls_Exposed -revA.txt." 21 Oct. 2012. Web. 12 Nov. 2012.

DvD Translations. "ReadMe-DvD_Translations-The_Portopia_Serial_Murder_Case -revB2.txt." 31 Oct. 2010. Web. 2 Nov. 2012.

Edge Staff. "THE MAKING OF… Japan's First RPG." *Edge*. 6 Mar. 2008. Web. 27 Aug. 2012.

Editorial & Business Headquarters. 1976. "Game Makers Plan Future." *Weekly Television Digest with Consumer Electronics* 16 (2): 12.

Edwards, Benj. "Inside Nintendo's Classic Game Console." *PCWorld*. 7 Aug. 2008. Web. 3 July 2012.

Edwards, Benj. "No More Blinkies: Replacing the NES's 72-Pin Cartridge Connector." *Vintage Computing and Gaming*. 7 Nov. 2005. Web. 6 June 2012.

Edwards, Benj. "VC&G Interview: Jerry Lawson, Black Video Game Pioneer." *Vintage Computing and Gaming*. 24 Feb. 2009. Web. 29 June 2012.

Electronic Code of Federal Regulations. "PART 1150—MARKING OF TOY, LOOK-ALIKE AND IMITATION FIREARMS." 1989.

Enix, Inc. "The Portopia Serial Murder Case Suspense Adventure Game Instruction Booklet (How to play)." Trans. harmony7. *DvD Translations*. 15 Nov. 2010. Web. 24 Oct. 2012. <http://dvdtranslations.eludevisibility.org/portopia/manual.html>

"Ensoniq Mirage." *Vintage Synth Explorer*. Web. 11 April 2013.

"Fairchild Channel F Commercial [1976]." *YouTube*. Uploaded 10 Nov. 2011. Video. 4 July 2012.

Famicom Disk System. "Disk Copy." Web. 9 April 2013. <famicomdisksystem.com>

Famicom Disk System. "Disks." Web. 7 Mar. 2012.

"Famicom Disc System CM (English)." Trans. Clyde Mandelin (aka matotree). *YouTube*. Uploaded 14 May 2011. Video. 4 July 2012.

"Famicom History Part 2: Japanese Famicom Slang 101." *Famicomblog*. 16 April 2011. Web. 13 June 2012.

Famicom World. "FDS Power Board Modifications." *Famicom World*. Web. 9 April 2013.

Famicom World. "Holy Grails." *Famicom World*. Web. 9 April 2013.

Famicom World. "Nintendo's Development Disks." *Famicom World*. Web. 9 April 2013.

Famicom World. "Product Codes: HVC." *Famicom World*. Web. 11 June 2012.

Famicom World. "Pulse Line Cartridges." *Famicom World*. Web. 30 June 2012.

Famicom World. "Topic: Famicom comic (1985) scanned" (xan_racketboy_fan). 16 Sept. 2011. Web. 7 July 2012.

Fayzullin, Marat. "iNES.doc (v 0.6)." *ai_lab*. 1 Jan. 1997. Web. 5 Apr. 2012. <http://147.91.177.212/extra/fileformat/emulator/nes/nes.txt>

Fayzullin, Marat. "iNES." *Marat Fayzullin*. 14 July 2011. Web. 16 Mar. 2012. <http://fms.komkon.org/iNES/>

Fayzullin, Marat. "Nintendo Entertainment System Architecture (version 1.4)." *NESHQ.com*. 9 Sept. 1996. Web. 4 Apr. 2012. <http://www.neshq.com/hardgen/nes-arc.txt>

"FCEUX." *Zophar's Domain*. 5 June 2011. Web. 13 July 2012. <http://www.zophar.net/nes/fceux.html>

Feldman, Vinny and Chett Walters. "Box Art Disparity: FDS vs. NES." *Time Warp Gamer*. 1 May 2011. Web. 7 June 2012.

Feldman, Vinny and Chett Walters. "Box Art Disparity: Showdown Between Regions." *Time Warp Gamer*. 19 Sept. 2010. Web. 7 June 2012.

Feldman, Vinny and Chett Walters. "Box Art Master: NES/Famicom." *Time Warp Gamer*. 23 Apr. 2010. Web. 7 June 2012.

Feldman, Vinny and Chett Walters. "Konami Box Art." *Time Warp Gamer*. 27 May 2012. Web. 7 June 2012.

Feldman, Vinny and Chett Walters. "NES Black Boxes." *Time Warp Gamer*. 28 Nov. 2010. Web. 7 June 2012.

Fieldsted, Jerry. (aka Wildcat). "Category Archives: Cultural Anxiety." *LVLs*. Web. 9 May 2012. <http://lvls.wordpress.com/category/features/cultural-anxiety-features/>

Firebug. "Comprehensive NES Mapper Document v0.80." *TuxNES*. 1998. Web.

Firestone, Mary. 2011. *Nintendo: The Company and Its Founders*. Edina: ABDO.

"First Nintendo Commercial." *YouTube*. Uploaded 23 Jan. 2007. Video. 4 July 2012.

Fromm, Randy. 1993. "Troubleshooting Flow Charts for Monitors." *RePlay*. Print.

Galoob. *Game Genie Programming Manual and Codebook*. Lewis Galoob Toys, 1991.

Game Developer Research Institute. "Company:Ikegami Tsushinki." *gdri*. 20 May 2012. Web. 4 July 2012.

GameMakr24. "Zelda Challenge: Outlands." *ROMhacking.net*. 15 May 2001. Web.

The Games Machine: Computer and Electronic Entertainment 1 (Oct./Nov. 1987).

GameSpite Quarterly 5 (Fall 2010). Print-on-demand.

Gardikis, Andrew. "Mario1_458 [*Super Mario Bros.* in 4:58]." *Speed Demos Archive*. 15 Dec. 2011. Video.

Gibbons, William. 2009. "Bip, Boop, Bach? Some Uses of Classical Music on the Nintendo Entertainment System." *Music and the Moving Image* 2 (1): 2–14.

Gifford, Kevin (aka tsr). "Aqui se faz aqui se paga: The NES in Brazil." *tsr's NES archive.* Web. 30 May 2012.

Gifford, Kevin. "Camerica's Aladdin Deck Enhancer." *tsr's NES archive.* Web. 26 Sept. 2012.

Gifford, Kevin. "Computer TV Game (Nintendo, April 1980)." *magweasel.com.* 21 March 2011. Web. 29 June 2012.

Gifford, Kevin. "Dragon Quest Composer Reflects on 24 Years of Games." *1up.com.* 24 Feb. 2010. Web. 1 Jan. 2013.

Gifford, Kevin. "Essential 50: Dragon Warrior." *1up.com.* Web. 1 Jan. 2013.

Gifford, Kevin. "Hacker International's Head Speaks." *magweasel.com.* 29 June 2010. Web. 12 Nov. 2012.

Gifford, Kevin. "Hidden Messagin'." *magweasel.com.* 29 Aug. 2009. Web. 8 May 2012.

Gifford, Kevin. "Mario Mania I (1985-6)." *magweasel.com.* 2 May 2011. Web. 12 Nov. 2012.

Gifford, Kevin. "Masayuki Uemura and the Family Computer project." *magweasel.com.* 30 April 2013. Web. 1 May 2013.

Gifford, Kevin. "More on Tokuma's Mario Guide." *magweasel.com.* 4 May 2011. Web. 12 Nov. 2012.

Gifford, Kevin. "The Road to Dragon Quest." *tsr's NES archive.* Web. 13 Nov. 2012.

Gifford, Kevin. "Super Mario Bros.' 25th: Miyamoto Reveals All." *1up.com.* 20 Oct. 2010. Web. 28 June 2012.

Gifford, Kevin. "Tetris...forever." *tsr's NES archive.* 1999. Web. 30 May 2012.

Galad, Gil. "NSF Ripper Guide." *Gil Galad.* 17 May 2007. Web. 1 April 2013. <http://gilgalad.arc-nova.org/intro.html>

Galad, Gil. "Video Game Source Code Repository." *Gil Galad.* Web. <http://gilgalad.arc-nova.org/>

godslabrat. "Any interest in NES ROB homebrews?" *Atari Age.* 15 Feb. 2011. Web.

Goldberg, Harold. 2011. *All Your Base Are Belong To Us: How Fifty Years Of Video Games Conquered Pop Culture.* New York: Three Rivers.

goroh. "Nesticle(ver 0.42) stafile infomation." *NesDev.* 12 Dec. 1997. Web.

Green, Matthew. "The Albatross on Parade." *Press the Buttons.* 18 May 2009. Web. 9 May 2012.

Greening, Chris. "Interview with the *Mega Man 1 & 2* Sound Team: Reunited 20 Years On." *Square Enix Music Online.* Web. 18 Feb. 2013.

Greetham, D. C. 1994. *Textual Scholarship: An Introduction.* New York: Garland.

Gross, Doug. "Nintendo seeks to trademark 'On like Donkey Kong'." *CNN.* 10 Nov. 2010. Web. 20 Mar. 2012.

"Gunpei Yokoi talks Donkey Kong in 'Gunpei Yokoi's House of Games'." *The End of Deep Layer.* 5 Dec. 2010. Web. 23 Feb. 2012.

Haanstra, John W., and Bob O. Evans, et al. 1983. Processor Products—Final Report of SPREAD Task Group, December 28, 1961. *Annals of the History of Computing* 5 (1): 6–26.

Hamman, Shaun. "The Tower of Druaga: Item Guide (v.1.11)." *GameFAQs.* 29 Apr. 2009. Web. 27 Aug. 2012.

Hansen, Kent. (aka SnowBro). "METROID MAP DATA FORMAT v1.0." *Snakeyes Gaming Corp.* 1998. Web. 19 Mar. 2012. <http://www.snakeyes.org/docs/files/met_map.txt>

"[HD] TAS: NES Super Mario Bros 3 (JPN) in 11:03.95 by Morimoto." *YouTube*. Uploaded 14 May 2011. Video. 4 July 2012.

Hayes, Michael, and Stuart Dinsey. 1995. *Games War*. London: Bowerdean.

Hayles, N. Katherine. 2008. *Electronic Literature*. Notre Dame: U of Notre Dame.

Hemnes, Thomas M. S. 1982. The Adaptation of Copyright Law to Video Games. *University of Pennsylvania Law Review* 131 (1):171–233.

Herman, Leonard. 2001. *Phoenix: The Fall & Rise of Home Videogames*. 3rd ed. Springfield: Rolenta.

Herrick, Clyde N. *Television Theory and Servicing: Black/White and Color. 2nd ed*. Reston: Reston, 1976.

Herz, J. C. 1997. *Joystick Nation*. Boston: Little, Brown and Co.

Hickman, Chris. "Interview with Landy on LandyNES." *Archaic Ruins*. 23 Dec. 1996. Web. 16 Mar. 2012. <http://patpend.net/articles/ar/lndy1223.html>

"History of the Floppy Disk." *Wikipedia*. 26 Jan. 2012. Web. 7 Mar. 2012.

Hodges, Don. "How High Can You Get?" *DonHodges.com*. 28 July 2011. Web. 21 Mar. 2012.

Holmes, Chris. "The Top 10 Chiptune Artists." *theNPCs*. 9 April 2010. Web. 11 April 2013.

Horton, Kevin (aka kevtris). "The FPGA Videogame Console." *kevtris.org*. 16 May 2005. Web. 20 March 2013.

Horton, Kevin. "HardNES." *kevtris.org*. Web.

Horton, Kevin. "NES Music Format Spec." *kevtris.org*. 27 June 2000. Web.

Horton, Kevin. "NES Video Voltage Levels." *NesDev*. 22 Sept. 2006. Web.

Horton, Kevin. "VRCVI CHIP INFO." *NesDev*. 31 Aug. 1999. Web.

Horton, Kevin. "VRCVII CHIP INFO." *kevtris.org*. 15 Nov. 1999. Web.

Hosokawa, Shuhei. 1984. The Walkman Effect. *Popular Music* 4: 165–180.

"How 'Adventure Mario' became The Legend Of Zelda." *CVG*. 18 Nov. 2011. Web. 4 Oct. 2012.

"HP 64000." *Wikipedia*. 15 Jan. 2012. Web. 29 Feb. 2012.

Hubbard, Rob. "Rob Hubbard - Golden Days of Computer Game Music." *YouTube*. Uploaded 5 Sept. 2007. Video.

Hughes, F. "'Super Mario Bros NES' R.Eng project." *ROMhacking.net*. 14 May 2008. Web. 11 April 2013.

Humble, Rod. "Game Rules as Art." *The Escapist*. 18 Apr. 2006. Web. 2 July 2012.

hydro (RiGaMoRTiS PRoDuCTioNZ). "TetaNES Program Documentation." *Snakeyes Gaming Corp*. 17 Sept. 1998. Web. 19 Mar. 2012. <http://www.snakeyes.org/util/files/tetanes.txt>

iFixit. "Nintendo Family Computer (Famicom) Teardown." *ifixit.com*. 01 July 2010. Web. 30 March 2014.

IKA. "Rockman No Constancy." *ROMhacking.net*. 21 Oct. 2007. Web.

Inoue, Osamu. 2010. *Nintendo Magic: Winning the Videogame Wars*. New York: Vertical.

Intellivision Productions, Inc. "1983 Intellivision/M Network Catalog." *intellivision-lives.com*. 1983. Web.

Intellivision Productions. "Intellivoice." *Intellivision Lives!* 10 Sept. 2011. Web. 16 April 2013.

Intellivision Productions. "M Network Colecovision." *Intellivision Lives!* Web. 16 April 2013.

Iwamoto, Yoshiyuki. 2006. *Japan on the Upswing: Why the Bubble Burst and Japan's Economic Renewal*. New York: Algora.

"Iwata Asks: Dragon Quest IX - Part 1: The History of Dragon Quest." *YouTube*. Uploaded 9 July 2010. Web. 10 April 2013.

Iz-Tavares, Gregg, and Dan Chang. "Programming M.C. Kids [1992]." *games .greggman.com*. 12 June 2003. Web.

Japan Industrial Designers' Association (JIDA). 1983. *Structure of Dexterity: Industrial Design Works in Japan*. Tokyo: Rikuyo-sha.

"Japanese Flock to Exhibit Focusing on the Future." *nytimes.com*. 30 March 1981. Web. 2 Nov. 2012.

Johnstone, Bob. 1999. *We Were Burning: Japanese Entrepreneurs and the Forging of the Electronic Age*. Boulder: Basic.

Jones, Steven E., and George K. Thiruvathukal. 2012. *Codename Revolution: The Nintendo Wii Platform*. Cambridge: MIT Press.

Kageyama, Masashi, and Naoki Kodaka. 2011. *Rom Cassette Disc in SUNSOFT*. Japan: City Connection. Compact Disc Set.

Kalata, Kurt. "American Dream." *Hardcore Gaming 101*. Web. 5 June 2012.

Kalata, Kurt. "The History of Dragon Quest." *Gamasutra*. 4 Feb. 2008. Web. 20 Oct. 2012.

Kaluszka, Aaron (aka MEGAßɎTE). "Computer Emulation." *kaluszka.com*. 14 Dec. 2001. Web. 14 Mar. 2012. <http://kaluszka.com/vt/emulation/>

Kaluszka, Aaron. "How the Super Mario Bros. extra lives system works (I think)." *The Mushroom Kingdom*. 24 May 2000. Web.

Kamermans, Michiel (aka Pomax). "The giongo/gitaigo dictionary." *Nihongoresources. com*. Web. 10 April 2013.

Kaneoka, Yukio. "Electronic Sound Synthesizer." Patent 4,783,812. 8 Nov. 1988.

Katayama, Osamu. 1996. *Japanese Business into the 21st Century*. London: Athlone.

Kean, Roger, ed. 1984. *Crash* No. 1: 51–2.

Kemps, Heidi. "Europe gets exclusive 'perfect version' of NES Donkey Kong in its Mario 25th Anniversary Wiis." *gamesradar*. 16 Nov. 2012. Web.

Kennedy, Sam. "We Track Down The Composer of Contra NES." *1up.com*. 20 Jan. 2009. Web. 30 Jan. 2013.

Kennedy, Sam and Thomas Puha. "Mario Maestro." *1up.com*. 19 Oct. 2007. Web. 28 June 2012.

Kent, Steven L. 2001. *The Ultimate History of Video Games*. Roseville: Prima.

Kerr, Alex. 2001. *Dogs and Demons: Tales from the Dark Side of Japan*. New York: Hill and Wang.

Kessler, Scott. "Super Mario Bros Tricks!" *Dman's Game Domain*. 21 Aug. 1999. Web. <http://www.elitecoder.com/smbtrick.html>

Kidder, Tracy. 1981. *The Soul of a New Machine*. Boston: Little, Brown and Co.

Kirn, Peter. "Prototype Nintendo Music Keyboard from 1984." *Create Digital Music*. 14 Sept. 2005. Web. 18 Apr. 2012.

Kirschenbaum, Matthew G. 2008. *Mechanisms: New Media and the Forensic Imagination*. Cambridge: MIT Press.

Kline, Stephen, Nick Dyer-Witheford, and Greig De Peuter. 2003. *Digital Play: The Interaction of Technology, Culture, and Marketing*. London: McGill-Queen's University Press.

Kodansha Ltd. 1987. *Best of Japan*. Tokyo: Kodansha.

Kodansha Ltd. 1980. *Japan Style*. Tokyo: Kodansha.

Kohler, Chris. 2005. *Power-Up: How Japanese Video Games Gave The World An Extra Life*. Bradygames.

Kohler, Chris. "The Secret History of *Super Mario Bros. 2*." *Wired Game|Life*. 1 Apr. 2011. Web. 8 May 2012.

Kohler, Chris. "Q&A: *Metroid* Creator's Early 8-Bit Days at Nintendo." *Wired Game|Life*. 7 Apr. 2010. Web. 10 May 2012.

Korth, Martin. (aka Nocash). "Everynes: Everything about NES and Famicom." 2004. Web. <http://nocash.emubase.de/everynes.htm>

Kowalski, John (aka Sock Master). "Sock Master's Donkey Kong Emulator for CoCo 3." *Sock Master's Web Page*. 31 Mar. 2007. Web.

Kraft, Emmitt R. (aka Gigafrost). "Submission #690: Gigafrost's NES Zelda 2: The Adventure of Link 'glitched' in 06:16.93." *TASVideos*. 28 May 2005. Web.

Kulczycki, Jeff. "Technical: What's with the Kill Screen." *Jeff's ROMHACK*. Web. 21 Mar. 2012.

Kulczycki, Jeff. "Donkey Kong Arcade Disassembly." Email to author. 29 Jan. 2012.

Kun, Ma Lam. "Funny Fantasy." *Algo's Home Page*. 20 Feb. 1996. Web. 4 July 2012. <http://www.ee.ust.hk/~algoma/music.html>

Kuntz, Jason (aka x_loto). "DRAGON QUEST Japanese Game Script and Mini Playing Guide v5.11." *GameFAQs*. 10 July 2010. Web. 14 Dec. 2012.

Lacey, Eugene. 1983. "Novelty Games - Cute is Crucial." *Computer & Video Games Book of Reviews* 10.

Laing, Gordon. 2004. *Digital Retro*. Cambridge: Ilex.

Lee, O-Young. 1982. *The Compact Culture: The Japanese Tradition of "Smaller is Better"*. Huey, Robert N., (trans.). Tokyo: Kodansha.

Leventhal, Lance A. 1979. *6502: Assembly Language Programming*. Berkeley: Osborne.

Levi, Antonia. 1996. *Samurai from Outer Space: Understanding Japanese Animation*. Chicago: Open Court.

Lewis, Peter H. "Commodore Introduces New Amiga." *nytimes.com*. 30 July 1985. Web. 13 Mar. 2012.

"List of Enix home computer games." *Wikipedia*. 9 May 2012. Web. 23 Oct. 2012.

Loguidice, Bill, and Matt Barton. 2009. *Vintage Games: An Insider Look at the History of Grand Theft Auto, Super Mario, and the Most Influential Games of All Time*. Amsterdam: Focal.

Loogaroo1. "Dragon Warrior: Enemy Territory Map." *GameFAQs*. 14 March 2010. Web. <http://www.gamefaqs.com/nes/563408-dragon-warrior/faqs/55534>

Lowood, Henry. 2006. "High-performance play: The making of machinima." *Journal of Media Practice* 7 (1): 25–42.

"Magnavox Odyssey TV Commercial - February 1973." *YouTube*. Uploaded 15 Dec. 2007. Video. 4 July 2012.

Maher, Jimmy. 2012. *The Future Was Here: The Commodore Amiga*. Cambridge: MIT Press.

Manbow-J. "MCKC: MML > MCK Converter Ver 0.14." Trans. virt. 1 Aug. 2002. Web.

Mandelin, Clyde (aka Mato). "A Look at the Metroid Series' Varia Suit." *legendsoflocalization.com*. 28 July 2013. Web.

Mandelin, Clyde. "Legends of Localization: Super Mario Bros." *matotree.com*. 28 Oct. 2011. Web.

"The Manual Project." *Vimm's Lair*. 4 May 2012. Web. 9 May 2012.

"Marionaire." 23 Aug. 2008. Web. <http://1st.geocities.jp/bysonshome/smb1/index.html>

Margetts, Chad and M. Noah Ward. "Lance Barr Interview." *Nintendojo*. Web. 16 Apr. 2012.

Markoff, John. "Making Computers Compatible." *nytimes.com*. 11 May 1988. Web. 13 Mar. 2012.

Marsland, T. A., and J. C. Demco. 1978. A Case Study of Computer Emulation. *INFOR* 16 (2): 112–131.

Maru-Chang. "Nintendo Hard Number: HVC." *maru-chang.com*. Web. 11 June 2012.

Matsuoka, Claudio. "Tracker History Graphing Project." *helllabs.org*. 4 Nov. 2007. Web. 23 Jan. 2013.

McCallum, John. "Memory Prices (1957-2013)." *jcmit.com*. 27 Feb. 2013. Web. 24 July 2013.

McCullough, J. J. "Nintendo's Era of Censorship." *Filibuster Cartoons*. Web. 28 Feb. 2012.

McFerran, Damien. "Slipped Disk - The History of the Famicom Disk System." *Nintendo Life*. 20 Nov. 2010. Web. 9 April 2013.

McGill, Douglas. "The ultimate video game: Nintendo vs Atari." *New Straits Times*. 23 March 1989. Web.

Memblers. "NES Music Authors List v3.8." *NesDev*. Nov. 2002. Web. 22 Feb. 2013.

Mentzer, Frank. 1983. *Dungeons & Dragons Dungeon Masters Rulebook*. Lake Geneva: TSR Hobbies, Inc.

MeteorStrike. "Dragon Warrior Hacking Analysis FAQ." *IGN Walkthroughs*. 20 May 2007. Web. 17 Dec. 2012.

Michael, Chris. "Videogame facts that blow your mind (SuperMarioBros. SHOCKING SECRET INSIDE p #70)." *NeoGAF*. Jan. 2008. Web. <http://www.neogaf.com/forum/showthread.php?p=9490699#post9490699>

"Microcode." *Wikipedia*. 16 Feb. 2012. Web. 27 Feb. 2012.

"Might and Magic: Oddities, Theories, and Unused Content." *Flying Omelette*. Web.

The Mighty Mike Master. "NES Game Genie Technical Notes." *TuxNES*. Web. 11 April 2013.

Mong, Nick (aka mmbossman). "Submission #2486: mmbossman's FDS Arumana no Kiseki in 08:26.67." *TASVideos*. 9 Dec. 2009. Web.

Montfort, Nick. "Continuous Paper: The Early Materiality and Workings of Electronic Literature." *nickm.com*. 28 Dec. 2004. Web.

Montfort, Nick. "Emulation as Game Facsimile (or Computer Edition?)." *post position*. 14 May 2011. Web. 18 June 2012.

Montfort, Nick, and Ian Bogost. 2009. *Racing The Beam: The Atari Video Computer System*. Cambridge: MIT Press.

More Strategies for Nintendo Games. 1989. New York: Beekman House.

Morimoto. "NES Super Mario Bros. 3 (JPN) in 11:03.95." *TASVideos*. 20 Nov. 2003. Web.

Morris-Suzuki, Tessa. 1988. *Beyond Computopia: Information, Automation and Democracy in Japan*. London: Kegan Paul International.

Nakagawa, Katsuya. "External memory having an authenticating processor and method of operating same." Patent 5,070,479. 3 Dec 1991.

Nakagawa, Katsuya. "Recordable Data Device Having Identification Symbols Formed Thereon and Cooperating Data Processing System Having Registering Symbols." Patent 4,860,128. 22 Aug. 1989.

Nakagawa, Katsuya. "System for determining authenticity of an external memory used in an information processing apparatus." Patent 4,799,635. 24 Jan. 1989.

Nakagawa, Katsuya, and Yoshiaki Nakanishi. "Memory cartridge having a multi-memory controller with memory bank switching capabilities and data processing apparatus." Patent 4,949,298. 14 Aug. 1990.

"Naohisa Morota." *Videogame Music Preservation Foundation*. 23 Jan. 2013. Web. 1 April 2013.

Napier, Susan J. 2007. *From Impressionism to Anime: Japan as Fantasy and Fan Cult in the Mind of the West*. New York: Palgrave Macmillan.

"Narpas Sword." *Wikitroid*. 11 April 2012. Web. 8 Nov. 2012.

National Programme on Technology Enhanced Learning. "Lecture - 3 Quantization, PCM and Delta Modulation." *YouTube*. Uploaded 27 Aug. 2008.

Nelson, Rob. "Nintendo Redivivus: how to resuscitate an old friend." *Ars Technica*. 12 Feb. 2003. Web. 6 June 2012.

Newman, James. 2008. *Playing with Videogames*. London: Routledge.

Newman, James. 2004. *Videogames*. London: Routledge.

NesDev. "$2001 8-pixel mask" (noattack). *NesDev* Forums. 5 March 2013. Web. 25 April 2013.

NesDev. "Big Bird's Hide and Speak sample compression" (rainwarrior). *NesDev* Forums. 3 March 2012. Web.

NesDev. "Cartridge and mappers' history." *NesDev Wiki*. 9 Nov. 2011. Web. 26 April 2014.

NesDev. "CIC lockout chip." *NesDev Wiki*. 13 July 2011. Web. 4 July 2012.

NesDev. "CIC lockout chip pinout." *NesDev Wiki*. 5 Apr. 2011. Web. 4 July 2012.

NesDev. "Clarification on OAM and palette locations" (noattack). *NesDev* Forums. 7 July 2012. Web.

NesDev. "Clock Rate." *NesDev Wiki*. 10 Jan. 2012. Web. 4 July 2012.

NesDev. "Composite out of a french PAL NES" (alex). *NesDev* Forums. 15 Oct. 2007. Web.

NesDev. "Docs on game genie hardware?" (jwdonal). *NesDev* Forums. 30 May 2010. Web.

NesDev. "How do I create a enhanced VDP/PPU?" (Hamtaro126). *NesDev* Forums. 25 Sept. 2011. Web.

NesDev. "NES expansion port pinout." *NesDev Wiki*. 7 Sept. 2011. Web. 4 July 2012.

NesDev. "Overscan." *NesDev Wiki*. 28 May 2012. Web. 7 July 2012.

NesDev. "PPU memory map." *NesDev Wiki*. 21 March 2014. Web. 7 May 2014.

NesDev. "PPU OAM." *NesDev Wiki*. 28 May 2012. Web. 4 July 2012.

NesDev. "PPU palettes." *NesDev Wiki*. 19 Oct. 2011. Web. 9 July 2012.

NesDev. "Question about coding for NES zapper" (kalzone). *NesDev* Forums. 4 July 2010. Web.

NesDev. "Tracker history" (noattack). *NesDev* Forums. 23 Jan. 2013. Web. 29 Jan. 2013.

NesDev. "Zelda dungeons" (cpow). *NesDev* Forums. 15 April 2009. Web. 9 April 2013.

NesDev. "Zelda FDS (and general disk-related questions)" (noattack). *NesDev* Forums. 24 Aug. 2012. Web.

NEVERMIND8. "The NESticle Movie Archive." *Emulation Zone*. 11 Feb. 2001. Web. 15 Mar. 2012. <http://www.emulationzone.org/savestates/nesticle/>

"NFG Games Presents: Nintendo Famicom Disk System Manual." Trans. Zumi and NFG. *NFG Games*. Web. <http://nfggames.com/games/famicomdisksystem/0>

"Nibble." *Wikipedia*. 31 May 2012. Web. 6 July 2012.

Nielson, Martin (aka NES World). "Aladdin Deck Enhancer." *NES World*. Web. 26 Sept. 2012.

Nielson, Martin. "Jon Valesh Interview." *NES World*. 1 Dec. 2007. Web. 29 May 2012.

Nielson, Martin. "The Nintendo Entertainment System (NES) FAQ v.1.12." 13 Oct. 1996. Web. 28 Mar. 2012. <http://nescene.tripod.com/articles/nes_art.txt>

Nielson, Martin. "The Nintendo Entertainment System." *NES World*. 19 Aug. 2005. Web.

"Nintendo Family Computer (Famicom) Teardown." *ifixit*. 2 Sept. 2010. Web. 11 June 2012.

Nintendo Ltd. 1985. *This is Family Computer!* Family Computer Compilation.

Nintendo Ltd. 1985. *This is Family Computer!* Disk System Guide.

Nintendo of America Inc. 1988. "Classified Information - Explore the mysterious minus world." *Nintendo Power* 3: 55.

Nintendo of America Inc. 1988. "Counselor's Corner - Super Mario Bros." *Nintendo Power* 1: 52.

Nintendo of America Inc. "Donkey Kong Operation Manual [Model No: TKG4-UP] (1981)." *Basement Arcade Classics*. 2 Oct. 2005. Web [PDF].

Nintendo of America Inc. *Dragon Warrior Instruction Booklet*. 1989.

Nintendo of America Inc. 1991. "Inside the NES." *Nintendo Power* 22: 60–62.

Nintendo of America Inc. "Iwata Asks - Club Nintendo: Game & Watch." *Nintendo. com*. 2011. Web.

Nintendo of America Inc. "Iwata Asks - New Super Mario Bros: Volume 1." *Nintendo.com*. 2011. Web.

Nintendo of America Inc. "Iwata Asks - New Super Mario Bros: Volume 2." *Nintendo. com*. 2011. Web.

Nintendo of America Inc. "Iwata Asks - Volume 1: Shigesato Itoi Asks in Place of Iwata." *Nintendo.com*. 2011. Web.

Nintendo of America Inc. "Iwata Asks - Volume 2: NES & Mario." *Nintendo.com*. 2011. Web.

Nintendo of America Inc. *The Legend of Zelda Instruction Booklet*. 1987.

Nintendo of America Inc. *Nintendo Fun Club News* 1.4 (Winter 1987).

Nintendo of America Inc. 1991. *NES Game Atlas*. Japan: Tokuma Shoten.

Nintendo of America Inc. *Nintendo Power* 6 (May/June 1989).

Nintendo of America Inc. *Nintendo Power* 7 (July/Aug. 1989).

Nintendo of America Inc. *Nintendo Power* 50 (July 1993).

Nintendo of America Inc. 1995. "Nintendo Times: Ten Years of NES History." *Nintendo Power* 77: 20–23.

Nintendo of America Inc. *Super Mario 64 Instruction Booklet*. 1996.

Nintendo of America Inc. *Super Mario Bros. / Duck Hunt Instruction Booklet*. 1988.

Nintendo of America Inc. 1989. *Super Mario Bros. 2 Inside out Part I*. Japan: Tokuma Shoten.

Nintendo of America Inc. *Super Mario Bros. 2 Instruction Booklet*. 1988.

Nintendo of America Inc. 1987. *The Official Nintendo Player's Guide*. Japan: Tokuma Shoten.

Nintendo of America Inc. 1992. *Top Secret Passwords Player's Guide*. Japan: Tokuma Shoten.

Nintendo of America Inc. "VIDEO ROBOTS." (Advertisement). *New York Times* (17 Nov. 1985): A29.

Nintendo of America Inc. 1991. "Why Your Game Paks Never Forget." *Nintendo Power* 20: 28–31.

Nintendo of Europe GmbH. 2010. *Iwata Asks*. vol. 8. "Flipnote Studio - An Animation Class." Web

Nintendo of Europe GmbH. "Iwata Asks: Zelda Handheld History." 2010. Web.

"Nintendo Online Magazine Shigeru Miyamoto Interview - August, 1998." *ZeldaDungeon.net*. Web. 9 April 2013.

"Nintendo Vs. Unisystem." *John's Arcade*. 3 Feb. 2013. Web. 9 April 2013.

Nisan, Noam, and Shimon Schocken. 2005. *The Elements of Computing Systems*. Cambridge: MIT Press.

nullsleep. "MCK/MML BEGINNERS GUIDE." *nullsleep.com*. 2003. Web.

"Object-oriented programming." *Wikipedia*. 5 July 2012. Web. 6 July 2012.

O'Donnell, Casey. 2010. "The Nintendo Entertainment System and the 10NES Chip: Carving the Video Game Industry in Silicon." *Games and Culture* 6 (1): 83–100.

O'Donnell, Casey. 2009. "Production Protection to Copy(right) Protection: From the 10NES to DVDs." *IEEE Annals of the History of Computing* 31 (3): 54–63.

Okada, Satoru. "Video Target Control and Sensing Circuit for Photosensitive Gun." Patent 4,813,682. 21 Mar. 1989.

Olmos, Davis. "Chip Shortage Strains Computer Makers." *latimes.com*. 3 Mar. 1988. Web.

OptimusPriNe. "Dragon Warrior Run." *Speed Demos Archive Forum*. 7 May 2009. Web.

Opulent. "The Doomed Speed Demos Archive." *Doomworld*. Web. 13 Mar. 2012. <http://www.doomworld.com/sda/doom_sda.htm>

Orland, Kyle. "Review: NES Remix is more evocative than transformative." *arstechnica.com*. 18 Dec. 2013. Web.

Osborne, Adam. 1980. *An Introduction to Microcomputers*, Volume 1: *Basic Concepts*. 2nd ed. Berkeley: Osborne.

Ostermayer, Markus. *The Radar Scope Pages*. Web. 24 Feb. 2012. <http://www.ostermayer.ch/>

Otero, Jose. "How Mario 3D World's Co-Director Gave NES Games a Second Life." *ign.com*. 23 April 2014. Web.

Owen, Patrick. "PC Ditto." 1988. *Page 6* 32: 38. Web. 13 Mar. 2012. <http://www.page6.org/archive/issue_32/page_38.htm>

Papp, Zilia. 2010. *Anime and its Roots in Early Japanese Monster Art*. Kent: Global Oriental.

Parish, Jeremy. "An interview with Konami's Hidenori Maezawa." *1up.com*. 13 Jan. 2009. Web. 30 Jan. 2013.

Parkin, Simon. "The Dragon Invasion: How the role-playing game came to Japan." *The Magazine*. 26 Sept. 2013. Web.

Patten, Fred. 2004. *Watching Anime, Reading Manga*. Berkeley: Stone Bridge.

Paumgarten, Nick. "Master of Play." *The New Yorker*. 20 Dec. 2010. Web. 12 April 2013.

Paumgarten, Nick. "Spelunking in Sonobe." *The New Yorker*. 13 Dec. 2010. Web. 12 April 2013.

pditincho. "Donkey Kong Disassembly Revision 4." 10 Mar. 2012. Web. 21 Mar. 2012. <http://www.romhacking.net/documents/540/>

pditincho. "Donkey Kong Disassembly Revision 5." 26 Mar. 2012. Web. 6 July 2012. <http://www.romhacking.net/documents/540/>

Peddle, Charles I., Wilbur Mathys, William Mensch, Jr., and Rodney Orgill. "Integrated circuit microprocessor with parallel binary adder having on-the-fly correction to provide decimal results." Patent 3,991,307. 9 Nov. 1976.

"Personal Computers: Fujitsu FM R Series." *Historical Computers in Japan*. IPSJ Computer Museum. Web. 29 Feb 2012.

Peterson, Jon. 2012. *Playing at the World*. San Diego: Unreason.

Phillips, George. 2010. "Simplicity Betrayed." *Communications of the ACM* 53 (6): 52–58.

Picard, Martin. 2013. "The Foundation of *Geemu*: A Brief History of Early Japanese video games." *Game Studies*. 13: 2. Web.

Pichugan, Igor. (Игорь Пичугин). "Steepler начал продавать Dendy (Steepler starts sales of Dendy)." Trans. Vera Brown. *kommersant.ru*. 18 Dec. 1992. Web. <http://www.kommersant.ru/doc/33856>

Pickford, Ste. "Ironsword Dragon King concept art." *The Pickford Bros' Website*. 20 Feb. 2009. Web. 10 April 2013.

Pickford, Ste "Ironsword Eagle working." *The Pickford Bros' Website*. 8 Jan. 2009. Web. 10 April 2013.

Pickford, Ste "Ironsword title screen working." *The Pickford Bros' Website*. 26 Feb. 2009. Web. 10 April 2013.

Pinch, Trevor, and Frank Trocco. 2002. *Analog Days: The Invention and Impact of the Moog Synthesizer*. Cambridge: Harvard University Press.

Pioneer4x4. "I got my Atari to control my Nintendo R.O.B. Robot!" *Atari Age*. 13 Nov. 2011. Web. 26 Apr. 2012. <http://www.atariage.com/forums/topic/190214-i-got -my-atari-to-control-my-nintendo-rob-robot/>

"Platform game." *Wikipedia*. 28 June 2012. Web. 4 July 2012.

Pollack, Andrew. "Shortage of Memory Chips Has Industry Scrambling." *nytimes.com*. 12 March 1988. Web.

Polsson, Ken. "Chronology of Nintendo Video Games." 18 May 2012. Web. 3 July 2012. <http://vidgame.info/nintendo/>

Ponce, Tony. "Untapped Potential: A true family computer." *Destructoid*. 26 June 2009. Web.

"Popeye." *Wikipedia*. 28 Feb. 2012. Web. 2 Mar. 2012.

"Popeye - You're A Sap, Mr Jap (1942)." *YouTube*. Uploaded 17 Mar. 2012. Video.

Provenzo, Eugene. 1991. *Video Kids: Making Sense of Nintendo*. Cambridge: Harvard.

Pugh, Emerson W., Lyle R. Johnson, and John H. Palmer. 1991. *IBM's 360 and Early 370 Systems*. Cambridge: MIT.

Quartermann. 1989. "Gaming Gossip. *Electronic Gaming Monthly* 3: 28.

Quietust. "Chip Images." *QMT Productions*. 28 Oct. 2012. Web. 19 Feb. 2013.

"Radar Scope (1980)." *The Arcade Flyer Archive*. 6 Apr. 2003. Web.

RaEJaE. "Translations." *Emulation Zone*. 24 Dec. 1998. Web. 15 Mar. 2012. <http://www.emulationzone.org/consoles/nes/translate.htm>

Rard, Joseph. "The Battle of Donkey Kong." *KAMINARIYA*. 11 Jan. 2011. Web.

Reckhard, Tobias (aka jester). "FREQUENTLY ASKED QUESTIONS (FAQ) LIST FOR ALT.BINARIES.SOUNDS.MODS." 25 Aug. 1997. Web. <http://www.koeln.netsurf.de/~michael.mey/faq1.txt>

Retro Synth Ads. "Yamaha GS1 (GS-1) and GS2 (GS-2), Keyboard 1982." 7 June 2010. Web. 17 March 2013.

"The Rise and Fall of Weekly Shonen Jump: A Look at the Circulation of Weekly Jump." ComiPress. 6 May 2007. Web. 12 April 2013.

Roach, Adam. "comp.emulators.misc Frequently Asked Questions (FAQ) [3/3]." Faqs.org. 25 Apr. 1997. Web. 5 Apr. 2012. <http://www.faqs.org/faqs/emulators-faq/part3/>

Roberts, R. S. 1981. Dictionary of Audio, Radio and Video. London: Butterworths.

Rosin, Robert F. 1969. "Contemporary Concepts of Microprogramming and Emulation." Computing Surveys 1 (4): 197–212.

Rosin, Robert F., and Richard H. Eckhouse, Jr. 1972. "An Environment for Research in Microprogramming and Emulation." Communications of the ACM 15 (8): 748–760.

Ryan, Jeff. 2011. Super Mario: How Nintendo Conquered America. New York: Portfolio/Penguin.

Ryan8bit. "Dragon Warrior (NES) Formulas v1.0." GameFAQs. 10 Jan. 2011. Web.

Sample, Mark. "What Comes before the Platform: The Refuse of Videogames." Play the Past. 17 Jan. 2012. Web. 11 Feb. 2013.

Sandberg-Diment, Ereik. "Competing for the Business Mind." Nytimes.com. 3 Nov. 1985. Web. 13 Mar. 2012.

Sandifer, Philip. "Am Error." The Nintendo Project: An 8-Bit Psychochronography. 7 Apr. 2011. Web. 10 Feb 2012.

Saponas, Thomas A. and Brian W. Kerr. 1980. "Logic Development System Accelerates Microcomputer System Design." Hewlett-Packard Journal 31 (10): 3–13.

Sarkeesian, Anita. "Damsel in Distress: Tropes vs Women in Video Games." Feminist Frequency. 7 March 2013. Video.

Scanlon, Leo J. 1980. 6502 Software Design. Indianapolis: Howard W. Sams & Co.

Schottstaedt, Bill. "An Introduction to FM." Center for Computer Research in Music and Acoustics. Web. 17 March 2013. <https://ccrma.stanford.edu/software/snd/snd/fm.html>

Scott, Dean. "Miyamoto: 'I am lazy.'" CVG. 9 Feb. 2004. Web. 9 April 2013.

Segher. "The weird and wonderful CIC." HackMii. 17 Jan. 2010. Web. 30 May 2012.

Sellers, John. 2001. Arcade Fever: The Fan's Guide to the Golden Age of Video Games. Philadelphia: Running Press.

Semrad, Edward J. "New Nintendo system way ahead of the field." Milwaukee Journal. 5 Oct. 1985. Web. 17 Apr. 2012.

Semrad, Edward J. "Nintendo fails to get its action together." Milwaukee Journal. 9 Aug. 1986. Web. 17 Apr. 2012.

SeRiAlKLR. "THE ROM HACKERS BIBLE vo.2." GameFAQs. 1997. Web.

Sheff, David. 1993. Game Over: How Nintendo Zapped an American Industry, Captured Your Dollars, and Enslaved Your Children. New York: Random House.

Shirai, Ichiro. "Multi-Directional Switch." Patent 4,687,200. 18 Aug. 1987.

Sir-Tech Software Inc. 1981. Wizardry (Instruction Manual). New York: Sir-Tech.

SKETCZ. "French NES - with RGB ouput." Hardcore Gaming 101 Blog. 11 Dec. 2009. Web. 12 June 2012.

Slade, Giles. 2006. *Made to Break: Technology and Obsolescence in America*. Cambridge: Harvard University Press.

Sliver X. "Hacking The Legend of Zelda NESticle save states." *Romhacking dot net*. 14 May 2008. Web. 15 Mar. 2012.

Sloan, Daniel. 2011. *Playing to Wiin: Nintendo and the Video Game Industry's Greatest Comeback*. Singapore: Wiley.

Slocum, Paul. "Atari 2600 Music And Sound Programming Guide." *qotile.net*. 19 Feb. 2003. Web. 29 Jan. 2013.

Smith, David. "Feature: What's in a Name?" *1UP.com*. 13 June 2005. Web. 13 Nov. 2012.

Smith, Patrick. 1997. *Japan: A Reinterpretation*. New York: Pantheon.

Snider, Mike. "Q&A: 'Mario' creator Shigeru Miyamoto." *USA Today*. 8 Nov. 2010. Web. 28 June 2012.

snowcon3. "RetroSnow: The Nintendo Famicom (Overview)." *YouTube*. Uploaded 20 Aug. 2011. Video. 4 July 2012.

Sopalin. "Miyamoto, la Wii U et le secret de la Triforce." *Gamekult*. 1 Nov. 2012. Web. 25 Jan. 2013.

Sparke, Penny. 1987. *Modern Japanese Design*. New York: E.P. Dutton.

Speirs, Akira (aka akira slime). "Dragon Warrior: Names/Stats/Levels FAQ." *GameFAQs*. 20 July 2002. Web.

Stanlaw, James. 1994. "'For Beautiful Human Life': The Use of English in Japan." *Re-Made in Japan*. Tobin, Joseph (ed.) New Haven: Yale University Press.

"Static RAM in the SNES carts" (FistOfFury). *ZSNES Board*. 19 Dec. 2004. Web. 10 April 2013.

Stengel, Steven. "Old Computer Ads [Amiga]" *The Obsolete Technology Website*. Web. 13 Mar. 2012. <http://oldcomputers.net/oldads/old-computer-ads.html>

Stern, Richard H. 1982. "Unloading ROMs: illegal piracy, an unfair trick, or free competition?" *IEEE Micro* 2 (2): 85–87.

"*Strafgesetzbuch* section 86a." *Wikipedia*. 17 June 2012. Web. 4 July 2012.

Stuart, Keith. "The game of art: a profile of digital artist Cory Arcangel." *The Guardian Games Blog*. 4 Dec. 2009. Web.

Swink, Steve. 2009. *Game Feel: A Game Designer's Guide to Virtual Sensation*. Burlington: Morgan Kaufmann.

T.M. (aka knbnitkr). "Submission #2836: knbnitkr's GB Makai Toushi SaGa in 01:47.17." *TASVideos*. 16 Sept. 2010. Web.

Takano, Masaharu. "How the Famicom was Born." *Nikkei Electronics* (1994–95). Reprinted at *Nikkei Trendy Net*. 2008. Web. <http://trendy.nikkeibp.co.jp/article/special/20080922/1018969/>

Takano, Masaharu. "Part 1 - The Dawn of Video Games." Trans. Aria Tanner. *GlitterBerri's Game Translations*. 14 Feb. 2012. Web.

Takano, Masaharu. "Part 6 - Making the Famicom a Reality." Trans. Aria Tanner. *GlitterBerri's Game Translations*. 28 Mar. 2012. Web.

Takano, Masaharu. "Part 7 – Deciding on the Specs." Trans. Aria Tanner. *GlitterBerri's Game Translations*. 21 Apr. 2012. Web.

Takano, Masaharu. "Part 8 – Synonymous With the Domestic Game Console." Trans. Aria Tanner. *GlitterBerri's Game Translations*. 21 Apr. 2012. Web.

Takano, Masaharu. "Part 9 – The Short-Lived Disk System." Trans. Aria Tanner. *GlitterBerri's Game Translations*. 12 June 2012. Web.

Takano, Masaharu. "Part 10 – Developing the Famicom Modem." Trans. Aria Tanner. *GlitterBerri's Game Translations*. 29 June 2012. Web.

Tanner, Aria (aka GlitterBerri). "Adventure of Link: Retranslation." *GlitterBerri's Game Translations*. 10 May 2011. Web.

Tanner, Aria. "Discussion Between Miyamoto & Horii." *GlitterBerri's Game Translations*. 20 Dec. 2011.

Tanner, Aria. "Konami: The Nintendo Era." *GlitterBerri's Game Translations*. 1 Jan. 2012. Web. 23 April 2013.

Tanner, Aria. "Making Mr. Gimmick!" *GlitterBerri's Game Translations*. 30 March 2012. Web.

Tanner, Aria. "The Music of Mr. Gimmick." *GlitterBerri's Game Translations*. 14 Aug. 2012. Web.

Tanner, Aria. Personal correspondence. 16 Aug. 2012.

TASVideos. "Emulator Resources." *TASVideos*. 7 June 2012. Web. 13 July 2012.

TASVideos. "Guidelines." *TASVideos*. 28 Mar. 2012. Web. 4 July 2012.

TASVideos. "Luck Manipulation." *TASVideos*. 13 Mar. 2011. Web. 13 July 2012.

Taylor, Brad. "2A03 Technical Reference." *NesDev*. 23 April 2004. Web. 19 Nov. 2012.

Taylor, Brad. "Delta modulation channel tutorial 1.0." *textfiles.com*. 20 Aug. 2000. Web. 8 March 2013.

Taylor, Brad. "Famicom Disk System Disk Drive/RAM Adaptor Technical Briefing." *NesDev*. Web. 23 Aug. 2012.

Taylor, Brad. "Famicom Disk System technical reference." *NesDev*. 23 Apr. 2004. Web. 6 Mar. 2012.

Taylor, Brad. "NTSC Delta Modulation Channel Documentation." *NesDev*. 19 Feb. 2003. Web. 15 Jan. 2013.

Teiser, Don. "Atari - Nintendo 1983 Deal." Interoffice memo. *The Atari Museum*. Web. 28 Feb. 2012.

Television Bureau of Advertising. "TV Basics." *TVB.org*. Dec. 2011. Web [PDF].

Texas Instruments. "TMS9918A/TMS9928A/TMS9929A Video Display Processors. (Microprocessor Series)." Houston: Texas Instruments Inc., Nov. 1982.

Tersigni, Dean. "Uncensored Religion in NES Games." *TheAlmightyGuru*. 2009. Web. 8 May 2012.

Teti, John. "As Fast as Impossible: 10 Insanely Thrilling Tool-Assisted Speedruns." *Crispy Gamer*. 20 Apr. 2009. Web. 6 Mar. 2012.

Théberge, Paul. 1997. *Any Sound You Can Imagine*. Hanover: Wesleyan University Press.

Thorpe, Patrick, ed. 2013. *The Legend of Zelda: Hyrule Historia*. Milwaukie: Dark Horse Comics.

"Tools-Assisted Speedruns." *Doomworld*. Web. 13 Mar. 2012. <www.doomworld.com/tas/>

Touvell, Dave. "Microsoft Softcard." *Apple2Info.Net*. 2006. Web. 9 Mar. 2012.

"Traditional colors of Japan." *Wikipedia*. 15 May 2012. Web. 12 June 2012.

Tran, Albert. "Game Genie: Video Game Enhancer FAQ [ver. 1]." *GameFAQs*. 28 Jan. 2003. Web.

"Transformer." *Personal Computer Museum*. Web. 13 Mar. 2012. <www.pcmuseum.ca>

Tucker, S. G. 1965. "Emulation of Large Systems." *Communications of the ACM* 8 (12): 753–761.

Turner, Benjamin and Christian Nutt. "Nintendo Famicom: 20 Years of Fun!" *gamespy*. 2003. Web.

United States Court of Appeals. "16 F. 3d 1032 - Nintendo of America Inc v. Lewis Galoob Toys Inc." *OpenJurist*. 17 Feb. 1994. Web. 11 April 2013.

United States Court of Appeals. "746 F.2d 112: Universal City Studios, Inc., Plaintiff-appellant, v. Nintendo Co., Ltd., Nintendo of America, Inc., Defendants-appellees." *Justia*. 4 Oct. 1984. Web.

United States Court of Appeals. "Atari Games Corp. v. Nintendo of America Inc." *Digital Law Online*. 10 Sept. 1992. Web.

United States District Court. "Lewis Galoob Toys, Inc. v. Nintendo of America, Inc." *Google Scholar*. 12 July 1991. Web. 11 April 2013.

United States District Court. "Nintendo of America, Inc. v. Elcon Industries, Inc." *Google Scholar*. 4 Oct. 1982. Web. 4 July 2012.

Unseen64staff. "The Legend Of Zelda [NES - Beta / Concept]." *unseen64.net*. 14 April 2008. Web. 9 April 2013.

V., Eric. "Label: Gunpei Yokoi." *beforemario: Nintendo Toys & Games 1965 – 1983*. Web. <http://blog.beforemario.com/search/label/Gunpei%20Yokoi>

V., Eric. "Nintendo Kousenjuu Duck Hunt (光線銃 ダックハント, 1976)." *beforemario: Nintendo Toys & Games 1965 – 1983*, 23 Sept. 2012. Web.

V., Eric. "Nintendo Ultra Hand (ウルトラ ハンド, 1966)." *beforemario: Nintendo Toys & Games 1965 – 1983*. 12 March 2011. Web. 13 June 2012.

Valesh, John. "Nintendo, America!" *valesh.com*. 1998. Web. 29 May 2012. URL only accessible via archive.org Wayback Machine. <http://www.valesh.com/~jon/computers/nintendo.html>

VmprHntrD. "iNES Header/Format Information File [ver. 2.0]." *EMU-DOCS*. 31 Jan 1998. Web.

VmprHntrD. "iNES Header/Format Information File [ver. 2.2]." *GameFAQs*. 4 Jan. 1999. Web.

Vreeland, Rich. (aka Disasterpeace). Tweet to author. 11 Apr. 2013. <https://twitter.com/Disasterpeace/status/322460562980212737>

W., Dan et al. "Exclusive Interview with Donkey Kong Creator Shigeru Miyamoto." [Reprinted from *Nintendo Online Magazine #18*. Feb. 2000.] *The Mushroom Kingdom*. 25 June 2012. Web. 29 June 2012.

W., Dan et al. "Interview with Shigeru Miyamoto Volumes 1 and 2." [Reprinted from *Nintendo Channel*. Dec. 2010]. *The Mushroom Kingdom*. 11 Apr. 2012. Web. 4 July 2012.

W., Dan et al. "Mario in Japan." *The Mushroom Kingdom*. 27 May 2012. Web. 4 July 2012.

W., Dan et al. "Reference - Oops!" *The Mushroom Kingdom*. 3 Jan. 2012. Web. 28 June 2012.

W., Dan et al. "Super Mario Bros. - From Japanese to English." *The Mushroom Kingdom*. 4 Mar. 2012. Web. 4 July 2012.

W., Lennart (aka Baxter). "Submission #1693: Baxter's NES Arkanoid in 12:26.8." *TASVideos*. 11 Sept. 2007. Web.

W., Lennart (aka Baxter) and AngerFist. "NES Mega Man 3, 4, 5 & 6 (USA) in 39:06.92 by Baxter & AngerFist." *TASVideos*. 23 May 2007. Web.

Warren, Richard M. 1999. *Auditory Perception: A New Analysis and Synthesis*. New York: Cambridge University Press.

Watanabe, Masao. 1975. "The Conception of Nature in Japanese Culture." *Project Physics Reader: Readings in Classical and Modern Physics*. New York: Holt, Rinehart and Winston.

Watkinson, John. 1996. *Television Fundamentals*. Oxford: Focal Press.

Webster, Andrew. "Mega Man 9 to feature intentional, optional glitches." *arstechnica. com*. 5 Aug 2008. Web. 21 May 2012.

Weil, Rachel Simone. "No Bad Memories (Or, Video-game nostalgia and the academic and popular discourses that shape it)." *Critical Proximity*. 16 March 2014. Video.

Wen, Howard. "Why emulators make video game makers quake." *Salon.com*. 4 June 1999. Web. 15 Mar. 2012.

Whalen, Zach. 2012. "Channel F for Forgotten." *Before the Crash: Early Video Game History*, ed. Mark J.P. Wolf. Detroit: Wayne State University Press.

"Why DO you have to hold reset while turning power off?" (Protoman). *Famicom World*. 30 Aug. 2011. Web. 10 April 2013.

"Why was the Famicom 'maroon'?" (ファミコンカラーが「アズキ色」だった理由 とは――?). *ITmedia Gamez*. 7 Oct. 2010. Web. 12 June 2012. <http://gamez. itmedia.co.jp/games/articles/1010/07/news098.html>

"Wild Gunman (1974)." *Internet Arcade Museum*. 2012. Web. 4 July 2012.

Williams, Dmitri. 2006. "A (Brief) Social History of Video Games." In *Playing Computer Games: Motives, Responses, and Consequences*, ed. P. Vorderer and J. Bryant. Mahwah: Lawrence Erlbaum.

Wizards of the Coast. "The History of TSR." *wizards.com*. 2003. Web. 11 April 2013.

Wirth, Jonathan. "Spotlight: Earthbound." *Lost Levels*. July 2004. Web. 10 May 2012.

Wolf, Mark J.P., ed. 2001. *The Medium of the Video Game*. Austin: University of Texas Press.

Wolf, Mark J.P., ed. 2008. *The Video Game Explosion: A History from PONG to PlayStation and Beyond*. Westport: Greenwood.

Wong, John J., and Paul S. Lui. "Computer Game Cartridge Security Circuit." Patent 5,004,232. 2 Apr. 1991.

Yamagishi, Takeshi. 1992. "Landscape and the human being." *Human Studies* 15: 95–115.

Yamaha Corporation of America. *Yamaha DX7 Digital Programmable Algorithm Synthesizer Operation Manual*. Buena Park: Yamaha, 1999.

"Yoshihiro Sakaguchi." *Videogame Music Preservation Foundation*. 15 Jan. 2013. Web. 1 April 2013.

Young, Sean. "Texas Instruments TMS9918A VDP: Almost complete description including undocumented features (Version 0.4.2)." *msxnet*. Sept. 2002. Web. 28 May 2012. <http://bifi.msxnet.org/msxnet/tech/tms9918a.txt>

Young, Sean "The Undocumented Z80 Documented (Version 0.91)." *Myquest*. 18 Sept. 2005. Web (PDF). 28 May 2012.

"YTMD - OMG, Hitler's Exploding on Bionic Commando!" ytmnd. Web. 4 July 2012.

Yukawa, Masayuki. 1987. "Cartridge for Game Machine." Patent Des. 292,399.

Yukawa, Masayuki. "Front Loading Apparatus for a Memory Cartridge Utilized for a Data Processing Machine." Patent 4,763,300. 9 Aug. 1988.

Zaks, Rodnay. 1983. *Programming The 6502*. 4th ed. Berkeley: Sybex.

Zazulak, Michael A. "NES SEALED GAME CONTENTS FAQ." *GameFAQs*. 20 July 2010. Web.

"Zelda no Video History of Zelda Documentary." *YouTube*. Uploaded 8 Jan. 2012. Video. 9 April 2013.

"Zoo Keeper." *The Arcade Flyer Archive*. 14 Feb. 2002.

Zophar. "NESticle: One Year Anniversary." *Patent Pending*. 3 Apr. 1998. Web. 15 Mar. 2012. <http://patpend.net/articles/zd/article1.html>

Index

on miniature gardens, 188–190, 192–193

on *Super Mario Bros.*, 117, 120–122, 132, 156, 161

Module (MOD) format, 283

Morota, Naohisa, 279

Moss, Larry, 296

MOS Technology,
6502 processor, 13–16, 27–31, 36, 243, 251–252, 298–299, 336
6507 processor, 28. See also Atari VCS

MSX, 16, 28, 30, 85, 200, 273, 357n60

Multi-memory controller (MMC). *See* Mapper

Mushroom Kingdom. *See* Kinoko Kingdom

Music Macro Language (MML), 385n79

Nakago, Toshihiko, 117, 123, 144–145, 170, 175, 177–178

Nakamura, Koichi, 201–202, 204–207, 209, 212, 216, 220, 225, 240

Nakatsuka, Akito, 265–268

Namco, 53–55, 119, 172, 274–276

Name table, 36–38, 42, 73, 76, 99, 123–124, 126, 130, 141, 234–235, 247
mirroring, 31–32, 38, 119, 143, 181–182, 221–224, 245–246, 306, 308, 311–312

NEC, 107, 172, 194, 200–201, 206, 211, 242, 273, 299, 301

NEC PC-Engine/TurboGrafx 16, 200, 275

NerdTracker 2, 283–284

NES. *See* Nintendo Entertainment System

NES Remix. See *Famicom Remix*

NES-001. *See* Nintendo Entertainment System, industrial design

NES-101. *See* Nintendo Entertainment System, redesign

NES-JOINT, 109

NESticle, 310–314, 317–319, 328, 330

Ninja Gaiden, 6, 100–101, 252, 289, 324

Nintendo,
censorship, 7, 62, 110–112, 114–115
licensing practices, 91–94, 105–107, 110, 115, 211, 241, 243, 302–303

R&D1, 22, 25, 53–54, 95, 211, 264

R&D2, 11–12, 15, 53, 79

R&D3, 211

seal of quality, 105, 110, 367n72

Nintendo Color TV Game consoles, 14, 17, 62, 200

Nintendo Entertainment System,
cartridges. *See* Game paks
in Europe, 92, 115, 198–199, 242–244, 316–318, 367n72
expansion port, 90, 94, 195, 364n26, 367n70, 383n37
holding reset during power-down, 185–188
industrial design, 85–89
light gun, 94–95, 100–104
PAL version, 49, 90, 252, 280, 330, 357n59, 381n3, 382n23
prototype. *See* Advanced Video System (AVS)
redesign, 94, 364n26, 379n96
toaster nickname, 364n23
zero insertion force (ZIF) mechanism, 88–89, 91, 94, 108, 186, 239

Nintendo Power, 157, 215, 230–232

Nintendo Service Center, 109

NSF (NES Sound Format), 277–281, 284–285

NSF player, 266, 280

nullsleep, 287

Nuts & Milk, 31, 70

Obarski, Karsten, 281, 283

Object Attribute Memory (OAM), 30, 40–45, 99, 130, 145–146, 357n69
cycling, 4, 71, 148–151, 223, 233, 235, 327

Otocky, 270–271

Overscan, See Cathode ray tube (CRT), overscan

Pac-Man, 13, 43, 54, 62, 64–65, 67, 83, 93, 110, 201

Palette swapping, 124, 144, 149, 313, 358n77

PasoFamicom (PasoFami), 303–304, 306–307, 309, 340

Printed in the United States
by Baker & Taylor Publisher Services